CRITICA

THE TRUTH

"Laura's underlying worldview, articulated as seven basic principles, coincides with natural science and philosophy. From that perspective, she shares a very personal journey through the history of supernatural religion. She finds constructive concepts, but its practice is found wanting. ... She envisions science open to the inner experiences of human consciousness, but grounded in a consensual reality. Her panetheism sees the wisdom and purposefulness of the original Creator throughout nature."
– **Paul Von Ward**, independent scholar, cosmologist, and author of *Gods, Genes & Consciousness* and *The Soul Genome: Science and Reincarnation*

"Laura reaches deep within the soul of the reader with her gift of blending inner knowing with scholarship – a true partnership of heart and mind, feminine and masculine. The strength of this book is that the Universal Truths that emerge from the author's earnest quest ring true for readers, because her quest is one they recognize as their own."
– **Susan S. Trout, Ph.D.**, President of the Institute for the Advancement of Service and author of *The Soul and Service Trilogy, The Awakened Leader,* and *The Clarion Call*

"The seven rules for judging the adequacy of any religious tradition are well chosen and persuasive. Intelligent and rational people ought to carefully consider how well their own beliefs and practices measure up to these guidelines."
– **Karen Lang, Ph.D.**, Professor of Religion at the University of Virginia.

"The Truth outlines the tenets of the five major religions as established by the original founders, prophets and teachers. Laura holds up a magnifying glass to see if they currently follow their founders' principles. She then evaluates seven well-grounded objectives against which any God-centered religion might be judged. A commanding read for anyone interested in religion or spirituality."
– **Reverend Lowell K. Smith**, MEE, MSCS, author of *Growing Up Psychic: What Every Parent & Child Should Know About Psychic Sensitivity*

"This fascinating account of Laura's burning desire to understand God takes the reader on an exploration that skillfully drives us through many unexpected avenues of thought as she challenges the dogma, doctrine, and politics of God and Truth. In the process she becomes suspicious of all attempts to control truth and to force her to conform to the truth of others. Time and again she demonstrates that just because someone of authority says something is true does not make it so. This captivating adventure is a must read for anyone who is seeking God and willing to ask hard questions in the pursuit of The Truth."
– **Elena Moreno**, Editor of *Empowerment Weekly Magazine* and author of *The Empowerment Series, The Right Living Mentoring Series,* and *Eight Lessons on the Art of Self Love*

"This is a tastefully designed book which in the course of its advocacy provides a useful summary of the 'divine messages' sent to us by God through the prophets, and explores the five religions – Hinduism, Judaism, Buddhism, Christianity, and Islam – to determine if any of these manmade religions 'have remained faithful to the Truth.'"
– **Gene Schwartz**, Editor at Large of *ForeWord Magazine*

THE PENTACLE

The Oracle Institute chose the Pentacle as a symbol for its humanitarian work after researching, designing, and considering dozens of potential logos. We selected the Pentacle because of its noble history and the fact that the Truth about this ancient symbol – like all Truth – needs to be revealed.

The oldest known use of the Pentacle dates to 3,000 B.C.E., when it was used by the Sumerians and Babylonians to depict angles and provide directional orientation. Scholars believe that these civilizations also used the Pentacle for astrological purposes, assigning the five points to the planets: Mercury, Mars, Jupiter, Saturn, and Venus.

The great Greek mathematician Pythagoras was fascinated by the Pentacle. He recognized in its geometry a division of lines which resulted in the "golden ratio," an emblem of perfection that was incorporated into Greek art and architecture. Pythagoras was the first person to refer to the harmony and balance of the Cosmos, and his followers embraced the mystical concept of the soul's eternal existence through the process of transmigration. His followers also ascribed the points of the Pentacle to the five classical elements: earth, air, fire, water, and ideas.

Later, Roman Emperor Constantine used the symbol as a seal and an amulet. When the Roman Catholic Church was formed, some Christians adopted the Pentacle as a representation of the five wounds of Jesus Christ, which pierced: his two hands, his two feet, and his side. Other Christians associated the Pentacle with the five senses: touch, taste, smell, hearing, and sight.

In medieval times, the Pentacle was associated with the legends of King Arthur and the Knights of the Round Table, who were said to possess five virtues: friendship, generosity, chastity, courtesy, and piety. During the Renaissance, Leonardo da Vinci revived the Pentacle when he illustrated that the proportions of the human body symmetrically align within this sublime shape.

Today, at the close of the Fourth Spiritual Paradigm, it is fair to say that the Pentacle represents the five primary religions: Hinduism, Judaism, Christianity, Buddhism, and Islam. May these now ancient religions update their teachings and unify their wisdom traditions in order to guide humanity toward the utopian state described by their prophets as "heaven on earth."

And at the dawn of the prophesied Fifth Spiritual Paradigm, may we recall the most glorious and enduring use of the Pentacle – as a symbol for Venus, the goddess of Love. We, at The Oracle Institute, believe that it is this very aspect of the Supreme Being and of our own Divine nature which will inspire each of us to seek the perennial promise of the Pentacle:

Spiritual Enlightenment

THE TRUTH:
ABOUT THE FIVE PRIMARY RELIGIONS

BOOK I OF A FOUNDATIONAL TRILOGY

WRITTEN IN ASSOCIATION WITH:
THE ORACLE INSTITUTE

CONTRIBUTED BY:
LAUREL
(PEN NAME OF LAURA M. GEORGE, J.D.)

BOOK II OF THE TRILOGY:
THE LOVE: OF THE FIFTH SPIRITUAL PARADIGM

BOOK III OF THE TRILOGY:
THE LIGHT: AND THE NEW HUMAN

THE ORACLE INSTITUTE PRESS, LLC

Published by:
The Oracle Institute Press, LLC

A Division of:
The Oracle Institute

P.O. Box 368
Hamilton, VA 20159
www.TheOralceInstitute.org

Publisher's Cataloging-in-Publication Data

    The truth : about the five primary religions / written in
      association with the Oracle Institute ; contributed by
      Laurel. -- 2nd ed.
        p. cm.
      Includes bibliographical references and index.
      Includes appendix: Brief history of the major events
    in human evolution, politics, and religion.
      LCCN: 2009923784
      ISBN-13: 978-0-9773929-1-9
      ISBN-10: 0-9773929-1-0

      1. Religions. 2. Religion. 3. Religion and
    politics. 4. Spiritual life. 5. Mythology.
    I. Laurel, 1961- II. Oracle Institute.

    BL80.3.T749 2010   200
                    QBI08-600262

Printed and bound in the United States

Cover by:
Sagetopia – www.Sagetopia.com

Interior design by:
Kate, Ink – www.KateInk.com

Fine Art by:
Bill Amos

Dedicated to my many teachers
Four of whom I will name:

My three children:

Erin, the kindest soul
Patrick, the wisest soul
Sean, the bravest soul

And to their loving father:

J.C., the most generous soul.

Additionally, all proceeds from the sale of this book
will be used to further our mission of promoting
religious freedom and spiritual evolution.

ACKNOWLEDGMENTS

This book would not be possible without the support of my soul group:

Specifically, I wish to thank my grandmother *Ruby*, who has given me so many gifts that I feel guilty naming just two: curiosity and courage. As a young woman, she questioned her birth religion and read *The Holy Bible*, which was forbidden at the time. Later, she rejected Catholicism when her quest for spiritual Truth led her to a better understanding of God. At age ninety-two, she remains a primary source of my inspiration.

I also am grateful for my mother *Patricia*, who encouraged me at a young age to explore all the world's religions and who helped me research this book. Frankly, our *karma* is so inexorably linked that at times I suspect we are the same soul. Her thirst for spiritual wisdom represents the purest embodiment of feminine energy I know.

Thanks also to my loving sister *Leslie*. As a social worker, her faith in humanity has been challenged over the last twenty years. Even so, she is determined to fulfill her mission in life and to support me during the critical moments of mine.

Additionally, I wish to thank the other members of my immediate soul group:

Sue (a/k/a *Nancy Drew*), who helped me interpret some Signs connected to this book;

Karen, who assisted with research and was always eager to debate religion with passion;

The "other" Leslie, whose balance and innate assuredness restored me at vital moments;

Siu, who brought Chinese mysticism into my life and tons of energy to help fuel me;

Molly, whose maiden energy kept me tethered to the material plane;

Patti, who played *Thelma & Louise* with me when I needed a break from writing;

John, whose intellect and wisdom provided me with another safe harbor in the wind;

Sharon & Brian, who show that feminine and masculine energy can be balanced;

Ellen & Toni, two childhood friends who reentered my life just when I needed them;

Karin, who, as the soul sister to my sister, has become one of my closest confidants;

The "other" Pat, who generously offered her editing skills to support this project;

Mary, the only person whose aura I've seen – a white glow that symbolizes her divinity;

Greg, my steadfast *karmic* companion and soul brother; and

Sam, the guru who taught me how to commence the *Saddha* process of soul growth.

Lastly, I wish to thank *Fenton*, who provided me with the love, privacy, and protection I needed to complete this work.

TABLE OF CONTENTS

INTRODUCTION vii

CHAPTER ONE
The Saddha Experience 1

CHAPTER TWO
The Major Prophets and What They Taught 25
    Hindu Prophets 30
    Jewish Prophets 37
    Buddhist Prophets 54
    Christian Prophets 63
    Muslim Prophets 146
    Early Philosophical Prophets 174
    Conclusions 177
    Comparative Religions Reference Table 181

CHAPTER THREE
The Seven Rules of Any Good Religion 183
    Rule Number 1 – Philosophy 185
    Rule Number 2 – Science 188
    Rule Number 3 – Morality 196
    Rule Number 4 – Justice 200
    Rule Number 5 – Inclusiveness 201
    Rule Number 6 – Openness 204
    Rule Number 7 – Spirituality 208
    Conclusions 212

CHAPTER FOUR
How the Major Religions Have Failed Us 215
    Hinduism 220
    Judaism 228
    Buddhism 252
    Christianity 265
    Islam 327
    Conclusions 356
    New Millennium Report Card 358

CHAPTER FIVE
The Great Cusp: Why We Are Spiritually Polarized 361

APPENDIX
Brief History of the Major Events in Human Evolution,
Politics, and Religion 391

BIBLIOGRAPHY
Twelve Years of Research 419

INDEX 425

INTRODUCTION

I began writing the first edition of this book in 2003. The horrific events of September 11, 2001, along with visions I was receiving in meditation, convinced me that the world was changing in an unprecedented manner and at an unpredictable pace. A major paradigm shift was in the air, and we would have little time to prepare for it. I also realized that orthodox religion – not just religious fanaticism – would determine our fate. In short, I saw that humanity had not evolved enough spiritually to solve the immense problems we were facing. It is now May of 2009, and it has become even more evident: *We must update our concept of God and self if we wish to enter the era of peace prophesied in our holy books, foretold by the mystics, and foreseen by indigenous cultures.*

But how could one woman's quest for spiritual wisdom possibly help elevate the collective consciousness? Was my spiritual journey worth sharing? So I hesitated to write, due to nagging self-doubt and the fear of taking on such a large project. Eventually, however, I felt compelled to present my research and obligated to relay the messages I was getting – all of which were based on three simple yet profound words: **Truth, Love, and Light**.

Ironically, though, it was a New Age seminar that frustrated and finally persuaded me to write this book. I won't name the group that sponsored the class. Suffice it to say that I found the day such a complete waste of time, I asked for a refund (which I received). I came home afterward determined to list what a "good" religion should do for the soul. In my personal journal, I wrote *"The Seven Rules of Any Good Religion,"* which are now contained in Chapter Three of this book. My project had officially begun.

But I get ahead of myself, as my quest for spiritual Truth really started fifteen years ago. My marriage had just ended and I was in so much pain that I simply *had* to make sense of it all. Why would God allow a human soul to feel such devastation? Where had I failed as a wife? How could I stem my children's suffering? And why had I lost a husband whom I still loved and who said he still loved me? Suddenly, nothing made sense and I desperately yearned for answers.

So I turned in earnest to religion, hoping to find solace and understanding. Having been raised a Catholic, I started my search by re-reading *The Holy Bible*. What a learning experience! The vengeful God of the *Old Testament* gave me flashbacks to Catechism class, and I started to recall my childhood fears and early sense of separation from that vindictive portrayal of God.

Additionally, I was confused by the inconsistent depiction of God in the *New Testament*, although years later I would come to understand the incongruity.

After finishing *The Holy Bible*, I realized that my childhood impressions of Christianity were fairly accurate in that either: (i) God is bi-polar, has a predilection for violence, and exhibits suicidal tendencies as evidenced by the voluntary death of his son/alter ego, Jesus Christ; or (ii) the *Bible* stories are mainly parables, meant to teach us important moral and spiritual lessons. Needless to say, I chose the second alternative explanation. I then proceeded to study the other four primary religions: Hinduism, Judaism, Buddhism, and Islam.

After studying all five of the primary religions, I still felt uncomfortable. I had not yet found a religion that both made sense to me *and* was being practiced today in a healthy manner. For instance, I found that a couple of the religions were fairly close to my own belief system regarding the nature of God, our duties toward each other, and our need for soul growth on the Earth plane, but their depictions of the afterlife were silly and therefore did not resonate with me. I also found that most of the religions enforce unnecessary man-made rules that actually hamper the soul's ability to seek spiritual Truth.

Admittedly, I was "trying on" different religions to see how they "fit." The result was that none of the five primary religions felt right to me. My faith and my "inner bell" were telling me that something was wrong with each one of them. It seemed to me that the man-made religions were overshadowing, even hiding, the Truth about God. As much as I tried, I simply could not avoid concluding that all five religions are flawed. Consequently I pressed on with my search.

By the late 1990s, I was reading "unorthodox" books, exploring the New Age movement, and even looking into Chinese mysticism and Wicca. At first, I found the New Age movement very appealing, given its emphasis on the abundance of the Universe and our innate ability to manifest positive results (i.e., "good" *karma*). However, by the fall of 2003 when I enrolled in the seminar, I already knew that the New Age movement was not my cup of tea.

To me, some of the New Age theories seem shallow in focus and self-centered in nature. In large part, the New Age movement consists of nothing more than standard motivational and self-improvement rhetoric. The movement places way too much emphasis on the "self" instead of on God and our obligations to our fellow man. Consequently, the New Age movement misses the main point of spirituality, which is dependent not only on personal soul growth, but also on our connection to God and to each other. Nevertheless, the movement should be applauded for attempting to update the Earth's religions and for reaching out to the many souls who have reached the painful yet accurate conclusion that orthodox religion is spiritually stagnant.

Thus, despite the best of intentions, most leaders of the New Age movement don't get "It" either. Primarily, the New Age movement is flawed because it focuses more on individual empowerment as opposed to the collective consciousness. This narrow focus easily leads to greed and hubris, which are the two cardinal sins identified in this book. For example, most of the people at the New Age seminar I attended asked for tips on how to "manifest wealth" – a goal specifically denounced by all the major prophets. Sadly, at the end of my fifteen year search, I am no closer to finding a compatible religion for my evolving spiritual belief system.

On the bright side, however, my long journey of religious study, personal introspection, and spiritual growth had greatly healed my heart and inspired my soul. As a result, even though I still craved communion with kindred souls, I thought it best to continue my quest for spiritual Truth in isolation. I was content that my spiritual work and meditation, a process I call *Saddha*, had brought me to a new and better understanding of myself and God. Consequently, I assumed that God would approve of my decision to continue researching, processing, and synthesizing spiritual Truth on my own. *God, however, had other plans for me.*

Please accept this book of Truth and trust that I have taken great care to ensure its accuracy. Please also understand my pure motive for writing this book. I simply want to share what I have learned about God, the prophets, mankind's checkered religious history, and the current state of the five primary religions: Hinduism, Judaism, Buddhism, Christianity, and Islam. The prophet Muhammad, speaking for God, explained this mission of Truth best:

> *Thus do We explain the Signs in detail; and perchance they may turn unto Us. Relate to them the story of the man to whom We sent Our signs, but he passed them by; So Satan followed him up, and he went astray.*
>
> *The Holy Quran*, Sura VII, Verses 174–175

Mankind erroneously has been led to believe that God's messengers delivered complete religions. That simply is not true. Each prophet brought and taught an additional layer of Truth to help humanity. We were supposed to accept these Truths and grow spiritually with the aid of each new message. God never intended for us to latch onto just one prophet. God also never intended for us to blindly follow just one religion. Remember, God did *not* create any of them. The religions were created by men *after* the major prophets died. And mankind is fallible.

I believe God wants us to synthesize *all* the messages brought to us by *all* the prophets, and God wants us to build and continuously update a spiritual database which includes *all* the Truths known to mankind.

Obviously, if God wanted to spoon-feed us the Truth, God would send a prophet who could perform such amazing miracles on the Earth plane that even nonbelievers would turn into devout followers. The most sinful among us would fall into line. But that is not God's plan.

> *Even if We did send unto them angels, and the dead did speak unto them, and We gathered together all things before their very eyes, they are not the ones to believe, unless it is in God's Plan. But most of them ignore the Truth.*

> *The Holy Quran, Sura VI, Verse 111*

God's plan for us requires both faith and hard work. In order to do this hard work, we need to demonstrate courage and openness. We must be brave enough to question the now ancient man-made religions, and we must be receptive enough to accept recent discoveries by mankind and new messages from God. The point is, God did not stop talking to us after the major prophets died. We have roughly 1,500 years worth of new information to assimilate.

Moreover, each of us is responsible for perfecting our own soul and attaining everlasting peace in heaven. We do not get to heaven based on which prophet or which religion we prefer. Rather, we earn the right to be with God in the Ethereal plane based on our interactions with our brothers and sisters on the Earth plane. In my opinion, Jesus stated this simple Truth the best:

> *The first is this: "Hear, O Israel! The Lord our God is Lord alone!*
> *You shall love the Lord your God with all your heart, with all your soul,*
> *with all your mind, and with all your strength."*
> *The second is this: "You shall love your neighbor as yourself."*
> *There is no other commandment greater than these.*

> *Gospel of Mark, Chapter 12:29*

Mankind seems to be moving in circles right now and religion is not helping steer us. Ironically, it appears that religion has become the greatest barrier to the fulfillment of God's plan. In my opinion, religion divides us unnecessarily and currently is the force on our planet which contributes the most to intolerance and hatred of our brothers and sisters who happen to live in different countries or who happen to subscribe to different religions.

Even though our souls are temporarily locked in human bodies, God still expects us to evolve spiritually by perfecting ourselves. The main way in which we perfect our souls is by recognizing our connection to each other. We're supposed to be helping each other, not focusing on our own selfish interests, be they racial, national, or purely the result of our basest emotions.

To understand God's plan better, I suggest three spiritual goals:

1. We should synthesize God's past messages of Truth, as originally told to us by the great prophets;

2. We should add the new Truths we have discovered on our own since the prophets died in order to build an updated "Tower of Truth"; and

3. We should try our hardest to transform ourselves into the loving and compassionate creatures God intended for us to one day become.

I am hopeful that this book will help shed light on these three critical goals. I also earnestly hope that this book resonates somewhere deep inside you. Most of you are ready for this book, are open to new information, and are hungry for Truth. Please open your hearts and minds and learn how each of the major prophets contributed to our collective wisdom about God.

Finally, please know that my intent is *not* to hurt or offend anyone who subscribes to one of the five primary religions. My intent is simply to help mankind achieve a greater understanding of God's lessons as taught by the major prophets, and illustrate how the man-made religions are dividing humanity. Consequently, if the information in this book makes you feel uncomfortable, please keep reading. The deplorable state of organized religion *is* an upsetting topic, and the inhumane actions being perpetrated in the name of God *are* shocking and disgraceful.

Quite simply, my goal is to help humanity ponder the perplexing but undeniable nexus between religion and intolerance.

May this book inspire everyone who reads it, and
May this book energize the Fifth Spiritual Paradigm.
For the good of All and according to the free will of All.

So it mote be.

If a woman is going to write a Book of Peace,
it is given her to know devastation.

Maxine Hong Kingston, *The Fifth Book of Peace*

O nce upon a time in 1961, a female child was born into a remarkable family of Truth seekers. The girl was born on a military base in Virginia, as her father was an ensign in the United States Navy. He had just graduated from the Naval Academy and was about to leave for the Vietnam War. The girl would later learn that her father's acceptance into the Naval Academy was considered a "miracle" by her family, since her father had none of the connections usually required in order to obtain an appointment letter from a United States senator or congressman.

You see, the girl's paternal grandfather was not born in the United States. He was born in Canada and then orphaned at age three. Thereafter, the girl's grandfather was placed in an orphanage along with his older brother, who was seven years old. The year was 1914, and on cold winter nights the older brother would read the younger one stories of "Cowboys and Indians." As the boys grew, they dreamed of joining Buffalo Bill Cody's *Wild West* show or fighting in World War I. To that end, the girl's grandfather and great uncle ran away from the orphanage! They were determined to become either cowboys or soldiers.

However, soon after the boys left the orphanage, both the Wild West and World War I were over. Undaunted, the brothers learned to ride horses and then worked as cowboys on ranches throughout western Canada. In fact, the girl's great uncle became such a good rider, he won a belt at the Calgary Stampede in 1929. Eventually, though, the girl's grandfather moved to the United States to start a new life and pursue his second dream. He joined the U.S. Army and went to Europe as a soldier in World War II. But first he had to say goodbye to his young son, the girl's father, whose earliest memory was of his father in uniform.

Similarly, the girl's earliest memory was of her father in Navy dress whites. She was only four years old at the time, and she wore a beautiful white dress which, in her vestal imagination, perfectly matched her father's immaculate uniform. She remembers that his hat was grandly positioned over his handsome face. She remembers that the brim of his hat cast a soft shadow over his radiant green eyes. And she remembers that he saluted other sailors as they saluted him, a poetic gesture of marked time, symmetry of motion, and mutual respect.

Her father held her small hand as they approached the gang plank to board a large ship, equipped with towers and gunnery. Suddenly, she was terrified of the ship and its steep walkway. She looked up at her father, hoping that he could read her mind and know her heart's deepest desire. To her surprise and delight, he could read her mind! Her father scooped her up into his strong arms and carried her on board the big ship. Rarely in her life since has the little girl felt that safe, that understood, and that loved by a man. *She learned that day that true love exists.*

The little girl would not see her father again until 1966, the day before his surgery for cancer of the larynx. She remembers wanting to play tic-tac-toe on his neck, where an ink grid had been drawn by the doctors to monitor radiation treatments. Yet, somehow the little girl knew that it was no time for games.

When next she saw her father, his neck and chest were bloody and raw and sewn together like a quilt with zippers. She remembers gurgling machines made of tubes and metal that were hooked into her father and that sucked red and yellow liquids from his body. She remembers hearing her father cry even though he could not speak. She no longer has a memory of her father's voice, but she imagines that it was strong and sure and always spoke the Truth.

She would learn many things from her father over the course of her life, as she watched him struggle with a disfigured body, a dismantled life, and a disintegrating relationship with God. To the outside world, her father appeared to overcome his life-altering affliction. Lacking speech after his operation, her father relied on his other talents and became a great writer. He focused his considerable intellect on resolving the Cold War and writing about the U.S. and Soviet Navies. At the zenith of his career, he was appointed a statesman by President Reagan and his books contributed to the fall of communism. Nevertheless, her father was haunted by what might have been and blamed God for taking his dream of a brilliant military career.

Somewhere deep inside, the girl, now a young woman, knew the Truth about her father. She knew that he never stepped foot inside a church again after his surgery. She knew that he accepted his handicap fearlessly, but that he never totally conquered the challenges that God handed him. She also knew that her father never forgave God for the loss of his military career.

In the year 2000, her father was buried at the cemetery at the Naval Academy in Annapolis, Maryland, an honor only bestowed upon admirals in the U.S. Navy. The woman, now a mother of three, reflected on the irony of her father's life and death. He was buried where his dream began. He wanted to be a naval officer and he ultimately received an admiral's burial. Therefore, did he not fulfill his mission on the Earth plane? She hoped that he was in heaven watching this tribute to his life and that he was proud of the twenty-one gun salute which ripped through the air and her heart just nine short years ago.

Signs have floated about this woman her entire life – indications of God's plan, hints of greater occurrences, and synchronous whispers of larger Truths.

So, too, on her mother's side of the family, did the little girl learn of God's ever-presence. Her mother's family had migrated to Canada from Hungary and Czechoslovakia before the start of the first World War. Everything was left behind, except for the money sewn into the children's skirts and knickers for safekeeping on the long boat ride from France to Canada. Eventually, the little girl's grandparents managed to buy a farm in Saskatchewan, and they scratched out a paltry existence based on hard work and faith in the Almighty. They made their underwear from sugar sacks and blood sausage from entrails. Nothing was wasted and nothing was taken for granted. Respite was found only one day a week – on Sunday in God's house.

The girl's mother grew up on that farm. In the fall, she dreamed of stone temples hidden underneath the wood pile. In the winter, she prayed that the hand-built, horse-drawn sleigh would reach the school; otherwise, she would be boarded in town for the winter, since education was deemed paramount. In the spring, her mother rejoiced at the arrival of the baby farm animals, although once, in her innocent zeal, she accidentally strangled a gosling that she pressed too close to her heart.

Yet, it was during the summer months away from school that her mother's imagination took flight and God was most available. Her mother, as a young girl, would play "crucifix" in the vegetable garden. She would stand for hours with her arms outstretched, wanting to know how Jesus felt on the cross. Her mother would stay in that position until her arms ached or until her parents ordered her to stop. Years later, the girl's mother would consider becoming a nun and devoting her life to God.

The little girl vividly remembers her grandmother's stories and her mother's lessons – Slavic myths and legends from the Old Country, which stood in glorious contrast to the *Children's Bible* stories read to her nightly by her mother. But sometimes her grandmother's tales of gypsies and magic had unhappy endings. To the girl's horror, evil sometimes prevailed in the *Bible*, as well. This confused the little girl. So when she started Catechism class she asked the nun why God would let bad people win. It was then that she learned: She was a sinner, too! The nun told her that when Eve disobeyed God, *everyone* became tainted. That is why God sent his only son to die on the cross. If Jesus hadn't paid for our sins, we would never get into heaven. These explanations only confused the girl more. She still wanted to believe that she was good, since God made her from his image. And she secretly hoped that God would judge her based on her own actions, not the mistakes or sacrifices of another.

Thus, the little girl wove her own tapestry of Truths about God – a colorful blending of ethnic fable mixed with Christian parable. And the more she learned about the heroes and heroines who fought in God's name to vanquish evil, the more she prayed for the chance to perform a great mission herself. The little girl was truly blessed to grow up in such a rich environment of feminine energy and spiritual devotion, with a mother and grandmother who gave her the gifts of love and wisdom. Additionally, the two women gave the girl yet another gift – a fantasy world in which she could escape from her father's painful recovery and emotional abandonment.

In the early 1970s, the girl, now a teenager, witnessed some unexpected changes in her mother. Suddenly, her mother was attending college and wearing go-go boots and hot pants. She saw her mother's anguish when Walter Cronkite reported nightly on the Vietnam War, and she watched her mother applaud when President Nixon resigned. Then, she noticed her mother reading strange books about God and talking to other grown-ups about reincarnation and a prophet named Buddha. The girl also heard her mother and a group of women arguing with a priest about birth control! Then, her mother stopped going to church altogether. When she asked her mother why they no longer went to church, her mother said that the Catholic Church had hurt many people and had purposely concealed important Truths about God. Rarely in her life since has the girl felt that curious, that inspired, and that proud of a woman. *She learned that day that it takes true grit to seek the Truth about God.*

The girl would not explore religion again for another twenty years – not until a great crisis arose in her own life. In the meantime, she would learn many things from her mother, as she watched her mother struggle with a domineering husband, a yearning for freedom, and a growing relationship with God. To the outside world, her mother appeared to betray her husband and her church, as she divorced them both. Lacking self-confidence after her divorce, her mother cloistered herself and became a great reader. She focused her considerable compassion on the Holy Wars and researched the barbaric history of religion. At the nadir of her studies, she was beyond despair and worried about the fate of humanity. Nevertheless, her mother was haunted by what should have been and asked God how she might contribute to the rise of true spirituality.

Somewhere deep inside, the girl, now a mother herself, knew the Truth about her own mother. She knew that her mother never stepped foot inside a church again after her divorce. She knew that her mother accepted her isolation bravely and that she eventually overcame the challenges that God handed her. She also knew that her mother's unshakable devotion to God helped restore her mother's fragile faith in mankind.

In the fall of 2003, the woman's mother was at work contemplating her upcoming retirement, when a strange message appeared on her computer monitor – one she had never seen. Unexpectedly, a puppy with a bone in its mouth ran across the screen. The bone turned into a scroll, which slowly started to unfurl. On the scroll was written a long list of career paths, arranged in alphabetical order. Her mother stared at the computer screen in amazement as the cursor lighted on "Archeology." The puppy then asked, "Are you interested in this career?"

As her mother stared at the question on her computer screen, the woman began to write a book on religion. She was secretly hoping that her mother, who was nearing retirement and loved to research religion, would help her "dig" into the five primary religions to "unearth" universal Truths about God.

Signs have floated about this woman her entire life – indications of God's plan, hints of greater occurrences, and synchronous whispers of larger Truths.

When my own marriage imploded in 1994, a renewed cycle of family pain commenced. Anyone who has gone through a divorce has their own excruciating story to tell, so I won't belabor mine, except to recall that I felt naked, raw, and exposed. Then I went numb. I had three small children who needed a mother, not a zombie. At some point, I bought a T-shirt which read, "What doesn't kill us makes us stronger." I wore that shirt as a mantra while I struggled to regain my courage and clarity. Exactly how, though, does a devastated soul start a new chapter in life?

In my case, I started my recovery by mimicking what I had been taught by my parents. Like my father, I felt depression and anger, and I viewed my involuntary isolation as a challenge from God. Like my mother, I felt guilt and fear, but I interpreted my newfound freedom as an opportunity to get to know myself and God better. However, in the early stages of my healing, my mind just ruminated and I realized I needed outside help.

Luckily, I found a very good therapist. Thank you, again, Georgeanne. She guided me until I saw how my past had contributed to the demise of my marriage, but also how it could strengthen me for my future. And she helped me reconnect with my inner self to resurrect buried talents and forgotten dreams.

I was fortunate because I had some freedom. I already had stopped practicing law after my third child was born. After the divorce, my ex-husband agreed that I should stay home with our youngest child until he started school. As a result, I had three glorious years to extend myself and explore the Universe. I used this time wisely and my soul began to flourish. I tried *anything* that allowed me to use my imagination. In my spare time, I acted, wrote plays, and started to paint. And I read voraciously, always choosing books on religion.

I started with *The Holy Bible*, and I read it cover to cover. Next, I focused on Buddhism, and I learned the seminal Four Noble Truths. Thereafter, I studied Hinduism and read the life-affirming poetry contained in *The Bhagavad Gita*. I also read about Mahatma Gandhi, the Hindu revolutionary who practiced Jesus' methods of non-violent social defiance. And for extra fun, I read fictionalized religious books like *The Celestine Prophesy*, by James Redfield. I absolutely adored this book in which the protagonist finds ancient manuscripts that date back to 600 B.C.E. The earliest manuscript contains the "First Insight," which states that humanity will reach the next level of spirituality "when we become conscious of the coincidences in our lives." It was at precisely this juncture in my life that I met an amazing man named Sam.

As a good starting point for the Truths contained in this book, I wish to underscore the fundamental Truth enunciated in *The Celestine Prophesy* and recognized by our greatest prophets, philosophers, and scientists:

There are no coincidences.

Psychologist Carl G. Jung came to accept this Truth after a lifetime of clinical work and after exploring the dream state and the unconscious aspects of the mind. Dr. Jung also studied the *I Ching*, a Chinese divination system created approximately 400 B.C.E., and utilized by the great Chinese philosopher Confucius. In his *Foreword* to the English translation of the *I Ching*, Dr. Jung explained the Truth of non-coincidence, which he called "synchronicity."

> *Synchronicity takes the coincidence of events in space and time*
> *as meaning something more than mere chance, namely, a peculiar*
> *interdependence of objective events among themselves as well as with*
> *the subjective (psychic) states of the observer.*

> *I Ching* or *Book of Changes,* Translated by Richard Wilhelm

In other words, apparent random acts or chance encounters which stem from a confluence of seemingly independent factors are really interdependent and related events. Consequently, we should pause at those unique moments of synchronicity and ponder the deeper meaning of what, at first blush, appears mere coincidence.

Regarding Sam, he came into my life at *exactly* the right moment to guide me to the next stage of my spiritual journey. As it happened, a mutual friend introduced me to Sam right after I finished reading *The Celestine Prophesy*. Immediately, I was taken by the kind nature and gentle wisdom of this Indian gentleman, so much, in fact, that I felt comfortable telling him that I was on a spiritual quest. Instinctively, I sought Sam's advice, somehow sensing that he was a teacher.

What is fascinating about my first encounter with Sam was its synchronicity. First, Sam was looking for a personal assistant, not a student, and I did not need to go back to work yet. Despite these crossed purposes (or because of them), the Universe brought us together. Second, to my surprise (but not coincidentally), I discovered that Sam lived in my neighborhood! Finally, I learned that Sam is a disciple of Zoroastrianism, the oldest monotheistic religion practiced today, and that he liked to teach Zoroastrian and other spiritual philosophies. *In sum, our paths crossed at a precise and pivotal moment due to the perfect alignment of interdependent events.*

Let us joyfully acknowledge that there are no coincidences in life. For instance, it is no coincidence that each of the major prophets came to Earth exactly when we needed them most. Nor is it a coincidence that each major civilization received its own unique prophet, who arrived in a specific region of the world and who spoke to people in their own language. It also is no coincidence that each prophet accepted and then expanded upon the message of his predecessor.

What skeptics call a coincidence, initiates call a sign, and believers call a miracle.

Furthermore, it is nothing short of miraculous that during the last century mankind has pieced together the course of evolution, reclaimed vast amounts of history, developed stupendous scientific advancements, and retrieved revealing ancient records, such as the *Dead Sea Scrolls*, all of which add to our "spiritual database." These recent discoveries, just like God's prophets, appeared at the very moment in time we needed further clarification and direction.

Similarly, Sam entered my life just when I wanted and needed further spiritual guidance. After meeting Sam, my soul took flight! We would get together once a week to study and meditate together. He had a vast library of books covering the five primary religions and the more mystical branches of each. He also had books on his religion, so I was able to learn about Zarathustra, who many scholars believe was the first prophet to renounce paganism and teach about the one true God. In fact, many Christian schol-ars believe that the three wise men who visited the baby Jesus were Zoroastrian priests.

During this time of intense spiritual awakening, I lovingly referred to Sam as my "guru." There is no doubt in my mind that I was meant to study with Sam and that he has enriched my life and my faith in God beyond measure. He would later say that he learned much from me as well, in accordance with the sage principle that the teacher also learns from the student. In Truth, however, he is yet another soul to whom I owe an enormous debt of gratitude. Thank you, Sam.

It was during this soulful time with Sam that I first came across the Buddhist term **Saddha.**

> *Thus it [Saddha] is faith .... Its characteristic is trusting. Its function is to clarify .... It is manifested as non-fogginess, or it is manifested as resolution.*

> *Visuddhimagga*, Chapter XIV, Verse 140

Saddha is often incorrectly translated into English as meaning "faith," but a more literal interpretation of the word is "trustful confidence." You see, Sam, as well as all the great prophets whom God sent to us, taught that one should not have blind faith in any of the man-made religions. To the contrary, the prophets all taught that the soul only grows through personal experience and actual contact with the Almighty. In other words, no one can "teach" you about God. Rather, you have to encounter and feel God's presence on your own, otherwise the soul learns nothing. Sure, the mind is capable of memorizing religious history and learning rote dogma about God. However, true spiritual enlightenment can only be achieved through: (i) careful study; (ii) prayer and meditation; and (iii) the loving practice of good works while the soul is on the Earth plane. *Saddha* also begs the question:

Are we human beings who occasionally have spiritual experiences, or are we spiritual beings who currently are having human experiences?

Saddha favors that latter interpretation of the human condition and offers a methodology for connecting with God while the soul is locked on the Earth plane. Thus, *Saddha* is a spiritual process that should never end until the moment we die. *Saddha* is faith based on personal growth and a desire to know God. It is faith that builds upon itself as new revelations are understood and mastered. It also is faith based on Truth, as opposed to faulty man-made constructs or outdated interpretations of God. In short, *Saddha* is a powerful and healthy mindset that compels the soul to embark on a quest for spiritual

Truth and which allows the soul to glimpse the multi-dimensional and multi-faceted primordial source we call God.

Most importantly, though, the *Saddha* process promotes a personal relationship with God. We should be talking to God one-on-one and without the intervention of third parties, regardless of their man-made credentials. We also should be open to new and more sophisticated information and experiences. The ultimate goal of *Saddha* is to reach an unshakable faith in God. We accomplish this goal through intellectual curiosity, spiritual freedom, inner peace, and collective harmony. Consequently, *Saddha*, in many ways, is the antitheses of an inherited religious belief system, since faith based on Truth and personal experience must necessarily supersede man-made ritual. The Hindus and Buddhists explain this well-worn path to Truth or *Dharma* thus:

> *A single oneness of pure love, of never-straying love for Me [God]; retiring to solitary places, and avoiding the noisy multitudes; a constant yearning to know the inner Spirit, and a vision of Truth which gives liberation: this is true wisdom leading to a vision. All against this is ignorance.*

The Bhagavad Gita, Chapter 13

Once I grasped the core concept of *Saddha*, I was ready to commence an advanced stage of my spiritual development. My curiosity and courage were at an all-time high and I no longer felt any lingering loyalty to my inherited religion of Catholicism. I was open to new information and Truth was now paramount. It was during this phase of my journey that I devoured the *Dead Sea Scrolls* and the "heretical" *Gnostic Gospels*, which the early Catholic bishops ordered burned. I also read about the prophet Muhammad and Islam. It seemed to me that none of the five primary religions were accomplishing either their explicit goal of teaching mankind about God, or their implicit goal of leading mankind to inner and outer harmony. During my meditations, I imagined that I was climbing a mountain of Truth with Sam by my side. I was happy and fulfilled. For the first time in my life, I felt at peace with myself and I knew that my life had real purpose. *And then my spiritual journey came to a screeching halt.*

Quite simply, I had run out of time. My youngest son was in first grade and my ex-husband had carried the family financially long enough. With tears of sadness and gratitude, I reluctantly said goodbye to Sam. Then, I put on my pantyhose and a Joe Banks suit and joined a small law firm in rural Virginia. After three glorious years of soul growth, I was a lawyer again.

To say that it was difficult for me to practice law again would be a gross understatement. I craved my lost freedom and spiritual connectedness. I could not even continue my soul quest at night, since my new boss wanted me to become proficient in two areas of the law I had never studied. Consequently, in my "spare time," when I wasn't at work or taking care of my children, I was reading massive treatises on immigration and bankruptcy law. Ugh! There wasn't time anymore to read about God. I started to feel trapped and anxious and I began to question the meaning of my life again. *Why was I here and what did God want of me?*

Since therapy had helped me in the past, I thought that it would be wise to explore my thoughts with a counselor. However, because I wanted to discuss spirituality, I decided to seek a therapist with a more holistic approach. Not coincidentally, I found her. She actually was a practitioner of Japanese Reiki. She used both massage techniques and counseling as a means to sift through the subconscious. In a nutshell, she believed that a soul in conflict can readily release internal strife if the different sources of discord are each given a separate "voice." Therefore, she instructed me to move about her living room and sit in different locations as I spoke, as a way of encouraging debate amongst those various parts of myself which were in conflict.

For example, Laura the Lawyer would sit in one chair and pronounce the importance of contributing financially to the family unit. Laura the Mother would sit on the couch and address the impact of work on the kids' scholastic and emotional needs. Then, Laura the Truth Seeker would sit cross-legged on the floor and decry the lack of time to focus on God and soul growth. Eventually, Laura the CEO spoke and wisely synthesized the divergent voices. That Laura was able to prioritize conflicting needs and create unity of purpose. In 1998, that Laura decided it was in everyone's best interest to move to the country.

> *The land into which you are crossing for conquest is a land of hills and valleys that drinks in rain from the heavens, a land which the Lord your God looks after; His eyes are upon it continually from the beginning of the year to the end.*
>
> *Deuteronomy*, Chapter 11:11

The farm was intended to serve and has to this day served many important purposes. First, the farm provides me and my children with a direct connection to the Earth. The land is rich with purple flowers and aromatic mint. The woods contain magical trees and a variety of wildlife. Even the soggy bottomland is special, as it brims with unseen spirits. When I am outside working on the farm – digging, planting, mowing, or building – time just flies. I am able to "Zen out" and become one with the Universe. In Truth, working on the farm is a form of meditation which I wanted to teach my children. I also wanted to instill in them a work ethic based on the fine discipline of physical labor. In sum, the farm has provided us with many adventures. Moreover, my children now have learned that nature is the best place to find and be with God.

It is no secret that Jesus held this same view. He loved to preach in the wilderness and, in particular, near the Sea of Galilee. He rejected the formal atmosphere of the Jewish Temple, which he felt had been tainted by the Roman occupation, the corrupt Jewish priests, and the merchants who were allowed to sell their wares on the Temple grounds. He also believed that the priests, acting as intermediaries between the people and God, were an impediment to Truth. Consequently, he encouraged his followers to seek God on their own, anytime and anywhere. Consider this quote attributed to Jesus in one of the more famous *Gnostic Gospels*:

> *Split a piece of wood, and I am there.*
> *Lift up the stone, and you will find me there.*

Gospel of Thomas, Verse 77

Second, the farm connects me and my family to the magical properties of flowing water. A major creek bisects the property and reminds me daily that I must stay in my "flow" and help my children find theirs. When Sam first taught me to meditate, he told me to envision myself floating down a river. He said that to find my particular flow, I shouldn't fight the current by trying to swim upstream, nor should I try to hurry downstream by swimming with the current. Instead, I should simply float with the current and enjoy my unique path to God. He also said that once in my flow, I would see the signs that are meant for me. Or, as my Chinese friend Siu says, the creek has major Feng Shui!

Third, the vast variety of wildlife and farm animals that we see on or near the farm provides us with yet another constant reminder of God's magnificence. I keep binoculars handy and not a day goes by that we don't see a cardinal, groundhog, owl, raccoon, fox, hawk, deer, beaver, horse, or praying mantis. Without overstating the matter, the farm is our own private Garden of Eden.

Lastly, my soul desperately needed the farm. During my modified Reiki sessions, one voice emerged above the rest. Laura the CEO knew what to do. If I had to practice law again, she was determined to make the best of the situation and the farm was a sensible compromise. It allowed me to retain my connection with God in the Ethereal plane even as I was forced to deal with my clients' problems on the Earth plane. During those years when my studies were temporarily suspended, the farm provided me with a spiritual sanctuary and a multitude of signs to remind me daily of my Creator. The prophet Muhammad explained the beauty of nature thus:

> *Do they not look at the birds, held poised in the midst of the air and the sky? Nothing holds them up but the power of God. Verily in this are Signs for those who believe.*

> *The Holy Quran*, Sura XVI, Verse 79

Let us segue for a moment to a topic that will help explain the critical importance of the farm to my spiritual growth. More importantly, however, this segue will explain why *everyone* needs a special place to be with God.

During college, I took some psychology classes and learned about Abraham Maslow's "Hierarchy of Needs." Basically, Dr. Maslow theorized that mankind cannot and does not reach higher level needs and goals until basic level needs are satisfied. Specifically, Dr. Maslow hypothesized that most of us cannot even approach self-actualization (i.e., spiritual growth), until our lower level needs, like physical comfort, are met. Here is a list of the Hierarchy of Needs in descending order:

Self-Actualization Needs
Self-Esteem Needs
Belonging and Love Needs
Safety Needs
Physiology Needs

Dr. Maslow believed that our basest needs stem from physiological or bodily functions. For example, if your belly is rumbling due to hunger, you don't care about going to the opera or watching a football game. You want food! Similarly, if your home isn't secure or you fear physical attack, you probably won't concern yourself with fellowship. In other words, it's pretty hard to love your neighbor if you fear him. It also is difficult to establish healthy self-esteem, which is dependent on loving relationships, unless you live with supportive and nurturing people.

Finally, in order to reach the top rung of the Hierarchy of Needs, Dr. Maslow asserted that you must first have all your material needs met, be in relative harmony with those around you, and feel your own self-worth. Only then will you have the energy, freedom, and trustful confidence to reach your full potential as a human being, insist on Truth in all matters, and commence a meaningful relationship with God – the process I call *Saddha*.

In large part, Dr. Maslow was right. For most people, inner and outer peace, the quest for spiritual Truth, and the yearning to know God are lofty goals that we have the luxury to embrace only *after* our lower level needs are completely satisfied. However, this is not always the case. Some people are able to self-actualize without the satiation of material plane needs. In fact, all of the prophets renounced material plane needs in order to focus exclusively on God.

For instance, Buddha almost starved himself to death during his quest for spiritual enlightenment, Jesus was practically a vagabond for three years during his ministry, and Muhammad constantly faced personal danger to accomplish his mission. In addition, many people in third world nations are able to self-actualize and maintain faith in God, despite a lack of basic resources and the presence of military conflict. Such people are exceptions to Dr. Maslow's theory, since they are able to self-actualize without having their physical and material needs met.

There is another exception to Dr. Maslow's theory worth mentioning. It is quite common for people to turn to God when they have hit "rock bottom." We all know someone who, in their darkest hour, relied exclusively on their faith in God when faced with total chaos and destruction. In such dramatic situations, it is irrelevant where you fall on Dr. Maslow's Hierarchy of Needs. People who have never given God a second thought often reach out to God to help them cope with overwhelming odds or insurmountable pain. In this way, total desolation sometimes prompts a person to "leapfrog" into the proper mindset for the *Saddha* experience. At such moments, a brave person looks at himself in the mirror, begins to explore the meaning of life, and either reaches out to God for assistance or rejects God altogether.

Regarding my own spiritual development, phantom childhood pain and a failed marriage threw me headlong into an abyss. My feelings of utter privation and abandonment prompted me to seek help and answers from God. The quote by Maxine Hong Kingston at the beginning of this chapter underscores the point that great loss necessarily pushes the soul into a debate with God. That is how I started my adult exploration into spirituality. I hit rock bottom and I turned to God. Fortunately, I was able to connect to God and to myself. As a result, I learned firsthand that I can rely on God and my higher self to recover from loss. And because I learned these lessons myself, I now know that God is ever available to me whenever I need additional strength. That is *Saddha* – a faith that grows through actual experience and the quest for spiritual Truth.

On the other hand, when I met Sam, I was primed to self-actualize for different reasons. For the most part, I had recovered from my divorce and my dysfunctional family history. I was no longer in crisis, my lower level needs were met, and I had the energy and freedom to meaningfully explore myself and the Universe. Therefore, I was the perfect candidate to model Dr. Maslow's theory. I was ripe for advanced spiritual work because I had the necessary foundation for self-actualization.

When I went back to work, however, I was afraid I would backslide down the Hierarchy of Needs, which is why I bought the farm. I was convinced that if I moved to a spiritual location on the Earth plane, I would stay in contact with my higher self and God in the Ethereal plane. Thankfully, my plan worked. The farm kept me in my flow and connected to God.

Consequently, I firmly believe that everyone needs a special place to commune with God. If you don't have a special place in your home that you can dedicate to meditation, try going outside and allow nature to connect you with the Almighty. Your spiritual juices will start to flow and you will become more open to the *Saddha* process of soul growth. This Truth is well known to Hindu and Buddhist masters:

> *Day after day, let the Yogi practice the harmony of soul: in a secret place,*
> *in deep solitude, master of his mind, hoping for nothing, desiring nothing.*
>
> The Bhagavad Gita, Chapter 6, Verse 10

By the turn of the millennium, I again found time to devote to my studies. I continued my research and focused heavily on the New Age movement. Initially, the New Age materials held my attention, since their central focus is that positive energy produces positive results. I enjoyed reading about those people who can tap into their own divinity and the power of the Universe to manifest whatever they seek, even while their souls are locked on the Earth plane. In fact, I have met such people and they truly are masters of the

Universe. Therefore, let us acknowledge another fundamental Truth relayed to us by our greatest prophets, philosophers, and scientists:

Our thoughts, words, and deeds create *karmic* consequences.

On a lesser scale, Sam had taught me how to manifest my desires through a variety of meditative techniques and the results were astounding. I lived in a beautiful oasis. My kids were happy, healthy, and excelled scholastically. My male partner enhanced my life in wondrous ways. My friendships were mutually loving and generous, and I started a women's group to generate even more positive energy. *What more could I possibly want or humbly ask from the Universe?*

Honestly, all I wanted was more time to devote to my spiritual quest and to God. So that is what I visualized during my meditations. Not coincidentally, by the end of 2001, a series of events intersected on my behalf which allowed me to stop practicing law – at least for a while. Talk about synchronicity! Once again, I was free to pursue Truth, explore my life's purpose, and connect with the Supreme Being.

It was at this juncture that I kicked my Saddha experience into overdrive. I dove back into my research and decided to focus exclusively on the major prophets. By this time, I had more than a strong suspicion that mankind had perverted the Truths relayed by God's messengers. So, I reread *The Holy Bible* to review the teachings of the Jewish and Christian prophets. I also revisited Hinduism in my quest for *Dharma*. Additionally, I studied the teachings of Buddha and of reincarnated *bodhisattvas*, like the Dalai Lama. Then, I read one of the most inspiring texts ever written: *The Holy Quran*. As we shall see in the next chapter, the horrific events of September 11, 2001, are the results of religious fanaticism, not the teachings of Muhammad.

After reading many of the holy scriptures, I focused on the next level of source material, which includes the records of those historians and religious leaders who lived contemporaneously with the prophets or during critical periods of religious history. It is important to understand that the holy books are just one source of information about the five primary religions. Indeed, there are many historical accounts that deserve further illumination. For example, the Roman historian Flavius Josephus chronicled the Jewish wars and the destruction of the Jewish Temple in 70 c.e. Additionally, the early Christian bishops, like Clement of Alexandria, Irenaeus, and Valentinus, wrote histories and letters which describe the early Christian sects. By comparing these accounts, one gets additional insight into the Jewish interpretation of Jesus' life as a false "Messiah," versus the Christian interpretation of Jesus' death as a divine "Savior."

After sifting through ancient historical records for spiritual Truth, I started reading the current research produced by our best *independent* scholars. The Truth is that vast amounts of recorded history have been tainted, destroyed, or fictionalized by church affiliated historians who were expected to support orthodox religious interpretations. As a result, the church sanctioned histories went unchallenged for thousands of years. Today, however, we have secular historians with academic freedom who are taking a fresh look at religious history. Not surprisingly, these unbiased scholars have different interpretations of critical religious events. Consequently, as a Truth seeker myself, I tend to favor the independent historians and trust that their accounts are more accurate.

Unfortunately, this new breed of religious scholar tends to produce exceedingly cerebral research. In other words, most independent historians write on an academic level for their peers. For example, there is a world-renowned scholar named Robert Eisenman who has dedicated himself to uncovering the Truth about Jesus' brother, James "the Just." Dr. Eisenman also is a foremost authority on the recently published *Dead Sea Scrolls*, some of which pertain to the era when Jesus and James lived. Contrary to the Catholic version of history, this new research proves that James was the *actual* brother of Jesus and that it was James, not Peter, who led the early Christians after the crucifixion. Unfortunately, this seminal work on James, which is entitled, *James the Brother of Jesus*, is more than one thousand pages long! Obviously, most people don't have the time to read this book, which is made even more difficult because the professor assumes we all have a total grasp of Roman, Jewish, and Christian history from 100 B.C.E. to 100 C.E. Thus, one of my goals in writing this book is to accurately summarize the work of the secular scholars so that more people may learn the Truth about orthodox religion.

By the end of 2003, my quest for spiritual Truth had led me to some startling conclusions regarding the five primary religions. Sadly, my suspicions had been born out, since much of the spiritual Truth professed by our greatest prophets is now buried under faulty man-made dogma. I was grateful, though, that I now understood how and why spiritual Truth was being smothered. And I began to share what I had learned with my friends and family, who also were astonished and appalled by my research.

By the end of 2003, my enchantment with the New Age movement had ended, as well. Although I still practiced many of the New Age methods for drawing positive energy into my life (i.e., classic Hindu and Buddhist techniques), I began to feel uncomfortable. New Age theology teaches that by raising our own consciousness, we vicariously elevate the Universe. However, based on my research, I knew that the self-centered focus of the New Age movement was undeniably at odds with the lessons of the major prophets, all of whom preached the Truth that selfless acts of charity for others is the true path to heaven. Frankly, I was starting to feel guilty. *Was it really "okay" to focus only on my own spiritual enlightenment?*

Let me give you a perfect example of how New Age teachers contradict God's prophets, all of whom taught that unconditional love and good works are required for salvation. Recently, I caught one of the most famous (and prosperous) New Age leaders giving a seminar on television. After proselytizing about the importance of allowing *only* positive influences to enter one's life, he proceeded to describe some techniques for blocking negative energy. He then recited the voice message that is recorded on his telephone answering machine, which goes something like this:

> *If you are calling with good news and positive energy, please leave your message at the tone and I will return your call. However, if you are calling with a problem that will ruin my day or create negative energy in my life, please call Dr. Phil.*

It seems to me that the New Age movement targets those people who are just starting spiritual quests. As a result, I worry that some New Age advocates take advantage of those souls who have recently left orthodox religions (for valid reasons), but who are unsure what to do next. Incidentally, I thank God that I met Sam at that stage of my spiritual journey. Otherwise, I might have been charged a fee to "connect to Source" or to "manifest the abundance of the Universe."

To summarize, I am uncomfortable with the New Age emphasis on individual attainment. The Truth is, self-empowerment is just one of the stages that a soul must pass through to reach spiritual enlightenment. I have witnessed firsthand how an emphasis on "self" can produce nothing more than an inflated ego or a desire for more material plane "stuff." Thus, I disagree with those New Age leaders who fail to teach that the ultimate goal of enlightenment is spiritual unity. For these reasons, I cannot align myself with the mainstream New Age movement either.

I suspect that Dr. Maslow also would take exception with the New Age emphasis on self. He would say that self-actualization occurs *after* a person satisfies his physical and material needs. He also would argue that self-actualization comes *after* a person attains positive self-esteem. Moreover, Dr. Maslow would say that enlightenment is attained only *after* a person releases ego, which is a human concept the soul willingly discards once it is ready to merge with the Sublime. In sum, the top rung of Dr. Maslow's Hierarchy of Needs seems to exceed and may even conflict with the goals of the New Age movement. More to the point, however, God's prophets would disapprove of this self-centered theology.

The great messengers of Truth all taught that mankind's Earth plane needs and desires are irrelevant at best, a huge distraction at least, and an evil temptation at worst.

We are not here for material plane gain. The holy books are quite clear on this score. Indeed, the way we graduate from this plane is by perfecting ourselves, not by indulging our desires or feeding our egos. If we wish to attain union with the Supreme Being, we must prove ourselves worthy by loving each other and sharing what we have with our less fortunate neighbors. So says Jesus, one of the ascended Masters:

> *Sell your belongings and give alms. Provide money bags for yourselves that do not wear out, an inexhaustible treasure in heaven that no thief can reach nor moth destroy. For where your treasure is, there also will your heart be.*

> *Gospel of Luke*, Chapter 12:33

My intent here is not to single out the New Age movement for scorn. On the contrary, I trust that the true leaders of the New Age will soon appear. Rather, my point is that I have searched high and low for fifteen years and I still cannot find one religion practiced by mankind today that has remained faithful to God's messages of Truth.

With regard to the five primary religions, it is apparent that none of them has updated the Truths relayed by the prophets. Strangely, it's as though time stood still after the prophets died. Consequently, most people are following religions that were created thousands of years ago by primitive, superstitious, and uneducated civilizations. We deserve much more from our religions. We deserve the Truth, as relayed thousands of years ago by the prophets plus all the new Truths that mankind has discovered since the prophets died. Hence, a "good" religion, just like faith, should evolve and grow via the *Saddha* process.

One of the happiest discoveries I made during the course of my research was that all the prophets agreed on the "basics." In fact, as we shall see in the next chapter, the prophets delivered many synchronous messages. For example, all the prophets taught that mankind has three basic obligations while on the Earth plane: (i) we should maintain faith in the one true God; (ii) we should obey universal Truths (a/k/a God's laws), such as the Jewish Ten Commandments; and (iii) we should love our fellow man by practicing charity and good works. Muhammad explained these obligations perfectly in *The Holy Quran*.

> *All who obey God and the Apostle are in the company of those on*
> *whom is the grace of God – the Prophets who teach, the sincere lovers*
> *of Truth, the witnesses who testify, and the righteous who do good;*
> *Ah!What a beautiful fellowship!*

> *The Holy Quran*, Sura IV, Verse 69

Another interesting observation I made during the course of my studies is that God disseminates Truth a little at a time. Indeed, I think God reveals Truth on a "need to know" basis. First, consider the fact that none of the prophets professed to have total knowledge. Rather, each of them humbly delivered mere pieces of the puzzle. Second, many teachers have provided us with astounding Truths. Thankfully, we have been blessed with great philosophers and scientists, in addition to the prophets. Thus, many souls have added to mankind's database of spiritual knowledge, which I will refer to as God's **Tower of Truth**.

Frankly, it only makes sense that God would deliver Truth to us piecemeal. Just consider how long it takes us to accept and adapt to new information (e.g., human evolution). Moreover, because we tend to receive and discover spiritual data on a sporadic basis, it also makes sense that it is our job to put all the puzzle pieces together. Thus, not only are we capable of formulating a cohesive and meaningful picture of Truth, I believe it is our sacred responsibility to do so.

During the last century, in particular, we have made incredible scientific discoveries. We also have systematically verified all sorts of historical information. At this point, we have proven that we are intellectually capable of solving many of life's mysteries on our own. However, the issue is whether we are morally and spiritually sophisticated enough to manage all this new data. Quite probably, our continued survival will depend on it.

Just as importantly, though, we need to assimilate and synthesize all these exciting new Truths so that we can fashion a more contemporary and sophisticated understanding of God. The time has come for us to update our Tower of Truth and adopt a new spiritual belief system. In fact, this work is long overdue. The Truth is that God granted us astounding intellectual abilities so that we could experience the thrill of creation ourselves. Mystics ascribe this divine power to the *"masculine half"* of God. In addition, God graced us with free will and a conscience so that we could assume the duty of making moral and wise decisions. Spiritualists associate this divine power with the *"feminine half"* of God. The bottom line is that instead of helping humanity understand and manage the divine gifts bestowed upon us by the Supreme Being, the five primary religions are creating confusion on the planet by refusing to accept new Truths from and about God.

In the remainder of this book, I will demonstrate how and why the man-made religions have either forgotten or are purposely ignoring their essential purpose, which is two-fold:

1. Religion was supposed to assist mankind in developing a personal relationship with God by encouraging the dissemination of Truth and by leading us toward higher spiritual vistas.

Instead, religion historically has attempted to control the masses by asserting an absolute right to interpret the holy scriptures, by instituting barriers to our individual communion with God, and by suppressing both ancient and new Truths.

2. Religion was supposed to model for us and remind us, on those occasions when we succumb to laziness or selfishness, that we should demonstrate compassion and love for each other by performing good deeds.

Instead, religion historically has attempted to divide mankind into separate theological camps by emphasizing trivial differences, by promoting intolerance, and by sanctioning the use of force to undermine opposing religions.

Until mankind is ready to admit that religion has failed to meet these two important goals, the majority of people on this planet will not progress spiritually. Sadly, most people are being led astray by the very institutions that should be preserving and protecting the Truth about God.

Truly, I have been unable to find one man-made religion that is fulfilling its mission.

Therefore, as a starting point for spiritual reform, we all need to be more educated about the five primary religions created by mankind. If I do my job properly, this book will help disseminate major Truths that have been purposely hidden or manipulated throughout history. Nothing is more important than the preservation of Truth, for it is ignorance that renders us blindly obedient and spiritually confused.

> *Under the influence or control of ignorance, there is no possibility of*
> *a permanent state of happiness. Some kind of trouble, some kind of*
> *problem, always arises. So long as we remain under the power of*
> *ignorance, that is, our fundamental misapprehension or confusion about*
> *the nature of things, then sufferings come one after another, like ripples*
> *on water.*

His Holiness the Dalai Lama, *The Four Noble Truths*

As I wound down my research, I began to meditate on why I had spent so many years pursuing spiritual Truth. Was it simply for my own benefit or my own curiosity? I should have been at peace, since I had achieved my goal of unearthing the Truth about the primary religions. But for some reason I felt anxious, as though I had missed something. So I asked God again, "What is my mission in this lifetime?" *And this time God answered.*

It is now clear to me, due to the extensive research I have conducted and the tremendous blessings God has bestowed upon me, that I am obligated to share what I have learned with as many people as possible. Therefore, I have accepted as my mission the task of showing how and why the five primary religions have become flawed and are now detrimental to our collective spiritual evolution. My earnest hope is that this book, which contains a condensed account of all my research, provides the critical information the reader needs in order to evaluate the current state of orthodox religion.

Thus, this book should prompt you to start questioning your religion, just as I began to question mine fifteen years ago. I respectfully submit that it is healthy to question your religion. It is *not* the same exercise as questioning God. In fact, exploring the underlying Truth of religion should help you expand your faith and bring you even closer to God.

As you begin this exercise, please realize that God did not create any of the religions. Rather, the five primary religions were crafted by men after the prophets died. Some of these men had pure motives, but others did not. I implore you to open your minds and your hearts to this regrettable yet undeniable Truth.

Finally, if the information contained in this book makes you feel unsettled or confused, please keep reading. Rest assured that I have undertaken this project with the utmost care and humility. At a minimum, please trust that I am a Truth seeker and have no ulterior motive for writing this book. In Truth, there have been many moments when I wanted to abort this mission, as it has taken its toll on me and those I love. Nevertheless, that which I have vowed I will pay.

> *And the Lord appointed a great fish to swallow Jonah, and Jonah was in the stomach of the fish three days and three nights.*
>
> *Then Jonah prayed to the Lord his God from the stomach of the fish, and he said, "I called out my distress to the Lord, and He answered me. ... For Thou hadst cast me into the deep, into the heart of the seas .... Water encompassed me to the point of death. ... While I was fainting away, I remembered the Lord; and my prayer came to Thee, into Thy holy temple. Those who regard vain idols forsake their faithfulness, but I will sacrifice to Thee with the voice of thanksgiving. That which I have vowed I will pay. Salvation is from the Lord.*
>
> *Then the Lord commanded the fish, and it vomited Jonah up onto the dry land.*
>
> Jonah, Chapter 2

CHAPTER

THE MAJOR PROPHETS AND WHAT THEY TAUGHT

But what is the mission of apostles but to preach the Clear Message? For We assuredly sent amongst every people an apostle, with the command, "Serve God and eschew Evil."

Of the people were some whom God guided, and some on whom error became inevitably established. So travel through the earth and see what was the end of those who denied Truth.

The Holy Quran, Sura XVI, Verses 35, 36

In today's world, we must face the sad reality that there exists massive confusion and outright war over the nature of God, God's plan for mankind, and mankind's obligations to God and to each other. It is my hope that this chapter, in particular, will provide a basic understanding of how mankind *should* have grown spiritually. God has not left us in the dark as to how we are supposed to be evolving. Rather, God has given us many signs and sent numerous prophets to help guide us toward the Truth. Frankly, there is no justification for our aberrant behavior.

For those of you who love history, now might be a good time to flip to the Appendix entitled *Brief History of the Major Events in Human Evolution, Politics, and Religion.* Others of you may find the Appendix tedious, but I encourage you to read it because it provides a quick historical backdrop for the amazing messengers we are about to study.

For those of you who may elect not to read the Appendix, allow me to summarize: Mankind's history is barbaric and terrifying. It is riddled with human weakness and human error. Moreover, if the "good guys" are winning, it is by a slim margin at best and at a very great cost. *The most disturbing fact of all, though, is that our greatest mistakes have involved lethal conflicts over which religion is the closest to God.*

Therefore, before we delve into the prophets and their incredible lessons of Truth, let us pause at the outset to begin contemplating *why* mankind has experienced so much division. Clearly, a loving God would not want us to be prejudiced, intolerant, malicious, or homicidal. Ideally, we should be using our intellect, empathy, and vast resources to create a utopian world. Why then are we so entrenched and isolated along ethnic, national, economic, and religious lines?

In my opinion, evil action is the direct result of perverse desires. Mostly, evil stems from two cardinal sins: greed and pride.

Unbridled greed leads to an obsession with money and material possessions. Undaunted pride leads to an obsession with power and world domination.

Whenever our most pathetic and self-serving instincts outstrip our best and most altruistic emotions, chaos reigns. History shows that we have repeatedly followed corrupt leaders down self-destructive paths. Certainly, there have been great bearers of light, such as the prophets we will soon discuss. However, history is replete with examples of mankind's failure to discern Truth and fractionalize along religious lines. This is not the path God intended for us. God wants us to recognize Truth and love each other. I suspect that we are a grave disappointment to our Creator at this juncture in time, as there simply is no excuse for the way we continue to treat each other.

As the Appendix shows, after the prophets died the manmade religions and political systems became corrupted over time by leaders who suffered from greed and hubris. In fact, religion and politics are so intertwined that it is practically impossible to separate the two. Religious leaders have used monarchs and even democratic leaders to spread their version of God's message to the exclusion of all others, while the nobility and politicians have used religion to perpetuate their control over the masses and advance new systems of government.

But the end never justifies the means, and therein lie the seeds of man's corruption. Too many religious and political leaders have used any means necessary to reach their goals and the Truth has been bastardized in the process.

Unfortunately, we, the laity and the governed, have followed these flawed leaders all too willingly. Only rarely do we revolt against injustice and lies. Throughout history, mankind has remained in tainted religious organizations and broken political systems rather than heed God's messages, take responsibility for ourselves and our world, and refuse to follow perverse orders. For this sin of laziness, we have been punished mightily.

We, the "common people," need to understand that many of our leaders are corrupt. Indeed, so many of them are unfit to lead that we must stop giving them unquestioned power. We need to turn inward for answers and then act for mankind's universal betterment. No longer can we afford to view each other as disconnected strangers who practice different religions or who live in foreign countries. Our world is getting smaller every day and we must start banding together or face dire consequences.

Luckily, God periodically sends us spiritual teachers whom I will refer to as "Prophets." These Prophets were sent to help us understand the nature of God, the meaning of our creation, our duty to achieve peace on the Earth plane, and how to attain salvation in the Ethereal plane. In addition, the Prophets were not sidetracked by the same material plane obsessions that pervert so many of our religious and political leaders. These souls were pure and, if you believe in reincarnation, were probably on their last visit to the Earth plane. They came with a mission and with God's blessing to help us learn how to control and master our lower emotions so that we could become worthy to join God in heaven.

If we go to source material and the research compiled by objective historians, we learn that *all* the major Prophets were divinely inspired beings who pronounced messages from God. Nevertheless, they did not deliver their messages in the same way. God sent us different Prophets so that each race would receive its own special message from a person they could trust and in a manner that would make sense to that particular culture. Also, since there was no mass communication at the time of the great Prophets, it seems logical that God would send multiple Prophets to different locations on the planet.

For example, Moses spoke to the Jewish people and Buddha spoke to people living in the Asian continent. Naturally, therefore, Jews are going to prefer the messages delivered by Moses and Asians are going to prefer the messages spoken to them by one of their brethren. Moreover, each culture is going to prefer a holy scripture written in a language and in a style that its people can readily understand. Hence, God sent various Prophets for different parts of the world, and God inspired multiple holy scriptures for different cultures.

> *We have, without doubt, sent down the Message: And We will assuredly guard it against corruption. We did send apostles before thee amongst the religious sects of old: But never came an apostle to them but they mocked him.*
>
> The Holy Quran, Sura XV, Verses 9–11

In addition, each successive Prophet built upon and improved the messages of the previous Prophets. So not only did God send us messengers to impact each major civilization, God also made sure that each Prophet further clarified and refined the lessons of his predecessors. Thus, as mankind became more enlightened, the Prophets' messages became more sophisticated.

It is fascinating to realize that every time a major Prophet came to us, we got another piece of the puzzle! And each time we got a piece of the puzzle, God wanted us to process the new information and add it to our collection of holy literature. God did not intend for each culture to develop in a vacuum, divided from or scornful of each other. God knew that one day we would improve our methods of communication and that we would debate and dissect religion. **Consequently, I believe we were supposed to build a spiritual Tower of Truth, which should include all of the Prophets' lessons.**

It is only logical to assume that God wants us to assimilate all of the Prophets' messages, since each Prophet added to the collective Truth about God. Similarly, it appears that God wants us to ponder additional holy texts, such as the fifty-two recently discovered *Gnostic Gospels* and the 870 fragmented *Dead Sea Scrolls*, some of which were written at the start of Christianity. Otherwise, why would these documents have been revealed to us? My argument is the same one used by Christians to defend the haphazard manner in which *The Holy Bible* was put together. Typically, Christians state that the "Holy Spirit" inspired the Catholic bishops to choose the four gospels of the *New Testament*. Fine. Maybe so. However, the fact that we now have unearthed additional religious texts which contain a different slant on Jesus' mission tells me:

1. God now wants us to read these newly discovered religious texts that have been safely stored and left untouched for two thousand years; and
2. Mankind now is ready to handle additional Truths and proceed to the next level of collective spiritual development.

Once we accept the harmonious concept that each Prophet built upon and improved the messages of his predecessors, we will be ready to embrace their combined wisdom. Moreover, we will come to realize that we already possess answers to many of our most complex questions. Just like Dorothy in *The Wizard of Oz,* who had magical ruby red slippers which could transport her home, we possess the tools we need to propel us closer to God. But first we need to synthesize the messages of the great Prophets and start building a unified spiritual belief system. It won't be an easy task, particularly given the divisiveness of the five primary religions. Nevertheless, it is a job we must undertake because we stand at a critical juncture in human history.

Therefore, as you read this chapter, consider how we might update our Tower of Truth. At a minimum, we should incorporate *all* the ancient religious texts and *all* the spiritual Truths preached by the major Prophets. Thereafter, we should add the philosophical and scientific Truths revealed to us since the beginning of recorded history. Finally, we should adopt a more contemporary definition of God and of God's plan for mankind which reflects the sophistication of the 21st Century. We will then experience a shift in the collective consciousness, otherwise known as a new **Spiritual Paradigm.**

My research has led me to conclude that humanity has passed through four Spiritual Paradigms and that we are on the verge of a fifth:

First Spiritual Paradigm:	All is One	pre-Big Bang
Second Spiritual Paradigm:	The Great Mother	25,000 B.C.E. – 5000 B.C.E.
Third Spiritual Paradigm:	Gods and Goddesses	5000 B.C.E. – 50 C.E.
Fourth Spiritual Paradigm:	God the Father	50 C.E. – 2000 C.E.
Fifth Spiritual Paradigm:	Era of Enlightenment	soon, hopefully!

We will discuss these Spiritual Paradigms in more detail throughout the book. For now, please enjoy this first chapter, which contains concise yet poignant summaries of what each of the major Prophets taught. These summaries also will show how, over time, God's messages have gotten clearer and clearer. As we shall see, all the Prophets agreed that the basic formula for salvation includes the commencement of a private journey of faith, the process I call *Saddha, plus* the performance of good works while on the Earth plane. May we all benefit from the following lessons of Truth, Love, and Light.

HINDU PROPHETS

The Hindu religion started approximately 2500 B.C.E. in the Indus Valley, which is located along the Indus River in the country now known as Pakistan. The name comes from the Persian word *hindu* and the Sanskrit word *sindu*, which mean "river." The Indus Valley settlement was one of four original great river civilizations, collectively referred to as the **Cradles of Civilization**. The early Hindus lived along this fertile river valley and worshiped a variety of deities, depending on their preference. As a result, the early Hindu gods and goddesses were quite varied. By 1500 B.C.E., people from central Asia, known as Aryans, migrated to the Indus Valley, bringing with them new customs and religious practices. The map in the Appendix shows the Indus Valley civilization circa 3000 B.C.E.

The Hindus have no records of their ancient Prophets but their oldest holy books, the *Vedas*, were composed over time beginning in 1500 B.C.E. The *Vedas* set out rituals and mantras for making sacrifices to the Hindu gods and goddesses. The *Vedas* also contain mankind's first record of the primary message imparted to us by all the Prophets: *Love thy neighbor.*

> *Bounteous is he who gives unto the beggar who comes to him in want of food and feeble. ... Let the rich satisfy the poor implorer, and bend his eye upon a longer pathway. Riches come now to one, now to another, and like wheels are ever rolling.*
> *The foolish man wins food with fruitless labor: that food – I speak the Truth – shall be his ruin. He feeds no trusty friend, no man to love him. All guilt is he who eats with no partaker.*

The Rig Veda, Hymn X, Verse 117

Thereafter, another series of Hindu holy scripture was written called the *Upanishads*. Historians believe that these texts were started around 800 B.C.E., about the same time that the Hebrews were writing the earliest books contained in the *Old Testament*. The *Upanishads* further refine the Hindu religion and teach how to develop an ideal inner state of being through meditation and yoga. Additionally, the *Upanishads* teach that there are four goals in life:

1. *Kama* – the pursuit of legitimate pleasure;
2. *Artha* – the pursuit of legitimate worldly success;
3. *Dharma* – the obligation to follow the religious laws and traditions and to seek the balance of the Universe (also translated as Truth); and
4. *Moksha* – release from the material plane and the end to reincarnation.

Hindus believe that the attainment of the higher self (*atman*), leads to wisdom (*jnana*), and to the Truth of the Universe (**Dharma**). However, in order to achieve this higher wisdom, the Hindus believe that the attractions and distractions of the Earth plane must first be satisfied. Sound familiar? That's because Abraham Maslow's Hierarchy of Needs closely mimics the ancient Hindu model of self-actualization.

Thus, the Hindus believe that the self eventually rises above the temptations of the material plane to seek the ultimate Truth about the life and death cycle and God. It is at this stage that Hindus renounce worldly interactions and detach from material obsession. By detaching entirely from the Earth plane, Hindus believe that the consequences and rebirths associated with action (*karma*) are neutralized. During this final stage of development, the self is firmly grounded in Truth (*Dharma*), reaches the status of an enlightened one (*brahmin*), and attains immortality. However, in order to achieve immortality, the self must undergo a learning process that sounds remarkably similar to the *Saddha* process of soul growth.

> There are three branches of the law: Sacrifice, study, and charity are the first; austerity the second; and to dwell as a brahmacharin [student] in the house of a tutor, always mortifying the body in the house of a tutor, is the third. All these obtain the worlds of the blessed; but the brahmin alone obtains immortality.

> *Chhandogya Upanishad*, 2 Prapathaka 23

Once liberation from the material plane is accomplished, the soul ascends to one of the multiple levels of heaven. However, the highest realms of heaven are reserved for the gods and goddesses. For instance, the paramount creator god, **Brahman** (a/k/a Prajapati or the "One"), resides in the highest heaven called *Bramaloka*.

Thus, the goal of Hinduism is to stop the cycle of reincarnation (*samsara*), and the way to attain release from the material world (*moksha*) is to perfect the self (*atman*).

The Bhagavad Gita is another text that forms part of the Hindu collection of holy books. It was written about 300 B.C.E., and is part of Book VI of an epic poem called the **Mahabharata**, the world's longest poem (100,000 verses). *The Bhagavad Gita* is a story about a warrior named Arjuna who questions the consequences of taking another person's life. The god Krishna explains to Arjuna that liberation from rebirth is based on *karma*. Krishna also explains that the holy path requires exploration of self, the use of pure reason and logic, and the absence of action based on improper desire (i.e, greed or pride). The essence of the poem is that God, in the form of the Hindu deity Krishna, resides in all things. This new concept – that we already are part of God and that God dwells in each of us – will be repeated later by all the major Prophets.

> *He who sees that the Lord of all is ever the same in all that is, immortal in the field of mortality – he sees the Truth. And when a man sees that the God in himself is the same God in all that is, he hurts not himself by hurting others: then he goes indeed to the highest Path.*

The Bhagavad Gita, Chapter 13, Verses 27, 28

Around 200 B.C.E., a legendary and perhaps mythical king named **Manu** added to the Hindu holy texts by composing a code called the *Manava-Dharma-Sastra* (the *Laws of Manu*). Manu's code contains additional rules for appropriate social behavior and sets forth the four stages of a man's life (the *asramas*). The first level of spiritual growth is the "student" stage, during which boys are assigned a mentor to study the *Vedas*. At the second stage, a young man is described as a "householder," and he is expected to marry and produce a son. The third level of spiritual development is called the "forest dweller" stage, when a man in old age should focus on religious obligations in isolation. The fourth level of enlightenment is called the "ascetic" stage, when a man may evolve into a priest (*brahmin*).

It is important to note that Manu's code only applied to men and only to the men in the top three social castes. During Manu's time, women were not deemed worthy of achieving spiritual enlightenment. In Chapter Four, we will discuss more thoroughly the negative import of these rules as they relate to women.

Manu also helped define the Hindu **caste system**, which separates humans into different social and spiritual categories. The Hindus divide people into hundreds of classifications, which can be summarized into five basic groups as follows:

1. *Brahmins* – The priests who enjoy the status of being in the highest caste;
2. *Ksatriyas* – The ruling class, governors, warriors, and landowners;
3. *Vaisyas* – The middle-class workers and merchants;
4. *Sudras* – The lower social class, whose members perform the most humble and menial tasks, such as farming and carpentry; and
5. *Dasyus* (a/k/a "untouchables") – This is the lowest class, whose members are permitted to perform only the dirtiest jobs, such as the handling of corpses and the removal of waste.

The caste system, which still exists today except in the more cosmopolitan areas of India, has many unfair rules. There are prohibitions against inter-caste marriage, eating or handling food outside of one's caste, and even making bodily contact with a person from a different caste. Additionally, a person may not attempt a vocation outside of his caste, although recently untouchables have been permitted to perform menial labor due to economic necessity. However, most Hindus still subscribe to the belief that once a person is born into a certain caste, he cannot change his social or spiritual status except through reincarnation which is based on *karma*.

> *Action, which springs from the mind, from speech, and from the body, produces either good or evil results [karma].*
>
> *In consequence of the many sinful acts committed ... a man becomes in the next birth something inanimate ... a bird, or a beast ... [or] he is re-born in a low caste.*

> *Manu Smrti*, Chapter 12, Verses 3, 11

The Hindus ascribe the many facets of God to a variety of deities. The earliest *Vedas* state that there are thirty-three gods, but hundreds more were added over time. Today, most Hindus worship: (i) **Brahma,** the god who created the Universe; (ii) **Vishnu,** the god who preserves the Universe and who also incarnated as **Krishna,** the god of love; and (iii) **Shiva,** the god of destruction and time, who represents the cycles of rebirth (*samsara*).

Hindus also believe that God has female aspects, and they worship a variety of goddesses known as *devas*. The primary goddesses include: (i) **Mahadevi,** the greatest goddess (considered Brahma's equal), who generates feminine energy (*shakti*); (ii) **Sarasvati** (consort to Brahma), the goddess of wisdom and intellectual pursuits; (iii) **Lakshmi** (consort to Vishnu), the goddess of wealth and prosperity; (iv) **Parvati** (wife of Shiva), a benevolent emanation of the *shakti* energy; (v) **Durga,** the most fierce goddess whose powers are invincible; and (vi) **Kali** (a/k/a Tara), another goddess who fights to destroy evil and who is invoked by practitioners of the ancient Hindu ritual known as *Tantra*, which involves the use of masculine and feminine sexual energy.

Even though Hinduism unnecessarily separates God's various aspects into multiple deities, the religion teaches the elementary Truth that God contains both masculine and feminine energies. As we shall soon see, the only other primary religion to grasp this fundamental concept is Islam. However, despite the fact that Hinduism celebrates the feminine half of God's energy by assigning certain deities the female gender, the religion does not fully honor the duality of God's energy. Instead, the Hindu religion patently favors men and accords women a second-class social and spiritual status. We will explore this theme in more detail in Chapter Four, since the subjugation of the feminine half of God is a systemic problem with each of the five major religions.

Before we depart Hinduism, there are two more Prophets of this religion well worth mentioning. The first is **Guru Nanuk,** who was born in 1469 C.E., in the area known as Punjab. Nanuk was raised in a Hindu family but he had a Muslim tutor. As a result, Nanuk studied both Hinduism and Islam. One day while walking in the forest, Nanuk had an encounter with God and returned three days later transformed. Thereafter, Nanuk reportedly could perform miracles and he once raised an elephant from the dead. At the age of thirty, Nanuk renounced all of his worldly possessions and began to preach the inclusive message, "There is no Hindu, there is no Muslim." By this, he meant that neither religion was entirely correct regarding the nature of God, and that mankind need not subscribe to any particular religion in order to attain salvation. Instead, Guru Nanuk taught that mankind attains enlightenment through perfection of the soul. After his death, the Guru's followers adopted a new religion called **Sikhism.**

Guru Nanuk greatly expanded upon the Hindu and Islamic concepts of God. He agreed with the Hindus that the soul reincarnates and that we have multiple opportunities to perfect ourselves prior to joining with God. Therefore, he disagreed with the Muslims on the issue of just one earthly experience for the soul. However, he rejected the multiple deities of Hinduism and agreed with the Muslims that there is only one God. He also denounced the Hindu caste system and the religious monopoly of the *brahmin* priests. Moreover, he chastised both religions for their unfair treatment of women.

Guru Nanuk is aces in my deck. In fact, the theology espoused by Guru Nanuk genuinely resonates with me – in my heart, my mind, and my soul. Unfortunately, the current resurgence of religious fundamentalism has not left the Sikhs in India and Pakistan unscathed, and there are reports of Sikh leaders who are undermining the most basic and precious tenets of this religion, such as the social and spiritual equality of its male and female members. Thus, like all of the manmade religions, this one would do well to follow the teachings of its Prophet, Guru Nanuk, who warned of five cardinal sins: (i) *kan* (lust); (ii) *krodh* (anger); (iii) *moh* (earthly attachment); (iv) *lobh* (greed); and (v) *ahankar* (pride).

As previously stated, I believe that greed and pride are mankind's two most destructive tendencies. Indeed, I have gone even further and labeled greed and pride the "two cardinal sins," since those who succumb to self-ishness and megalomania harm not just themselves, but also the rest of us. Sadly, anyone who is obsessed with material plane rewards has yet to start the *Saddha* process of enlightenment, which is the surest path for attaining spiritual salvation. The unknown author of *The Bhagavad Gita* stated this Truth succinctly and beautifully:

> *When a man dwells in the solitude of silence, and meditation and contemplation are ever with him; when too much food does not disturb his health, and his thoughts and words and body are in peace; when freedom from passion is his constant will, and his selfishness and violence and pride are gone; when lust and anger and greediness are no more, and he is free from the thought "this is mine"; then this man has risen on the mountain of the Highest: he is worthy to be one with Brahman, with God.*

The Bhagavad Gita, Chapter18, Verses 52, 53

The other important Hindu Prophet I want to mention is **Mahatma Gandhi,** who was born in 1869 C.E. Although historians have yet to accord Gandhi Prophet status, I think he has earned this distinction, as evidenced by his rare spiritual gifts and his insightful leadership skills. Gandhi was born into an Indian family that was part of the Hindu *vaisya* caste (i.e., merchants). He was raised in India but was educated as a lawyer in Great Britain. He lived during a critical time in India's history and led a passive revolt against the British to regain India's independence.

More importantly for our purposes, however, Gandhi defied the Hindu caste system, which he viewed as unfair to the lower classes and to women. Thus, he realized that the Hindu religion needed to be updated, and he devoted himself to improving and modernizing Hinduism. His favorite saying was, "God is Truth." By this he meant that God is the foundation for moral righteousness. He also believed that we each have a piece of God's divine authority within us, which he attributed to the conscience. He often spoke of the "inner voice" that keeps us on the path to Truth. He also said that if each of us shared our inner voice with our perceived enemy, Truth would be revealed and we would never fight.

> *Truth is said to be the one unequaled means of purification of the soul. Truth is the ladder by which man ascends to heaven, as a ferry flies from one bank of a river to the other. ... It is Truth which makes the Earth bear all beings, Truth which makes the sun rise. It is through Truth that winds blow and that waters flow. Truth is the greatest gift, Truth is the*

most efficacious kind of austerity, Truth is the highest duty in the world,
thus it has been revealed to us .... Speak Truth and discard falsehood. It
is through Truth that thou shalt attain heaven.

Narada-Smrti, Chapter 1, Verse 210

In addition to studying Hindu holy scripture, which includes the above passage entitled *The Power of Truth*, Gandhi studied *The Holy Bible.* In particular, Gandhi loved to read the Christian *New Testament,* as he greatly admired the non-violent reform methods utilized by Jesus. Gandhi ultimately adopted Jesus' passive approach to encouraging social and spiritual reform. As a result, the occupying British government and the highest caste members of his own religion were no match for the political and spiritual liberation movement led by Gandhi.

Incidentally, even though Gandhi cherished the *New Testament* lessons, he did not convert to Christianity. Therefore, Gandhi is not in heaven according to fundamentalist Christians. They argue that Gandhi had the opportunity to accept Jesus as a personal savior, but declined. Indeed, even for those Christians who believe in a "back door" to heaven – for people who have never heard of Jesus but who lead good lives (i.e., the "Aborigine exception") – Gandhi does not cut the mustard because he knew about Jesus but did not convert to Christianity. It is sad that so many people are confused about how a soul achieves everlasting peace. With regard to Gandhi, he certainly has ascended to the Ethereal plane to be with Jesus and all the other masters who lovingly performed good works and attained spiritual enlightenment while on the Earth plane.

Lastly, it is important to note that during the 20th Century there was an influx of Hindu teachers (*yogis*) to the western world. These *yogis* greatly impacted the spiritual growth of many Americans and helped to shape the New Age movement. An example of such a *yogi* is **Swami Satchidananda** (1914–2002), who immigrated to the United States in the 1960s and became a famous teacher of Hindu philosophy and yoga. In fact, Swami Satchidananda became so popular that in 1969 he was the opening speaker at Woodstock. And in 1986, he opened the Light of Truth Universal Shrine (LOTUS) in Virginia, a spiritual community dedicated to teaching advanced Hindu philosophies. True *yogis* are not necessarily Prophets, but they do reach the sublime state of enlightenment while on the Earth plane.

JEWISH PROPHETS

For theological reasons, I am listing the Persian Prophet **Zarathustra** after Hinduism and before Judaism because many religious scholars credit Zarathustra with being the first Prophet to record his belief in one god and because his teachings undoubtedly influenced the Jewish religion. Zarathustra was born in Persia, the land now known as Iran, at a time when his people and the neighboring Semites (i.e., Arabs) still believed in multiple deities. Unfortunately, there is much debate amongst scholars regarding when Zarathustra was born. His legendary birth date is 6000 B.C.E., but most historians now believe that he lived between 2000 and 1500 B.C.E., based on the style of his literature. Despite the uncertainty concerning his birth date, Zarathustra is acknowledged as being one of the first or second Prophets to worship God, whom he called **Ahura Mazda**.

Although Zarathustra believed in God, he also taught that there is an evil force at work in the Universe. He believed that we have the innate ability to overcome evil by taking personal responsibility for our own development and by performing good works. In addition, Zarathustra predicted the end of the Earth and he taught that a divine leader named Saoshyant would come to lead the righteous in a final battle against evil. Thus, some historians also credit Zarathustra with being the first Prophet of a monotheistic religion to predict a Messiah figure. Moreover, Zarathustra preached that mankind would be judged by God after an apocalyptic battle to determine the soul's afterlife. At the time of judgment, if good deeds predominate the soul would go to paradise, but if bad deeds predominate the soul would go to a place of torment.

When the Persian Empire flourished in 500 B.C.E., **Zoroastrianism** became the official religion of the empire. The Persians were quite tolerant of other faiths and allowed the Jews to return to Jerusalem and rebuild their Temple. As a result of this intermingling of cultures, historians believe that Zoroastrianism further influenced the Jewish (and later Christian) religions, since it is around this time period that certain sects within the Jewish faith started to believe in a Messiah and an after-life. Additionally, scholars think that the three wise men who visited the baby Jesus were Zoroastrian priests (*magi*).

Zoroastrianism was almost stamped out when the Muslims invaded Iran in 638 C.E. Some Zoroastrians sought refuge in India and became known as the **Parsis**. Historically, Zoroastrians have been very tolerant toward other religions and my guru Sam is no exception. Finally, it is interesting to note that

Zoroastrianism appears to be making a huge comeback in Iran among the younger and more cosmopolitan Iranians.

The Jews have many "official" Prophets, all of whom are described in vivid detail in the *Tanach*, which is the Jewish version of the *Old Testament*. It is important to note, however, that the *Tanach* and the Christian *Old Testament* are slightly different. Therefore, in order to explain the significance of the Jewish Prophets, we will delve into their *Old Testament*. First, however, we need to review the most current research on how the *Old Testament* scripture was preserved, written, and eventually compiled into one collection.

The Jewish *Old Testament* is broken into three main groupings: (i) the *Torah*, which contains the first five books supposedly written by **Moses**; (ii) the *Nevi'im*, which consists of historical accounts and the books of the Prophets; and (iii) the *Ketuvim*, which is comprised of the psalms and the wisdom books. Orthodox Jews accept as fact that Moses, their most revered Prophet, wrote the *Torah* and that the history contained in the *Old Testament* is accurate. Additionally, Orthodox Jews still believe in the literal meaning of the *Old Testament* parables and wisdom books. However, many Jews have come to accept the research of independent historians, who now agree that Moses did *not* author these five books. In fact, secular scholars believe that Moses was long gone by the time the first *Old Testament* stories were written.

The first book of the *Old Testament* is called *Genesis*. It purports to describe how God created the Earth and mankind, which the early Jews believed occurred in 3761 B.C.E. Originally, historians believed Moses lived around 1250 B.C.E., but there is new evidence to suggest he lived as early as 1450 B.C.E. Moreover, some scholars think Moses may have been the **Pharoah Akhenaten** (*circa* 1350 B.C.), who tried to convert the Egyptians to monotheism. Regardless, most scholars concur that the earliest possible dating for the *Torah's* composition is 900 B.C.E., well after Moses' death. Historians also seem to concur that the *Old Testament* was not put together into one collection of scripture until roughly 90 C.E. Therefore, the Jewish part of *The Holy Bible* was written over the course of one thousand years and was based, primarily, on oral history. That means the authors of the *Old Testament* were describing events more remote in time to them (i.e., the book of *Genesis*) than we are to the time of Jesus! Needless to say, we should assume that many of the stories contained in the *Old Testament* changed throughout the centuries prior to being recorded. Therefore, these stories should be read with a very careful and critical eye.

Now, let's look at some of the most famous and important sections of the *Old Testament. Genesis* starts with the creation of the Universe, the Earth, the seas, the plants, and the animals, which supposedly took God six days. Additionally, on the sixth day God created mankind.

> *Then God said, "Let **Us** make man in **Our** image, after **Our** likeness; and let **them** have dominion ...." And God created man in His own image; in the image of God created He him; **male and female** created He **them**. [Emphasis added]*
>
> *Genesis*, Chapter 1:26

To begin with, it is interesting to note that in the first Jewish version of creation, God was viewed as a *plural* entity and that man and woman were created *at the same time*. As we shall soon see, God also uses the plural mode throughout *The Holy Quran*. Some religious scholars have interpreted this plural and genderless reference as merely connoting the "royal We." However, I suspect that ancient man recorded the story of creation using the plural pronoun for a different reason – either as a remnant of the pagan belief in multiple deities, or in recognition of God's dualistic masculine and feminine energies, an elementary Truth that we will explore later.

In Chapter 3 of *Genesis*, a serpent tempts the woman into eating the forbidden fruit from the "tree of knowledge." He convinces her that, contrary to what God has said, she will not die if she eats the fruit. After **Adam** and **Eve** eat the fruit, "then the eyes of them both were opened," and they learn the difference between good and evil. Thereafter, God banishes Adam and Eve from the Garden of Eden so that they cannot also eat from the "tree of life" and become immortal. From this ancient story, the Christians will later adopt the view that mankind is inherently sinful. However, that is *not* the Jewish interpretation. Rather, most Jews understand that this parable merely illustrates: (i) God gave us the ability to seek knowledge and discern right from wrong; (ii) God gave us free will; and (iii) God holds us accountable whenever we choose evil over good.

The next main character in *Genesis* is **Noah**, who is nine generations removed from Adam, the first man. By Noah's time, mankind had grown so wicked that God decides to destroy all of mankind except for Noah, whom God describes as the only just man alive. God then instructs Noah to build an ark and only Noah, his family, and the creatures that Noah herds onto the ark are allowed to survive a world-wide flood. Thereafter, Noah's sons repopulate the Earth.

> *The sons of Noah who came out of the ark were Shem, Ham and*
> *Japeth. These three were the sons of Noah, and from them the whole*
> *earth was peopled.*
>
> *Genesis*, Chapter 9:18

Incidentally, at this point in the *Old Testament*, there is no mention yet of Judaism or any other religion, as Noah's descendants all appear to believe in God. It also is important to note that *all* of mankind is descendant from Noah according to this Jewish legend.

The next major event occurs hundreds of years later, when a man named **Abram** is born in Ur, a city located in the Arabian territory of Mesopotamia (present day Iraq). The time now is approximately 2000 B.C.E. Abram, who is ten generations removed from Noah and descendant from Noah's son Shem, is the man whom the Jews believe fathered their race and their religion. However, as just mentioned, the *Old Testament* reports that after the flood, Noah's sons repopulated the Earth, which would mean that *all* of mankind is from the same race. Consequently, the Christians and the Muslims view Abram as the patriarch of their religions also.

In *Genesis* Chapter 17, God directly communicates with Abram and enters into a covenant with him. God's agreement with Abram can be summarized as follows: *If Abram will follow God's instructions and acknowledge that God is the Supreme Being, then God will make Abram the father of a multitude of nations.* God also tells Abram that the entire world will be blessed because of the covenant God is willing to make with him. Abram accepts the terms of the covenant and God changes his name to **Abraham**, which means "father of nations." It is critical to know that in the *Old Testament*, God repeatedly refers to Abraham as the father of "nations," indicating, quite plainly, that Abraham would father more than one culture.

It also is important to know the historical backdrop of this era, so another peek at the Appendix is in order. In 2000 B.C.E., the Egyptian Empire was thriving. The Egyptians already had built the Sphinx and the great pyramids at Giza. Their multi-faceted religion was dominant and they controlled the northern African continent and the Middle East. At this time, there still was no Jewish religion; however, the term "Hebrew" was in use. **Hebrew** comes from the word *habiru*, which means "wandering people." Thus, during Abraham's time, the people who lived around Egypt were either Egyptians or Hebrews (wandering non-Egyptians), and most of the

Hebrews lived a tribal or nomadic existence. Most notably, though, the early Hebrews believed in multiple deities, just like the Egyptians.

In *Genesis* Chapter 12, God instructs Abraham to leave his home in Mesopotamia and travel to Canaan, which God states he will grant to Abraham and his descendants. Abraham takes his wife and his nephew Lot with him to Canaan. Eventually, Lot settles in the nearby land of Sodom, which God later destroys because of the sinful conduct of its inhabitants. However, God spares Lot and certain members of his family from the annihilation.

Meanwhile, Abraham and his wife Sarah have grown old and have remained childless. Sarah concludes that Abraham should have a child with their servant Hagar, an Egyptian woman. To Abraham and Hagar is born a son named **Ishmael**. God tells Abraham that he will bless Ishmael and make him the father of a great nation. The Muslims believe that they are descendant from Ishmael, as we will discuss in more detail at the end of this chapter.

Next, God tells Abraham and Sarah that they will bear a son, which they find hard to believe because of their advanced age. Yet, when Abraham is one hundred years old, Sarah miraculously gives birth to a son named **Isaac**. God then states that the covenant he made with Abraham will be continued through Isaac. Thereafter, Sarah becomes jealous of Hagar and Ishmael, and she demands that Abraham banish them. Although Abraham concedes, that is not the end of Ishmael. Indeed, God reaffirms his love for Ishmael and repeats that Ishmael shall father a great nation.

> And God said unto Abraham … "And also of the son of the bondswoman will I make a nation, because he is thy seed." And Abraham … took bread and a bottle of water, and gave it unto Hagar, putting it on her shoulder, and the child, and sent her away; and she departed, and strayed in the wilderness of Beer-sheba. And the water in the bottle was spent, and she cast the child under one of the shrubs. And she … lifted up her voice, and wept.
>
> And God heard the voice of the lad; and the angel of God called to Hagar out of heaven, and said unto her, "What aileth thee, Hagar? Fear not; for God hath heard the voice of the lad where he is. Arise, lift up the lad, and hold him fast by thy hand; for I will make him a great nation."
>
> *Genesis*, Chapter 21:12–18

I am very visual. If you are like me, a family tree will be exceedingly helpful in learning basic Jewish history. In the genealogy charts contained in this book, I will use dotted lines to indicate the passage of multiple generations and solid lines to show direct descendants.

JEWISH FAMILY TREE

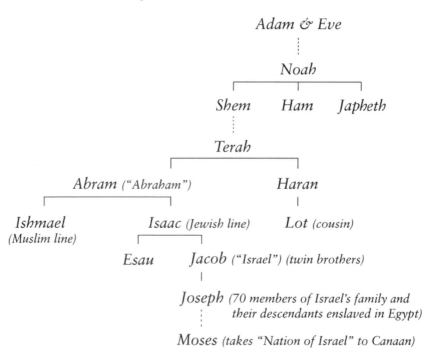

The story continues with Abraham's grandson **Jacob,** whom God again addresses directly. In *Genesis* Chapter 35, God tells Jacob that he shall benefit from the covenant made with Abraham and that Jacob's descendants shall multiply to create an "assembly of nations." Note that the *Old Testament* still is reciting that multiple nations will be honored by the Hebrew God. God then renames Jacob "**Israel,**" which means "one who prevails with God," and Jacob's sons and grandsons became the patriarchs of the **Twelve Tribes of Israel.**

One of Israel's sons, **Joseph,** later is appointed Governor of Egypt by the pharaoh after Joseph accurately predicts a great famine. As a result of the famine, Israel's family becomes destitute in Canaan. With the pharaoh's permission, Joseph grants his father and brothers some of the best land in Egypt to farm. Israel accepts the land grant and seventy members of the family migrate from Canaan to Goshen, part of the Egyptian Empire.

Unfortunately, the great famine continues after Israel's tribe settles in Goshen, causing even more problems for the family. Israel decides to strike a bargain with the pharaoh whereby Israel will give Goshen back to the

Egyptians in exchange for food and protection. As a result, Israel's family becomes serfs (i.e., tenant farmers). When the pharaoh dies, the new pharaoh enslaves the Jews. *So begins roughly four hundred years of slavery for the descendants of Israel.*

Enter **Moses**, who first appears in the next book of the *Old Testament* entitled ***Exodus***, wherein the Hebrew slaves are referred to for the first time as "the people of Israel." However, Israel is not yet a place, but a continued reference to Jacob, the grandson of Abraham. Moses supposedly authored *Exodus* and the other four books of the **Pentateuch**, which is another name for the first five books of the *Old Testament*. Today, though, even Jewish scholars will admit that the *Pentateuch* was written by rabbis and Prophets who lived between 950 and 450 B.C.E., and that the editing and compilation of the *Pentateuch* was not completed until 444 B.C.E.

Historians are unsure when Moses actually lived, but most place him around 1250 B.C.E. When Moses is born, the pharaoh orders the killing of all Hebrew baby boys, reportedly due to a Hebrew population explosion. Moses' mother places him in the Nile River and the pharaoh's daughter finds Moses and raises him as an Egyptian. After Moses is grown, he witnesses an Egyptian guard mistreating Hebrew slaves, which incites Moses to kill the guard. As a result, Moses must either flee Egypt or be exposed as a Hebrew and face certain death. So Moses escapes, joins a Hebrew tribe in Midian, and marries the Midian priest's daughter.

Detailed research has led scholars to conclude that Moses' new father-in-law, Jethro, worshiped a pagan god named El Shaddai (a/k/a Baal or El). El was a mountain god whom the Midians believed reigned over lesser gods. Some historians believe that Moses adopted this name for God because Moses associated God with mountaintops. For instance, Moses was on top of Mount Horeb when God first spoke to him, and Moses was on top of Mount Sinai when God gave him the Ten Commandments. Additional evidence for this theory comes from the Hebrew word for God, **Elohim**, which may be a derivative of the name El. Elohim and the Hebrew name for God, **Yahweh,** are used interchangeably for God's name throughout *Exodus*. Yahweh was later translated as **Jehovah**, the name most of us recognize. In sum, independent historians find it quite likely that when Moses married into the Midian Hebrew tribe, he adopted their name for God, which has now been handed down to us for over three thousand years.

In *Exodus* Chapter 3, God appears to Moses through an angel in a burning bush as Moses is tending sheep. God instructs Moses to return to Egypt, free the Hebrew slaves, and lead them back to Canaan. Moses and his brother **Aaron** eventually are successful in convincing pharaoh to release the Hebrew slaves, purportedly due to the miraculous powers given to Moses, including the ability to unleash a series of ten plagues on Egypt. The last of the ten plagues is the death of the first-born, during which God kills all the first-born Egyptian children. In *Exodus* Chapter 12, God instructs Moses to use lambs' blood to mark the Hebrew doors so that the plague will bypass the Hebrew families. The Jewish holiday of **Passover** commemorates this event.

After his son dies, the pharaoh relents and agrees to let the Hebrew slaves leave Egypt. Moses then parts the Red Sea and leads the freed slaves toward Canaan. During the journey, Moses reunites with his father-in-law, Jethro the Midian priest, and with his wife and children. *Exodus* Chapter 18 discloses that when Moses tells Jethro the story of their escape from Egypt, Jethro acknowledges that the Hebrew God is the greatest god of all. This is quite a revealing passage, as it indicates that other Hebrews still are pagan and worship multiple deities.

Moses then stops at the base of Mount Sinai. It is on this mountaintop that God speaks again to Moses and provides him with the **Ten Commandments** etched in stone. In the classic Hebrew translation, the Ten Commandments read as follows:

1. *I am the Lord thy God, who brought you out of the land of Egypt, out of the house of bondage.*
2. *You shall have no other gods besides Me. You shall not make a graven image, nor any manner of likeness of anything that is in heaven above or that is in the earth below, or that is in the water under the earth. You shall not bow down unto them, nor serve them. For I, the Lord thy God, am a jealous God.*
3. *You shall not take the name of the Lord thy God in vain.*
4. *You shall keep the Sabbath day holy.*
5. *You shall honor your father and mother.*
6. *You shall not murder.*
7. *You shall not commit adultery.*
8. *You shall not steal.*
9. *You shall not bear false witness against your neighbor.*
10. *You shall not covet your neighbor's house. You shall not covet your neighbor's wife, nor his male or female slaves, nor his ox or his ass, nor anything else that belongs to him.*

Exodus, Chapter 20:2–14

Thereafter, the Hebrews will place the stone tablets containing the Ten Commandments in a gilded box called the **Ark of the Covenant**. Later, when the Jews build the Temple in Jerusalem, the Ark of the Covenant will be kept in the "Holy of Holies," which is the innermost sanctum of the Temple. Today, the location of the Ark of the Covenant is unknown, but many legends have evolved regarding its secret location and its awesome powers.

In *Leviticus*, the third book of the *Old Testament*, God provides Moses with additional laws and instructions on almost every facet of daily life. The entire collection of Hebrew rules, which includes the Ten Commandments and the other instructions from God, is known as the "Mosaic laws." The Mosaic laws pertain to such diverse topics as: (i) marriage (men could have more than one wife); (ii) the treatment of slaves (Hebrews could even enslave other Hebrews); (iii) food preparation and ritual washing of the body; (iv) childbirth and sex; (v) property laws; (vi) specifications for the Temple that God wanted built in his honor; (vii) animal sacrifices; and (viii) criminal punishments (the penalty for blasphemy and working on the Sabbath was death). Incidentally, the Jewish **Sabbath** is Saturday, which is the seventh day of the Jewish week, not Sunday as practiced by Christians. Lastly, according to Jewish tradition, God continued to inspire devout rabbis who recorded their insights and modern interpretations of Jewish law in two other holy books called the *Talmud* (compiled in 1100 C.E. by **Rabbi Alfasi**), and the *Mishna Torah* (another codification of the *Talmud* written in 1200 C.E. by **Rabbi Maimonides**).

In *Numbers* and *Deuteronomy*, the last two of the five holy books included in the *Torah*, God leads the Hebrews, now called the "Nation of Israel," near the banks of the Jordan River, across from which is the "promised land" of Canaan. At God's command, Moses takes a census and identifies the twelve tribes of Israel and the land they shall receive. However, God states that Moses will not be allowed to enter Canaan because Moses once defied God during the forty year journey to Canaan. Thus, God instructs Moses to hand over leadership of the tribes to **Joshua**, who is charged with responsibility for fighting the other Arab tribes already living in Canaan. Thereafter, Moses dies at the age of one hundred twenty years, the last Jewish Prophet to ever see God.

> *Since then no prophet has arisen in Israel like Moses, whom the Lord knew face to face. He had no equal in all the signs and wonders the Lord sent him to perform in the land of Egypt against Pharaoh and all*

his servants and against all his land, and for the might and the terrifying
power that Moses exhibited in the sight of all Israel.

Deuteronomy, Chapter 34:10

In *Joshua*, the sixth book of the *Old Testament*, the Hebrews cross the Jordan River and commence fighting for Canaan. It is fascinating to note that God instructs the Hebrews *not* to fight some of the other nations that are descendant from Noah. Thus, certain nations are spared during the wars because they are viewed by the Hebrews as brethren (e.g., the nations descendant from Lot, Abraham's nephew). Strangely, God actively assists the Hebrews in taking the region. Literally, God helps the Hebrews conquer and vanquish their enemies.

> *Thus Joshua struck all the land, the hill country and the Negeb and the*
> *lowlands and all their kings. He left no survivor, but he utterly destroyed*
> *all who breathed, just as the Lord, the God of Israel, had commanded.*
> *And Joshua struck them from Kadesh-barnea even as far as Gaza, and*
> *all the country of Goshen even as far as Gibeon. Joshua conquered all*
> *these kings and their lands at one time, because the Lord, the God of*
> *Israel, fought for Israel.*

Joshua, Chapter 10:40

As a result of this first campaign, which lasts approximately seven years, many of the other Arab tribes already populating the area are displaced. Notably, however, the Philistines, who are known today as the **Palestinians,** are not conquered and manage to retain a strip of land along the Mediterranean Sea, the area still known as **Gaza.** It is truly tragic that today, three thousand years later, the Jews and the Palestinians still are fighting over this land.

In the next book of the *Old Testament* called *Judges*, God instructs the Hebrews to recommence fighting and take the remainder of the land around Canaan. However, instead of destroying the remaining inhabitants, the Hebrews spare their lives and make pacts with them. Eventually, the Hebrews start to intermarry with the pagan Arabs and even start to worship the pagan god Baal. God is furious that his instructions have been ignored and he decides to punish the Hebrews. Thereafter, the Jews are tormented and taken as slaves by their enemies, including the Philistines. In addition, the tribes of Israel start to fight amongst themselves. The result is that the Jews begin to form two kingdoms, the **Kingdom of Israel** in the north and the **Kingdom of Judah** in the south.

So the anger of the Lord burned against Israel, and He said, "Because this nation has transgressed My covenant which I commanded their fathers, and has not listened to My voice, I also will no longer drive out before them any of the nations which Joshua left when he died."

Judges, Chapter 2:20

After suffering years of torment for abandoning God, including the temporary loss of the Ark of Covenant to the Philistines, the children of Israel plead to God for assistance. In response, God chooses a young Hebrew man named David to rule over the Jewish tribes, which still are feuding amongst themselves. In approximately 1000 B.C.E., David is born into the tribe of Judah in the town of Bethlehem. As a young man, David kills a Philistine giant named Goliath, and he is crowned King of Judah. Eventually, **King David** unifies all the Hebrew tribes into one nation. King David also captures the holy city of Jerusalem. Lastly, King David is important for yet another reason: *As we will soon see, Christians believe Jesus is descendant from King David.*

Thereafter, around 950 B.C.E., David's son, **King Solomon**, builds the first Jewish Temple in Jerusalem and the Ark of the Covenant is moved inside. During much of King Solomon's reign, the united Kingdom of Israel prospers. However, after Solomon marries wives from other cultures, he commits sin in God's eyes by building altars to the pagan gods and goddesses worshiped by his wives. As a result, God punishes Solomon and the kingdom splits once again. The House of David loses control over the northern nation of Israel but continues to rule over the southern nation of Judah. The reader may want to refer to the Appendix again, which includes a Middle East map for this period.

Thereafter, the fighting between the two Jewish nations continues and calamities plague the children of Israel. In the north, the nation of Israel continues to worship idols; whereas, the House of David, which rules the nation of Judah in the south, remains loyal to God. Eventually, both nations are severely weakened by their civil wars. As a result, in 722 B.C.E., the Assyrians (Arabs) conquer Israel in the north and deport the Jews, who become the **"Ten Lost Tribes of Israel. "** Next, in 586 B.C.E., the Babylonians (also Arabs) conquer the nation of Judah and destroy the Temple in Jerusalem. It is during this time period that the Ark of the Covenant probably was lost.

In 538 B.C.E., the Persian Empire (Aryans) takes control of the region, which is now called **Palestine.** The Persians, who practice the Zoroastrian faith, are remarkably tolerant of other religions, and they permit the Jews to return to Jerusalem. By 516 B.C.E., the Jews have rebuilt the Temple and live in relative harmony with the Persians. However, when the Romans conquer Palestine in 63 B.C.E., the Jews, once again, lose control of their homeland. *Except for a brief period of time during a revolt against the Romans, the Jews will not regain control of Palestine until 1948 C.E., when the nation of Israel is created at the end of World War II.*

The adversity of the Jewish people was predicted by many Jewish Prophets. One of the first Prophets to predict internal conflict amongst the Jewish tribes was **Elijah,** who lived approximately 800 B.C.E., after the death of King Solomon when the Kingdom split again into the northern nation of Israel and the southern nation of Judah. Elijah opposed the rule of the northern King Ahab, who rebelled against the House of David, married a pagan woman named Jezebel, and started worshiping her god Baal. Elijah predicted a great drought and famine as God's punishment for King Ahab's return to pagan worship. A later Jewish Prophet named **Malachi,** would foresee Elijah's return immediately preceding the arrival of the Messiah.

One of the most revered Jewish Prophets is **Isaiah,** who lived approximately 750 B.C.E. Prior to the Assyrian invasion in 722 B.C.E., Isaiah predicted the fall of Jerusalem due to the wickedness of the people during the time that the Kingdom of Israel and the Kingdom of Judah were fighting. He also predicted that the Temple would be destroyed, which indeed happened. The Temple was destroyed twice: first, by the Babylonians in 586 B.C.E.; then, after being rebuilt, the Temple was destroyed for the final time by the Romans in 70 C.E. Today, only the western wall of the Temple survives ("**Wailing Wall**"), which the Jews consider the most holy site on Earth. Additionally, Isaiah prophesied that the Jews would eventually regain their kingdom on Earth and that God would send them a "Prince of Peace" from the House of David who would renew the covenant.

> *For a child is born to us, a son is given us; upon his shoulder dominion rests. They name him Wonder-Counselor, God-Hero, Father-Forever, Prince of Peace. His dominion is vast and forever peaceful, from David's throne, and over his kingdom, which he confirms and sustains by judgment and justice, both now and forever.*
>
> Isaiah, Chapter 9:5

The next major Jewish Prophet is **Jeremiah,** who was born approximately 650 B.C.E. Jeremiah lived during the fall of the Assyrian Empire when the House of David was temporarily restored to power. Nevertheless, he predicted that the Temple would be destroyed, which happened in 586 B.C.E., when the Babylonians invaded the southern Kingdom of Judah. He, too, prophesied that a descendant from the House of David would one day reunite Israel.

Around 600 B.C.E., the Jewish Prophet **Ezekiel** also foretold the Temple's destruction and lived to see it decimated by the Babylonians. Additionally, Ezekiel predicted that after God punished the Jews for idolatry, the Temple would be rebuilt, which happened in 516 B.C.E. Also, he described an apocalyptic period of war during which the Jews would be exiled and the world would experience great plagues and destruction. Similar to Zarathustra's prophesy, Ezekiel predicted that God would return to help the Jews vanquish their enemies and to judge mankind. Moreover, Ezekiel stated that God would be sending a "servant David their prince forever" to reunify Israel and rule over the world. He also indicated that this prince would enter the Temple through the east gate which, interestingly enough, is where Jesus later entered the rebuilt Temple. Finally, Ezekiel introduced the concept of "**resurrection**" to the Jews, by stating that the dead would resurrect and that the righteous would live in a renewed Garden of Eden here on Earth.

> The hand of the Lord came upon me, and he led me out ... and set me in the center of the plain, which was now filled with bones. ... He asked me, "Son of man, can these bones come to life?"
>
> "Lord, God," I answered, "you alone know that."
>
> Then he said to me, "Prophesy over these bones .... I will bring spirit into you, that you may come to life. I will put sinews upon you, make flesh grow over you, cover you with skin, and put spirit in you so that you may come to life and know I am Lord."

> *Ezekiel*, Chapter 37:1–6

Another important Jewish Prophet is **Zechariah,** who lived approximately 550 B.C.E. Zechariah was alive when the Persian Empire conquered Palestine and allowed the Jews to return to Jerusalem and rebuild the Temple. Although the Jews seemed safe during this era, Zechariah predicted another great conflict, during which there would be war, massive Earth changes, and mystical signs from heaven. The Christians will later borrow this vision for the *New Testament.*

> Again I raised my eyes and saw four chariots coming out from between two mountains .... I asked the angel who spoke to me, "What are these, my Lord?" The angel said to me in reply, "These are the four winds of the heavens, which are coming forth after being reviewed by the Lord of all the earth ...."

> Then the Lord shall go forth and fight against those nations .... The
> Mount of Olives shall be cleft in two .... On that day, living waters shall
> flow from Jerusalem .... And this shall be the plague with which the
> Lord shall strike all the nations that have fought against Jerusalem: their
> flesh shall rot while they stand on their feet, and their eyes shall rot in
> their sockets, and their tongues shall rot in their mouths.
>
> Zechariah, Chapters 6:1–14:3

In addition, Zechariah wrote that a "king shall come ... meek and riding on an ass" who would lead the Jews during this final conflict. Again, it is interesting to note that Jesus rode a donkey into Jerusalem to attend his last Passover celebration. Although Zechariah's description of the final battle between good and evil is similar to the Christian prophecy about the Apocalypse (contained in the *New Testament* book entitled *The Revelation to John*), the Jewish version is fundamentally different for two reasons. First, the Messiah described by Zechariah does not die. Second, the Messiah ushers in a new age of worldwide peace here on Earth.

Thus, the Jewish Old Testament ends with a collection of prophecies which can be summarized as follows: As a consequence of mankind's failure to follow God's laws, mankind will be punished by great wars, plagues, and Earth changes. In particular, the Jewish prophecies suggest severe punishment for those Jews who have broken their covenant with God. Thereafter, a king who is descendant from the House of David will arise to restore order and vanquish evil. This **Messiah,** which literally means "anointed one" in Hebrew, will lead the Jews back to the promised land to reclaim Jerusalem, assume his throne, and lead mankind into a new age of peace and harmony, referred to as the "**Messianic Age.**" In the end, those good people who died before or during the conflict will resurrect to join the survivors of Armageddon, and the Earth will again be like the like the Garden of Eden where the righteous will live in peace and abundance forever.

Therefore, contrary to the Christian version of the Apocalypse, the Jews believe that the Earth will *not* be destroyed during the final conflict between good and evil. Rather, the Jews believe that once the Messiah arrives, he will vanquish evil, he will reign as King of Jesusalem, and mankind will again experience heaven on Earth.

Although most of the Jewish Prophets predicted a Messiah who survives the final battle between good and evil, one of the Prophets described a "servant of God" who would die during the conflict and prior to the fulfillment of peace on Earth.

*See, my servant shall prosper, he shall be raised high and greatly exalted.
… So shall he startle many nations, because of him kings shall stand
speechless …. Yet it was our infirmities that he bore, our sufferings he
endured …. But he was pierced for our offenses, crushed for our sins ….
We had all gone astray like sheep, each following his own way; But the
Lord laid upon him the guilt of us all. Though he was harshly treated,
he submitted and opened not his mouth; Like a lamb led to the
slaughter or a sheep before the shearers, he was silent and opened not
his mouth. Oppressed and condemned, he was taken away, and who
would have thought any more of his destiny?*

Isaiah, Chapters 52:13, 53:4

The Christians will later assert that this prophecy supports their position
that Jesus was the Messiah. However, this is not the accepted Jewish position.
Jewish scholars are quick to point out the fact that four separate "servants" are
described at the end of *Isaiah*, and that the Prophet probably did not write
Chapters 40 through 66, the final chapters of this *Old Testament* book.

*It also is important to realize that the Jewish interpretation of God's final
judgment and the after-life have nothing to do with the soul ascending to heaven.*
Most Jews do not accept the notion that mankind may join with God in heaven,
as they continue to believe that mankind is not worthy of being with God. The
Prophets Enoch and Elijah are the only exceptions I have found. God took Enoch
according to *Genesis* Chapter 5, and Elijah went to heaven in a whirlwind in
Kings 2, Chapter 2. Strangely, there is no mention in the *Old Testament* of Moses
being worthy of or ascending to heaven. Instead, the Jews believe that after the
Messiah arrives, he will usher in a new age of enlightenment and universal peace
here on Earth where righteous Jews and Gentiles will be immortal and live in harmony. Similarly, for those good people who have died, after the Messiah arrives,
they will resurrect, receive new bodies, and then share in paradise.

As we will discover shortly, some Jews will later reinterpret these prophecies and change the meanings of Jewish terms, like "Messiah," "resurrection,"
and "final judgment," in order to adapt the prophecies to fit the circumstances surrounding Jesus' death. The result will be a brand new religion.

**In short, Christians believe that the Messiah prophecies were fulfilled by
Jesus, even though he was not crowned a king on Earth, failed to bring world-
wide peace, and died. The Jews, on the other hand, are still waiting for the
Messiah because according to the original prophecies, the Messiah will be
crowned King of Jerusalem, establish everlasting peace and abundance on
Earth, and live forever.**

Before we leave Judaism, I want to impress upon the reader that the Jewish faith is more than a religion. It also is a way of life and a code of ethics which is intended to bring one closer to God. Abraham, the Jewish patriarch, was chosen by God to promote righteousness and justice and to pass these values on to his descendants. Therefore, like the earlier religions of Hinduism and Zoroastrianism, the Jewish religion shares a belief in the necessity of spiritual development and perfection of the soul. In other words, one must have more than faith to be pleasing to God. We also must adhere to God's laws, act in compliance with these Truths, and love each other by performing acts of charity and other good works.

Lastly, although most Jews do not think that mankind is worthy of joining God in heaven, one mystical branch of Judaism, called **Kabbalah**, goes beyond the *Torah* and the *Talmud* lessons by suggesting that it is possible for mankind to attain a higher wisdom and closeness to God. Kabbalists rely on a holy text called the **Zohar**, which was probably written by **Moses of Leon**, a Jewish philosopher who lived around 1300 C.E. The *Zohar* describes a spiritual path which helps a soul commune and unite with God. Thus, this mystical branch of Judaism suggests that heaven is not a place but a state of mind, a fundamental Truth more fully described by our next Prophet.

However, the advanced path of Kabbalah requires great faith and hard work to master. Consequently, it is very similar in nature to the *Saddha* process of spiritual enlightenment and, therefore, contrary in most ways to the type of religion prescribed to the masses. In other words, one must be willing to embark on a solitary journey and suspend preconceived notions about God. In addition, Kabbalah correctly teaches that God is comprised of both masculine and feminine energies, another fundamental Truth universally acknowledged by the mystics. Sadly, this Truth is rarely discussed by the masses, who strangely prefer to accept the orthodox man-made doctrine that God is male.

Unfortunately, some Jews also continue to conceptualize God only in male terms. Indeed, *Genesis* contains two conflicting creation legends, one of which seems to purposely minimize women. Orthodox Jews favor the mythology of *Genesis* Chapter 2, in which God creates Adam in his image, then the animals as companions for Adam, and lastly Eve. Because the primary focus of this creation myth is Adam and because the fable later relates that a serpent successfully tempts Eve, women in the Jewish and Christian faiths historically have been denied equal status with men. For instance, in ancient times Jewish women were considered unworthy to pray inside the Temple, since the female role was limited to keeping the home and raising the children. Today in orthodox congregations, women still sit in segregated areas of the Temple and may not pray with men. Thus, for many Jews, a patriarchal view of God continues to this day. Moreover, although a few women have been ordained as rabbis in more progressive congregations, orthodox Jews view this positive change as sacrilegious.

In sum, even though Judaism backtracks by failing to recognize and glorify the feminine half of God, the religion is a logical advancement over Hinduism because it acknowledges this basic Truth: *There is only one God, despite being multi-faceted and beyond our comprehension.* Therefore, Judaism may be viewed as adding to our Tower of Truth, since most of mankind now realizes that there is just one Supreme Being from which our existence and our reality stem. Thus, Judaism, as the first of the five primary religions to accept monotheism, represents a pivotal addition to mankind's collective spiritual database. Now, let us examine how our next Prophet further enhances our understanding of God.

BUDDHIST PROPHETS

Siddhartha Gautama was born in 563 B.C.E. in the country now known as Nepal near the border of India. He was born a prince into a noble Hindu family of the warrior (*ksatriya*) caste. Legend has it that his mother, **Maya,** was impregnated in heaven by a white elephant, a holy animal to the Hindus and strikingly similar to the white dove which represents the Holy Spirit to Christians. Siddhartha was not born of the womb, reportedly emerging from his mother's side. Immediately after being born, Siddhartha could walk and took seven steps.

> When the Bodhisattva [Siddhartha] had descended into his mother's womb, no sensual thought arose in her concerning men, and she was inaccessible to any man having a lustful mind.

Majjhima Nikaya, Sutra 123, Verse 10

It is interesting to note that Siddhartha, just like Jesus, was born in a miraculous manner. Like Jesus' father Joseph, Siddhartha's mortal father was not given credit for producing his offspring. Also, Siddhartha's mother Maya, just like the virgin Mary, was "unsullied" by the physical act of intercourse. Siddhartha's mother died seven days after his birth, reportedly in a "purified" state, another legend that mirrors the Christian stories about the Virgin Mary. Thereafter, Siddhartha was raised by his aunt **Mahaprajapati,** who also was his stepmother after she married Siddhartha's father, who was king.

After his son's birth, the king summoned fortune tellers who foresaw two possible futures for Siddhartha: (i) the prince could unify India, conquer many other kingdoms, and become a great king on the Earth plane; or (ii) the prince could forsake his earthly throne and become a great leader on the spiritual or Ethereal plane.

> The long-haired sage looked at the baby and with great joy he picked him up. Now the Buddha was in the arms of a man who had waited for him, a man who could recognize all the signs on his body – a man who now, filled with delight, raised his voice to say these words: "There is nothing to compare with this: this is the ultimate, this is the perfect man!"

Sutra-Nipata, Verses 689–691

It is interesting to note, once again, the similarities between the Buddhist and Christian parables surrounding their Prophets. Compare the story of the three *magi* who attended the birth of Jesus with the fortunetellers who predicted Siddhartha's sterling destiny.

The king was determined that Siddhartha should fulfill the first of the possible destinies, so he isolated his son from the outside world in an attempt to prevent Siddhartha from witnessing any human suffering. One day, however, Siddhartha snuck outside the palace gates and witnessed the misery of his people. First, Siddhartha saw an old man ravaged by time and infirmity; thus, the prince learned the reality of physical decay. Second, Siddhartha saw a man racked by disease lying helpless on the side of the road; so the prince learned of physical illness. Third, Siddhartha saw a corpse; thereby learning about death. Fourth, the prince saw a monk meditating in peace. It was then that the prince learned of the ascetic life and that true happiness comes after we detach from the physical plane. Although Siddhartha's own life was filled with blessings, including a beautiful wife and healthy son, he was tormented by the pain he had seen in the world.

At the age of twenty-nine, Siddhartha decided to renounce his life of privilege and opulence, forsake his family, and flee the artificial existence within the palace gates. He then began his quest for Truth (*Dharma*). He started by studying with two Hindu monks, but he did not reach enlightenment while under their tutelage. Next, he decided to study with a group of ascetics, and he almost starved himself to death in an attempt to learn the Truth about God. However, this path did not produce enlightenment either. Finally, Siddhartha concluded that he should take the "middle path" and he set off to seek the Truth on his own.

It was during this solitary search that Siddhartha finally achieved a state of enlightenment called **nirvana**. While meditating under a Bo tree, he grasped the Truth about the nature of life on the Earth plane. He realized that mankind's existence is based on fear of physical suffering and fraught with desire for material gain. Once he conquered these Earth plane illusions, Siddhartha was emancipated and ready to merge with the Ethereal plane. In a nutshell, Truth set him free.

> Then the Lord sat cross-legged in one posture for seven days at the foot of the tree of awakening, experiencing the bliss of freedom [nirvana].
>
> *Vinaya Mahavagga*, Sutra I, Verse 1

Once again, it is interesting to note the parallels between this Buddhist legend, which involves a tree of enlightenment, and the Jewish parable concerning a tree of knowledge. Furthermore, the Buddhist belief that spiritual illumination follows from solitary meditation corresponds to Jesus' reclusive journey into the desert for forty days before he started his ministry.

After this period of enlightenment, which lasted a total of forty-nine days, Siddhartha was transformed into **Buddha**. For the next fifty years, Buddha spread his messages of Truth and founded a new religion called **Buddhism**. At first, only men were welcome to study this new religion. Then, Buddha's stepmother, Mahaprajapati, requested permission to study with him. Initially, Buddha refused to allow her to participate, but his cousin and closest disciple, **Ananda**, convinced him that women should be welcome too. Although reluctant at first, Buddha eventually acknowledged that it was possible for women to become enlightened.

Buddha set up a monastery (*sangha*) where both male monks and female nuns could study the new religion, and during Buddha's lifetime, both men and women were ordained. There were few rules regarding monastic life at the *sangha*, although the rules for nuns were more detailed and restrictive than the rules pertaining to monks. Everyone had to assume an ascetic lifestyle and renounce all worldly possessions. In order to maintain his own spiritual purity and state of *nirvana*, Buddha would retire to the forest in solitude for three months out of every year.

Buddha dissected all the social and spiritual problems presented to him in an acutely analytical, logical, and impartial manner. During his lifetime, Buddha was considered a wise sage and a great philosopher, in the same ranks as Confucius and Socrates. He also is reported to have been a most generous and tender teacher. In addition, there are accounts of him performing miracles, such as walking on water, feeding multitudes with just a few cakes, and healing the sick. Again, the miracles performed by Buddha seem to mirror the powers ascribed to Jesus.

In 483 B.C.E., Buddha died at the age of eighty. Legend has it that he ate his last meal in the presence of friends and then laid down on his side and died. According to Buddhist scriptures, his final words included these: "Hold fast to the Truth as a lamp. Hold fast as a refuge to the Truth." After Buddha died, the skies rumbled with thunder and the Earth shook. Some of his followers attempted to deify him, as would be done with Jesus. However, Buddha made clear during his lifetime that anyone may achieve the state of *nirvana*. Specifically, he taught that freedom from Earth plane illusions may be achieved by anyone who is disciplined and pursues the *Dharma*. Additionally,

Buddha paid little worship to the Hindu gods and goddesses, even though he continued to believe in the supreme creator god Brahma. Instead, Buddha encouraged his followers to undergo a personal quest for God (*Saddha*), in order to attain the bliss of *nirvana*.

Prior to his death, Buddha did not appoint a successor. Instead, Buddha had indicated during his life that the *sangha* lifestyle should continue, holding assemblies whenever major communal issues arose. This lack of structure presented problems after Buddha's death, such as the emergence of different interpretations of Buddha's lessons. One of his closest disciples, Mahakasvapa, proposed a meeting amongst the *arhats* (monks in the state of *nirvana*), in order to officially compile the teachings of Buddha. As a result, roughly five hundred monks convened at the **First Buddhist Council** around 470 B.C.E. During the meeting, Ananda recited sixty thousand words relayed by Buddha. The *arhats* agreed that the recitation was accurate and began to record Buddha's teachings into a collection of holy scriptures, collectively known as the **Pali Canon**.

The *Pali Canon* was compiled over the next three hundred years. Inevitably, differences started to emerge between the *Pali* and *Sanskrit* versions, since various ancient Indian languages were used to record the canons. Today, historians are unsure which version is the oldest and purest. The first series of books of the *Pali Canon* is called the **Sutra Pitaka** ("Basket of Discourses"), which contains the original sayings of Buddha (including the holy text called the **Dhammapada**). The second series is called the **Vinaya Pitaka** ("Basket of Discipline"), which sets forth a code for the *sangha*. The third group of texts is the **Abhidharma Pitaka** ("Basket of Higher Teachings"), which lists the mental and physical requirements needed for spiritual enlightenment.

By 100 B.C.E., the Buddhist holy text known as the **Tripitaka** was compiled. To most historians, the *Tripitaka* is considered the most definitive translation of the *Pali Canon*. However, one must bear in mind that just like the Jewish holy texts, the Buddhist holy scriptures are based on hundreds of years of oral tradition. Nevertheless, the Buddhist scriptures were recorded much faster than were the Jewish parables and history. Recall that the Jews based significant portions of the *Old Testament* on oral history covering more than two thousand years.

The *Tripitaka* lists the three levels of knowledge that Buddha attained in order to reach the state of full enlightenment (*nirvana*):

1. He was able to recollect all his previous lives and the results of his prior lives' actions (*akasha*);
2. He was able to see all beings in their true state depending on their *karma* (i.e., their states of pleasure or pain based on their actions); and
3. He was able to free himself from the limitations and impurities of a *karmic* existence, which meant that he would not have to be reborn.

The *Tripitaka* also sets forth the **Four Noble Truths**, which to Buddha represent the realities of the Earth plane. The Four Noble Truths can be summarized as follows:

1. Suffering is inherent in life and is the natural order of the Earth plane;
2. Suffering arises from man's craving for power and sensual delight, which then results in rebirth;
3. Suffering can only be ended when man stops craving earthly pleasure and when no passion remains for the material plane; only then is man liberated and released from false needs; and
4. *Nirvana* and the end of reincarnation are attained by adhering to the following **Eight-Fold Path:**

(i) Right views;	(v) Right livelihood;
(ii) Right resolve;	(vi) Right effort;
(iii) Right speech;	(vii) Right mindfulness; and
(iv) Right conduct;	(viii) Right concentration.

When the Four Noble Truths are fully understood, then enlightenment is possible. That is why the Buddhists believe that blind faith, as practiced by some religions, cannot lead to or access the ultimate Truth about God. Rather, Truth must be learned gradually and internally by each of us on an incremental and individualized basis. *This progression of soul growth is called Saddha.*

During his lifetime, Buddha broke from many Hindu traditions. *To begin with, Buddha rejected the Hindu caste system and the authority of the Hindu priests (brahmins).* Buddha viewed the caste system as corrupt and not in keeping with the natural law of *karma*. Buddha also challenged the absolute authority that the Hindu priests historically had wielded over the masses. He believed that the priests were no better positioned to attain enlightenment than any other soul. As a result, Buddha was castigated by the *brahmin* class, just as Jesus later would be feared by the Jewish Sanhedrin. Thus, Buddha's views were a radical departure from Hinduism, which asserts that a soul is locked into just one caste during each lifetime and cannot assume a higher caste or reach enlightenment except by reincarnating into the *brahmin* caste.

When these brahmins teach a path that they do not know or see, saying, "This is the only straight path," this cannot possibly be right. Just as a file of blind men go on, clinging to each other, and the first one sees nothing, the middle one sees nothing, and the last one sees nothing – so it is with the talk of these brahmins.

Digha Nikaya, Sutra XIII, Verse 15

Buddha also had little use for rules and rituals, and he taught that enlightenment was not dependent on such trivial and man-made concepts. Consequently, Buddhism is not a religion based on strict dogma or tradition. In fact, many Buddhists follow a simple creed known as the "**Three Jewels**," which merely instructs practitioners to take refuge in the Buddha, the *Dharma*, and the *sangha*. Buddha also encouraged his laity to avoid the Hindu temples, seek solitude, and meditate in private, just as Jesus would later do with his followers. As a result, the Hindu temples and rituals were slowly undermined. This change angered the *brahmin* priests, who began to lose their authority and control over the people. Nevertheless, Buddha's followers enjoyed a newfound freedom that both inspired and supported them on their personal quest for *Dharma*.

If one, though reciting little of texts, lives a life in accord with Dharma, having discarded passion, ill will, and unawareness, knowing full well, the mind well freed; He, not grasping here, neither hereafter, is a partaker of the religious quest.

The Dhammapada, Sutra I, Verse 20

Buddha also renounced the importance of the Hindu multiple deities. He taught that guidance should come from within, rather than from the super-stitious and external supplication to Brahma or the lesser gods and god-desses. He taught that we each have the ability to become Divine ourselves and that the gods merely help us on our private spiritual journey. Buddha also taught that we access our higher nature through meditation and by detaching from the physical plane. For some people, enlightenment may take many lifetimes to achieve. However, *nirvana* can occur at any time, even while the soul appears locked inside a healthy body.

It also is important to understand that Buddhism does not recognize the concept of a permanent self or soul. That is because the "self" is and should be ever-changing and evolving toward the Truth of the Universe (*Dharma*). Faith gained through personal experience (*Saddha*) is a process which changes the soul. As one gains new insight, the self is modified and elevated. In sum, because the soul is not the same after enlightenment, the self is not permanent or static.

A childish person becomes anxious,
Thinking, "Sons are mine! Wealth is mine!"
Not even a self is there to call one's own.
Whence sons? Whence wealth?

Childish ones, of little intelligence,
Go about with a self that is truly an enemy;
Performing the deed that is bad,
Which is of bitter fruit.

The Dhammapada, Sutra V, Verses 62, 66

Finally, Buddhism suggests that enlightenment may not lead to a union with God. Although Buddhism presents a radically different view of the soul's ascendence, the religion still seems to view mankind as unworthy of joining with God, just like Hinduism and Judaism. *Nirvana* simply means that the cycle of reincarnation ends and the self is extinguished. Buddha never explained whether, after attaining *nirvana*, the soul joins with God in the Ethereal plane. His lessons suggest, however, that the soul is merely released or extinguished. Unfortunately, Buddha did not offer much insight on what, if anything, happens next.

In whom the influxes are fully extinct,
Who is not attached to sustenance,
And whose pasture is freedom that is empty and signless,
His track is hard to trace,
As that of birds in the sky.

The Dhammapada, Sutra VII, Verse 93

Some are born in a womb,
Wrongdoers, in hell.
Those of good course go to heaven,
To nirvana those without influxes.

The Dhammapada, Sutra IX, Verse 126

Consequently, the state of *nirvana* cannot be compared to the Christian concept of heaven, which most Christians think of as a "place" where God resides. Some Buddhist followers have questioned the "nothingness" that the state of *nirvana* suggests. Yet, permanent separation from God seems to be a central tenet of Buddhism even after the soul reaches *nirvana.*

Those who are intent on meditating, the wise ones,
Delighting in the calm of going out,
Even the gods long for them,
The Fully Enlightened Ones, the mindful.
Forbearing patience is the highest austerity;
Nirvana is supreme, the Awakened Ones say.

The Dhammapada, Sutra XIV, Verses 181, 184

To his followers, Buddha's extreme departure from Hinduism was refreshing, empowering, and inspiring. As a result, the religion spread rapidly both during and after Buddha's lifetime. Additionally, it is important to reiterate that Buddha allowed women to join his order and study with the male monks. Pause to realize that this had never been done before. *Buddhism was the first of the five primary religions to truly embrace feminine energy.*

Thanks to Buddha, women were finally being accorded the right to study religion, participate in the daily religious activities, and even teach religious doctrine. While it is true that Buddha restricted women's involvement in the religion, Buddha still gets credit for being the first Prophet to accept women into active religious practice. Buddha also deserves praise for acknowledging that women can reach enlightenment and become *buddhas*, just like men!

Unfortunately, when the **Second Buddhist Council** met in 383 B.C.E., the fair treatment of women and much of the appreciation for feminine energy ended. Women were no longer ordained, they were separated from men at the monasteries, and they were permanently relegated to "nun" status. Today, Buddhist women may actively participate in the religion as "mother monks" (*mae chi*), but the rules which were created after Buddha's death clearly place women in a second-class status within the religious hierarchy. Only in a few countries where Buddhism is practiced, like Japan, are women ordained and treated on par with male monks.

Putting Buddha's contributions in historical perspective, it is evident that Buddha further refined and expanded the spiritual Truths taught by the Hindu and Jewish Prophets. Consistent with my theory that all the Prophets successively added to our Tower of Truth, Buddha made tremendous contributions to our understanding of God and the solitary path that the soul must undertake in order to reach the Ethereal plane. Buddha also clarified that the soul will not achieve enlightenment through the use of outworn and arcane ritual. Consequently, Buddha was disdainful of organized temple worship in supplication to the priests and the Hindu gods and goddesses, since mere prayer in the absence of true comprehension is unproductive.

In sum, Buddha taught that each individual must work privately in meditation to achieve spiritual enlightenment. Only through the *Saddha* process of soul development, may a person gradually learn the Truth of the Universe, grasp the fullness of God's power, and become worthy of ascending to an Ethereal plane existence.

Buddha also taught that contentment during our Earth plane existence depends on relinquishing irrelevant and harmful material plane desires and distractions. In other words, mankind will continue to suffer so long as we place greater value on Earth plane rewards than we do on spiritual growth. Thus, the key to true happiness and harmony is perfection of the soul, a quest that requires dedication and hard work. Mankind owes much to Buddha's teachings, as they constitute a tremendous addition to our Tower of Truth.

Finally, I want to underscore the fact that both before and after his death, Buddha's followers wanted to deify him. However, Buddha clearly rejected the suggestion that he was a god and would not assume a godlike title, special living arrangements, or any other indicia of supremacy or worldly gain. In many ways, Buddha did not even view himself as "special." *Remember, Buddha taught that everyone has the innate ability to attain the state of nirvana.*

Moreover, Buddha believed that *arhat* monks, those who reach the state of *nirvana*, may elect to return to the Earth Plane as **bodhisattvas**. Buddhists believe that *bodhisattvas* are *buddhas* who elect to postpone their Ethereal plane existence in favor of reincarnating again to help mankind. This belief in *bodhisattvas* further highlights the Buddhist core tenet that death is irrelevant to attaining spiritual enlightenment.

One well-known *bodhisattva* is **His Holiness the Dalai Lama**, the Tibetan *arhat* who has reincarnated fourteen times. The current Dalai Lama was born in 1935 and named Tenzin Gyatso. Tibetan Buddhists believe that when the Dalai Lama dies, his soul reincarnates and that monks are able to identify the teacher during his next childhood. The current Dalai Lama has been exiled from Tibet since 1951, when Communist China invaded his homeland, destroyed Buddhist temples, and banished the monks. The Dalai Lama won the Nobel Peace Prize in 1989 for his lifelong dedication to world peace. It is interesting to note, though, that there has never been a female Dalai Lama. Sadly, Buddhist literature mentions only a few female *bodhisattvas*.

Our next Prophet, like Buddha, repeatedly opposed the suggestion that he was a god. Nevertheless, the early Christians, who were heavily influenced by the harsh politics and pagan religion of the Roman Empire, would deify him anyway. For those of you who come from Christian backgrounds, this section of the book will be exceedingly interesting but also unsettling. Please, try to keep an open mind and a sincere heart as we delve into the historical and legendary figure known as Jesus of Nazareth. Please also trust that I have no religious or other agenda. *Truth is our shared goal in this book.*

CHRISTIAN PROPHETS

B efore I begin the Christianity section of this chapter, I feel compelled to interject a few personal thoughts. I was raised in a Christian family – Catholic to be specific – and initially it was hard for me to give myself permission to commence a spiritual journey outside of Christianity. Moreover, it was difficult for me at first to open up my heart and mind to new ideas about God. During the initial phase of my journey, I had to consciously shove aside my Catholic upbringing in order to adopt a mindset conducive to acquiring new information. Later, as I learned about all the Prophets, it became easier for me to recognize Truth. I was excited about what I was learning, and I could feel myself getting closer to God. Eventually, I was able to analyze new information without bias, as my goal was pure and simple: I wanted to learn the Truth about God (or as much Truth as humanly possible, recognizing that my perception of the Earth plane and the Ethereal plane would necessarily be sculpted by my own gifts and shortcomings).

After a few years, I reached the point where I no longer cared in which direction my search took me. I was in *Saddha* mode and grateful to God that I had the intellect, motivation, time, and the proper mindset to study the five primary religions, synthesize what I was learning, and extract Truths from each religion to create a heathy framework for living. Best of all, though, I learned how to commune with my higher self and with God during my meditations. I decided to write this book in order to share what I had learned during my twelve year quest. However, that decision has forced me, once again, to face my Christian roots and wrestle with an old belief system that was instilled in me as a child and which will forever linger in my psyche. Consequently, as I write and rewrite this section, I must admit to feeling phantom pain from the orthodox Christian dogma and Catholic demons I amputated years ago.

The first of these demons is the unnecessary mythology that the early Church adopted, despite the overtly simple and practical lessons of its primary Prophet. Thus, my first challenge is to properly distinguish between Christian fact and fiction. The second demon is the confusion caused by varied sources of historical information and the public's lack of knowledge concerning recent biblical finds, like the *Dead Sea Scrolls*. My second challenge, then, is to synthesize massive quantities of conflicting and previously unknown data and draw appropriate conclusions when possible. Yet, by far the scariest demon is the third: *my own ego*, as influenced by my Christian heritage, my life history, and my sometimes unpredictable spiritual growth. The Truth is that we all filter information to some degree, based on unconquered fears and repressed desires. Thus, the most I can do is acknowledge this Truth and pledge to be honest and forthright.

Therefore, please accept the following as my best and truest understanding of Christianity. I will strive to be as unbiased and balanced as I can be. Also, please know that I feel an incredible responsibility in writing this section of the book, as Christianity is both the most popular religion in the world and the religion that has strayed the most from the teachings of its primary Prophet. It is my sincere hope that the Truth you are about to read will encourage you to start or renew your own spiritual journey toward the Supreme Being. Here we go.

I am listing **John the Baptist** as a Christian Prophet, even though he was Jewish and would die well before the start of the Christian movement. John was born approximately 7 B.C.E., and is described in the *New Testament* as Jesus' cousin from his mother's side of the family. The *Gospel of Luke* gives the best account of John's life and recites that John paved the way for the Messiah by preaching to the Jews that he would be arriving soon.

Recall that the Jewish Prophets had predicted a Messiah who would: (i) be a member of the Tribe of Judah and descendant from the House of David; (ii) reunify the Jews; (iii) lead the Jews through an apocalyptic period of war; (iv) take back Jerusalem and rebuild the Temple; and (v) reign as king over the entire Earth, which would again be like the Garden of Eden. Furthermore, recall that the Prophet Malachi had predicted that the Prophet Elijah would reappear (i.e., reincarnate), to announce the arrival of the Messiah. Based on these prophecies, some of the Jews thought that John the Baptist was Elijah, and some even thought that he was the Messiah. In the *Gospel of John*, Jewish priests ask John who he is, and John answers that he is neither Elijah nor the Messiah. However, in Chapters 11 and 17 of the *Gospel of Matthew*, Jesus states that John is Elijah, the precursor to the arrival of the Messiah.

By all accounts, John's ministry was quite successful. He baptized many devout Jews in the River Jordan and he even had his own disciples by the time Jesus entered the picture. In fact, according to the *Gospel of John*, Simon (a/k/a Saint Peter) and Andrew were at first John's disciples, and they met Jesus for the first time while they were with John. On the other hand, the *Gospel of Matthew* and the *Gospel of Mark* state that Jesus enlisted Peter and Andrew *after* John was imprisoned by King Herod Antipas, the son of Herod the Great. As we shall soon see, the four gospels in the *New Testament* often contradict each other-sometimes on matters of grave historical importance. In those instances, I will provide both my own analysis and that of independent scholars and historians. With regard to John the Baptist, though, the gospels seem to agree on the charismatic nature of this pious man who paved the way for a religious revolution.

> *John the Baptist appeared in the desert proclaiming a baptism of repentance for the forgiveness of sins. People of the whole Judean countryside and all the inhabitants of Jerusalem were going out to him and were being baptized by him in the River Jordan as they acknowledged their sins … And this is what he proclaimed: "One mightier than I is coming after me. I am not worthy to stoop and loosen the thongs of his sandals. I have baptized you with water; he will baptize you with the holy Spirit." It happened in those days that Jesus came from Nazareth of Galilee and was baptized in the Jordan by John.*

Gospel of Mark, Chapter 1:4–9

I always have found it curious that Jesus wanted to be baptized by John. The ritual of baptism was not a new one. To the Jews it represented a purification of the soul and the washing away of sins, the same meaning the Christians ascribe to the ritual today. All four gospels recite the baptismal story in their early chapters. Consequently, the *New Testament* seems to immediately contradict the orthodox Christian view that Jesus was without sin and was a human manifestation of God. In other words, why would Jesus submit to baptism if he were without sin? Additionally, I find it strange that Jesus would submit to baptism if he foresaw that his mortal death on the cross was the only way to wipe away the sins of mankind.

But I get ahead of myself, as there is so much confusion surrounding the Christian religion and their most revered Prophet that I hardly know where to start. As a rational starting point, let us list **Jesus** as a Christian Prophet, even though he, just like John the Baptist, was a devout Jew. Moreover, let us acknowledge at the outset that at no time during his ministry did Jesus advocate the start of a new religion. To the contrary, Jesus was a Jewish *rabbi* (religious teacher) who was singularly focused on reforming Judaism, a religion that had gone seriously awry due to the political corruption of the Roman Empire and the spiritual degradation of the Jewish high priests, known collectively as the **Sanhedrin Council**. Please understand that this basic information about Jesus is not conjecture. Rather, it is based on the four gospels of the *New Testament* and it also is supported by apocryphal (i.e., outside *The Holy Bible*) sources of historical information. *The Truth is that there is absolutely no evidence that Jesus wanted to start a new religion.*

In order to properly understand Jesus, one must grasp the complex era in which he lived. At the time of Jesus' birth, the Roman Empire had conquered

Palestine but had not placed the region under the exclusive dominion of the Roman government. Instead, most of the power was held by a terrifying monarch named **Herod the Great**. King Herod ruled the Roman province of Judea from 37 B.C.E. to 4 B.C.E. He was a ruthless man and was universally hated by the Jews for a variety of reasons which we shall explore in a moment. Most notably, though, the Jews hated King Herod because he collaborated with the Romans and killed over forty members of the Sanhedrin Council, the Jewish elders who ruled the religious aspects of daily life in Jerusalem. King Herod then replaced the devout priests he murdered with an assorted collection of his own cronies. As a result, the Jews felt that the sacred Sanhedrin had been corrupted by King Herod. By the time Jesus was born, tempers were flaring and the Jews were on the verge of a revolt.

Going a little further back in time will be even more helpful to our analysis. After Moses led the Jews to Canaan, God appointed Moses' brother, Aaron, and his tribe, the Tribe of Levi, to be the Jewish priests and to manage the Temple. Recall, though, that the Jewish Temple was destroyed by the Babylonians in 586 B.C.E. Thereafter, the Persians conquered Palestine and allowed the Jews to return and rebuild their Temple. However, the region soon was at war again, as the Persians, the Greeks, and the Romans all fought for control of this land. It was during this mayhem in 167 B.C.E., that a Jewish man named Judas Maccabee led a revolt and managed to regain control of Jerusalem. For the next 100 years, the **Maccabee Dynasty** ruled Jerusalem, as both kings and high priests of the Temple, in consort with a strictly orthodox Sanhedrin Council. Today, the Jewish holiday **Hanukkah** commemorates the Maccabees' rededication of the Temple.

Then, in 63 B.C.E., the Roman Republic conquered Palestine. As a result, the power of the Maccabee Dynasty started to wane, as the Roman Republic morphed into the Roman Empire, which was consolidated in 27 B.C.E. by Augustus Caesar. Thereafter, the Romans placed Herod in the Roman province of Judea and made him King of Jews, as a reward for his service during the wars along side Mark Antony and against the Maccabees. King Herod claimed to be part Jewish, but there is little evidence for this assertion. In any event, the remaining Maccabean priests and their pious followers resented Herod's rule in Jerusalem and viewed his appointment by the Romans as a critical blow to their independence. Thus, the Jews, once again, lost their ability to self-rule and were antagonistic toward Herod even at the start of his reign.

As a result, some Jews left Jerusalem to protest the pagan rites and Roman taxes that Herod imposed on them. One radical sect set up camp near the Dead Sea at **Qumran**, which is where the *Dead Sea Scrolls* later would be found. We will discuss the *Dead Sea Scrolls* in more detail later. For now, it is important to realize that the Jews at Qumran who opposed Herod were *not* the peaceful "**Essene**" sect initially described by the Catholics, who for over forty years exercised exclusive dominion over the *Scrolls* and who repeatedly misinformed the public of their astounding content. Rather, as many independent historians now agree, the Jews at the Qumran community were "**Ossene**," which translated means "the doers of the law." In other words, the Jews at Qumran were religious fundamentalists or "Zealots," who not only opposed King Herod, but who also may have been planning a revolt. Indeed, if we accept the latest research that indicates the Qumran community was comprised of Jewish Zealots, what happened next makes total sense. Sometime around 36 B.C.E., Herod the Great destroyed Qumran, in a calculated move to demonstrate total domination over and complete intolerance of any social disturbance. As independent scholars logically point out, Herod the Great would not have bothered suppressing the Jews at Qumran if they were peace loving Essenes.

Yet, this first slaughter at Qumran is nothing compared to what Herod the Great did next. In a futile attempt to garner Jewish support, King Herod decided to marry into the Maccabee family. He married their last Jewish princess, who was named Mariam. In addition to marrying into the Maccabee family, Herod attempted to ingratiate himself with the Jews by remodeling and refurbishing the Jewish Temple, which some scholars have described as an unprecedented architectural achievement that qualified the Temple as the eighth Wonder of the World. Even so, the gesture won Herod few admirers, for he soon proved himself to be a raging despot and a true enemy of the Jewish people.

After he married Mariam, who was one of ten wives, King Herod killed her grandfather Hyrcanus, high priest to the Sanhedrin. Herod also killed Miriam's mother Alexandra. Next, Herod killed Miriam's youngest brother Aristobulus, immediately after the boy reached the age of thirteen and assumed the role of High Priest to the Sanhedrin. Even yet, King Herod was not done. He then proceeded to kill his own two sons by Miriam, apparently concerned that the Jews might favor his sons who had Maccabean blood. Lastly, Herod the Great killed Miriam, thereby completely wiping out the Maccabees and the last royal and priestly family in Jewish history.

By this point, the Jews were beyond rage. The Zealot movement was gaining massive support and many Jews were preparing for a revolt. Meanwhile, King Herod continued to stack the Sanhedrin Council with priests who were willing to support his despotic reign in return for wealth and power. The new priests were despised by the people, and many more joined the ranks of the Zealots. By the time King Herod died in 4 B.C., the Zealots had rebuilt their fortress at Qumran and were preparing for eventual war with Rome. In addition, many Jews thought that God would send the Messiah, as prophesied in the *Old Testament*. They believed the time was ripe for the Messiah to stop the desecration of the Temple, cast off the yoke of Roman rule, and take the throne as the rightful King of Israel.

Consequently, by the time Jesus began his ministry, Jewish unrest was at a fever pitch. The aggressive Jewish Zealots already had moved back to Qumran and were documenting their religious struggles against the corrupt Sanhedrin priests in the *Dead Sea Scrolls*. In addition, a second Zealot community, identified as the first "Zionists," set up camp at a fortress in **Masada**. They, too, were contemplating outright rebellion against the Romans and the degenerate rabbis. It was at this point in the unfolding drama that John the Baptist, a vocal critic of the Sanhedrin and of King Herod's son and heir, **Herod Antipas**, began preaching that the Messiah would be arriving soon. In retaliation, Herod Antipas would have John's head cut off as punishment for inciting the Jews and criticizing Herod Antipas' incestuous marriage to his niece. John's murder only served to further enrage the Jews, who now were convinced that Armageddon was imminent and that the Messiah would arrive at any moment to save them. In short, Jerusalem was a powder keg waiting for a spark. Enter Jesus, who held a torch lit by Truth, Love, and Light.

Before we begin to explore the awe-inspiring messages from God communicated by Jesus, let's learn what we can about Jesus' family of origin and his poorly documented childhood. To begin with, we must accept that the exact date of Jesus' birth is a mystery that probably will never be solved. The *Gospel of Matthew* states that Jesus was born during the reign of King Herod, which would mean that Jesus was born sometime before Herod the Great's death in 4 B.C.E. Alternatively, the *Gospel of Luke* states that Jesus was born at the time of a Roman census, which the records indicate occurred sometime in 6 C.E. Thus, the massive confusion regarding this Prophet starts immediately with the year of his birth which, contrary to common myth, does *not* mark the beginning of the calendar used by most of the world today. That is why historians no longer use the incorrect Catholic designations "B.C." to demarcate the time "before Christ," nor the designation "A.D." which stands for the Latin phrase *anno domini* and translated means the "year of our Lord." Rather, historians now use the terminology "B.C.E." (before common era) and "C.E." (common era) to reference historical events.

Adding to the confusion created by the gospel records is the fact that the Romans used a different calendar than the Jews. In 45 B.C.E., Julius Caesar created a new Roman calendar, called the "Julian Calendar" to memorialize his rise to power. The new calendar featured a twelve month schedule and the concept of a leap year. However, the Romans mistakenly added a leap year every three years instead of every four, so the Julian Calendar slowly was gaining time.

In 523 C.E., the Roman Catholic Church decided to update the Julian Calendar. Easter was beginning to fall during the winter months, and the Catholics wanted it to be celebrated near the vernal equinox (March 21), the purported date of Jesus' death. A Catholic monk named Dionysius Exiguus was given the tasks of: (i) correcting the leap year error; (ii) creating a table of future Easter dates; and (iii) restarting the calendar based on the year of Jesus' birth. However, the monk made an error in his calculations and his calendar was six years off from his target date of year one (there was no year zero). Therefore, assuming the monk was correct in his dating of Jesus' birth and merely made an error with his calendar, Jesus was born in 6 B.C.E. Some scholars believe, though, that Dionysius also was wrong about his target year. Based on current research, some scholars believe that Jesus was born as late as 4 B.C.E., the same year King Herod died.

There is also astronomical evidence to support the proposition that Jesus was born either in 6 B.C.E. or 4 B.C.E. The *Gospel of Matthew* reports that a bright star appeared on the night Jesus was born, as foretold in the "Star Prophecy" of the *Old Testament* and the *Mormon Bible*. The gospel also asserts that three wise men, probably Zoroastrian priests, followed the star to Bethlehem. Yet, we know that Jesus' parents, **Mary** and **Joseph**, did *not* reside there. Scholars have three possible explanations for the Bethlehem story: (i) the Romans may have ordered an earlier census which required Jews to register in Bethlehem; (ii) the family traveled to Bethlehem for Passover; or (iii) the family was never there at all and the story was fabricated to satisfy the Star and Messiah prophecies (i.e., King David was born in Bethlehem). Regardless of these theories, I think Jesus was born in Bethlehem. Present day astronomers have confirmed via computer modeling that in 6 B.C.E., the planet Jupiter was basked in early dawn sunlight, making it appear like a huge star over Bethlehem. Additionally, Chinese astronomical charts show that a supernova occurred in 4 B.C.E., which would have been highly visible in Bethlehem. Thus, scientific data seems to corroborate that Jesus was born in Bethlehem either in 6 B.C.E. or 4 B.C.E.

In 1572 C.E., the Catholics updated the calendar again to the Gregorian Calendar, which the American colonies adopted in 1752 C.E. Today, Easter always falls on the first Sunday after the first full moon, after the vernal equinox. This formula creates a span of possible Easter dates between March 22 through April 25 each year. **Easter** is the Christian celebration of Jesus' resurrection, which occurred three days after his crucifixion. Recall, though, that the Jews believed in an Earth plane bodily resurrection for righteous people who died before the arrival of the Messiah, not for the Messiah himself. Thus, Jesus' resurrection and ascendence to the Ethereal plane constitute radical departures from the original meaning of the Jewish prophecies.

Incidentally, there is another reason why the early Christian leaders decided to place Easter close to the vernal equinox. As we shall soon see, the early Christians had an uphill struggle converting pagans (a/k/a Gentiles) to the new religion and often accommodated them rather than lose converts. With regard to Easter, there already existed a pagan festival that was celebrated at the vernal equinox. **Eostre** was a pagan goddess who represented dawn and fertility. The word "Easter" comes from this pagan holiday, which was celebrated *before* the Christians decided to celebrate the death and resurrection of Jesus. Eostre was honored with painted eggs and the rabbit was her mascot, as these symbols represented the dawn of springtime and fertility.

For similar reasons, the Christians decided to celebrate Jesus' birthday on December 25. Historians agree that Jesus was *not* born on December 25. Rather, that was the date the Romans celebrated the winter solstice and worshiped **Mithras**, god of the Sun. Many such concessions were made to pacify the Romans, the Greeks, and the other pagan cults, all of whom believed that a variety of deities controlled various aspects of the Universe.

Now let us turn to yet another source of confusion caused by the conflicting gospels. Sadly, the *New Testament* accounts do not even agree on Jesus' genealogy, other than the fact that his parents were Mary and Joseph. Even more disturbing is that much of the confusion stems from purposeful editing and extraction of valuable information, especially regarding Jesus' family.

Let us start, though, by going *up* Jesus' family tree, to determine, if possible, Jesus' ancestors.

According to the *Gospel of Matthew*, Jesus is descendant from the House of David through King Solomon, who was King David's favorite son and heir. However, according to the *Gospel of Luke*, Jesus was descendant from King David's ninth son, Nathan. *This is the first problem with Jesus' genealogy.* There really is no rational way to account for this discrepancy, nor the fact that these two gospels list completely different men as Joseph's father (i.e., *Matthew* identifies Jacob as Joseph's father, and *Luke* names Heli). For now, let us ignore this problem and view the genealogy chart according to the *Gospel of Matthew*. Again, I have used doted lines to indicate the passage of multiple generations, and straight lines to indicate successive generations.

JESUS' ANCESTORS

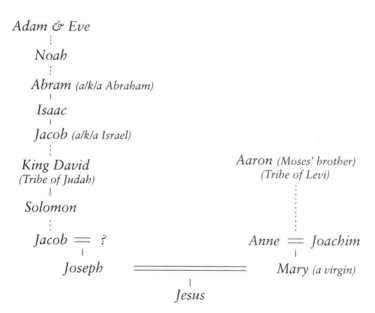

In this family tree, Jesus is descendant from two of the most revered families in Jewish history. On his father's side, he is from the Tribe of Judah and a descendant of King David through David's son, Solomon. Recall from the *Old Testament* that King David unified the northern and southern Jewish Kingdoms and made Jerusalem the capitol of the new kingdom, where his son Solomon later built the first Temple.

On his mother's side, Jesus is descendant from the Tribe of Levi, which is the tribe of Moses' brother Aaron. Recall that after the Exodus, God appointed Aaron's tribe, the Levites, to be the priests and manage the Temple. While the *New Testament* itself never bothers to mention Mary's parents, Christian scholars believe she is a Levite because: (i) Mary's cousin Elizabeth, the mother of John the Baptist, is described in the *Gospel of Luke* as descendant from Aaron; and (ii) in the apocryphal gospel ***Protevangelium of James***, in which Mary's parents are identified as Anne and Joachim, Mary is dedicated to a temple and lives there from age three to twelve, a story which Christians view as proof of her priestly connections (while independent scholars dismiss the story completely, since women were not allowed inside Jewish temples).

Despite the gospels' disagreement over the identity of Joseph's father, the early Christians initially were content with this genealogy, since Jesus was descendant from a Jewish king on his father's side of the family and a Jewish priest on his mother's side. *However, the Christians soon realized that there were two more problems with this family tree*: (i) Mary supposedly was impregnated by God, which left open the question of how Jesus was related to King David; and (ii) they wanted Mary to be a "perpetual virgin," which left open the question of how to deal with Jesus' brothers and sisters, referenced as such in multiple sources. Thus, the Christians now had three problems to resolve. Below is their extremely creative solution to all three issues.

Jesus' First "Official" Family Tree

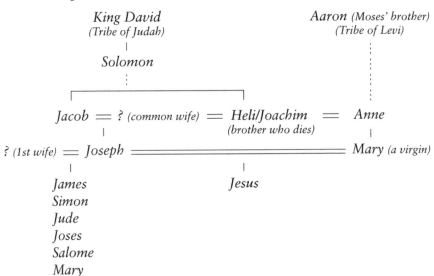

King David
(Tribe of Judah)

Aaron (Moses' brother)
(Tribe of Levi)

Solomon

Jacob ═ ? (common wife) ═ Heli/Joachim ═ Anne
(brother who dies)

? (1st wife) ═ Joseph ═══════════════ Mary (a virgin)

James
Simon
Jude
Joses
Salome
Mary

Jesus

With this family tree, the Christians solved all three of their problems. It's pretty confusing, so let me clarify. First, they found an ingenious way to deal with the conflict between the different men named as Joseph's fathers in the *Gospel of Matthew* and the *Gospel of Luke*. They assert that Jacob (the father specified in *Matthew*) and Heli (the father identified in *Luke*) were brothers. Next, they assert that Heli died and that Jacob married Heli's widow, based on the Jewish tradition that a man is obligated to marry his brother's widow. Jacob and the unnamed widow then had Joseph. Thus, Joseph's natural father was Jacob and his step-father was Heli.

Second, the Christians devised a way to make Mary a member of the Tribe of Levi *and* the Tribe of Judah. They do this by arguing that Heli and Joachim were really the same person! Therefore, when Anne married Heli/Joachim, she became a member of the Tribe of Judah through marriage. Once Mary's mother Anne was a member of the Tribe of Judah, Jesus was Davidic on his mother's side, too. Thus, Joseph becomes irrelevant, although it is a bonus that Jesus' adoptive father also was descendant from the House of David. Incidentally, this family tree makes Mary and Joseph cousins.

Third, the Christians came up with a solution to the pesky brother and sister problem. Over time, the early Church leaders declared that Mary was a virgin when Jesus was born *and* that she stayed one forever. They accomplished this goal by claiming that Joseph had an unnamed first wife with whom he had all the children identified as Jesus' brothers and sisters both in the *New Testament* and in numerous apocryphal gospels and historical records. The net result: Mary is a perpetual virgin and Jesus' brothers and sisters are relabeled step-brothers and step-sisters.

Although this family tree at first solved all three of the problems identified by the early Christian leaders, a fourth problem soon arose. It all started in 325 C.E., when **Roman Emperor Constantine** convened the **Council of Nicaea** and ordered the Christians to stop fighting. After Jesus died there were *dozens* of sects all claiming to understand his messages from God the best. Unfortunately, some of these sects were overtaken by men who craved power and who began vying for supremacy. In fact, the early bishops could not even agree on whether Jesus was a god, let alone God himself. The deification of Jesus will be discussed in more detail later. For now, realize that the early Christians were a divergent group that Constantine wanted under control. Thus, the purpose of the Council of Nicaea was to put an end to the incessant battles amongst the differing Christian sects and to consolidate and reinforce

Constantine's power over the pagans, the Jews, and the rapidly expanding Christian population.

Incidentally, historians still debate whether Constantine truly converted to Christianity, since he continued to worship the pagan god Mithras. It is true, though, that he politically endorsed Christianity by removing legal impediments against the religion, and that he submitted to baptism on his death bed. However, many scholars believe that he organized the Christians to consolidate his empire, and that he was baptized for superstitious reasons rather than true faith. Indeed, Constantine did not behave as a Christian. He murdered his wife, his son, and numerous other relatives. Moreover, it was **Roman Emperor Theodosius** who, in 380 c.e., made Christianity the official religion of the Roman Empire.

Nevertheless, Constantine does deserve credit (or blame, depending on your viewpoint), for convening the Council of Nicaea, creating the **Roman Catholic Church,** and temporarily suppressing the many divergent Christian beliefs. One of the first things the new Church did was address, yet again, the perceived problem with Jesus' family history. Around 400 c.e., a Catholic monk named Saint Jerome proposed a revised family tree. Moreover, three Catholic popes of that era, Damasus, Innocent I, and Gelasius, endorsed Saint Jerome's theory, called the "Trinubium," which is based on Mary's mother Anne having three husbands. Apparently, the newly formed Catholic Church really loved the concept of virginity (or hated sex), since Saint Jerome added two new concepts – Joseph's virginity and Mary's birth by Immaculate Conception. Here it is, folks: Jesus' family tree according to the Catholics.

Jesus' Second "Official" Family Tree

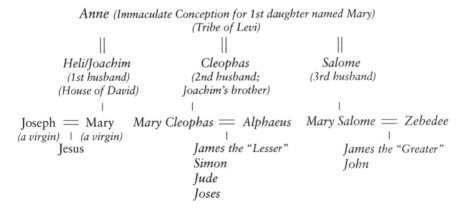

Anne (Immaculate Conception for 1st daughter named Mary)
(Tribe of Levi)

Heli/Joachim
(1st husband)
(House of David)

Cleophas
(2nd husband;
Joachim's brother)

Salome
(3rd husband)

Joseph = Mary   Mary Cleophas = Alphaeus   Mary Salome = Zebedee
(a virgin) | (a virgin)
Jesus

James the "Lesser"   James the "Greater"
Simon   John
Jude
Joses

In this family tree, Anne is married three times, a remarkable feat given that women rarely outlived men at that time. Through Anne's first husband, Jesus ultimately is born into the two most important Jewish tribes and the House of David. Through Anne's second husband, the brothers and sisters of Jesus, described as such in multiple sources, now are turned into cousins. Lastly, through Anne's third husband, the Catholics scramble the identity of Jesus' most important brother James by calling the marginal character James of Zebedee "the Greater."

We shall study **James the Just** (a/k/a James "the Lesser") in great detail later. For now, know that Jesus' blood brother James was an exceedingly important and pivotal historical figure. In fact, James was the undisputed Bishop of Jerusalem for thirty years after the crucifixion, and he died trying to keep the Christian movement in line with his brother's teachings. Nevertheless, a vastly different form of Christianity would emerge victorious after the Council of Nicaea, which is why the Catholics purposely minimized James in the *New Testament* and in the revised family tree. Tragically, they turned James into Jesus' cousin and nicknamed him the "Lesser" to the hardly mentioned apostle James of Zebedee. The Catholics also employed this technique to scramble the identities of the "Marys" in the *New Testament*. In the case of the Marys, the Catholics wanted to conceal the immense importance of **Mary Magdalene**, whom we will also discuss in detail later.

The early Catholics accepted the above genealogy chart for over one thousand years. The net result of this historically fallacious family tree is the following: (i) Joseph gets to be a virgin too; (ii) Jesus' brothers, the very men who lived through and helped shape the outcome of the Christian movement, get turned into Jesus' cousins, which further aids in camouflaging their historical significance; and (iii) Jesus' two sisters, Salome and Mary, are combined into one person who gives birth to James "the Greater," an apostle who one prominent scholar believes never even existed. I have to say, though, that my favorite twist (and it is hard to pick a favorite), is that Jesus' grandmother Anne now has three daughters, the first of whom is born miraculously, but all three of whom are named Mary.

Before we depart the topic of Jesus' genealogy, I should comment on the Catholic edict that Mary was the **Immaculate Conception**. Many people think this term applies to Jesus' birth. However, the term actually refers to Anne's conception of Mary, and it means that Mary was born "without the stain of original sin." In other words, not only was Mary impregnated by God and a perpetual virgin, she also was the only woman (other than Eve) born without sin. To this dogma, the Catholics later added the myth that Anne was a virgin, too. Eventually, the Catholics dismissed this fiction and officially went with the Trinubium theory, including the concept of the Immaculate Conception. Thus, in 1854 C.E., **Pope Pius IX** officially decreed that Mary was the Immaculate Conception, dicta now accepted as fact by Catholics who also believe that their popes are infallible and somehow directly ordained by God.

Needless to say, the early Christians did a superb job of creating complete mayhem with Jesus' genealogy. The inclusion of multiple Mary and multiple James characters was pure genius and a topic that we will study in more detail later. For now, though, we absolutely must move on or we will never get to the most important gift Jesus gave us – *his ministry*. Although most Christians point to Jesus' tragic and untimely death as his crowning achievement, I beg to differ. *It was Jesus' inspirational words and compassionate deeds that provide mankind with glorious and revolutionary lessons of Truth.*

Because I believe it was Jesus' life, not his death, that should have further enlightened mankind and contributed to God's Tower of Truth, I am eager to explore and analyze the dichotomy between Jesus' complicated political life versus his remarkably simple spiritual lessons. More importantly, though, I am anxious to remind as many people as possible exactly what Jesus said and did while he was alive, as it appears that most people have forgotten his messages. However, in order to flesh out the man behind the myth, we have to look at *all* the available information, including Roman, Jewish, and Christian source materials. While I have not read every document which mentions Jesus, I have read and painfully pondered all the holy texts, many relevant ancient documents, and compilations from some of our most respected religious scholars. Allow me one more short detour, then, to explain the evolution of *The Holy Bible* and to list the other source material that is at our disposal, particularly since some of the more recent discoveries have dramatically altered Christian history but have yet to make their way into mainstream Christian awareness.

To start with, it is absolutely critical to accept the fact that when Jesus was alive and for roughly three hundred years after his death, there were dozens of different Jewish and later Christian sects all claiming superior knowledge about Jesus. It also is critical to realize that these factions *never* would have agreed on one *catholic* interpretation (Greek for "universal"), if the Roman Empire had not intervened. In fact, even after Emperor Constantine convened the Council of Nicaea, the Christian bishops continued to fight over doctrine, including, most notably, the divinity of Jesus and which gospels to canonize in *The Holy Bible*. Indeed, Christian in-fighting has never stopped. As we shall see in Chapter Four, the Catholic Church has splintered many times, starting with the **Great Schism** of 1054 C.E., which resulted in a new sect called the **Eastern Orthodox Church**.

The point to remember is that there has *never* been a consensus amongst Jesus' followers on the central tenets of Christianity, a fact which, in and of itself, provides startling evidence that Jesus never intended to start a brand new religion. However, Jesus' earliest devotees did manage to grasp one important Truth: *Judaism needed to be updated*.

Consequently, the first "Christians," all of whom were Jewish, began to record what they had learned from Jesus. Scholars believe that by 50 C.E., the apostles had recorded Jesus' lessons into a teaching manual, which they refer to as the *Sayings Source*, even though the text has never been found. In the 1980s, an international team of historians cross-referenced all of the available scripture for Jesus' most repeated quotes, which they then compiled in *The Book of Q* (the "Q" stands for *quelle*, which is German for "source"). Today, you can buy *The Book of Q* at almost any book store and experience for yourself the few verifiable quotes attributable to Jesus.

Based on the *Sayings Source*, Jesus' followers started to write gospels which contained his quotes *plus* details of his life and his tragic death. As time passed, the gospels became more "magical" in nature, and Jesus' status as a human Messiah was elevated to include the concept that he was the "son of God." Eventually, some of the gospels began to equate Jesus with God, as though they were one entity. In total, historians have catalogued over one hundred gospels and other ancient texts written by Jesus' followers over the course of roughly three hundred years. Consequently, there is a plethora of information at our disposal to help piece together the mystery of Jesus.

Now, let us take a look at *The Holy Bible*. The *Bible* contains the four canonical gospels, twenty-one letters, a choppy history of the thirty years after Jesus' death called *Acts of the Apostles*, and an apocalyptic scripture entitled *The Revelation to John*. Historical records indicate that the early church leaders vigorously debated which gospels should be incorporated into the *New Testament*. In fact, the bishops passionately argued over which gospels were authentic and which were "heretical," a term that would later sentence millions to oppression and death and which still is used by the Catholic Church to silence unorthodox theologians. It was not until 364 C.E., at the **Council of Laodicea,** that the bishops reached a consensus on which gospels were "orthodox." Even so, the Christians continued to bicker with each other and tinker with the *Bible* until making a final determination regarding its content at the **Council of Trent** in 1545 C.E. Needless to say, the Christian *New Testament,* just like the Jewish *Old Testament,* should not be accepted by an intelligent Truth seeker without the aid of further research materials.

Here is a closer look at the four gospels of the *New Testament* in order of appearance:

1. The *Gospel of Matthew* was written approximately 90 C.E. By tradition, the Catholics credited this gospel to the apostle Matthew, but even the Catholics now agree with the modern scholars who assert that the unknown author used Matthew's name as a pseudonym, which was a common practice in gospel writing. This gospel was based on the *Sayings Source* and on the *Gospel of Mark.* Scholars agree that it was intended for a Jewish audience, as it closely parallels the Jewish view that salvation is dependent on righteousness and good works.

2. The *Gospel of Mark* was written around 70 C.E. It is the oldest of the canonical gospels and was written for a Gentile (i.e., pagan) audience. Some historians believe that it was written in Rome by an assistant who knew Paul or Peter. Different versions of this scripture exist, and scholars believe that two different endings were added to this gospel (one in the 300s and one in the 600s C.E.).

3. The *Gospel of Luke* was written about 90 C.E. The author of this gospel also is unknown, although in his letters, Paul mentions a physician named Luke with whom he traveled. This author also wrote *Acts of the Apostles.* He intended his work for a Gentile audience and he relied on the *Sayings Source.* This is the gospel which was the most palatable to the Romans (and perhaps the most offensive to the Jews), as the Roman governor tries three times to release Jesus.

4. The *Gospel of John* was written sometime after 100 C.E. Traditionally, the Catholics ascribed this gospel to the apostle John, but even they now agree with the modern scholars that the author is unknown. This gospel, too, has been edited a number of times over the centuries. It is the most magical of the gospels and the only one in which Jesus states that he is the "son of God."

To summarize, historians now agree that none of the four canonical gospels were written by the apostles or anyone else who walked with Jesus or knew him firsthand. Moreover, of the twent-one letters contained in the *New Testament* (fourteen of which were written by Paul), only Paul's letters are thought to be authentic and, as we shall see, Paul never met Jesus and seems totally unaware of the *Sayings Source*, which contained Jesus' quotes. Instead, Paul develops his own theory, that faith in Jesus as a unique son of God is the only requirement for salvation. Sadly, even the letter attributable to Jesus' brother James is suspect, although the content of the letter is consistent with James' view that blind faith without good works never brings salvation.

Thus, I need to stress two important points before referencing the *New Testament* for any reliable information: (i) none of the four canonical gospels were written by the apostles or anyone else who knew Jesus firsthand; and (ii) three of the gospels were written for a Gentile audience – pagans who believed in gods and goddesses with magical powers.

Once the Christian bishops decided on the material to be included in the *New Testament*, they banned the rest. Researchers refer to these banned scriptures as the **Lost Gospels**. Some bishops even went so far as to order the "heretical" texts destroyed. Fortunately, some unknown defenders of Truth defied the orthodox bishops. These brave unsung heroes somehow managed to hide and preserve the apocryphal gospels. During the last millennia, the *Lost Gospels* have slowly started to surface and probably will continue to surface to mankind's benefit and to the Church's horror. Even so, no one could have predicted the dramatic turn of events which occurred in the middle of the 20th Century.

In 1945 C.E., an Egyptian local in Nag Hammadi, Egypt uncovered an amazing treasure trove of information when he accidentally discovered books that appeared to be quite ancient. These books, which historians refer to as the **Gnostic Gospels**, tell some of the same stories about Jesus as relayed in the *New Testament*, plus they contain some new information. Moreover, some of the *Gnostic Gospels* are older than the four sanctioned gospels, and they confirm the immense importance of Jesus' two most trusted apostles, James the Just and Mary Magdalene.

Then, in 1947 C.E. and just as the the nation of Israel was reforming, even more ancient documents were found at the site of the old Jewish settlement at Qumran near the Dead Sea. Historians refer to these documents as the **Dead Sea Scrolls**, and most independent scholars now think that the *Scrolls* were written by the Jews during the reign of Herod the Great and through the period of time when Jesus and his brother James were preaching. Consequently, during the last sixty years we have discovered and now have at our disposal much more information about Jesus, James, Mary Magdalene, and the many divergent Jewish and early Christian sects.

More exciting still is the fact that this new data has now been reviewed and analyzed by independent historians. After the *Dead Sea Scrolls* were found, the Catholic Church obtained unfettered control over all but seven of them until 1991, when microfiche copies of the *Scrolls* finally were made available to the public. Prior to 1991, the Catholic priest who headed the "international" research team refused anyone else access to the *Scrolls*. In fact, there was only one member of the team who wasn't Catholic, and he eventually blew the whistle on the panel's purposeful concealment and misinterpretations of the *Scrolls*. Some scholars have even suggested that the Catholics may have hidden or destroyed some of the more sensitive *Scrolls*, as there are numerous accounts of missing parchments. Regardless of these accusations, the Truth is that independent scholars were denied access to the *Scrolls* for over forty years, a scandal that will be discussed later. *At any rate, we now have fifty-two Gnostic Gospels and remnants of over eight hundred Dead Sea Scrolls to add to our pool of available information about Jesus.*

As you can imagine, independent scholars are having a field day with these ancient texts. Unfortunately, it appears that little of this new information is reaching the masses, another reason why I decided to write this book. Frankly, if you are Christian and you don't know about the *Lost Gospels,* the *Gnostic Gospels,* or the *Dead Sea Scrolls,* then you are missing out on the most revealing information we have on Jesus. Moreover, if your church leaders have failed to address and explain these important texts, they are not serving their purported function.

Let us start our analysis, though, with the four "orthodox" gospels. After Jesus was born, the *New Testament* gospels are frustratingly silent regarding Jesus' childhood and his religious training. In fact, the sanctioned gospels contain only two stories about Jesus' childhood.

The first story appears in Chapter 2 of the *Gospel of Matthew,* when the three wise men follow the star and visit the holy family in Bethlehem. Herod the Great is outraged to learn that the *magi* intend to honor the "king of the Jews," so he tells the *magi* to report back to him the exact location of the baby so that he "may go and do him homage." In reality, though, Herod wants to kill Jesus, which the priests realize through a dream. Then, an angel appears to Joseph and instructs him to take the family to Egypt for safekeeping. When the *magi* fail to report back to Herod, he orders the massacre of all the baby boys who live in and around Bethlehem.

The only other childhood story appears in Chapter 2 of the *Gospel of Luke*. When Jesus is twelve years old, he and his parents travel to the Temple in Jerusalem for the Passover festivities. During the return trip to Nazareth, Joseph and Mary discover that Jesus is missing. After three days of searching, Joseph and Mary find Jesus at the Temple talking to the rabbis, who are astounded by the breadth of his knowledge. His parents admonish him for his behavior and Jesus replies, "Did you not know that I must be in my Father's house?"

That's it. Those are the only two stories related to Jesus' childhood in *The Holy Bible*. Christians who rely solely on the *Bible* stories often refer to Jesus' childhood and young adulthood as the "lost years" of his life. Yet, were they lost?

Based on *all* the early Christian texts now available to us, a much fuller picture of Jesus' childhood emerges. For example, the *Lost Gospels* include two scriptures entirely dedicated to his childhood. In these scriptures, the **Infancy Gospel of James** and the **Infancy Gospel of Thomas** (traditionally credited to Jesus' brothers James and Judas Thomas, respectively, but probably written in pseudonym), Jesus is described as performing miracles as an infant, just like Buddha. For instance, the water that Mary uses to bathe the baby Jesus contains all sorts of powers, including the ability to cure leprosy and a deadly fever. In addition, Jesus' swaddling blanket and clothes contain amazing powers, as these garments can repel demons and even raise the dead. One of the more amusing stories relates that Jesus' mere presence cures a new bridegroom of impotency, since prior to seeing Jesus the man "could not enjoy his wife."

According to the *Infancy* gospels, after Herod the Great dies, the holy family returns to Judea. When Jesus is seven years old, he and his friends are playing in mud puddles and making animals and birds out of clay. Jesus makes his clay figures walk and fly. When the other children see these wonders they report the events to their parents, who thereafter keep their children at home. Jesus gets angry that his playmates are hiding from him, so he temporarily turns them into kid goats! Other versions of these stories are even more dramatic. In one episode, Jesus kills a boy who destroys his mud pond. Jesus also kills a child who knocks him down and a teacher who tries to whip him. Distressed at the increasing violence, Joseph declares to Mary, "henceforth, we will not allow him to go out of the house; for everyone who displeases him is killed."

After relaying these amazing tales of how Jesus learned to use and, eventually, control his mystical powers, the *Infancy Gospel of James* ends on a very serious note. After causing the deaths mentioned above, Jesus is secluded by his parents until the trip to the Temple in Jerusalem when Jesus is twelve. The *James* version of the Temple story is similar to the rendition contained in the *Gospel of Luke*, but much more vivid and haunting, as Jesus has greatly matured in the intervening five years and now seems to realize his life mission. Ponder the intensity of the following responses given by Jesus to his elders' questions.

> [To the rabbis] And he explained to them the books of the law, and precepts, and statutes: and the mysteries that were contained in the books of the prophets; things which the mind of no creature could reach....
>
> [To an astronomer] The Lord Jesus replied, and told him the number of heavenly bodies, as also their triangular, square, and sextile aspect; their progressive and retrograde motion; their size and several prognostications; and other things which the reason of man had never discovered....
>
> [To a philosopher] He replied, and explained to him physics and metaphysics. Also those things which were above and below the power of nature; The powers also of the body, its humours, and their effects. Also the number of its members, and bones, veins, arteries, and nerves .... How the soul operated upon the body; What its various sensations and faculties were; The faculty of speaking, anger, desire; And lastly the manner of its composition and dissolution; and other things, which the understanding of no creature had ever reached.

Infancy Gospel of James, Chapter 21

The above passage is absolutely mind bending. Clearly, Jesus had received training from some source and is no longer operating as a child. The gospel goes on to report that after Joseph and Mary find Jesus and return to Nazareth, Jesus "obeyed them in all things." Thereafter, the gospel states that Jesus "began to conceal his miracles and secret works." Finally, the gospel states that Jesus continued his studies in earnest until he turned fourteen, at which point Jewish boys are deemed men.

Although portions of the *Infancy* gospels may seem silly or overly magical, the reality is that *all* the gospels likely suffer from the ills of exaggeration and poetic license to some degree, and to a degree that we will never be able to accurately judge. For instance, is it any harder to believe that Jesus at age seven flew into a childhood rage and accidentally killed a friend, than it is to believe that Jesus at age thirty-three raised his friend Lazarus from the dead? The point is, Christians accept the Lazarus story because it is contained in one of the four "orthodox" gospels. However, with over sixty gospels now available to us, why would we limit our search for Truth to just four? The answer is, we shouldn't. However, once we start studying the apocryphal materials, the search for Truth does become more complicated. The issue is how to discern which of the ancient texts is the most accurate versus which of them have been altered to promote a man-made agenda completely unrelated to Jesus' ministry, such as the acquisition of wealth and power.

Let me explain how I have approached this dilemma. As I read and study the four gospels in the *New Testament*, the *Lost Gospels*, the *Gnostic Gospels*, and the *Dead Seas Scrolls*, I first pause to consider which texts resonate with me as valid expressions of Truth. Incidentally, because I believe in miracles, I have no trouble accepting that God imbued his messengers with special powers. Next, I consider the age of the text and the manner of its creation. In this way, I attempt to put the document into its respective historical context, as the politics of each century greatly affected what Jesus' followers were safely reading and writing. Therefore, as I read the ancient texts, I factor in all these considerations and then attempt to draw rational conclusions. There really is no other way to make sense of the vast amount of conflicting source material.

For example, any Christian gospel that offended the Romans would have been immediately confiscated and destroyed. That is why most historians believe that the earliest Christian texts, except for the closely guarded *Dead Sea Scrolls*, were all written with the Romans in mind. The fearsome oppression of the Roman Empire always was a consideration, as the Christians were persecuted mercilessly by numerous caesars, most notably Roman Emperor Nero. This constant threat to the survival of the Jesus movement explains the ludicrous portrayal of **Pontius Pilate** in the canonical gospels as a champion for Jesus' innocence and a pawn of the Sanhedrin Council. The Truth is that Pontius Pilate was a ruthless governor who crucified thousands.

Alternatively, one can assume that the Christian forefathers were better equipped to judge the authenticity of the gospels. That has been the traditional Christian view, plus the notion that the early Christian bishops possessed some sort of divine insight from God. However, even if you believe that the early church leaders somehow knew which gospels God preferred (after centuries of debate, editing sessions, and violence to ensure God's result), that still doesn't explain why all of a sudden the *Lost Gospels*, the *Gnostic Gospels*, and the *Dead Sea Scrolls* have surfaced. Moreover, it is difficult to explain why certain banned gospels, like the *Infancy Gospel of James*, initially were accepted as valid scripture well into the 4th Century and still are deemed orthodox by the Eastern Orthodox Church in Istanbul and the Coptic Christian Church in Egypt where many of the infancy *Bible* stories took place.

May I humbly suggest that the reappearance of these precious documents is no mere coincidence. Remember our good friend Carl Jung and his theory on synchronicity? I find it both synchronous and nothing short of miraculous that just as mankind is on the brink of a massive paradigm shift (or self-extinction), God has allowed these lost records about Jesus to surface. Thus, it appears to me that God now is *insisting* that we update our Tower of Truth, a process we should have been tending to all along. Moreover, to me it is obvious that most of the world has forgotten what the Prophets said, particularly the messages of Jesus. So what did Jesus say? Finally, we are ready to discuss the heart of Christianity and I can barely contain my excitement!

After the Temple visit, which happened when Jesus was twelve, the *New Testament* gospels immediately jump to Jesus' ministry, which started when he was in his early thirties. Tragically, Jesus only was able to teach for about three years before being brutally executed. It is these three action-packed years that are the most important in terms of providing mankind with a template for compassionate living – the true path to salvation. Indeed, during these three years, Jesus explicitly told us how to reach God in heaven. As we shall see, Jesus was crystal clear on this score. In Truth, it is tantamount to blasphemy how Jesus' prescription for salvation has been twisted by foolish and corrupt men over the last two thousand years. Let us begin, then, to study the ministry of Jesus and remove all doubt about how we achieve union with the Supreme Being.

According to three of the *New Testament* gospels, Jesus begins his mission with a solitary journey into the desert. For forty days, Jesus isolates himself to commune with God, which was a common and necessary practice for all the Prophets. During this contemplative sojourn, Jesus squares-off against **Satan**, a lesser deity created by the Christians as we shall see in Chapter Four. Satan tempts Jesus and tries to deter him from his mission. This sort of temptation also seems to be a prerequisite for an advanced spiritual journey, as all the Prophets contended with "demons."

In Jesus' case, Satan proposes three challenges to trick Jesus into aborting God's mission. First, Satan appeals to Jesus' bodily needs to test his detachment from the physical plane. After fasting for forty days, Jesus is starving so the Devil taunts him by suggesting that Jesus turn rocks into bread. Jesus swiftly replies, "One does not live by bread alone, but by every word that comes forth from the mouth of God." This statement shows two things: (i) Jesus had adopted an ascetic lifestyle and had overcome his material plane needs, just as Buddha starved himself underneath the Bo tree to reach enlightenment; and (ii) Jesus had forsaken Earth plane attachments in favor of perfecting his relationship with God in the Ethereal plane, also in compliance with the earlier teachings of Hinduism and Buddhism. In short, Jesus had totally embraced the *Saddha* process.

Second, the Devil takes Jesus to the Temple and dares him to prove he is the son of God by jumping off the parapet and flying. Jesus responds by declaring that it is wrong to "put the Lord, your God, to the test." Christians sometimes point to this passage as evidence that Jesus realized he was God and that he was refusing to display his powers for Satan, but that is not how this passage reads. The test was not whether Jesus could fly, but whether Jesus would ask God to "command his angels" to support Jesus while he tried to fly. Thus, by denying Satan, Jesus was refusing to test his relationship with God or ask God for any favors, which is our first evidence that Jesus viewed himself as a separate entity from God.

Third, Satan offers Jesus consummate power over all the world if Jesus will agree to worship him instead of God. Jesus responds by restating the Second Commandment, "The Lord, your God, shall you worship and him alone shall you serve." This quote is highly significant for two reasons, as it further explains these basic Truths: (i) Jesus and God are separate entities; and (ii) Earth plane power not only is meaningless in the sight of God and real men of faith, the desire for control over others is a selfish and egotistical goal more aligned with the satanic principles than with the true messengers of God.

After Jesus returns from his trial in the desert, the gospels suggest that Jesus has a plan which he immediately starts to execute. First, Jesus picks his twelve apostles. Some scholars doubt that Jesus had twelve apostles because the *New Testament* never adequately identifies who some of these men were or how they contributed to the mission. For example, one very respected historian has argued that James of Zebedee (whose only reference in *Acts of the Apostles* is his untimely death by the second King Herod in 44 C.E.), never even existed, and that this so-called James "the Greater" was fabricated to confuse and undermine the historical contributions of Jesus' brother James. Indeed, the popular theory amongst independent historians is that the reported number of apostles is mere allegory for the twelve tribes of Israel. Additionally, researchers point to the fact that at Qumran, the sanctuary for the Jewish sect which authored the *Dead Sea Scrolls*, twelve priests ran the community. Some historians postulate that the twelve priests at Qumran were Jesus' twelve apostles. Thus, there currently is a *huge* debate raging amongst scholars about who the apostles were and even whether there were twelve of them.

Furthermore, it is important to note that not even the four gospels of the *New Testament* agree on the identity of the twelve apostles. Here is the collected list according to: the *Gospel of Matthew* (Chapter 10:1); the *Gospel of Mark* (Chapter 3:16); the *Gospel of Luke* (Chapter 6:14); and the *Gospel of John* (Chapters 1:37–1:45; 6:71; 11:16; 13:23; and 14:22).

1. **Simon** (a/k/a **Peter** and nicknamed **Cephas** by Jesus, which means "rock"): According to Paul's letters, Peter is one of the "three pillars" of the Jerusalem church after Jesus dies. His leadership also is stressed in *Acts of the Apostles*. Later, Peter will be labeled the first Bishop of Rome, even though there is no mention of him going to Rome in the *New Testament*. Later still, he will be retroactively named the first pope by the Roman Catholic Church, which sought control of the religion and dominion over the Eastern Orthodox Church, which officially separated from the Catholics during the Great Schism of 1054 C.E.

2. **Andrew** (Peter's brother): He neither ministers nor contributes to the mission in any significant way. In fact, he is hardly mentioned in the *New Testament*. Consequently, Andrew is one of the "shadow figures" in the list of apostles.

3. **James, son of Zebedee** (a/k/a **James "the Greater"**): His ministry also is never mentioned in the *New Testament*, thereby providing zero support for his nickname "the Greater." Moreover, his early death in 44 C.E. makes him another shadow figure in the cause.

4. **John, son of Zebedee** (brother of James): John no longer is considered the author of any *New Testament* work. However, he is one of the

"three pillars" of the church after Jesus dies, according to Paul's letters. Traditionally, he was thought to be the mysterious "beloved disciple" in the *Gospel of John*, although new research casts serious doubt on this supposition, to be discussed later.

5. **Philip:** Another shadow figure, since his ministry is never mentioned.

6. **Bartholomew** (a/k/a **Nathanael**): Another shadow figure of no apparent consequence, as he is rarely discussed in the *New Testament*.

7. **Matthew** (a/k/a **Levi**): He is described as a Jewish tax collector for the Romans whom Jesus nevertheless embraces. However, his ministry is never mentioned and he is no longer considered the author of the *Gospel of Matthew*. Hence, he is another shadow figure in the apostolic mission.

Now, here is where it gets interesting:

8. **James, son of Alphaeus** (a/k/a **James "the Just"**; a/k/a **James "the Lesser"**): Based on: (i) Paul in his *New Testament* letters; (ii) *Acts of the Apostles*; and (iii) the Roman historian Josephus in *Antiquities*, independent theologians now believe that James of Alphaeus is James the Just, the real brother of Jesus. Moreover, not only is James clearly identified by Paul as one of the "three pillars" of the Jerusalem church after Jesus' death, James also is identified in numerous historical records as the undisputed first Bishop of Jerusalem and legitimate heir to his brother's mission. Lastly, James traditionally is thought to be the author of the **Letter of James**, which is found in the *New Testament* and which attacks Paul's version of Christianity. In sum, James is the most important historical figure other than Jesus in the Christian movement, a fact purposely suppressed by the Catholic Church for nearly two thousand years after they decided Paul's version of Christianity was "orthodox."

9. Simon, the Cananean (a/k/a Simon "the Zealot"): If we rely solely on the New Testament for information about this apostle, we certainly would relegate him to the shadows, as he is listed as an apostle in all the gospels but hardly mentioned again. However, independent scholars now believe that he is none other than Jesus' second brother and identified as Simeon bar Cleophas in numerous historical documents, which makes him the second Bishop of Jerusalem. Thus, some scholars now assert that: (i) Simon assumed control of the Jesus movement after James was killed in 62 C.E.;

(ii) Simon was the second Bishop of Jerusalem during the riots which led to the Roman destruction of Jerusalem in 70 C.E. and the scattering of the both the Jews and early Christians; and (iii) Simon survived the riots and was still in control of the Jesus movement when the Jews and early Christians fled to their fortress at Qumran, which ultimately fell to the Romans in 134 C.E.

10. **Thomas** (a/k/a **Thomas Didymus**; a/k/a **Thomas "the Twin"**; a/k/a **Judas Thomas**): Based on one *New Testament* gospel, Thomas was absent when Jesus resurrected and refused to believe it happened until he touched Jesus' wounds. This "doubting Thomas" story is rejected by serious theologians, who now believe that Thomas was Jesus' third brother, Jude, and the author of the now famous *Gnostic Gospel*, the *Gospel of Thomas*, which is based on the *Sayings Source* and contains amazing information about Jesus that predates the canonical gospels.

11. **Thaddeus** (a/k/a **Judas "not Iscariot"**; a/k/a **Judas Thomas**): Traditionally, he is considered the author of the *New Testament* **Letter of Jude**. Scholars now suspect that he is the same Jude as apostle number 10, the third brother of Jesus, and that his identity got thoroughly and intentionally scrambled to further hide the fact that Jesus had siblings. Recently, a few theologians have speculated that Jesus' third brother, Jude, is none other than our next apostle, the infamous Judas.

12. **Judas Iscariot** (a/k/a **Judas, son of Simon the Iscariot**): This is the maligned apostle who, by tradition and according to the *New Testament* gospels, betrayed the movement by reporting to the corrupt Sanhedrin Council where to arrest Jesus. Not surprisingly, new research is creating quite a stir with the theory that this Judas is another alias for Jesus' third brother Jude. Thus, apostles 10, 11, and 12 may all be the same person which, if true, dramatically alters the meaning of Jesus' command to Judas at the Last Supper, "What you are going to do, do quickly." (*Gospel of John*, Chapter 13:27).

Now, just for fun, let's compare the above list of apostles to "Jesus' Second 'Official' Family Tree," after the Catholic Church decided to turn Jesus' brothers and sisters into cousins (See also, *Gospel of Matthew*, Chapter 13:55). In particular, note that three of Jesus' "cousins" have the same names as the last five apostles.

JESUS' SECOND "OFFICIAL" FAMILY TREE

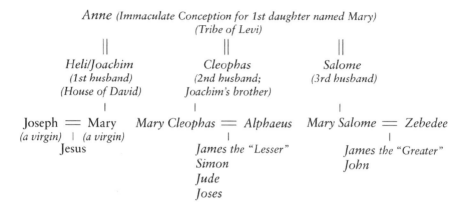

Anne (Immaculate Conception for 1st daughter named Mary)
(Tribe of Levi)

Heli/Joachim	Cleophas	Salome
(1st husband)	*(2nd husband;*	*(3rd husband)*
(House of David)	*Joachim's brother)*	

Joseph = Mary   Mary Cleophas = Alphaeus   Mary Salome = Zebedee
(a virgin) | *(a virgin)*
  Jesus   James the *"Lesser"*   James the *"Greater"*
                       Simon   John
                       Jude
                       Joses

The reader now has all the available information to judge whether the most important apostles were Jesus' step-brothers, cousins, or real brothers. At a minimum, it is clear that at some point Jesus' mission became a family affair. Indeed, one scholar, Dr. Robert Eisenman, refers to Jesus' spiritual dynasty as similar to the Kennedy political dynasty, assassinations and all. Although this may be a lot of new information, please bear the above facts and theories in mind as we continue to unravel the many riddles surrounding the Prophet Jesus.

The *New Testament* gospels report that after he chooses his apostles, Jesus formally begins preaching to his Jewish brethren. In the beginning, Jesus preaches in the area known as Galilee, north of his alleged home town of Nazareth. It is interesting to note, however, that the gospels usually refer to him as Jesus the "**Nazorean**," *not* Jesus of "Nazareth" (See *Gospel of Matthew*, Chapter 2:23). This is an important distinction because researchers now believe that the term Nazorean is a reference to a Jewish sect, *not* people from the town of Nazareth. Pliny, another Roman historian of the 1st Century, reports that there were dozens of Jewish sects in existence during this era. The Roman invasion of Palestine and the corruption of the Sanhedrin Council caused the Jews to splinter into many groups, including the Pharisees, Sadducees, Essenes, Daily Baptists, Samaritans, the Sons of Zodak at Qumran, and the Nazoreans. Thus, Judaism, just like early Christianity, was chock full of divergent sects, all of which thought they understood God the best.

Specifically, the Nazoreans were a sect that lived near Galilee and who believed that they were the preservers of the true faith of Israel. Some historians believe that the Nazoreans and the Essenes were related sects and closely allied to, if not part of, the "**Sons of Zodak,**" the authors of certain *Dead Sea Scrolls*. The bottom line is that the Nazoreans were fundamentalists and most were *not* pacifists. In fact, this region of the Roman Empire was a hotbed of discontent, and many of the Jews who lived there were Zionists who supported going to war to regain their national independence. Consequently, modern scholars believe that Jesus grew up near or in a radical sect that was disgusted with the Sanhedrin priests and was planning a revolt against Rome.

In this politically charged climate, Jesus elects to start his ministry of peace. He chooses a village called Bethsaida and travels to the outskirts of this town where the Jewish outcasts, such as the sick, the handicapped, the lepers, and the prostitutes are forced to live. Thus, Jesus initially reaches out to those Jews who comprise the lowest element of society, including the tax collectors who are scorned and branded traitors by their Jewish brethren. Jesus also preaches in Capernaum, where he performs many of his healing miracles, feeds five thousand people with five loaves of bread and two fish, and walks on water in the Sea of Galilee. It appears that Jesus purposely chooses the Galilee region to start his ministry in order to reach the "common people." By all accounts, Jesus' plan for reaching the masses is a smashing success. It is not long before he wins their support with his revolutionary messages of total acceptance, sharing, and love.

However, there is one town that rejects him. In Chapter 4 of the *Gospel of Luke*, Jesus goes to Nazareth to preach and he is recognized as Joseph's son. When Jesus refuses to perform a miracle and states that "no prophet is accepted in his home town," the crowd becomes incensed and tries to hurl him down a hill. Similarly, in Chapter 3 of the *Gospel of Mark*, Jesus goes home to preach, but "when his relatives heard of this they set out to seize him, for they said, 'He is out of his mind.'" This section also recites that Jesus snubs his mother and brothers when they call to him from the crowd, saying, "Who are my mother and my brothers? ... Whoever does the will of God is my brother and sister and mother." These stories are revealing for a couple reasons, since they show: (i) Jesus was not afraid to defy either his family or the Zealots, who disagreed with his peaceful attempts to bring about change; and (ii) Jesus' family initially denied his ministry, which comports with the theory that Jesus' brothers did not join the mission until later.

So why did the disenfranchised and the truly pious embrace Jesus' messages of Truth, while certain members of his family, the Jewish Zealots, and even the orthodox priests were reluctant to follow him? The answer is simple. Jesus was a hero to those who were despised, disillusioned, utterly destitute, but able to recognize his messages of Truth; and Jesus was a threat to those who were angry, violent, wealthy, hypocritically pious, and perversely powerful.

In sum, Jesus assured God's salvation for souls who love their neighbor by sharing, living compassionately, exercising forgiveness, and searching for Ethereal plane Truth; and Jesus reaffirmed God's judgment on souls who harm their neighbor by hoarding wealth, living selfishly, judging others, and exploiting positions of Earth plane power.

Let us now study Jesus' *exact* teachings in minute detail. A perfect place to start is with the glorious **Sermon on the Mount,** in which Jesus begins to explain how a soul attains salvation.

> *Blessed are the **meek**, for they will inherit the earth.*
> *Blessed are those who hunger and thirst for righteousness,*
> *for they will be filled.*
> *Blessed are the **merciful**, for they will be shown mercy.*
> *Blessed are the **pure** in heart, for they will see God.*
> *Blessed are the **peacemakers**, for they will be called sons of God.*
> *Blessed are those who are persecuted because of*
> *righteousness, for theirs is the kingdom of heaven.*
> *[Emphasis added]*
>
> Gospel of Matthew, Chapter 5:5

I have highlighted certain words above to underscore the two critical points of the sermon. *First, Jesus emphasizes that righteousness and pacifism are the keys to salvation.* We shall see that Jesus repeats this theme of love and forgiveness over and over again to drive home the point that it takes great effort to achieve salvation. In fact, Jesus *never* asserts that faith alone, either in him or in God, earns a person a place in heaven. This fundamental point needs to be stressed, since many Christians have been incorrectly taught that blind faith in Jesus as a savior, or as a god, or as a human manifestation of God, entitles them to automatic admittance in heaven. The Truth is that Jesus consistently upheld the Jewish definition of righteousness, which includes both faith *and* good works. Unfortunately, Paul will later assert the "blind faith" formula for salvation, which the Catholic bishops later seize upon as a tool to manipulate and control the masses.

Second, Jesus emphasizes that each of us has the innate potential to be "children of God." Indeed, he repeats this message of personal responsibility over and over again to let us know that we can perfect our divinity, just as he did. Originally, the Jewish phrase "son of God" meant a member of the nation of Israel. However, Jesus uses this term to refer to himself and anyone who accepts his messages of Truth. As we shall see, Jesus never claimed to be a unique "son of God." This is another point that needs to be stressed, since most Christians have been taught that Jesus is the only son of God, which somehow makes Jesus and God synonymous.

Let us return for a moment to Jesus' central theme regarding good works and forgiveness. In these enlightening quotes, it appears that Jesus is setting a pretty high standard for those who aspire to be "children of the Most High." Certainly, more than faith is required.

> *But to you who hear I say, love your enemies, do good to those who hate you, bless those who curse you, pray for those who mistreat you. To the person who strikes you on one cheek, offer the other one as well, and from the person who takes your cloak, do not withhold even your tunic. Give to everyone who asks of you, and from the one who takes what is yours do not demand it back.* **Do unto others as you would have them do to you.**
>
> *For if you love those who love you, what credit is that to you? Even sinners love those who love them. And if you do good to those who do good to you, what credit is that to you? Even sinners do the same. ... But rather, love your enemies and do good to them ...; then your reward will be great and you will be children of the Most High. [Emphasis added]*
>
> *Gospel of Luke, Chapter 6:27–35*

Paul will later assert that Jesus' martyrdom does away with all the pesky Jewish laws and that all we have to do in order to go to heaven is believe that Jesus died for our sins and accept him as our savior. As we shall see, Paul will go so far as to abandon the Ten Commandments, asserting that blind faith in "Christ Jesus" is all that is expected of us. Jesus, on the other hand, seems to hold a different view.

> *[A man] asked him, "Good Teacher, what must I do to inherit eternal life?" Jesus answered him, "Why do you call me good? No one is good but God alone. You know the commandments: You shall not kill, you shall not commit adultery; you shall not steal; you shall not bear false witness; you shall not defraud; honor your father and your mother."*
>
> *He replied and said to him, "Teacher, all of these I have observed in my youth." Jesus ... said to him, "You are lacking in one thing. Go, sell what you have and give to the poor and you will have treasure in heaven ...."*

> *Jesus looked around and said to his disciples, "How hard it is for those who have wealth to enter the kingdom of God! ... It is easier for a camel to pass through the eye of a needle than for one who is rich to enter the kingdom of God."*
>
> *Gospel of Mark*, Chapter 10:17–25

So far, at least, Jesus seems to be providing us with clear and ample advice on how to join God in heaven. Conversely, Jesus also is pretty clear on who is *not* a child of God and who will *not* be admitted into the kingdom of heaven. In the following verses, Jesus reiterates the primary lesson of Buddha, that attachment to Earth plane temptations, such as wealth, excess in food, shallow amusement, or perverse use of power, are incompatible with spiritual enlightenment. Therefore, one cannot honestly commence a journey of Truth toward God and the Ethereal plane until one begins to detach from the Earth plane and its many distractions and illusions. In short, the *Saddha* process demands devotion to perfecting self.

> *But woe to you who are rich, for you have already received your comfort.*
> *Woe to you who are well fed now, for you will go hungry.*
> *Woe to you who laugh now, for you will mourn and weep.*
> *Woe to you when all men speak well of you, for that is how their fathers treated the false prophets.*
>
> *Gospel of Luke*, Chapter 6:24

At the beginning of this chapter, I grouped all of mankind's shortcomings into two main categories, which I call the cardinal sins of greed and pride. These cardinal sins are "evil" because they interfere with and, in the case of many souls, totally block spiritual development. To recap:

Unbridled greed leads to an obsession with money and material possessions.
Undaunted pride leads to an obsession with power and world domination.

I cannot take credit for reducing evil to these two sins. Rather, it was the Tower of Truth, built with the lessons of all the Prophets, that led me to this conclusion. If you carefully read the *New Testament* or *The Book of Q*, which contains the verifiable quotes of Jesus, you will find that Jesus clearly summarized this Truth. First, Jesus synthesized all of the Ten Commandments by telling us to love our neighbors as ourselves. Second, he condensed all of mankind's sins by telling us not to be greedy or power hungry.

Let us consider these Earth plane distractions or "sins" one at a time, starting with Jesus' messages regarding material plane riches. Wealth, in particular, seemed to disturb Jesus, and he condemns rich people often in his lessons. Most of us are familiar with the parable about the camel and the eye of the needle, but check out these other quotes which chastise the wealthy.

> No one can serve two masters. He will either hate one and love the other, or be devoted to one and despise the other. **You cannot serve God and money.** [Emphasis added]
>
> *Gospel of Matthew*, Chapter 6:24

For those who subscribe to the greedy motto "more is better," Jesus' obvious disgust with excess money and possessions should cause severe internal conflict. And make no mistake, Jesus is not at all ambivalent on this subject. *Jesus clearly states that charity is mandatary for his true followers and for anyone who seeks to join with God.*

> Sell your belongings and give alms. Provide money bags for yourselves that do not wear out, an exhaustible treasure in heaven that no thief can reach nor moth destroy. For where your treasure is, there also will your heart be. ... In the same way, **everyone of you who does not renounce his possessions cannot be my disciple.** [Emphasis added]
>
> *Gospel of Luke*, Chapter 12:33, 14:33

Moreover, Christians should not assume that rote almsgiving, particularly at church in the presence of others, satisfies this charity obligation.

> Take care not to perform righteous deeds in order that people may see them; otherwise, you will have no recompense from your heavenly Father. When you give alms, do not blow a trumpet before you, as the hypocrites do in the synagogue and in the streets to win the praise of others. ... But when you give alms, do ... so that your almsgiving may be secret. And your Father who sees in secret will repay you.
>
> *Gospel of Matthew*, Chapter 6:1

Thus, charity and the performance of good works for the benefit of others, as directly opposed to amassing wealth and ignoring our less fortunate brothers and sisters, is a central component of Jesus' teachings and one which we must always remember.

Next, let's examine Jesus' view on the second cardinal sin, the assertion of Earth plane power to control, exploit, or judge the masses. Nothing seemed to make Jesus angrier than the corrupt rabbis who wielded immense power and abused their positions of authority.

The scribes and the Pharisees have taken their seat on the chair of Moses. Therefore, do and observe all things they tell you, but do not follow their example. For they preach, but they do not practice. ... They love places of honor at banquets, seats of honor at synagogues .... As for you, do not be called "Rabbi." You have but one teacher, and you are all brothers.

Gospel of Matthew, Chapter 23:2–10

It is obvious from all the available sources, that Jesus was outraged with the Jewish rabbis who mistreated and misinformed their laity. In fact, Jesus often used the term "Hypocrite" to describe men of power who fake their piousness and use the cloak of religion to exploit others. On one occasion, Jesus healed a cripple on the Sabbath and the rabbis criticized the act as a violation of Mosaic law. Not one to tolerate form over function, Jesus denounced the rabbis for such a ridiculous and strict interpretation of Jewish law.

Hypocrites! Does not each of you on the Sabbath untie his ox or his ass from the manger and lead it out for watering? This daughter of Abraham, whom Satan has bound for eighteen years now, ought she not to have been set free on the Sabbath day from this bondage?

Gospel of Luke, Chapter 13:15

Eventually, Jesus' public attacks on the Sanhedrin would be his undoing, as he continued to unleash his frustration with their failed leadership. It makes me wonder what would happen if Jesus returned and, once again, criticized those "men of faith" who abuse their positions of power. *Would his life be in jeopardy for exposing the corrupt religious leaders of our time?*

*Woe to you scribes and Pharisees, you **hypocrites**! You lock the kingdom of heaven before human beings. You do not enter yourselves, nor do you allow entrance to those trying to enter.*

Woe to you scribes and Pharisees, you hypocrites! You traverse sea and land to make one convert, and when that happens you make him a child of Gehenna [a pagan tribe that made human sacrifices] twice as much as yourselves.

Woe to you scribes and Pharisees, you hypocrites! You pay tithes of mint and dill and cummin, and have neglected the weightier things of the law: judgment and mercy and fidelity.... Blind guides, who strain out the gnat and swallow the camel!...

Woe to you scribes and Pharisees, you hypocrites! You are like whitewashed tombs, which appear beautiful on the outside, but inside are full of dead men's bones and every kind of filth. Even so, on the outside you appear righteous, but inside you are filled with hypocrisy and evildoing. [Emphasis added]

Gospel of Matthew, Chapter 23, 13–27

Thus, leadership and the exercise of authority for the benefit of the masses, as directly opposed to using power to manipulate, subjugate, control, and herd our less fortunate brothers and sisters, is a central tenet of Jesus' lessons and one which all of us, particularly our religious and political leaders, must never forget.

Later in this section, we will revisit the *Sayings Source*, as recorded in the *New Testament* gospels and *The Book of Q*. In addition, we will explore some of the apocryphal quotes contained in the *Lost Gospels*, the *Gnostic Gospels*, and the *Dead Sea Scrolls*, all of which further clarify and illustrate Jesus' central theme that getting to heaven requires charity toward others and perfection of self. For now, though, let us pick up with the *New Testament* accounts of the tragic events that occur at the end of Jesus' short yet action-packed life.

The disputed date falls between 27 C.E. and 36 C.E., in the Hebrew lunar month Nissan. The historical records indicate that Jesus had been preaching for three years, and they suggest that his followers numbered in the thousands. Jesus' actual brothers, even if not original apostles, were now part of the inner circle of disciples. Additionally, the source material indicates that there were at least seven women who regularly accompanied Jesus and the apostles when they traveled, with most of them described as wives or relatives of the apostles. One of these women is Mary Magdalene, who has been mercilessly vilified and relegated to the shadows by the jealous and petty men who later absconded with the Jesus movement. Mary Magdalene has been labeled everything from a lunatic to a prostitute. In Truth, she was a devout companion of Jesus and, quite possibly, his wife. We will study Mary Magdalene in greater detail in Chapter Four. For the time being, simply realize that Jesus and Mary Magdalene had a very special relationship, that Jesus often stayed in her home when he visited Bethany, a town on the outskirts of Jerusalem, and that Jesus especially loved her sister Martha and her brother Lazarus, as well.

By 30 C.E., near the end of his ministry, Jesus' followers already were calling him the Messiah. This is an important point, as Christians tend to think that Jesus' followers dubbed him the Messiah after his death and resurrection. *On the contrary, it was Jesus' death that caused some of his followers and most of the other Jews to doubt that he was the Messiah.*

Recall from the Jewish section of this chapter what the term Messiah meant to the Jews, including Jesus. The *Old Testament* Prophets predicted that God would send the Jews a king or "anointed one" (Messiah in Hebrew) from the House of David, who would unify the twelve tribes of Israel. In addition, the Messiah would vanquish the enemies of the Jews, take back Jerusalem, establish his kingdom there, and oversee God's final judgment on mankind. Ultimately, the Messiah would usher in and oversee a new age of peace and enlightenment, during which the righteous who were dead would resurrect to join the righteous who were still living, all of whom would then be immortal. The anticipated result was that the entire Earth would resemble the Garden of Eden and be our final resting place, since the Jews did not believe that mankind was worthy of joining God in heaven.

Now, picture Jesus and his supporters against this backdrop of social unrest in Judea. Recall that the devout Maccabean priests of the Sanhedrin had been killed by Herod the Great and replaced with corrupt rabbis who loved riches and power more than their purported religion. Also, we know that the Roman occupation of Palestine, then in its 93rd year, was abhorrent to the Jews who passionately sought to regain their independence. In addition, we know that the Jews had splintered into a vast array of sects, some of which were radical and potentially violent.

Lastly, we know that Jesus was a Nazorean, which means he came from a fairly radical sect in Galilee. We also know that at least two of the apostles, Simon and Judas, were nicknamed "Zealot" and "Iscariot," terms related to Jewish sects that were more radical than the Nazoreans. In fact, Iscariot stems from the Hebrew word *sicarii*, which means "assassin." Thus, not only did Jesus' inner circle believe that he was the Messiah, they also were anxious for him to stake his claim as King of Jerusalem, and some were willing to fight for him. In sum, Jesus' followers desperately wanted him to prove he was the Messiah. After all, the signs were pointing to the fulfillment of the ancient Jewish prophecies.

Realize, too, that the Jews weren't the only ones aware of how neatly Jesus seemed to be fulfilling the Messiah prophesies. Let us not forget that Herod the Great had tried to kill Jesus when he was a baby. Moreover, John the Baptist had identified Jesus as the Messiah three years earlier at the beginning of Jesus' ministry. It is only logical to conclude, therefore, that Jesus was a marked man, probably from birth. In fact, some researchers have gone so far as to suggest that Jesus was so well known that, even as a teenager, his parents were worried about his safety. These scholars theorize that the "lost years" were the result of a plan to hide Jesus and protect him until he reached maturity. In any event, it is rational to assume that Jesus was being watched by the Sanhedrin and the Romans. Indeed, the *Gospel of Matthew* and the

Gospel of Luke both report that word of Jesus' popularity and his miraculous healings had reached Herod Antipas, the then current ruler of Judea. Consequently, Jesus had to know that his life was in danger, which makes his next move all the more bold and ... curious.

Most revealing for our purposes, however, is that Jesus seems to have believed that he was the Messiah. Consider first that Jesus must have known about his lineage and that he was descendant from the House of David. The Jews had been waiting nearly eight hundred years for the Messiah prophecies to be fulfilled, and every generation hoped that he would come during their lifetime. Moreover, Jesus was a well trained rabbi who appeared to know more about the *Old Testament* and the prophecies than any of the other rabbis he encountered. In addition, Jesus would have been acutely aware of his divine powers, which he displayed only when overwhelmed with compassion and never as a stunt to please the crowds. Finally, the gospels indicate that Jesus admitted to his inner circle that he was the Messiah.

> *Now Jesus and his disciples set out for the villages of Caesarea Philippi. Along the way he asked his disciples, "Who do people say that I am?" They said in reply, "John the Baptist, others Elijah, still others one of the prophets." And then he asked them, "But who do you say that I am?" Peter said to him in reply, "You are the Messiah." Then he warned them not to tell anyone about him.*
>
> *Gospel of Mark*, Chapter 8:27–30

It is at this juncture that Jesus decides to confront the orthodox Jewish establishment, with a move calculated both to challenge the Sanhedrin priests and to fulfill the Messiah prophecies. Whether because of his notoriety or in spite of it, Jesus concludes that he is ready for the ultimate contest, so he elects to attend the Passover festivities at the Temple in Jerusalem, a place he seems to have purposely avoided during his ministry. Make no mistake, Jesus knows what he is doing. He intentionally and methodically orchestrates a face-off between himself and the rabbis. By way of comparison, Jesus' showdown with the Sanhedrin at the Temple makes the altercation between Wyatt Earp and the Clanton brothers at the OK Corral look like mere child's play.

First, Jesus chooses to enter Jerusalem on Passover, the most revered Jewish holiday, when over a million Jews are present to hear him preach. Second, Jesus rides through the city on a donkey to fulfill the *Old Testament* Messiah prophecy according to *Zechariah*, and he enters the Temple through its east gate in order to comply with the Messiah prophecy contained in *Ezekiel*. Third, Jesus creates a scene by upsetting the tables of the merchants and moneychangers who are allowed to operate inside the Temple. Fourth, as previously mentioned, Jesus accuses the Sanhedrin of desecrating the Temple and exploiting the masses. Lastly, Jesus predicts the destruction of the Temple, which later will be interpreted at his trial as a blasphemous threat.

It is extremely important that we fully appreciate the level of Jesus' disgust with and defiance against the Sanhedrin Council. He publically accuses the rabbis of defiling the very Temple they're entrusted to consecrate, and he denounces them for exploiting the very people whose souls they're obligated to protect. Allow me to drive this point home with an apt analogy: Imagine an outspoken yet well respected dissident Catholic priest entering St. Peter's Cathedral on Easter Sunday and accusing the pope and the Vatican council of purposely misleading their laity about the nature of God, concealing the true path to salvation by promoting blind faith, amassing wealth to support their grand institutions and cozy lifestyle rather than helping the poor, focusing on meaningless ritual and arcane dogma to divert attention from their obsolete functions, and exploiting the masses for the sake of Earth plane power. I stand in total awe of Jesus' integrity, his courage, and his unwavering sense of Truth.

After the Temple incident, Jesus retires with his apostles and partakes of the **Last Supper**. According to the *New Testament*, Judas leaves the dinner and betrays Jesus by reporting his whereabouts to the Sanhedrin. Based on the recently discovered Gnostic *Gospel of Judas*, many scholars now think that Jesus *wanted* Judas to turn him in, and that Judas has gotten a bum rap for simply following orders. In many respects, this version of the tale makes more sense, since: (i) Jesus purposely baited the priests by staging the scene at the Temple; (ii) Jesus obviously sought a confrontation with the rabbis; and (iii) Judas may well have been Jesus' younger brother or close relative. All of these factors weigh heavily against betrayal.

In any event, Jesus ultimately is tried and found guilty by the Sanhedrin priests. He then is sent to the Roman governor, Pontius Pilate, who sentences Jesus to death, apparently for sedition. Scholars hotly disagree over whether **High Priest Caiaphas** had the power to order an execution, even though Jewish law states that the penalty for blasphemy is death by stoning. However, theologians agree that Caiaphas could not have sentenced Jesus to death for the charge of sedition against the Roman Empire, which would explain why Caiaphas sent Jesus to Pilate.

Thus, the *New Testament* accounts illustrate that Jesus was prepared to die for his cause. Indeed, it appears that Jesus actually welcomed the opportunity to confront the Sanhedrin priests. Furthermore, in all four gospels, Jesus tells the apostles during the Last Supper that he will be leaving them, and in three of the gospels Jesus predicts his death and resurrection with specificity.

> *Behold, we are going up to Jerusalem, and the Son of Man will be handed over to the chief priests and the scribes, and they will condemn him to death, and hand him over to the Gentiles to be mocked and scourged and crucified, and he will be raised on the third day.*
>
> *Gospel of Matthew*, Chapter 20:18

Based on this prediction, Christians believe that Jesus saw into the future. They also think that God wanted Jesus to die and that Jesus was a willing participant in this preordained outcome. To this belief system, they add the dogma that Jesus' death washed away the sins of mankind and that his resurrection opened up the gates of heaven. Thus, they view Jesus as the prophesied Messiah even though he failed to fulfill critical elements of the Messiah prophecies, such as leading the Jews to freedom and bringing everlasting peace to Earth. Finally, in 325 C.E. and by a very narrow majority, the Christian bishops adopted the **Nicene Creed**, which states that God is a tripartite entity, comprised of God, Jesus, and the Holy Spirit.

With all due respect to my Christian readers, this "faith-based" interpretation of Jesus' life and death does not pass muster under close scrutiny. Quite frankly, the historical records contain such a startling number of opposing facts and enough contrary quotes from Jesus himself, that the orthodox Christian position that Jesus is God cannot be sustained. However, in the spirit of Truth and in order to fairly explore the Christian belief system, we should examine *all* possibilities, including two other interpretations of Jesus' life, the crucifixion, and the resurrection, which are much more reasonable and consistent with the facts.

First, we will look at the evidence which supports the proposition that Jesus was nothing more nor less than one of the greatest Prophets the world has ever seen. Under this hypothesis: (i) Jesus still possessed special knowledge about God, including an understanding of how to attain salvation in the Ethereal plane; and (ii) Jesus died trying to educate the rest of us, thereby sacrificing his life rather than abandoning us or his mission.

Second, we will explore the theory that Jesus did not die on the cross at all, but instead survived the crucifixion. Please bear with me, as this theory isn't as far fetched as you may think. I'm willing to bet that most Christians aren't aware of this hypothesis, which was first advanced by Hugh Schonfield in his book *The Passover Plot*. The Truth is that there are a lot of unusual and suspicious occurrences surrounding the crucifixion and resurrection, and that these bizarre events tend to undermine the very foundation of Christian orthodoxy.

Let us start with the more outlandish theory first – that Jesus survived the crucifixion. Today, some respected academics believe that Jesus may have staged the entire week of Passover, including his own crucifixion. While I am not prepared to side with the "Passover Plot" scholars, I feel it is important to summarize their findings, as their arguments are fairly convincing and prove, at a minimum, that Jesus orchestrated quite a finale to his life. Indeed, it appears that Jesus staged much of "Passion" week, including his donkey ride into Jerusalem, although the apostles seem oblivious to the plan until Jesus gives them the code words to collect the waiting prop.

> As he [Jesus] drew near to Bethphage and Bethany at the place called the Mount of Olives, he sent two of his disciples. He said, "Go into the village opposite you, and as you enter it you will find a colt tethered on which no one has ever sat. Untie it and bring it here. And if anyone should ask you, 'Why are you untying it?' you will answer, 'The Master has need of it.'"
>
> So those who had been sent off found everything just as he had told them. And as they were untying the colt, its owners said to them, "Why are you untying the colt?" They answered, "The Master has need of it."
>
> *Gospel of Luke*, Chapter 19:29–34

Similarly, Jesus makes advanced plans for the Last Supper. Once again, he instructs the apostles at the last minute on what they need to do.

> He [Jesus] sent two of his disciples and said to them, "Go into the city and a man will meet you, carrying a jar of water. Follow him. Wherever he enters, say to the master of the house, 'The Teacher says, "Where is my guest room where I may eat the Passover with my disciples?"' Then he will show you a large upper room furnished and ready."
>
> *Gospel of Mark*, Chapter 14:13–15

We already have discussed the next act of the Passover Plot. Many scholars now surmise that during the Last Supper, Jesus instructed Judas to tip-off the Sanhedrin so that Jesus could control the timing of the showdown. Perhaps Jesus thought that a majority of the council would acknowledge him as the Messiah, a title he already assumed in private. Or maybe Jesus figured that Caiaphas wouldn't have the nerve to convict him, in which case he could go on preaching. Regardless of whether Jesus thought he could control the outcome of the trial or not, proponents of the Passover Plot believe that Jesus had a back up plan. In the event that the Sanhedrin denied Jesus' status as the Messiah and turned him over to the Roman authorities, Jesus and his closest followers had a plan to simulate Jesus' death on the cross, stage his burial in a private tomb, and ensure his resurrection and later escape from Jerusalem.

Impossible you say? You're probably right. Still, try to keep an open mind as we walk through the plan that may have been activated after Jesus was officially rejected as the Messiah. First, almost all the independent theologians agree that there was no Roman or Hebrew "custom" that would have prompted Pontius Pilate to spare a Jewish criminal's life in deference to Passover. *Why on Earth, then, do the gospels report that Pilate offered to free either Jesus or Barabbas?*

Well, what if Pilate was in on the Passover Plot from the beginning? Or, what if Pilate was tricked into abetting the plan after Jesus appeared dead? For such a plan to work, Pilate would have to be bribed or convinced that Jesus was worthy of special treatment after his crucifixion. Let's suppose, for the sake of argument, that Jesus had a rich sponsor who managed to bribe Pilate into releasing Jesus. Wouldn't that explain the bizarre gospel accounts of Pilate trying to persuade the crowd to free Jesus? It also would explain why Pilate, after failing to convince the crowd to release Jesus, would "wash his hands" of the whole affair. So, was there a rich benefactor who might have interceded on Jesus' behalf, either before or after the crucifixion? Yes, there was such a man.

Enter **Joseph of Arimathea**, a relatively minor character in the *New Testament*, but the key player in the Passover Plot. The *Gospel of Mark* and the *Gospel of Luke* both recite that Joseph of Arimathea was one of the seventy-one rabbis on the Sanhedrin Council. In addition, the gospels agree that after the crucifixion, Joseph of Arimathea convinced Pilate to turn over Jesus' body. Moreover, one of the gospels lets slip that Joseph of Arimathea was wealthy.

> When it was evening, there came a **rich man** from Arimathea named
> Joseph, who was himself a disciple of Jesus. He went to Pilate and asked
> for the body of Jesus: then Pilate ordered it to be handed over. Taking
> the body, Joseph wrapped it in clean linen and laid it in **his new tomb**
> that he had hewn in rock. Then he rolled a huge stone across the
> entrance to the tomb and departed. But Mary Magdalene and the other
> Mary remained sitting there, facing the tomb. [Emphasis added]

Gospel of Matthew, Chapter 27:57–61

There is another interesting tidbit in this passage: Jesus' body is taken to Joseph's private tomb. In addition, the *Gospel of John* indicates that the tomb is located next to the area where Jesus was crucified. This entire episode is strange for a whole host of reasons. To begin with, death by crucifixion was designed and intended to be a public warning to others not to violate Roman law. Therefore, victims not only died on the cross, their bodies were left on the cross to rot, sometimes for weeks. The Romans wanted the putrefied bodies to serve as a future deterrent to crime. So why was Jesus' corpse given preferential treatment by immediately being taken off the cross? And why was Jesus crucified next to a private cemetery? Scholars contend that these events are completely unfathomable and that Pilate never would have allowed any of this to occur unless he was a friend of Joseph of Arimathea or he was paid for these favors.

Even more mysterious is how quickly Jesus died, since death by crucifixion normally took several days. Two of the gospels report that Jesus was on the cross for only three hours, and one gospel recites that he died in six hours. It also is worth noting that if Jesus' legs had been broken, he certainly would have died from asphyxiation.

> So the soldiers came and broke the legs of the first and then the other one who was crucified with Jesus. But when they came to Jesus and saw that he was already dead, they did not break his legs, but one soldier thrust his lance into his side, and immediately blood and water flowed out.
>
> Gospel of John, Chapter 19:32

Probably the most titillating evidence supporting the mock crucifixion hypotheses is that all four gospels agree Jesus was offered wine during the crucifixion process. Moreover, three of the gospels state that the wine was mixed with a narcotic and that Jesus was offered the drug twice. Immediately before he dies, Jesus accepts the potion which, if administered in a hefty enough dosage, could have caused Jesus to appear dead while in an unconscious state.

> They gave Jesus wine to drink mixed with gall. But when he had tasted it, he refused to drink. ... From noon onward, darkness came over the whole land until three in the afternoon. And about three o'clock Jesus cried ..., "My God, my God, why have you forsaken me?"...
>   Immediately, one of them ran to get a sponge; he soaked it in wine, and putting it on a reed, gave it to him to drink. ... But Jesus cried out again in a loud voice, and gave up his spirit.
>
> Gospel of Matthew, Chapter 27:34–50

After Joseph retrieves Jesus' body, a man named **Nicodemus**, who is described in the gospels as "a ruler of the Jews" and a member of the Sanhedrin, meets Joseph at the private tomb. Nicodemus brings with him what appears to be a cache of herbs, aloes, and medicines to treat Jesus. Thus, it is possible that Jesus was drugged during the crucifixion to simulate death and that he immediately received medical treatment before being placed in the tomb to recuperate.

> Nicodemus, the one who had first come to him at night, also came
> bringing *a mixture of myrrh and aloes weighing one hundred pounds.*
> So they took the body of Jesus and bound it with burial cloths along
> with the spices, according to the Jewish burial custom.
> [Emphasis added]
>
> Gospel of John, Chapter 19:39

After Jesus was buried, the gospels report that Jesus arose on the third day, even though no one witnessed the resurrection. It also is frustrating that none of the gospel writers agree on who saw Jesus first after the resurrection, so let us examine the endings of the gospels in turn. We will skip the *Gospel of Mark* because the original ending has been lost. Scholars now agree that the Christians added a new ending, which was adopted at the Council of Trent in 1545 C.E.

In the *Gospel of Matthew*, Mary Magdalene and the "other Mary" (probably Jesus' mother), come to the tomb and an angel descends from heaven. The angel rolls back the stone, tells them that Jesus is gone, then instructs them to tell the disciples that Jesus will see them in Galilee.

> Then they went away quickly from the tomb, fearful yet overjoyed, and
> ran to announce this to his disciples. And behold, Jesus met them on
> their way and greeted them. They approached, **embraced his feet,** and
> did him homage. ...
> The eleven disciples went to Galilee, to the mountain to which Jesus
> had ordered them. When they saw him, they worshiped, but some
> doubted. Then Jesus approached and said to them, "All power in heaven
> and on earth has been given to me, Go, therefore, and make disciples of
> all nations ...." [Emphasis added]
>
> Gospel of Matthew, Chapter 28:8–19

This account is fascinating for a few reasons. First, Jesus is tangible, not an apparition, as the women can physically touch him. This report not only fits with the Jewish view of resurrection (i.e., the righteous receive a new body), it also supports the Passover Plot theory. Thereafter, Jesus meets with his apostles and some of them have doubts, but about what exactly? Do they doubt the resurrection? Do they doubt Jesus' instruction to expand the ministry to "make disciples of all nations?" It is quite odd that some have doubt *after* the resurrection.

In the *Gospel of Luke*, Mary Magdalene, Joanna, and Mary "the mother of James" (probably Jesus' mother), go to the empty tomb and find two angels, who tell them that Jesus has been raised. The women report this news to the apostles who refuse to believe them. Thereafter, two of the apostles encounter Jesus while leaving Jerusalem.

> *Jesus drew near and walked with them, but their eyes did not recognize him. He asked them, "What are you discussing as you walk along?" ... One of them, named **Cleopas**, said to him in reply, "Are you the only visitor in Jerusalem who does not know of the things ... that happened to **Jesus the Nazarene, who was a prophet** mighty in deed and word before God and all the people ...." [Emphasis added]*

> *Gospel of Luke*, Chapter 24:15–19

It is very odd that the two apostles fail to recognize Jesus who, interestingly enough, they describe as a "prophet." Even after Jesus speaks they don't recognize him. Christians explain this anomaly by saying that the Holy Spirit had not yet entered the apostles, but the Passover Plot team has a much simpler and more rational answer: *Jesus looked different.* Why? Because he had been beaten, scourged, nailed to a cross, and cut about the head and face by a crown of thorns. Therefore, it is only logical to assume: (i) his face was disfigured and scarred; (ii) his body was skinny and frail; (iii) he probably limped or hunched over when he walked; and (iv) in order to go about unnoticed, he probably covered his face in public. Behind closed doors, though, the apostles finally recognize Jesus.

> *So he [Jesus] went to stay with them. And it happened that, while he was with them at the table, he took the bread, said the blessing, broke it, and gave it to them. With that their eyes were opened and they recognized him ....*
>
> *So they set out at once and returned to Jerusalem where they found and gathered together the eleven and those with them who were saying, "The Lord has truly been raised and has appeared to Simon!" ... While they were still speaking about this, he stood in their midst and said to them, "Peace be with you." But they were startled and terrified and thought that they were seeing a ghost.*

> *Then he said to them, "... Touch me and see, because a ghost does not have flesh and bones as you can see I have." ... While they were still incredulous for joy and were amazed, he asked them, "Have you anything here to eat?" They gave him a piece of baked fish; he took it and ate it in front of them. [Emphasis added]*
>
> Gospel of Luke, Chapter 24:29–43

I don't know about you, but if I saw someone walking and talking, being embraced and touched by others, and eating baked fish, my mind would conclude that the person is human *and* an Earth plane being. In other words, it seems a little inconsistent to me that if Jesus were on his way to the Ethereal plane to join God that he would be at all hungry. Score ten points for the Passover Plot team.

Incidentally, the two apostles who meet Jesus on the road were probably his brothers, James and Simon. In "Jesus' Second 'Official' Family Tree," James is identified as the son of Cleophas, a name remarkably similar to "Cleopas." Remember, Paul and the Catholics tried to undermine James "the Lesser," who properly taught that blind faith, absent good works, is irrelevant. Therefore, James is minimized at every available turn, as is done in this story. Keep this in mind as we attempt to identify the mysterious "beloved disciple," whose identity is purposely concealed in the last gospel's account of the resurrection.

Lastly, let us examine the *Gospel of John*, which provides even more clues. In *John*, Mary Magdalene comes to the tomb alone and finds Jesus' body missing. She then tells Peter and the "disciple whom Jesus loved" that the body is gone. Next, the men rush to the tomb but after seeing nothing, they leave. Mary Magdalene remains outside and is crying when she notices two angels inside the cave. While the angels comfort her, she turns around and sees a strange man. Once again, Jesus is unrecognizable yet a physical entity whom Mary can hug. It is interesting to note that Jesus takes the time to clarify, for the umpteenth time, that he and God are not the same, by explaining to Mary that God is Father and God to all of mankind, Jesus included.

> *Jesus said to her, "Woman, why are you weeping? Whom are you looking for?" She thought it was the gardener and said to him, "Sir, if you carried him away, tell me where you laid him, and I will take him."*
>
> *Jesus said to her, "Mary!" She turned and said to him in Hebrew, "Rabbouni!," which means Teacher. Jesus said to her, "Stop holding on to me, for I have not yet ascended to the Father. But go to my brothers and tell them, 'I am going to my Father and your Father, to my God and your God.'" [Emphasis added]*
>
> Gospel of John, Chapter 20: 15–17

Thereafter, the *Gospel of John* reports that Jesus appears three more times. During the last encounter, Jesus appears while the disciples are fishing and the beloved disciple is the first to recognize him. After Jesus eats breakfast with the disciples (he is hungry, again), Jesus talks privately with Peter and rebukes him for being jealous of the beloved disciple.

> Peter turned and saw the disciple following whom Jesus loved, the one who had also reclined upon his [Jesus'] chest during the last suppera .... When Peter saw him, he said to Jesus, "Lord, what about him?" Jesus said to him, "What if I want him to remain until I come? What concern is it of yours?"

> *Gospel of John*, Chapter 21:20–22

The *Gospel of John* ends with this uncomfortable scene involving Jesus, Peter, and the beloved disciple. From *Acts of the Apostles*, we learn that James, Peter, and John became the "three pillars" of the Jesus movement. However, contrary to Christian tradition, John of Zebedee *cannot* be the beloved disciple based on the following deductive reasoning. The gospel lists seven apostles who are present at the last encounter with Jesus: (i) Peter; (ii) Thomas; (iii) Nathanael; (iv) James of Zebedee; (v) John of Zebedee; (vi) the "beloved disciple;" and (vii) another who is purposely unnamed. Consequently, unless you count John twice in the list of the seven disciples, someone else must be the beloved disciple. In all likelihood and for the reasons previously cited, the beloved and unnamed disciples are, once again, Jesus' brothers James and Simon.

In summary, the *Gospel of John* adds to the Passover Plot hypothesis in a unique way. The encounters after the resurrection illustrate that Jesus had not finished preparing the apostles for discipleship. In short, the guys needed a few more lessons. In *Acts of the Apostles*, Jesus provides them with additional instructions on how to spread the message that humanity has the potential to join God in heaven. Indeed, *Acts* reports that after the resurrection, Jesus lingers for forty more days "speaking about the kingdom of God," a startling message considering that almost everyone, including the Jews, the Hindus, the Buddhists, and the pagans, believed that man was not worthy of joining God in heaven. Moreover, Paul states in Chapter 15:6 of *Corinthians I*, that over five hundred people heard Jesus preach after the resurrection. No wonder the Passover Plot adherents question whether Jesus really died.

Now let's examine the other possible explanation for Jesus' life, death, and resurrection, namely, that Jesus was a mere mortal, albeit a very special one, and that he was chosen by God as our next major Prophet. This is my personal take on Jesus' mission. It also happens to be the interpretation favored by the vast majority of people on this planet who know about Jesus but who reject orthodox Christianity. Moreover, as we shall see, it is the same view held by Jesus' own apostles and almost all the early Christian sects. Consequently, I hope my Christian readers do not perceive me as prejudiced, for I am not. I am a Truth seeker. Furthermore, because of my Christian roots, it has taken me many years and tons of research to grasp the Truth about Jesus. Therefore, please allow me to explain, as best I can, how and why I arrived at the conclusion that Jesus was a Prophet and not God.

Before we proceed, however, I want to underscore the shared foundation which exists between the "Prophet" theory of Jesus' life and the "Jesus as God" theory accepted by Christians.

I believe that when all of the source material is digested and fairly analyzed, the texts support the following conclusions, which also happen to be part of orthodox Christian theology:

1. Jesus was born to a virgin who was miraculously impregnated by God;
2. Jesus was born with a special mission to reveal the next layer of spiritual Truth: *Mankind is worthy of joining God in heaven*;
3. Jesus was determined to accomplish this mission, even if it meant he had to die;
4. Jesus did die in the performance of his mission;
5. Jesus resurrected to further clarify his teachings before ascending to heaven;
6. Jesus did join with God in heaven, the destination of every enlightened soul;
7. Jesus promised that he or another Prophet would come to Earth at a critical moment in history to remind us and further enlighten us about the nature of God, the nature of mankind, our obligations to each other, and how we may achieve a permanent home in the Ethereal plane; and
8. Jesus was the Messiah predicted by the Jews even though he never unified them, his passive revolt started a chain reaction that led to the destruction of the Temple and the scattering of the Jews, and he failed to bring peace to the Earth.

Since we already have examined the major events of Jesus' life history, I won't belabor those accounts, except to point out that they are consistent with the current hypothesis that Jesus was a mortal Prophet. So let's skip to the crucifixion and the resurrection, since those events are at the heart of the Christian religion as currently practiced. It is important to keep in mind, though, that it was one Christian sect, the Catholic Church, which ultimately gained enough power to: (i) officially interpret Jesus' life and death; (ii) deify Jesus and make him equal to God; (iii) decide which of the ancient texts were "orthodox" (i.e., in line with the deification theory); (iii) package the selected materials into *The Holy Bible*; and (iv) decree that the remaining gospels were "heretical." Thus, after all my research, it is my earnest yet profoundly sad conclusion that the Catholic Church successfully slanted history to deify Jesus in the Ethereal plane, while at the same time elevating their own status on the Earth plane.

At this point, most of my Christian readers may be distraught and probably disagree with my conclusion that Jesus was a mortal Prophet. However, most Christians have not had the chance or the time to read all of the available source material that may change their view of Jesus. Consequently, this is an opportune time to explore the fascinating and illuminating scriptures that were rejected by the Catholics because they threatened the orthodox interpretation of Jesus' life and death. However, even without the *Lost Gospels*, the *Gnostic Gospels*, and the *Dead Sea Scrolls*, the official Catholic interpretation rests on shaky ground. To prove this point, we first will delve into the accepted accounts of Jesus' trials, during which he was asked to explain himself. As a retired attorney, I feel the trial records merit special attention. Old habits die hard, I guess.

The *New Testament* relates that during his trials, Jesus was asked by High Priest Caiaphas, King Herod Antipas, and Roman Governor Pontius Pilate whether he was: (i) the Messiah; (ii) the King of the Jews; or (iii) the son of God. In the *Gospel of Mark*, Jesus clearly admits that he is the Messiah (although he is answering a compound question). In the *Gospel of Matthew* and the *Gospel of Luke*, when asked if he is the "King of the Jews," Jesus vaguely replies, "You say so." In the *Gospel of Mark* and the *Gospel of Luke*, Jesus refers to himself as the "**Son of Man**" and states, "From this time on the Son of Man will be seated at the right hand of the Power of God." Unfortunately, this affirmative statement is not very helpful, since the Jewish phrase "Son of Man" is just another term for the mortal Messiah. (See *Daniel*, Chapter 7.) *Thus, despite repeated questioning, Jesus only ever claims to be the Messiah.*

However, in the *Gospel of John* Jesus seems willing to clarify who he is for the record.

> *So Pilate went back into the praetorium and summoned Jesus and said to him, "Are you the King of the Jews?" ...*
>
> *Jesus answered, "My kingdom does not belong to this world. If my kingdom did belong to this world, my attendants would be fighting to keep me from being handed over to the Jews. But as it is, my kingdom is not here."*
>
> Gospel of John, Chapter 18:33–36

This exchange is exceedingly important, as it provides relevant clues into how Jesus viewed himself. First, Pilate asks Jesus whether he is the "King of the Jews," meaning a mortal king in the normal sense of the word. It is obvious from Jesus' answer that he no longer thinks he will be king, a view he formerly held if the other transcripts are to be believed. Additionally, Jesus admits that he does not have sufficient servants to become a king on Earth, otherwise his "attendants would be fighting to keep me from being handed over." Thus, Jesus appears to know that he is not the same Messiah predicted by the Jewish Prophets. To me, there is a melancholy quality to Jesus' answer, since it almost seems that Jesus wishes he could be that Messiah. *Nevertheless, the question remains, if Jesus isn't the Jewish Messiah, who is he?*

Pilate, too, is confused, particularly since Jesus mysteriously refers to some other kingdom that "does not belong to this world." So Pilate modifies his question to try to determine whether Jesus is *any* kind of king. Jesus gives his standard response, "You say I am a king," which isn't very helpful to our inquiry. However, what Jesus says next is extremely enlightening.

> *So Pilate said to him, "Then you are a king?"*
>
> *Jesus answered, "You say I am a king. For this I was born and for this I came into the world, to testify to the Truth. Everyone who belongs to the Truth listens to my voice."*
>
> *Pilate said to him, "What is Truth?"* [Emphasis added]
>
> Gospel of John, Chapter 18:37–38

Thus, Jesus states unequivocally that he was born to convey the Truth and that everyone who listens to him by following God's updated instruction – *Love thy neighbor as thyself* – also will belong to the Truth. And it's just that simple: *Jesus came here to add the next layer to God's Tower of Truth, which is exactly what Prophets do.* Kings, on the other hand, rule over others. In addition, kings manage empires, conquer enemies, reward servants, and condemn the wicked. In Truth, there is only one heavenly King and the rest of us, including Jesus, are mere servants until we earn our salvation. Jesus was an obedient son of God, which explains how he earned divine, not deified, status in heaven. In fact, to drive this point home, Jesus warned his followers that neither worship of him nor good deeds done in his name would help them reach heaven.

> *Not everyone who says to me, "Lord, Lord," will enter the kingdom of heaven, but only the one who does the will of my Father in heaven. Many will say to me on that day, "Lord, Lord, did we not prophesy in your name? Did we not drive out demons in your name? Did we not do mighty deeds in your name?" Then I will declare to them solemnly, "I never knew you." [Emphasis added]*

Gospel of Matthew, Chapter 7:21–23

Please read the above passage again, for these are Jesus' words, not mine. In this passage, Jesus emphasizes, yet again, that he and God are not the same entity and are not to be compared. Jesus also indicates that the mere act of calling him "Lord" (i.e., worshiping him instead of God) is totally irrelevant at best. Furthermore, anyone who teaches in his name or does good deeds in his name will be gravely disappointed. What matters, then, is whether we act in compliance with God's will, as explained to us by all the Prophets. Thus, just like Buddha and our next Prophet Muhammad, Jesus repeatedly corrected those followers who wanted to deify him. Moreover, Jesus even resisted his apostles' attempts to call him "master," since he believed that anyone who seeks God and comes to understands himself (i.e., the *Saddha* process) will be worthy of joining God in heaven. Thus, a person who understands Jesus' messages is no longer a slave to ignorance but has the ability to become a master himself.

> *I no longer call you slaves, because a slave does not know what his master is doing. I have called you friends, because I have told you everything I have heard from my Father.*

Gospel of John, Chapter 15:15

Now, let's compare some quotes from Jesus contained in the *Gospel of Thomas*, one of the *Gnostic Gospels*, which most scholars think predates the four gospels of the *New Testament* and which may have been written by Jesus' third brother, Judas Thomas.

Whoever finds the interpretation of these [Jesus'] sayings will not experience death. ...

Let him who seeks continue seeking until he finds. When he finds, he will become troubled. When he becomes troubled, he will be astonished, and he will rule over the all. ...

If those who lead you say, "See, the kingdom is in the sky," then the birds of the sky will precede you. If they say, "It is in the sea," then the fish will proceed you. Rather, the kingdom is inside of you, and it is outside of you. When you come to know yourselves, then you will become known, and you will realize that it is you who are the sons of the living Father. But if you will not know yourselves, you dwell in poverty and it is you who are that poverty. ...

I am not your master. Because you have drunk, you have become intoxicated from the bubbling spring which I have measured out." [Emphasis added]

Gospel of Thomas, Verses 1–3, 13

The Greek term for "knowledge" is **gnosis**. The *Gnostic Gospels* were cherished by a sect of early Christians whom scholars refer to as the **Gnostic Christians**. The Gnostic Christians flourished until approximately 300 C.E., when the Catholic Church started gaining momentum. The Gnostics believed that Jesus was speaking about joining God through the accumulation of spiritual Truth. Consequently, the Gnostic Christians did not believe that blind faith in Jesus brings salvation, nor did they believe that Jesus opened the gates of heaven by dying for our sins. Rather, they understood that Jesus was a great Prophet who explained to us *how* to reach heaven, a message that no other Prophet had yet delivered.

Come to hate hypocrisy and the evil thought; for it is the [evil] thought that gives birth to hypocrisy; but hypocrisy is far from truth. ... Become earnest about the word! For as to the word, its first path is faith; the second, love; the third, works; for from these comes life. ...

So also can you yourselves receive the kingdom of heaven; unless you receive through knowledge, you will not be able to find it. [Emphasis added]

Apocryphon of James, Verse 8

In the *Gnostic Gospels*, Jesus describes the same path to enlightenment that Buddha taught and which I call the *Saddha* process of reaching God. It is a personal journey of Truth.

Farming in the world requires the cooperation of four essential elements ... water, earth, wind, and light. God's farming likewise has four elements – faith, hope, love, and knowledge. Faith is our earth, that in which we

take root. Hope is the water through which we are nourished. Love is
the wind through which we grow. Knowledge then is the light through
which we ripen.

Gospel of Phillip, Verse 79

For the Gnostics, the key to salvation was going inward for Truth and then going outward with love. Ignorance was considered the enemy of enlightenment and the antithesis of God.

For he who is ignorant is in need, and what he lacks is great, since he
lacks that which will make him perfect. ... For he who is ignorant until
the end is a creature of oblivion, and he will vanish along with it. ...
Therefore, if one has knowledge, he is from above. Having knowledge,
he does the will of the one who called him, he wishes to be pleasing to
him, he receives rest.

Gospel of Truth, Verses 21, 22

Additionally, the Gnostic Christians followed Jesus' example by preserving a respect for the Jewish Ten Commandments but abandoning the ancient Jewish traditions that Jesus taught were unnecessary and counterproductive to spiritual growth. Consequently, the Gnostics met outside the confines of the Jewish temples, which continued to adhere to arcane Jewish rituals such as burnt offerings and animal sacrifices. Instead, the Gnostic Christians met in their homes to pray, since the vast majority of the Roman Empire still was pagan and no Christian churches had yet been built. In sum, the Gnostic sect came to agree with Jesus that we do not need priests, temples, authoritarian rules, nor silly rituals to help us commune with God, which explains why the Catholic Church later banned their books. Here is a passage from another *Gnostic Gospel* that the Catholics ordered destroyed and which they hoped would never again see the light of day.

The foolish – *thinking in their hearts that if they confess, "We are*
Christians," in word only but not with power, while giving themselves
over to ignorance, to a human death, not knowing where they are going
nor who Christ is, thinking that they will live, when they are really in
error – **hasten towards the principalities and the authorities. They fall**
into their clutches because of the ignorance that is in them.
For if only words which bear testimony were effecting salvation, the
whole world would endure this thing and would be saved. But it is in
this way that they draw error to themselves, they do not know that they
will destroy themselves. If the Father were to desire a human sacrifice
[Jesus], he would become vainglorious. [Emphasis added]

The Testimony of Truth, Verses 31, 32

As we shall explore in detail in Chapter Four, the Catholic sect was more concerned with accumulating money and power than disseminating Truth. Eventually, their Earth plane obsessions made them slaves to the cardinal sins of greed and pride.

To summarize, it is my belief that Jesus came to the world to deliver a revolutionary message of Truth about how we achieve salvation and join with God. Since most of mankind still believed that man was innately sinful or not worthy of joining God in heaven, Jesus' message was blasphemous to the Jews and initially mind-boggling to the pagans. Recall, though, that Buddha already had broached this same Truth. Buddha taught that perfection of self and detachment from the Earth plane lead to spiritual enlightenment, and that such growth is humanly possible during any lifetime. Yet, Buddha stopped short of defining *nirvana* as going to heaven. *Hence, Jesus was the first Prophet to declare this next layer of spiritual Truth from God:*

It is possible for mankind to earn salvation in the Ethereal plane but only if we are willing to follow Jesus' example on the Earth plane, by searching inside ourselves for Truth and then by performing outward acts of compassion and love toward others.

So what happened to this simple message of Truth? How did our roadmap for salvation, the next layer of our Tower of Truth, get so warped? Jesus clearly told us that the first step to salvation is true knowledge of ourselves, not blind faith in others. Jesus also clearly stated that the second step to salvation is loving our neighbors and forgiving our enemies, not frivolous worship of Jesus as another god. So what happened after Jesus died that so dramatically altered and drastically undermined the fruits of his mission?

To begin with, after Jesus died there were literally dozens of Christian sects, all claiming to understand Jesus the best. Ironically, these sects did not agree on some very basic concepts, such as whether Jesus' resurrection signified bodily reincarnation or his ascension into heaven, whether compassionate living or mere faith in Jesus as a divine creature was the path to salvation, or whether Jesus was a mortal man, another god, or God himself. Moreover, the early Christians could not agree on the role of women within the church, despite Jesus' explicit and undeniable inclusion of women in his inner circle. How quickly man forgets!

Historians classify the early Christian sects into three basic categories:

1. **Jewish Christians.** The earliest Christian sect was led by Jesus' closest apostles, referred to in the *New Testament* as the "**three**

pillars of the church." The three leaders were: (i) **James,** the true brother of Jesus and the acknowledged first Bishop of Jerusalem after Jesus died, which makes James heir of the Jesus movement; (ii) **Peter,** the apostle who denied Jesus three times after his arrest but whom Jesus identifies as the "rock," a quote which later will provide fodder for the fallacy that Peter was the first Roman pope and in command of the movement after Jesus died; and (iii) **John,** the apostle who historically has been considered the mysterious "beloved disciple" and the author of the *Gospel of John*, but who historians now agree did not author either that gospel or *The Revelation to John*. The Jewish Christians originally did not want to spread Jesus' messages to the Gentiles, since Jesus himself only preached to the Jews. *Thus, this sect was reluctant to view Jesus as anything other than the predicted Jewish Messiah.*

2. **Gentile Christians.** This sect was led by a Jewish man named **Saul of Tarsus** (a/k/a **Saint Paul**), who also had the good fortune to be a Roman citizen educated in the Jewish religion, Greek philosophy, and Roman mythology. Paul never met Jesus, as he readily admits in his *New Testament* letters. Moreover, *Acts of the Apostles* makes clear that Paul never was accepted into the Christian church in Jerusalem, since he was both hated and feared by the Jewish Christians. Paul claimed he had a "vision" in which Jesus commanded him to stop persecuting the Jewish Christians. This vision prompted Paul to join the Christian movement, although he never was accepted or trusted by James or Peter. So Paul started the Gentile Christian sect, by preaching that salvation is derived *exclusively* from faith in Jesus as the divine "son of God." This sect eventually gained Roman acceptance and the power to define orthodox Christianity. *Hence, Paul began the deification of Jesus.*

3. **Gnostic Christians.** This sect flourished outside of Jerusalem at the same time the Gentile Christian sect was gaining steam. The Gnostics believed that Jesus taught on multiple levels and that they alone understood the true depths of his teachings. Thus, the Gnostics agreed that faith in God was important, but that this was only the first level of Truth. They believed that Jesus was advocating a much deeper spiritual journey which involved internal growth and soul development. Some Gnostics thought that Jesus was preaching about reincarnation and that his resurrection was proof that a soul

must perfect itself before attaining salvation. Consequently, they did not think that Jesus' death was they key to *their* salvation. *Rather, they understood that they had to earn the right to go to heaven, which meant they viewed Jesus as a great Prophet but did not deify him.* Additionally, they rejected church ritual and irrelevant Jewish laws, such as food restrictions and temple sacrifices. They also acknowledged Mary Magdalene as one of Jesus' closest apostles, and allowed women to teach the word of God. Historians credit this sect with preserving the original quotes of Jesus, the *Sayings Source*, and including Jesus' quotes in many *Gnostic Gospels*, such as the *Gospel of Thomas*.

Personally, I believe that the Gnostic Christians were the closest followers of Jesus, since they accurately interpreted the finer points of his life mission and refused to accept the childish interpretation which Paul preached to the masses. They comprehended that Jesus was sent here to provide updated instructions on how to join with the Supreme Being, and that we should glorify Jesus based on his life teachings, not his untimely and tragic death.

> The pharisees and the scribes have taken the keys of gnosis and hidden them. They themselves have not entered, nor have they allowed to enter those who wish to. You, however, be as wise as serpents and as innocent as doves. Blessed are the solitary and elect, for you will find the kingdom. For you are from it, and to it you will return.
>
> Gospel of Thomas, Verses 39, 49

Unfortunately, the Gnostic Christians were labeled heretics, ostracized, and eventually snuffed out by the ultimate victors in the race to own and package Jesus – the Catholic Church. Practically speaking, the Gnostics didn't stand a chance. They lacked political clout and they rejected those who tried to control them. Instead, they followed Jesus' advice and were deeply suspicious of manmade rules and authority figures. They also preferred private meditation, as they trusted Jesus when he said that God is everywhere and the Holy Spirit is within each of us.

> Split a piece of wood, and I am there. Lift up the stone, and you will find me there.
>
> Gospel of Thomas, Verse 77

The Jewish Christians, on the other hand, were holding fast to the Ten Commandments and the ancient Jewish laws and rituals. The heart of this sect remained in Jerusalem and was led by James, Peter, and John. However, contrary to orthodox Christian history, Peter was *not* in charge of the church after Jesus died. Rather, Jesus' brother James was the first "Bishop" of the new religion and he remained in charge of the Jewish Christians for approximately thirty years.

> *The disciples said to Jesus, "We know that you will depart from us. Who is to be our leader?"*
>
> *Jesus said to them, "Wherever you are, you are to go to James the Just, for whose sake heaven and earth came into being."*

> *Gospel of Thomas*, Verse 12

It is now universally accepted by all independent historians that James was the heir of his brother's ministry and the titular head of the earliest "Christian" church, although that term was not yet in use. All of Jesus' original apostles, including Peter and John, deferred to James in accordance with Jesus' instructions. Therefore, let us take a moment to understand what James and the earliest Christians believed about Jesus, as their beliefs are quite surprising and revealing.

First, the Jewish Christians believed that Jesus was the predicted Messiah, even though he failed to fulfill the Jewish prophesies. Remember, Jesus was supposed to unify the twelve tribes of Israel, take back the Holy Land, lead the Jews through an apocalyptic period of war, and emerge victorious as an Earthly king to rule over a renewed Garden of Eden – none of which happened. Nevertheless, the Jewish apostles concluded that Jesus was the Messiah. Therefore, they started to reinterpret the prophesies in a symbolic manner to comport with actual events.

Second, the Jewish Christians believed that Jesus was a mortal man, as they continued to honor the Second Commandment: There is only one God. The apostles were all Jewish, they believed in only one God, and they never would have blasphemed God by deifying Jesus. Consequently, the earliest Christians viewed Jesus as a special servant of God, who became Divine after the resurrection. These are Peter's words.

> *You who are Israelites, hear these words. **Jesus the Nazorean was a man** commended to you by God with mighty deeds, wonders, and signs, which God worked through him in our midst, as you yourselves know.*

> This **man**, delivered up by the set plan and foreknowledge of God, you
> killed, using lawless men to crucify him. … The God of Abraham, of
> Isaac, and of Jacob, the God of your ancestors, has glorified his **servant**
> Jesus whom you handed over and denied in Pilot's presence, when he
> had decided to release him. [Emphasis added]

Acts of the Apostles, Chapters 2:22; 3:13

Third, as the above quote makes clear, the Jewish Christians still viewed Jesus as a Jewish Messiah, and they insisted that anyone who wanted to benefit from the renewed covenant with God had to convert to Judaism. This meant that male converts had to agree to circumcision, a huge impediment to those pagans who were tempted to join the new religion but who wanted to keep their family jewels intact. This tender topic would soon be addressed by Paul, a latecomer to the Jesus movement and the founder of the Gentile Christian sect.

Fourth, the Jewish Christians believed that God intended for Jesus to die on the cross, that Jesus submitted to God's will, and that the crucifixion opened the gates of heaven. Remember, the Jews still believed in Temple sacrifice, so the idea that Jesus' crucifixion was a "sacrifice," was in keeping with their traditions. More important, though, is the revolutionary concept that the Jewish Christians preached. Never before had mankind felt worthy of joining God in heaven.

Recall that Buddha had stopped short of declaring that spiritual enlightenment brings union with God. Thus, the Jewish Christians correctly heard the next layer of spiritual Truth: *Reaching heaven is humanly possible.* However, the Jewish Christians did not presume they could go to heaven automatically. Here is Peter's view of the crucifixion, as he testified to during one of his trials before the Sanhedrin, which continued to persecute Jesus' followers.

> When they had brought them in and made them stand before the
> Sanhedrin, the high priest questioned them, "We gave you strict orders
> to stop teaching in that [Jesus'] name. Yet you have filled Jerusalem with
> your teaching and want to bring that man's blood upon us."
>
> But Peter and the apostles said in reply, "We must obey God rather
> than men. The God of our ancestors raised Jesus, though you had him
> killed by hanging him on a tree. God exalted him at his right hand as a
> leader and savior to grant Israel repentance and forgiveness of sins. We
> are witnesses of these things, as is the holy Spirit that God has given to
> those who obey him."

Acts of the Apostles, Chapter 5:27

Fifth, even though the Jewish Christians believed Jesus had made it possible for them to get into heaven, they still thought they had to earn salvation themselves. In other words, they did not think that Jesus' sacrifice had wiped away their sins completely. Rather, they thought that Jesus' death somehow nullified original sin and that the ritual of baptism purified them. However, they still felt susceptible to sin *after* baptism, and they knew that they should stay pure and do the will of God if they wanted to get into heaven. Remember, the Jewish Christians had heard Jesus preach. They understood that heaven was in no way guaranteed simply because they believed Jesus was the Messiah. Therefore, they continued to honor Mosaic law, including the Ten Commandments. They also understood that Jesus had charged them with a new **"Eleventh Commandment"**: *Love thy neighbor as thyself.*

Sixth, the early Christians were so aware of this new commandment that they required all church members to practice the Golden Rule. As a result, members were expected to sell everything they owned and share the proceeds with the other members of the church. In essence, the earliest Christians lived in communes.

> *The community of believers was of one heart and mind, and no one claimed that any of his possessions was his own, but they had everything in common. ... There was no needy person among them, for those who owned property or houses would sell them, bring the proceeds of the sale, and put them at the feet of the apostles, and they were distributed to each according to need.*
>
> *Acts of the Apostles,* Chapter 4:32–35

In addition, there were stiff penalties for failing to share as Jesus had instructed. Indeed, the earliest Christian sect strictly followed Jesus' teachings in Jerusalem until 70 C.E., when the Romans leveled the Holy City and massacred both the Jews and the Jewish Christians.

> *A man named Ananias ... sold a piece of property. He retained for himself, with his wife's knowledge, some of the purchase price, took the remainder, and put it at the feet of the apostles. But Peter said, "Ananias, why has Satan filled your heart so that you lied to the holy Spirit and retained part of the price of the land? ..." When Ananias heard these words, he fell down and breathed his last .... The young men came and wrapped him up, then carried him out and buried him.*
>
>   *After an interval of about three hours, his wife came in .... Peter said to her, "Why did you agree to test the Spirit of the Lord? Listen,*

the footsteps of those who have buried your husband are at the door,
and they will carry you out." At once, she fell down at his feet and
breathed her last.

Acts of the Apostles, Chapter 5:1–10

Seventh, the Jewish Christians believed that Jesus would return to Earth to judge them prior to their entrance into heaven. The Jewish Christians did not believe they could go to heaven immediately upon their death, even if they kept all of the Ten Commandments and even if they observed the new commandment regarding loving their fellow man. They still thought the dead would stay buried until Jesus returned to Earth to judge mankind, in keeping with the ancient Messiah prophecies.

> *When the Son of Man comes in his glory, and all the angels with him, he*
> *will sit on his glorious throne, and all the nations will be assembled*
> *before him. And he will separate them from one another, as the*
> *shepherd separates the sheep from the goats. He will place the sheep on*
> *his right, and the goats on his left.*
>   *Then the king will say to those on his right, "Come, you who are*
> *blessed of my Father. Inherit the kingdom prepared for you from the*
> *foundation of the world. For I was hungry and you gave me food, I was*
> *thirsty and you gave me drink, a stranger and you welcomed me, naked*
> *and you clothed me, ill and you cared for me, in prison and you visited*
> *me." ...*
>   *Then he will say to those on his left, "Depart from me, accursed*
> *ones, into the eternal fire prepared for the devil and his angels. For I*
> *was hungry and you gave me no food, I was thirsty and you gave me no*
> *drink, a stranger and you gave me no welcome, naked and you gave me*
> *no clothing, ill and in prison, and you did not care for me." ...*
>   *He will answer them, "Amen, I say to you, what you did not do for*
> *one of these least ones, you did not do for me." And these will go off to*
> *eternal punishment, but the righteous to eternal life. [Emphasis added]*

Gospel of Matthew, Chapter 25:31–46

Based on this famous passage, the early Christians retained the Jewish concept that the Messiah would come to Earth during an apocalyptic war to judge mankind. They also deduced that God had set a very high standard for salvation, which depends on how we treat each other, including, especially, the poor, the sick, and the enemies of peace. Additionally, they thought that God had appointed Jesus as his representative on Earth to judge mankind and decide which souls deserve to go to heaven. Thus, the early Christians were anticipating a day when Jesus would return and pass final judgment on mankind (a/k/a **"Judgment Day"**). At that time, the righteous who were still living would go straight to heaven, and the righteous who were dead would resurrect and then ascend to heaven, just as Jesus had done.

Eighth, the Jewish Christians were certain that Jesus would return during their lifetime. In fact, they were obsessed with the timing of Judgment Day since they thought it was imminent. By my count, there are over a dozen apocalyptic gospels, including the *Revelation to John* and the numerous apocalyptic tales contained in the *Gnostic Gospels* and *Dead Sea Scrolls*. Because they thought they were living during the final hours of human history (a/k/a **"End Times"**), the Jewish Christians piously devoted themselves to meeting the new Golden Rule standard. Indeed, they were not about to question the Eleventh Commandment proclaimed by God through his servant Jesus. Frankly, the Jewish Christians were the most "Christian" religious group the world has ever seen, and we would do well to follow their example.

To understand the End Times mania of the 1st Century, we must appreciate the historical backdrop of the post-crucifixion era. Jesus had just been killed for allegedly inciting the Jews to rebel against the corrupt Sanhedrin rabbis and the Roman occupation. However, Jesus' death had not put an end to the social unrest. On the contrary, the Jewish leaders still had a huge problem on their hands, and the rabbis were terrified that Jesus' followers would continue to oppose them. Their worst fears came true, as James, Peter, and John committed to continuing Jesus' mission. While he was alive, Jesus preached a mere overhaul of Judaism. But after Jesus died, the apostles started promoting an entirely new theology. Indeed, the Sanhedrin now faced a full-fledged new religion, which seemed opposed to Judaism and which seriously threatened their authority.

In addition, the Jews still sought their independence from Rome, and Jesus' execution only served to fuel the Zealots. Consequently, the Sanhedrin priests were even more frustrated after Jesus died, since the crucifixion had failed to extinguish the Christian movement and it also had failed to snuff the Zealot movement. In sum, the Sanhedrin now had two rebellious groups to contend with: (i) the Jewish Christians, who were deferring to James the Just instead of them; and (ii) the Jewish Zealots, who were ready to go to war against Rome to reclaim Israel. As a result, the chaos in Jerusalem actually became *worse* after the crucifixion.

It was at this juncture, that the Sanhedrin decided to implement more extreme measures of crowd control. First, the orthodox Jewish leaders began to persecute the new Christian sect by publicly condemning the apostles in Jerusalem. *Acts of the Apostles* reports that the apostles were tried twice by the Sanhedrin and even imprisoned for a while. When these measures failed to stifle the Jewish Christians, the Sanhedrin became even more aggressive. This time, however, they did not seek Roman assistance as they had done when they wanted to get rid of Jesus. Instead, the Sanhedrin decided to deal with the conflict themselves, by establishing their own private hit squad.

Enter the mysterious **Saul of Tarsus**, who is introduced in the *New Testament* as an agent of the Sanhedrin. It appears from all the source material that **Paul**, as he later came to be known, was engaged by the Sanhedrin to eliminate the Jewish Christians in Jerusalem. That's right, folks. *Paul was hired to undermine the Christians*. In fact, the *New Testament* introduces Paul by noting his involvement in the execution of Stephan, a devout disciple of the Jesus movement and, according to the Catholics, the "first martyr" and a Saint.

> Now Saul was consenting to his execution. On that day, there broke out a
> severe persecution of the church in Jerusalem, and all were scattered
> throughout the countryside of Judea and Samaria, except the apostles.
> Devout men buried Stephan and made loud lament over him. Saul,
> meanwhile, was trying to destroy the church; entering house after house
> and dragging out men and women, he handed them over for imprisonment.
>
> *Acts of the Apostles*, Chapter 8:1–3

Paul is a fascinating character for many reasons, most notably because he ultimately won the race to define and market Jesus. *How did this happen, you may ask? How did a man who hated the early Christians come to represent orthodox Christianity?* Historians are not certain, although Paul's victory had a lot to do with the fact that he was a Roman citizen, readily equipped with Roman rights and privileges such as the ability to move about the Roman Empire more freely than the apostles. Unfortunately, there are gaps and inconsistences in Paul's life history, which means we may never solve the riddle of how Paul came to be the most influential spokesman for the Christian movement during the post-resurrection era.

Here is what we do know about Paul. He was born in Tarsus, an area now known as southern Turkey, around 10 C.E. Paul was well-educated and received his Jewish training from a highly respected rabbi in Jerusalem named Gamaliel. Paul was Jewish, but his family had somehow managed to acquire the mantle of Roman citizenship. Some historians think he may have been related to Herod, which would explain his early persecution of the Jewish Christians.

Other scholars believe that Paul started out as a member of the violent Shammaite Pharasees, a fundamentalist Jewish sect that aggressively opposed any threat to Jewish law. Either way, we know that Paul was violently opposed to the Jewish Christians and was retained by the Sanhedrin, probably by High Priest Caiaphas himself, to eliminate the Christians in Jerusalem.

It also is widely accepted by scholars that Paul was hired by the Sanhedrin to undermine James, specifically. Academics rely on an historical account written in the 1st Century by **Bishop Clement** of Rome, who was a disciple of Peter (and retroactively named the fourth pope by the Catholic Church). Clement relates that during a seven day debate at the Temple between James and the high priest, James won the hearts of the Jews, who were ready to convert to Christianity. When Paul realized that the Sanhedrin had lost the debate, he started a riot, during which James was thrown down the Temple stairs. As a result of this attack, James' legs were broken and the Christians fled to Damascus for safety. Based on this account, historians suspect that James also was taken to Damascus to recuperate and that Paul followed him there, for it is on the road to Damascus to arrest Christians that Paul receives his "vision."

> *Now Saul, still breathing murderous threats against the disciples of the Lord, went to the high priest and asked him for letters to the synagogues in Damascus, that, if he should find any men or women who belonged to **the Way**, he might bring them back to Jerusalem in chains.*
>
> *On his journey, as he was nearing Damascus, a light from the sky suddenly flashed around him. He fell to the ground and heard a voice saying, "Saul, Saul, why are you persecuting me?" He said, "Who are you, sir?" The reply came, "I am Jesus, whom you are persecuting. Now get up and go into the city and you will be told what you must do."* [Emphasis added]

Acts of the Apostles, Chapter 9:1–6

Numerous historical accounts, including Paul's own letters, reveal that after Jesus died, the Sanhedrin commissioned Paul to go to Damascus to arrest seditious Jews who were part of the **"Way,"** a sect of Jesus followers which we will discuss shortly. Historians used to take for granted the notion that Paul traveled to the city of Damascus located in Syria. However, since the public release of the *Dead Sea Scrolls*, historians have been reevaluating this assumption. In fact, the discovery of the *Dead Sea Scrolls* may be the greatest archeological find in modern history, as the *Scrolls* contain the additional information we need to make sense out of the post-crucifixion characters and events.

Recall that the *Dead Sea Scrolls* originally were found in 1947, but they were sequestered by a team of Catholic priests until their unofficial public release in 1991. Contrary to the early interpretations provided by the Catholics, historians now know that some of the *Scrolls* relate to a sect that practiced a religion known as the Way, the same sect targeted by Paul in the above passage from *Acts of the Apostles*. In fact, the *Scrolls* contain numerous references to the Way, which independent historians have concluded is another term for the "Sons of Zadok" and the "Nazoreans," who were closely aligned with the Jewish Zealots who followed Jesus. Thus, researchers no longer believe that all the *Scrolls* were written by the pacifist Jewish sect known as the Essenes, whom the Catholics erroneously identified as the authors of *all* eight hundred *Scrolls*. In Truth, the *Dead Sea Scrolls* represent a massive library of Jewish history, accumulated over hundreds of years, which the Jews hid at Qumran after the Temple was destroyed by the Romans in 70 C.E. Therefore, no one sect wrote all the *Scrolls*.

For our purposes, the *Dead Sea Scrolls* reveal that the place we now call Qumran used to be called Damascus. Hence, it is very likely that Paul was on his way to Qumran, not Syria, when he was hunting the Jewish Christians. Furthermore, scholars point out that the Sanhedrin's arrest warrant would not have been enforceable in Syria, which was a separate Roman province not under Jewish rule. However, the Jewish warrant would have been binding at Qumran, which was within the Sanhedrin's jurisdiction. In putting all of these puzzle pieces together, independent scholars now believe that the Jewish Christians established a community at Qumran to practice their religion, which they called the Way, and to hide from the Sanhedrin and the Romans whenever they were persecuted and forced to flee Jerusalem.

In summary, it appears that some of the *Dead Sea Scrolls* are directly related to the earliest Christian movement and were written by the Jews who followed James the Just, the actual brother of Jesus and the uncontested leader of the new religion.

Thus, the *Dead Sea Scrolls* help tremendously in sorting out the mystery of how Paul – a man who never met Jesus and sought to assassinate the official leader of the first Christian sect – managed to usurp all of the apostles and change the course of Christian history. For now, though, we will return to the canonical biblical accounts of the ongoing conflict between James, the leader of the Jewish Christian sect, and Paul, the founder of the Gentile Christian sect.

Just try to imagine James' dismay over Paul's conversion! In the midst of the turmoil he helped to create, Paul decides to switch teams and wants to "help" James prepare the Jews for the second coming of Jesus. James had to wonder whether Paul was a double agent or a mole for the Sanhedrin, particularly since it appears that the Sanhedrin entered into a temporary truce with the Jewish Christians. It is extremely odd that there is no further mention in *Acts of the Apostles* of the Sanhedein persecuting the Christians after Paul's conversion. Thereafter, the Sanhedrin basically left James alone, although they ultimately would be responsible for his death. It also is bizarre that despite their justified suspicions of Paul, the apostles in Jerusalem tolerated their new Christian convert. Clearly, James was a righteous man who practiced the new commandment to "love thy enemy." Even so, *Acts* reveals that not all of James' followers were willing to "turn the other cheek." In fact, *Acts* reports that the Jewish Christians attempted to kill Paul twice while he was preaching in Jerusalem. It is at this point in the story that James steps in and instructs Paul to leave Jerusalem. *So starts the Gentile mission of Paul.*

In all likelihood, James probably thought that nothing more would come of the perplexing and complicated Saul of Tarsus. Indeed, after James banished Paul to the outskirts of the Roman Empire, he probably thought that Paul would fade into the background where he belonged. However, the historical records indicate that Paul's first mission was successful. Apparently, the Romans were ready for a Spiritual Paradigm shift, since Paul was able to convince some of them to abandon their many gods and goddesses in favor of just two: God and his son "Christ Jesus."

Frankly, it is difficult to know the Truth about Paul. Did Paul really receive a vision from Jesus and faithfully carry out an important mission? Was Paul a legitimate but flawed messenger who inadvertently ruined the Christian movement? Or was Paul a double agent for the Sanhedrin who purposely undermined Jesus? Honestly, after all my research I still am not sure about Paul. On the other hand, I am sure about James, who fully met his obligations to God, to his brother, and to mankind. *Hence, James is worthy of Prophet status in my book.*

Control of the church passed to the apostles, together with the Lord's brother James, whom everyone from the Lord's time till our own has called the Righteous, for there were many Jameses, but this one was holy from his birth; he drank no wine or intoxicating liquor and ate no animal food; no razor came near his head; he did not smear himself with oil, and took no baths. He alone was permitted to enter the Holy Place, for his garments were not of wool but of linen. He used to enter the Sanctuary alone, and was often found on his knees beseeching forgiveness for the people, so that his knees grew hard like a camel's from his continually bending them in worship of God and beseeching forgiveness for the people.

Because of his unsurpassable righteousness he was called the Righteous *and Oblias – in our own language "Bulwark of the People, and Righteousness" – fulfilling the declarations of the prophets regarding him. [Emphasis added]*

The above quote is contained in a multi-volume work entitled *Ecclesiastical History*, which was written around 320 C.E. by Bishop Eusebius, who was the Bishop of Caesarea and is recognized by the Catholic Church as the "father of Church history." Bishop Eusebius based his account of James on an earlier five volume treatise entitled *Memoirs*, written by another respected Church historian named Hegesippus around 150 C.E.

Clearly, James was a holy man and worthy of his assignment from Jesus to continue teaching the Jews how to reach God in heaven. However, the nagging question still remains: *Was Paul also a sanctioned spokesman for God?* We may never know for sure what motivated Paul, as great minds have pondered this mystery for two thousand years without consensus. However, as we shall see, the Catholic Church ultimately backed Paul's watered-down version of Christianity over James' more rigorous interpretation for two very calculated reasons:

1. Paul's simplistic view of Christianity was more appealing to the masses because it required no real work and actually fostered intellectual and spiritual laziness; and

2. Paul's success in convincing the masses to place blind faith in Jesus as a savior god later helped the Church leaders persuade the masses to place blind faith in them.

Therefore, let us pause to consider in what ways Paul modified the central messages preached by Jesus and James, and how **blind faith** got substituted for **good works** as orthodox Christianity.

First, Paul abandoned the Jewish Christian belief that Jesus was a mortal Messiah and instead preached that Jesus literally was the son of God, thereby suggesting that Jesus, just like his Father, must be a deity. In order to fully comprehend the history of Christianity as it exists today, we must first acknowledge that Paul is the *only* character in the *New Testament* who consistently refers to

Jesus as the son of God. The apostles, on the other hand, consistently refer to Jesus as either the "Son of Man" or the Messiah ("Christ" in Greek). Thus, most of the apostles believed that Jesus occupied a separate and subservient status with regard to God even after the resurrection. However, when Paul writes about Jesus and God, he seems to give them equal billing as though they are partners in the Ethereal plane. Moreover, it is difficult to tell where one entity begins and the other one ends, when Paul writes about Jesus and God.

> *Blessed be the God and Father of our Lord Jesus Christ, the Father of compassion and God of all encouragement, who encourages us in our every affliction, so that we may be able to encourage those who are in any affliction with the encouragement with which we ourselves are encouraged by God. For as Christ's sufferings overflow to us, so through Christ does our encouragement also overflow.*

> *2nd Letter to the Corinthians*, Chapter 1:3

As the above passage illustrates, Paul was the first person to blur the line between God and Jesus, a catastrophic error of judgment and completely contrary to Jesus' admonition against calling him lord and master in derogation of God. Nevertheless, Paul starts the deification of Jesus by upgrading him from Messiah to "son of God" and equating him with the Supreme Being. Paul also scrambles some of the most famous *Old Testament* parables in an attempt to distinguish Jesus from other Jewish Prophets and explain why God would send and then kill his own son. Primarily, Paul uses two *Genesis* stories to make his case for blind faith in Jesus as a savior god: (i) the covenant story between God and Abraham; and (ii) the story of God testing Abraham to see if he will kill his son Isaac.

Paul begins the deification of Jesus by asserting that God wanted to make a new covenant with mankind because we failed to live up to the original contract between God and Abraham. Why God would reward us for failing to honor the first covenant is beyond me. Anyway, Paul says that under the terms of the new covenant, anyone who believes that Jesus is the son of God is entitled to a heavenly reward. As a result, Paul misconstrues the original covenant parable, since he treats it like an expired contract between God and the Jews as opposed to a metaphor for mankind's realization that there is only one God in the Universe who is worthy of our worship.

Next, Paul cites the story of God asking Abraham to sacrifice his son as proof that faith in Jesus is all that is required under the new covenant. He also uses the story to prove that God would sacrifice his own son. Never mind that in the story, God stops Abraham from killing Isaac. And never mind that this parable, which is over four thousand years old, was intended to end the barbaric practice of human sacrifice by teaching our pagan ancestors that such rituals are irrelevant to God (the interpretation universally accepted by mythology experts). Instead, Paul revives the pagan concept of human sacrifice and casts Jesus as the "Passover Lamb" of the *New Testament*.

Thus, according to Paul, Jesus was killed as consideration for the new covenant between God and mankind. He also implies that God has abandoned the covenant with the Jewish people. Once again, the logic behind Paul's assertion that God would take *anyone's* life as payment for the totality of mankind's sins, totally escapes me. Paul either failed to grasp the *Old Testament* parables or he purposely misconstrued them to manipulate his Gentile audience. Regardless of the reason, Paul totally butchers some of the most important Jewish holy scripture in his struggle to deify Jesus. Additionally, Paul begins to sound exceedingly anti-Semitic.

> *I ask, then, has God rejected his people? Of course not! ... But through their transgressions salvation has come to the Gentiles, so as to make them jealous. ... Now I am speaking to you Gentiles. Inasmuch then as I am the apostle to the Gentiles, I glory in my ministry in order to make my race jealous and thus save some of them. For if their rejection is the reconciliation of the world, what will their acceptance be but life from the dead?*
>
> Letter to the Romans, Chapter 11:1–15

Although I internally recoil from Paul's machinations of *Old Testament* parables and his lack of respect for the finer points of the Jewish tradition, I find it absolutely fascinating how he placates his Roman audience by dangling two pagan concepts in front of them: (i) the previously extinct custom of human sacrifice; and (ii) the spiritually immature need to create and personify separate deities with distinct functions. Consider that Paul replaces the Egyptian god **Ra** and the Greek god **Zeus** with "God the Father." Similarly, he transforms Jesus into the "Son of God" as a substitute for Ra's son **Osiris** (who also resurrected from the dead), and for Zeus' son **Apollo**. Finally, Paul manages to sideline the wisdom goddesses, the Egyptian **Isis** and the Greek **Athena**, and inculcate the Gentiles with a third genderless deity, the amorphous Holy Spirit.

The second way Paul's theology differed from the Jewish Christians, was his belief that Jesus' death not only neutralized original sin but also eliminated our obligation to avoid sin. Indeed, Paul goes even further and argues that Jesus' sacrifice released us from observing the Mosaic laws, since we need only have faith in Jesus as a savior god in order to reach heaven.

> *Before faith came, we were held in custody under the law, confined for*
> *the faith that was to be revealed. Consequently, the law was our*
> *disciplinarian for Christ, that we might be justified by faith. But now*
> *that faith has come, we are no longer under a disciplinarian.*

> *Letter to the Galatians, Chapter 3:23*

Even more mind-numbing is Paul's argument that the Ten Commandments make us *more* prone to sin by focusing our attention on what we should *not* do. I vaguely remember my children passing through this early stage of emotional development. I knew if I said to them, "Don't you dare touch that," their attention might switch to the forbidden item.

> *Yet I do not know sin except through the law, and I did not know what*
> *it is to covet except that the law said, "You shall not covet." But sin,*
> *finding an opportunity in the commandment, produced in me every kind*
> *of covetousness. ... For sin, seizing an opportunity in the*
> *commandment, deceived me and through it put me to death.*

> *Letter to the Romans, Chapter 7:7–11*

Third, Paul believed that because we're all sinners, the only way to get to heaven is through faith in Jesus. In addition, Paul preached that our good works are irrelevant under the new covenant. Thus, despite Jesus' insistence that the Golden Rule is the key to salvation, Paul proposes an alternative formula – blind faith. It is a tragedy that most Christians, particularly fundamentalists, have adopted Paul's formula for salvation. It explains, though, why being a Christian today is a mere label and no longer a description of one who lives a compassionate life.

> *But now the righteousness of God has been manifested apart from the*
> *law ... the righteousness of God through faith in Jesus Christ for all*
> *who believe. For there is no distinction; all have sinned and are deprived*
> *of the glory of God. ...*
>   *What occasion then is there for boasting? It is ruled out. **On what***
> ***principle, that of works? No, rather on the principle of faith. For we***
> ***consider that a person is justified by faith apart from works of the law.***
> *[Emphasis added]*

> *Letter to the Romans, Chapter 3:21; 27*

Sadly, Paul's childish belief that Jesus will forgive our sins and rescue us in exchange for blind worship could not be further from the Truth. In fact, Paul's substitution of blind faith for good works is the most disturbing of all of his flawed lessons and the one that must have made James the Just absolutely nuts. In his *New Testament* letter, James tries to correct Paul's mistaken theology. Unfortunately, though, James was unable to stem the tide of "Paulianity."

> *What good is it, my brothers, if someone says he has faith but does not have works? Can that faith save him? If a brother or sister has nothing to wear and has no food for the day, and one of you says to them, "Go in peace, keep warm, and eat well," but you do not give them the necessities of the body, what good is it? So also faith of itself, if it does not have works, is dead. ... For just as a body without a spirit is dead, so also faith without works is dead.*

> *Letter of James, Chapter 2:14–26*

Finally, in the event that my Christian readers still think that blind faith is the path to salvation, let me close this debate once and for all by quoting a Prophet who knows the Truth.

> *Do not think that I have come to abolish the law or the prophets. I have come not to abolish but to fulfill. Amen, I say to you, until heaven and earth pass away, not the smallest letter or the smallest part of a letter will pass from the law, until all things have taken place. Therefore, whoever breaks one of the least of these commandments and teaches others to do so will be called least in the kingdom of heaven. But whoever obeys and teaches these commandments will be called greatest in the kingdom of heaven. I tell you, unless your righteousness surpasses that of the scribes and Pharisees, you will not enter the kingdom of heaven.*

> *Gospel of Matthew, Chapter 5:17–20*

If only Paul had bothered to read the *Sayings Source*, he would have learned that Jesus revered the laws of Moses. Furthermore, if Paul had taken the time to study with the apostles, he would have understood that Jesus delivered a new law from God: *Love thy neighbor as thyself.* It is easy to understand Paul's zeal, particularly given the dramatic nature of his own conversion. Even so, there is no excuse for Paul's failure to do his homework. He should have paused long enough to fully digest the next layer of the Tower of Truth which Jesus pronounced to the world: *Mankind is worthy of joining with God, but only through the exercise of love and good works.*

The fourth lesson Paul taught that differed from the Jewish Christian sect, was that everyone has the ability to join God in heaven. Finally, a tenet of Paul's worthy of applause, and resounding applause at that! Recall that before Jesus died, he had not yet expanded his mission outside of Judea, and he never once broke bread with Gentiles. Thus, it may be that Jesus spoke to Paul from heaven and asked Paul to spread the gospel to the Gentiles, since: (i) Paul was a Roman Jew, specially equipped for such an assignment; and (ii) Jesus had not made it clear during his lifetime that the next layer of spiritual Truth should be shared with all cultures.

However, it looks as though Paul was so excited about spreading the word that mankind can achieve union with God, that he failed to memorize the right formula for salvation. It also appears that Paul would modify the formula depending on his audience's taste. In other words, Paul tried to "please all of the people all of the time," a posture which is *not* conducive to Truth.

> *Although I am free in regard to all, I have made myself a slave to all so as to win over as many as possible. To the Jews I became like a Jew to win over Jews; to those under the law I became like under the law – though I myself am not under the law – to win over those under the law. To those outside the law I became like one outside the law – though I am not outside God's law but within the law of Christ – to win over those outside the law. To the weak I became weak, to win over the weak. I have become all things to all, to save at least some. All this I do for the sake of the gospel, so that I too may have a share in it.* [Emphasis added]

1st Letter to the Corinthians, Chapter 9:19

The fifth thing Paul did which was different than the Jewish Christians, was to introduce the topic of church hierarchy. Indeed, Paul seemed obsessed with ranking early church leaders and subjugating the laity. Before Paul started preaching, none of the apostles questioned James' authority as the sole leader of the church. By all accounts, Peter was second in command and quite content with that role. However, after Paul and some of the apostles started preaching to the Gentiles, they started to establish churches outside of Jerusalem in major cities such as Antioch, Alexandria, and Rome. The leaders of these churches had no official titles as yet, and everyone continued to defer to James in Jerusalem. Only Paul sought to challenge James and, in the process, began setting the stage for a later church hierarchy.

Not surprisingly, the reason Paul was concerned with the upper echelons of the church was because he was at the bottom rung of the ladder. James never trusted Paul and apparently would not issue him "letters" authorizing him to represent the church, which meant that Paul lacked the indicia of authority when he was about church business abroad. Additionally, Peter wrote to the outlying priests instructing them not to accept any disciple who did not have a letter signed by James. As a result, Paul became obsessed with his standing within the Jesus movement and he started challenging the "super-apostles," as he sarcastically called them.

> And even if I should boast a little too much of our authority, which the Lord gave for building you up and not for tearing you down, I shall not be put to shame. **May I not seem as one frightening you through letters.** For someone will say, "His letters are severe and forceful, but his bodily presence is weak, and his speech contemptible." Such a person must understand that what we are in word through letters when absent, that we also are in action when present. ...
>
> For I think that I am not in any way inferior to these **"superapostles."** Even if I am untrained in speaking, I am not so in knowledge; in every way we made this plain to you in all things. [Emphasis added]

> *2nd Letter to the Corinthians*, Chapters 10:8, 11:5

Paul came back to Jerusalem twice to meet with the apostles. The first time was around 50 C.E., and historians refer to this meeting as the **First Jerusalem Council.** During the Council, the apostles debated whether Christian converts needed to be circumcised. Paul won this debate, and James issued a decree from the Council allowing Gentile converts to remain uncircumcised. (See *Acts of the Apostles*, Chapter 15:19).

> Then after fourteen years I again went up to Jerusalem .... Moreover, not even Titus, who was with me, although he is Greek, was compelled to be circumcised .... **But from those who were reputed to be important – what they once were makes no difference to me;** God shows no partiality – those of repute made me add nothing. On the contrary, when they saw that I had been entrusted with the gospel to the uncircumcised, just as Peter to the circumcised, for the one who worked in Peter for an apostolate to the circumcised worked also in me for the Gentiles, and when they recognized the grace bestowed upon me, **James and Cephas** [Peter] **and John,** who were **reputed to be pillars,** gave me and Barnabas their right hands in partnership, that we should go to the Gentiles and they to the circumcised. [Emphasis added]

> *Letter to the Galatians*, Chapter 2:1–9

Clearly, Paul was a man with a huge ego and an attachment to Earth plane power. He was not about to let James hamper his mission or question his authority, which he claimed came directly from Jesus. Indeed, after the First Jerusalem Council, Paul defied anyone to question his authority, and he even assumed the power to send others to preach in his name.

*I am writing you this not to shame you, but to admonish you as my beloved children. Even if you should have countless guides to Christ, yet you do not have many fathers, for I became your father in Christ Jesus through the gospel. **Therefore, I urge you, be imitators of me.** For this reason I am sending you Timothy, who is my beloved and faithful son in the Lord; he will remind you of **my ways in Christ,** just as I teach them everywhere in every church. [Emphasis added]*

1st Letter to the Corinthians, Chapter 4:14–17

It was at this juncture that Paul began to proselytize on how church meetings should be conducted and how congregations should be structured and managed. He even had the audacity to state that his ideas on church hierarchy were commanded by Jesus.

So what is to be done brother? When you assemble, one has a psalm, another an instruction, a revelation, a tongue, or an interpretation. ... Two or three prophets should speak, and the others discern. ...

*As in all churches of the holy ones, **women should keep silent in the churches,** for they are not allowed to speak, but should be subordinate, as even the law says. But if they want to learn anything, they should ask their husbands at home. For it is improper for a woman to speak in the church. ...*

*If anyone thinks that he is prophet or a spiritual person, he should recognize that **what I am writing you is a commandment of the Lord.** If anyone does not acknowledge this, he is not acknowledged. [Emphasis added]*

1st Letter to the Corinthians, Chapter 14:26–38

Thus, Paul recognized, as all men of power do, that in order to seize control of an organization, authority must be firmly established and that the fastest way to impose authority over others is to fabricate layers of structure and insist on strict discipline. Ideally, the most effective type of discipline is blind allegiance, in which the masses never think to question their "chosen" leaders. Check out how ingeniously Paul starts to prepare the masses for their later domination by men of power.

*Let every person be subordinate to the higher authorities, for there is no authority except from God, and those that exist have been established by God. **Therefore; whoever resists authority opposes what God has appointed, and those who oppose it will bring judgment on themselves.** For rulers are not a cause of fear to good conduct, but to evil.*

*Do you wish to have no fear of authority? Then do what is good and you will receive approval from it, for it is a servant of God for your good. **But if you do evil, be afraid, for it does not bear the sword without purpose; it is the servant of God to inflict wrath on the evildoer.***

> *Therefore, it is necessary to be subject not only because of wrath but
> also because of conscience. **This is why you also pay taxes, for the
> authorities are ministers of God**, devoting themselves to this very thing.
> [Emphasis added]*

Letter to the Romans, Chapter 13:1–6

Thus, Paul employed a two-pronged approach to seize power: (i) with
regard to the Jewish Christians, he purposely and methodically undermined
those whom he perceived to be a threat to his mission, including James and the
apostles in Jerusalem; and (ii) with the Gentiles, he introduced the notion of
total obedience to church leaders, yet another conflict with Jesus' views. Please
also note Paul's assertion that church authorities are directly appointed by
God, a sacred concept to Catholics who think their popes are so ordained.
Additionally, Paul suggests that church authorities have the right to punish
"evildoers." As we shall discuss in Chapter Four, the Catholics used this passage to buttress the six hundred year killing spree known as the Holy
Inquisition.

*The sixth doctrine that Paul interjected into the Christian belief system
was misogyny.* As with Paul's other character flaws, the Catholic Church
would soon come to embrace Paul's disdain of women, which is completely
anathema to the teachings of Jesus. As we shall see in Chapter Four, the
Catholic Church relentlessly purged feminine energy in the name of orthodoxy.

> *But I want you to know that Christ is the head of every man, and a
> husband the head of his wife, and God the head of Christ. ... For if a
> woman does not have her head veiled, she may as well have her hair cut
> off. ... A man, on the other hand, should not cover his head, because he
> is the image and glory of God, but woman is the glory of man. For man
> did not come from woman, but woman from man; nor was man created
> for woman, but woman for man; for this reason a woman should have a
> sign of authority on her head, because of the angels.*

1st Letter to the Corinthians, Chapter 11:3–10

Needless to say, by the end of his ministry, around 60 C.E., Paul had lost all
semblance of righteousness himself, as he became more concerned with Earth
plane power than with spreading the actual messages of Jesus. Tragically, Paul
undermined most of Jesus' lessons, including the fundamental Truth that God
does not reside in any religious institution but, rather, in our hearts. In fact,
Jesus was so determined to spread this important Truth that he martyred himself rather than placate the corrupt Temple priests. Most disturbing, though,
is that Paul never accepted *the* central tenet of Christianity: *Love thy neighbor.* In his letters, Paul instructs his Gentile laity to ostracize "those who are

different" and to "purge the evil person from your midst," in direct opposition to the Eleventh Commandment. No wonder, then, that so many independent scholars have concluded that Paul was either a Jewish or Roman spy sent to destroy the Jesus movement.

Today, however, we call Paul's version of Christianity "orthodox." When you contrast of Paul's simplistic message (i.e., faith in Jesus as a god is the key to salvation), against the rigorous Jewish Christian belief (i.e., we must submit to God's will and love our neighbor to get into heaven), and the more advanced Gnostic Christian view (i.e., faith and compassion are mere starting points for spiritual enlightenment), it becomes fairly clear that Paul was not interested in figuring out the deeper meaning behind Jesus' life and death. The spiritual journey embraced by the Jewish Christians and the Gnostics was much more complicated. Indeed, it required hard work! The only thing I can say in Paul's defense is that he, just like the Jewish Christians, thought that the end of the world was near. Perhaps Paul thought that he didn't have time to thoroughly explain Jesus' spiritual Truths prior to Judgment Day. Nevertheless, over the past two thousand years Christian leaders have had plenty of time to correct Paul's mistakes and have declined to do so.

Unfortunately, Paul's views on Jesus have rarely been questioned, which means that Christianity still is based on a pagan view of God that takes us a step backward spiritually. Quite simply, Paul relied on Jewish tradition, Greek mythology, Roman deification of rulers, and pagan imagery in a blatant attempt to convert his Gentile audience. Paul kept the *Old Testament* stories alive to appease the Jews. He added a dash of mythology and a pinch of paganism to turn Jesus into God's begotten son, a familiar image to the Gentiles as Zeus had many such children. And he carried the ball over the finish line by shamelessly using the momentum of the true heirs of the Jesus movement, James and the apostles, with little or no regard for the actual words of Jesus.

Yet, what I find the most unforgivable is Paul's deification of Jesus, since it was a myth that was completely unnecessary to teach the masses about Jesus' lessons of love. As proof that Jesus' deification was unnecessary to amass followers, simply count the multitudes throughout history who have sought to emulate Jesus' life while still viewing him as a Prophet. I am talking about people from other religions, like Gandhi, and those who reject ritualistic religion, like me, who aspire to Jesus' high standards and cherish the Truth he taught, without feeling any need to worship him as a god. Incidentally, the

First and Second Commandments emphatically state that there is only one God and that the worship of any other god or idol is strictly forbidden. In sum, it is tragic that Paul added an inconsistent and frivolous layer of pagan fantasy to Jesus' divine mission. *Ironically, Paul's view of Jesus serves to minimize, rather than glorify, God's plan, since Jesus came here to teach us how to earn our own divinity, not to worship his.*

Paul's ministry not only is outrageous in retrospect, it also was horrific to the Jews and Jewish Christians who lived during Jesus' time and who knew first-hand what Jesus preached. The *Lost Gospels* and the *Gnostic Gospels* are full of scriptures and letters which directly attack Paul and his grossly flawed theology. Likewise, the authors of the later *Dead Sea Scrolls* recorded their displeasure with Paul. Today, many historians believe that the characters in the most famous *Dead Sea Scrolls* – the *Damascus Document*, the *Habakkuk Pesher*, and the *Manual of Discipline* – are none other than James and Paul. These *Scrolls* chronicle the life and lessons of a person called the **Righteous Teacher** as juxtaposed against his two nemeses – the **Spouter of Lies** and the **Wicked Priest**. Although the *Scrolls* do not use proper names, they describe people and events in vivid detail. Some historians now think that James the Just is the Righteous Teacher, who is the leader of the Way and who insists that good works, rather than mere faith, are required in order to achieve salvation.

Another main character in the *Dead Sea Scrolls* is the Spouter of Lies. Again, there is a growing consensus amongst historians that Paul may be the Spouter of Lies, since this character is reported as defying the sacred laws of Moses, leading people astray with lies, and raising a congregation based on deceit. The Spouter of Lies also is the enemy of the Righteous Teacher. Considering that the Qumran Zealots never trusted or accepted Paul and that Paul remained an adversary of James til their deaths, it is logical that the *Dead Sea Scrolls* would refer to Paul as the Spouter of Lies.

The final showdown between James and Paul occurred sometime around 60 C.E., during the **Second Jerusalem Council**. *Acts of the Apostles* reveals that during Paul's last visit to Jerusalem to meet with James, his very presence causes a riot. Paul is rescued by Roman guards (who just happen to be nearby), and he then is tried in a variety of tribunals on the charges of blasphemy and treason. During Paul's trials before the Sanhedrin, Jewish King Agrippa, and the new Roman Governor Felix, Paul eloquently admits to his sordid history. He confesses that he chased members of the Way to Damascus but was ordered by Jesus to stop the persecutions. Thus, even the sketchy history contained in *Acts* provides the careful reader with critical pieces of the puzzle. In the end, Paul is sent to Rome for a final trial that results in nothing more than house arrest. The Catholic Church asserts that Paul was martyred in Rome in 64 C.E., but there is little evidence to support this claim.

The other main character referred to in the *Scrolls* is the Wicked Priest, who kills the Righteous Teacher. Some Scholars think the Wicked Priest was Ananias, the high priest who succeeded Caiaphas to the Sanhedrin. Roman records suggest that Ananias was responsible for James' death in 62 C.E. The motive for this murder is easy to glean, since there are multiple accounts of James usurping the role of the High Priest, going into the Holy of Holies (the inner chamber of the Temple), and speaking God's name, which was strictly forbidden. Thus, scholars think James was tried for blasphemy before the Sanhedrin, just like his brother, and that the corrupt rabbis were responsible for his death as well. Thereafter, rioting crowds killed Ananias in retaliation for James' murder, according to the historian Josephus. Similarly, the *Scrolls* report that the Righteous Teacher's followers took their revenge by killing the Wicked Priest.

After James' death in 62 C.E., the Jewish Christians made Simon (a/k/a Simon Cleophas) the second Bishop of Jerusalem. If you refer back to Jesus' family trees for a minute, you'll see that Simon was Jesus' second brother, although the Catholic Church would have us believe that Simon was Jesus' cousin. Nevertheless, some of our best scholars now think that Simon, the second Bishop of Jerusalem, was actually Jesus' second brother. During Simon's tenure as leader of the Jewish Christians, the chaos in Jerusalem reached its zenith. Historians believe that as a result of continuing riots over the death of James, the Romans finally intervened. In 70 C.E., the Romans massacred the Jews and leveled the Temple for the final time.

Prior to the Roman onslaught, some of the Jews and Jewish Christians managed to escape to their fortress at Qumran and another one at Masada. After regaining control of Jerusalem, the Romans followed the Jews who went to Masada and attacked the fortress. By 74 C.E., the Jewish situation was hopeless and, rather than be taken by the Romans, about one thousand Jews committed mass suicide. Given their belief in an earthly resurrection and, perhaps, their newfound faith in a heavenly afterlife, the Jews at Masada chose to die rather than defile themselves before the Romans, who would have killed the men and children and sent the women to Roman brothels. With stoic passion, the Jewish men killed their wives and children and then drew lots to kill each other, leaving the remaining man responsible for burning the fortress and committing suicide.

Meanwhile at Qumran, the Jews plotted against the Romans and held fast to their precious *Dead Sea Scrolls*. The fortress at Qumran was the final stronghold for the Zealot wing of the Jewish Christians, including Jesus' Nazorean sect. In 132 C.E., the Zealots attacked the Romans and actually recaptured Jerusalem and held it for two years. But by 134 C.E., the Roman legions were able to retake Jerusalem and the remaining Zealots were beaten back to Battir and Qumran. In 135 C.E., the Romans finally conquered the Zealots, but not before they had safely concealed the *Dead Sea Scrolls*. It is nothing short of miraculous that the *Scrolls* were found in 1947. Clearly, God wants us to learn all that we can from these precious texts, which so many died to protect and which contain our oldest copies of some *Old Testament* books and historical accounts written at the time of Jesus and his brother James.

With regard to the *Gnostic Gospels*, the story is even more ominous, since it was the Catholic Church, as opposed to pagans, who purposely tried to destroy them. After the Romans decimated the Jewish Christians, there were two major Christian sects left: the Gentile Christians and the Gnostic Christians. At first, the Gentiles and the Gnostics coexisted rather peacefully and left each other alone. Sure, there was the occasional nasty letter and the rare physical scuffle, but basically the two sects lived side by side with neither sect trying to assert anything more than intellectual dominance over the other. Eventually, though, the Gentile Christians gained greater momentum, since their magical view of Jesus as a savior god was a lot easier to understand and more popular with the common people. The other reason the Gentile Christians gained popularity is because they followed Paul's lead and started to impose structure on their unsuspecting laity. The following passage illustrates how the Gnostic Christians viewed the emerging church leaders of the more powerful Gentile Christian sect and their naive followers.

> And they praise the men of the propagation of falsehood, those who come after you. And they will cleave to the name of a dead man [Jesus], thinking that they will become pure. But they will become greatly defiled and they will fall into a name of error, and into the hand of an evil, cunning man and a manifold dogma, and they will be ruled heretically. ...
> And there shall be others of those who are outside our number who name themselves bishop and also deacons, as if they have received their

authority from God. They bend themselves under the judgment of the
leaders. Those people are dry canals."

Apocalypse of Peter, Verses 74, 79

Indeed, the Gnostics' personal approach to God was no match for those who promoted blind faith and sought to impose a new church hierarchy with bishops, priests, and deacons. Like lambs to the slaughter, the ranks of the Gentile Christian laity swelled. By 180 C.E., the Gnostics were in serious trouble, as the Gentile Christians made a full frontal attack on them and their cherished scriptures. That year, the powerful **Bishop Irenaeus** of Lyons published his five volume treatise *The Destruction and Overthrow of Falsely So-Called Knowledge*, which directly attacked the Gnostic Christians and their gospels. For the next 150 years, the gospel debate and the infighting amongst the various Christian sects raged until Roman Emperor Constantine stepped into the fray and convened the Council of Nicaea in 325 C.E.

Because no one bishop had the power to declare dominance over the other Christian bishops, it was Roman Emperor Constantine who orchestrated this first meeting of the Christians, to which he summoned 250 bishops. Constantine was disturbed that the bishops' infighting over Christian doctrine, particularly the issue of whether Jesus was a god, would rip his empire apart. Essentially, Constantine ordered the bishops to stop fighting and create one universal (*"catholic"* in Greek) church, because he wanted to consolidate his shaky empire.

Hence, it was a pagan Roman ruler who: (i) convened the first Christian council, known as the Council of Nicaea; (ii) ordered the bishops to stop fighting and forced them to adopt just one version of Christianity; and (iii) thereafter declared that this "orthodox" version of Christianity be known as the Roman Catholic Church.

Thus, at the Council of Nicaea the bishops discussed the problematic Gnostic Christians (a/k/a the "Cathari" or the "Cathars"). They also argued and then voted on such fundamental issues as whether: (i) Jesus commenced his life as a human; (ii) Jesus was a god both before and after the crucifixion; (iii) Jesus was a lesser god who was "begotten" by the Father; (iv) Jesus was pre-existent, just like God, and therefore equal to God; or (v) Jesus was simply a Prophet, a position held by a large theological faction. Yet, by the end of the Council the bishops managed to agree on the **Nicene Creed**, which is the edict that created the now famous **Holy Trinity** of "God the Father, God the Son, and God the Holy Ghost."

Not surprisingly, the Holy Trinity was an on-going concern for those Christian bishops who knew that there is only one God. Indeed, over the next eighty years the bishops continued to debate Jesus' divinity. In 359 C.E., Constantine's son, **Emperor Constantius**, summoned the bishops to additional councils, during which they abandoned the Nicene Creed in favor of the **Creed of Rimini-Selucia** (a/k/a the "Dated Creed"). *Thus, for a while the Catholics adopted a different theology in which Jesus was not the same as God, but simply like the Father in nature.*

Thereafter, the bishops met yet again to settle the gospel debate. In 364 C.E., they convened the Council of Laodicea and made a first cut in determining which gospels would be deemed "orthodox" and which would be labeled "heretical." However, some Eastern bishops never accepted the council's decision to exclude certain *Lost Gospels* and *Gnostic Gospels*. Finally, as unbelievable as it may sound, not until the Council of Trent in 1545 C.E., did the Christians officially decree which gospels and letters would be included in *The Holy Bible*.

However, around 450 C.E., **Pope Leo I** (who was actually the Bishop of Rome but who started calling himself "*Pontifex Maximus*," to the utter dismay of the Eastern bishops), concluded that the *Gnostic Gospels* had to be suppressed. Thus, he declared the *Gnostic Gospels* heretical and ordered that they "should not only be forbidden, but entirely destroyed and burned with fire." Fortunately, some brave soul in the Eastern branch of the Church disobeyed Leo's order and hid a set of the *Gnostic Gospels* in a jar. Surely, the preservation and later discovery of these ancient texts is nothing short of Divine intervention. There simply is no other interpretation for this archeological find, except that God thinks we now are ready for Jesus' deeper messages of Truth regarding the path to salvation.

In Chapter Four, we will explore the evolution of the Catholic Church from the fall of the Roman Empire onward, to see how this institution continued to amass power and wealth at the expense of Jesus' spiritual messages of Truth. Before I close this section, however, I want to summarize the actual teachings of Jesus, now that our discussion of the earliest Jewish, Gentile, and Gnostic Christian sects is completed.

The primary reason that Jesus was a revolutionary Prophet is that he changed our concept of God. The God of the *Old Testament* was fierce, judgmental and, oftentimes, brutal, and he expected strict obedience, as reflected in the Mosaic laws. Moreover, the Jewish God was hard even with his own people and punished them repeatedly for breaking his laws and returning to paganism. Although Jesus never advocated breaking from the Jewish laws and, in fact, made it clear that the Ten Commandments still apply to us, he described God in totally new terms.

Jesus described God as a father figure, who is nurturing, protective, and forgiving. Moreover, the God whom Jesus described provides comfort and salvation *if* we continue to adhere to his plan for mankind. Consequently, this God is much more approachable and compassionate. Personally, I feel much more comfortable and aligned with this updated image of God, and I am grateful that God sent Jesus to explain this next layer of Truth and to help me better understand God's true nature.

Jesus also was a revolutionary Prophet because he fearlessly protested against the corrupt leaders and outworn rituals of his own religion. He brazenly defied the Jewish hierarchy by claiming that God is everywhere and in all things, not just in the Temple. He also stressed that the Jewish Temple had been defiled by the priests who were claiming dominion over the people, taking money for selfish purposes, and claiming ultimate authority from God. Moreover, just as Buddha had done with the *brahmin* priests, Jesus rebutted the existing notion that only the rabbis were worthy of communing with God. Instead, he taught that God is available to all of us and that we need only turn inward to grasp spiritual Truth and be with God. Also like Buddha, Jesus ignored some of the outworn rituals of his religion that conflicted with God's new message regarding compassionate living. For instance, Jesus healed the sick on the Sabbath in defiance of the archaic Jewish law that no work can be done on that day.

Most importantly, though, Jesus taught that God's love and salvation are available to all. Despite the fact that Jesus preached almost exclusively to the Jews, he never rejected people outside of his religion whom he encountered and who sought his help. Jesus' parable about the good Samaritan who helps a hurt Jew on the side of the road was meant to show that a person of any religion who performs good acts is a child of God. He used a Samaritan in the story because they were considered foreigners and enemies of the Jews. Additionally, if you believe that Jesus chose Paul to spread his inclusive teachings to the Gentiles, it is even more evident that Jesus wanted his message of love and spiritual insight to reach everyone.

Thus, it is safe to conclude that, just like Buddha, Jesus wanted each of us to experience God's Truth and achieve spiritual enlightenment for ourselves. Jesus also taught, as did Buddha, that we attain release from the Earth plane through faith in God and in ourselves, since we cannot attain an Ethereal plane existence until we perfect our soul. Even more specifically, Jesus taught that we earn salvation in heaven by performing compassionate acts while on Earth.

> I will show you what someone is like who comes to me, listens to my words, and **acts on them**. That one is like a person building a house, who dug deeply and laid the foundation on rock; when the flood came, the river burst against the house but could not shake it because it had been well built. But the one who listens and **does not act** is like a person who built a house on the ground without foundation. When the river burst against it, it collapsed at once and was completely destroyed. [Emphasis added]
>
> Gospel of Luke, Chapter 6:47–49

The above passage not only emphasizes that faith without good works is meaningless, it also is the perfect metaphor for the *Saddha* process of spiritual growth, which results in firm, not blind, faith. In sum, Buddha and Jesus agree on the following formula for spiritual enlightenment: (i) faith in God and our ability to perfect ourselves; (ii) going inward for the light of Truth; then (iii) moving outward with love and charity for our less fortunate neighbors, including our enemies.

Jesus also taught that the less you have on the Earth plane, the more likely you are to join God in the Ethereal plane. Like Buddha before him, Jesus taught that mankind's desire for wealth and power is sinful in God's eyes. Compassionate acts toward our neighbors hold the key to salvation. Moreover, to the Ten Commandments he added one global edict: *Do unto others as you would have them do unto you.* Therefore, let us acknowledge how hard it is to get into heaven. Not only must we continue to follow the Jewish Ten Commandments, we also must treat others with total love and forgiveness by sharing what we have for the collective good of mankind.

In sum, the Prophet Jesus brought us the next layer of spiritual Truth from God, that mankind has the ability to achieve salvation and join with God in the Ethereal plane.

Remember, the Prophets of the earlier religions – Hinduism, Judaism, and Buddhism – did not believe that mankind was worthy of joining God. Jesus, however, taught that we may unite with God *if* we perfect ourselves. Thus, he expanded on Buddha's concept of *nirvana*, which simply meant liberation from the Earth plane. *It is interesting to note, though, that Jesus agreed with Buddha that the kingdom of God is a state of being, as opposed to a place.*

Rather, the kingdom is inside of you, and it is outside of you. When you come to know yourselves, then you will become known, and you will realize that it is you who are the sons of the living Father. But if you will not know yourselves, you dwell in poverty and it is you who are that poverty.

Rather, the kingdom of the father is spread out upon the earth, and men do not see it.

Gospel of Thomas, Verses 3, 113

When asked by the Pharisees when the kingdom of God would come, he said in reply, "The coming of the kingdom of God cannot be observed, and no one will announce, 'Look, here it is,' or 'There it is.' For behold, the kingdom of God is within you."

Gospel of Luke, Chapter 17:20

The above quotes by Jesus could be interpreted as holding fast to the Jewish notion of a bodily resurrection on Earth. However, after analyzing the available source material, I have concluded that Jesus was positing a brand new belief system. In addition, it makes sense that Jesus came to Earth to add the next layer to our Tower of Truth by expanding upon Buddha's concept of *nirvana*. Indeed, it appears that Jesus had already attained the state of *nirvana*, continued on his spiritual journey by uniting with God in heaven, and then decided to come back to Earth to teach the rest of us how to achieve salvation too. *Therefore, Jesus may have been our first bodhisattva which, if you recall, is a buddha who ascends to the Ethereal plane but then elects to come back to the Earth plane to further edify mankind.*

Lastly, Jesus included women in his inner circle and defied Jewish laws which prohibited praying with women. Once again, Jesus went beyond Buddha's teachings in this regard and willingly embraced feminine energy. Not only did Jesus believe that women should share in the unveiling of Truth about God, he also sought female input and valued the opinions of women. Indeed, when all the source material is studied and analyzed, it appears that Mary Magdalene was, at a minimum, Jesus' closest follower and confidant.

Additionally, there is a mounting body of evidence which suggests that Jesus and Mary Magdalene may have been husband and wife. Putting aside Dan Brown's *The Da Vinci Code*, there are many independent scholars who now believe that Jesus and Mary were married and that the wedding at Cana, described in the *Gospel of John*, was Jesus' own wedding reception. Regardless of whether Jesus and Mary were married or simply close spiritual companions, it is now evident that Jesus greatly respected her mind and preferred her over the other apostles.

Even the canonical gospels support this fact. The *Gospel of Matthew*, *Gospel of Mark*, and *Gospel of John* all agree that Jesus appeared to Mary Magdalene first after the resurrection. Jesus also returned to Bethany to resurrect Mary's brother Lazarus after he suddenly died, and Jesus often stayed with Mary Magdalene's family when he visited Jerusalem. Also, Mary was *not* the "sinful woman" described in Chapter 7 of the *Gospel of Luke*. Rather she was one of the women listed by name in Chapter 8 of *Luke*, who regularly accompanied Jesus. Thank God the Catholic Church finally had the decency to retract their fallacious and reprehensible teachings about this holy woman. Unfortunately, however, it was not until 1969 C.E., that Pope Paul VI finally admitted that the Church had unduly and erroneously stigmatized Mary Magdalene and retracted all negative dicta about this disciple.

In addition to the significant evidence of Mary's stature contained in the *New Testament*, the *Gnostic Gospels* are replete with examples of Jesus preferring Mary's company over that of the male apostles. In the following passage, I have used the symbol ^ to indicate missing text. However, even with some words missing, it is obvious that Jesus loved Mary very very much.

> *There were three who always walked with the Lord: Mary his mother*
> *and her sister and Magdalene, the one who was called his companion.*
> *His sister and his mother and his companion were each a Mary. ...*
> *And the companion of the ^ Mary Magdalene ^ loved her more than*
> *all the disciples and used to kiss her often on her ^ The rest of the*
> *disciples ^ They said to him, "Why do you love her more than all of us?"*
> *The savior answered and said to them, "Why do I not love you like her?"*
>
> *Gospel of Philip,* Verses 59, 64

Furthermore, in the *Gnostic Gospels*, it is Mary Magdalene who speaks the most often with Jesus, indicating that she understood his deeper teachings much better than the men. The following passage relates to a dispute between Mary and Peter because Peter refuses to believe that Jesus would share secret thoughts with a woman.

> *Peter said to Mary, "Sister, we know that the Savior loved you more*
> *than the rest of women. Tell us the words of the Savior which you*
> *remember – which you know but we do not, nor have heard them."*
> *Mary answered and said, "What is hidden from you I will proclaim*
> *to you." And she began to speak to them these words: ... "Lord, I saw*
> *you today in a vision."*

He [Jesus] answered and said to me, "Blessed are you, that you did not waver at the sight of me. For where the mind is, there is the treasure."

I said to him, "Lord, now does he who sees the vision see it through the soul or through the spirit?"

The Savior answered and said, "He does not see through the soul nor through the spirit, but the mind which is between the two – that is what sees the vision and it is ^" ...

Peter answered and spoke concerning these same things. He questioned them about the Savior, "Did he really speak with a woman without our knowledge and not openly? Are we to turn about and all listen to her? Did he prefer her to us?"

Then Mary wept and said to Peter, "My brother Peter, what do you think? Do you think that I thought this up myself in my heart, or that I am lying about the Savior?"

Levi answered and said to Peter, "Peter, you have always been hot-tempered. Now I see you contending against the woman like the adversaries. But if the Savior made her worthy, who are you indeed to reject her? Surely the Savior knows her very well. That is why he loved her more than us. Rather let us be ashamed and put on the perfect man and acquire him for ourselves as he commanded us, and preach the gospel, not laying down another rule or other law beyond what the Savior said." [Emphasis added]

Gospel of Mary, Verse 18, 19

Unfortunately, men of power did lay down rules and laws "beyond what the Savior said," which subjugate women and which contradict the *Saddha* process of enlightenment. Truly, if the Gentile Christians had understood Christ, our world would be a very different place. Now, let us turn to our next Prophet to see if the people of his culture heard his messages of Truth any better.

MUSLIM PROPHETS

Muhammad ibn Abdullah was born in 570 C.E. in Mecca, which today is a city located in Saudi Arabia. In that region of the Middle East, which was then called Arabia, the influential religions were Zoroastrianism, Judaism, and Christianity. However, the vast majority of the Arabs worshiped multiple deities, believing that the most powerful god of all was **Allah.**

In Mecca, there was a holy building named the **Ka'ba,** which the Arabs believed was built by Abraham, the patriarch of the Jewish religion, and Ishmael, who was Abraham's son by his Egyptian wife, Hagar. The Arabs believed that they were descendant from Adam, the first man, through Abraham's oldest son, Ishmael. Although the Arabs practiced many religions, the people were not at peace. In fact, at the time of Muhammad's birth, social conditions were chaotic and tribal feuding was common. The fourteen Arab tribes in Mecca paid strict allegiance to their specific clans, while other Arabs lived in nomadic tribes outside the city.

Muhammad's early life was tragic. He belonged to one of the weakest tribes in Mecca called the Hashim. Muhammad lost his father a few days before he was born, his mother died when he was six, and the grandfather who took over his care died when Muhammad was only eight years old. Muhammad then went to live with his uncle, who became head of the Hashim. Nevertheless, his uncle's family was of humble means and Muhammad grew up tending animals. Consequently, Muhammad was never formally educated and could not read or write.

Occasionally, Muhammad traveled with his uncle along the merchant trade routes between Mecca and Syria. As a result, Muhammad was able to learn about life outside of Mecca. Reportedly, Muhammad was fascinated by religion and sought out holy men of various faiths whenever he traveled. Through these encounters, Muhammad started to learn about the monotheistic God worshiped by the Jews and the Christians, even though his people still practiced paganism by worshiping multiple deities.

On one such trip, Muhammad met a Christian monk named Bahira, who knew of Jesus' promise to send another Prophet to repeat and more fully explain God's lessons of Truth.

If you love me, you will keep the commandments. And I will ask the
Father, and He will give you another Advocate to be with you always,
the Spirit of Truth .... The Advocate, the holy Spirit that the Father will

send in my name – he will teach you everything and remind you of all that I told you.

Gospel of John, Chapter 14:15–26

When Bahira saw Muhammad, he excitedly exclaimed that the Christian prophecy was fulfilled. Bahira declared that Muhammad, the boy tending the caravan's animals, was the teacher of Truth predicted by Jesus and sent by God.

When Muhammad was a young man, he began to work for a wealthy widow named **Khadija**, who was fifteen years his senior. Muhammad tended to her business affairs and managed merchandise along a variety of trade routes throughout Arabia. Consequently, Muhammad was exposed even more to the Jewish and Christian religions, and he began to wonder why there was so much religious divisiveness in the world. It was during a caravan expedition for Khadija that another Christian holy man approached Muhammad and, once again, identified Muhammad as the next Prophet sent by God. When the news of this trip reached Khadija, she proposed marriage to Muhammad. Already, she believed in his greatness. Muhammad was twenty-five years old when he and Khadija were married, but nothing as yet had prompted the young man into spiritual action.

Muhammad's life changed forever in 610 C.E. when he was forty years old. By all accounts, Muhammad was an extremely contemplative soul and he habitually sought privacy in a cave located on Mount Hira near Mecca. While mediating in the cave one day, Muhammad saw an angel who told him to recite Allah's messages to the people. Muhammad was terrified and reported to his wife that he might be going crazy! However, Khadija trusted him and encouraged him to accept his holy mission. The following is one of the earliest messages relayed by God and recited by Muhammad:

He is Allah, the One and Only; Allah the Eternal, Absolute; He begetteth not, nor is He begotten: And there is none like unto Him.

The Holy Quran, Sura CXII, Verses 1–4

Muhammad then realized that Allah was not the most powerful of many gods, but that Allah was the only God. Muhammad also realized that Allah was the same God worshiped by the Jews and Christians.

It is interesting to note the similarities between Muhammad's story of spiritual awakening and the epiphany of Moses. Recall that Moses originally believed that there were multiple gods and that the supreme god was Elohim. After God spoke to him, however, Moses realized that Elohim was the *only*

God. Also, historians are quick to note the similarity in the names ascribed to the Hebrew and Islamic God. When the plural ending is dropped from Elohim, God's name is Eloh in Hebrew. Eloh and Allah are fascinatingly similar. Additionally, it is interesting to note that both of these Prophets talked to God on mountaintops.

Muhammad received most of his messages from Allah through an angel, whom Muhammad believed to be the Archangel Gabriel. For almost two years, Muhammad was afraid to share the messages with anyone other than his wife, Khadija. Eventually, the angel ordered Muhammad to "Recite!" Muhammad finally obeyed the command and, at the age of forty-two, began his ministry.

Incidentally, Jesus referred to a future Prophet numerous times in the *New Testament*, where the Greek term "*Paraclete*" is used to describe the next messenger from God. This term is often translated as "Comforter," but it is more properly translated as "Advocate" or "Counselor." Christians assert that the Advocate is the Holy Spirit, an intangible entity connoting the spirit or word of God. However, the passages related to the Advocate plainly reveal that Jesus was describing a flesh and blood person, not a ghost. Moreover, when the word *Paraclete* is translated into Arabic, the word becomes *Ahmad* (i.e., Muhammad). In sum, Muslims think Jesus fore-saw Muhammad. As an impartial seeker of Truth, I tend to agree with the Muslims. Indeed, Jesus even predicted *how* the next Prophet would receive and share God's messages.

> *I have much more to tell you, but you cannot bear it now. But when he comes, the Spirit of Truth, he will guide you to all truth.* **He will not speak on his own, but he will speak what he hears, and will declare to you the things that are coming.** *He will glorify me, because he will take from what is mine and declare it to you. [Emphasis added]*
>
> Gospel of John, Chapter 16:12–14

When Muhammad began reciting Allah's messages, there was no consoli-dated form of government in Arabia. The brutal warlords who controlled the Arab populace staunchly rejected Muhammad's messages of brotherly love and charity toward the poor. The Arab chieftains had little concern for their less fortunate brethren and prospered in an environment where only the strong sur-vived. Muhammad labeled the pagan nobles "Unbelievers" and "Hypocrites."

> *O ye men! If ye are in doubt as to my religion, behold! I worship not what ye worship, other than Allah! But I worship Allah – who will take*

your souls at death. I am commanded to be in the ranks of the Believers,
and further: Set thy face towards Religion with true piety, and never in
any wise be of the Unbelievers; Nor call on any other than Allah – such
will neither profit thee nor hurt thee. If thou dost, Behold! Thou shalt
certainly be of those who do wrong.

The Holy Quran, Sura X, Verses 104–106

For three years, Muhammad proclaimed Allah's messages to the people of Mecca, but to little avail. Muhammad taught that mankind should surrender to Allah, the source of all life both on Earth and in heaven. He called the new religion Islam, which means "submission," and his followers were called Muslims or "those who surrender." Muhammad also preached that we should express our gratitude and love of Allah by giving generously to our less fortunate neighbors. Based on the belief that Allah is the same God worshiped by the Jews and Christians, Muhammad also taught that mankind should unite under one shared religion.

Oh ye Apostles! Enjoy all things good and pure, and work
righteousness: For I am well-acquainted with all that ye do. And verily
this Brotherhood of yours is a single Brotherhood, and I am your Lord
and Cherisher: therefore, fear me and no other.
  But people have cut off their affair of unity, between them, into
sects: Each party rejoices in that which is with itself. But leave them in
their confused ignorance for a time.

The Holy Quran, Sura XXIII, Verses 51–54

Despite this simple message of brotherly love and unity, the powerful Meccan leaders refused to renounce their pagan deities. Moreover, the warlords encouraged their clansmen to ostracize the Muslims, and many of them were ridiculed, tortured, and even killed. Nevertheless, Muhammad continued to teach that there is only one God and that we are all brothers and sisters, a simple message that eventually gained support amongst the poorest members of Arab society.

As tensions mounted, some of Muhammad's most vulnerable followers left Mecca for fear that they would be killed. After this exodus of slaves and lower-class tribe members, the Meccan nobles officially ordered Muhammad to stop preaching, as they were losing their work force. Muhammad refused to obey their command and, in retaliation, the chieftains imposed a boycott on Muhammad's tribe. Thereafter, none of the other tribes would do business with the Hashim. As a result, food and other necessities became scarce and the territory occupied by the Hashim was reduced to a ghetto. Historians think that

Khadija starved to death during the boycott, since she passed away just as the ban against the Hashim was lifted. Soon thereafter, Muhammad's uncle, the head of the Hashim tribe, also died. Muhammad was inconsolable over the loss of his wife and devastated by his uncle's death. He faced the darkest hour of his mission. Ultimately, Muhammad managed to overcome these setbacks and inspire more followers. This time, the Meccan nobles decided to propose a compromise: If Muhammad would agree to worship Allah and just three of their favorite goddesses, then they would join his new religion. Muhammad refused this compromise and reasserted that only Allah should be paid homage, especially at the sacred Ka'ba. Muhammad's stubborn dedication to his mission infuriated the Meccan leaders, who began to contemplate full-scale war against the Muslims. But first, the chieftains tried to assassinate Muhammad, in an attempt to thwart the impending revolution.

While civil war brewed in Mecca, leaders from another Arab town called Yathrib decided to invite Muhammad to their city to act as a mediator. The Yathrib tribes continuously fought, and the chieftains hoped that Muhammad would act as an impartial judge to resolve the conflicts. Allah instructed Muhammad to accept the invitation, so Muhammad made secret plans for the Muslims to move to Yathrib. Before departing himself, Muhammad waited until his followers made a mass exodus toward Yathrib. Miraculously, Muhammad managed to escape from Mecca in the dark of night with his most trusted ally, **Abu Bakr.**

Muhammad moved to Yathrib, later renamed Medina, in 622 c.e., and started preaching to great numbers of people. The Muslims call the migration from Mecca to Medina the **Hijra**, and they began a new calender starting from 622 c.e. in honor of the exodus. While in Medina, Muhammad operated as both a religious and political leader. As a Prophet of God, Muhammad continued to recite scripture whenever Allah revealed new suras. As a statesman, Muhammad harmonized relations between the city's five tribes, three of which were Jewish. As a result, the Muslims from Mecca, the Muslim converts in Medina, and the Jewish tribes all coexisted peacefully in Medina. Thus, Muhammad's dream of creating one community (*ummah*), based on spiritual unity (i.e., a belief in one God), rather than tribal kinship, had become a reality.

At first, the *ummah* in Medina seemed quite serene. All the pagans converted to Islam, along with some of the Jews. Most of the Jews, however, chose to maintain their distinct religious beliefs and traditions. Although

Muhammad was frustrated that many of the Jews refused to convert to Islam, he never tried to force or coerce them into joining the new religion. Indeed, tolerance toward the other monotheistic religions is a central tenant of Islam, which explains how Muhammad was able to create an environment in which both Jews and Muslims could coexist.

It is critical to understand that Muhammad viewed Islam as an ordained extension of Judaism and Christianity. Moreover, Muhammad taught that **The Holy Quran** was the culmination of God's "Book," which included the *Old Testament* and the *New Testament.* Consequently, even though Muhammad was upset that some of the Jews in Medina refused to accept the *Quran* as part of their holy scripture, he allowed the Jewish tribes to remain in Medina provided that they remained loyal to the *ummah* and made charitable donations for the poor.

> *We gave Moses the Book and followed him up with a succession of Apostles; We gave Jesus the son of Mary clear Signs and strengthened him with the holy spirit. ...*
> *And when there came to them an Apostle from Allah, confirming what was with them, a party of the People of the Book threw away the Book of Allah behind their backs, as if it had been something they did not know!*
>
> *The Holy Quran*, Sura II, Verses 87, 101

While Muhammad accepted the Jews who refused to convert to Islam, he had no patience for the pagan clans in Mecca, their selfish rivalries, or their inhumane treatment of the poor. Moreover, Muhammad had absolutely no compunction about raiding the Meccan caravans and stealing their goods. In fact, he frequently authorized such raids. Consequently, the Arab nobles' hatred of Muhammad intensified, since his raids cut into their profits and threatened their livelihood as traders. During the early attacks on the Meccans, the violence was relatively contained because Muhammad instructed the Median raiders not to kill the pagans. Realistically, however, it was only a matter of time before the raids escalated into full-scale war.

In addition to the caravan raids, Muhammad attacked the Meccan leaders by continuing to criticize their immoral and brutal practices. For instance, the Meccan tribes customarily engaged in gambling, abuse of women, and murder of female babies. These immoral practices were common in and around Mecca, and Muhammad preached against all these sins.

And they assign daughters for God! Glory be to Him! And for
themselves sons they desire! When news is brought to one of them of the
birth of a female child, his face darkens .... Shall he retain it on
contempt or bury it in the dust? Ah! What an evil choice they decide on!

The Holy Quran, Sura XVI, Verses 57–59

Thus, just like Jesus before him, Muhammad focused on the inhumane
treatment of the most vulnerable members of society. Not surprisingly,
slaves, women, and the downtrodden were drawn to Muhammad's messages of brotherly love and unity. Indeed, some of the disenfranchised
Meccans managed to defect to Medina, where they were welcomed with
open arms. In addition, the nomadic Bedouin tribes that lived nearby began
to pledge allegiance to the new religion. Consequently, the Meccans not only
were losing slave labor, they also were losing the support of the Bedouin
clansmen. These defections posed a grave threat to the Meccan way of life.

As tensions mounted between the Muslims in Medina and the pagans in
Mecca, war became inevitable. The first war occurred in 624 C.E., and it is
known as the **Battle of Badr.** During this campaign, Muhammad's men were
outnumbered but were victorious nevertheless. Also, it was during the Battle
of Badr that Muhammad first recited verses related to war and the treatment
of prisoners. We will study Muslim ethics and their code of war shortly. For
now, know that Muhammad sought and honored all peace treaties and
returned all prisoners of war.

But if the enemy incline towards peace, do thou also incline towards peace,
and trust in Allah: for He is the One that heareth and knoweth all things. ...
It is not fitting for an Apostle that he should have prisoners of war
until he hath thoroughly subdued the land.

The Holy Quran, Sura VIII, Verses 61, 67

If one amongst the Pagans ask thee for asylum, grant it to him, so that
he may hear the Word of Allah; and then escort him to where he can be
secure. That is because they are men without knowledge.

The Holy Quran, Sura IX, Verses 4–6

To commemorate the victory at the Battle of Badr, Muhammad patterned
a holiday after the Jewish Passover and declared the fast of **Ramadan,** which
Muslims still celebrate today. However, after the battle, Muhammad learned
that one of the Jewish tribes in Medina had secretly aided the Meccans.
Muhammad asked the Jews to reaffirm their allegiance to the *ummah* but

they refused. With a heavy heart, Muhammad expelled the traitorous Jewish tribe from Medina.

The next time the Muslims and the Meccans went to war, Muhammad was not so lucky. In 625 C.E., the Meccans marched toward Medina seeking revenge for their previous losses. Once again, Muhammad faced incredible odds, but this time he lost at the **Battle of Uhud.** Primarily, the Meccans won the war because two of the Medina tribes, including one of the remaining Jewish tribes, refused to fight. As a result, Muhammad's forces were hopelessly depleted before the battle began. Afterward, Muhammad expelled the Jewish tribe from Medina for refusing to defend the *ummah.* This left just one Jewish tribe remaining in Medina.

In 627 C.E., the Meccans and Muslims faced off again. This time, the Meccans attacked Medina with the intent of taking the city. However, Muhammad knew the pagans would return so he had a deep trench dug around Medina to fortify it. As a result, the **Battle of the Trench** resulted in a stalemate and the Meccans returned home without a victory. They had, however, infiltrated the third Jewish tribe in Medina, which secretly aligned with the pagans. Upon learning of the last Jewish tribe's treachery, Muhammad failed to contain his anger. He ordered all the Jewish men killed and he expelled all the Jewish women and children from the *ummah.*

While critics of Muhammad like to point to this period of Muslim history as evidence that Muhammad was not a man of God, let us pause for a moment to recall the many "holy wars" started at the behest of Jewish Prophets, as amply recorded in the *Old Testament.* Therefore, the Battle of the Trench, although an example of brutality, may be fairly understood for four reasons. First, Muhammad already had been betrayed twice by the Jews in Medina. In the previous cases, he demonstrated remarkable restraint and mercy by releasing the Jews, particularly considering the brutality of that era. Thus, if you stop to consider the barbaric nature of tribal warfare and the heinous code of ethics that reigned at the time, Muhammad's decision to "turn the other cheek" and spare the first two Jewish tribes was an unprecedented act of compassion and forgiveness.

Second, each time he was betrayed, Muhammad gave the remaining Jewish residents in Medina the benefit of the doubt. He continued to operate under the assumption that he could trust those Jews who chose to remain part of the *ummah.* Moreover, the Jews in Medina could leave at any time. Instead, they chose to betray Muhammad and the *ummah*, which would be considered criminal treason even by today's standards.

Third, Muhammad had learned the hard way that if he released traitors of the *ummah*, he might meet them again on the battlefield. He had no desire to release the third tribe of Jews just to fight them later, and it was evident that the Muslims and the Meccans would continue fighting until one group was dominant. From a strategic standpoint, therefore, it would have been foolish for Muhammad to release yet another tribe of defectors who might hurt his people in the future.

Fourth, despite this early disaster between the Jews and Muslims, the Jews would soon enjoy peace and prosperity in Muslim lands. As illustrated in the Appendix, the Muslim spirit of religious tolerance soon would produce a safe haven for the Jews, who were free to practice their religion wherever the Muslims reigned. Ironically, it was the Christians who became the primary Jewish antagonists. For the next thousand years, the Catholic popes and the Christian nations demoralized, expelled, and slaughtered millions of Jews and other "heretics." *Thus, despite the current tensions between the Muslims and Jews, it would be wise for us to remember that historically, it is the Muslims who have been the Jews' greatest defenders and protectors.*

Finally in 630 C.E., Muhammad "conquered" the Meccan nobility and consolidated all the Arab tribes. Impressively, he accomplished this goal not by fighting another war, but by shaving his head, donning the white robe of a holy man, and peacefully approaching the sacred Ka'ba. Apparently, after the Battle of the Trench and his failure to win the hearts of the Jews in Medina, Muhammad's vision of his mission took another turn. He simply asked the Meccans if he could visit the Ka'ba during the holy time known as the **Hajj** in order to pray to Allah.

At first, the Meccans refused him access to the city and prepared for battle, even though all Arabs subscribed to the sacred custom that fighting is forbidden near the Ka'ba, especially during the *Hajj*. Yet, when the Meccans saw Muhammad approaching the city without arms and prepared for worship, the pagan adversaries finally accepted Muhammad's message of Truth: *There is only one God and we are all connected.* Thus, Muhammad returned to Mecca, the place of his birth, as a hero and a great Prophet. The following year the Ka'ba was rededicated to Allah alone, the 360 statues of other deities were removed, and Mecca became the religious capital for the Islamic religion for all time.

Muhammad died two years later in 632 C.E., leaving numerous wives but having fathered no male heir. However, he left behind an astonishing legacy of unity for the Arab people, which they have never relinquished. The Appendix illustrates the great breadth of the Muslim Empire. By 750 C.E., the Muslim Empire was the largest nation on the face of the Earth, well exceeding the expanse of the Roman Empire. The Muslims controlled the entire Middle East and parts of eastern Asia. The empire also included the northern African continent and all of Spain. Indeed, scholars view the Muslim Empire as the greatest civilization in mankind's history.

In total, Muhammad received messages from Allah for twenty-three years. While *The Holy Bible* primarily recites historical events, there is little history in *The Holy Quran*. Instead, the *Quran* contains explicit moral instructions from Allah, who often speaks in the first person. Additionally, the *suras* in the *Quran* were written contemporaneously by Muhammad's followers as he spoke, whereas major sections of the *Bible* were written hundreds and even thousands of years after the events described therein and rarely by the Prophets themselves. Thus, Muslims believe that the *Quran* contains God's clearest instructions, since Muhammad's quotes came directly from Allah, were recorded immediately, and have never been altered by man. In fact, the *suras* of the *Quran* were compiled into one text by 650 C.E., a mere eighteen years after Muhammad's death. Therefore, the *Quran* may very well be the most accurate of the holy texts available to mankind.

> *This Quran is not such as can be produced by other than Allah; On the contrary it is a confirmation of revelations that went before it, and a fuller explanation of the Book – wherein there is no doubt – from the Lord of the Worlds.*

> *The Holy Quran*, Sura X, Verse 37

One of the first messages relayed to Muhammad is the following central tenet of Islam: *There is only one Allah, and Allah is the same God worshiped by the Jews and the Christians.* However, unlike Jews and Christians, Muslims believe that Allah resembles nothing in creation that we can understand or envision. Consequently, no idols or other depictions of God in human form are permitted, and none will be found in mosques. The Islamic prohibition against idiolatry is based on the Second Commandment God gave to Moses.

> *You shall not make for yourself an idol, or any likeness of what is in heaven above or on the earth beneath or in the water under the earth.*

> *Exodus*, Chapter 20:4

Muhammad also correctly revealed that Allah is neither male nor female.
Although the male pronoun is used in *The Holy Quran* whenever God is written about in the third person, the plural pronoun is used whenever God speaks.

> What is with you must vanish; what is with Allah will endure. And **We** will certainly bestow, on those who patiently persevere, their reward according to the best of their actions.
>
> Whoever works righteousness, man or woman, and has Faith, verily, to him **We** give a new Life, a life that is good and pure, and **We** will bestow on such their reward according to the best of their actions. [Emphasis added]
>
> *The Holy Quran*, Sura XVI, Verse 97

Thus, Islam suggests that God, although one entity, is comprised of both male and female energies. However, it probably is more accurate to say that Muslims view God as genderless. Recall that the Jews also used the plural pronoun in parts of the *Old Testament* to describe God, which later helped the Jewish Kabbalists comprehend God's masculine and feminine components. In Truth, though, it is because the Jews lived safely and comfortably within the Muslim Empire, particularly the Jews in Spain, that this more mystical branch of Judaism was allowed to blossom. Indeed, Moses of Leon, the famous Jewish rabbi and reputed author of the Kabbalah holy text, the *Zohar*, lived in Muslim Spain in the late 1200s, where he was exposed to and influenced by the more progressive Muslim theology regarding the nature of God.

Contrary to the misinformation propagated in the West, Muhammad revered not only the Jewish and Christian holy books, he also revered their Prophets. The Holy Quran makes clear that all the Jewish and Christian Prophets were divinely inspired messengers from God.

> That was the reasoning about Us, which We gave to Abraham to use against his people: We raise whom We will, degree after degree: For thy Lord is full of wisdom and knowledge.
>
> We gave him Isaac and Jacob: all three We guided: And before him We guided Noah, and among his progeny, David, Solomon, Job, Joseph, Moses, and Aaron: Thus do We reward those who do good. And Zechariah and John, and Jesus and Elijah: All in the ranks of the Righteous: And Ishmael and Elisha, and Jonah and Lot:
>
> And to all We gave favor above the nations: To them and to their fathers, and progeny and brethren: We chose them, and We guided them to a straight Way.

> *These were the men to whom We gave the Book, and Authority,*
> *and Prophethood: If these their descendants reject them, Behold! We*
> *shall entrust their charge to a new People who reject them not.*

> *The Holy Quran,* Sura VI, Verses 83–89

Muhammad also revered Mary, the mother of Jesus, and believed in the miracle of the virgin birth.

> *And remember her [Mary] who guarded her chastity; We breathed into*
> *her of Our Spirit, and We made her and her son a Sign for all peoples.*

> *The Holy Quran,* Sura XXI, Verse 91

In fact, Muhammad taught that Jesus' birth was a miraculous act, in the same league as God's creation of Adam, the first man. Therefore, Jesus is very dear to Muslims, and he is considered the only human other than Adam whom God specially created.

> *Behold! Thy Lord said to the angels: "I am about to create man, from*
> *sounding clay from mud moulded into shape; When I have fashioned*
> *him in due proportion and breathed into him My Spirit, fall ye down in*
> *obeisance unto him."*

> *The Holy Quran,* Sura XV, Verse 28

However, Muslims do not accept the Christian deification of Jesus, nor the view that Jesus was literally the "son" of God, nor that Jesus was a partially human manifestation of God. Muhammad found these notions blasphemous, since God would never "beget" a human child. Muhammad also pointed out that the worship of Jesus as a god violates the proscription contained in the Jewish Second Commandment, that mankind should not worship anything other than God. Consequently, Muhammad denounced the Christian authorities who wielded so much power over the masses and who had convinced their laity that Jesus was a god.

> *They take their priests and their authorities to be their lords in derogation of*
> *Allah; And they take as their Lord, Christ, the son of Mary; Yet they were*
> *commanded to worship but one God: There is no god but He. Praise and*
> *glory to Him: Far is He from having the partners they associate with Him.*

> *The Holy Quran,* Sura IX, Verse 31

Muhammad also staunchly rejected the Roman Catholic Holy Trinity (i.e., God the Father, God the Son, and God the Holy Spirit). Muhammad taught that this tri-deity belief system was: (i) sheer paganism; (ii) created by men after Jesus died and never espoused by Jesus himself; and (iii) a clear violation of the Second Commandment given to Moses, that there is only one God. There are at least a dozen passages in *The Holy Quran* which renounce the Christian deification of Jesus. The following *sura* is one such example.

> They do blaspheme who say: "God is one of three in a Trinity." For there is no god except one Allah. ...
>
> Christ the son of Mary was no more than an apostle; many were the apostles that passed away before him. His mother was a woman of Truth. They had both to eat their daily food. See how Allah doth make his Signs clear to them; Yet see in what ways they are deluded away from the Truth!
>
> *The Holy Quran*, Sura V, Verses 76–78

In sum, Islam logically asserts that turning Jesus into a god contradicts the basic tenet espoused by most modern religions – that God is a singular entity. Muslims have rationally deduced that if Jesus is deemed a god or even another manifestation of God, then there would be two gods and we would be right back to a pagan belief system. In keeping with this core tenet, Muhammad discouraged his followers from trying to deify him. Recall that Buddha also had to chastise members of his laity who wanted to deify him, just as Jesus corrected his disciples whenever they compared him to God.

Muhammad also taught that all Semitic people, including both the Arabs and the Jews, are brothers because they are descendant from Abraham, and that it was time for the three religions of Abraham to unify. Recall that Abraham had two sons: Isaac, who then had a son named Jacob (later renamed Israel by God), who fathered the Jewish nation; and Ishmael, who traveled to Arabia and fathered the Muslim nation. In addition, the Muslims believe that Abraham and Ishmael built the Ka'ba, the holy structure located in Mecca, Saudi Arabia. During his life, Muhammad made it clear that he admired the Jewish and Christian religions. He felt, however, that it was time for the Jews, the Christians, and the Muslims to join together due to their common heritage and their shared belief in one God. Consequently, it was frustrating to Muhammad that the religions never totally merged.

> The Jews say: "The Christians have naught to stand upon"; And the Christians say; "The Jews have naught to stand upon." Yet they profess to study the same Book. Like unto their word is what those say who know not; But Allah will judge between them in their quarrel on the Day of Judgment.
>
> *The Holy Quran*, Sura II, Verse 113

Muhammad also showed extreme deference to Jerusalem and viewed it as a holy city for all three of the religions which stemmed from Abraham. One night, Muhammad had a vision which took him to Jerusalem. In the vision, he went to heaven and spoke with Allah, who instructed him that the devout should pray fifty times each day. Moses then interceded, so God reduced the number to five times a day, which is how often Muslims are supposed to pray.

After the Muslims captured Jerusalem, they built two important structures which still stand today. In 691 C.E., they built the **Dome of the Rock,** which is a shrine commemorating Muhammad's trip to heaven, and in 720 C.E., they built the **Al Aqsa Mosque.** Both of these structures were built on top of the Jewish Temple mount and together, they are the third most holy Muslim site in the world, second only to the Ka'ba in Mecca and the holy mosque in Medina. However, because the mosque and the Dome of the Rock are located right beside the holiest place on Earth to the Jews, namely the Wailing Wall, horrendous religious tensions currently exist in Jerusalem between the Muslims and Jews.

Additionally, Muhammad taught that mankind is innately good. Although Jesus strove to spread this Truth, it was Muhammad who asserted the principle clearly enough that the message finally was recorded. Muhammad disagreed with the orthodox Jewish and Christian positions regarding the sinful nature of mankind. Instead, Muhammad stated that because Allah is perfect, mankind's design must reflect that perfection. Thus, Muhammad taught that Allah gave mankind free will as a gift, not as a set-up for failure. He also taught that Adam and Eve chose to disobey God at *their* peril, not ours. As a result, Muslims do not subscribe to the self-denigrating psychology that Adam and Eve's mythical indiscretion tainted all of mankind with original sin.

In this way, Muhammad preached the Truth of self-responsibility. He proclaimed that we each have the ability and the duty to choose good over evil, and he taught that we should use our inner moral compass (*fitrah*), to pursue goodness and Truth in order to please Allah. In essence, Muhammad was describing the Eastern philosophy of *karma*, since he believed that choosing evil is the "cause" which produces the "effect" of sin.

> *And if anyone earns a sin, he earns it against his own soul: for Allah is full of knowledge and wisdom.*
>
> The Holy Quran, Sura IV, Verse 111

Specifically, Muhammad taught that Allah maintains a "Book of Deeds" in which is recorded both our good deeds and our sins. Muhammad taught that God will review everyone's record on Judgment Day, which he described in vivid terms which mirror the Judeo-Christian prophecies. Moreover, Muhammad taught the inclusive doctrine that, regardless of our professed religion, all of us are worthy of joining God in heaven provided that our good deeds outweigh our bad ones.

> *This Our Record speaks about you with Truth: For We were wont to put on record all that ye did.*
> *Then, as to those who believed and did righteous deeds, their Lord will admit them to His mercy: That will be the achievement for all to see.*
> *But as to those who rejected Allah, to them will be said: "Were not Our Signs rehearsed to you? But ye were arrogant and were a people given to sin!"*

The Holy Quran, Sura XLV, Verses 29–31

Again, it is interesting to note the similarities between the Islamic belief system, that each soul has a record of good and bad deeds, and the Hindu and Buddhist belief system, that each soul has a *karmic* record that is acquired through many lifetimes (*akasha*). Recall that Hindus and Buddhists believe that our *akasha* determines how and in what form our soul will reincarnate. Although Muhammad did not subscribe to the multiple life theory of transmigration, he clearly felt that the soul acquires a *karmic* record during the current life that will be judged by God at death.

Muhammad also taught that God is predisposed to forgive sin. Because mankind is viewed as inherently good, in contrast to Judeo-Christian theology, Muslims believe that we are prone to goodness. Nevertheless, Muslims believe that if a person chooses to sin, he can atone for the sinful behavior (*tawba*). A person achieves *tawba* by repenting, making restitution, and resolving never to repeat the mistake. Even though each soul is responsible for making the right choices and will be held strictly accountable on Judgment Day, Allah will take into account the extent of our shame and our attempts to eradicate our flaws and correct bad behavior. In sum, Muslims view Allah as extremely benevolent and forgiving.

> *If any one does evil or wrongs his own soul but afterwards seeks Allah's forgiveness, he will find Allah Oft-forgiving, most Merciful.*

The Holy Quran, Sura IV, Verse 110

Additionally, Muhammad preached that mankind is worthy of joining Allah in heaven. Thus, Muhammad disagreed with the Jewish view of the afterlife, that mankind will experience a mere bodily resurrection on Earth. He also would have disagreed with Buddha and rejected the sad notion that the emptiness of *nirvana* is the ultimate spiritual state that mankind can achieve. And he certainly disagreed with the Christian view, that Jesus was a savior god who opened the gates of heaven by dying for our sins.

Instead, Muhammad taught that each of us has the innate ability to earn our own salvation. In addition, he taught that heaven is a definite and sublime destination which Allah will make available to worthy souls after everyone passes through the rigors of Judgment Day. Therefore, Muslims do not believe that anyone has the power to intercede on our behalf on Judgment Day, and they have accepted the Truth that their own record of deeds will save or condemn them.

> And Allah will judge with justice and Truth: But those whom men invoke besides Him, will not be in a position to judge at all. Verily, it is Allah alone who sees and hears all things.

> *The Holy Quran*, Sura XL, Verse 20

However, Muslims believe that the Prophets have played a great role in guiding mankind toward ultimate union with Allah. Muslims also believe that *The Holy Quran* sets forth the path for attaining salvation. Specifically, the *Quran* announces mankind's affirmative obligation to provide charity to the poor and prescribes the correct form of prayer, the two primary means for reaching heaven, according to Muhammad. Thus, just like Moses, Buddha, and Jesus before him, Muhammad taught that it is our actions on the Earth plane which will determine whether we attain salvation in the Ethereal plane. Thus, heaven is by no means an automatic reward in Islam.

> Leave alone those who take their religion to be mere play and amusement, and are deceived by the life of this world. But proclaim to them this Truth: that every soul delivers itself to ruin by its own acts: It will find for itself no protector or intercessor except Allah.

> *The Holy Quran*, Sura VI, Verse 70

In sum, Muhammad taught that each soul reaches heaven based on its own merit, and that the Prophets are mere guides sent to instruct us but with no power to save us.

Consequently, Muhammad condemned the Christian doctrine that anyone who has faith in Jesus as a god is entitled to everlasting life. Indeed, if Muhammad were alive today, he would cringe at the evangelical extension of this dogma, that anyone who accepts Jesus as his personal savior is *guaran-*

teed a place in heaven. Muhammad correctly explains in *The Holy Quran* that Jesus never claimed to have any such power and that Jesus never asked to be worshiped.

> *And behold! Allah will say: "O Jesus the son of Mary! Didst thou say unto men, 'Worship me and my mother as gods in derogation of God?'"*
>
> *He [Jesus] will say: "Glory to Thee! Never could I say what I had no right to say. ... Never said I to them aught except what Thou didst command me to say, to wit, 'Worship Allah, my Lord and your Lord ....' If Thou dost punish them, they are Thy servants: If Thou dost forgive them, Thou art the Exalted in power, the Wise."*
>
> *Allah will say: "This is a day on which the truthful will profit from their truth: theirs are Gardens, with rivers flowing beneath – their eternal home: Allah well-pleased with them, and they with Allah: That is the great Salvation."*
>
> The Holy Quran, Sura V, Verses 119–122

Thus, Muhammad agreed with the Jews that God alone has the power to decide our fate, but he agreed with the Christians that God may grant us a heavenly salvation if we are worthy. Additionally, Muhammad agreed with the Christians that the world would one day end. In fact, *The Holy Quran* vividly describes Judgment Day, the punishment that will meet evildoers, and the rewards that await the righteous. The *Quran* also depicts Judgment Day as a joyous time for the worthy souls who will enter heaven naked and in new bodies. Finally, Muhammad taught that each of us will await final judgment behind our respective Prophet (i.e., Jews with Moses; Christians with Jesus; and Muslims lined up behind Muhammad).

> *One day We shall remove the mountains, and thou wilt see the earth as a level stretch, and We shall gather them all together, nor shall we leave out any one of them.*
>
> *And they will be marshaled before thy Lord in ranks .... And the Book of Deeds will be placed before you; And thou wilt see the sinful in great terror because of what is recorded therein; They will say, "Ah! Woe to us! What a book is this! It leaves out nothing small or great, but takes account thereof!" They will find all that they did, placed before them: And not one will thy Lord treat with injustice.*
>
> The Holy Quran, Sura XVIII, Verses 47–49

Muhammad also recited strict religious laws which were intended to help the Arabs live in accordance with the will of Allah. *Shariah* is the Arabic word that means the path of correct or straight behavior. It is a code of conduct that evolved over time, in many ways similar to the Jewish *Mishna*, which contains learned rabbis' interpretations of the laws of Moses. Formally, *Shariah* is based on four authorities: (i) *The Holy Quran*; (ii) the words of the Prophet (**Hadith**); (iii) the deeds of the Prophet (**Sunnah**); and (iv) the exercise of sound judgment (*ijtihad*) by religious scholars (*ulama*), who are expected to interpret the first three sources in new situations to arrive at a consensus (*ijma*) and sound extensions of the law (*qiyas*).

The Holy Quran is the paramount source of Islamic law and it contains rules which govern individual obligations and laws designed to maintain social order. The religious rules which encourage personal responsibility and spiritual growth are called the **Five Pillars of Islam**:

1. *Shahadah* – Declaring allegiance to Allah;
2. *Salat* – Daily prayer;
3. *Zakat* – Annual charity;
4. *Saum* – Month-long fasting for Ramadan; and
5. *Hajj* – Pilgrimage to Mecca.

As part of their daily prayer ritual (*salat*), Muslims declare that Allah is the only God (*shahadah*). In addition, Muslims repeat their prayers five times a day in accordance with Allah's instructions to Muhammad during his night journey to Jerusalem, and they face the Ka'ba in Mecca when praying. Charity for the poor (*zakat*) is mandatary and contributions are not used to maintain religious institutions or church leaders, which, arguably, is the primary purpose of tithing in other religions. For the month of Ramadan, Muslims fast from dawn to dusk (*saum*), in order to learn self-discipline and to sensitize themselves to the plight of the poor. Lastly, Muslims are encouraged to make the annual pilgrimage to the Ka'ba (*Hajj*), at least once in their lifetime. Everyone who makes the pilgrimage wears white robes to eliminate outward signs of social class, to signify unity, and to show absolute love for Allah.

The Islamic laws pertaining to social behavior can be broken down into three basic categories as follows: (i) economic laws; (ii) laws regulating relationships with other cultures and religions; and (iii) laws regulating relationships between men and women, all of which are expected to be followed without fail. The first group of laws on economics relate to charity and business practices, such as the lending of money and inheritance laws. As already discussed, Muslim charity goes directly to the poor, which results in an atmosphere of sharing through the partial redistribution of wealth. In other words,

Muslims habitually practice the Golden Rule. With regard to business, *Shariah* forbids the charging of interest on loans. The original intent of this law was to stop enslavement when debtors defaulted on loans. Today, loans are made but the lender and borrower are deemed partners in the enterprise. In addition, *The Holy Quran* outlaws primogeniture, the practice of the eldest male inheriting all the family wealth. As a result, under Islamic law all relatives share in an inheritance, including women. This law was revolutionary for its time and for centuries produced the most progressive and pro-feminist society in the world.

Second, Islamic law dictates how Muslims should treat others outside of their religion. One of their core beliefs is that Abraham married an Egyptian woman who fathered Ishmael, the patriarch of their nation. Consequently, Muhammad took pride in both his Arab and Hebrew heritage which, coupled with his fair treatment of Jews and Christians, tempered race relations. Additionally, *The Holy Quran* instructs Muslims never to force religious conversion on others, since every soul must arrive at spiritual Truth on its own in accordance with the will of Allah.

> *Let there be no compulsion in religion: Truth stands out clear from error: whoever rejects evil and believes in Allah hath grasped the most trustworthy hand-hold, that never breaks. [Emphasis added]*
>
> The Holy Quran, Sura II, Verse 256

Consequently, when the Muslim Empire conquered a new territory, conversion to Islam was not mandatory. In fact, the standard practice of Muslim rulers was to show respect toward acquired nations and leave the local people in peace, provided that they agree to cease hostilities and make the required tithing to the poor (*jizya*). As a result, the existing religious practices and holy sites of other cultures were almost always left intact and unharmed under Islamic rule.

> *O ye who believe! Truly the Pagans are unclean; So let them not, after this year of theirs, approach the Sacred Mosque [Ka'ba].... Fight those who believe not in Allah nor the Last Day, nor hold that forbidden which hath been forbidden by Allah and his Apostle, nor acknowledged the Religion of Truth of the people of the Book;* **Until they pay the jizya with willing submission, and feel themselves subdued.** *[Emphasis added]*
>
> The Holy Quran, Sura IX, Verses 28, 29

Thus, history shows that Muslims have been quite accepting of other religions. Indeed, historians credit the Muslim Empire as being the most tolerant of all societies that have risen to worldwide domination. As we shall see in Chapter Four when we study the Christian Crusades and the Catholic Inquisition, it was the Christian rulers who consistently instituted inhumane policies and practices against people of other faiths and who demanded religious conversion from conquered nations. Unfortunately, given the sordid state of world politics today and the terrifying tactics employed by some Islamic fundamentalists, many people now suffer from deep misconceptions about Muhammad and the original tenets of Islam. Consequently, I am eager to debunk some of the myths surrounding this religion. At this point, it already should be evident to the reader that Muhammad was a moral leader. His greatest accomplishments resulted from spiritual debate and passive revolts, as has been the case with all holy men. Thus, we cannot blame Muhammad for the evil committed by Islamic terrorists any more than we can blame Jesus for the sinful acts perpetrated by corrupt leaders of the Catholic Church.

Next, it would behoove Westerners to learn the true definition of the Arabic word *jihad*. The word does *not* mean "holy war." It means to struggle or to strive for some altruistic end and to put forth effort in accordance with the will of Allah. Therefore, a person can initiate *jihad* against any unjust situation. For example, contributing more to the underprivileged than is required by *jizya* is a type of *jihad*, since it is a moral act undertaken to eradicate an evil. Similarly, Jesus promoted *jihad* when he instructed his disciples to leave their families and sacrifice their personal comfort and safety to travel to distant lands and spread the word of God.

With regard to actual war, *The Holy Quran* sets forth clear instructions. Admittedly, the *Quran* refers to war as a type of *jihad*, but only if properly sanctioned and morally justified. However, the *Quran* clearly states, in accordance with the Jewish Sixth Commandment, that murder is a sin. Thus, Islamic law unequivocally bans criminal murder.

> *Nor take a life – which Allah has made sacred – except for just cause. And if anyone is slain wrongfully, We have given his heir authority to demand qisas or to forgive: but let him not exceed the bounds in the matter of taking life; for he is helped by the Law.*

> *The Holy Quran*, Sura XVII, Verse 33

The Arabic term *qisas* is defined as "equal retaliation." *Qisas* can be compared to the "eye for an eye" justice prescribed by the Jewish *Old Testament*. Frankly, this system of justice is no more barbaric than the death penalty, which still is meted out as the ultimate punishment for murder in the United States. The important point is that Muhammad limited the penalty for murder to *one* execution in order to stop the Arab tradition of large scale clan retaliation. However, Muhammad stressed that forgiveness is the better path.

> *O ye who believe! The law of equality is prescribed to you in cases of murder: The free for the free, the slave for the slave, the woman for the woman. But if any remission is made by the brother of the slain, then grant any reasonable demand, and compensate him with handsome gratitude. This is a concession and a Mercy from your Lord. After this whoever exceeds the limits shall be in grave penalty.*
>
> The Holy Quran, Sura II, Verse 178

Thus, under Islamic law the family of the deceased may demand equal justice for a murder or accept an alternate remedy, although the family is encouraged to exercise forgiveness and seek some type of compensation. Just imagine having the right to choose a remedy if your loved one were murdered. Moreover, imagine how your decision would impact your relationship with God. How long would you search your conscience and ask God for help before choosing a punishment? Truly, Muhammad had the wisdom of Solomon.

While I respect Islamic law on murder, I must profess a certain amount of discomfort with Muhammad's rules of war. Although *The Holy Quran* never says "kill the Unbelievers" or "wage holy war against the Infidels," it does contain violent passages that can be interpreted as promoting religious warfare. Here is one of the more disturbing *suras*.

> *Let those fight in the cause of Allah who sell the life of this world for the Hereafter. To him who fighteth in the cause of Allah – whether he is slain or gets victory – soon shall We give him a reward of great value.*
> *Those who believe fight in the cause of Allah, and those who reject Faith fight in the cause of evil: So fight ye against the friends of Satan: feeble indeed is the cunning of Satan.*
>
> The Holy Quran, Sura IV, Verses 74, 76

Despite such evocative language, *The Holy Quran* carefully limits the circumstances under which war is justified. Additionally, the *Quran* forbids the killing of women, children, and the elderly. It also prohibits the killing of herd animals and the destruction of crops and trees. Compared to the *Old Testament*, in which God directs the Jews to slay the women and children of their enemies (or take them as slaves), Muhammad's rules on war are quite humane. Thus, a fair reading of the *Quran* makes clear that Muhammad viewed war as an extreme measure to be undertaken only under rare circumstances. For instance, the *Quran* states that war is justified to protect the weak or to help other Muslims who ask for assistance against oppressive overlords.

> *And why should ye not fight in the cause of Allah and of those who, being weak, are ill-treated and oppressed? – Men, women, and children whose cry is: "Our Lord! Rescue us from this town, whose people are oppressors; and raise for us from thee one who will protect; And raise for us from Thee one who will help!"*
>
> *The Holy Quran*, Sura IV, Verse 75

In addition, war is deemed appropriate as a means of self-defense. Therefore, Muslims may fight to defend their way of life or whenever they are attacked first. However, Muhammad instructed his people to cease hostilities as soon as the enemy wants a truce.

> *Fight in the cause of Allah against those who fight you, but do not transgress limits; For Allah loveth not transgressors. And fight them on until there is no more tumult or oppression, and there prevail justice and faith in Allah; But if they cease, let there be no hostility except to those who practice oppression.*
>
> *The Holy Quran*, Sura II, Verses 190–191

The primary reason *The Holy Quran* deals with war is because of the ongoing conflict between the pagan chieftains in Mecca and Muhammad's followers in Medina. Moreover, the references to war in the *Quran* pale in comparison to the violent initiatives supposedly ordered by God in *The Holy Bible*. In fact, a many of the stories in the *Old Testament* relate to the horrors of war, with God inciting and approving many of the conquests. Therefore, it is neither rational nor accurate for Christians to view the *Quran* as a book condoning war or encouraging bloodshed. Unfortunately, the same cannot be said of the *Bible*, in which God repeatedly sanctions violence.

To summarize, it seems evident to me, at a minimum, that *The Holy Quran* is no more obsessed with war than is *The Holy Bible*. Indeed, the *Bible* promotes war on more occasions and for a broader set of reasons than does the *Quran*. While I personally prefer Jesus' tactics of passive resistance to thwart evil, I am grateful that my own country's laws allow me to use force if my own life is threatened. Moreover, the citizens of the United States would not hesitate to defend themselves if attacked or declare war on an invader who tried to "reform" our way of life. I conclude, therefore, that Islam is not an inherently violent religion.

The third grouping of Islamic laws, which concern marriage and the treatment of women, were initially shocking to the Arab men, who were accustomed to treating women like chattel who could be bought through marriage. In fact, before Muhammad's time, Arab women had no rights. Moreover, the birth of a girl was viewed as a tragedy and female infants were routinely killed. Not only did Muhammad ban female infanticide, he also declared that women should have affirmative legal rights. *Thus, despite the misogynist culture of his time, Muhammad elevated the status of Muslim women far beyond the treatment of women in any other contemporary culture.*

> *O mankind! We created you from a single pair of a male and a female, and made you into nations and tribes, that ye may know each other, not that ye may despise each other.*
>
> The Holy Quran, Sura XLIX, Verse 13

In addition, Islamic law protects women by firmly establishing the sanctity of marriage. Sex is only permitted between a husband and wife, which effectively outlaws prostitution and adultery. Under Islamic law, the punishment for adultery and fornication is flogging. Moreover, flogging is the punishment if a man makes a false charge against a woman and cannot back up the charge with at least four witnesses.

> *And those who launch a charge against a chaste woman, and produce not four witnesses to support their allegations – flog them with eighty stripes; and reject their evidence ever after: for such men are wicked transgressors.*
>
> The Holy Quran, Sura XXIV, Verse 4

Muhammad also banned arranged marriages by giving women the right to reject a suitor. As a result, Islamic law put an end to women being sold like animals. Interestingly enough, the concept of dowry was retained, but *Shariah* requires that the woman's dowry be kept separate in the event of divorce, in which case the woman gets her money back. Furthermore, Muslim women have the right to seek a divorce, just like men, and obtain custody of children. However, the divorce procedure is quite cumbersome, it is geared toward promoting a reconciliation, and fathers are favored when deciding custody issues involving older children. For these and other cultural reasons, divorce in Islamic countries is very rare.

If you fear a breach between them twain, appoint two arbitrators, one from his family, and the other from hers; If they wish for peace, Allah will cause their reconciliation: For Allah hath full knowledge and is acquainted with all things.

The Holy Quran, Sura IV, Verse 35

In addition, *Shariah* requires that a woman receive one-half the inheritance of her brothers, which is very generous considering that Muslim men are financially responsible for their families. Islamic law also mandates that financial support be paid to a woman from her husband's family in the case of widowhood, and from the husband in the event of divorce.

Those of you who die and leave widows should bequeath for their widows a year's maintenance and residence.
For a divorced woman maintenance should be provided on a reasonable scale. This is a duty of the righteous.

The Holy Quran, Sura II, Verses 240, 241

In sum, Muhammad granted women rights that were practically inconceivable by the standards of his day. Even so, one of these laws deserves special attention, since it blatantly offends most 21st Century women. Under Islamic law, men are allowed to have up to four wives. Realize, however, that prior to the new law, men could have as many wives (and concubines) as they wanted. Therefore, Muhammad's limitation on marriage was a vast improvement over the Arabian mores of the 7th Century. Moreover, a man may not take more than one wife unless he can provide each of them with separate quarters (i.e., bedrooms), and treat them all fairly. Today, it is common for Muslim couples to enter into marriage contracts that preclude polygamy.

Marry women of your choice, two, or three, or four; But if ye fear that ye shall not be able to deal justly with them, then only one .... That will be more suitable, to prevent you from doing injustice.

The Holy Quran, Sura IV, Verse 3

It also is interesting to note that Muhammad exempted himself from the new law and took a total of ten wives during his lifetime. Muslims are quick to point out, though, that Muhammad did not marry another woman until his first wife, Khadija, died. Additionally, he did not marry his later wives for ignominious reasons. Rather, he married to forge alliances with other tribal chiefs, as was the custom of that era. For example, Muhammad married a Jewish girl named **Safiyah** from one of the

Jewish tribes he expelled from Medina, to soften old wounds and reignite Jewish alliances. Likewise, Muhammad married some older women who were widowed during the wars. His dearest wife after Khadija was **Aisha**, the daughter of his most trusted ally, Abu Bakr, and it is reported that Muhammad died in Aisha's arms. Aisha would later compose much of the *Hadith*, based on her close and devoted relationship to the Prophet. Thus, it appears that in addition to his other talents, Muhammad was able to successfully manage multiple wives.

As a final note on this topic, I want to reiterate that the current ill-treatment of women by some Arab regimes and fundamentalist Muslim sects finds little support in *The Holy Quran*. Rather, the misogyny expressed today in Arab countries is the direct result of male aggression and the desire for dominance. We will explore the current mistreatment of women in Chapter Four. For now, it is important to understand that Islamic law, as originally stated and enforced, protected Muslim women and improved their lives immensely. In fact, Muhammad went further than any other Prophet in creating a gender-neutral environment in which everyone could flourish.

When Muhammad died in 632 C.E., Islam was a firmly established religion. However, just as the Christians fractured after Jesus died, the Muslims split after Muhammad's death. At first, the Muslims were able to agree on who should lead the *ummah* and the first four "rightly guided" *caliphs* were chosen with minimal dissension. Abu Bakr was appointed the first *caliph* and Muhammad's cousin and son-in-law, **Ali ibn Abi Talib**, became the fourth *caliph*. In 661 C.E., Ali was assassinated and civil war broke out. Those who wanted Ali's sons to rule became known as **Shiite Muslims**. Shiites believe that only Muhammad's descendants – specifically, the bloodline of Ali and Fatimah (Muhammad's youngest daughter by Khadija) – should rule. They also believe that Muhammad's descendants are divinely chosen leaders who possess enhanced spiritual insight. Thus, Shiites subscribe to the view that the *ummah* is best served by an *imam* (not a *caliph*), who is both related by blood to the Prophet and who has the wisdom to act as a religious leader. Today, most of the Muslims in Iraq, Iran, and Afghanistan are Shiite.

After Ali was assassinated, another group known as **Sunni Muslims** seized power. Sunnis reject the idea that Muhammad's relatives are necessarily the best leaders of the *ummah*. Instead, Sunnis believe that Islamic political leaders should be selected based on merit and that learned clerics (*ulama*) should help govern by handling questions of a religious nature. Thus, Sunni Muslims are loyal both to the *ulama* and to the *caliph*, and they feel obligated to depose any politician who proves unworthy to lead. Sunnis ruled during the heyday of the Muslim Empire and generally are more tolerant of foreigners than the Shiites. Thus, it was during the Sunni reign that Muslims, Jews, and Christians lived in relative peace. Today, most Muslims in Saudi Arabia, Egypt, Syria, Jordan, and Palestine are Sunni.

Although the Shiites and Sunnis have yet to reconcile some of their religious differences, both sects believe that a Messiah figure called the **Mahdi** (the "expected one") will appear prior to Judgment Day to unite all true believers. There also is a prophecy in the *Hadith* which states that Jesus will return as an *imam*. Most Muslims believe that the Mahdi and Jesus will arrive separately to mark the advent of End Times. Not surprisingly, the Shiites believe that the Mahdi is descendant from Muhammad and is their long-lost Twelfth Imam, Muhammad al Mahdi.

In the late 1700s C.E., a group known as **Wahhabi Muslims** branched off from the Sunnis to form a more radical sect of Islam. Wahhabis denounce all changes to the *Shariah* and reject manmade civil law. **Osama bin Laden** is a Wahhabi, and he believes that some Muslim leaders, including the King of Saudi Arabia, have become puppets of the United States and, therefore, unfit to lead. Bin Laden's terrorist group, **Al Qaeda**, opposes Muslim leaders who amass great personal wealth in contravention of the rules on charity and who fail to adhere to a fundamentalist version of Islamic law. Moreover, as we are all painfully aware, Al Qaeda targets those countries which it views as meddling in Arab politics, including any nation that supports Israel.

Lastly, let us briefly discuss the mystical sect of **Sufi Muslims**. Like the Gnostic Christian followers of Jesus, the Sufis are Muslims who believe Muhammad taught on multiple levels. While *The Holy Quran* sets forth detailed laws regarding moral conduct and the straight path, there are other portions of the *Quran* which are exceedingly esoteric and open to interpretation. For example, the *Quran* describes a three-fold process of enlightenment that one must undergo in order to comport with the will of Allah. This process requires a person to understand and master: (i) the animal self (base instincts and desires); (ii) the accusing self (higher level questioning of our soul's purpose); and (iii) the restful self (state of mind that transcends our Earth-bound focus). Sufis believe that once a soul reaches this final state of spiritual awareness, it may join with Allah.

Therefore, unlike orthodox Muslims who believe that the soul retains an individuality separate from God until and even after death, the Sufis believe that the self can be extinguished and temporarily merge with Allah prior to Judgment Day. This powerful and joyous belief system is considered blasphemous by most Muslims. Consequently, Sufis historically have been treated with suspicion by other Muslims who believe that the path to Allah is explicitly and completely set forth in *The Holy Quran*. Nevertheless, Sufis seek spiritual enlightenment prior to death which, as we have seen, is the life-long goal of all mystics. It is unfortunate that orthodox preachers continue to tell their laity that death is a prerequisite for such a divine state.

Not surprisingly, the Sufi approach to mastering the base emotions, the ego, and then the spiritual self comports seamlessly with the mystical teachings of the other religions. Specifically, it parallels the advanced spiritual methods employed by Buddha and the more profound lessons taught by Jesus in the *Gnostic Gospels*. The Sufi model for spiritual enlightenment also tracks Maslow's Hierarchy of Needs. At its foundation, the Sufi belief system encourages the development of an evolving faith based on personal experience and continuous soul growth. *Once again, it appears that the more advanced members of each religion subscribe to the spiritual process known as Saddha.*

Probably the most famous Sufi mystic is **Jalaluddin Rumi** (1207–1273), who is credited with inspiring the Order of Whirling Dervishes, famous for their Sufi dance ceremony. Rumi was a prolific writer, poet, musician, and teacher, and his body of work is considered by Persians to be divinely inspired. In fact, many accord him Prophet status based on his life-long quest to perfect his own soul and his years at a renowned *madrassah* (Muslim school), where he taught others how to achieve enlightenment. Not surprisingly, Rumi encouraged his students to pursue Truth at all cost, even if it meant defying religious orthodoxy.

> There's courage involved if you want to become Truth.
> There is a broken-open place in a lover.
> Where are those qualities of bravery and sharp compassion in this group?
> What's the use of old and frozen thought?

> *Soul of Rumi*, Translated by Coleman Barks

Lastly, it is worth noting that the early Sufis were singularly dedicated to their quest to reach Allah and lived remarkably ascetic and impoverished lives as a result. Two of the most famous early Sufis are **Hasan al Basri** and a woman named **Rabia al Adawiyya,** both of whom lived in the 700s C.E. I hesitate to call these incredible messengers "prophets," since Muslims believe that Muhammad was the last Prophet that God will ever send. Nevertheless, as with Rumi, I choose to accord these teachers Prophet status, as they relayed important Truths about God and about mankind.

Rabia, in particular, is an inspiration to me because she grasped the Truth about the masculine and feminine halves of God. She expressed through her poetry a haunting love of Allah and a compassionate yearning for Truth that epitomizes **Sophia,** the mythological Greek goddess of wisdom. Nevertheless, Rabia was often challenged by the male clerics of her time, who liked to taunt her and question the authenticity of her divine mission. In one famous exchange, an *imam* sought to humble Rabia with this acute observation:

> All the great virtues belong to men: the crown of being prophets has
> been placed on their heads, the belt of authority has been fastened round
> their waists: no woman has ever been a prophet.

To which Rabia responded:

> All that is true. But the total selfishness and pride in their own
> achievements, and words like "I am your lord and master," never came
> from women. ... All these things are the special concern of men.

Today, it is regrettable that so many Muslim countries have fallen prey to fanatical regimes that are clearly oppressive and harmful to women. Indeed, Muslim fundamentalists now terrorize their own women and children more than their avowed enemies. We must keep in mind, however, that the sorry state of some Islamic nations does not stem from Muhammad's teachings nor the sublime messages contained in *The Holy Quran.* Rather, men of power are to blame for the continued unrest in the Muslim world.

Tragically, the full breadth of God's glory is being suppressed to some degree by each one of the five primary religions. This subjugation of half of God's energy – what mystics call the **Sacred Feminine** – is not the fault of the Prophets who inspired mankind to create religions. Instead, it is the shameful legacy of those men of power whom Jesus and Muhammad labeled "hypocrites," and whom I would define as corrupt souls who use religion as a tool to acquire wealth and as a weapon to amass power. In Chapter Four, we will study the negative impact of such hypocrites on the five major religions. For now, though, let us close this chapter on a high note and cleanse our palate on some additional Truths that were conveyed by our earliest and perhaps greatest philosophers.

EARLY PHILOSOPHICAL PROPHETS

From our beginning, mankind has contemplated the nature of and our relationship to God. This inquiry has never been the exclusive province of theologians. Indeed, some of our greatest philosophers have probed and pondered
the meaning of life and the concept of a Supreme Being. Let us briefly consider
the theories proposed by the following Greek and Chinese philosophers, since,
just like the religious Prophets, these men sought and grasped spiritual Truth.

Socrates (469–399 B.C.E.) is the legendary Greek professor who taught that
open debate and constant questioning are the *only* means to knowledge and
Truth (i.e., the Socratic Method). Socrates also was responsible for shifting his
contemporaries' focus from nature and the universe to man and humanity. He
believed that knowledge is virtue and that mankind's ability to reason holds
the key to the principles of human behavior. Socrates also asserted that we
each have a soul and that the cultivation of the soul is our greatest duty in
working toward the ethical ideals of temperance, justice, courage, nobility,
and Truth. He optimistically declared, "Wherefore I say, let a man be of good
cheer about his soul."

Unfortunately, Socrates was considered a threat to Athenian society
because he was scornful of the incompetent democratic leaders of his day and
because he encouraged his students to build a more evolved and tolerant
society. In addition, Socrates rejected the pagan Greek religion and the deification of Greek rulers, which further infuriated his more powerful contemporaries. As punishment for his heretical thinking and "corruption of
youth," Socrates was condemned to death. Rather than submit to tyranny
and the suppression of Truth, Socrates committed suicide by drinking poisonous hemlock.

Plato (427–347 B.C.E.) was a student of Socrates, and he started an academy in Greece to advance his mentor's philosophy about the relationship
between knowledge and virtue. Like Socrates, Plato had faith in mankind
and he asserted that the ultimate goal of society is to "elevate the highest
principle in the soul to the contemplation of that which is best in existence."
Plato also said that a person meets this goal when he "starts on the discovery of the absolute by light of reason only, and without any assistance of
sense, and perseveres until by pure intelligence he arrives at the perception of
the absolute good." Thus, Plato agreed with Socrates that mankind has the
innate ability to perceive Truth and, thereby, perfect the soul.

In addition, Plato found universal Truth in what he called "Ideas," which he described as intangible realities that only the mind can understand. Plato postulated that in order for mankind to move toward goodness, which he defined as a state which benefits all, we must first question what type of knowledge is required for goodness. Thus, Plato believed that education was the only stimulus which moves a person toward the highest good, which he likened to God. Hence, Plato viewed knowledge as the path to understanding the greatest of all Ideas – the nature of God. Not surprisingly, Plato's description of the process required for a soul to reach God is nearly the same as the spiritual quest described by the mystics and the journey of Truth which I call *Saddha*.

Aristotle (384–322 B.C.E.) was one of Plato's students and he founded a school that taught ethics, philosophy, and science. Later, Aristotle tutored Alexander the Great, who expanded the Greek Empire to its zenith. However, unlike Socrates and Plato, Aristotle was a pragmatic man who was more vested in observation and experience than with abstract notions of how the world ought to function. Although he agreed that mankind should strive toward Truth to perfect the intellect and the soul, Aristotle feared that most of mankind might be too weak to attain true enlightenment. Thus, even though he taught his students to aim for a virtuous life and strive for goodness, Aristotle concluded that most people require moderation to stay grounded, which is a philosophy remarkably similar to the "middle path" espoused by Buddha.

> *Virtue... is a mean between two vices, that which depends on excess and that which depends on defect.... With regard to feelings of fear and confidence, courage is the mean.... With regard to pleasures and pains, the mean is temperance.... With regard to honor and dishonor, the mean is proper pride....*

> *Ethica Nicomachea*

Confucius (551–478 B.C.E.), like the Greek philosophers, was a teacher who greatly influenced his culture. Confucius believed that everyone deserves an education regardless of class (except women), and he promoted a moral code that was standard curriculum in Chinese classrooms until the Communists took control of the country in 1949 C.E. Confucius taught that human nature is innately good, that mankind possesses free will, and that our fate is not predetermined. He also viewed virtue as its own reward and believed that each person should do his best regardless of circumstances. To advance his views, Confucius proposed rules intended to harmonize various relationships, such as the relationship between a ruler and his subjects, fathers and sons, husbands and wives, and between friends. However, because he felt that the morality of the populace depends on the well-being of the state, Confucius taught that only leaders who achieve a state of love and propriety (*ren*), are worthy of governing. His basic lesson should sound very familiar: "What you do not want others to do unto you, do not do unto them."

Lao Tzu (*circa* 550 B.C.E.), by some accounts, taught Confucius and Buddha. He also is credited with writing a wisdom book entitled *Tao De Ching*, which started the philosophical movement called **Taoism** (a/k/a Daoism). Lao Tzu believed that everything stems from one source called *Tao* (the "Way"), an undefinable source of energy which eludes discovery. Although Lao Tzu did not worship *Tao* as a god, he believed that *Tao* gives rise to all matter and all life and that *Tao* consists of a dual nature called **Yin** and **Yang**. Taoism asserts that harmony is achieved when Yin energy (e.g., the Earth, unconscious mind, darkness, night, *female energy*), contrasts and unites with Yang energy (e.g., the Sun, conscious action, light, day, *male energy*). Unless both aspects are allowed to operate freely and synchronously, life cannot be in balance and *Tao* cannot be experienced. Lastly, it is interesting to note that five hundred years before Jesus arrived, Lao Tzu coined the "Way" phraseology used in the *New Testament* and the *Dead Sea Scrolls*, and he also prophetically updated the Golden Rule by instructing, "Recompense injury with kindness."

CONCLUSIONS

After studying the original and untainted lessons of our greatest Prophets, my faith in mankind is restored ... almost. Chapter Four contains a summary of my reservations. For now, though, let's recap what we have learned from the Prophets. Here is a skeletal framework for the amazing Tower of Truth which they built.

1. **One God** – All the Prophets believed that there is one God who created an abundant Universe out of love for us. Even Hindus, who worship multiple deities, agree that there is one supreme God, Brahman.

2. **God's Nature** – The early Prophets believed that God is primarily demanding, intolerant, vengeful, and judgmental. The Hindus divided these traits amongst their various gods and goddesses. The early Prophets also believed that God has racial, religious, and gender preferences. On the other hand, the later Prophets described a God that is nurturing, loving, tolerant, and forgiving. They also realized that God is fair, just, and impartial, and that God would not play favorites.

3. **Mankind's Nature** – The early Prophets believed that mankind is inherently sinful, particularly women. The later Prophets started to view mankind as innately good and preached that women are worthy of grace as well.

4. **Free Will** – All the Prophets viewed mankind as having the ability to achieve greater closeness to God, but they also recognized that mankind has free will and may elect not to pursue this goal.

5. *Karma* – All the Prophets taught that our actions (good and bad) have direct consequences on our current life, if/when we reincarnate, and in the after-life. Moreover, the Prophets all agreed that we are responsible for our behavior and that we will be held accountable for our actions.

6. **Faith** – All the Prophets asserted that faith is a necessary component to attaining spiritual enlightenment, and they all had perfected this quality.

7. **Good Works** – All the Prophets stressed that higher levels of spirituality may only be achieved by performing the following tasks: (i) reducing or eliminating our attachment to material plane desires (e.g., money, power, greed, lust, hatred); and (ii) practicing acts of kindness and generosity toward others (i.e., the Golden Rule).

8. **Divinity** – The early Prophets viewed mankind as incapable of becoming divine, either during the current life or after death, which explains why they thought man was unworthy of joining God. The later Prophets taught that we have the potential to perfect our own divinity and become worthy of a heavenly afterlife.

9. *Saddha* – The later Prophets (and all the mystics) described a spiritual process whereby they learned greater Truths about God and were able to perfect their souls. Such a journey entails the gradual building of one's own divinity through study, faith, meditation, devotion, experience, charity, love, and, most importantly, *openness to the Truth of God's mysteries*.

10. **Heaven** – The early Prophets thought that heaven was off-limits to mankind and that the best we can hope for is a bodily resurrection or a lesser heavenly abode. The later Prophets taught that we all possess a piece of God's divine nature and, therefore, that mankind is worthy of joining with God in the Ethereal plane once that blissful state of existence is duly earned.

In conclusion, it seems to me that we have all the spiritual information we need in order to live on this planet in a compassionate, healthy, and joyous manner. If I am correct, then each Prophet came to Earth with God's blessing to teach spiritual Truth. Moreover, God sent new Prophets whenever we were ready to comprehend additional Truths. Assuming that each of them accurately relayed God's messages, then each successive Prophet added to our Tower of Truth. Nevertheless, it is painfully evident that mankind has failed to achieve the level of harmony envisioned and promoted by the Prophets. This lamentable Truth begs the question:

Why are we not living in a more peaceful and purposeful world?

As far as I can see, there are three possible reasons for our continued deviant behavior. Either: (i) God did not provide us with the wisdom we need in order to live compassionately; (ii) the Prophets were lousy teachers; or (iii) we are using our free will to ignore God's plan.

Under the first scenario, those of us who view mankind as inherently divine would have to accept the pessimistic view that God made us lacking in wisdom from the outset, in which case mankind is constitutionally incapable of spiritual enlightenment. As sad as this possibility sounds, there is one upside: We then could blame God for our dismal human record.

Alternatively, perhaps mankind is intelligent and moral enough to acquire wisdom – it then would make sense that God sent numerous Prophets to teach us how to build a utopian society. But maybe the Prophets scrambled God's messages. Under this scenario, we could blame our sordid history on the Prophets by indicting them as bad teachers. After all, if the Prophets had done a good job infusing us with wisdom, wouldn't we comprehend God's plan by now and be able to embrace the loving Spiritual Paradigm of the prophesied New Age?

I suspect, however, that we are operating under the third scenerio: It is our fault that we have failed to recreate the Garden of Eden. There really is no other rational conclusion, if you have faith that God created us with love and from a perfect image, and if you trust that we know how to express love and make wise decisions. Moreover, there should be no doubt that the major Prophets fulfilled their respective missions by educating us and inspiring us to follow God's plan. Therefore, we must reject the first two possible explanations and admit that our collective apathy and frequent cruelty is not the result of a design error made by God or due to the Prophets' ineffectiveness. Rather, it is time we face the Truth:

We are choosing to ignore God's plan.

Not all of us, of course. There are many bearers of light who are attempting to usher in the next Spiritual Paradigm. Luckily, some of these enlightened souls may be found in Hindu temples, Jewish synagogues, Buddhist retreats, Christian churches, and Islamic mosques. Others are members of the Unitarian and New Age movements. And some, like me, prefer to work alone.

Unfortunately, our efforts are being stymied by those lost souls who have succumbed to the two cardinal sins: *greed and pride.* Typically, these are men of power who are obsessively attached to the Earth plane. Oftentimes, they try to mask their bad intent and selfish deeds by feigning interest in the public's welfare or by pretending to do God's work. In Truth, however, men of power seek riches and dominance. To that end, men of power affirmatively manipulate and control the masses to ensure their continued authority. Tragically, most of these dark souls are enshrined in leadership positions, either in politics or within the five primary religions, and – just like the "hypocrites" who Jesus confronted – they prevent others from finding Truth.

In the final analysis, though, it is our responsibility to choose a valid spiritual path and an authentic spiritual guide. Make no mistake, these are important decisions, as our salvation depends on what path we choose. Consequently, we should ensure that our religion meets some basic requirements. And we should insist that our spiritual counselor comprehends the fundamental Truth that God is a single entity comprised of both masculine and feminine energies. Such a mentor can readily explain to us why the collective consciousness has yet to embrace God's evolutionary plan and experience the next Spiritual Paradigm.

In my opinion, the next stage of our spiritual evolution will arrive when we allow the Sacred Feminine half of God's energy to inform us.

As we shall see in Chapter Four, each of the five primary religions has at this point strayed from God's plan, as set forth by the Prophets. It is this failure by our religious institutions to lead us toward spiritual Truth that is the primary cause of discontent and disease on Earth. Thus, our problem is *not* that we lack the wisdom to comprehend or complete God's plan. Rather, our problem is that men of power have bastardized our houses of worship and are leading us astray, particularly through the use of arcane, outdated, and fundamentalist rhetoric that misconstrues the Prophets' simple messages of love.

Yet, before we examine the current state of the five primary religions, we should first try to reach a consensus on what constitutes the appropriate goals of any good and healthy religion. Then, we'll be able to analyze whether and to what extent each of the five primary religions is doing a satisfactory job. Therefore, in the next chapter, I will attempt to define what a good religion should do for the soul by developing an objective template which we later will use to grade the five primary religions.

Lastly, I have included a *Comparative Religions Reference Table* at the end of this chapter, which summarizes the basic lessons of the major Prophets and footnotes the later manmade deviations. This table will serve as a quick reference guide throughout the remainder of the book. It also will help us determine whether mankind built a Tower of Babel or a Tower of Truth with God's messages.

COMPARATIVE RELIGIONS REFERENCE TABLE

	Hinduism	Judaism	Buddhism	Christianity	Islam
Number of Deities	multiple	one*	multiple**	four***	one
God Personification	male & female	male*	male & female	male	genderless
Nature of God	varied	judgmental	neutral	benevolent	benevolent
Nature of Man	attachment	responsible	suffering	sinful***	good
Number of Lives	reincarnation	one	reincarnation	one	one
Path to Salvation	perfect karma	good works	perfect karma	Jesus***	submission & charity
Nature of After Life	lower heavens	Earth plane	*nirvana***	heaven	heaven
Ability to join God	no	no	maybe**	yes	yes

* The *Old Testament* opens with a reference to God as a plural entity and with the statement that both Adam and Eve are made in "Our" image. The Ten Commandments also suggest that early Jews believed in multiple deities, as the Second Commandment recites that God is "jealous" and that there should be no other gods "besides" God. These inconsistencies later are resolved as the Jews accept a single God with predominantly male attributes.

** To Buddha, the multiple gods and goddesses of Hinduism were of secondary importance, since true enlightenment can only be achieved by pursuing a solitary journey of Truth. Buddha described *nirvana* as a state of enlightenment in which the soul is released from the Earth plane. However, Buddha never clarified whether, after achieving *buddhahood*, the soul joins with God in the Ethereal plane.

*** Jesus taught that there is one God. However, the Roman Catholic Church created the mythological Holy Trinity (i.e., God the Father, God the Son, and God the Holy Ghost), and an evil deity known as Satan, thereby reviving the pagan belief in multiple gods. Jesus also taught that mankind is inherently good and capable of earning salvation, but the Catholic Church expanded the Jewish concept of sin, that man is responsible for his own actions, and decreed that mankind is innately sinful. Lastly, Jesus taught that the path to salvation is faith in God *plus* good works, which means following the Ten Commandments and the Golden Rule (i.e. the Eleventh Commandment). However, many Christians believe that Jesus is a deity who will grant salvation to his worshipers, regardless of good works.

*The same religion has He established for you as that which
He enjoined on Noah, which we have sent by inspiration to thee.
And that which We enjoined on Abraham, Moses, and Jesus:
Namely, that ye should remain steadfast in Religion and make no
divisions therein ... . And they became divided only after knowledge
reached them – through selfish envy as between themselves.*

The Holy Quran, Sura XLII, Verses 13, 14

I began this book by explaining why I started researching religion in the first place: I was disenchanted with my birth religion and I wanted to see if one of the other major religions better meshed with my evolving spiritual belief system. Thus, I began a quest to find a religion that both made sense to me and inspired me. At first, I subconsciously measured each religion in a fairly undefined manner, just based on a rough idea of what a good religion should do for the soul. Eventually, though, I arrived at a concrete set of criteria which I used to evaluate the different religions I was studying. It was against this objective template that I first began to realize that *none* of the man-made organized religions passed spiritual muster.

What I propose to do in this chapter is set forth seven objective standards that any good and healthy religion should easily satisfy. The chosen criteria were not selected at random. Rather, each of the seven rules is based on explicit instructions sent by God through the Prophets to teach mankind how to achieve spiritual enlightenment.

In addition, the seven rules are based on the more stringent methodology utilized by mystics, philosophers, and scientists who bravely embark on journeys of Truth. Therefore, the following rules not only will help us clarify whether the five man-made religions are sound, they also will guide anyone who is ready to commence the *Saddha* process of soul growth. Here, then, are seven indispensable pathways to spiritual Truth.

THE SEVEN RULES OF ANY GOOD RELIGION

Rule 1 – *Philosophy*
The religion must be logical and intellectually satisfying. If the religion asks you to make a leap of faith that seems irrational or if it requires you to sublimate your brain in favor of blind obedience, then there is a problem.

Rule 2 – *Science*
The religion must comport with physical realities as we presently understand them. If the religion rejects established scientific principles or if it fails to accept the natural laws of the Universe, then there is a problem.

Rule 3 – *Morality*
The religion must have fixed standards of right and wrong. If the tenets of the religion include violence or hate or if the religion promotes or tolerates unethical behavior, then there is a problem.

Rule 4 – *Justice*
The rules of the religion must apply to all souls fairly and uniformly, as no soul is "better" than another. Also, the religion must adhere to God's laws, as revealed by the Prophets, over man-made laws. If the religion asserts that members of its group are superior or if the religion's rules conflict with God's law, then there is a problem.

Rule 5 – *Inclusiveness*
The religion must welcome everyone. If the religion or its concept of God in any way discriminates against or excludes those who hold different beliefs or views on heaven, then there is a problem.

Rule 6 – *Openness*

The religion must welcome new information with excitement and anticipation of what is to be learned next through the grace of God. If the religion rejects or attempts to undermine new scientific data, or if it tries to suppress newly discovered history or religious texts, then there is a problem.

Rule 7 – *Spirituality*

The religion must inspire the human soul and assist its members in feeling positive emotional states, such as confidence, joy, and love. If the religion uses fear, retribution, or suppression to control or subjugate all or some of its members, then there is a problem.

Lastly, and most importantly, no man-made religion has all the answers about God. Therefore, any religion or any person who asserts absolute knowledge about the nature of God or God's plan for mankind should be ignored absolutely. Notwithstanding that peremptory warning, it is possible to identify the appropriate goal of a wholesome religion: spiritual Truth. Thus, a good religion creates an environment in which its members feel inspired to pursue this goal.

RULE NUMBER 1 – PHILOSOPHY

God gave us our incredible brain power for a reason and we should not hesitate to use it. In particular, we should apply our intellect when evaluating a religious belief system, and we should insist upon a strong philosophical foundation for any religion we choose to join. To do otherwise would be to ignore one of the greatest gifts that God gave us – *the power to reason.* Indeed, if we refuse to exert intellectual effort to explore and perfect our relationship with God, not only are we wasting our greatest faculty, we also may be guilty of sacrilege. In other words, it only makes sense that God wants and expects us to utilize our own power of reason when we question the meaning of our existence. *Why else would God have granted us this gift?*

Scientists now know that both our brain size and brain power increase slowly but measurably via the process of evolution. Consequently, in 100,000 years, our descendants will be smarter than we are right now! Therefore, it is folly to fear the power of the human mind, since our intellectual capacity will continue to evolve and expand whether we like it or not. Instead, let us be thankful for the gift of intelligence and rejoice at our apparently unique ability to conceive, contemplate, and comprehend Truth. Furthermore, let us eagerly draw on our genius and wisdom to reflect on the Supreme Being and give thanks for the rare gift of reason.

In a similar vein, we should evaluate our religion from time to time to ensure that it, too, is evolving in a rational direction. Simply being born into a family that follows a certain religion does not mean we should consider that religion correct when it comes to spiritual Truth. Consequently, we should be using our power of deductive reasoning to study and meditate on the nature of God, the nature of mankind, our obligations to each other, our connection to the Earth plane, and how we may join the Almighty in the Ethereal plane. In sum, we should be trying to solve the mysteries of life and death for ourselves. A good religion assists its members who embark on spiritual quests.

Conversely, a bad religion hampers its members who seek spiritual Truth. The English philosopher Sir Francis Bacon observed that knowledge is power, which explains why unhealthy religions only preach ancient recycled dogma and hide the deeper spiritual revelations of the mystics. If you were born into a religion that doesn't resonate with you on an intellectual level – which is what happened to me – don't be afraid to question that religion. It would be a grave mistake to bend your mind to accommodate a belief system that does not make sense to you. Instead, accept that your religion may be flawed and seek higher ground. If your mind whispers, "but this doesn't make sense," your higher self is speaking the Truth. It doesn't make sense!

Furthermore, no one should feel guilty for evaluating religion. Remember, God would not have given us the power to reason unless he wanted us to ponder the meaning of our existence. Moreover, unless we suffer from a cerebral or emotional impairment, we each possess enough wisdom to analyze the merits and mistakes of the man-made religions. Therefore, faith should not be considered an inherited attribute, like eye color, nor a learned behavior, like good manners. Instead, we should develop our own belief system as we mature, since each person's faith is as unique as a thumb print.

Suppose, for the sake of illustration, that you were born into a family with a history of child sexual abuse, which is a pathology that is very hard to break. In fact, psychologists estimate that it usually takes *seven* generations to rid a family of this horrid legacy. Now, imagine that as a child you were the victim of this type of abuse. If you were born into such a devastating situation, you would have an important choice to make as you matured. You could choose to reject the destructive family pattern and replace it with a healthy model, or you could choose to claim abuse as your heritage and, thereby, perpetuate the aberrant behavior.

The point is, we should not adopt a flawed belief system merely because it was handed down to us by our ancestors. Upon reaching adulthood, we must assume responsibility for our spiritual growth. Furthermore, we should view spiritual introspection as another adult obligation, like voting or good parenting, which, if properly exercised, will lead humanity to a brighter future. Luckily, we have the intellectual capacity to solve our problems, break bad family patterns, and create a better world for ourselves and for our children. We also possess the intellectual might to tackle and wrestle with the most complex philosophical question of all time – the nature of God.

In sum, we all have the duty, as children of God, to explore religion for ourselves. Moreover, God will know if we shirk this obligation. Consequently, if you are born into a religion that is philosophically suspect, then it is incumbent upon you to explore alternative belief systems. Your parents may not have had the freedom to question their religion; however, if this book has made its way into your hands, then you do have such freedom.

So, take the time to reevaluate your religion. Start by meeting with the clergy of your local church. If you don't feel comfortable approaching a church elder, then there is a problem. Similarly, if your pastor provides you with answers but the answers lack substance, then there's still a problem. And if he tells you simply to have "faith" in rote answers, there's a huge problem. Also, if the doctrine of your religion seems irrational to you, don't be afraid to reject it as faulty. Then start searching, as I did, until you find a spiritual belief system that is more intellectually satisfying and challenging.

If you doubt that philosophy and religion should naturally complement each other, ask yourself these questions. First, what is the primary attribute which separates mankind from the other living organisms on this planet? Intelligence. Second, would God give us the unique power to reason but expect us not to use it? No. God would not have given us enhanced brain capacity unless God wanted us to utilize it. Frankly, it would be absurd to argue, as some religions assert, that God does not want us to question man-made religion. Doubtless, the Supreme Being wants and expects us to search for spiritual Truth and reach enlightenment.

In sum, we should have the intellectual freedom to seek a better understanding of God. Indeed, we should examine our religion like a prism in the Sun, to see whether it catches the light. Thereafter, if we find that our religion is philosophically suspect, we must not be afraid to reject it and find another belief system that appeases the logical side of our brain. We must also have faith that upon discovering spiritual Truth our higher self will let us know by screaming, "Eureka!"

RULE NUMBER 2 – SCIENCE

Second only to the rule that a good religion should have a solid philosophical foundation is the requirement that a sound religion should fully comport with science. Indeed, science may very well lead us to the ultimate Truth of our existence and God's plan, since the implicit goal of science is to probe the mysterious connection between the Earth plane and the Ethereal plane. Consequently, we should thank the many scientists who have contributed to our understanding of the seen and unseen worlds, and we should acknowledge that our greatest scientists, such as Albert Einstein, are *en par* with our major Prophets, as both groups of teachers have glimpsed and imparted revolutionary lessons of Truth from and about God.

Because we owe scientists such an immense debt of gratitude, we should be horrified at how the man-made religions have treated them. My God, Leonardo Da Vinci had to write in code (backwards and in reversed script) in order to hide his discoveries from the Catholic Church, while other scientists were imprisoned, tortured, and killed for challenging arcane religious dicta. These souls were brave during the dark times. They defied orthodox religion for our betterment and they were persecuted and martyred on our behalf, just like the saints. I cannot praise our scientific masters enough and I applaud their tenacity and strength.

Thankfully, most scientists today operate in unrestricted environments, as the church no longer wields enough power to seriously threaten research or impede developing technologies. In my opinion, however, mankind won't proceed into the next Spiritual Paradigm until we face the undeniable connection between science and God. Thus, two keys are needed to unlock the ultimate Truth of the Universe: **trust in science and faith in God.**

The problem, though, is that science and religion have been operating at cross purposes for thousands of years, particularly during the last century. As we shall see in Chapter Four, religion declared war on science the minute the natural world was proven to be in conflict with *The Holy Bible*. As a result, scientists have valid reasons for fearing the church. Moreover, Christian fundamentalists recently have increased their attacks on science, thereby posing new challenges to our scientific and spiritual progress. Nevertheless, scientists should not overreact when God is introduced into discussions about the origins of life, just as clerics should stop claiming sole dominion over God's mysteries. The bottom line is, if we wish to create the utopian society described by the Prophets, we must end the inane battle between science and religion. Just as the collective consciousness won't grasp the prophesied New Age until we learn how to blend masculine and feminine energy, we won't progress into the next Spiritual Paradigm until we learn how to meaningfully integrate science and spirituality.

Unfortunately, there is an ever-increasing difference between orthodox religion and true spirituality. That is why so many people, including myself, fear losing the Constitutional barrier which separates church and state. Those of us who are spiritual but who think and operate independently of man-made religious dogma still believe that God is responsible for all of creation. We simply reject the outdated creation mythology contained in the ancient holy books.

For those readers who were taught the ancient Jewish tale of creation, which classically states that God created the Earth, the animals, and the first humans within a six-day time frame in 3761 B.C.E., please recognize that the *Old Testament* is a mixture of mythology and symbolism, proverb and prophecy, and fantasy and fiction. In short, the *Old Testament* is not a history book, it is a wisdom book. As such, the *Old Testament* was written to provide the early Hebrews with basic spiritual lessons, such as the Truth of monotheism, and fundamental moral lessons, such as the Ten Commandments. The *Old Testament* also kept the Jewish rulers humble by juxtaposing the imperfect nature of mankind against the utter magnificence of God.

The Truth is that all the early civilizations composed myths in an attempt to understand how God created the Universe, and the parable about Adam and Eve is nothing more than one ancient culture's simple explanation for the complex relationship between God and mankind. Therefore, we should not view the Jewish creation myth as a literal explanation for our existence, any more than we should adopt Egyptian, Greek, or Native American mythology for true science. In fact, historians now know that the Jewish story of creation is nothing more than a restatement of Sumerian legends, which the Sumerians began to record around 2700 B.C.E. Thus, the Jews heard the Sumerian tales, as recorded in such epics as the *Atrahasis*, the *Epic of Gilgamesh*, and the *Enuma Elish*, and they verbally altered the stories over time. Eventually, the Jews recorded the modified fables in their first holy book, *Genesis*, around 950 B.C.E.

In the original Sumerian tale of creation, gods and goddesses descend to Earth with two of the gods, brothers named **Enki** and **Enlil**, vying for supremacy. After a while, the gods decide that they need servants, so Enki makes a man out of clay. Unbeknownst to Enlil, however, Enki endows the man with godlike attributes, just as God does with Adam (*Genesis* 2). Thereafter, Enlil finds the humans too rebellious, so he decrees that mankind should perish in a great flood. Fortunately for us, Enki defies his brother and warns a man named **Atrahasis** about the impending flood, just as God warns Noah (*Genesis* 6). In response, Atrahasis builds a ship large enough to hold his family and the animals. After the deluge, Atrahasis releases a dove to determine if there is dry land, just as Noah does (*Genesis* 8).

The Sumerians invented the first written language by 3000 B.C.E. They carved clay tablets that contain their creation legends. These tablets are some of the oldest records on the planet, pre-dating Genesis by roughly 1,800 years. Consequently, many scholars wonder whether the early Hebrews heard the Sumerian tales about Enki and Enlil and combined them into one god named Yahweh. This is a fascinating theory because it would explain why Yahweh appears confused and even schizophrenic in Genesis (i.e., nurturing one minute, wrathful the next). Consider that Enki/God initially loves mankind enough to give us free will and the power to discern right from wrong. Yet, upon learning the full extent of our abilities, Enlil/God rejects mankind. Not long thereafter, Enlil/God becomes so appalled by our rebellious nature that he wants to destroy mankind with a great flood. Enki/God then decides that one pious man should survive to repopulate the Earth. Based on these and other striking similarities between the ancient Sumerian and Hebrew tales, scholars now think that the Judeo-Christian story of creation, which was originally intended to promote monotheism, actually may have evolved from the mythology of a polytheistic culture.

The important point is that every ancient civilization had a creation myth. In the case of the Hebrews, they likely inherited their creation myth from the Sumerians about 5,000 years ago. To put this into perspective, realize that the people who believed in the Sumerian/Jewish version of creation also believed in animal sacrifice, slavery, polygamy, ritualistic sex, food restrictions, and the death penalty for working on Saturdays. Moreover, the final draft of this parable was introduced with the avowed purpose of converting people to monotheism. Consequently, it is fair to say that the most famous mythological couple in recorded history was fabricated in order to convert pagans to a new religion, later called Judaism. Incidentally, although rarely discussed, *Genesis* Chapter 6 presents yet another tale of creation. This chapter lets slip a pagan reference to male gods mating with human females to produce superior offspring called **Nephilim.**

Despite the inaccurate and simplistic nature of the Jewish tale of creation, the parable contains some revolutionary spiritual messages which still apply to us today, such as:

1. The Truth that only one God exists;
2. The Truth that God is responsible for creation;
3. The Truth that we are all children of God;
4. The Truth that mankind is imperfect as compared to God;
5. The Truth that mankind, while in an imperfect state, is unworthy of reentering the Garden of Eden (i.e., heaven);
6. The Truth that mankind has the innate ability to become Divine; and
7. The Truth that mankind may return to the Garden (i.e., rejoin God in the Ethereal plane), once we perfect ourselves by conquering the challenges of the Earth plane.

For these reasons, the Jewish creation myth should be preserved and taught to our children, just like any other piece of great fiction that conveys sound moral, ethical, and spiritual lessons. But, the fable should be studied in a history, philosophy, literature, or ethics class – not science class – since science now has proven all the ancient creation myths to be grossly inaccurate.

Thankfully, most people in the world today understand that *The Holy Bible* contains nothing more than one ancient culture's attempt to explain the mystery of mankind's existence. As a result, educated people accept the fact that science is further along in explaining the origins of life, than is organized religion. However, this may no longer be the case in the United States, where Christian fundamentalism is taking hold of the populace at an alarming rate, almost as quickly as Muslim fundamentalism is spreading in the Middle East. In fact, a 2005 poll has revealed that more than half of all Americans believe the *Genesis* account of creation, including the fiction that God made the Universe in six days and fashioned Adam and Eve as full blown *Homo sapiens.*

This rejection of science is nothing short of tragic. Modern astronomers and physicists have estimated the age of the Universe at 13.7 billion years and

Earth at roughly 4.6 billion years. Moreover, archeologists and anthropologists have established that human evolution started approximately 5 million years ago and that modern man evolved from less sophisticated *hominids*. Nevertheless, public school districts all over the country are under assault from Christian fundamentalists who believe that God created the Universe in 3761 B.C.E. *Therefore, given that religious fundamentalism is on the rise worldwide, dare we attempt to blend science and spirituality?*

In my opinion, we stand at a proverbial crossroad and have a very big decision to make. We can either drop the artificial wall between science and spirituality and leap into the unknown, in which case we must be prepared for the chaos that always precedes transformative change, or we can allow the animosity and mistrust between science and religion to continue festering, in which case the collective consciousness will suffer as both sides claim Earth plane superiority. May I humbly suggest that in the 21st Century, we finally are scientifically and spiritually advanced enough to admit the obvious: **God is science.**

Moreover, although it probably has served us well to temporarily divorce natural science from orthodox religion, the Truth is that the deepest mysteries of the Universe will only be solved if we mate scientific imagination with spiritual mysticism. Consequently, it is my sincere hope that mankind now is mature enough to study the complex topic of creation without being hamstrung by ancient mythology or distracted by past prejudices. Furthermore, let us end the egocentric debate between scientists and clerics over who is best qualified to interpret the mysteries of the Universe, since both professions share in that distinct honor.

Let us presume, therefore, that mankind is ready to think about God and science in unison, and that it is the right moment in history to inject spirituality and mysticism back into science. We still would need to draw a clear distinction between the esoteric Truths relayed by the Prophets and the man-made dogma that evolved after these messengers died. Thus, just to be clear, let me reiterate that I am not proposing that we eliminate the separation between church and state, since without Constitutional protection Christianity might well become a state-sponsored religion. *Rather, I am proposing that we eliminate the barrier between spirituality and state.*

On the surface, the objectively benign concept of **Intelligent Design** falls within the scope of my proposal. In a nutshell, the theory of Intelligent Design holds that the process of evolution, as originally proposed by Charles

Darwin (and subsequently proven via empirical methods such as carbon dating and DNA testing), does not fully explain either the origins of life or the complexity of life on Earth. There are a few reputable scientists who have joined this cause and who honestly wish to fill the gaps in evolution. Unfortunately, however, the founders of this movement are religious fanatics who privately contend that the *Genesis* account of creation is accurate. Consequently, I have mixed feelings about Intelligent Design. It makes me nervous, since religious fundamentalism in any form provokes in me extreme discomfort bordering on paranoia. But it also excites me, since the thought of solving the mysteries of life evokes in me untold joy bordering on euphoria. As a person of faith, I may reject the creation mythology of my ancient ancestors, but I still wish to credit the Supreme Being that made it all possible.

In sum, even though I am not a scientist and likely am incapable of understanding the more complex issues involved in this debate, it is obvious to me that there are many mysteries which neither our science books nor our holy books currently can explain. Furthermore, it seems apparent that mankind will achieve greater enlightenment once science and spirituality are allowed to interface in the name of Truth.

As a final cautionary note, we need to ensure that political and religious men of power, who have a vested interest in keeping the masses misinformed, are not permitted to monopolize the Intelligent Design movement or use it to promote "Christian values." This is a red herring issue, folks – just a phrase that gets media traction. The Truth is that men of power use the phrase "Christian values" to distract us while they tend to business. It is classic sleight of hand, intended to misdirect us while they indulge in the two cardinal sins – greed and pride. Therefore, if the Christian right (or any other religious group) seizes control of the Intelligent Design movement, our courts should reinstate their previously strict policy of separation between church and state.

Despite these concerns, I earnestly believe and pray that the time has come to set our scientists and spiritualists free to search for Truth together. Along those lines, and as a perfect example of the type of beneficial research that will result once we acknowledge the nexus between science and spirituality, scientists recently asked Tibetan monks to participate in a study designed to explore how Buddhist meditation impacts brain activity and other parts of the human body. Researchers were able to track physical changes in the monks' neurological, respiratory, and pulmonary systems. The results indicate that the monks are able to self-direct physiological changes and truly achieve uninterrupted periods of mental stability and intense concentration. This research also buttresses the claims of doctors and patients who use visualization techniques, holistic practices, and semi-mystical Eastern traditions, such as acupuncture, to fight disease.

The bottom line is that mankind's pursuit of scientific knowledge is noble and deserves our support. The many physical realities pertaining to the human condition, planet Earth, and our place in the Universe continue to unfold before our eyes, as old scientific theories quickly become new scientific facts. Therefore, a good religion incorporates proven science in its belief system and also interjects theoretical science into theological discussions.

On the other hand, any religion that refuses to acknowledge proven science or expresses apprehension over scientific breakthroughs undermines mankind's collective spiritual progress. Such a religion also suppresses Truth. And while I would like to believe that those fundamentalist religious clerics who devalue science do so because of their own lack of education and ignorance, I am not that naive. Most fundamentalist leaders are men of power who are intent on preserving their positions of authority and maintaining the *status quo*, which in some cases means no change for thousands of years. Conversely, the majority of people who yield to fundamentalist rhetoric, including prohibitions against modern science, are victims of tainted man-made religion. Perhaps they lack education or they reject contemporary science out of fear of the unknown. Either way, it is a tragedy that so many people are following religions which reject or fear science.

Ironically, today's scientific advancements and interpretation of religious parables can eliminate our fears by explaining the Truths which underlie yesterday's mysteries and mythologies. Change is scary, but a good religion leads its members into the future in a fearless manner. I have often wondered whether fundamentalists fear science for the same reason I dislike computers – because such complex technologies are way beyond my comprehension. In other words, no one likes to feel intellectually inferior, stupid, or even confused. I also suspect that fundamentalists view major breakthroughs, such as stem cell research and cloning, as somehow challenging or usurping God's role as the only omnipotent and omniscient force in the Universe. However, such a perspective contradicts our innate human desire to explore and seek answers.

Therefore, instead of feeling belittled by scientific advancements, we should take comfort in the fact that science is getting us closer to comprehending the full breadth of God's glory. Similarly, in those rare instances when science contravenes our holy books, we should be grateful that science is getting us closer to comprehending God's plan for mankind. Regarding evolution, for example, just because mankind evolved from a more primitive life form does not mean God loves us any less or that we are somehow less special. Rather, the science of human evolution simply illuminates the fact that God intended for us to slowly develop into our current species, instead of making us full blown *Homo sapiens* from the start. Obviously, God must have wanted us to eventually walk upright, speak, and think. Moreover, God must have intended for us to master our base instincts, love each other, and one day build a utopian world; otherwise, why would God have sent the Prophets with such difficult and yet beautiful instructions? If we view human evolution in this way, there is no inconsistency between science and our holy books.

Thus, anthropology merely highlights and explains the full glory of God's creative power as focused on mankind. Other areas of science are equally illuminating. For example, archeology unearthed the dinosaurs, lost civilizations, and buried holy texts. Geography led to the mapping of our planet, while astronomy revealed that the Earth moves around the Sun, the extent of our solar system, the vastness of our Milky Way Galaxy, and that the stars are other suns which may support life. Ecology explained the Earth's atmosphere and the frightening reality that our ecosystem now is out of balance. Physics led to the creation of industrialized machinery, ships, cars, planes, rockets, computers, and the luxury items which were invented to "simplify" our lives. Biology led to the charting of the human body, including our entire DNA code, and the surgical procedures we now take for granted. Chemistry generated lifesaving drugs and the current cloning and stem cell technologies that are so controversial. And the science of psychology revealed the complexities of the subconscious mind, including vivid proof that faith has the power to alter physical realities and produce ... *miracles*.

And now we have come full circle. Science brings us back to an acknowledgment of God, since there are too many "miracles" and other enigmatic occurrences that science cannot explain. That doesn't mean, though, that science won't be able to explain such mysteries in the future.

RULE NUMBER 3 – MORALITY

The proposition that a good religion should encompass a pure moral imperative is so basic that I think we can safely assume universal agreement on this point. For the sake of providence, I think we also should assume that the vast majority of us share a common moral belief system and generally agree on which human attributes are "virtuous." Lastly, let us waste no time debating the regrettable yet obvious fact that evil exists in the world. One quick look at the Appendix would convince even the most optimistic soul that mankind has the capacity to commit unspeakable atrocities. Undeniably, much of our history is barbaric and loathsome.

Thus, mankind has the power to act morally or immorally, which means that each of us has an important choice to make. We can either pretend this choice doesn't exist, based on the misplaced notion that mankind is innately sinful and therefore doomed as a race, or we can pledge to do our best to make energetic progress in the good and thereby ensure our long-term survival, both physically and spiritually. But the second choice requires our *collective* moral vigilance. Regardless of our nationality, our status in life, or our preferred religion, we need to acknowledge our shared obligation to promote good and reject evil. We also need to heed Edmund Burke's profound warning, "All that is necessary for the triumph of evil is that good men do nothing."

Luckily, God gave us an incredible gift to help keep us morally strong: **the conscience.** Absent a psychological pathology, our conscience acts as a private barometer that tells us when we are doing right and when we are doing wrong. It can't always filter the negative thoughts that pop into our heads, but a properly functioning conscience does help us to control our actions. Self control is paramount and anger management is mandatory if one wants to live according to the Golden Rule. Indeed, it is easy to identify those souls who have mastered their base instincts to become spiritually enlightened. Such souls consistently treat others with love and compassion.

The good news is that all of the five primary religions being practiced by mankind endorse the Golden Rule. The bad news is that most of these religions don't practice what they preach. Just because a religion cites the Golden Rule as a central tenet of its belief system does not mean that its religious leaders are adhering to it. Consequently, it is very important to periodically examine the man-made religions to determine whether they are morally fit to guide us.

To the extent that a particular religion helps its laity maintain moral focus, it is a good religion. However, any religion that fails to endorse or model irreproachable standards of right and wrong not only is defective, it also is dangerous because it creates moral confusion in the minds of its members. Typically, this happens when a religion initially espouses a moral goal but then turns a blind eye to the use of unethical or violent conduct to achieve the stated mission. In such a case, the religion harms itself and its laity by condoning the use of devious or diabolical tactics in order to accomplish what otherwise was a virtuous goal. Frankly, hypocritical religions actually help the dark force in the Universe destroy the forces of light. *When will our religious (and political) leaders finally accept the Truth that the ends never justify the means?*

Here are two illustrations of how otherwise moral religious objectives can turn repugnant. Throughout history, the Catholic Church has asserted the altruistic goal of spreading the teachings of Jesus, which, as we saw in Chapter Two, were predicated on unconditional love and generosity. Today, the Catholic Church employs missionaries and other relatively peaceful means to achieve this objective. However, as we shall see in Chapter Four, for over six hundred years the Catholic Church used a horrifying tribunal called the Holy Inquisition to forcibly convert others to Christianity and keep its own laity submissive. As a result, millions of people were dispossessed, banished, tortured, and killed, in furtherance of the seemingly benign goal of promoting Christianity. Similarly, today some Islamic leaders have authorized deadly force to promote the otherwise altruistic goal of preserving their religion in the face of western encroachment and corruption. These Muslim zealots believe they are justified in brutally attacking others and that Allah will forgive and even reward their sinful transgressions, but they are woefully mistaken.

The Truth is that any religion which fosters hatred or employs violence to achieve an objective, including even a virtuous goal, has completely lost its moral footing.

Oftentimes, members stay in broken religions hoping that the problems will be fixed by the very clergy who are passively condoning or actively encouraging the immoral behavior. Unfortunately, such misplaced loyalty usually backfires for a variety of reasons. To start with, anyone who stays in a corrupted religion or continues to listen to an unethical cleric is not receiving true spiritual sanctuary, which completely negates the purpose for joining an organized religion in the first place. In other words, there is no point in attending a church that offers invalid or even questionable moral guidance. In fact, you're better off on your own.

Second, families that remain in tainted religious institutions are putting their younger and more gullible family members at risk, since children are easy prey for corrupt authority figures, especially clergy. The Muslim boys and young men who "voluntarily" commit suicidal acts in the name of Allah are prime examples of the danger associated with allowing corrupt clerics access to the impressionable and trustful minds of our youth.

Third, when serious problems arise within religious organizations, they are rarely dealt with openly or quickly. Indeed, troubled religions appear more concerned with maintaining the appearance of propriety and integrity than actually exercising such virtues. Take, for example, the Catholic Church's denial then mishandling of thousands of sexual abuse claims against priests. This decades-old scandal perfectly illustrates how religious men of power will choose to ignore and thereby perpetuate immoral behavior rather than protect and serve the needs of their laity.

Finally, staying aligned with a tainted religion only serves to mask problems and further empower and embolden corrupt clergy. Such misplaced loyalty actually fuels men of power, since immoral leaders rarely clean up their act unless and until the masses hold them accountable. Therefore, if your house of worship has become tainted by religious leaders who passively permit or, God forbid, affirmatively promote the suppression or persecution of others, or if your clergy are not healthy role models for you and your children, you should consider leaving your religion.

My point is that your very presence in a flawed religion, even if you protest the errors of judgment made by fallen church leaders, only serves to give the religion and those who run it the indicia of spiritual authority. Corrupt leaders thrive under the cloak of respectability and they will seize upon your loyalty as a justification for continuing their bad deeds. And if some "bad apples" are caught, don't be fooled into thinking that the issue is resolved. The Truth is that there must be pervasive evil in the top ranks of the religion or the bad apples would not have acquired power. *Consequently, people need to start grasping the painful reality that it is better to leave a corrupted religion than to stay involved, either actively or passively, in the hopes of fixing it.*

To drive this point home, let's flip the argument upside down and ask whether anyone would join a club with a suspect belief system or unethical leaders. Imagine that you are a woman and a friend asks you to join his charitable organization. You probably would feel flattered and offer to help. You soon learn, however, that only men may be elected to the Board of Trustees, only men may speak at meetings, and only men may determine how to allocate charitable contributions. Imagine further that female members may only participate in fundraisers as the cooks and clean-up crew for charitable events. Lastly, suppose that some of the male Trustees have just been indicted for embezzling money from the charity. Would you join such a club?

Obviously, you would hesitate joining such a club even if it were originally founded by good people with pure motives. Why? Because your efforts would be better spent working for another organization that operates ethically and morally. In sum, we are best served by a religion that has uncompromising standards of right and wrong, never tolerates hypocrisy in its leadership, and always exhibits moral strength, particularly when tested by complex social or political issues.

Similarly, leaving a flawed religion doesn't make you a "quitter." Rather, it shows you have the moral fiber and the courage to insist on Truth. In fact, that is how all revolutions start. The moral members of a group separate from the members who have lost their moral compass. The ones who leave aren't quitters. On the contrary, they are brave enough to fight for what they believe in by maintaining their high ideals and forming a better organization. Soon, like-minded souls are drawn to the new and improved organization. Ultimately, the new entity flourishes, whether a club, a country, or a church, because its leaders truly practice what they preach.

Consider the fact that every time a major Prophet came to Earth, a new religion started. That's because every time God sent us such a messenger, we realized that we had new information to process. First, pious followers of the Prophet would record God's updated messages to preserve the new spiritual lessons. Next, devotees of the Prophet would teach the more sophisticated belief system. Inevitably, these spiritual leaders would formalize the updated doctrine and create a new religion. For example, many Hindus decided to leave their religion for Buddhism after Buddha relayed his glorious lessons. Similarly, after Jesus died, some of his followers decided to leave Judaism and create a new religion called Christianity. Thereafter, some Jews and Christians converted to Islam once Muhammad recited his divine messages. And so it goes. Every time a new Prophet clarifies the nature of God, some of us move on to a "better" religion, which I would simply define as a spiritual belief system that is closer to the ultimate Truth.

RULE NUMBER 4 – JUSTICE

This section will be brief since, as part of my twelve-step recovery plan to stop practicing law, I'm supposed to avoid "legal" debates. Nevertheless, the omniscience of God's law versus the fallibility of man-made law is an important topic, so I must make an exception. At the outset, there are two points about man-made laws to keep in mind. First, man-made rules should be objectively beneficial and not necessarily geared toward pleasing or protecting a majority of the citizenry. In other words, man-made laws should comport with universal standards of morality and fairness. Second, a just society will adhere to man-made laws on a long-term basis only if the rules comply with universal principles. If the rules restrict fundamental personal rights or violate innate human freedoms, the citizenry rightfully will protest the rules (or their unfair application), and the fabric of society will unravel. In the spiritual context, a good religion only promulgates rules that flow naturally from God's laws as cited by the Prophets, including love, acceptance, and forgiveness.

Let me add a quick note regarding mankind's obsession with structure. Structure within certain organizations is crucially important, particularly when order and discipline are mandatory for the successful completion of the organization's goals (e.g., the military). However, structure that segregates people, subjugates the human soul, or requires blind obedience, has no place in religious institutions. Therefore, if your religion has adopted a top heavy structure or a ritualistic set of rules, make sure that its man-made constructs are fair to everyone and uniformly applied. Moreover, ensure that the religion's rules allow for fluid and frank communication between the clergy and the laity. Everyone's voice is heard in a good religion.

Most importantly, though, religious rules and dicta should never usurp the individual's innate ability and personal duty to use his power of reason and his conscience to arrive at sound moral and spiritual decisions. Religious leaders should never try to take away one's right to exercise free will, which is another gift from God. Any religion that teaches its members that they aren't worthy or smart enough to understand or communicate with God is making a power play and is trying to undermine its members' free will. Moreover, none of us have the right to abdicate our intellectual reasoning, our conscience, or our free will to our religious leaders. In fact, that is what cult religions seek – complete dominion over their members. Hence, bad rules are the hallmark of bad institutions, especially when dealing with political and

religious organizations. Therefore, make sure that your religion is not imposing rules that are unnecessary, nonsensical, designed to keep current leaders in
positions of power, or vigorously enforced to control the laity.

The Truth is we have but one Judge. Therefore, we should not rely exclusively on clergy to interpret the world, and no ordinary cleric should presume
to speak for God. Instead, we must weigh issues for ourselves with the help of
our God-given powers: our intellect and conscience. Then, we must use
another of our God-given gifts, free will, to implement our moral conclusions.
We did not get these divine gifts from any man or any man-made religion.
Consequently, it is not appropriate for a religion to promulgate rules designed
to control us or even mold us if such rules conflict with God's laws. Rather, a
good religion merely provides moral guidance and spiritual sanctuary to help
its laity explore the depth and dimension of universal principles on their own.

RULE NUMBER 5 – INCLUSIVENESS

A good religion is available to everyone, including those who subscribe to
different faiths. At a minimum, inclusiveness requires this twofold commitment: (i) the religion should welcome and respect people who hold different views on the mysteries surrounding the Universe and God; and (ii) as a
central tenet of faith, the religion should endorse the Truth that all good people have the potential to join with God in heaven, regardless of their religious
affiliation or lack thereof. This rule is simple in concept, yet rarely practiced
by organized religions. *The issue is tolerance.*

Most religions would have us believe that they welcome everyone. That
simply isn't true, at least not in the sense of inviting people to church to debate
the nature of God or the afterlife. Rather, most religious institutions are pre-
occupied with sustaining or increasing their membership. Thus, most religions
merely feign tolerance in an attempt to convert their invited guests. I am
reminded of the young people who knock at my door every so often and tell
me that they are on a "mission." I usually invite these young adults into my
house, as I am grateful for the opportunity to discuss my favorite topic.
However, I sense that they don't really enjoy theoretical debates on the nature
of man as related to the nature of God. Nor do they seem willing to consider
that other spiritual paths are valid, unless based on the premise that Jesus is a
deity who doles out salvation. Quite frankly, they do have a mission: to
convert me. The irony is that they ask me to be "open" to them, but they are
"closed" to any theology except their own.

Similarly, what happens at a dinner party when someone brings up the topic of religion? Everyone runs for the hills! Remember, God must have given us our acute intellect for a reason. Consequently, it is contrary to our Divine spirit not to ponder and talk about God; indeed, it may even be sacrilegious. Thus, we each have an obligation to analyze our faith, study our religion, and periodically update our belief system as we grow and learn new spiritual Truths, even if those Truths come to us from sources outside of our inherited or chosen religion.

Most disturbing, though, is the assertion by some religious leaders that you can join God in the Ethereal plane only if you subscribe to their religion. A prime example of such an exclusionary religion is fundamentalist Christianity, which asserts that a person can reach heaven only by accepting Jesus Christ as a savior deity. In Chapter Two, we studied the *New Testament*, the *Lost Gospels*, the *Gnostic Gospels*, and the *Dead Sea Scrolls* to properly interpret Jesus' life. Recall that Jesus never promised even his devout Jewish followers salvation unless they strictly observed the Ten Commandments *plus* the Golden Rule. Consequently, it is quite a stretch for Christians to posit that Jesus promised salvation to anyone who worshiped him as God. Nevertheless, the fundamentalist Christian movement seems to grow daily, proof that people are easily fooled into believing they can get something for nothing. But I have learned the opposite: nothing in this life (or the afterlife) is free. Remember, it was Paul, a man who never met Jesus, who crafted the auto-redemption sales pitch to persuade Gentiles to convert to Christianity. James the Just, who actually heard and understood his brother's lessons, tried to correct Paul by clarifying that blind faith in the absence of good works is meaningless, but to no avail.

In sum, any religion that represents itself as the only path to God is fatally flawed for a number of reasons. First, such religions do their laity a huge disservice by coddling their members and convincing them that they are somehow special and deserving of God's grace simply because they attend a certain church and recite certain prayers. Second, intolerant religions cause division in the world, thereby helping the dark side to splinter humanity into meaningless and, oftentimes, menacing factions. Third, extreme fundamentalist religions are prone to commit affirmative acts of evil, since the leaders of such religions preach discriminatory ideology designed to incite their followers to ostracize, pity, suppress, or hurt their neighbors who subscribe to different religions. Tragically, fundamentalist sects of the three Abrahamic religions – Judaism, Christianity, and Islam – have fallen victim to this last stage of religious zealotry and madness.

To avoid such extreme religious fundamentalism, the prudent and spiritually mature soul periodically examines his religion to ensure that negative influences have not taken hold of its leaders or members. Inclusiveness is an easy and effective litmus test for determining whether a religion is healthy, since intolerance is the antithesis of the Golden Rule. Thus, a good religion welcomes everyone, not to worship necessarily, but to a safe environment in which to debate and dissect theology. It may seem like a fine line to walk, since many people become upset when they perceive that their religion is being criticized. However, because religion is the single force responsible for most of the conflict on this planet, it is incumbent upon us to entertain theological discussions and close the ever-widening gaps between the five primary religions.

The bottom line is that a good religion fosters respect toward people who practice other faiths. Moreover, a positive religion attempts to minimize, not exacerbate, religious differences. Discrimination is anathema to spirituality. Therefore, a healthy religion engages in meaningful discussions about the mysteries of the Universe with people who hold different belief systems. Humility is another important factor in spreading spiritual Truth. Because none of the man-made religions may rightfully claim perfect knowledge of all spiritual Truth, it is absolute arrogance for any religion to assert itself as superior to another religion. God intended for mankind to build a Tower of Truth based on the accumulated wisdom of all the Prophets. Tragically, as we shall see in Chapter Four, we built a Tower of Babel instead.

Finally, it has been my experience that spiritual Truth comes from many sources other than religious institutions and theology books, such as philosophy, science, literature, and the arts. In addition, I have learned some of my most profound spiritual lessons from my children. When emotionally present, I am able to see the Universe through my children's eyes and feel God's presence in its purest form. Thus, it is hard to predict exactly when, where, how, or why some critical piece of spiritual Truth may fall into our lap. It also is hard to guess who may impart an important insight. What a shame, then, that so many religious leaders herd their flocks into fenced pastures. Religion should not restrict us in this manner. We were not meant to stay in separate religious camps forever. So don't be afraid to peek into neighboring pastures for a kindred spirit who has found a different path to God. We grow whenever we make new friends, explore new ideas, and discover new pathways to the Supreme Being. When in doubt, remember this inclusive Truth: **We are all children of God.**

RULE NUMBER 6 – OPENNESS

A good religion accepts as a central tenet that spiritual growth is an evolving process that never stops, even after we take our last breath. Most of the man-made religions teach this Truth, which means that most of us know that death represents just the expiration of the physical body, not the termination of the soul. Except for a few powerful mystics, however, none of us really knows what happens to the soul in the unseen realm (a/k/a heaven). People of faith will agree, though, that the soul undertakes both an Earth and an Ethereal plane journey. Unfortunately, because the exact nature of the soul's Ethereal plane quest remains a mystery, mankind has been unable to agree on which religion best explains how and why the soul seeks reunion with the primordial source (a/k/a God). Wouldn't it be great if instead of arguing about these mysteries, many of which science may one day solve, the five primary religions acknowledged their common belief that God created our souls for adventure?

Admittedly, as we saw in Chapter Two, some of the Prophets attempted to describe what happens to the soul after it leaves the Earth plane. God gave these great teachers information about the Ethereal plane and the Prophets did their best to relay this information in terms that both they and ancient man could understand. However, we need to remember that the five major religions practiced today were founded on messages relayed thousands of years ago and during eras when most of mankind was incapable of understanding the complex nature of either the natural or supernatural world. Consequently, the level of knowledge given to and disseminated by the Prophets was tailored to meet the intellectual and spiritual needs of their specific audiences. In other words, God spoon-fed us some elementary Truths to get us pointed in the right direction. Since then, mankind has continued to search for and uncover additional Truths, and we have discovered much about both the seen and unseen worlds by using the amazing gifts God gave us. As a result, it would be ridiculous for us to continue clinging to the simple explanations provided to our ancestors or to blindly follow outdated belief systems for the mere sake of tradition.

As the Appendix illustrates, much has transpired in human history since the Prophets died and the five primary religions were formed. Indeed, because of the hard work and ingenuity of many stellar individuals, mankind has acquired additional Truths and our collective consciousness has continued to evolve. Thus, mankind has amassed vast quantities of new data in such diverse fields as history, philosophy, and science. This new data has astounding spiritual significance which necessarily impacts how we view ourselves, our planet, and our Creator. Consequently, the five primary religions should have incorporated these new Truths into our spiritual database, alongside the spiritual lessons taught by the Prophets.

In sum, a good religion is open to new revelations, regardless of the source. Moreover, a healthy religion does not fear change but welcomes any new information which helps its members mature spiritually. Thus, the issue is whether the five "modern" religions still practiced by mankind now have become "ancient." Just as we should evaluate our religion to ensure that it retains a clear moral focus, we also should monitor our religion to ensure that it stays abreast of recent historical finds, current science, and enlightened spiritual theories.

Unfortunately, as we shall see in Chapter Four, most of the man-made religions have demonstrated a reluctance to synthesize and assimilate new information over the past two thousand years. In general, religion now serves as a barrier to Truth. *The irony, of course, is that religion was supposed to increase our understanding of the seen and unseen realms.*

Sadly, some religions doggedly refuse to update their belief system even when science mandates that we reevaluate our understanding of the origin of mankind. For example, in 2005 on Flores Island near Indonesia, another hominid species was discovered which scientists have named *Homo floresiensis*. This three foot tall human walked the Earth roughly twenty thousand years ago and could make tools and build fire. One anthropologist from George Washington University stated, "It is arguably the most significant discovery concerning our own genus in my lifetime." Nevertheless, I doubt that many religious leaders even bothered to address this exhilarating find with their laity. A good cleric not only would have discussed the importance of the discovery but also would have encouraged his laity to ponder how mankind's physical and spiritual evolution fits into the broader context of God's plan.

In sum, closed religions impede the soul's journey by suppressing or ignoring new Truths and by blocking the soul's quest to reach God. As a result, those people who crave knowledge about the natural world and who seek understanding of the supernatural world often feel pulled in contradictory directions. Religion often forces them to choose between: (i) their curiosity for intellectual and spiritual enlightenment; and (ii) their loyalty to an outdated view of the Universe and an archaic view of God. This is the tragic consequence of closed or fear-based religions. Those who remain in repressive religions are spoon-fed simple and incomplete answers to complicated questions, while those who bravely reject such sects begin to uncover Truth. In a nutshell, that is why I left my birth religion. I wanted to commence a deeper spiritual journey, unfettered by a religion that still taught ancient and erroneous lessons, such as the self-destructive fallacy that mankind is innately sinful.

For anyone who still believes his religion has all the answers, consider these two reasons why each of us must learn spiritual Truth on our own. First, even if you think there is a "right" religion, we do not become spiritual via osmosis. Thus, despite the best of intentions, no one can attain enlightenment simply by attending the "correct" church once a week or reciting "proper" prayers. As my grandfather used to say, "If it seems too good to be true, it isn't." In other words, the only real path to God is personal soul growth, which is fostered by the *Saddha* process and evidenced by our acts of love.

The other reason we have to learn Truth for ourselves is that our understanding of the Universe is necessarily limited by our unique perception of reality. As we acquire knowledge, Truth *appears* to change. In reality, though, Truth is a constant that we haven't discovered yet. For instance, the United States recently sent an advanced probe to Mars that is sending back amazing data, including evidence that Mars once had water. Consequently, it is likely that life once existed on Mars. This would constitute a new Truth to us even though God, as the omniscient force in the Universe, would consider this old news or, rather, no news at all.

Similarly, every star in the sky is a sun, potentially with its own solar system. Therefore, the Universe may encompass another planet like Earth that can sustain life. God already knows whether or not this is so, but to us it would be a new Truth if we found alien life. Indeed, there are some scholars who believe that aliens already have visited Earth, as evidenced by amazing astronomical sites built over four thousand years ago, such as Stonehenge and the Great Pyramid at Giza. These ancient structures prove that early man knew more about our solar system than did Copernicus, who merely rediscovered in 1543 C.E. that the Earth moves around the Sun. In addition, the ancient Ziggurat in Baalbek, Lebanon contains eight hundred ton boulders that experts say even modern machinery could not move across the desert. Even more startling is one current theory on the evolutionary "missing link." Some scholars are wondering whether Enki – who, if you will recall, is described in the ancient Sumerian texts as the god who created the first man – may have been an alien visitor who provided our ancestor *Homo habilis* with an intelligence boost. This seemingly far-fetched theory would account for the unprecedented increase in our brain capacity around 200,000 B.C.E., the period that anthropologists say we morphed into *Homo sapiens*.

Regardless of whether you believe we already have been visited by aliens or may be visited in the future, a healthy religion would entertain a discussion of these novel theories. Conversely, any religion that continues to perpetuate the mythological tale that God created Adam and Eve in 3761 B.C.E., is not only denying the scientific fact of human evolution, but also is preventing an unfettered discussion of whether intelligent life may exist on other planets. Perhaps the new theory of Intelligent Design will provide a positive bridge between the Christian fundamentalists, who still cling to the antiquated fable of creation contained in *Genesis,* and those scientists who acknowledge that Darwinism does not adequately explain how human beings developed faster than the other species on planet Earth.

To summarize, any religion that is based on a snapshot of our world taken thousands of years ago is hopelessly out of date and constitutes a serious impediment to learning. Moreover, none of us fully understands God's plan for mankind as yet, nor the full measure of God's glory. As a result, the Truth as we know it is constantly changing and evolving. It is therefore absurd for any religion or cleric either to assert absolute knowledge or suppress new information which may help us better comprehend the full breadth of God's magnificence. Clearly, God made us smart and curious for sound reasons. **We are here to learn.**

Consequently, a healthy religion acknowledges that each of us is a child of God and that each of us yearns to rejoin our Creator. A good religion also understands that the only way a soul reaches the Supreme Being is by undertaking a personal journey, communicating one-on-one with God, and contemplating the deeper Truths of the Universe. In addition, a positive religion acknowledges that soul growth is possible only in a supportive, nurturing, and open environment, as is all learning. This is the *Saddha* process of soul growth. Openness is both a prerequisite to and a byproduct of this methodology. Once a soul commits to such a quest, it is open to Truth regardless of the source. Eventually, answers start to unfold in mystical and synchronous ways. Ultimately, the soul attains enlightenment and earns salvation in the Ethereal plane.

RULE NUMBER 7 – SPIRITUALITY

Because we are made in God's image, we each possess some of God's divine nature. Therefore, we can utilize our power of reason to discern philosophical Truth, we can employ our genius to discover scientific Truth, we can - listen to our conscience to identify virtue, and we can exercise our free will to act in harmony with the Universal laws created by God. In addition to these gifts, God gave mankind another important attribute which my friend Sam calls the "inner bell." The inner bell is the most subtle and fragile aspect of our divinity, but also the most potent once perfected. It is our higher self – that piece of us which, if properly attuned, can commune with God.

Our inner bell is comprised of our Earth plane instincts, which we naturally possess, and our Ethereal plane intuition, which we accumulate both subconsciously and through practice. Moreover, it is a tool for analyzing the world, since it supplies us with important information we need to survive both physically and spiritually. When our inner bell is functioning properly, we literally can "feel" our surroundings. It causes an internal emotional reaction that lets us know whether an environment is healthy and safe for our physical body and also whether a situation is inspirational and nurturing to our soul. If a religion asserts a theological tenet or a man-made rule that causes a negative reaction inside the body or disturbs the spirit, our inner bell should start ringing to warn us there is danger. In this way, our inner bell is yet another God-given mechanism that helps us judge matters for ourselves and achieve true enlightenment.

It is very important to draw a clear distinction between the negative emotions we feel when we have done something wrong versus the negative emotions we feel when we witness a wrong committed by another person. We must take care not to confuse these two negative but different internal reactions. For example, if we act improperly, our conscience (as opposed to our inner bell), should activate the emotions of guilt and shame within us. That is as it should be, since a properly functioning conscience should make us feel bad when we do something wrong. In such a case, we should embrace the negative emotion, not "pivot away" from it as suggested by one New Age leader, since healthy shame compels us to use our free will to correct our errors.

On the other hand, if another person does something wrong, our inner bell should go off. Next, we naturally should experience a negative emotion like fear, sorrow, or anger. In this case, we need not utilize our conscience to evoke guilt or remorse, as we have done nothing wrong. We should, however, use our inner bell to analyze the situation and determine whether we have a duty to intervene, either to protect someone who has been harmed or to prevent further injustice.

Unfortunately, it is relatively easy for our inner bell to get out of whack. In extreme cases, people may be brainwashed to react in unnatural ways to dangerous situations. A prime example is the Jim Jones cult that thrived in the 1970s. Jones exerted such influence over his followers that he convinced them to commit mass suicide by drinking Kool-Aid laced with cyanide. Hundreds of people, including children, were killed in the incident. The moral of the story is that people in dysfunctional environments, such as religious cults, often lose their ability to hear their inner bell. In such a weakened state, a person is easy prey for religious fanaticism.

However, even members of less extreme religions may be victimized and lose their spirit. For instance, some religions restrict their female laity by asserting that they have fewer rights than the men. A perfect example is the right to obtain a divorce. Suppose for a moment that you are a woman in a bad marriage and that your husband physically abuses you. If your inner bell were working properly, you initially would feel anger toward your husband and your survival instinct would prompt you to escape such a sick environment. However, if your religion teaches that divorce is a sin, then your anger toward your husband might unnaturally and irrationally transform into guilt or depression, which psychologists define as anger turned inward. Such a religion harms the spirit of its female laity by forcing them to ignore their inner bell and sublimate their natural responses. In extreme cases, fanatical religious dogma may usurp the individual's ability to intuit what is safe and proper, resulting in emotional despondency and spiritual hopelessness. Then, the inner bell rings no more.

Another common way in which bad religions manipulate their laity is by portraying God as a judgmental "fire and brimstone" character who is always watching and waiting for us to fail. This model presupposes the innate sinfulness of mankind and our inability to perfect ourselves. This model also rejects the notion of personal responsibility and views salvation as something we "win" by selecting the "right" religion, as opposed to something we earn through spiritual growth. Additionally, this model actually helps tainted religions mislead and control their laity, who begin to accept the self-loathing and self-destructive idea that they are sinful and completely incapable of reaching heaven without clerical assistance. It is at this pathetically sad juncture that religion, to quote Karl Marx, becomes the "opiate of the masses." And we lose our connection to God.

The Truth is that we are responsible for our own actions, our own spiritual growth, and our own salvation. Betting on the childish dream that God, as a father figure, will forgive us for our sinful actions and let us into heaven anyway seems pretty risky to me. Even more destructive is the erroneous premise that mankind is innately sinful. It is nothing but a huge cop-out to posit that mankind is incapable of spiritual perfection but that God will forgive us our sins anyway. Such a belief system merely provides weak and corrupt souls with the excuse they crave to justify their aberrant behavior. Religions that still cling to the arcane model of the tragically flawed human being are outdated and counterproductive to positive spiritual growth. They also are based on early man's superstitious, unsophisticated, and limited understanding of the Universe. Today, most of us are not that weak, scared, or uneducated. We also are not that helpless.

Let's face it, God would not have given us so many divine gifts unless God wanted us to use these tools to better ourselves. Obviously, God expects us to use our intellect, conscience, free will, and inner bell to grow and to learn spiritual Truths. The bottom line is that we are responsible for our own salvation, which we must earn by and for ourselves. Going to church once a week or confessing sins to a priest isn't good enough. Praying for forgiveness after committing a bad act doesn't cut the mustard either. God expects more from us. If we choose to ignore our divine faculties or abdicate control of our spiritual growth, we do so at our own peril. *Spiritual laziness is not a path to heaven.*

Luckily, the Prophets explained to us, in progressive and increasing detail, everything we need to know to achieve salvation. Tough as it my be to accept, they taught that the path to heaven is narrow and that we must work hard for spiritual enlightenment. On the bright side, though, the Prophets also explained and modeled for us how to achieve perfection of the soul. They literally charted the course for us. Thanks to the Prophets, the path to heaven is fairly well marked and easy to navigate, provided that we earnestly and honestly do our best to love God, ourselves, and our fellow man. Thus, the Prophets gave us all the information and inspiration we need to perfect ourselves and join with God – just as they did.

To quickly recap, the Prophets taught that the surest way to fuse our spirit with God is by looking inward for direction and answers, as we all have a connection to the Divine, and then by acting outward with the inspiration gained from such sacred encounters. Thus, if we properly employ our intellect, our conscience, our free will, and our inner bell, we will feel the euphoria of acting in accordance with God's most basic law – **Love**. This is the *Saddha* process. It is as rewarding as it is exciting, since it inspires the soul to achieve inner peace and outer harmony.

Therefore, a good religion encourages and enhances spiritual ecstacy by providing its members with an inspirational environment in which to perfect a personal relationship with God.

Conversely, a flawed religion is one which causes its laity emotional confusion or spiritual discomfort. Taken one step further, a religion premised on fear is an abomination. There should be no fear of church clergy or church rules, no fear of reprisal for leaving the faith, and certainly no fear of God. At a minimum, then, a decent religion provides all of its members with basic comfort and support. In addition, a good religion inspires its members to commence true spiritual journeys or *Saddha* quests. And at the top of the scale, a great religion guides its members in determining their respective life missions, the only way to attain true bliss on the Earth plane and prepare the soul for the Ethereal plane. When in doubt, listen to your inner bell. It will tell you whether your place of worship is truly spiritual or whether your religious environment is unduly restrictive, emotionally repressive, physically perilous, or even life threatening.

Lastly, many people today find the male definition of God to be emotionally uninspiring and spiritually crippling. Fortunately, this two thousand year old myth is losing its luster – as it should. Mankind will never attain spiritual equilibrium until God's feminine attributes are worshiped alongside God's masculine characteristics. In this regard, the New Age movement deserves praise for reintroducing the primordial Truth that God's nature includes both male and female energies. Fortunately, there are many of us who welcome the long awaited return of the Sacred Feminine, which mystics describe as the wisdom half of God or the "should do" energy. Equally important is the masculine half of God, classically defined as containing the creation or "can do" energy. Until both of these energies are appreciated and understood, mankind will never attain peace.

As soon as we reaffirm the elementary Truth that God is half feminine energy, the herculean task of creating a truly spiritual religion for all of humanity will be feasible.

CONCLUSIONS

A smart religion comports with sound philosophical observations (*Rule Number 1*) and empirical scientific discoveries (*Rule Number 2*). A virtuous religion has fixed moral standards which are never compromised, especially when unpredictable or evil forces challenge humanity (*Rule Number 3*). A just religion guides its laity by imposing minimal rules, applying the rules fairly and uniformly, and ensuring that the rules mirror but never usurp the Universal laws established by God (*Rule Number 4*). A compassionate religion accepts and respects other faiths and exercises humility and tolerance whenever theological differences arise (*Rule Number 5*). And a brave religion fearlessly leads its laity into previously uncharted territory, by appreciating recent historical discoveries, entertaining new scientific theories, solving contemporary social ills, and incorporating such novel and advanced information into its spiritual database, all for the sheer joy of learning (*Rule Number 6*).

Most importantly, though, a healthy and vibrant religion provides its followers with a spiritual environment so that they may safely explore their own mystical connection to the Supreme Being and, thereby, reach true enlightenment (*Rule Number 7*). In other words, it is nearly impossible for the soul to attain a purified state without the aid of an inspirational and peaceful forum in which to meditate and pray. Thus, while all seven of the rules discussed in this chapter are essential to the establishment or maintenance of a good religion, it is this last component – spirituality – that is a prerequisite to the soul finding God and comprehending Truth, including the primordial and everlasting Truth that the Supreme Being is comprised of both masculine *and* feminine energies.

In sum, all seven of *The Seven Rules of Any Good Religion* are necessary for a religion to qualify as a sound theological institution. When taken as a whole, the seven rules promote intellectual and scientific application, moral and ethical behavior, patience and tolerance, and the desire to learn more about ourselves and God by undertaking a soul-searching journey of Truth. By subscribing to these seven rules, a religion also acknowledges that God gave mankind all the divine gifts needed to learn more profound Truths than were handed to our ancient ancestors. With all due respect to the Prophets and the revolutionary lessons they taught, it is now time for modern man and woman to assume responsibility for their own salvation.

Quite frankly, our physical and spiritual survival may now depend on how quickly and accurately we assimilate and manage the complex realities of the

21st Century. Until we recognize that God graced our species with the predilection and power to determine our own fate, we will continue to make lame excuses for our barbaric and nihilistic behavior (e.g., innate sinfulness). Thus, we must stop viewing ourselves as pawns on God's chess board. God surely has a plan and although it may be too intricate for us to fully comprehend at this juncture, it doesn't mean that we're trapped in some cosmic matrix that's fated for disaster. Indeed, the opposite is true. Remember, we're made from divine design and infused with spiritual spark.

We have the innate ability to elevate both our own and the collective consciousness – if we can muster the will.

Therefore, I suspect that the next stage of God's plan is for mankind to become free from the false precepts perpetuated by certain man-made religions. As we shall see in the next chapter, none of the five primary religions, as currently practiced, can satisfy the objective template represented by *The Seven Rules of Any Good Religion*. Perhaps, once we free ourselves of the arcane religious dogma that still restricts so many souls on the Earth plane, we will be ready to proceed to the next level of God's apparently multi-staged, multi-faceted, and multi-dimensional plan for our souls. Consequently, although we face perilous adventure in the 21st Century, we also hold at our fingertips the possibility of a glorious future, here on Earth and in the afterlife. However, in order for us to successfully navigate the next leg of our collective journey, we must have faith in God, in ourselves, and in each other.

By the way, some of you may be wondering why I chose not to include "faith" in the list of *The Seven Rules of Any Good Religion*. The reason that faith is not a mandatory requirement for a good religion is because faith is what each of us must bring to the table. We are responsible for ensuring that our faith coincides with our chosen religion and its approach to God. Additionally, only we can determine whether our faith is strong enough to commence a true spiritual journey. Thus, I hope that all who read this book have enough faith in God and in themselves to tackle the next chapter, which may be quite difficult for some people.

In the next chapter, I will use *The Seven Rules of Any Good Religion* to determine which, if any, of the five primary religions truly foster spiritual growth. Remember, a good religion must satisfy all seven rules. In addition, I will use *The Seven Rules of Any Good Religion* to grade the five primary religions to see how well they currently are performing and how ready they are to embrace and help birth the prophesied **New Millennium**.

*And the Lord came down to see the city and the tower which the
sons of men had built. And the Lord said: ... "Come, let Us go
down and there confuse their language, that they may not understand one another's speech." So the Lord scattered them abroad from
there over the face of the whole earth; and they stopped building
the city. Therefore its name was called Babel, because there the
Lord confused the language of the whole earth; and from there the
Lord scattered them abroad over the face of the whole earth.*

The Holy Bible, *Genesis*, Chapter 11:5–9

Hopefully, at this stage of my work, I have adequately presented two
Truths with which we all can agree. First, all the major Prophets
described in Chapter Two were sent to us by God. Second, all the
man-made religions which were started after the Prophets died should comply
with *The Seven Rules of Any Good Religion* listed in Chapter Three. In this
chapter, we will delve more deeply into the five primary religions to see
whether they evolved as God intended, based on the Prophets' lessons and the
objective criteria of *The Seven Rules of Any Good Religion*.

With regard to the Prophets, it seems obvious to me after all my research
that each of them came to Earth with God's blessing and with a two-fold purpose: (i) to help us comprehend the awesome energy and abundant love of

God; and (ii) to help us understand our own divinity, which we have the potential to achieve once we fully accept our sacred connection to God and to each other. Thus, we were supposed to assimilate the messages of all the Prophets and build a spiritual database (i.e., a religion), that would lead us in a *unified* manner in the direction of Truth. Unfortunately, rather than build a Tower of Truth, mankind started to build a Tower of Babel, as illustrated by the parable in the *Old Testament*.

In my opinion, the Prophets fulfilled their missions, but we have failed ours.

As primary proof that humanity has failed to adhere to or synthesize the Prophets' lessons, I present the tragic fact that in the 21st Century mankind still has been unable to reach a state of world-wide peace and global harmony. As further evidence that mankind has failed to properly assimilate God's prescription of unconditional love, I offer the Appendix at the end of this book. It succinctly summarizes the vast physical, emotional, and spiritual carnage that religion has generated throughout the ages. Ironically, history shows that it is religion that has posed the greatest impediment to mankind's collective mission.

And what exactly is mankind's mission while on the Earth plane? We need only recall the successive lessons of the Prophets and the wisdom contained in our holy books. They all refer to the **First Spiritual Paradigm** – the primordial period during which we were one with God. It is this perfect (some might say mythological) paradigm that beckons and inspires us. And it is our sacred task and solemn duty to seek reunion – with God and with our highest self – that will make us whole again.

Thus, by now mankind should have arrived at the following Truths:

1. We are all children of God;
2. We are supposed to evolve spiritually; and
3. We will enter the prophesied New Millennium (a/k/a the **Fifth Spiritual Paradigm**) as soon as the majority of us accept our own Divine nature.

At this point, we should know that our physical survival (i.e., non-extinction) depends on our using proper modes of conflict resolution without resorting to barbaric tactics of suppression, domination, or bloodshed. We also should know by now that our spiritual survival (i.e., salvation) depends on our practicing compassion and charity toward friends and enemies alike. In short, we have all the Earth plane experience and Ethereal plane lessons we need to understand and accomplish the task of creating heaven here on Earth. We cannot rightfully or honestly expect any more help from God.

Indeed, God's plan for the next stage of mankind's spiritual evolution seems pretty clear. At this stage of our spiritual development, we should be experiencing **Unity**. After all, the vast majority of us share a common belief in the Supreme Being and a common code of conduct. In addition, most of us agree with the universal Truths relayed by God's Prophets. As we learned in Chapter Two, the *Vedas*, the *Old Testament*, the *Dhammapada*, the *New Testament*, and *The Holy Quran* all recite nearly identical versions of the Golden Rule. So why have we failed to enter the Fifth Spiritual Paradigm? Two words: *free will*.

At the risk of sounding simplistic, allow me to state the obvious: *God gave us the ability to control our destiny because God wants us to control our destiny*. As we enter the 21st Century, may I humbly suggest that a critical component of God's plan for mankind is freedom of choice wisely executed. In other words, if we want the prophesied New Millennium to materialize, we will have to exercise our power of self-determination to make it happen. Only then will we demonstrate that we are enlightened enough to join with God.

In sum, it is our collective mission to create a utopia on the Earth plane. By doing so, we will prepare ourselves and our neighbors for afterlife in the Ethereal plane.

Sadly, some religions refuse to accept the fundamental Truth that mankind possesses the Divine power to alter the course of human history. Instead, some orthodox religions still teach that mankind has little or no control over events. In essence, such religions are regurgitating archaic superstitions – common in ancient mythology and lore – that God has never been happy with his creation (e.g., the Greeks believed that Zeus threw lightening bolts to punish humans). Evangelical Christians take this fatalistic mythology to an extreme and assert that the *Revelation to John*, the last book of *The Holy Bible*, describes God's future destruction of the Earth as punishment for our sinful conduct. This erroneous interpretation of a 2nd Century prophecy (which stems from an even older Jewish prophecy), is a prime example of how orthodox religion unwittingly prevents us from reaching our collective spiritual potential.

As we shall see in this chapter, not only have the five primary religions failed to adequately update God's Tower of Truth by excluding the lessons of all but their favored Prophet and by ignoring the modern revelations of the 21st Century, they also have periodically produced degenerate leaders who purposely block us from reaching the utopian goal of unity. Like sheep, many of us still follow religious leaders who selfishly accumulate material possessions or who insanely crave power over the rest of us. Therefore, we would be wise to focus our attention on the following inquiry: *How have a few misguided and perverted religious leaders managed to thwart God's plan and prevent the rest of us from claiming our God-given right to pursue material plane freedom and divine spiritual growth?*

At the outset, let us acknowledge that education is the best way to reach those souls who are hindered by archaic belief systems. Luckily, independent theologians, historians, and scientists have assumed the solemn task of helping humanity reach a more sophisticated understanding of God, our own nature, and our place in the Universe. The more difficult problem, though, is how to counteract those religious leaders who crave Earth plane power. These men know that they're teaching spiritual falsehoods and they don't care. They likely will never tell the Truth, not if it means losing control of their laity.

Unfortunately, the arsenal of weaponry employed by such corrupt souls is vast, efficient, and lethal. Men of power tend to be very dangerous individuals, even in the religious realm. Nevertheless, the only way to expose these hypocrites is by calling "a spade a spade," which is exactly what Jesus did. Thus, I am not suggesting the use of force, since the ends never justify the means. In fact, the use of violence only benefits the dark element in the Universe. Rather, those of us who wish to help humanity move toward the light of God will prevail only if we constantly remind ourselves that evil stems from ignorance.

Thus, if our goal is to weed out those religious leaders who are blocking our spiritual progress, either due to their own ignorance or their Earth plane attachments, we must remember that the best way to counteract darkness is by spreading Truth. Once we come to this realization, a simple and efficient answer to the problem becomes clear:

All we need do is stop building the Tower of Babel.

One of my primary motivations for writing this book is my fear that mankind has foolishly initiated another cycle of religious intolerance. Specifically, I am worried that history is repeating itself and that depraved men of power have commenced yet another "holy war." Unquestionably, many of our current political and religious leaders are now using religion to acquire great wealth and dominate the masses. These leaders have forsaken us because they have succumbed to the cardinal sins of greed and pride. These material plane demons always seem to strike our leaders the hardest. Hence, it seems a truism that power corrupts and absolute power corrupts absolutely.

Even more disturbing, though, is our apparent inability to identify and reject those leaders who use the facade of religion to commit evil acts. As we shall see in this chapter, corrupt men have used religion throughout the ages to accumulate possessions and power. Indeed, religion has been the favorite tool of greedy and prideful men throughout history and remains the weapon of choice even in the 21st Century. The question is: *Why are the rest of us blindly following men who crave money and power down a path toward darkness?*

Some of you may be offended by the condensed history and frank analysis contained in this chapter. I ask only that you keep an open mind and keep reading. Remember, the first step in solving a problem is admitting that a problem exists. Thus, it is for our collective benefit that I ask you to suspend whatever historical or inherited defenses you may have used in the past to fend off or discount criticism of your religion. For many people this will be difficult, since most of us were taught at an early age by our parents and church leaders to view our religion as sacred and inviolable. Moreover, most of us were taught that our religion is "right" and the other religions are "wrong."

Instead, please try to accept the fact that God did not create any of the religions we are about to examine. Rather, God sent Prophets as glorious beacons of Truth and it was their followers who crafted the religions we practice today. Consequently, while the Prophets deserve our utmost reverence, we do not owe a duty of loyalty to the man-made religions if they are based on inaccurate or incorrect interpretations of the Prophets' messages. The Truth is that all five of the primary religions are flawed at this point and that each of them is contributing to mankind's dissension and suffering. It is my heartfelt belief that if you finish reading this book, you will agree with my painful conclusion: *The man-made religions are failing in their essential purpose.*

As a final introductory note, I need to underscore the fact that some of our most critical religious history has been lost due to the purposeful destruction of great works by misguided religious leaders and by victorious political regimes. To historians, it is a well known and frustrating fact that to the "victor" not only go the "spoils," but also the recordation and, oftentimes, the reformation of history. As a result, even some of our best and most independent scholars cannot agree on a few aspects of religious history. Be assured that in those limited instances, I have attempted to provide balanced reporting of the scholars' disagreements and of my own educated guess as to the most reasonable interpretation of important historical events.

HINDUISM

In keeping with the order set forth in Chapter Two, we will start our analysis of the five primary religions with Hinduism. Recall that at the time the Indus Valley was settled, around 4000 B.C.E., mankind believed in multiple gods and goddesses. That was not always the case, however, as archaeologists agree that early man believed in just one deity – Goddess. We will refer to this early belief in female monotheism as the **Second Spiritual Paradigm.** Later, mankind abandoned goddess worship and embraced polytheism, which is a belief in multiple male and female deities. This shift into the **Third Spiritual Paradigm** was a logical development, since mankind correctly deduced that God must have both male and female energies. Thereafter, the four river valley civilizations, the Greeks and Romans, and many tribal cultures believed in a variety of deities. Indeed, it wasn't until Judaism, Christianity, and Islam took hold that the theology of monotheism again became popular, at which point most of mankind started to believe in one male God and we passed into the current **Fourth Spiritual Paradigm.**

Despite the fact that the vast majority of people now have concluded that monotheism provides the most rational framework for comprehending the Supreme Being, Hindus continue to prefer their polytheistic approach to understanding the Universe. As a result, Hindus still believe that their gods and goddesses perform distinct functions and control different aspects of both mankind's existence on the Earth plane and the higher realms of existence in the Ethereal plane.

To some extent, though, the Hindus have consolidated their pantheon of deities, which grew over the millennia to include hundreds of gods and goddesses. Today, most Hindus seem to agree that there is a supreme god called Brahma who created the Universe. Even so, many Hindus prefer to pay homage to Vishnu, the god who sustains the Universe, or to Shiva, the god who controls time and the cycles of rebirth. In addition, just as some Catholics like to pray to saints, some Hindus prefer to worship lesser gods, such as Varuna, who controls the sky, seasons, and rainfall, or the goddess Lalita, who gives her followers the power to manifest their desires.

The fact that Hindus continue to ascribe divine powers to multiple gods and goddesses presents a problem for those of us who believe that there truly is only one God. Additionally, the Hindu belief that the gods and goddesses intervene in our daily affairs is a superstitious construct to educated minds, as is the ancient practice of sacrificing food and other items to the gods. Additionally, the fact that Hindus often choose a lesser deity as their primary focus for prayer, sacrifice, and absolution, seems strange to those of us who believe that there is just one primordial Source for all of creation. For all these reasons, I must concur with the prevailing theology of monotheism and conclude that Hinduism unnecessarily separates the various facets of God's energy.

Therefore, according to the philosophical standards of the 21st Century, Hinduism violates *Rule Number 1* of *The Seven Rules of Any Good Religion* because the religion illogically splits God's energy amongst a variety of limited deities and because the religion is premised on the superstitious construct that mankind must appease the gods in order to gain favor and good fortune.

This dissecting of God's energy into artificial categories also makes no sense from a scientific standpoint. Early man separated God's attributes in an attempt to understand the natural forces within the Universe. They imagined that different gods and goddesses were responsible for rainfall, crop growth, fertility, and death. Our ancestors also believed that the gods and goddesses vied for supremacy and fought amongst themselves for power. Thus, they concocted Sun versus Moon gods, healing versus destructive goddesses, and benevolent versus judgmental gods. Scientifically, we now understand natural phenomena and we no longer are puzzled by weather patterns, for instance, even though we sometimes are surprised.

In addition, each of the Hindu gods and goddesses has his or her own legendary tale from which we learn how they received their special powers. For example, there is the legend of a god named Ganesha, who is the son of the god Shiva and the goddess Parvati. According to legend, Ganesha made his father angry by favoring his mother. A fight ensued between father and son and Ganesha's head was cut off! Parvati was so grief stricken that Shiva grabbed the first head he could find – that of an elephant – and placed it on top of Ganesha's body. Thereafter, Ganesha had the head of an elephant and is pictured that way today in Hindu art. This story is meant to inspire believers by glorifying wisdom and success over adversity. Today, Ganesha is one of the most popular gods worshiped by Hindus.

While I hesitate to poke fun at any religion and much prefer to attack inconsistencies on a more objective and intellectual plane, I find it hard not to giggle at this story. To take such a myth literally is silly, and I am sure that there are many Hindus who do not interpret it literally. The point, however, is that the Hindu legends, just like the parables in *The Holy Bible*, should rarely, if ever, be read literally. We should look at these stories as containing moral lessons and foreshadowing greater Truths. Unfortunately, many Hindus today still literally interpret the ancient legends and continue to worship gods who, like Ganesha with his elephant head, defy the laws of nature rather than help explain them. More troubling, though, is the fact that many Hindus continue to believe that numerous deities actually manipulate the elements of nature and actively intercede in our lives.

Consequently, the Hindu religion violates *Rule Number 2* regarding acceptance of and adherence to scientific principles because the religion tries to explain natural phenomena and sophisticated science via archaic tales and superstitious legends.

Nevertheless, I am eager to qualify my criticism of Hinduism for a very important reason: *Hinduism was the first religion to recognize and accept the Universal principle of karma.* Indeed, the Hindu construct of *karma* deserves our utmost respect. Recall that *karma* is the belief that our actions, both good and bad, impact our soul's growth and our ability to reach God in heaven. In fact, *karma* is one of God's laws which cannot be avoided, whether we believe in it or not. Consequently, the Hindus' indoctrination of *karma* as a philosophical and scientific approach to spiritual enlightenment constitutes a revolutionary spiritual advancement. As we shall see, the elementary Truth of *karma* was then adopted, at least to some degree, by all the later religions.

> I [Krishna] will reveal again a supreme wisdom, of all wisdom the highest: sages which have known it have gone hence to supreme perfection. ...
>
> If the soul meets death when Sattva [intelligence and goodness] prevails, then it goes to the pure regions of those who are seeking Truth.
>
> If a man meets death in a state of Rajas [impure desire], he is reborn amongst those who are bound by their restless activity;
>
> And if he dies in Tamas [ignorance or laziness], he is reborn in the wombs of the irrational. ...
>
> Those who are in Sattva climb the path that leads on high, those who are in Rajas follow the level path, and those who are in Tamas sink downwards on the lower path. ...
>
> And when he goes beyond the three conditions of nature which constitute his mortal body then, free from birth, old age, death, and sorrow, he enters Immortality.
>
> *The Bhagavad Gita*, Chapter 14, Verses 1–20

Thus, although Hinduism in some respects offends the philosophical and scientific mandates of *Rule Number 1* and *Rule Number 2* of *The Seven Rules of Any Good Religion*, Hinduism logically and empirically comports with the Universal law of *karma*, an essential component of any valid spiritual belief system.

Unfortunately, the primordial principle of spiritual *karma* became twisted over time and devolved into the man-made monster known as the Hindu caste system. Without question, the caste system is an abomination. To understand how the caste system was formed, we need to go back in time to approximately 1500 B.C.E., when the Aryan people from central Asia started to migrate eastward to India. Thereafter, the Aryans spread westward into Arabia and Europe, as the formidable Persian Empire. The Aryans were lighter skinned than the indigenous population and they viewed themselves as superior to the Indians (i.e., the Aryan reference of Hitler fame). After the Aryans conquered the local Indus Valley civilization, they wanted to retain racial purity, so the Aryans instituted a social system which discouraged intermingling with the Indians. Hence, the start of the caste system and endemic discrimination within the Hindu religion.

The earliest reference to the caste system is found in the *Vedas*, which were most likely written by the Aryans around 1500 B.C.E. The following passage describes the sacrifice and physical dismemberment of the first man, a giant named Purusa, whose severed body parts were used to create the Universe, including the various levels of the Hindu hierarchical society.

> When they [the gods] divided Purusa, how many portions did they make? What do they call his mouth, his arms? What do they call his thighs and feet?
> The Brahmin [priest] was his mouth, of both his arms was the rajanya [prince] made. His thighs became the viasya [commoner], from his feet the sudra [serf] was produced.

The Rig Veda, Book X, Hymn 90

From this verse, Hindus initially created four classes of society, forever separated by their assigned roles: (i) the *brahmins*, who were the priests; (ii) the *rajanyas* (a/k/a *ksatriyas*), the aristocratic caste who served as rulers and warriors; (iii) the *viasyas*, who were the largest class and worked as merchants, traders, and farmers; and (iv) the *sudras*, who performed the most humble tasks and who later assumed the agricultural role. Under this system, a person's caste was inherited from his or her parents and it was not possible to outgrow or promote oneself into a higher caste during the current life.

However, a member of a higher caste could work at a lower caste's occupation in order to earn money without losing status. In addition, marriage between men and women of different castes was strictly forbidden.

Later, around 200 B.C.E., these four classes of humanity were further refined in scriptures credited to Manu, a legendary figure who taught a holy code called the *Manava-Dharma-Sastra*. The *Laws of Manu* set forth even more classes for mankind, including the lowest *dasyus* class, an impure group whose hereditary work revolved around death and the most unclean jobs. The "untouchables," as they were later called, were the hunters, fishermen, leather workers, executioners, and corpse handlers. Furthermore, under the caste system the untouchables could not be educated and were forced to live outside the villages. For all intents and purposes, the untouchables were outcasts and, although not technically slaves, they were forced to carry out the wishes of higher caste members.

This systemic discrimination was not challenged openly until the social revolutionary Mahatma Gandhi entered the scene. By the time Gandhi was born, Hindus had developed over one thousand castes! Gandhi believed that man-made rules should be peacefully ignored when morally wrong according to our conscience. He believed that we should follow an inner knowing regarding Truth, and he fought against both the unfair Hindu caste system and the British occupation of India. He renamed the untouchables the *harijans*, which means "children of God." He also welcomed the untouchables into his social reform movement, an act which horrified the elite Hindu caste members. Hence, the great teacher Gandhi, who was himself a Hindu, believed that the Hindu caste system was immoral, anathema to spiritual growth, and contrary to God's plan for mankind.

Therefore, I quite easily conclude that the Hindu religion violates *Rule Number 3*, which mandates that a good religion espouse irreproachable standards of morality.

In addition to being manifestly immoral, the Hindu caste system is patently unfair. Indeed, it is a man-made construct designed to keep the masses poor and powerless. As such, it cannot be from divine origins, as God's laws are just, balanced, and apply equally to everyone.

Thus, Hinduism also violates *Rule Number 4* because the caste system, by definition, creates distinct classes of people and then treats each class differently, thereby substituting unjust man-made laws in place of God's uniform principles.

Furthermore, the caste system creates yet another soul-damaging consequence. It fosters the crushing mindset that certain souls are not worthy of reaching spiritual enlightenment, a theological error that Buddha would later correct. The Truth is that everyone has the innate potential to reach advanced stages of spirituality. Therefore, a sound religion includes everyone and welcomes everyone to participate in spiritual exaltation.

Because the caste system denies the fact that lower caste members are worthy of attaining spiritual growth and joining with God in the present lifetime, the religion effectively excludes lower caste members in direct contravention of *Rule Number 5* of *The Seven Rules of Any Good Religion*.

Sadly, Gandhi did not live long enough to see the positive results of his protests against the caste system, as he was killed by a Hindu extremist in 1948. It also is unfortunate that Gandhi's hard work produced only limited results in abating the caste system. In 1950, India finally passed a law making it illegal for businesses to discriminate based on caste. However, the law does not ban the caste system and the law is rarely enforced. Consequently, the caste system still is alive and well in India.

With regard to India's independence, Gandhi did live long enough to see the British relinquish control of his country. However, before turning over control of India in 1947, the British partitioned India and created the new country of Pakistan. Despite the British partitioning, strife in the region continued due to conflicts among three different religious groups – Hindus, Muslims, and Sikhs. The creation of Muslim Pakistan did not resolve the conflict for two basic reasons: (i) the Sikhs were not given a homeland; and (ii) the new borders were not approved by both the Muslims and Hindus (e.g., Kashmir was given to India but had been a Muslim province). As a result of the boundary dispute and Gandhi's refusal to take sides in the conflict, Gandhi was assassinated by a national extremist. The map in the Appendix shows the new boundaries, which still are a source of tension. Consequently, the world lives with the frightening reality that both India and Pakistan have nuclear weapons. As of this writing, Pakistan is in danger of falling into the hands of the **Taliban**, Muslim extremists who may be harboring Osama bin Laden. Thus, it appears that this region of the world will continue to suffer at the hands of religious zealots.

Because the Hindus have not been able to make peace with their Muslim neighbors and because they doggedly refuse to eliminate the caste system, Hinduism also runs afoul of *Rule Number 6*, which requires openness to change.

Lastly, we need to address the ingrained Hindu bias against women which continues to this day. Recall that the *Laws of Manu* contain a description of the four stages of a man's life. These laws only apply to men, since women were not deemed capable of achieving any of the four stages of spiritual growth. This misogynist position was further embellished by the following rules regarding the role of women:

> *In childhood a female must be subject to her father, in youth to her husband. When her lord is dead, to her sons.* **A woman must never be independent.**
>
> *Him to whom her father may give her, or her brother with the father's permission, she shall obey as long as he lives, and when he is dead, she must not insult his memory.*
>
> *Though destitute of virtue, or seeking pleasure elsewhere, or devoid of good qualities, yet a husband must be constantly worshiped as a god by a faithful wife.* [Emphasis added]

> Manu Smrti, Chapter 5, Verses 148, 151, 154

Unbelievably, these rules have not changed much over the millennia, although in the 1800s my Indian sisters were thankfully released from the ancient custom of committing suicide by throwing themselves on their dead husband's funeral pyres. Even today, Hindu women rarely are allowed to select their own mates. In addition, Hindu wives are expected to serve their husbands and abandon careers after marriage. It also still is customary for Hindu women to stay indoors unless given permission to leave the house. Indeed, there is a resurgence in India of fundamentalist values and a current trend for women to attend "finishing schools" to prepare them for married life. For example, the Manju Institute in Bhopal still teaches that a husband should be treated like a "god." Instructors also caution women against assuming that they will be equal partners with their husbands. In sum, Manu's two thousand year old misogynist dogma about women continues to be enforced within the Hindu culture.

In conclusion, the ancient Hindu belief that women are not worthy of spiritual enlightenment violates *Rule Number 4* regarding the fair application of God's laws. Moreover, the systemic subjugation of women violates *Rule Number 5* on inclusiveness.

Finally, it seems obvious to me that any religion which consistently castigates its female laity cannot claim to provide a healthy or even safe environment for women. Despite the fact that goddess worship is common in India, Hindu women are not revered nor respected in the same manner as men. Thus, it is easy to conclude that Hinduism is emotionally and inspirationally harmful to women.

Because Hinduism fails to provide women with a joyful and nurturing environment in which to spiritually prosper, Hinduism does not pass muster with *Rule Number 7.*

Sadly, I conclude that the Hindu religion runs afoul of every one of *The Seven Rules of Any Good Religion.* To quickly recap, the fractured nature of the Hindu multiple-deity system fails to promote a meaningful union between the earthbound soul and the one true God. As a result, Hinduism is not compatible with modern philosophical or scientific theories and data. Moreover, Hinduism continues to perpetrate the immoral caste system, thereby undermining mankind's innate desire for freedom of thought and spiritual growth. Indeed, Hinduism is such a harsh religion that it even castigates its own followers who happen to be members of lower castes. Such ingrained discrimination also helps to create in the minds of the highest Hindu caste members an attitude of disdain toward people of other cultures and faiths. In sum, Hinduism is so divisive that it promotes unnatural and harmful messages concerning the nature of God and of humanity.

Yet, these fundamental flaws with the Hindu religion are easily understood, considering that Hinduism is the oldest of the five primary religions. Realistically, we cannot expect a religion that was created 4,500 years ago to satisfy or comport with the level of sophistication reached by modern men and women. And that is exactly the point of this chapter.

As with all the religions, Hinduism is woefully in need of change and should be updated to reflect the progressed state of mankind's understanding of God and the many new Truths mankind has discovered and catalogued over the last few thousand years. Therefore, please do not view this chapter as an attack on any of the five major religions. Rather, this chapter is intended to be an honest and fair-handed critique of how and why the ancient religions have become a burden to humanity and an impediment to our continued spiritual growth.

Let us now explore whether Judaism, commonly assumed to be the earliest monotheistic religion, meets our objective criteria for a spiritually sound and healthy religion.

JUDAISM

Judaism is the second oldest of the five primary religions practiced by mankind, being at this juncture in history roughly four thousand years old. Recall that the Jewish patriarch Abraham lived approximately 2000 B.C.E., and that the stories recorded in the *Old Testament* supposedly date back to 3761 B.C.E., when God created the Universe according to the early Hebrews. Today, however, most Jewish and independent historians concur that the *Pentateuch*, which contains the first five books of the *Old Testament*, was not authored by Moses but by Jewish priests who lived around 950 B.C.E., during the era of King Solomon. In addition, independent scholars are quick to point out the numerous inconsistencies contained in the *Old Testament*. In fact, the confusion begins immediately because the first two chapters of *Genesis* propose patently irreconcilable creation myths.

Chapter 2 of *Genesis* opens on the seventh day of creation by declaring that God has finished making the Universe and is now resting. Next, there is a "flashback" to the day when God made the first man ("*adam*" in Hebrew). This chapter states that God used clay to fashion Adam and then breathed life into his nostrils. As previously mentioned, the Hebrews most likely inherited this myth from the Sumerians, who believed that their god Enki also used clay to make the first human. However, the Sumerians recorded their tales about creation and the great flood nearly two thousand years before the Jews.

The next thing God does in *Genesis* Chapter 2 is plant vegetation in the Garden of Eden, including *two special trees*: the "tree of knowledge of good and bad" and the "tree of life." Then, God places Adam in the garden with explicit instructions not to eat from the tree of knowledge, or else he will die. Thereafter, God decides that Adam should not be alone, so he creates animals and birds as companions for the man. Later, God realizes that none of the animals have "proved to be the suitable partner for Adam," so God creates a woman from Adam's rib. *Thus, in this version of creation, Eve is tantamount to a mere afterthought.*

Now, compare the order of events as detailed in Chapter 1 of *Genesis*. On the first day of creation, God makes light to separate day from night. On the second day God makes the sky. On day three, God makes the seas, the land, and then the vegetation. Day four consists of making the heavens, the Sun, and the Moon. On day five, God makes the fish and the birds. And on the sixth day of creation, God makes the land animals before fashioning two humans in God's image. *Thus, in this version, God's last act of creation is to make a man and a woman – both of whom are born at the same time and both of whom are fashioned in God's gender-plural image.*

> Then God said, "Let Us make man in **Our image**, after **Our likeness**. Let **them** have dominion over the fish of the sea, the birds of the air, and the cattle, and over all the wild animals and all the creatures that crawl on the ground." God created man in His image; in the divine image He created him; **male and female He created them.** [Emphasis added]
>
> Genesis, Chapter 1:26–27

Chapter 1 of *Genesis* then ends with God's blessing upon humanity: "Be fruitful and multiply, and replenish the earth and subdue it." In addition, God generously tells Adam and Eve, "I give you ... every tree that has seed bearing fruit on it to be your food." Consequently, in this tale of creation, rather than instruct Adam and Eve that there is a tree that is off-limits, God invites them to enjoy the abundance of the Garden of Eden.

Thus, the first two chapters of *Genesis* contain numerous inconsistencies, as universally recognized by biblical scholars. Specifically, the two chapters disagree on whether: (i) Adam and Eve were made separately or at the same time; (ii) special trees did or did not exist in the Garden; and (iii) God forbade or permitted Adam and Eve to eat from any tree they wished. Nevertheless, the Jews (and later the Christians) adopted the Chapter Two creation myth, in which Eve is relegated to an inferior status relative to Adam and both of them are warned not to touch the tree of knowledge. As a result, Jews will come to view mankind as disobedient and fallible (although not innately sinful), and they will come to view their women as lacking the same level of divinity that God granted to men, as evidenced by such man-made customs as segregating women at Temple and restricting them from becoming rabbis.

Chapter 3 of *Genesis* relates the infamous parable about the "fall of mankind." Recall that in Chapter 2, God tells Adam that he will die if he eats fruit from the tree of knowledge. However, in Chapter 3, a serpent encourages Eve to eat the forbidden fruit by convincing her that she will *not* die. The snake explains to Eve that if she eats the fruit, she will become like a god herself because she will know the difference between good and evil. Eve takes her chances and follows the serpent's advice. Lo and behold, the serpent was right! Eve survives her taste of the forbidden fruit but she does pay a price: *She is no longer innocent.* In other words, Eve now understands the difference between right and wrong. Thereafter, God has quite a negative reaction to Adam and Eve eating the fruit. Indeed, God becomes so angry that he decides to punish all of the involved parties. First, God condemns the serpent:

> *Because you have done this, cursed are you more than all cattle, and*
> *more than every beast of the field. On your belly shall you go, and dust*
> *shall you eat all the days of your life.*
>
> Genesis, Chapter 3:14

As a child, I used to wonder how the snake knew the Truth about the tree of knowledge and why God was mistaken. For a short while, I accepted the Catholic explanation, that God allowed Satan to tempt Eve to see if she would sin. Putting aside the classic Catholic interpretation, a careful reading of this parable reveals a totally different story, especially when the tale is put into historical context. To begin with, a fair reading of *Genesis* shows that God portrays the serpent as nothing more than an animal. In fact, Chapter 3 opens with the following description of the serpent:

> *Now, the serpent was the most cunning of all the **animals** that the Lord*
> *God had made. [Emphasis added]*
>
> Genesis, Chapter 3:1

Furthermore, the word "satan" does not appear in *Genesis*. That's because the evil deity known as **Satan** (a/k/a the Devil) is a later Christian invention. Just for the record, the Hebrew word *satan* simply means "enemy" or "accuser." Moreover, the word is used only four times in the *Old Testament*. The first reference to satan, which appears in *Chronicles* 1, Chapter 21, simply states, "a satan rose up against Israel." Similarly, the word is used in *Psalm* 109, Verse 6, to describe someone who is "a lying witness, a satan ... that he may be judged and found guilty." The term also appears in the *Book of Job* and in *Zechariah*, both of which were written around 500 B.C.E. In these later Jewish texts, the amorphous enemy of Israel has evolved into a singular entity called Satan, who now tries to harm mankind. But even in these scriptures, Satan merely represents an enemy of man, not God. Nevertheless, in the *New Testament* the Christians will elevate Satan and depict him as a lesser deity akin to **Hades**, god of the underworld in Greek mythology. Still not content, the Christians will ascribe even more power to Satan in the last book of the *New Testament*, called the *Revelation to John*, by giving Satan a critical role in humanity's ultimate demise.

The Truth is that all the ancient civilizations believed that the snake represented wisdom, not evil. In fact, the snake initially was associated with the Great Mother, who early man believed was the only Supreme Being for approximately twenty thousand years. Then, when mankind adopted polytheism around 5000 B.C.E. and progressed into the Third Spiritual Paradigm, the snake continued to be associated with goddesses, such as the Babylonian goddess **Ishtar,** the Egyptian goddess **Isis,** and the Greek goddess **Athena,** all of whom represented wisdom. As previously noted, the Gnostic Christians retained the concept of the feminine half of God and called her **Sophia,** which is Greek for "wisdom." Not surprisingly, the Gnostic Christians sometimes used live snakes in their mystical ceremonies.

Therefore, the Jewish parable of creation reinforces the mythology that snakes represent wisdom, as the serpent in *Genesis* seems to know all about the powers of the forbidden tree. Consider that the snake is correct on both counts: (i) Eve does not die when she eats the fruit; and (ii) God admits that Adam and Eve have become like "Us" (i.e., godlike), after they eat from the tree of knowledge of good and bad.

> *Then the Lord God said: "See! The man has become like one of Us, knowing what is good and what is bad!"*
>
> Genesis, Chapter 3:22

After cursing the serpent, God curses Eve by pronouncing that her labor pains shall intensify and that her husband shall be her master. God then curses Adam by decreeing that the Earth will be full of thorns and that planting and gathering food will require toil and sweat. Lastly, God tells Adam that he shall return to the ground from whence he came (i.e., die).

Finally, it is fascinating to note how Chapter 3 of *Genesis* actually ends, since most of us were taught as children that God ejects Adam and Eve from the Garden of Eden due to their disobedience. That is *not* how the parable reads, however. God does not spurn mankind for exercising free will or for acquiring the capacity to discern right from wrong, although God clearly is not happy that Adam and Eve have attained such advanced powers. *Rather, God is worried that Adam and Eve might also eat from the tree of life and become immortal.*

> *Then the Lord God said, "[T]herefore, he must not be allowed to put out his hand to take fruit from the tree of life also, and thus eat of it and live forever." The Lord God therefore banished him from the Garden of Eden, to till the ground from which he had been taken. When He expelled the man, He settled him east of the Garden of Eden; and He stationed the cherubim and the fiery revolving sword, to guard the way to the tree of life.*
>
> Genesis, Chapter 3:22–24

Ironically, the reason God gives for expelling Adam and Eve from the Garden of Eden is practically the opposite reason provided by the classic Jewish and Christian interpretation. God does not reject Adam and Eve because they succumbed to evil. He banishes them because they were becoming too godlike! Despite this more accurate reading of *Genesis*, most Jews and Christians continue to believe that God punished Adam and Eve for their disobedience.

Consider that after Adam and Eve ate from the tree of knowledge, they could discern right from wrong. In other words, they attained the ability to grasp Truth by and for themselves and, as a result, were well on their way to perfecting their own divinity. Unfortunately, God felt threatened by Adam and Eve's heightened state of awareness, just as the Sumerian god Enlil began to fear the endowed human beings crafted by his brother, the god Enki. Consequently, God decided to throw Adam and Eve out of the garden to prevent them from also eating from the tree of life and becoming immortal, as God did not want them to achieve total divinity. Hence, the true meaning behind the Jewish/Sumerian parable of creation centers on the mystical powers contained in the two magical trees. One tree offered humanity the intellectual capacity needed to comprehend Truth, the burden of which Eve accepted when she chose wisdom over ignorance. And the other tree continues to offer humanity the spiritual immortality needed to join with God, which is a benefit that is much more difficult to achieve.

In sum, the Jewish creation myth contains very important lessons, almost all of which have been misinterpreted. Here is an alternative interpretation of the parable:

1. From the ether of the First Spiritual Paradigm, God created mankind based on a Divine image. The masculine half of God, which represents the ability to create, made both man and woman "after Our image." In the Jewish creation myth, the Garden of Eden represents this primordial and perfect paradigm – a time when humanity and God were one.

2. The serpent, who symbolizes wisdom and the feminine half of God, gave mankind the option of an autonomous existence ... life outside the ether. Eve chose to eat from the tree of knowledge because she sought Truth about herself and God. Hence, her act was not a sin. Rather, her choice is a metaphor for our unique gifts from God:

free will and intellect. And the "fall of mankind" represents the shift from the First to the Second Spiritual Paradigm (i.e., our perceived separation from God, a/k/a the Big Bang).

3. Mankind has the ability to achieve immortality, just like God, but only if we eat from the tree of life. Originally, God blocked us from reaching this goal, not because we are sinful, but because we have to earn this right. We earn immortality (i.e., salvation) by perfecting our soul. And we perfect our soul by returning again and again to the tree of knowledge. *In other words, we first must undergo the Saddha process of soul growth.* That is how we enter the Fifth Spiritual Paradigm and achieve enlightenment. Luckily, because all of us were created by and from God, we all have the potential to become Divine. But it takes hard work.

Because the Jewish interpretation of their own creation myth does not flow logically from the text of the *Old Testament*, core tenets of Judaism are philosophically suspect and, therefore, violate *Rule Number 1* of *The Seven Rules of Any Good Religion.*

Moreover, some Jews still believe in a literal interpretation of this creation myth. Indeed, much of the world is holding fast to the simplistic and uneducated notion that God created the Universe in six days and that this all happened around 4000 B.C.E. Specifically, orthodox Jews (and fundamentalist Christians) continue to deny the science of evolution. This refusal to accept modern science is a yoke around the neck of mankind, as it denies the Truth of our planet's long history and mankind's complex physical and spiritual ascent. As summarized in the Appendix, scientists have concluded that the Earth is roughly 4.6 billion years old and that mankind evolved just like every other creature on this planet.

Consequently, the orthodox Jewish religion and all other fundamentalist religions that fail to recognize the scientific fact of evolution violate *Rule Number 2*, which requires us to utilize our stupendous intellect to better understand the full breadth of God's glory.

Some of you may ask why this matters. What harm can there be in an ancient religion holding on to some patently unscientific mythology regarding the creation of Earth and mankind? *The answer is that incredible harm always results from the denial or subversion of Truth.*

First, the denial of scientific Truth constitutes a great sin, given our God-given intellect and the advanced state of our scientific research. God gave us our amazing brain power to utilize in a methodical and rational fashion. Failing to use our intellect is a shameful waste of one of God's primary gifts to us – the very gift that separates us from the other living creatures on Earth. It is simply wrong, on a very fundamental level, not to apply our intellect to its full capacity.

Second, by failing to acknowledge the now elementary science of evolution, orthodox Jews and evangelical Christians have demonstrated a willingness to suppress Truth. And while we could blame church leaders for stubbornly promoting traditional interpretations of creation myths, it is the laity's lack of intellectual processing that implicitly gives clerics permission to both misinterpret ancient scripture and suppress new scientific discoveries. Put simply, intellectual laziness by the masses almost always leads to an abuse of power by those in positions of authority. Frankly, if they can convince you today that mankind – unlike every other species on Earth – escaped the evolutionary process, what will they be able to convince you of tomorrow?

Third, even feigned ignorance by only part of this planet's inhabitants affects everyone. Conversely, enhanced knowledge benefits us all, since it raises the collective consciousness. Therefore, another way to add to God's Tower of Truth is by educating those who are scaling a man-made Tower of Babel. The Truth is that every ancient civilization composed a creation myth. Why on Earth, then, would we give more credence to the Jewish version than to the Chinese? What I find interesting, however, are the legends' similarities. For instance, many of the tales foreshadowed the Truth that life sprang from water. Today, scientists know that all forms of life on Earth began in the oceans, as outlined in the Appendix. Thus, even though God did not author any of the creation myths, it is evident that many of them were divinely inspired.

Fourth, once we all accept the science of evolution, we will have one less point of conflict. The more we share in terms of common beliefs, the better. Our species tends to fight when we disagree on basic precepts. Let us be done with this issue, as it is a waste of time, energy, money, school board hearings, and judicial resources. If there is a "missing link" in mankind's evolution, it occurred around 200,000 B.C.E., and its eventual discovery will not undermine the science of evolution. Therefore, let us apply our passion to purposeful debates on authentic topics of worldwide concern, such as our unjust and inadequate distribution of resources to the poor and our negligent destruction of our planet's ecosystem. These are the issues we should be discussing in the 21st Century, not human evolution, a topic which enlightened man resolved a century ago.

Fortunately, the vast majority of Jews are open to new scientific discoveries, are willing to revisit and reinterpret their wisdom parables in light of modern circumstances, and are eager to synthesize new information which brings us closer to the ultimate Truth, which means that the Jewish religion, on the whole, passes muster with *Rule Number 6.*

Before we leave the topic of creation and the parable about Adam and Eve, we should explore the concept of sin in a little more detail so that we understand the slight yet critical difference between the Jewish and Christian interpretations of this fable. First, most Jews believe that Adam and Eve sinned when they disobeyed God. However, Jews do *not* believe that this sin forever tainted mankind. Instead, the Jewish tradition correctly teaches that God gave each of us the freedom to choose good or evil. Second, it is customary for Jews to ponder and then judge their own actions to determine if they are living in accordance with God's commandments. Specifically, during the Jewish **High Holy Days**, which is a ten day period beginning with **Rosh Hashanah** (the Jewish New Year), and culminating with **Yom Kippur** (the Day of Atonement), Jews repent for the sins they committed over the past year and make a pledge to themselves and to God to improve spiritually in the upcoming year. Thus, Jews comprehend an essential Truth: *We are solely responsible for our spiritual destiny.*

Unfortunately, the Catholic Church embellished the Jewish creation myth by adopting the fiction of **"Original Sin,"** which attaches to all new souls at birth. In addition, Christians retroactively ascribed to Jesus the task of opening the gates of heaven by dying for mankind's original and accumulated sins. *The net result is that sin became a defining characteristic in both the Jewish and Christian traditions, although much more damning in Christian theology.*

This core Judeo-Christian belief, that mankind is inherently unworthy of joining with God, necessarily impacts how we view ourselves. It also impedes our spiritual growth. Therefore, let us examine the interplay between free will and sin to determine whether the Judeo-Christian legacy of sin has in any way dampened our spirit or limited our perception of our own divinity.

The premise of the Judeo-Christian belief system is that mankind was somehow defective at the outset; otherwise, Eve would not have disobeyed God. But what does this supposition about mankind's nature say about God? Simple logic dictates only a few possible axioms concerning mankind's nature as juxtaposed against God's nature, each of which we will consider:

1. Mankind is sinful because God is fallible (pagan view);
2. Mankind is sinful but God is perfect (Jewish and Christian view); or
3. Mankind is good because God is perfect (Buddhist and Muslim view).

Regarding the first possible scenario, the vast majority of the human race now correctly views God as omniscient (i.e., all knowing) and omnipotent (i.e., all powerful). Recall, though, that the pagans believed that their deities possessed human emotions and acted out their shortcomings on humans (e.g., anger and lust). Consequently, it is conceivable that a pagan god might mis-create Adam and then be shocked at the outcome. However, it is simply impossible that the Supreme Being would unintentionally imbue Adam with the power to choose evil over good. Therefore, just because we find it hard to understand our own nature and tame it does not mean that God is surprised by our actions. For these reasons, I think we can safely rule out the first expla-nation for mankind's intermittent bad behavior and agree, at a minimum, that God is perfect.

Next, let us consider the Judeo-Christian view that mankind is prone to sin. If we agree that God is omniscient, then God knows everything, includ-ing our nature. Moreover, if we agree that God is omnipotent, then logically mankind cannot be sinful unless God wanted us that way. Therefore, if God is perfect but God designed us to be imperfect, then, by definition, God's design for us still is perfect in the sense that it was fully intended and engi-neered by God.

Consequently, any religion which teaches that God is perfect but that mankind is sinful by nature must logically conclude that God *wanted* mankind to be sinful. Otherwise, we're right back to the first explanation for our bad behavior – that God is fallible. Inevitably, then, the Judeo-Christian tenet that mankind is sinful begs the question: *Why would God create crea-tures who have a predominantly sinful nature?*

The only semi-rational answer to this question is that God made us sin-ful because God wanted our default mode to be evil. In other words, we wouldn't be sinful unless God wanted us to be bad or unless God expected us to use our free will to choose evil over good. Either way, this scenario produces a paradox, since it suggests that God *prefers* evil. In addition, this would mean that we are doomed as a race. Not surprisingly, fundamental-ist Christians think that Jesus (no longer a pacifist) will return to Earth to play an instrumental role in destroying and judging the human race. Logically, then, the position that mankind is prone to sin but that God is perfect makes no sense, unless you accept the bizarre conclusion that: (i) God designed us to be evil; and (ii) God created us with the intention of destroying us sometime in the future.

Now, let's examine the third possible alternative – that mankind is inherently good. Admittedly, God made us fallible. Therefore, as with the second scenario, we need to assume that mankind is imperfect by design. Unlike the second supposition, however, we now are assuming that mankind is inherently good. If mankind is imperfect but innately good, then mankind is only *susceptible* to sin, not *prone* to it. Furthermore, if mankind is inherently good, then our default mode is love, not hate. Now, we're being positive! Rather than seeing the glass as half empty, we see it as half full ... and more. Yet, even this axiom begs difficult questions: *Why would God want us even to be tempted by evil? Why not make us immune to such temptation and totally good?*

The answer is that God intended for us to seek, learn, stretch, and grow in order to earn our own divinity. Unless and until we perfect our souls, we are not worthy of joining with God, who is perfect. Thus, despite the Judeo-Christian interpretation of creation, God knew for a certainty that Adam and Eve would eat from the tree of knowledge of good and bad. God also knew that they would want to eat from the tree of life. Consequently, this parable is merely a metaphor for mankind's desire for intellectual and spiritual growth – the *Saddha* experience.

The Truth is: (i) God is omniscient and omnipotent; (ii) Mankind is inherently good because God gave us the innate ability to perfect ourselves; (iii) God wants and expects us to reach our Divine potential; and (iv) No one else can do this hard work for us.

During the course of my studies, I have read the footnotes to the Jewish *Torah* and I have spoken with Jewish friends about the creation parable. As a result, I have learned that Reform Jews have reached the same conclusions I have about the nature of mankind and the nature of God. Generally speaking, the Jews have a love of education and are willing to reexamine their parables based on the enlightened state of the human condition and craft contemporary interpretations.

Nevertheless, some of the traditional Jewish tenets leave me feeling sad and alienated from the God of the *Old Testament*. First, there's the belief that God is male and that only Adam was created in God's image. Then there's the view that mankind, although not innately sinful, is not worthy of joining God.

There also are the *Old Testament* stories in which God wreaks mayhem whenever mankind fails to obey him. Honestly, it is hard for me to feel inspired by a figure that is so fearsome, vindictive, and merciless. Consider these examples of God's wrath, first toward the Jews (who supposedly are his "chosen" or favorite people), and then against one of their enemies.

> *When Solomon was old his wives had turned his heart to strange gods ....*
> *By adoring Astarte, the goddess of the Sidonians, and Milcom, the idol*
> *of the Ammonites, Solomon did evil in the sight of the Lord .... So the*
> *Lord said to Solomon: "Since this is what you want, and you have not*
> *kept my covenant and my statutes which I enjoined on you, I will*
> *deprive you of the kingdom and give it to your servant."*

> *Kings 1*, Chapter 11:4–11

> *That night the angel of the Lord went forth and struck down one*
> *hundred and eighty-five thousand men in the Assyrian camp. Early the*
> *next morning, there they were, all the corpses of the dead.*

> *Kings 2*, Chapter 19:35

Frankly, I find the God of the *Old Testament* so vengeful that I become detached when I read it. God repeatedly exhibits unpredictable anger, pronounces harsh judgment, and doles out ruthless punishment on humanity. Overall, God's reaction to mankind's flaws is unforgiving. Indeed, the temperament of the ancient Jewish God is very close to the pagan gods and goddesses worshiped by the Babylonians, the Egyptians, the Greeks, and the Romans, which were the dominant societies at the time the Jewish scripture was written. Recall that the Gentiles believed in pantheons of deities who constantly meddled in human affairs. If angered, a god might cast down a lightning bolt from heaven or stir the oceans and flood the land. If bored, a goddess might assume the form of an animal and mingle with humans. And if they felt lustful, the gods and goddesses were known to consort with humans and even beget children. For example, the Greeks believed that **Zeus** had a son named **Hercules** by a mortal princess, and the Romans thought that Julius Caesar was descendant from **Venus** and a human mate named Prince Anchises.

To my 21st Century mind, these myths are amusing and show how desperately ancient man wanted to personify God. Intuitively, though, most of us now know that God's nature is balanced, nurturing, tolerant, and forgiving. Also, I don't think we need to worry anymore about God taking sexual liberties with human females. Therefore, it is not surprising that as mankind evolved spiritually, the later Prophets began to describe God as merciful and compassionate. Most notably, Jesus preached that we are all children of God and that God is always available to comfort us, particularly when we are lost. This is the God depicted in the *New Testament* and in *The Holy Quran*. And it is this updated image of God, as a benevolent force, which has the potential to inspire us.

In sum, because the Jewish portrayal of the Supreme Being includes many negative human emotions, such as anger, disdain, and vindictiveness, rather than Divine traits, such as compassion, acceptance, and forgiveness, the Jewish religion fails to pass *Rule Number 7*, which requires an inspirational atmosphere in which to build faith. Likewise, to the extent that Judaism portrays mankind as prone to sin or unworthy of joining God in heaven, the religion violates the positive spiritual mandates of *Rule Number 7*.

Genesis continues with the story of Abraham, whose sons Ishmael and Isaac are the ancestral fathers of Islam and Judaism, respectively. When God first talks to Abraham, God instructs him to leave his homeland and start a new nation (i.e., new religion), that will benefit all of civilization.

> *The Lord said to Abram, "Go forth from the land of your kinsfolk ... to a land that I will show you. I will make of you a great nation, and I will bless you; I will make your name great, so that you will be a blessing. I will bless those who bless you and curse those who curse you. **All the communities of the earth shall find blessing in you.**" [Emphasis added]*

Genesis, Chapter 12:1–3

Thereafter, God formalizes his promise to mankind by making a "covenant" with Abraham.

> *My covenant with you is this: You are to become the father of a **host of nations**. No longer shall you be called Abram; your name shall be Abraham, for I am making you the father of a host of nations. I will render you exceedingly fertile. **I will make nations of you**; kings shall stem from you. I will maintain my covenant with you and your descendants after you as an everlasting pact, to be your God and the God of your descendants after you. [Emphasis added]*

Genesis, Chapter 17:4–7

Thus, God tells Abraham that he will father multiple nations. Specifically, God says in *Genesis* Chapter 17 that Ishmael, Abraham's first born son by an Egyptian woman, will father a "great nation." The Jews believe that Hagar was a servant, but the Muslims believe she was Abraham's second wife. God even repeats the pledge to Ishmael in Chapter 21, when Abraham's wife,

Sarah, has a second son named Isaac. Thus, God tells Abraham that *both* of his sons will father great nations. Incidentally, Abraham marries a third time and has even more children.

Thereafter, *Genesis* focuses exclusively on Abraham's second son, Isaac, and his progeny. The "chieftains" spawned by Ishmael are briefly mentioned in Chapter 25 and then dismissed. This theme of preferring the second-born son is repeated in Chapter 27, when Isaac's second son, Jacob, tricks his blind father into giving him the family blessing. Consequently, Isaac's first son, Esau, is disinherited. Esau implores his father to retract the blessing, but Isaac seems powerless to correct the mistake. The bizarre result is that the dishonest Jacob becomes heir to the covenant between God and Abraham. Apparently content with this twist of fate, God changes Jacob's name to Israel and then pledges the promised land of Canaan to Israel and his descendants. To help keep everyone straight, let's look at the Jewish genealogy chart one more time.

JEWISH FAMILY TREE

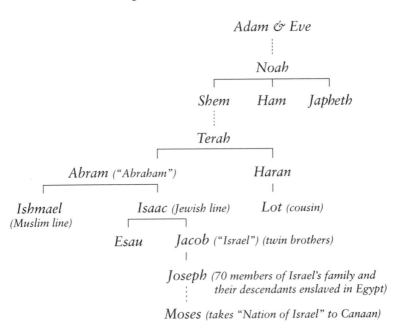

Adam & Eve

Noah

Shem   *Ham*   *Japheth*

Terah

Abram ("Abraham")   *Haran*

Ishmael   *Isaac (Jewish line)*   *Lot (cousin)*
(Muslim line)

Esau   *Jacob ("Israel") (twin brothers)*

*Joseph (70 members of Israel's family and
      their descendants enslaved in Egypt)*

Moses (takes "Nation of Israel" to Canaan)

I find the above passages fascinating because the Jews will later interpret them as meaning that God was creating only one nation for only one of Abraham's many sons. However, that is not how *Genesis* reads. Rather, God declares in *Genesis* that he will give Abraham millions of descendants who will form many nations which will be ruled by many kings. *Therefore, a more reasonable interpretation of Genesis is that God spoke with Abraham regarding his connection to all people and that all nations which accept God as the Supreme Being shall be blessed.*

Despite this fairer reading of *Genesis*, Jews have traditionally interpreted these passages as stating that God favored Abraham, then his second son Isaac, and then Isaac's second son Jacob. Moreover, the Jews completely discount the pledge God makes to Ishmael, Abraham's first son and patriarch of the Islamic religion. Admittedly, God says to Abraham in Chapter 12 of *Genesis* that he will lead Abraham to the promised land in Canaan, and God repeats this promise to Isaac in Chapter 26 and to Jacob in Chapter 28. However, God does not forsake the other members of Abraham's family, nor Noah's other descendants. For example, God plainly states that Ishmael also will father a great nation (*Genesis* 17:20; 21:13). God forbids Moses from making war against the Edomites because they are descendant from Esau (*Deuteronomy* 2:4). God also forbids Moses from attacking the Moabites because they are descendant from Abraham's nephew, Lot (*Deuteronomy* 2:9).

Consequently, I take huge exception with the core Jewish belief that God made a covenant with only one branch of Abraham's descendants. The *Old Testament* itself contradicts the assertion that only Jacob's descendants (i.e., the Jews who were enslaved in Egypt and who later were called the "nation of Israel") were meant to benefit from the covenant. Clearly, God made the promise to multiple patriarchs and, more logically, to all the Hebrew (i.e., non-Egyptian) nations that were willing to accept God as the one and only Supreme Being.

Furthermore, it is incomprehensible to me that God would "prefer" one race or even one monotheistic religion over another, and I find little basis for this tenet when I read the relevant passages of the *Old Testament*. It was the pagan religions that offended God. The other tribes in the *Old Testament* that believed in God also received God's protection, and the Jews were told not to make war against them.

Therefore, the myopic Jewish interpretation of *Genesis*, that God is only interested in the spiritual growth of one of many Hebrew tribes, patently violates *Rule Number 4* regarding the uniform and fair application of God's law.

Most Jews still believe that God will send them a human Messiah who will lead the Jewish people for a final time to the promised land. As a result, some

Jews believe that the present nation of Israel, created through war in 1948 C.E., is not sanctioned by God because they did not wait for the Messiah to appear. The forced taking of Palestine by the Jews also has not produced the peace and harmony predicted in the *Old Testament* prophecies. Recall that the Jewish Prophets envisioned worldwide peace after the Jews return to Israel. While the scope of this book does not permit me to indulge in proposing a solution to the Israeli-Palestinian conflict, a solution must be found ... and fast. For now, though, let us ponder the notion that God wants the Jews to have a special home and that when the Jews finally are settled, the rest of us will enjoy worldwide harmony.

While the world certainly would be more peaceful without the Israeli-Palestinian conflict, that is not the main focus of the Jewish prophecies regarding the Messianic Age. Rather, the Jewish version of the final conflict between good and evil presupposes a favored status for the Jews after the dust settles. The *Old Testament* prophecies state that there will be great wars and massive Earth changes, as the righteous fight the evildoers. Then the Messiah, who is from the House of David, will appear to lead the children of Israel back to the Holy Land. In addition, those righteous people who died before the Messiah arrives will resurrect. Once installed on his throne in Jerusalem, the Messiah will rule and the righteous will live forever. Finally, the Earth will be transformed once again into the Garden of Eden and mankind finally will witness the dawn of everlasting peace due to God's renewed covenant with Israel. Thus, most Jews believe that only they and their Messiah can lead mankind to everlasting peace.

Again, it is hard for me to imagine God having a preference for just one race or religion. Fortunately, when I read the *Old Testament* for myself, I find numerous inconsistencies with the Jewish predictions about the Messianic Age, which lead me to conclude, once again, that the Jews have not correctly interpreted their own prophecies. For example, the later Jewish prophets make clear that *everyone* who is good will survive the final conflict and be entitled to partake in an Earth plane paradise. Even though Jerusalem and the House of David remain special to God, all nations which accept God and are righteous will receive the same treatment on Judgment Day. Thus, the prophecies state that God will renew his covenant with all of mankind, not just the surviving Jews.

> *Many peoples and strong nations shall come to seek the Lord of hosts in Jerusalem and to implore the favor of the Lord. Thus says the Lord*

of hosts: In those days **ten men of every nationality,** *speaking different tongues, shall take hold, yes, take hold of every Jew by the edge of his garment and say, "Let us go with you, for we have heard that God is with you." [Emphasis added]*

Zechariah, Chapter 8:22

The above passage and many others from the *Old Testament* verify God's intent to treat all of mankind fairly and equitably. To me, the Jewish prophecies, when correctly interpreted, provide ample proof that God loves all of us the same and that all of us may benefit from the covenant originally made with Abraham. Furthermore, I don't believe we have to wait for a Messiah, or Armageddon, or Jesus in order to renew our covenant with God. As previously discussed in Chapter Two, the later Prophets all clarified that God is always available to anyone who seeks spiritual Truth.

Nevertheless, many Jews continue to believe that they are God's "chosen people" and that they enjoy a special relationship with God that the rest of us can neither fully understand nor share. Moreover, when the Messiah finally appears, some Jews still believe that they will receive preferential treatment in paradise. Consequently, I must conclude that the core Jewish tenet, that God chose just one Hebrew tribe for special treatment, smacks of cultural prejudice.

Because many Jews still believe that they enjoy an elevated status with God as the "chosen people," that they were given the "promised land," and that ultimately a Jewish Messiah will rule mankind, the religion is premised on an egocentric as opposed to an inclusive foundation, in direct violation of *Rule Number 5.*

While I cannot accept the notion that God prefers the Jews, I can accept the Jewish belief that God chose Abraham as a messenger to impart the Truth of monotheism. The later Prophets agreed with Abraham that there is only one God, and almost all human beings now accept the fact that one form of intelligent energy is responsible for creating the Universe. Thus, Abraham deserves credit for bravely affirming the Truth of monotheism in the face of incredible opposition from the pagan Hebrews and Egyptians. However, contrary to what most of us have been taught, Abraham was not the first person in history to believe in a single deity. Rather, Abraham (or Zarathustra or Akhenaten) was the first person in *recorded history* to discover this Truth.

Archeological evidence from statuary, carvings, and cave drawings shows that prior to recorded history, early man believed in the Great Mother (i.e., that God is female). This was a logical conclusion for humans to reach, based on their uneducated assumption that women are the sole creators of life. The time now is approximately 25,000 B.C.E. During this relatively late stage of mankind's evolution, humans lived in small groups and worked as "hunter/gatherers" to sustain themselves. At that time, there was little distinction between male and female "roles." Basically, our species was in survival mode and everyone worked full time to put food on the proverbial table. To the extent that the earliest tribes contemplated God at all, they concluded that God must be female because women carry and give birth to children. Therefore, they deduced that Goddess must be the Supreme Creator. It was a fairly rational conclusion based on the state of their reproductive knowledge.

Later, mankind learned that both sexes physically contribute to the creation of offspring. In addition, sociologists believe that when mankind learned to grow food, the nomadic hunter lifestyle slowly succumbed to the **Age of Agriculture**. Thereafter, a more clearly defined division of labor started to evolve between the sexes. The result was that women started to tend to permanent home sites and men worked in the fields and raised livestock. Eventually, nomadic tribes turned into true communities, as people put down roots, both literally and figuratively. The Appendix contains a map showing the four great river valleys which supported mankind's earliest organized societies, collectively referred to as the Cradles of Civilization.

Once true communities formed, another sociological pattern developed. People were less likely to abandon their homes. In the event of a threat, tribes would choose to fight and protect their territory rather than seek safer ground, as they were more apt to do when they lived a nomadic lifestyle. Eventually, during times of war, men defended their communities and women stayed at home. Over time, women's contributions to society were discounted by men, and women were deemed the "weaker" sex. It was at this juncture that mankind went through its first paradigm shift and abandoned the monotheism of Goddess in favor of polytheism, a spiritual belief system based on multiple male and female deities.

As the Appendix shows, mankind believed in Goddess for roughly twenty thousand years. In fact, some archeologists date Goddess worship to 200,000 B.C.E. Then, with the advent of the Third Spiritual Paradigm, mankind believed in multiple gods and goddesses and adopted a pagan theology for about five thousand years. Finally, Zarathustra, Abraham, and the Chinese and Greek philosophers reintroduced the notion of a single God force, but it took a while for this concept to supplant polytheism. Not until well after Jesus died, did mankind start to accept one Supreme Being again. It was at this juncture that humanity entered the Fourth Spiritual Paradigm.

Unfortunately, the early Hebrews could not resist the urge to personify God. Remember, they started out as and were surrounded by pagans. As a result, the early Jews often reverted to polytheism and used masculine terminology to refer to God. Consequently, it is worth pausing for a moment to ponder why the first Jews, who brilliantly anticipated the Fourth Spiritual Paradigm, had a hard time believing that one God could have both masculine and feminine energies. *Why did Abraham correctly surmise that there is only one God, but then treat God as a male deity?*

Historians suggest that mankind personified God based on the mistaken belief that the Earth is the center of the Universe and the narcissistic assumption that God must look like us. Psychologists would add that during the early phases of child development, we all pass through a cognitive stage in which we myopically perceive ourselves as the focal point of existence. Hence, babies are naturally egocentric because the newborn brain is wired only to project physical needs. Even as toddlers, we still respond to the immediacy of bodily functions and to the yearnings of emotional needs. Only later, as the brain develops, do children learn how to think abstractly and in a compassionate manner. It may be helpful to recall Maslow's Hierarchy of Needs. In essence, children operate at the lowest tiers of Maslow's chart, since their overriding concern is to secure their own physical and emotional comfort.

Similarly, people who feel the need to personify God are at a lower tier of spiritual comprehension. While it may make sense initially to teach children that God is like a "father" in order to help them build faith, feel secure, and start connecting to God, it is a very different matter when adults view God as a parental figure. Thus, when an adult personifies the Supreme Being, he too is succumbing to childish fears and insecurities. It may make us feel special to imagine God as a benevolent and forgiving father figure. Nevertheless, it is tantamount to viewing God as a child views the stuffed animal he takes to bed at night. Spiritually mature souls know this Truth: *The Supreme Being is not humanlike and is far beyond our comprehension, even today.*

Ironically, Abraham's inclination to personify and attach the male gender to God has *not* brought us comfort in the long run. Rather, it has caused undue pain to the women worldwide who now seek their just position as full partners on the Earth plane. Making God male may have worked for thousands of years to herd humanity onto a more correct path, but the path to Truth should not have stopped there. I suppose, though, that it would have been too much to expect the early Hebrews to depart totally from their pagan roots and their cultural male bias and simply view God as a positive energy source.

Today, many Jews realize that God, although a single entity, contains both masculine and feminine energies. However, some Jews continue to view God as a masculine force. This lingering male preference, combined with the notion that Eve committed the first sin, has led to a multitude of problems for Jewish women and for women born into the other two religions of Abraham. As we shall soon see, the misogyny planted by Judaism later took root in both Christianity and Islam. Thus, the patriarchal image of God, first introduced by the Jewish religion around 2000 B.C.E., has negatively impacted women for thousands of years and still constitutes a serious impediment to mankind's collective spiritual growth.

In sum, the systemic misogyny which still pervades orthodox Judaism is offensive to enlightened 21st Century men and women and violates three of *The Seven Rules of Any Good Religion*. First, treating God as a male deity has resulted in the separate and unequal treatment of women, in direct contravention to *Rule Number 4*, which requires a religion to treat all souls fairly and uniformly. Second, continuing to view God as masculine energy, particularly after the Jewish Kabbalists rediscovered the concept of Divine feminine energy, shows that some Jews are not open to change and have yet to update their belief system as mandated by *Rule Number 6*. Third, glorifying God as a predominantly male force is overtly harmful to women and contravenes *Rule Number 7*, which requires a religion to spiritually nurture all of its members.

In conclusion, the Jewish religion, particularly as practiced by orthodox Jews, violates many of *The Seven Rules of Any Good Religion*. We can attribute this low score to the fact that Judaism, as arguably the oldest surviving monotheistic religion on Earth, is now four thousand years old. Thus, just as with Hinduism, the Jewish religion at this point is in need of a major overhaul. Otherwise, Judaism will not be ready to contend with the complex realities and intense challenges facing mankind in the 21st Century.

I readily and happily concede, however, that the Reform Jewish movement is much more open to change and actually promotes healthy theological debate. Indeed, some Jews no longer are waiting for a human Messiah.

Instead, they believe that the Messianic Age will arrive when humanity finally embraces the prophesied Fifth Spiritual Paradigm. We will discuss the upcoming Fifth Spiritual Paradigm in more detail when we get to Chapter Five. With regard to Judaism and the other four man-made religions, though, we should not be surprised that these now ancient religions no longer satisfy those men and women who crave a more accurate and sophisticated spiritual belief system.

Finally, I want to underscore the horrid state of civilization during the eras in which Abraham and Moses lived. At the time the Jewish religion was formed, the Arab world was chaotic and violent. Outside the ordered confines of the Egyptian Empire, the Hebrew tribes lived a harsh nomadic lifestyle, and their pagan gods and goddesses provided little spiritual guidance.

On the other hand, the new Hebrew God provided ordered rules for a moral society. The Ten Commandments and the other laws that God gave Moses were more than practical. Indeed, Mosaic law was morally and ethically superior to the standards followed by the other cultures of that time. For instance, not only did the Jewish laws promote a healthy and civilized environment, they also provided a reference point for compassionate living. Generally speaking, then, the Jewish laws constitute a sound code of conduct that the Jewish people still follow today. Moreover, Mosaic law provides Jewish families with a strong foundation for moral and spiritual growth. Specifically, the Jewish tradition teaches that the only way to pass God's final judgment is to perform *good works*.

Therefore, the Jewish religion comports with *Rule Number 3* because it provides fixed standards of moral and ethical behavior, and it correctly affirms that each soul is personally responsible for attaining spiritual enlightenment in accordance with God's laws.

Thus, the ancient Hebrew belief that God favored the Jews is not that disturbing when viewed in the relevant historical context. In ancient times, your gods and goddesses protected you, just as other tribes' gods and goddesses protected them. In fact, tribal wars often started over whose gods were stronger, and warlords thought their deities led them into battle. Consequently, if a tribe lost a war, they thought it was because the other tribe's gods were more powerful. Therefore, the Jewish belief that Yahweh loved only them was a common notion for that era.

It also was normal at that time for mankind to feel unworthy of joining the gods and goddesses in heaven. Many cultures believed in an afterlife, but most of them thought they would remain on the Earth plane. The Egyptians are a prime example. They believed in a physical afterlife based on a bodily existence, which explains why they mummified themselves and buried their treasures with them. As George Carlin would say, they wanted their "stuff" for the afterlife. Thus, the Jewish belief in a bodily resurrection also was consistent with the era.

Today, however, many of the Jewish precepts seem irrational and untenable for all the reasons we have explored. To further prove my point, just imagine what your reaction would be to a new "prophet" who told you that God now prefers a different race and a new religion. Imagine how you would respond to this new "messenger from God" if he claimed that only followers of his religion could get into heaven. Most of us would either laugh or be appalled, and we wouldn't give this person or his new religion the time of day. Yet, many of us stay in religions that assert this exact belief! The Judeo-Christian legacy is the most disturbing in this regard. None of the other five primary religions maintain such exclusionary dogma.

However, once we update and correctly interpret the Jewish parables, we find that the basic tenet of Judaism is that everyone will be judged by God according to the same standards. Thus, in the end it's not about which religious label we wear (or whether we wear one at all), it's about our spiritual accomplishments. *Boiled down to its bare essence, then, Judaism stands for the proposition that what matters most to God is how we treat each other on the Earth plane.*

Having thus reduced Judaism to its most beautiful core belief, I still must briefly address the ongoing Israeli-Palestinian conflict, which is a direct result of the worst core tenet of Judaism – the belief that the Jews are God's "chosen people." Honestly, I see no way to logically separate the Israeli-Palestinian conflict from the Jewish belief that God promised them land in Palestine. *This war between Arab brothers has raged on-and-off for over three thousand years.* Moreover, this conflict has been a holy war from the start. It began the day that Moses announced his intent to seize land from the other tribes who lived in the region originally known as Canaan.

It is unfortunate that many of us in the western part of the world have been led to believe that the Muslims declared military *jihad* without provocation. Blaming the Muslims also is counterproductive to arriving at a just solution to this never-ending conflict. Therefore, let us face the following Truths, all of which are chronologically discussed and mapped in the Appendix:

1. Even if you believe that God "gave" Abraham the land known as Canaan around 2000 B.C.E., the *Old Testament* reports that Abraham periodically abandoned the territory during periods of famine.

2. In approximately 1800 B.C.E., Abraham's descendants completely abandoned the territory and moved to Goshen, which was part of the Egyptian Empire. Thereafter, the Egyptians betrayed and enslaved the Jews.

3. Sometime around 1250 B.C.E., the Jews, led by Moses, escaped Egypt and started a holy war by fighting and conquering some of the other Arab tribes that already had settled in the "promised land."

4. The Jews lost Canaan repeatedly over the course of the next fifteen hundred years. They lost it for the final time when the Romans destroyed Jerusalem in 70 C.E., decimated the Jewish community, and banished the surviving Jews.

5. The Jews revived the ancient holy war when they seized Palestinian land by force in 1948 C.E. The net result is that the Jews did not have control of this region for 1,878 years, during which time various Arab nations lived in Palestine.

In sum, the reason the conflict in the Middle East constitutes a holy war is because the Jews feel that their religion entitles them to the land. The religious conviction that God promised Abraham this land four thousand years ago is one of the primary justifications for the Jews taking the land back by force in 1948. Additionally, the Jews feel entitled to this land even though they historically were unable to defend their nation and despite the fact that they were absent from, or at least not communally organized within, the region for almost two thousand years.

My point is that the Middle East conflict is not a holy war because Muslims have been struggling to get the land back for the past sixty years. Consequently, it is hypocritical for Jews to blame Muslims for this conflict or to label Muslim aggression a holy war. Without a doubt, Jews "deserve" a homeland. The question, though, is whether Palestinians "deserve" to be dispossessed.

The Truth is that both the Jews and the Muslims are to blame for the continuation of the holy war in the Middle East and for the worldwide terrorism that their religious conflict has spawned and inflicted upon the rest of us.

Today, most of us are aware that Muslim extremists have escalated the Middle East conflict, which now threatens the United States and the rest of the world. Even so, I encourage the reader to study the chronology and maps contained in the Appendix for a fuller version of this sordid tale. Suffice it to say, there is no "good guy" in this ongoing nightmare, a theme we will explore in greater detail in the Islam section of this chapter.

For now, let us simply recognize that, until recently, the Israelis have failed to return any of the land they seized in 1948, despite their informal and formal promises to make reparations to the Palestinian Arabs. Specifically, in 1993, the **Oslo Peace Accord** was signed and in 1995, **Oslo II** was signed, both of which obligated the Jews to return the Gaza Strip and the West Bank to the Palestinians, although final borders were not addressed. In contravention of these agreements, the Israeli government continues to allow Jewish settlers to move to the West Bank. In addition, the Israelis are building a 450 mile wall around Jerusalem which cuts into Palestinian marked territories. This concrete and wire barrier does not correspond to any accepted borders, and it has caused untold misery and chaos to those Muslim families, farms, and villages that have been haphazardly divided. In response, Palestinian fighters have further degraded the peace process by continuing to attack Israel.

Here is a summary of recent developments, most of which – both positive and negative – relate to the actions of Israel.

1. The Israeli people have begun to seriously protest their own government's stubborn stance in not releasing land to the Palestinians. A clear majority of Israelis (some polls indicate 70%) now want the land that has been promised to the Palestinians returned and Israeli settlers moved out of Palestinian areas.

2. In 2003, thirteen Israeli reservists from the elite Military Commando Unit wrote a letter to the Israeli prime minister demanding that the Israeli government make peace with the Palestinians. The letter states in part:

> We have long ago crossed the line between fighters fighting a just cause and oppressing another people. ... [The Israeli government is] depriving the rights of millions of Palestinians [and using soldiers as] human shields for settlements .... We will no longer butcher our humanity by taking part in an occupying army's missions .... [This letter is written] out of deep fear for the future of the state of Israel as a democratic, Zionist and Jewish country and out of concern for its moral and ethical image.

3. In 2004, the Israeli Supreme Court ruled that the wall being built around Jerusalem and into the West Bank violates the rights of Palestinians, although the Court did not indicate a new path for the wall.

4. In 2004, the International Court of Justice (a/k/a the "World Court") ruled 14 to 1 that the wall around Jerusalem violates Palestinian rights and must be torn down. The single vote in favor of the Israeli position was cast by the American judge. The United Nations passed a resolution demanding that Israel comply with the court ruling and tear down the barrier. The resolution passed 150 to 6, with Israel, the U.S., Australia, Micronesia, Palau, and the Marshal Islands opposed.

5. In 2005, after the death of Palestinian leader **Yasser Arafat**, Israeli Prime Minister **Ariel Sharon** and the new Palestinian leader **Mahmoud Abbas** agreed to a truce.

6. In 2005, Israel unilaterally withdrew from the Gaza Strip and a small part of the West Bank. Prime Minister Sharon also has promised to redirect the wall around Jerusalem, although it still will cut into the West Bank.

7. In 2006, Lebanon kidnapped two Israeli solders. In response, Israel invaded Lebanon, resulting in the death of 1,700 and the displacement of 1.1 million civilians. As a result, the Muslim fundamentalist group **Hezbollah** has gained strength in Lebanon.

8. In 2008, Israel invaded Gaza in response to **Hamas** bombings. As a result, 1,400 Palestinians were killed and 51,000 were displaced.

9. In the West Bank, Israeli settlements increased 69% in 2008, and over the past three years, the Jewish population in the West Bank has grown from 35,000 to 285,000.

10. In Jerusalem, 60,000 Palestinians (1/4 of the city's Muslim population) are at risk of eviction based on legal claims that their homes are not properly permitted.

Thus, although it appears that the Jewish people are realizing that they are morally obligated to return some land to the Palestinians, peace still is not at hand. In the Islam section of this chapter, we will probe the genesis and the current state of this holy war in more detail. For now, though, let us see whether the religion spawned by Buddha is faring better than Hinduism and Judaism in the 21st Century.

BUDDHISM

From Chapter Two, we learned that Buddha was born into a Hindu family but found Hinduism lacking in terms of spiritual substance. Consequently, Buddha broke away from Hinduism and started a new religion called Buddhism, which is more focused on spiritual attainment during the current life cycle. In other words, Buddha believed that death was not a precursor to the soul's evolution. Instead, he taught that spiritual enlightenment may come at any time.

In general, Buddhism asserts that spiritual salvation (*nirvana*) depends on the following three factors: (i) Earth plane acts and their consequences (*karma*); (ii) personal spiritual work (*Saddha*); and (iii) enlightenment which comes from knowing the Truth (*Dharma*). For these reasons alone, Buddhism is a revolutionary advancement over the earlier religions, since Buddhism recognizes that salvation requires personal dedication to Truth and selfless acts of kindness. Thus, Buddhists believe that faith in God is not good enough to attain *nirvana. Rather, spiritual enlightenment depends on learning the Truth about God and the Universe, which requires more work than worship.*

In sum, Buddha taught that we must save ourselves. He also taught that blind faith, without true understanding, keeps us forever locked on the Earth plane. Thus, in order to attain *nirvana*, we must perfect ourselves, and no one, not even our favorite Prophet, can accomplish this mission for us.

> *Oneself indeed is patron of oneself.*
> *Who else indeed could be one's patron?*
> *With oneself well restrained,*
> *One gets a patron hard to get.*
> *By oneself is wrong done;*
> *By oneself is one defiled.*
> *By oneself wrong is not done;*
> *By oneself, surely, one is cleansed.*
> *One cannot purify another;*
> *Purity and impurity are in oneself alone.*

The Dhammapada, Sutra XII, Verses 160, 165

The Buddhist belief system constitutes a radical departure from Hinduism and Judaism, which focus primarily on the worship of external deities who have the power to grant humans redemption (i.e., gods, goddesses, and God). Thus, to Hindus and Jews, ritualistic worship is more than half of the equation for attaining salvation. To Buddhists, however, faith in a particular god, goddess, or even in God is a secondary concern. *Specifically, Buddhists believe that release from the Earth plane is a hard won privilege that must be earned by each individual soul.*

> *Few are they among humans,*
> *The people who reach the shore beyond.*
> *But these other folk only run along the hither bank.*
> *But those who live according to Dharma -*
> *In Dharma well proclaimed -*
> *Those people will reach the shore beyond.*
> *The realm of death is hard to cross.*

> *The Dhammapada*, Sutra VI, Verses 85–86

That is not to say that Buddha lacked faith in God. Like the Jews, Buddha expressed a belief in one main God, whom he called Brahma. Also like the Jews, Buddha believed that good works and the accumulation of positive *karma* is very important. But unlike the Jews, Buddha taught that *Dharma* is the key to eternal release from the Earth plane and spiritual *nirvana*. Consequently, Buddha correctly deemed irrelevant all man-made rules, rituals, and religions. Instead, Buddha taught this logical and essential Truth: *In order to meet God, a soul must learn and experience Dharma by and for itself.*

> *Anyone who withdraws into meditation on compassion can see Brahma with his own eyes, talk to him face to face and consult with him.*

> *Digha Nikaya*, Chapter 19, Verse 43

Because Buddha understood that the process of acquiring faith (*Saddha*), requires a personal relationship with God and a quest for Truth, and because he clearly explained how this process leads to *nirvana*, Buddhism more than passes muster with the philosophical mandates of *Rule Number 1* of *The Seven Rules of Any Good Religion*.

Buddha also believed in the scientific principle called *karma* – that all action produces a result, both in the seen and unseen worlds. In a metaphysical sense, then, Buddha's understanding of *karma* is an earlier statement of Sir Isaac Newton's theory regarding the science of physics: "For every action, there is an equal and opposite reaction."

Thus, the scientific basis for *karma* is not only completely logical, it also has been accepted, endorsed, and taught by all the great Prophets, philosophers, and scientists. Rational minds may debate whether *karma* impacts only one life (as the Jews, the Christians, and the Muslims believe), or whether *karma* impacts and determines the nature of multiple lives (as the Hindus and Buddhists believe). Nevertheless, the Buddhist belief in the Universal Law of *karma*, that for every cause there is an effect, is a proven scientific fact on the Earth plane.

Consequently, it is only logical to assume that *karma* also applies to the Ethereal plane. Undoubtedly, our actions must impact our ability to achieve salvation. Therefore, if we assume that *karma* impacts our soul in some way, then the issue becomes how and to what degree our actions affect our spiritual development. That mystery then begs this question about the afterlife: *Does accumulated karma render one worthy or unworthy to go to heaven after just one life, or does karma determine successive incarnations and, ultimately, our ability to reach nirvana?*

Those who subscribe to the three religions of Abraham believe in only one Earth plane experience for each soul prior to God's redemption. Consider, though, that reincarnation makes more philosophical sense once we accept the responsibility of achieving God's grace on our own. In other words, a benevolent God would grant us multiple opportunities to perfect ourselves.

> *Should a person do a wrong,*
> *Let him not do it again and again.*
> *Let him not form a desire toward it.*
> *A suffering is the accumulation of wrong.*
>
> *Should a person do some good,*
> *Let him do it again and again.*
> *Let him form a desire toward it.*
> *A happiness is the accumulation of good.*
>
> *Think not trifling of good,*
> *'It will not come to me!'*
> *With falling drops of water,*
> *Even a waterpot is filled.*
> *A wise one is filled with good,*
> *Acquiring bit by bit.*
>
> *Some are born in a womb,*
> *Wrongdoers, in hell.*
> *Those of good courses go to heaven,*
> *To Nirvana those without influxes.*

The Dhammapada, Sutra IX, Verses 117, 118, 122

Reincarnation also makes sense from a scientific standpoint. First, scientists know that energy can change form and even gain strength (e.g., nuclear fission). Likewise, transfiguration accounts for the apparent loss of body energy at death. Second, there are well-documented case histories of prior life recollections at major universities and research centers throughout the world. Most notably, the Association for Research and Enlightenment, located at Virginia Beach, contains hundreds of readings given by **Edgar Cayce**, a 20th Century healer and psychic who, among other things, dated the Great Pyramid to 10,000 B.C.E., the date now being considered by some scientists.

Regardless of whether you think God gives us just one shot or multiple chances to earn a place in heaven, the law of *karma* is incorporated, to some degree, in almost every religion. Buddha merely clarified that our *karma* dictates how quickly (or slowly) we spiritually evolve. Thus, it is our Earth plane actions, not our religious affiliation, that God will judge when deciding whether we are worthy of a permanent Ethereal plane existence.

Let us applaud Buddhism, then, for being the first of the primary religions to pass the logical and scientific requirements of *Rule Number 1* and *Rule Number 2*, by correctly teaching that *nirvana* is dependent on the *karmic* results of our thoughts, words, and deeds.

Unlike Hinduism and Judaism, Buddhism makes no distinction between the different races, man-made nations, or social status. Buddha and his followers always have believed that God's love and the Universal law of *karma* apply to us all, regardless of our race, our nationality, our politics, our caste, or our chosen religion. Moreover, Buddhists know that God's laws apply equally to everyone, regardless of whether one believes this to be so. Thus, God will judge each of us according to the same set of rules, notwithstanding the preposterous assertion by some religions that God prefers their man-made creed. In Truth, God makes no distinction between us and will judge us based on our *karmic* record alone. Thus, the Buddhists were the first to believe that the principles related to spiritual progression are the same for every soul and, thankfully, they have managed to hold fast to this glorious and egalitarian precept.

Consequently, Buddhism satisfies *Rule Number 4*, because the religion holds as its basic tenet that God's laws apply to everyone fairly, uniformly, and equally.

Not only do the principles of Buddhism apply equally to everyone, everyone is welcome to join this religion. Indeed, of the five primary religions, Buddhism probably is the most inviting. Consequently, anyone who feels secure enough to embark on a private journey of the soul is ready to study Buddhism, as there are no formalities to getting started. In fact, this religion really has no rules. Rather, the heart of this religion is the quest for Truth, and followers are permitted to pursue *Dharma* in their own way. Hence, initiates are encouraged to begin the *Saddha* process and then allow the Truth about God and the unity of humanity to miraculously unfold.

Because the leaders of Buddhism foster an environment of acceptance and love, Buddhism also is the first of the five primary religions to comport with *Rule Number 5,* **which obligates a religion to welcome and respect people of other faiths.**

Unlike the Christian faith which splintered into competing and, at times, warring factions after Jesus died, Buddhism experienced no such chaos upon Buddha's death. As we shall see, some of the early monks disagreed on portions of Buddha's lessons after he was gone, but they openly and respectfully debated their differences. In other words, the monks never violated the very principles that Buddha had taught them, like non-violence. As a result, divergent Buddhist factions managed to separate peacefully and thereafter practiced tolerance toward one another, which is an unprecedented feat in the annals of religious history.

For example, after Buddha died in 483 B.C.E., numerous monks believed they understood Buddha the best. Sound familiar? Consequently, the religion did undergo a philosophically turbulent period. A number of councils were convened and, in 250 B.C.E., the **Third Buddhist Council** met in an attempt to consolidate the religion. The early followers of Buddha were arguing over rules involving discipline and doctrine. The monks were unable to agree on a few issues which revolved around whether lay people should be included in the movement. Some monks thought that only the ascetic lifestyle within their community (*sangha*) could produce enlightenment, so they sought to limit lay persons' access to Buddha's teachings. Other monks expressed a greater commitment to teaching all who seek *Dharma*, so they were more open to doctrinal innovation.

As a result of this conflict, a schism occurred, which resulted in the splitting of the religion into two main branches: **Hinayana** (a/k/a Theravada) and **Mahayana** Buddhism. The Hinayana Buddhists stress the monastic lifestyle and are more focused on their personal quest for liberation from the material plane. Consequently, the Hinayana branch of Buddhism is known as the "Lesser Vehicle." The other main branch of Buddhism, Mahayana, is referred to as the "Greater Vehicle" because practitioners seek to help those sentient beings who are tied to the Earth plane. The Mahayana monks emphasize the role of the *bodhisattvas*, who are enlightened monks (*arhats*) in the state of *nirvana*. Recall that *bodhisattvas* are *arhats* or *buddhas* who elect to return to the Earth plane to teach *Dharma* to the rest of mankind. Thanks to the initial openness of the Mahayana branch, many sects of Buddhism are flourishing today.

The important point is that the divergence in Buddhist theology did not result in war or bloodshed. The differing monks simply went their separate ways and proceeded to practice their respective brands of Buddhism. As a footnote, though, I should mention the legendary story of Buddha's rogue cousin, Devadatta, who supposedly tried to assassinate Buddha by unleashing a wild elephant in Buddha's path. The plan failed, however, when the elephant stopped his charge and bowed at Buddha's feet. It appears that every Prophet faces a moment of betrayel in his or her life.

To this day, Buddhists have rarely fought with each other and have never gone to war to force the religious conversion of other people. Admittedly, there were Buddhist rulers who conquered other territories and, thereby, were instrumental in spreading the Buddhist religion. For example, the **Mongolian Emperor Kublai Khan** conquered many Muslim territories and, in 1253 C.E., adopted Buddhism as the official religion of the Mongolian Empire. However, Khan's thirst for increasing the size of his empire has never been viewed by historians as a religious crusade or holy war. Rather, the Khan dynasty was simply power hungry and wanted more land. By way of stark contrast, we soon will explore the abject horror of the Christian Crusades.

Because the Buddhists rarely, if ever, initiated a war in the name of religion and have never condoned the use of force to acquire either wealth or power, Buddhism passes moral muster and is the only religion practiced today that easily satisfies *Rule Number 3*, which states that a good religion must never compromise its moral standards.

If you remain unconvinced that Buddhists are pacifists in the face of political change and man's despicable quest for power, it may be helpful to refer again to the Appendix. Historically, Buddhism's greatest enemy has been Communism. The wars that have taken place in the Asian continent have, at times, threatened the very existence of the Buddhist religion. Here is a short list of some of the more egregious attacks on Buddhist monks, nuns, and their laity:

1. In 1911, the last Chinese Emperor is exiled and the suppression of Buddhism begins. By 1928, the new Chinese government destroys most of the Buddhist Temples and kills thousands of Buddhists.
2. In 1949, the People's Republic of China is officially established by the Communist Party and all religion is suppressed.

3. In 1950, Communist China invades Tibet and the **14th Dalai Lama** is forced into exile. The Chinese then destroy all the Buddhist Temples in Tibet and kill over one million Buddhist followers. In 1989, the Dalai Lama is awarded the Nobel Peace Prize.

4. In 1962, socialist army officer Ne Win stages a coup and becomes dictator of Burma. He is responsible for the 1947 assassination of General Aung San, whose efforts led to Burma's independence from Great Britain in 1948. Since 1988, General Aung San's daughter, **Aung San Suu Kyi,** has led a resistance movement against the repressive Burma Socialist Party, which has killed thousands of Buddhist and pro-democracy supporters. In 1989, the socialist government arrests Aung San Suu Kyi. She has been imprisoned for most of the past twenty years and is under house arrest at this time. In 1991, she is awarded the Nobel Peace Prize.

5. In the 1970s, the Khmer Rouge in Cambodia massacre one-quarter of the Cambodian people and almost obliterate the Buddhist religion.

6. In 1995, Communist Chinese authorities abduct and imprison a six year child, Gedhun Choekyi Nyima, who is the **11th Panchen Lama** (a *bodhisattva*), and replace him with another child whom the Communists control.

7. In 2000, the reincarnated **Gyalwa Karmapa** (a 17th generation *bodhisattva*) is forced into exile by Communist China.

The point is that Buddhism is an extremely passive religion which has rarely been tarnished by internal corruption or external conflict. If anything, the Buddhists err on the side of being too passive, thereby allowing greedy and corrupt souls to thrive. Their courage and composure in the face of abject evil is truly amazing.

However, before you get the impression that I am completely enchanted with Buddhism, I want to express a few reservations I have concerning this ancient religion. *To begin with, Buddhism has never fully extended its egalitarian principles to include women.* During his life, Buddha was reluctant to allow women to join his order. He also initially opposed women living in the same community (*sangha*) with the male monks. Additionally, he implemented rules within the *sangha* that placed women in an inferior position to the male monks.

The first decree imposed by Buddha against women was the rule that women had no seniority in the *sangha*. A woman's rank didn't matter because she was expected to pay homage even to newly ordained male monks. Second, monks were permitted to criticize nuns, but nuns could never criticize monks. Third, a woman could not join the *sangha* without permission from her father or husband, but a man could leave his wife to become a monk without recourse.

Additionally, the *Tripitaka* contains explicit descriptions of the polluted nature of the female body and specific denunciations of sexual relations with women. It is reported that when Buddha met with a monk who had returned temporarily to his family, Buddha said it would have been better for the monk to have inserted his penis into the mouth of a poisonous snake than to have placed it in the vagina of a woman. Buddhist scripture seems particularly disgusted by a woman's menstruation cycle and by the "filth" accompanying childbirth. The scripture also states that if a *bodhisattva* is born, his mother's womb may never again be polluted by sexual relations. Hence, according to the legend of Buddha's birth through the immaculate conception of Maya, his mother, Buddha's mother had to die so that her womb could not thereafter be polluted.

Even more disturbing is that leaders of the Theravada school, one of the main branches of Buddhism, affirmatively rejected the Buddha's teachings that women may attain enlightenment. Recall that Buddha taught that both men and women may become *bodhisattvas* and *buddhas*. However, after Buddha died the nuns were permanently separated from the monks. In addition, Theravada Buddhists believe that in order to become a *buddha* a person must:

1. Be in a human incarnation;
2. Be *male*;
3. Be able to achieve enlightenment in the current lifetime;
4. Make a vow to seek enlightenment through a living *buddha*;
5. Renounce worldly attractions and bodily desires, such as sex;
6. Possess yogic powers;
7. Be capable of sacrificing his own life;
8. Have a great passion for spiritual growth.

Needless to say, this branch of Buddhism violates *Rule Number 4* due to its unequal and unfair treatment of women, and it also violates *Rule Number 5*, which prescribes full participation for all members, regardless of sex.

Buddhism's disparate treatment of women also negatively impacts our assessment of the spiritual aspects of this religion under *Rule Number 7*. Consider that there are thousands of male *bodhisattvas* and *buddhas*, but only a handful of females who have been accorded such a status. Therefore, despite Buddha's relatively progressive views on female participation, many branches of Buddhism have failed to follow or expand upon his example. Indeed, the religion is more repressive toward women than it was 2,500 years ago when Buddha lived.

Generally speaking then, it is fair to criticize male Buddhist leaders for their continued subjugation of women. Nevertheless, I would be remiss if I failed to mention that in a few dramatic instances women have been elevated to the top ranks of Buddhism, including the goddess realm. Most notably, Buddhists believe that the goddess **Tara** (a/k/a Kali in Hinduism) was initially a human woman who took the *bodhisattva* vows and eventually achieved *buddhahood*. Thereafter, Tara was credited as being both a *buddha* herself and the mother of all future *buddhas*.

> *Finally, ... she [Tara] awoke to the first concepts of Bodhi-Mind. At that time some monks said to her, "If you pray that your deeds accord with the teachings, then indeed on that account you will change your form to that of a man, as is befitting."*
>
> *After much discourse she finally replied, "In this life ... attachment to ideas of 'male' and 'female' is quite worthless. Weak-minded worldlings are always deluded by this."*
>
> *And so she vowed, "There are many who wish to gain enlightenment in a man's form, and there are but few who wish to work for the welfare of sentient beings in a female form. Therefore may I, in a female body, work for the welfare of beings right until Samsara has been emptied."*
>
> *Then she remained in the palace for ten million and 100,000 years in a state of meditation. ... As a result of this she gained success in the realization that Dharmas are non-originating and also perfected the meditation known as "saving all sentient beings," by the power of which, every morning she released ten million and 100,000 beings from the bondage of their worldly minds. ...*
>
> *Then her former name was changed and she became known as the Saviouress ... [and] as Goddess Tara. [Emphasis added]*
>
> Jo Nang Taranatha, *The Origin of Tara Tantra*

Other than Tara, only a few women have ever been declared *bodhisattvas*. Moreover, until recently, all of them have come from the East. However, in 1985 a remarkable meeting occurred and an American woman was recognized as the reincarnation of Ahkon Lhamo, the female *yogini* who co-founded the Palyul sect of Tibetan Buddhism in 1652 C.E. She is now known as **Jetsunma**, and she is the only woman in the Western world ever to be named a *lama*. She was first recognized by **His Holiness Pema Norbu Rinpoche**, who was visiting from India and who is himself a *bodhisattva*, forced to flee Tibet in 1959 when Communist China invaded. In 1988, Jetsunma was officially enthroned, at which time she was already on her way to establishing one of the largest

Buddhist congregations in the United States. She maintains two Buddhist centers: one in Maryland, which houses the biggest crystal collection outside of the Smithsonian Museum and contains a sixty-five acre *stupa* park; and a second in Arizona, which was officially opened in 2005. May Jetsunma eradicate the lingering sexism in the Buddhist religion and lead all sentient beings toward the upcoming Fifth Spiritual Paradigm.

The mandatory practice of celibacy is another way in which Buddhism artificially separates men and women. The practice also seems to contradict the theory of the "middle path" espoused by Buddha himself. Recall that Buddha chose the "middle path" to attain enlightenment, after discovering that neither obsessive indulging in earthly delights nor obsessive austerity help one to grow spiritually. Despite his belief that we should balance our lives in order to attain *nirvana*, Buddha required absolute celibacy from his monks and nuns. He obviously viewed sex as a spiritual distraction and saw no middle ground on this issue.

Nevertheless, I humbly submit that appropriate sexual relations actually foster our spiritual development. Indeed, the union of male and female energies during intercourse is probably the most sacred act human beings can perform. Consequently, I think Buddha was wrong about sex. Obviously, a person can become obsessed with the physical plane and, thereby, start down a destructive path toward various sins, including sexual gluttony. However, Buddha should not have banned sex nor viewed sex as an impediment to spiritual growth, since the blending of male and female spirit helps us experience the unity of God's compound nature.

In sum, celibacy inevitably harms both sexes. It may start simply enough, with men merely segregating women, but it always ends with men subjugating women. Thereafter, celibacy attacks both the male and female spirit because it denies the innate sexuality of our species. As a result, celibacy produces unnecessary sexual frustration, which itself distracts us in our search for God. Darker still, celibacy can lead to inappropriate sexual relations, as evidenced by the cancer of pedophilia which has now ravaged the Catholic Church. In Truth, celibacy is a needless and painful sacrifice that God never asked of us.

Consequently, Buddhism runs afoul of *Rule Number 7* because the religion fails to fully honor its female members and because it denigrates the most awe inspiring of our God-given powers: our ability to generate sexual energy and to create new life.

Yet, by far the most disturbing aspect of Buddhism is the implication that we do not join with God after spiritual enlightenment is attained. Recall that *nirvana* is not heaven. Rather, Buddha defined *nirvana* as a state of being in which the soul becomes fully detached from the material plane and eventually is completely extinguished. In other words, we no longer exist after we reach *nirvana*, unless we elect to return to assist mankind as a *bodhisattva*.

Consequently, I find the Buddhist view on the afterlife just as sad as the Jewish concept of a mere bodily resurrection. It leaves me feeling isolated from God and forever adrift. Moreover, I see no point to searching for understanding and spiritual Truth if, in the end, I merely evaporate. Therefore, it makes more logical and spiritual sense that in the last stage of our soul development we are united with the Supreme Being. Also, as we learned in Chapter Two, the later Prophets verified that mankind is worthy of returning to the Creator, provided that we earn our salvation.

Thus, when it comes to the afterlife, Buddhism only slightly adds to our Tower of Truth. Recall that the oldest of the five primary religions, Hinduism, teaches that there are multiple layers to heaven with Brahman alone in the highest realm. Next came Judaism, which asserts that mankind is not worthy of an Ethereal plane afterlife, but that after the Messiah comes, the dead may resurrect to enjoy a newly established heaven on Earth with the living. Then came Buddhism, which posits that the state of *nirvana* – total enlightenment – is the highest ideal.

> Who, having abandoned the human bond,
> Has transcended the heavenly bond;
> Who is released from all bonds,
> That one I call a Brahmin.
>
> Whose course gods, gandhabbas [semi-divine beings],
> and humans do not know,
> Whose intoxicants are extinct, an Arhat [monk in Nirvana];
> That one I call a Brahmin.

> The Dhammapada, Sutra XXVI, Verses 417, 420

Buddha never clarified whether the soul, after reaching *nirvana*, may join with God, but there is little in Buddhist holy texts to support this conclusion. Instead, Buddha seems to suggest the complete annihilation and expiration of "self" as the final reward for learning the *Dharma*. Nevertheless, some Buddhists believe that the soul does reach heaven after attaining *nirvana*, which is a welcome update to this religion. However, this more modern interpretation is not universally accepted. Therefore, Buddhism still stands for the proposition that mankind is not worthy of joining God and that the most we can hope for is release from material plane suffering.

Regrettably, I find that Buddhism does not fully comport with the spiritual mandates of *Rule Number 7*, because the religion fails to acknowledge mankind's primordial instinct and predominant intuition that we will one day join with God in the Ethereal plane.

Lastly, I disagree with the Buddhist precept that total detachment from the Earth plane is required in order to achieve spiritual enlightenment. Certainly, it is beneficial for the soul to extinguish all *harmful* Earth plane desires in order to purify and prepare for the Ethereal plane. But it seems obvious to me that we are on this glorious planet and in these amazing bodies for a very important reason: *God wants us to explore and enjoy the abundance of the Earth plane while we are in physical form.*

Thus, instead of enjoying the many gifts given to us by God, Buddha would have us cut ourselves off from the beauty of this planet, our sensory delights, and our personal relationships. In fact, Buddha would have us detach even from our closest loved ones.

> *Let one not be together with the dear;*
> *Nor ever with those that are dear;*
> *Not to see the dear is a misery,*
> *So too is it to see the non-dear.*
>
> *Therefore, let one not make endearment,*
> *For separation from the dear is bad.*
> *For whom there is neither the dear nor non-dear,*
> *For them are bonds not found.*
>
> *From the dear arises grief.*
> *From the dear arises fear.*
> *For one set free from endearments,*
> *There is no grief. Whence fear?*

The Dhammapada, Sutra XVI, Verses 211–213

How utterly sad. And how uninspiring for those of us who have unbounded love to share. Hence, the Buddhist emphasis on detachment seems diametrically opposed to God's design of our bodies, emotions, and instincts, including the survival instinct, the mothering instinct, and the overriding instinct to perpetuate the species. *Innately, mankind is wired for attachments.*

Consequently, how can these instincts be bad, unhealthy, or a barrier to spiritual growth? If morally checked, our needs and desires not only protect us, they also promote love and unity. Besides, to suppress our nature is to question God's design for us at a very fundamental level. Instead, we should accept that God is omniscient and that our design, which is still evolving, was fully intended and accords perfectly with the ultimate plan for mankind.

Thus, the core Buddhist tenet, that enlightenment is achieved through detachment, discourages the expression of some of mankind's most basic but also most spiritual needs, such as the innate desire to join with each other in a state of abundance, joy, and love, in direct opposition to the inspirational requirements of *Rule Number 7*.

Although there are flaws in a few of his lessons, Buddha was the first Prophet to teach the seminal Truth that we all have the ability to grow spiritually and perfect ourselves. Moreover, Buddha gave us the necessary formula for spiritual success – *Saddha*. It is through the *Saddha* process that we commence a personal journey of faith, talk with God on an individualized basis, and learn this *Dharma*: *Compassionate living on the Earth plane leads to eternal bliss in the Ethereal plane.*

In sum, although Buddhism lacks certain spiritual components, the religion on the whole comports with *Rule Number 7* because it provides its members with an inspirational environment in which to seek direct communion with the Almighty.

In many ways, Buddhism is more of a philosophy than a religion, since the goal is personal soul growth as opposed to mundane worship. Hence, Buddhism presents a methodology for connecting to our higher self through meditation, perfecting our own divinity by helping others, and ultimately reaching the Truth about God. As a direct result of this inquisitive and experiential philosophy, Buddhism is more open to change than the other four primary religions. Hopefully, Buddhist leaders are primed and ready to help guide humanity through the current paradigm shift, as there are many confused souls who are resisting the Fifth Spiritual Paradigm.

Because this religion is less focused on ancient rules and arcane dogma from the past and more concerned with spiritual growth and spreading unity in the future, Buddhism satisfies *Rule Number 6* of *The Seven Rules of Any Good Religion*, which encourages all religions to be open to the inevitable discovery of higher and more advanced Truths.

Now, let us see whether Christianity has properly honored and retained the lessons of its glorious teacher, who described an afterlife shared with God and, thereby, greatly advanced our understanding of the Ethereal plane.

CHRISTIANITY

This is going to be a very challenging section for a variety of reasons. First, almost none of the sects which claim to practice Christianity are in keeping with the original teachings of Jesus. This Truth is a direct result of the fact that corrupt souls hijacked the Jesus movement early on and repackaged this Prophet and his messages to obtain power over the masses. Consequently, at this moment in history there is no shining example of a true "Christian" religion.

Second, there are so many Christian sects in existence today that I have to be careful not to generalize too much. Therefore, I periodically will compare and contrast the different groups so as to not lump all Christians together unnecessarily, as some Christians are closer to the Truth than others. However, given the number of Christian sects around the world, it is impossible within the context of this book to account for all the variations of purported Jesus followers.

Third, and most importantly, I will do my best to draw a clear distinction between the religion that *should* have started after Jesus died and the very different religion that Paul started and which gained enough traction to be adopted as "orthodox" Christianity. Indeed, all modes of Christianity practiced today have been affected by one group's faulty interpretation of Jesus, regardless of whether the later sects thought they were preserving the best tenets of this flawed foundation or rebelling against its worst practices. Thus, to the extent that I critique Christianity, please be aware that most of my analysis is directed at the unfortunate common denominator which permeates *all* the Christian sects and which exercised a monopoly over the mass marketing of Jesus for one thousand years: **the Roman Catholic Church.**

Starting with *Rule Number 1* of *The Seven Rules of Any Good Religion*, let us analyze whether the teachings of Jesus are philosophically sustainable. Based on my study of the available source material, including the records that the Catholic Church did not want us to see, such as the *Lost Gospels*, the *Gnostic Gospels*, and the *Dead Sea Scrolls*, I find that the lessons directly attributable to Jesus and for which we have an accurate historical account are both logical and intellectually satisfying. In other words, I don't need to strain nor bend my mind in an unnatural manner in order to comprehend and accept Jesus' lessons. To the contrary, Jesus' arguments are fluid, integrated, and rational. Moreover, even when speaking in parable, Jesus presented coherent and practical examples to underscore his lessons.

In addition, Jesus' sermons were in keeping with the needs of his audience and their capacity to understand. Jesus tailored his arguments to reach the common people of his day, although there is substantial evidence that Jesus also engaged in deeper discussions with his closest apostles and the Jewish elders whom he challenged. Thus, not only were Jesus' spiritual lessons intellectually comprehensible for the masses and philosophically probative for the learned, his approach in getting out the "Word" was highly effective, as he successfully touched all sorts of people with his messages of Truth.

Let us not forget that the Jews of the 1st Century were overrun with oppression and corruption, both within the occupying Roman government and amongst their own cultural and religious leaders. Jesus cut through the fabric of this harsh and immoral society by clearly and rationally leading his followers to the conclusion that something had to be done to reinstate godliness into their lives. Philosophically, then, Jesus' lessons were immensely probative and intellectually satisfying, which should come as no surprise to us given that he spoke for God.

> I came into the world as light, so that everyone who believes in me might not remain in darkness. And if anyone hears my words and does not observe them, I do not condemn him, for I did not come to condemn the world but to save the world. Whoever rejects me and does not accept my words has something to judge him: the word that I spoke, it will condemn him on the last day, because I did not speak on my own, but the Father who sent me commanded me what to say and speak.
>
> Gospel of John, Chapter 12:46–49

Moreover, Jesus' view of God, as a loving and compassionate figure, makes much more sense than the God envisioned by the three earlier religions. To recap quickly, recall that the Hindu gods and goddesses, who are too numerous to name, represent a fragmentation of the Universe, including creation energy, destructive forces, manifestations of nature, and various aspects of human emotions and experience . Additionally, the Hindu deities reside in various levels of heaven and are able to wreak havoc with our lives if not appeased, similar to the pagan Roman gods and goddesses. The Hindu deities also emulate a set of mind-bending rules, such as the horrendous caste system.

Next in time is the Jewish version of a single God, who is harsh, judgmental, and quite vindictive. Additionally, the Jewish God prefers one race and has a predilection for inane rules of worship that no longer make sense today, such as animal sacrifice and rituals for food and sex. The Jewish God also is unobtainable and unreachable, as reflected in the Jewish belief that mankind may not join with God in heaven.

Lastly, the Buddhist God, Brahma, is presented as a neutral force with few benevolent attributes. Just like the Jewish God, Brahma is so remote from us that we never get to reach him, even after attaining enlightenment. However, Buddhism posits the glorious Truth that mankind has the innate ability to achieve total enlightenment and perfection.

To this Buddhist concept of God and the afterlife, Jesus added the next layer of Truth: *Not only does mankind have the ability to attain freedom from the material plane and experience spiritual salvation, we also have the potential to join with God in heaven.* Thus, by explaining the loving nature of God and underscoring our own divine nature, Jesus added another story to our Tower of Truth.

In sum, I find the Christian view of God more reasonable and logical than the views espoused by the earlier religions. It just makes more sense that God loves us completely, as evidenced by the generous gifts we have received, including the life breathed into our lungs, the intelligence imbued in our minds, the abundance of planet Earth, and the great Prophets who have been sent by God to teach us Truth. Those of us who have undertaken the *Saddha* process of soul growth also are fortunate to receive daily reminders of God's love through the amazing people with whom we share our lives and via the many signs we receive from God.

Therefore, Jesus' view of God, as generally adopted by all the Christian sects, is philosophically based, intellectually satisfying, and in full compliance with *Rule Number 1* of *The Seven Rules of Any Good Religion*.

Let us now move along to the topic of science and the objective standard that religion should never violate nor contradict valid scientific principles. Unwittingly, fundamentalist Christians have yet to embrace the full majesty of God's glory. They don't appreciate the scientific wonders that unfold about us daily because they refuse to accept that our best and brightest scientists are able to correctly interpret and document these yielding mysteries.

I do not wish to beat a dead horse, but it is time for all of us to accept the *fact* of evolution. The mythological description of creation contained in *The Holy Bible* was meant for people who lived four thousand years ago. This parable is no longer worthy of holding us spell-bound. The Truth behind God's formation of the Universe and mankind's unique development far exceeds the simplistic view of creation contained in *Genesis*. The Christian fundamentalists' refusal to accept evolution has become an untenable barrier to our collective understanding of the ultimate Truth.

Without overstating the matter, we sit at the dawn of the 21st Century and the future of the human race may very well hinge on how we elect to interpret and manage scientific discoveries. Sadly, the advancement of the human race is being hamstrung by souls who, because of their fear-based attachment to man-made religion, believe that God created Adam and Eve as full-blown *Homo sapiens* about six thousand years ago. Strangely, these otherwise intelligent souls have reached the incorrect conclusion that mankind would somehow be less special or play a less critical role in God's plan if humans evolved gradually as science has proven.

We no longer can afford to indulge our brothers and sisters who feel more comfortable with fairy tales than with fact, as the stakes are too high now. Not only are our public schools at risk, but the collective spiritual development and the preservation of our planet also are in jeopardy. Science is not going to hurt us, but our refusal to fully grasp and properly manage science may very well kill us. Honestly, I will never understand how or why fundamentalist Christians believe that scientists from every culture and religious affiliation, every country and accredited university, would collectively lie about evolution. Notwithstanding this paranoia, the fundamentalists are correct about one thing: *There has been a conspiracy involving science, but the misinformation did not stem from the scientific community.*

Not surprisingly, the Catholic Church is mostly to blame for convincing otherwise intelligent human beings that evolution is some sort of worldwide scientific conspiracy. Indeed, this is an opportune time to more closely examine the seemingly perpetual war against science initiated by the Catholic Church.

The Catholic Church has created two institutions with the stated mission of counteracting all scientific and historical discoveries that conflict with orthodox Christian interpretations of The Holy Bible. The first institution is the **Pontifical Biblical Commission** (the "**PBC**"). In 1902 C.E., **Pope Leo XIII** created the PBC to defend against then current archeological discoveries which raised questions about the historical life of Jesus. Additionally, the PBC was established to undermine the scientific discoveries which directly contradicted the creation myth contained in *The Holy Bible*. Specifically, the PBC was formed to suppress the Truth contained in four extremely controversial books, all of which were published at the end of the 19th Century:

1. *The Origin of Species*, written in 1859 C.E. by **Charles Darwin,** which set out what was *then* the scientific theory of evolution;

2. *The Life of Jesus*, written in 1863 C.E. by a Catholic ex-seminarian and theologian named **Ernest Renan**, who traitorously asserted that there was no historical evidence for the deification of Jesus nor the virginity of Mary;

3. *The Descent of Man*, written in 1871 C.E., also by Charles Darwin, which fully asserted that man evolved from ape-like ancestors in a fashion consistent with the evolution of all life on planet Earth; and

4. *The History of the Origins of Christianity*, written in 1883 C.E., also by Ernest Renan, which further analyzed Biblical scripture and highlighted inconsistencies with other historical accounts of the period, including, most notably, a copy of the *Damascus Document*, which would later be found at Qumran with the other *Dead Sea Scrolls*.

The Vatican was shaken to its core by these objectively written works and wasted no time in protecting itself. In 1870 C.E., **Pope Pius IX**, in an obvious attempt to declare a monopoly on just who is authorized to speak on all matters concerning God's creation of mankind and Jesus' status as a deity, issued the infamous declaration of "**Papal Infallibility.**" This doctrine holds that: (i) the pope is never wrong in matters of faith, since he is chosen by God; and (ii) the pope has the ultimate and final word on all religious issues, including, apparently, interpreting mankind's sordid history and evaluating new scientific discoveries. Even members of the Christian community scoffed at this offensive grab for power, which only prompted the Vatican to further fortify itself against the inevitable onslaught of science.

As a result, the Vatican created the PBC and charged its brainchild with the task of educating young priests to effectively counter the rapidly mounting historic and scientific findings of the 20th Century. A special monastery was set up for this very purpose in Jerusalem, and the school was named the **Ecole Biblique**. The brightest monks were sent to the Ecole Biblique to study the relationship between *The Holy Bible* and recent scientific and historical discoveries. Not surprisingly, many of the young monks found inconsistencies between the *Bible* on the one hand, and science and history on the other. Troublemakers were summarily dismissed from the monastery and replaced with more dutiful seminarians. Eventually, the Ecole Biblique became the preeminent site for Catholic approved "research." Moreover, the school's journal became the Vatican's favorite propaganda machine. To this day, the *Revue Biblique* still publishes the official Catholic interpretations of current scientific and historic discoveries.

The second Catholic institution charged with "correctly" interpreting new scientific and historical discoveries is the **Congregation for the Doctrine of Faith** (the "**CDF**"). Although the CDF was officially formed in 1965 C.E. by **Pope Paul VI**, the CDF has a much more long and sordid history. The CDF used to be called the Holy Office and the Holy Office used to be called the **Holy Inquisition**. Yes, *that* Inquisition. The name may have changed, but not to protect the innocent. This entity, which still convenes "judicial" tribunals and still submits priests to "trials" on charges of heresy, remains the Catholic Church's favorite ministry of misinformation and suppression. This institution also maintains a list of heretical books which are off-limits to all Catholics, especially priests who teach at universities and monks who study at seminaries.

One notorious example of a fairly recent CDF trial involved a Catholic theologian named **Hans Kung**, who was head of the Department of Theology at the University of Tubingen in Switzerland. In 1970 C.E., Kung wrote a book entitled *Infallible?* Kung respectfully questioned the Catholic doctrine of Papal Infallibility, and he concluded his thesis by asserting the obvious: *No one is infallible except God.* In 1979 C.E., the CDF stripped Kung of his position at the University, declared that he was no longer qualified to teach Catholic doctrine, and ordered him to stop publishing his research. The CDF's decision was officially ratified by **Pope John Paul II**.

Another infamous CDF trial involved the Catholic ban against the birth control pill. In 1959 C.E., the pill was made available to the public. Ironically, one of the doctors who helped develop the pill was a Catholic named John Rock. Dr. Rock argued that the pill would not violate the Church's stance against birth control because it merely functions within the framework of the female body's own endocrine system as an extension of the rhythm method. However, the Catholic Church disagreed and officially denounced this medical breakthrough in *Humanae Vitae*, an encyclical published by Pope Paul VI in 1968. **Father Charles Curran,** a professor of theology at Catholic University, dissented from the decree and asserted that the doctrine of Papal Infallibility should not apply to this sort of medical decision. Nevertheless, the CDF convened and reviewed Dr. Curran's teachings. In 1986, then **Cardinal Joseph Ratzinger** requested that Catholic University terminate Father Curran, who was summarily dismissed in 1988. Thereafter, Cardinal Ratizinger continued to oversee the CDF until his election as **Pope Benedict XVI** in 2005.

Lastly, let's consider what many scholars view as the greatest Catholic conspiracy of all time. When the *Dead Sea Scrolls* were found in 1947, all but seven of them were taken to the Ecole Biblique and placed under the exclusive control of a Catholic priest named Roland de Vaux. Not only was Father de Vaux head of the Ecole Biblique, he also was a governing member of the PBC, the institution charged with undermining any new historical find or scientific discovery that potentially threatens Catholic Church doctrine. Please, just pause for a moment to fully appreciate the irony of this situation and the stupendous synchronicity involved: *The Dead Sea Scrolls literally were locked inside the one place on Earth dedicated to the suppression – if not outright destruction – of any and all anti-Christian history and science.*

Needless to say, the Catholics' receipt of the *Dead Sea Scrolls* was a sign from God. Father de Vaux and the Catholic Church were presented with a monumental test to see if they would honestly decipher and disseminate the Truth about the *Scrolls*. And the results of this test? The Roman Catholic Church failed miserably ... yet again. Rather than admit that the *Scrolls* contain revealing information pertaining to the time when Jesus and James walked the Earth and the Jewish Temple was destroyed, the Catholics chose to protect their version of early Christian history at all costs. As we shall see, the Catholics purposely and methodically charted a course designed to suppress the amazing revelations contained in the *Dead Sea Scrolls*.

To begin with, Father de Vaux allowed only one non-Catholic researcher on his "international" team. This isolated yet brave soul was John Allegro, who was openly agnostic in his belief about God. Save for this one independent historian, no other scholars were allowed to see the *Scrolls* or even photos of the *Scrolls*. The academic world was in an uproar, particularly since Jewish historians fluent in the Aramaic and Hebrew languages used in the *Scrolls* were readily available and begging to join the team. Nevertheless, the Catholics were adamant that only they were qualified to properly translate and interpret the *Scrolls*. This refusal to include Jewish academics was an outrage, especially given the fact that the Ecole Biblique is located in Jerusalem. Moreover, various accounts reveal that Father de Vaux was anti-Semitic. He should have been disqualified from analyzing the *Scrolls* based on that character flaw alone.

Years passed with the Catholic team publishing only scraps of the least revealing *Scrolls*. The Catholics asserted that all the *Scrolls* were written by the Essene Jewish sect around 200 B.C.E., thereby creating the false impression that the *Scrolls* were unrelated to the era and events surrounding the birth of Christianity. By 1956, Allegro was sick of the stonewalling, so he openly defied Father de Vaux by publishing a book and publicly discussing the

Copper Scroll, which lists the contents of the Jewish treasury, including an inventory of gold, silver, and important records hidden by the Jews prior to the destruction of the Temple in 70 C.E. A scandal ensued, as the Catholics insisted that the *Copper Scroll* was a mere collection of buried treasure legends. Finally, Allegro affirmatively accused the Catholic team members of lying about the contents and the dating of the *Copper Scroll*. In retaliation, the Catholics issued a written statement in the London newspaper *The Times*, effectively discrediting Allegro and forcing him off the team.

With Allegro gone, the Catholic Church had complete control over the *Dead Sea Scrolls*. Whenever one of the Catholic members of the research team retired or died, he was allowed to appoint his successor or heir, as though the *Scrolls* were personal property. This unconventional method for appointing successors to the team further enraged the academic world. Eventually, U.S. and British newspapers drew attention to the scandal by publishing numerous editorials in the 1980s. Nevertheless, the Catholic Church still refused to publish the bulk of the *Scrolls*.

Finally in 1991, the *Scrolls* were made available to all interested scholars, compliments of the Bechtel Corporation. Somehow, Elizabeth Bechtel managed to get photographs of the *Scrolls* and deposited the negatives at the Huntington Library in California. Thereafter, the library offered microfiche copies of the *Dead Sea Scrolls* to anyone willing to pay a $10 fee. At last, the *Scrolls* were liberated! The Catholic team tried but was unable to stop the release of the *Scrolls*. It is a disgraceful fact that the Catholic research team published less than 25% of the *Dead Sea Scrolls* during their forty year monopoly over them.

Since 1991, independent historians have been relishing what they describe as the most important theological find in the last two thousand years. Today, almost all independent scholars agree with Allegro that the *Scrolls* represent a vast collection of literature spanning roughly three hundred years, starting with the reign of the Maccabees and ending with the destruction of the Temple. Sadly, Allegro died in 1988, while still suffering from disgrace at the hands of the Catholic conspiracy machine and before being dubbed a hero by the academic world. To his immense credit, Allegro was the only member of the team to translate and publish all the *Scrolls* entrusted to his care.

For all the above reasons, I quite easily conclude that the Catholic Church is guilty of purposely suppressing and undermining science in direct violation of *Rule Number 2* of *The Seven Rules of Any Good Religion*.

In stark contrast to the oppressive and closed-minded practices of the Catholic Church, stand the early Christians' views on science and the mysteries surrounding creation. In the *Gnostic Gospels*, Jesus plainly speaks of greater mysteries that are available to those who seek understanding and are capable of accepting Truth.

> If one does not understand how fire came into existence, he will burn in it, because he does not know the root of it. If one does not first understand water, he knows nothing. For what use is there for him to be baptized in it? If one does not understand how blowing wind came into existence, he will blow away with it. If one does not understand how body, which he bears, came into existence, he will perish with it.
>
> *The Dialogue of the Savior*, Verse 35

Thus, the *Gnostic Gospels* typically contain deeper and more complex interpretations of Jesus' lessons. Ponder the following language which examines the critical interplay between knowledge of Truth and freedom from the material plane. This passage also indicates that love is the secret to achieving ultimate freedom.

> He who has knowledge of the Truth is a free man, but the free man does not sin, for "he who sins is the slave of sin." Truth is the mother, knowledge the father. ...
>
> But "love builds up." In fact, he who is really free through knowledge is a slave because of love for those who have not yet been able to attain to the freedom of knowledge. Knowledge makes them capable of becoming free.
>
> *Gospel of Phillip*, Verse 77

Similarly, the *Dead Sea Scrolls* plainly show that early Jewish Christians were, in fact, eager to understand the Truth of creation and the nature of God. They did not think it was sacrilegious to seek such higher Truths. Indeed, they believed that God wanted them to search for understanding and Truth as revealed in this incredible passage from one of the *Scrolls*.

> The dark places will be made light because of Your abundance, and Eternal Being shall be the lot of the Seekers of Truth and the witnesses of Your judgments. ... You will be the Elect of Truth and pursuers after insight with judgment . ... Would they ever say, "We have grown weary in the ministries of Truth?"...
>
> Does not God give knowledge of ^ on Truth, to discern all mysteries, and understanding did He apportion to those who inherited Truth. ...
> And they pursue all the roots of understanding, and diligently ^ according to their knowledge, one man will be glorified over another ....

Day and night meditate on the Mystery of Existence ^ concerning the knowledge of the Secret of Truth .... Then you will gain knowledge of His inheritance and walk in righteousness .... Bend your back to all discipline, and through all wisdom, purify your heart, and in the abundance of your intellectual potential, investigate the Mystery of Existence. And ponder all the ways of Truth, and consider all the roots of evil.

Children of Salvation and the Mystery of Existence

Frankly, I don't think these men could have been any clearer regarding their love of Truth and their quest for understanding. Indeed, they assumed it was their duty to ponder the meaning of creation, the elements of existence, and the parameters of both the seen and unseen worlds.

Consequently, I find that Jesus' lessons and the interpretation of those lessons by Jesus' earliest followers – the Jewish and Gnostic Christians – comport in every way with *Rule Number 2*, which requires a healthy religion to bolster, as opposed to interfere with, our love of science and commitment to Truth. Moreover, I easily conclude that Jesus and his most devout followers fully complied with *Rule Number 6*, which demands that all new information be received and reviewed in an honest and open environment.

The Catholic Church, on the other hand, has a long and unrepentant history of suppressing scientific discoveries and also quashing any other data that in any way threatens their orthodox view of God, creation, the nature of man, or their claim to spiritual superiority. Indeed, the Catholic Church has methodically and systematically destroyed anyone, including their own priests and nuns, who threatens the Church's authority. I have mentioned a few current examples of how the Vatican deals with renegade priests. Now, let's take a few moments to ponder some of the more egregious examples of how the Church historically has eliminated some of our greatest scientists, philosophers, and spiritualists throughout the ages.

In 1543 c.e., Mikolaj Kopernik (a/k/a **Copernicus**), a Polish/Prussian scientist, was the first man to contradict the Christian scriptures which state that the Earth is the center of creation. Copernicus' theory was astounding, as it not only contradicted *The Holy Bible*, it also signaled the birth of empirical science, which historians call the **Age of Enlightenment**. Previously, European science included the study of alchemy, astrology, and the magical arts. However, the 16th Century was a time of scientific reawakening for Europe, as many fields of study had been lost during the Middle Ages, although safely preserved by the Muslim Empire. Thus, Copernicus was instrumental in leading Europeans back to true science. Shortly before his death, Copernicus published a book entitled *Of the Revolution of Celestial Spheres*. Ironically, Copernicus dedicated his book to **Pope Paul III**.

Luckily for Copernicus, he died before the Catholic Church condemned his findings. Nevertheless, the Church decided that something must be done to restrict scientific publications and books of literature which contradicted orthodox Christian theology. To solve the problem, the Vatican created a list of heretical books in 1565 C.E., called the **Tridentine Index**, and placed Copernicus' book on the list. *In total, the Tridentine Index banned nearly three-quarters of all the books then in print in Europe.* Incidentally, although the Vatican "officially" suspended the *Tridentine Index* in 1966 (at which time it contained roughly four thousand titles), the CDF still maintains a list of banned books which are off limits to "good" Catholics.

Despite the ban on Copernicus' work, an Italian scientist named **Galileo Galilei** bravely pursued astronomy. The Holy Inquisition was in full swing at this time, having officially begun in 1231 C.E., pursuant to a papal bull decreed by **Pope Gregory IX** entitled *Excommunicanus*. Thus, Galileo knew that his life would be in jeopardy. Nevertheless, in 1610 C.E., Galileo used a new invention called the telescope to further Copernicus' research. Galileo was able to confirm Copernicus' theory that the Earth moves around the Sun, and he published his results. He also wrote that *The Holy Bible* should not restrict research into the natural world.

By 1633 C.E., Galileo could no longer avoid the wrath of the Catholic Church and he was brought before the Inquisition. Galileo was threatened with torture, but he recanted his findings in time to be spared physical harm. Even so, he was sentenced to indefinite house arrest and remained incarcerated until his death in 1642 C.E. Just for the record, in 1992 Pope John Paul II commissioned an inquiry into the Inquisition's treatment of Galileo. Eleven years later, in 2003, the Vatican concluded that Galileo's inquisitors were guilty of "subjective error."

In addition to condemning scientific geniuses, the Inquisition also destroyed the lives of some of our best philosophers. In 1619 C.E., French philosopher **René Descartes** started the "Rationalist Movement," which adopted a more systematic approach to evaluating the wonders of the world. Rationalists did not start their analysis with the revered "truths" of Christianity, but rather proceeded from a position of doubt and utmost scrutiny until real Truths emerged through the use of both deductive and inductive reasoning (i.e., the scientific method). In short, Descartes questioned the basis for mankind's existence and the nature of man in a manner that had not been done since the time of the Greek and Chinese philosophers.

> *But I immediately became aware that while I was thus disposed to think that all was false, it was absolutely necessary that I who thus thought should be somewhat; and noting that this Truth,* **I think, therefore I am,** *was so steadfast and so assured that the suppositions of the skeptics, to whatever extreme they might all be carried, could not avail to shake it, I concluded that I might without scruple accept it as being the first principle of the philosophy I was seeking. [Emphasis added]*

René Descartes, *Discourse on Method*, Part IV

Although a Catholic, Descartes concluded that human beings while still alive can attain a state of perfection based on mankind's own ability to reason, similar to the Christian concept of "grace" but independent of the Christian notion of salvation. If I thought Descartes had access to the *Dhammapada*, I would swear that he had plagiarized Buddha, who first posited this Truth when he described how mankind may attain the enlightened state of *nirvana*.

Needless to say, the Catholic Church decided that Descartes was a very dangerous man. The Inquisition targeted him, but he managed to escape punishment by fleeing to Holland. Descartes remained in exile for twenty-one years and his books were included in the *Tridentine Index*. Indeed, almost all of the books written during the Age of Enlightenment which contained progressive theories on science, philosophy, or spirituality were added to the Catholic list of banned books.

Even **Sir Isaac Newton** (1642 – 1727) was condemned by the Catholic Church and his publications added to the *Tridentine Index*. In addition to attacking his greatest scientific discoveries, including his work on the gravitational properties of the planets, the physics of matter, and the optics of light, the Church declared his theological beliefs heretical. Some researchers have speculated that the Church may have feared Newton for another reason, as well. He may have been a grand master of the **Priory of Sion**, a secret society purportedly created to preserve the true history of Jesus.

The best-selling novel *The Da Vinci Code* contains a fictionalized account of this legend. There is a body of evidence that the Priory of Sion was formed in 1099 C.E. to protect the biggest secret of all time: *Jesus was a man who was married to and had a child with Mary Magdalene.* Assuming for a moment that this tale is true, it is fairly easy to understand why this secret would be closely guarded. Indeed, if the legend could be proven, it would completely unravel the very fabric of orthodox Christianity. Moreover, anyone who lived during the time of the Inquisition and believed in the legend would have been vulnerable to attack by the Catholic Church.

Leonardo Da Vinci (1452 – 1519) also may have been a grand master of the Priory of Sion. We know, at a minimum, that he was watched very closely by the Catholic Church and that he wrote in his journals using a code in an attempt to protect his ideas. Some scholars believe that Da Vinci's paintings, such as the *Mona Lisa*, contain clues which prove that he was a member of the Priory of Sion. Even conventional art historians agree that the *Mona Lisa* is a self portrait of Da Vinci which he femininized. Legend scholars add that Da Vinci intended for the *Mona Lisa* to depict a basic Truth about God: *The Supreme Being is comprised of both masculine and feminine energy.* Thus, the *Mona Lisa's* smile, the most famous smile on the planet, may signify Da Vinci's wry conviction that Jesus was a human Prophet and not God. Similarly, many people now believe that the feminine figure sitting beside Jesus in Da Vinci's *Last Supper* is Mary Magdalene, not the male apostle John.

Lastly, in addition to terrorizing some of our greatest scientists and philosophers, the Vatican used the Inquisition to silence some of the most devout Christian spiritualists to ever live, such as **John Wycliffe** of England (1329–1384) and **John Hus** of Czechoslovakia (1369–1415). Wycliffe was a brilliant scholar who taught at Oxford University and who firmly believed that the only basis for Christian doctrine is *The Holy Bible*. Consequently, he staunchly rejected the man-made rules which the Church imposed on the uneducated masses, since such rules violate the very heart of Jesus' lessons. Wycliffe also denied that the pope was ordained by God and openly expressed his disgust at the wealth and power the clergy accumulated by taxing and collecting penance money from the poor. Additionally, Wycliffe felt that everyone should be allowed to read the *Bible*. To that end, he set about translating the Latin *Bible* into English for the masses, a defiant move fiercely opposed by the pope, who did not want the common people to know that Jesus had condemned the Sanhedrin priests for the very same acts being perpetrated by the Catholic clergy.

Finally, in 1376 C.E., Wycliffe openly attacked the pope by writing that the pope was the "most cursed of dippers and purse heavers ... [who] vilified, nullified and utterly defaced" God's Ten Commandments. Wycliffe also wrote that Church properties should be seized and turned over to the poor. Then, he argued that the 1215 C.E. papal decree regarding the **Doctrine of Transubstantiation**, which states that the bread Eucharist is literally the body of Christ, was not biblically justified and was just another man-made ritual of no spiritual significance.

In response to these "heresies," **Pope Gregory XI** ordered the English king to imprison Wycliffe. However, before this sentence could be carried out, Pope Gregory XI died and three new popes simultaneously tried to seize power. The internal strife and corruption within the Church only served to buttress Wycliffe's claims that the Catholic clergy were morally and spiritually unfit to lead. In 1382 C.E., the Archbishop of Canterbury officially condemned Wycliffe, who then was forced into hiding. Eight years after his death, Wycliffe's devotees completed his work and an English translation of *The Holy Bible* finally was made available to the public. The Vatican was so outraged that he had accomplished his mission, that in 1428 C.E. the Inquisition extracted retroactive revenge against Wycliffe by exhuming his corpse and burning it!

When I first read how the Catholic Church responded to the widespread publication of *The Holy Bible*, I was shocked and could not fathom why they would want to suppress scripture. One would assume that such a sharing of spiritual information would have pleased the Church. Nevertheless, the Vatican decreed at the Council of Trent in 1545 C.E., that the laity should not read scripture. *Moreover, the Church's overt policy of keeping the masses ignorant of the actual teachings of Jesus was to continue for the next four hundred years.* Not until 1962 C.E., at the ecumenical council **Vatican II**, did the Catholic Church give its laity permission to read the *Bible*. Indeed, my grandmother begged her priest in the 1940s to get her a translated copy of the *Bible*, which he did after making her promise to use it only as a prayer book. Eventually, my grandmother left the Catholic Church after she read firsthand how Jesus viewed the religious hypocrites of his day. Now I understand why the Catholics fear dissemination of Truth.

As a final example of how the Inquisition destroyed good Catholics who spread the true teachings of Jesus, stands the tragic case of John Hus, a brilliant scholar and Dean of Philosophy at the Charles University in Prague. Hus criticized the Church for selling **Indulgences**, a payment to the clergy that was supposed to guarantee a person a smooth ride to heaven. Regarding Indulgences he wrote, "They cannot rid themselves of fleas and flies, and yet want to rid others of the torments of hell." He also attacked the Church for amassing material possessions at the expense of the common people and in derogation of Jesus' admonition against wealth. Moreover,

Hus denied the infallibility of the pope and the notion that the pope is ordained by God, which was a fairly obvious conclusion, since at the time, three different popes were vying for supremacy. Hus explained, "As for the argument that the pope is the most holy father who cannot sin ... be it known to you that papal power is limited by God's law."

Eventually, **Pope John XXIII,** one of the three popes at the time, excommunicated Hus. In addition, Pope John XXIII convened the **Council of Constance** in 1414 C.E. (which the other two popes skipped), during which Hus was declared a heretic and condemned to death by fire. During his trial before the Inquisition, Hus was accused of forty-seven heresies, with six warranting mortal death: (i) failing to believe in Transubstantiation; (ii) denying the infallibility of the pope; (iii) refuting the power of priests to absolve sin; (iv) refusing to subject himself to the "absolute authority of his worldly superiors"; (v) rejecting the prohibition of marriage for priests; and (vi) comparing Indulgences paid to priests with bribery. Facing certain death, Hus never recanted. Rather, he stated in his defense that: (i) Jesus was able to turn water into wine, but mere priests were incapable of turning wine into blood or dough into flesh; (ii) the pope was subject to the same temptations and sins as any other man; (iii) only God can forgive sins, as plainly set forth in the scriptures; (iv) Jesus clearly taught that we should never obey priests over the word of God; (v) God himself sanctified the institution of marriage; and (vi) "Nothing appears more godless to me than to commercialize the forgiveness of sins, to deceive the poor and miserable people that heaven might be bought with a few farthings."

Because Hus was an ordained priest himself, the inquisitors decided to strip him of his consecration prior to execution. Seven bishops forcibly dressed Hus in his priestly vestments and then defrocked him while also cursing him as "Judas." They then placed a paper crown on his head. Able to fully comprehend the irony of his situation, Hus openly exclaimed, "My Lord Jesus on account of me, a miserable wretch, bore a much heavier and harsher crown of thorns." Hus was then paraded in the market square, where he and his books were publicly burned. His last words were, "Jesus Christ, son of the Living God, have mercy upon me."

It is interesting to note the fate of Pope John XXIII, the man primarily responsible for Hus' murder. During the Council of Constance, the Pope miscalculated and lost control over the six hundred bishops in attendance, who decided they would rather back one of the other two popes, either **Pope**

Gregory XII or **Pope Benedict XIII.** After pulling their support, the bishops charged Pope John XXIII with fifty-four counts of immoral and illegal conduct, although by the time of his trial the charges were reduced to just five offenses: piracy, murder, rape, sodomy, and incest. Incidentally, in what may have been the first instance of the Church relocating a sex offender, Pope John XXIII was appointed Cardinal of Tusculum after serving a three year prison term. He was later denounced as an "anti-pope," and in 1958 C.E. a new pope assumed his title – the second Pope John XXIII – in yet another attempt to erase our memory banks and rewrite history.

Because the Roman Catholic Church has a long-standing and unrepentant history of suppressing important scientific, historical, and biblical information, and also of persecuting those who attempt to spread such knowledge, I quite easily conclude that Catholicism violates *Rule Number 6*, **which requires a religion to openly and honestly contend with new theories and discoveries. Likewise, those fundamentalist Christian sects which prefer ancient mythology over current science, edited archives over actual history, and religious orthodoxy over advanced spiritual growth, also violate** *Rule Number 6.*

Next, let's consider the dual prescriptions that a good religion should be moral, which I have identified as *Rule Number 3*, and also that a sound religion must be just, which I have labeled *Rule Number 4*. There is an important reason for us to ponder these two requirements together: *Jesus himself taught that moral and ethical standards may not be separated from God's law, which is and shall forever remain paramount.*

In other words, morality naturally flows when we follow God's laws, including the most important Mosaic laws (i.e., the Ten Commandments) and the Golden Rule (a/k/a the Eleventh Commandment). Thus, even though Christian fundamentalists believe that salvation is based on blind faith in Jesus as a savior, Jesus instructed us otherwise. After delivering the Eleventh Commandment, Jesus clarified that we must obey all of God's laws if we wish to reach heaven, especially the moral mandate to love and care for our less fortunate brothers and sisters.

As previously discussed in Chapter Two, this is a tragic point of divergence between the actual teachings of Jesus and the man-made dogma adopted by the Catholic Church. Recall that it was Paul – a man who never met Jesus and persecuted the original apostles – who first asserted that mere faith in Jesus as the son of God qualifies a soul for heaven. And in the process, Paul relegated God's eleven sacred principles to the shadows.

> *We, who are Jews by nature and not sinners from among the Gentiles, who know that a **man is not justified by works of the law but through faith in Jesus Christ**, even we have believed in Christ Jesus that we may be justified by faith in Christ and not by works of the law, because by works of the law no one will be justified. [Emphasis added]*

Letter to the Galatians, Chapter 2:15

This aberration of Jesus' lessons was officially adopted by the Roman Catholic Church and has remained the cornerstone of nearly all Christian sects to this day. Hence, the common error, "Accept Jesus Christ as your personal savior or you won't get into heaven." We explored the misplaced origin of this theological tenet at great length in Chapter Two, so let me simply restate the obvious: The soul is neither justified nor seriously advanced through faith alone. Rather, faith in *any* deity is merely the first step to spiritual enlightenment.

Likewise, faith in Jesus as a Prophet, a savior, a lesser deity, or God himself, will do nothing for the soul except get one started on the path to heaven. On Judgment Day, our ability to join with God will be based on whether we assimilated the lessons of all the Prophets and, especially, how well we adhered to Jesus' grand model of a loving human being. In sum, Jesus was crystal clear on how we attain everlasting salvation: *We will be judged based on whether we obeyed God's laws.*

> *Do not think that I have come to abolish the law or the prophets, I have not come to abolish but to fulfill. ... I tell you, unless your righteousness surpasses that of the scribes and Pharasees, you will not enter into the kingdom of heaven.*
>
> *You have heard that it was said to your ancestors, "You shall not kill; and whoever kills will be liable for judgment." But I say to you, whoever is angry with his brother will be liable to judgment ... and whoever says, "You fool," will be liable to fiery Gehenna [a place that practiced child sacrifice; i.e., hell]. ...*
>
> *You have heard that it was said, "You shall not commit adultery." But I say to you, everyone who looks at a woman with lust has already committed adultery with her in his heart. ...*
>
> *It was also said, "Whoever divorces his wife must give her a bill of divorce." But I say to you, whoever divorces his wife causes her to commit adultery ....*
>
> *Again you have heard that it was said to your ancestors, "Do not take a false oath, but make good to the Lord all that you vow." But I say to you ... Let your "Yes" mean "Yes," and your "No" mean "No." Anything more is from the evil one.*
>
> *You have heard that it was said, "An eye for an eye and a tooth for a tooth." But I say to you, offer no resistance to one who is evil. When*

someone strikes you on your right cheek, turn the other one to him as well. ... Give to the one who asks of you, and do not turn your back on one who wants to borrow.

You have heard that it was said, "You shall love your neighbor and hate your enemy." But I say to you, love your enemies, and pray for those who persecute you, that you may be children of your heavenly Father, for he makes the sun to rise on the bad and the good, and he causes rain to fall on the just and the unjust. ... So be perfect, just as your heavenly Father is perfect. [Emphasis added]

Gospel of Matthew, Chapter 5:17–48

As the above quote makes plain, Jesus taught that adherence to the Ten Commandments is the *minimum* standard of behavior required in order for a soul to gain admittance into heaven. Obeying the Eleventh Commandment is the only guaranteed route. Jesus also demonstrated that it is okay to ignore man-made rules that conflict with God's laws or which defy common sense. Indeed, Jesus challenged the leaders of his own religion and chose to die a martyr's death rather than submit to the religious hypocrites of his day. Hence, people like John Hus are true heroes. Hus fully grasped Jesus' message that God's laws always trump man-made rules. Moreover, Hus was brave enough to defy the Catholic Church and put his life on the line for this Truth – the same price Jesus paid for refusing to submit to man-made dogma.

Without question, therefore, Jesus and his true followers meet the requirements set forth in *Rule Number 3* and *Rule Number 4* of *The Seven Rules of Any Good Religion*, because they understand that salvation is the just reward for those who obey God's laws, including the basic Ten Commandments and the much more challenging Golden Rule, even if such obedience means defying hypocritical clergy or abandoning misguided religions.

Unfortunately, the Catholic Church and most fundamentalist Christian sects have adopted the untenable position that salvation is gained through a cursory belief that Jesus is God and that he died for our sins, thereby promoting blind faith as opposed to moral and ethical responsibility. This shocking over-simplification of the true path to heaven is an effrontery to the very Truths revealed to us by Jesus, who both fully explained and demonstrated for mankind how difficult it is to attain union with God in heaven.

Therefore, I regretfully conclude that the Catholic and fundamentalist Christian concept of salvation is anathema to the moral and ethical lessons taught by Jesus and a flagrant violation of *Rule Number 3* and *Rule Number 4*.

The moral criterion set forth in *Rule Number 3* also requires that a religion have fixed standards of right and wrong. The oppression of others, either through insidious messages of hate or through an actual show of force, is patently offensive to spiritual human beings and to God. From all the historical evidence, it appears that Jesus was a pacifist, even though some of his followers, including some apostles, subscribed to the more violent doctrines promoted by the Jewish Zealots, who eventually went to war against the Romans and were massacred. In sum, there is absolutely no evidence that Jesus ever advocated the use of force to achieve his goals.

In fact, my research proves the opposite. It appears that Jesus voluntarily submitted to the jurisdiction of the Sanhedrin court, either because he thought he was the prophesied Messiah and the priests would not dare harm him, or because he was a divine Prophet who was willing to die in order to spread the message that we are worthy of uniting with God. Regardless of his reason, Jesus allowed the Sanhedrin to capture him and he chose not to physically resist the authorities either during his Jewish trial for blasphemy or his Roman trial for sedition.

Thus, Jesus perfectly modeled for us how to "love your enemy," in total compliance with *Rule Number 3*, since he proved his steadfast moral character even in the face of his own torture and death.

It is now time to properly and solemnly revisit the horror of the Holy Inquisition. In my opinion, the Inquisition was the most morally bankrupt institution created by man. The fact that it still exists – in the more modest form of the Congregation for the Doctrine of Faith – makes me shudder. For those of you who do not know the history of the Inquisition, you are in for a shock. Although Catholics like to pretend that it was some sort of aberration and label it "ancient history," the Truth is that the leaders of the Catholic Church used the Inquisition for over six hundred years to terrorize, torture, and kill people from all religions, including their own, who opposed them. *Even more horrific is the fact that numerous and successive popes supported the Inquisition through papal decrees enacted and enforced in God's name.*

As previously mentioned, the Holy Inquisition was officially spawned by Pope Gregory IX in 1231 C.E., pursuant to a papal bull entitled *Excommunicamus*. However, by the 13th Century the Catholic Church already had a long history of imprisoning, torturing, and killing its enemies. In 1184 C.E., **Pope Lucius III** granted bishops the right to try heretics and turn unrepentant sinners over to the civil authorities for execution, since the Catholic Church wanted to preserve the fiction that it never sheds blood. Then, in 1199 C.E., **Pope Innocent III** officially declared that heresy was "treason against God." Thus, earlier popes already had set the stage for the Church to commit mass murder and mayhem by the time Pope Gregory IX was ordained.

Nevertheless, even if we use the Inquisition's official birthdate of 1231 C.E., it would mean that the Inquisition continued in full force and effect for 585 interminable years until 1816 C.E., when **Pope Pius VII** issued an edict forbidding torture in Inquisition tribunals. One should note, however, that Spain continued to use its Inquisition tribunals to kill heretics through 1834 C.E. Moreover, in 1856 C.E., **Pope Pius IX** issued an edict clarifying that "excommunication, confiscation (of property), banishment, imprisonment for life, as well as secret executions in heinous cases" still were permitted Inquisition practices. Thus, it is well documented that the Church used physical torture and murder to reform wayward Christians and convert people from other religions as recently as 150 years ago. Consequently, it is both impossible and preposterous to relegate the Inquisition to a "minor" event in Catholic Church history.

A logical starting point for our own inquisition is: *Why did so many European monarchs assist the Catholic Church in eliminating "heretics"?* The answer lies in the very genesis of Catholicism, when Roman Emperor Constantine embraced Christianity and forced the creation of one "catholic" (i.e. universal) church. In sum, monarchs throughout history have backed the Catholic Church in order to consolidate their own power. For example, in 476 C.E. after the fall of the Roman Empire, the fledgling European monarchies utilized the power of the Church for protection, and *vice versa*. Later, the European nobles realized that the Inquisition was an effective tool to control the masses. Civil resistance was futile, since the Catholic Church was given free reign to publicly conduct the Inquisition. The cardinal sins of greed and pride, now firmly entrenched in both the Church and the European monarchies, were mercilessly unleashed on the perpetually abused and beaten common people. Consequently, a symbiotic, political, and mutually rewarding relationship evolved between the Vatican and national leaders, which started with the European monarchs but later included elected leaders.

The actual death count from the Inquisition is incalculable, but most historians agree that millions of people were killed at the direction of the Catholic bishops who oversaw the tribunals. The Inquisition process was a nightmare, not just for those who were accused of heresy, but also for every inhabitant of the targeted town. When the inquisitor arrived, he would call the congregation together and instruct the laity to report any suspected heretics. There was a grace period, usually a week, during which heretics were encouraged to confess on their own in exchange for leniency. Penalties for heresy ranged from fines and confiscation of property to imprisonment, torture, and death at the stake. A suspected heretic was not allowed to call a witness in his defense or to know the identity of his accuser. Because prosecution witnesses were guaranteed anonymity and protection, trumped-up charges based on personal malice and greed were commonplace. If a suspect failed to confess immediately, he was tortured into submission, usually on a rack or by a system of pulleys, both of which stretched the appendages of the body and frequently caused dislocation of the joints.

In 1252 C.E., **Pope Innocent IV** issued a new papal bull entitled *Ad Extirpanda*, which further condoned the use of torture. He said that, "bodily torture has ever been found the most salutary and efficient means of leading to spiritual repentance." This edict led to more brutality, as the inquisitors started to torture witnesses as well. In fact, the only exemptions from torture under the new rules were for pregnant women until they gave birth, girls under the age of twelve, and boys under the age of fourteen.

Thereafter, as accusations of "witchcraft" became popular, women were particularly suspect and vulnerable. In 1484 C.E., **Pope Innocent VIII** condemned witchcraft in his papal bull *Summis Desiderantes*. An Inquisition handbook that was based on the new edict rhetorically asked, "What else is a woman but a foe to friendship, an inescapable punishment, a necessary evil, a natural temptation, a desirable calamity, a domestic danger, a delectable detriment, an evil of nature, painted in fair colours?" In total, historians estimate that 80% of the witch trials targeted women – usually spinsters, widows, and midwives – who had no male protection.

To summarize: Over the span of more than six hundred years, a continuous succession of more than eighty Catholic popes authorized and condoned the use of physical torture and execution by fire in the name of the Almighty.

To the murders sanctioned by the Catholic Church via its Inquisition, I would add the millions of Christians and Muslims killed during the **Christian Crusades,** which spanned 175 years, from 1095 C.E. to 1270 C.E. These crusades were brutal and inhumane wars, usually begun at the direction of the Catholic pope. In total, the Christians launched eight crusades, as detailed in the Appendix. These wars were fought in God's name and were intended to retake the Holy Land from the Muslim Empire. Ironically, the Christians might have been able to hold on to

Jerusalem if they had stuck together. However, the in-fighting between the popes who controlled the Western branch of the Catholic Church in Rome and the patriarchs who governed the Eastern branch of the Church in Constantinople ensured that the Christians would lose the Holy Land.

The fighting within the Catholic Church actually dates back to the **Arian Controversy**, which was a theological debate that pitted the Eastern and Western bishops against one another. After Jesus died and the Pauline version of Christianity started to take hold, there still raged a huge debate about whether Jesus started out as a man, whether he was divine from the start, or whether Jesus and God were one entity (the view that ultimately prevailed).

The debate intensified in 314 C.E., when a Catholic priest from Alexandria named **Arius** proposed a thoughtful interpretation of Jesus' life and death. Arius was troubled by the emerging concept of the Holy Trinity (i.e., God the Father, God the Son, and God the Holy Ghost), since he believed that Jesus started out as a man. Arius argued that Jesus was a human being who became so sublime that God adopted him as his son, sacrificed him in order to redeem humanity, raised him from the dead, and then granted him divine status in heaven. Additionally, Arius surmised that if Jesus and God were the same entity, then God himself was subjected to the crucifixion at the hands of mankind, a preposterous notion to most of the bishops of that era. Thus, Arius correctly deduced that Jesus was inferior and subordinate to God, and Arius' viewpoint gained a lot of support from the bishops in the Eastern Catholic churches.

Nevertheless, a vocal minority of bishops in the West continued to argue that Jesus and God were one in the same. As mentioned in Chapter Two, the debate came to a head in 325 C.E. at the Council of Nicaea, which was attended by 250 bishops and which Roman Emperor Constantine called specifically to put an end to the Arian Controversy. Even though most of the bishops agreed with Arius – that Jesus was born a human and was subordinate to God – pressure from Emperor Constantine to reach a consensus prevailed. Unfortunately, by the end of the Council, the Holy Trinity was adopted as "orthodox" Christianity and the Arian position was officially banned. *The net result was that the bishops turned Jesus into a deity and granted him a divine status equivalent to God, in direct opposition to the Second Commandment, which states that there is only one God.*

The wounds from the Council of Nicaea never truly healed. Indeed, the fighting continued for centuries, as the bishops in the East continued to question the veracity of the Holy Trinity, which they viewed as a man-made convention.

Incidentally, the Bishop of Rome did not attend the Council of Nicaea. Recall that Constantinople had become the capitol of the Roman Empire. Consequently, Rome was not considered a major center of Christian thought at the time, and none of the bishops who attended the Council of Nicaea claimed superiority over any other bishop. Moreover, the term "Pope" would not come into common usage until approximately 450 C.E., when **Leo the Great**, the Bishop of Rome, unilaterally adopted this designation. Thereafter, successive Roman bishops, now calling themselves popes, began to assert that Rome should be the center of the Christian world and have the final say on matters of Church dogma. Not surprisingly, the response from successive Constantinople bishops, called "Patriarchs," was disdainful and unyielding. The patriarchs of Constantinople ignored the popes of Rome and continued to teach that Jesus had two natures, human and divine, and that Jesus was subordinate to God. Thus, the two branches of the Catholic Church never really agreed on Jesus' status.

In addition to continuing the debate over the Arian Controversy, the Eastern and Western branches of the Catholic Church began to argue over whether the pope in Rome or the patriarch in Constantinople should have ultimate authority over the Church. In 870 C.E., tensions between the two branches of the Church escalated further when **Pope Nicholas II** attempted to control the election of the patriarch of Constantinople and "excommunicated" **Patriarch Photius**, who was elected by the Eastern bishops. In response, Patriarch Photius excommunicated Pope Nicholas II. This in-fighting would continue for another few hundred years, as the Roman popes continued to seek dominance over the Constantinople patriarchs.

Finally, in 1054 C.E., the **Great Schism** occurred, when the Eastern bishops of the Catholic Church officially broke away from the Western bishops and formally rejected Rome's claim to superiority. Hence, the birth of the **Eastern Orthodox Church**. Thereafter, each church excommunicated the other, claiming that their version of Christianity was "orthodox." Today the two churches remain separate, with the Eastern Orthodox Church under the control of the Patriarch of Istanbul, Turkey (the current name for Constantinople), and the Catholic Church under the control of the Pope of Rome. Incidentally, in a rather amusing gesture of reconciliation, the Eastern Orthodox Church and the Catholic Church finally lifted their mutual excommunication of each other in 1965, in a joint statement read simultaneously in Istanbul and Rome.

The Great Schism dramatically altered the course of the Christian Crusades. The power hungry Catholic Church and the greedy European monarchs began to view the crusades as opportunities to undermine the newly formed Eastern Orthodox Church. Specifically, Western crusaders became more concerned with acquiring land and wealth than retaking Jerusalem. As a result, the Vatican surreptitiously undermined the **Fourth Crusade**, which Pope Innocent III sanctioned in 1201 C.E. During the Fourth Crusade, the knights from western Europe actually turned on the Christian residents of Constantinople, who were now members of the Eastern Orthodox Church. The Catholic knights burned and totally destroyed the beautiful city of Constantinople, which was home to the most impressive Christian cathedrals and which for nine hundred years had been the jewel of the Christian world.

The carnage wrought upon the city and people of Constantinople was recorded for our collective posterity and serves as yet another example of the corruption of the Catholic Church. Villehardouin, a contemporary historian of that time, wrote, "So much booty had never been gained in any city since the creation of the world." The Catholic crusaders not only decimated the city of Constantinople, they also slaughtered the Eastern Orthodox Christians. The Catholic knights then totally aborted the crusade in favor of taking their stolen riches home to the West. The result of this massacre was that Constantinople – the mightiest Christian outpost in the East – no longer was strong enough to fend off the Muslim Empire, which later expanded into Europe to become the greatest civilization in recorded history.

The Catholic Church split again after **Martin Luther**, a Catholic monk and professor of divinity at the University of Wittenburg in Germany, denounced the Church's corrupt practices. Luther visited Rome in 1510 C.E. and was shocked by the conduct of the Catholic priests, whom he viewed as greedy and immoral. Specifically, Luther was distressed over the religious rules and dogma which he believed exploited the uneducated masses. In addition, Luther believed that the Catholic Church could only be reformed if the man-made canon law was abandoned. To that end, in 1517 C.E. Luther tacked his famous *Ninety-five Theses* to the door of Wittenburg Church, attacking as "human doctrine" many of the Catholic canons, including the Indulgence, which was a payment of money that supposedly allowed the soul to skip purgatory and proceed directly to heaven. At the time, the Church was collecting Indulgences in order to build St. Peter's Basilica in Rome. The Vatican was quick to act and convicted Luther of heresy in *absentia* in 1518 C.E.

For a while, Luther went into hiding to evade the Inquisition. Later, he continued his attack on the Church and defended the works of Wycliffe and Hus, referring to Hus as a "Saint." In 1520 C.E., Luther publicly burned the Catholic canon law and the papal bull which excommunicated him. In retaliation, the Vatican commanded King Charles V of Germany to imprison Luther and hold him for an Inquisition. However, Elector Frederick, the governor of Luther's town, staged a kidnaping and hid Luther in a castle. While in hiding, Luther continued to write blistering books attacking the man-made rules on celibacy, confession, and communion. Luther also began to translate the *New Testament* into German. Eventually, Luther's protests started the **Reformation,** which spread throughout western Europe and which prompted many Christians to leave the Catholic Church for new sects, such as the **Lutheran Church.** Regrettably, as various Protestant churches took shape, they continued to rely on the Pauline version of Christianity, since Luther perpetuated the fallacy that faith alone, without good works or active compassion for others, is all that is required for a soul to gain access to heaven.

Ultimately, then, the Catholic Church was unable to prevent the Reformation movement. Even so, the Church continued to use the Inquisition to silence those who opposed its authority. The parallels between the Catholic Inquisition and the Sanhedrin Council are noteworthy, as true followers of Jesus were persecuted by corrupt Catholic bishops in the same manner that Jesus was condemned by corrupt Jewish rabbis. However, in my opinion the Inquisition constitutes the single greatest hypocrisy in religious history for the simple reason that its stated mission was to protect the "true" teachings of Jesus. The irony, of course, is that the very religion which claimed to revere Jesus the most sold him out for mere Earth plane riches and power.

Perhaps the acute pain I feel when I read about the Inquisition stems from the fact that I was raised a Catholic and feel some inner shame at my involuntary association with this religion. Or maybe I'm obsessed with the Catholic Church because I have yet to overcome all the damage that it inflicted upon me. Regardless of the motive my readers (or a psychiatrist) might assign me, I would be remiss if I failed to address what many consider to be the most egregious of all the Catholic Church betrayals. Indeed, what you are about to read is the real story of how and why the Inquisition was created in the first place. Here it is then: *The history of the Cathar Christians, who were pious followers of Jesus and the first victims of the Holy Inquisition.*

The **Cathars** were a puritan sect of Christians that flourished for hundreds of years in southern France until roughly 1300 C.E., when they were exterminated by the Catholic Church. The Cathars were spiritually descendant from the Gnostic Christians and believed that Jesus came to Earth to spread a new Truth about the benevolent nature of God that was not contained in the *Old Testament*. Consequently, the Cathars refused to attend the Catholic mass, which they viewed as tainted by man-made rules, ritual, and dogma. Instead, they preferred to worship God in their own homes or outside. In addition, the Cathars worshiped the mysterious **Black Madonna**.

The Cathars strictly followed Jesus' example of love and charity. They lived a communal existence, just as Jesus' chosen apostles lived in Jerusalem after the crucifixion. Moreover, they lived very simply, they adhered to a vegetarian diet, and they established a welfare system for the poor, including free schools and hospitals. They also invited anyone to join them and allowed women to both teach and preach about God. In fact, the Cathars were so highly regarded throughout France that they even had the support of Saint Bernard, who reported on their behalf, "No sermons are more Christian than theirs and their morals are pure." Nevertheless, for the reasons we are about to explore, the Catholic Church was so threatened by this small group of devout Christians that the Inquisition was created to eliminate them.

To fully appreciate this slice of Catholic history, we must first understand the connection between the Cathar Christians and the **Merovingian Dynasty** (a/k/a the "Fisher Kings"), who were rumored to be Jewish descendants from the House of David. Merovingian kings ruled Francia, an area now known as France, from 457 C.E. to 751 C.E. In the southern region of this kingdom along the Mediterranean Sea was a province called **Septimania** composed of Jewish settlers. In 719, C.E., the Muslim Empire conquered Spain and also Septimania. Despite the turbulence caused by this period of religious warfare, the Muslims were careful to leave Septimania unharmed. In fact, the Merovingians and the other Jewish leaders of Septimania enjoyed the support of the most powerful rulers of that era, including successive kings of France, popes in Rome, and Muslim caliphs in Baghdad.

Why, you may ask, did the minor Kingdom of Septimania merit such renown and universal support in the midst of medieval feuding and religious mayhem? The answer is quite astonishing and will help us understand why the Inquisition later targeted the peaceful Cathars. *The reason the Merovingian Dynasty was revered by the French monarchy, the Catholic Church, and the Muslim Empire is because the Merovingians were thought to be Jewish royalty descendant from the House of David.*

The Merovingian Dynasty also is connected to the **Legend of the Holy Grail**. In the classic tale, the Holy Grail is the cup that Jesus used at the Last Supper. Recently, however, historians have pieced together more of the facts which underlie this legend. As we shall see, the endless rumors, plays, art-work, ballads, and books regarding the Holy Grail not only involve Jesus, but also connect him to the Merovingian kings and the Cathars. Consequently, some scholars now believe that the legend further explains why the Catholic Church created the Inquisition and why the peaceful Cathars were singled out as Catholic "Enemy Number One."

Let us start this fascinating story against a known historical backdrop. In 632 C.E., the Prophet Muhammad died and within a few short years the Muslim Empire was fueled into action. The Arabs were zealous for their new religion and eager to acquire new lands, particularly since the Roman Empire lay in ruins and Palestine was vulnerable. Thus, the Arab tribes which united under Islam were eager to reclaim this sacred territory. By 638 C.E., the Muslim Empire had acquired Palestine and Jerusalem with it.

Meanwhile, the Christian world was plunged into darkness. The Roman order had been abolished and new monarchies were forming throughout Europe with varied alliances. A new Christian continent was slowly taking form and remapping itself for posterity. It was during this era that the Jewish principality of Septimania was formed. As already noted, the rulers of this region received protection from the French monarchy, the Catholic Church, and the Muslim Empire. But the rest of the world seemed permanently at war.

Historians refer to this period of relentless feuding as the **Dark Ages** because so much history was lost and so much went unrecorded. As it hap-pened, the Catholic Church thrived in this wasteland. The popes used this dark time to extend their control over the exhausted and pathetically impov-erished masses. In fact, the corruption within the Catholic Church was so rampant, the Church itself was in the midst of crisis. Pious clergy began to question the blatant avarice of the popes and the bishops. Consequently, much of the history of this time was purposely destroyed by the Catholic Church. Scholars are accustomed to this painful reality, as usurpers often destroy or rewrite history in order to justify their barbaric actions and conquests. Nevertheless, researchers have painstakingly recovered sufficient information about this period to now explain why the Catholic Church feared the Cathars. May God bless and protect all pursuers of Truth.

Over the next four hundred years, while rival European monarchs fought over territory and the Pope of Rome and the Patriarch of Constantinople split the Catholic Church in the Great Schism, the Muslims managed to build the largest lasting empire in recorded history. Eventually, the Christians regrouped and decided to challenge the Arabs. In 1095 C.E., **Pope Urban II** called for the **First Crusade,** a holy war to take Jerusalem from the Muslim Empire. The European lords consented to the war and ordered their knights, known as "crusaders," to the Holy Land. In 1099 C.E., the crusaders successfully captured Jerusalem, and Crusader States were established in Palestine.

After the war, a French nobleman named **Godfroi de Bouillon** was appointed the ruler of the new **Kingdom of Jerusalem,** with the blessing of the pope. The new monarch rejected the title of king and instead took the title Defender Bouillon of the Holy Sepulcher. The term "sepulcher" refers to the tomb of Jesus. Researchers now have evidence that Defender Bouillon was related to the Merovingian Dynasty. *Thus, if the rumors about the Merovingian Dynasty are true, then a descendant from the House of David was once again the King of Jerusalem.* This also would explain why the pope agreed that Defender Bouillon was qualified to rule Jerusalem. Immediately after assuming the crown, Defender Bouillon built a Catholic abbey on Mt. Zion called the **Abbey of Sion.** Interestingly enough, the monks of the new **Order of Sion** worshiped the mysterious Black Madonna, just like the Cathars.

In 1100 C.E., Defender Bouillon died and his younger brother became **King Baudouin I** of Jerusalem. In 1118 C.E., King Baudouin I was approached by a man named Hugh de Payen, who requested permission to start an order of warrior monks called the **Knights Templar.** The stated purpose of the Knights Templar was to protect the roads between the Palestine coast and Jerusalem so that pilgrims could travel safely to the Holy City. King Baudouin I granted the order, which originally consisted of only nine knights. Strangely, however, the knights did not protect the roads and would not admit anyone else into their order. Instead, they immediately set up a permanent camp at the Jewish Temple ruins and started to dig. In 1127 C.E., after nine years of digging, the knights returned to France as though their mission was completed.

So what was the real mission of the Knights Templar? Historians have speculated for centuries that the knights were searching for something of immense value that may have been buried by the Jews prior to the destruction of the Temple in 70 C.E. British engineers were able to excavate the site for the first time in 1867 C.E., and what they found was astounding. Underneath the

Temple ruins, there is an eighty foot vertical shaft. From this vertical tunnel, multiple horizontal tunnels fan out, with one of them leading to the Dome of the Rock, the Muslim mosque built in 639 C.E. on the Temple mount. However, the British found nothing of value in the empty tunnels.

Therefore, the question remains: *Did the Knights Templar find something of value under the Jewish Temple ruins?* Luckily, the *Dead Sea Scrolls* hold a clue. If you will recall, one of the members of the international team, John Allegro, believed that the *Copper Scroll* was an inventory of the Jewish treasury. Archeologists have never been able to find the treasure, which included gold, silver, and the Ark of Covenant, which supposedly housed the Ten Commandments. Today, however, historians have collected enough circumstantial evidence from verifiable sources that the weight of the evidence is overwhelming. In sum, many historians now think that the Knights Templar unearthed the Jewish treasury and then brought their booty back to France. Thus, the legend of the Holy Grail states that the Knights Templar found the Jewish treasury, which included not only gold and silver, but also the Holy Grail.

For now, however, let's stick with known facts. The next important event occurred in 1128 C.E., a year after the knights stopped digging at the Temple ruins and returned to France. The knights were greeted with great fanfare, and Saint Bernard convened a Church council in France to laud the knights and officially recognize them as a religious order. Hugh de Payon was named the first Grand Master of the Knights Templar. Then, in 1139 C.E., **Pope Innocent II** issued a papal bull acknowledging the knights as an official order of the Catholic Church. As a result, their ranks swelled and thousands of knights were sent to defend the Crusader States. What is peculiar about the pope's decree, though, is that the grand master was given complete autonomy. No Catholic bishop and no monarch had any control over the order. The end result was that the Knights Templar became the independent military arm of the Catholic Church.

The knights were sworn to poverty, chastity, and obedience, and they followed stringent rules that controlled their diet, grooming, and dress. They wore white tunics with a red cross emblazoned on the front, and their creed was to fight to the death for Christ. Even though the knights themselves lived simply, their unexplained wealth and influence spawned rumors that they had found a great treasure in Jerusalem that included the Holy Grail. Moreover, some knights worshiped the Black Madonna, just like the Cathars and the monks at the Order of Sion. Also, the knights were headquartered in southern

France and closely aligned with the Cathars. In fact, some of the knights were Cathars, including some of the grand masters.

After receiving the pope's blessing, the Knights Templar were very busy. To start with, the order was granted lands by European nobility on which to build and live. In exchange, the knights granted protection to Christian monarchies. Because it was considered a great honor to be admitted into the Knights Templar, most royal families requested membership in the order. As a result, the number of knights soared and they soon were able to control both the land and sea around the Christian world. In fact, the knights had their own navy composed of both war ships and commercial vessels. The knights were universally praised as being brave, fair, and noble, and there is no evidence that they ever abused their power.

The Knights Templar also were prolific builders. They built hundreds of castles and forts for the European monarchs and the Catholic Church. In total, the Knights Templar built over three hundred churches. Some of the Templar cathedrals are astounding, both in scale and due to their unique architecture. In order to build on such a scale, the knights trained their own stone masons, who were called the **Children of Solomon**, after Jewish King Solomon who built the first Temple in Jerusalem. It was rumored that the geometry and physics used by the masons was based on mathematical formulas taught by the Egyptians and known by the Muslims. The **Freemasons**, a secret society that still exists today, is descendant from the Children of Solomon.

Over time, the Templar real estate holdings and businesses grew to include farms, mines, and stone quarries. The knights also owned lodges and merchandising operations. In England alone, they owned over five thousand properties. The knights also established their own banking system and invented the world's first credit card. In fact, the bank operated by the Knights Templar was used by the entire Christian world, and the knights often lent money to the nobility and the Catholic Church. Additionally, the knights were responsible for communications in the Christian world, as their fleet of ships carried both merchandise and mail. Thus, historians also credit the knights with creating the first public post office.

In sum, the Order of the Knights Templar was the world's first business conglomerate. Without question, during the 12th and 13th Centuries the Knights Templar was the wealthiest and most advanced organization on the face of the Earth. However, despite their amazing accomplishments and their reputation for honesty and hard work, the knights frequently are referred to in the history books as "illiterate warriors." Shortly, you will understand why the Catholic Church tried to erase the Knights Templar from our history books ... and also how the Catholic Church managed to acquire much of its staggering wealth.

In 1187 C.E., the Knights Templar lost Jerusalem to the Muslim Empire. It was a crushing blow and it caused internal conflict within the order. As a result, the Knights Templar and the Order of Sion appear to have split from each other. Thereafter, the Order of Sion became known as the **Priory of Sion,** a secret organization which allegedly separated from the Catholic Church and which may still exist today. However, the Knights Templar stayed loyal to the pope and, for the next hundred years, attempted to regain the Holy Land. As the Appendix shows, though, the knights were unable to permanently recapture Jerusalem, which caused them to lose prestige and eventually the support of the pope and the King of France.

While the Order of the Knights Templar was busy licking its wounds over the loss of Jerusalem and mounting multiple crusades to retake the Holy Land, a different storm was brewing in southern France. The Cathars continued to defy the authority of the Catholic Church, although not in a confrontational manner. As previously noted, the Cathars simply wanted to conduct their own religious services in their homes or fields. They also continued to worship the enigmatic Black Madonna. Then suddenly, and with no apparent provocation, the pope took aim at the Cathars and let fly such wrath that scholars still are scratching their heads in disbelief.

In 1209 C.E., Pope Innocent III issued a papal bull against the Cathars, declaring them heretics and condemning them to death. The pope called for a full scale crusade against the Cathars, called the **Albigensian Crusade.** In order to entice the European nobility to participate in the slaughter, the pope decreed that the crusaders would receive Indulgences for heaven and that they could seize Cathar property. Approximately thirty thousand crusaders descended on the pacifist Cathars and went to work. In the southern French city of Beziers, over twenty thousand Cathars were slain. Indeed, in their zeal to wipe out the Cathar Christians, the crusaders also killed many Catholics. The papal legate in charge of the mass extermination, Arnald Amalric, callously declared to his troops, "Kill them all, God will recognize his own."

This purge continued for years. In 1229 C.E., the King of France joined the fray, as he saw an opportunity to annex the southern province of Languedoc. However, the Cathars had the support of the Knights Templar, who knew the

Cathars well because most of them lived in southern France where the knights were headquartered. Moreover, some of the knights were Cathars themselves. History reveals that a few knights actually hid Cathars to help them escape, but most of the knights were engaged in the crusades against the Muslim Empire. Although the Knights Templar never openly confronted the Catholic Church, the entity they were sworn to protect, it is clear that the knights refused to participate in the Cathar persecutions.

Then in 1231 C.E., Pope Gregory IX officially created the Inquisition to eliminate heresy, defined as a "deliberate denial of a Catholic article of truth and a public persistence in that error." The Cathars still were the primary target. The standing order to the inquisitors was, "Show mercy neither to order, nor to age, nor to sex." One of the final scenes of devastation occurred at the Seminary of Montsegur in 1244 C.E. More than two hundred Cathars refused to renounce their faith and were burned alive at the stake. The net result of this genocide is that by the early 1300s C.E., the Cathars had been completely wiped out by the Catholic Church.

The history books list a variety of reasons for the Catholic Church's purge of the Cathars. First, the Cathars rejected the notion that Jesus was God. Instead, the Cathars believed that Jesus was a divine soul sent to teach mankind how to achieve union with God. Second, the Cathars were spiritually similar to the Gnostic Christians, who believed that Jesus passed secret knowledge to his closest disciples, such as Mary Magdalene, that was not being taught by the Catholic Church. Third, the Carthars wanted to personally commune with God, without a priest acting as intermediary. Lastly, the Cathars did not believe that blind faith would save their souls. Rather, they understood the lessons of Christ and knew that salvation is won through the exercise of compassionate acts toward others.

While such a difference of opinion on how to reach God might explain why the Catholics sought to eliminate the Cathars, new research suggests a much stronger motive. Indeed, those independent scholars who have focused on the legend of the Holy Grail have a new theory on why the Church attacked the Cathars. The key to the mystery is the relationship between the Cathars and the Knights Templar. Some historians now think that the Cathars knew of the sacred items found by the Knights at the Jewish Temple – including precious manuscripts that detailed the true nature of the Holy Grail. If this is true, then the fates of the Cathars and the knights were inexorably linked, which would explain what happened next.

When the knights refused to participate in the massacre of the Cathars, **Pope Clement V** began to question their loyalty. The pope also had to be covetous of the knights' wealth and jealous of their prestige. Moreover, in addition to being the richest men on Earth, the knights also were rumored to possess important and potentially embarrassing documentation proving that Jesus was directly related to the Merovingian Dynasty. Add to these strong conjectures the fact that the Vatican was heavily in debt to the knights. Likewise, **King Phillip IV** of France was hopelessly in debt to the order. The king also hated the Knights Templar because he had been refused admittance into the order as a young man, a humiliation he never forgot. *Thus, based on the most current research, many historians now believe that King Philip IV and Pope Clement V conspired to exterminate both the Cathars and the Knights Templar.*

On **Friday the 13th**, in October of 1307 C.E., the Inquisition backed by King Philip IV arrested the grand master and the principal knights of the Order of the Knights Templar. The knights were accused of being sympathetic to the heretical Cathars and failing to protect the Holy Land by colluding with the Muslim Empire. In addition, the inquisitors charged the knights with sodomy, heresy, and witchcraft. It is much more likely, however, especially given the recent research, that the pope and the king feared the knights' influence with the common people, and that they wanted to confiscate the knights' real estate holdings and massive treasury.

It is fascinating to me that the one piece of this story which everyone knows is the day that the Knights Templar were seized by the Inquisition. Indeed, more than seven hundred years have passed since the pope betrayed the Knights Templar. And still, Friday the 13th is imprinted on our brains. For anyone who doubts it, this is proof positive that mankind has a collective consciousness. Each of us is aware that evil won a huge victory on that ominous date.

Thereafter, the grand master and hundreds of the knights were killed by the Inquisition. **Grand Master Jacques de Molay** was publically burned to death over a slow fire. Before he died, de Molay cursed Pope Clement V and King Philip IV and prophesied their deaths. Not coincidentally, both the pope and the king died within a year of de Molay's curse. As my own personal epitaph to Pope Clement V, may I express my sincere doubts that the pope's faith in Jesus as a personal savior got him anywhere close to heaven.

Incidentally, before King Philip IV died, he attempted to steal the knights' treasury, but his plan was foiled. The main treasury of the Knights Templar had been emptied and most of the knights' naval fleet had vanished. Thus, some of the knights managed to escape and records indicate that the surviving knights landed in Scotland with their treasure. The pope fared far better than the king, however. The Catholic Church confiscated the majority of the real estate owned by the Knights Templar. *Indeed, the Church's theft of the knights' holdings is one of the reasons why the Catholic Church is the wealthiest institution on the planet.*

Thus, most historians still believe that the reason that the pope and the king attacked the knights was to acquire their wealth and undermine their influence with the common people – the cardinal sins of greed and pride. However, new research suggests there is more to the story. Some scholars now suspect that the primary reason the pope destroyed and disbanded the Knights Templar is that the knights knew the Truth about the Holy Grail. *Specifically, the updated legend is that the Merovingian line of monarchs, rumored to be descendant from the House of David, were literally descendant from the union between Jesus and Mary Magdalene.*

At this juncture, allow me to summarize the most recent research on the legend of the Holy Grail. The updated legend starts with the secret marriage of Jesus and Mary Magdalene (hereafter referred to as Mary). Biblical scholars agree that Jesus was from the Tribe of Judah and somehow descendant from Jewish King David. In the *New Testament*, Mary also is identified as Mary of Bethany, which would make her a member of the Tribe of Benjamin. Researchers have theorized that a match between Jesus and Mary would have been quite powerful and would have further bonded the tribes of Judah and Benjamin, which traditionally had been allies.

Those who subscribe to this legend also have a ready answer for why the *New Testament* is silent about such an important wedding. They claim that the marriage was purposely kept secret to avoid unnecessary attention on such a dynastic couple. As discussed in Chapter Two, it is very likely that Jesus was considered royalty at birth, as the canonical gospels suggest that many people knew of his heritage. Therefore, Jesus was likely a high profile personality, especially after he started to minister. Consequently, Mary may have needed protection. Recall that Jesus was being attacked on all fronts, as the Romans, the Sanhedrin priests, their minion Saul of Tarsus (i.e., Paul), and King Herod Antipas, all opposed the Jesus movement.

Legend researchers also suspect that Mary's last name was not a reference to the town of Magdala, but to the Hebrew word *"Magdaleder."* In the *Old*

Testament, the Prophet **Micah** predicted that a *Magdaleder*, which is Hebrew for "Tower of the Flock," would help restore the Jewish Kingdom. Also, this scripture states that a "***Batgader***" which means "fenced-in Maiden," would give birth to a new ruler from the House of David.

> In days to come the mount of the Lord's house shall be established higher than the mountains; it shall rise high above the hills, and peoples shall stream to it. ...
>
> And you, O Magdaleder, hillock of daughter Zion! Unto you shall it come: the former dominion shall be restored, the kingdom of daughter Jerusalem.
>
> Now why do you cry out so? Are you without a king? Or has your counselor perished, that you are seized with pains like a woman in travail? ... For now shall you go forth from the city and dwell in the fields; To Babylon shall you go, there shall you be rescued. ... How many nations are gathered against you! They say, "Let her be profaned, let our eyes see Zion's downfall!" ...
>
> Now fence yourself in, Batgader! They have laid siege against us! With the rod they strike on the cheek the ruler of Israel. ... Therefore the Lord will give them up, until the time when she who is to give birth has borne, and the rest of his brethren shall return to the children of Israel. [Emphasis added]
>
> *Micah*, Chapters 4, 5

In the above passage, which Christians have interpreted as referring to the Virgin Mary, there are at least four reasons why the "mother" figure cannot be Jesus' mother. To begin with, the *Magdaleder* is told to go forth from the city (of Jerusalem) and hide as "many nations are gathered against you." With regard to the Virgin Mary, there is no evidence that she was ever in danger or that she went into hiding and then had to be rescued. Second, the passage indicates that the mother will be "profaned," but the Virgin Mary is revered by all the other religions. Third, the mother is instructed to, "fence yourself in" because a siege has started. This passage logically relates to the time after Jesus is crucified, as evidenced by the earlier question, "Are you without a king?" Fourth, the last sentence makes clear that Jesus is not the prophesied child, since before the mother gives birth to the unknown child the enemies already have persecuted the "ruler of Israel."

Based on this *Old Testament* prophesy, some scholars believe that the *New Testament* references to Mary Magdalene are garbled records of her formal title, "Mary the Magdaleder." Additionally, we learn from the *New Testament* that Mary had a brother named Lazarus and a sister named

Martha, and that Jesus often stayed at their home in Bethany, not Magdala. Furthermore, some historians believe that the town of Magdala did not exist until the 2nd or 3rd Century.

Moreover, legend scholars believe that the canonical gospels do cite the wedding between Jesus and Mary, namely, the wedding at Cana. This wedding must have been an important event in the life of Jesus because it is carefully described in the *Gospel of John*. The following evidence suggests that the wedding at Cana may have been for Jesus and Mary: (i) the wedding took place right after Jesus collected his twelve apostles and immediately before the start of his ministry, which indicates that Jesus was getting married in anticipation of a new chapter in his life, similar to the timing of wartime weddings as soldiers leave for battle; (ii) Jesus' mother attended the wedding; (iii) all the apostles were present; (iv) Jesus' mother came to him for help when the wine ran out, as though it was their obligation to attend to the guests; (v) Jesus took command of the situation by instructing the waiters to serve guests from the water jugs; (vi) Jesus' act of turning water into wine was the first miracle reported in the *Gospel of John*; (vii) Jesus brought Mary's brother Lazarus back from the dead; and (viii) Mary traveled with Jesus according to the *Gospel of Luke*, a privilege that an unmarried woman would not have assumed in the Jewish culture of that era.

The updated legend continues with Mary's pregnancy. Researchers speculate that before Jesus was crucified, Mary conceived a child and that the pregnancy, just like the marriage, was kept a secret. The gospels tell us that after Jesus was killed, his body was taken to a tomb belonging to Joseph of Arimathea, a wealthy patron who also may have been a family member. There is an oral tradition that Joseph took Mary and the unborn child to Alexandria on the northern coast of Egypt. According to these stories, Mary delivered a baby girl in Alexandria and then fled across the Mediterranean Sea to the southern coast of France.

Traditionally, the legend of the Holy Grail has centered on the cup that Jesus used at the Last Supper and passed around to the apostles. In the gospels, Jesus told the apostles that the wine in the chalice was symbolic of his blood, which would be shed for mankind. After the crucifixion, Joseph of Arimathea supposedly took the chalice to Europe. In the earliest renditions of the tale, including the romances about King Arthur, the chalice is referred to as the *"Sangreal."* Throughout history, this French word has been translated "Holy Grail." Legend scholars suggest that this translation is based on separating the word thus, "San-Grael." However, if the word is separated in this manner, "Sang-Real," the meaning of the word changes to "Royal Blood." Thus, the updated legend holds that the grail is a metaphor for Mary's womb, the actual vessel which contained the royal blood (i.e., bloodline) of Jesus. Ironically, if this version of the story is true, it would mean that another Joseph protected another Mary who carried yet another royal descendant from the House of David.

Unfortunately, we may never know the Truth behind the legend, either the original tale about the chalice or the updated version made famous in Dan Brown's novel *The Da Vinci Code*. Nevertheless, the new evidence involving Mary Magdalene is persuasive. For instance, there is a little French town along the Mediterranean coastline called *Les Saints Maries de la Mer*, which means, "Saint Mary of the Sea." Also in this town is a shrine to **"Saint Sarah the Egyptian,"** even though there is no Saint Sarah in the Catholic Church. However, in Hebrew *sarah* means "princess." To this day, the town celebrates a festival dedicated to a "Black Queen" and her daughter Sarah.

In trying to put all of these puzzle pieces together, researchers have formed an interesting hypothesis. *They believe that Jesus and Mary had a daughter, a Jewish princess named Sarah.* In addition, they believe that Mary Magdalene is both the Black Queen worshiped in France and the Black Madonna worshiped by the monks at the Order of Sion, the Knights Templar, and the Cathars. Thus, they suspect that the statues of the Black Madonna and child found in numerous Catholic Churches are depictions of Mary Magdalene and Sarah, not the Virgin Mary and Jesus.

The legend of the Holy Grail continues with Sarah, who supposedly married into another royal family – the Merovingian Dynasty. Recall that Merovingian kings ruled in the region now known as France from 457 C.E. to 751 C.E. Their reign ended when the last of the Merovingian kings was deposed by **Pepin III** (a/k/a Pepin the Short), who then assumed the crown. Thereafter, a new royal line ruled the Franks, known as the **Carolingian Dynasty**. However, legend scholars assert that this was not the end of the Merovingian story.

Trouble actually started for the Merovingians in 679 C.E. when **King Dagobert II** was assassinated, possibly at the hands of his mayor **Pepin II** (a/k/a Pepin of Herstal), Pepin II was Pepin III's grandfather. Consequently, many historians believe that Pepin II conspired with the Vatican to assassinate Dagobert II, since Pepin III later was crowned King of the Franks and anointed by **Pope Stephan II**. This coronation was significant because it was the first time a monarch was anointed by a pope of the Roman Catholic Church. Thereafter,

Pepin III's son and heir, **Charlemagne**, would go a step further. In 800 C.E., **Pope Leo III** crowned him **Charles I**, the first **Holy Roman Emperor**. *This obsequious act by Charlemagne would result in the Vatican assuming both religious and political authority over the entire Christian world.*

To recap, historians universally accept that in 751 C.E., Pepin III ended the Merovingian Dynasty and started his own Carolingian Dynasty. However, the legend scholars assert that the Merovingian line continued. In fact, Carolingian family records reveal that Pepin III's sister Auda married one or possibly two men – both named Theodoric (a/k/a Thierry IV; a/k/a Makir Theodoric). Legend proponents believe that one of her husbands (or both if the personages were purposely scrambled) is none other than Merovingian **King Therodoric IV**, who reigned from 720 C.E. until his death in 737 C.E. Genealogy charts also indicate that the couple had a son who some researchers believe was **Guilhelm de Gellone** (a/k/a Count Guilhem de Toulouse), another dynastic figure.

In addition, after Emperor Charlemagne inherited the throne, there is evidence that he wanted (or needed) to appease the Jewish populace of Septimania, who still were loyal to the Merovingians. Therefore, in order to heal old wounds and foster a new loyalty to the Carolingians, legend scholars assert that Emperor Charlemagne appointed his Merovingian cousin, Guilhelm de Gellone, to be the King of Septimania. These historians point to evidence that Guilhelm lived in the region, started a Jewish academy in nearby Narbonne, and adopted the "Lion of Judah" as his new royal crest, which was the same crest used by King David and the Tribe of Judah. If true, then this is one branch of the Merovingian line through which the legend of the Holy Grail continues.

Next, recall that after the Knights Templar acquired the Holy City in 1099 C.E., Defender Bouillon was appointed by the pope to rule the new Kingdom of Jerusalem. Legend researchers have compiled a family history which shows that Defender Bouillon was related to two of the Merovingian kings: King Theodoric IV on his mother's side and King Dagobert II on his father's side. So this constitutes a second branch of the Merovingian line through which the legend progresses

In addition to this family history, legend scholars have researched the old Merovingian estate located in the southern French town of Rennes le Chateau and the church dedicated to Mary Magdalene. In fact, King Dagobert II was married in the church and his son, **Sigebert IV**, supposedly hid in the church to evade Pepin II when his father and the other male members of the family were murdered. Researchers have uncovered some bizarre events involving the estate. Most notably, in 1891 C.E., a Catholic priest by the name of **Father Sauniere** was assigned to the thousand year old church. According to the legend, Father Sauniere found documents hidden inside the church which prove the continued existence of the secret society known as the Priory of Sion and its connection to the Knights Templar, the Cathars, and the Merovingian Dynasty.

Soon thereafter, Father Sauniere reportedly received a great sum of money which he used to completely rebuild the Tower of Magdalene, which is part of the church at Rennes le Chateau. At the time, it was rumored that Father Sauniere was paid by the Catholic Church to keep quiet about the documents he had found. Moreover, it was reported that when Father Sauniere was on his death bed making his last confession, the attending priest would not absolve him of a great sin and also refused to administer him the last rites. So the question is: *Did Father Sauniere find something of value at the Merovingian church dedicated to Mary Magdalene?*

Legend researchers believe that Father Sauniere found documents which include genealogy charts for the Merovingian Dynasty and other documents which prove a link between the House of David and current monarchs and aristocrats around the world. Legend proponents also point to the notorious *Dossiers Secret*, a collection of documents and genealogy charts discovered in the National Library of Paris in the 1960s, some of which purport to list the grand masters of the Knights Templar, including Leonardo Da Vinci, Isaac Newton, and Victor Hugo. At the time of this discovery, both sets of documents made quite a splash and, along with Dan Brown's best-selling novel *The Da Vinci Code*, furthered the legend of the Holy Grail as it relates to the bloodline of Christ. Today, however, these documents have been shown to be forgeries created by a man who desired to establish a relationship between his own family and the Merovingian line.

As a result of these recent forgeries and the assault by the Catholic Church on Dan Brown, most people have concluded that the legend of the secret marriage and progeny of Jesus and Mary Magdalene is a farce. And perhaps they are right … maybe it is just a fairytale. Yet, even when we exclude the recent forgeries related to this mystery, there still exists historical evidence of nefarious conduct on the part of the Vatican and the numerous monarchs of Europe who conspired against the Merovingians, the Cathar Christians, the Jews, and any other "heretical" group that claimed to have superior knowledge about or a special relationship with Jesus. And there still exists genealogical evidence that a royal Jewish bloodline existed and may still exist today. Here is the family tree which supports this hypothesis.

GRAIL FAMILY TREE

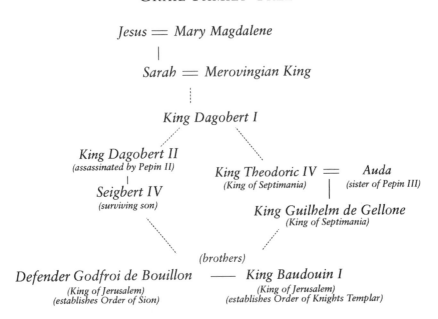

Jesus = Mary Magdalene
|
Sarah = Merovingian King
⋮
King Dagobert I

King Dagobert II
(assassinated by Pepin II)
|
Seigbert IV
(surviving son)

King Theodoric IV = Auda
(King of Septimania) | *(sister of Pepin III)*

King Guilhelm de Gellone
(King of Septimania)

(brothers)

Defender Godfroi de Bouillon —— King Baudouin I
(King of Jerusalem)   *(King of Jerusalem)*
(establishes Order of Sion)   *(establishes Order of Knights Templar)*

Therefore, let us suppose for the sake of argument that King Dagobert II truly was related to Jesus. This would explain why the pope feared him and wanted him eliminated. Thereafter, perhaps the Catholic Church became comfortable with the Merovingian secret. Or maybe the Church was given assurances that the secret would remain hidden for all time in exchange for a truce. After all, if the Church believed that the Merovingians were related to Jesus, one would think that the pope might hesitate to kill them. Thus, a secret compact would explain why Charlemagne and the pope might agree to place Guilhelm on the throne in the new Jewish Kingdom of Septimania. This theory also would explain why multiple popes, kings of France, and even the caliphs of the Muslim Empire thereafter honored this minor kingdom. The pope's complicity also would explain why Defender Bouillon was uncontested as the rightful King of Jerusalem after the First Crusade.

On some level, however, the Catholic Church probably realized that this secret would one day leak out. If it were ever revealed, the secret would destroy the very bedrock of Christianity. Moreover, assuming the Knights

Templar unearthed actual proof of the secret when they dug under the Temple ruins, the Church and the Carolingian Dynasty might reconsider their secret pact with the Merovingian heirs. Thus, the more people learned the Truth about Jesus, the more the Church's vulnerability and fear increased.

Most likely, the original nine knights already knew the secret, which is why they went digging for treasure in the first place. Stories about the Holy Grail abounded throughout Europe. So even if they didn't know about the secret before their expedition, the knights appear to have found something of extreme value, including, possibly, documents which supported the legend. That would explain why the pope was eager to bring the knights into the fold and also why he agreed to let the knights be autonomous. Remember, "knowledge is power." In other words, the knights had become major players in this drama and commanded respect. To their credit, though, it appears that the knights never abused their power and kept their end of the bargain by protecting the pope and orthodox Christianity.

At this point, however, too many people knew the secret behind the legend. The Cathars knew it, since they maintained that Jesus was human and they worshiped the Black Madonna who was Mary Magdalene. Additionally, the monks at the Abbey of Sion knew the secret, as they, too, paid homage to the Black Madonna. Finally, once the Order of the Knights Templar split from the Order of Sion and established the secret Priory of Sion, it is likely that even more people learned the Truth about the progeny of Jesus and Mary.

Let us also not forget that whatever the knights possessed – whether booty or information – they did not hand it over to the Vatican. Instead, the knights took their riches and discoveries to the Cathar region of southern France. This had to make the Catholic Church even more nervous, which would explain why the pope conspired with the King of France to get rid of the Cathars and the knights. Moreover, the pope and the king were heavily in debt to the knights, yet another motive for murder. Thus, not only was the Merovingian secret on the brink of being exposed, the knights now had evidence to prove the true meaning of the legend of the Holy Grail. Consequently, the Catholic Church needed a plan to make the secret disappear forever.

As it turns out, the pope would have to wait a while for an opportune moment to attack the knights, since they grew more powerful and wealthy with every passing year. Besides which, the knights still served an important purpose – protecting the Holy Land. However, when the knights lost Jerusalem, the defeat presented an opportunity. Finally, the knights were vulnerable. Moreover, while the knights were busy trying to recover Jerusalem, the pope saw his chance to deal with the problematic Cathars. They, too, knew the secret and had to be eliminated. Hence, the time was ripe. So the pope and the King of France conspired to exterminate the Cathars. Once the Cathars were gone, the pope turned on the Knights. The rest, as they say, is history.

Or not ... since much of the history which the Catholic Church modified or obliterated to conform to their version of events has now been called into question by a new generation of historians. If the legend is true and if it ever can be proved, then one day we may know for certain whether Jesus and Mary Magdalene have descendants who are walking the Earth right now.

In sum, given all the attention being paid to the updated legend of the Holy Grail in books, movies, television specials, internet sites, and church lectures, I suspect we are nearing the time when mankind will finally learn and accept the Truth about Jesus – that he was a man, not a god. In the end, though, it doesn't really matter whether Jesus was married or had children. *What matters is the Truth and mankind's embrace of the Fifth Spiritual Paradigm which Jesus described.*

Lastly, before we conclude this section on the morality of Christianity, I feel compelled to address the embedded anti-Semitism that has plagued the Christian religion. From the start, Christians have abused Jews, as evidenced by the biblical account of Pontius Pilate first condemning Jesus to death, then trying to save his life. This story makes no sense and serious scholars reject it. Nevertheless, according to all four canonical gospels, Pilate tried to save Jesus. Moreover, in three of the gospels Pilate offers to release Jesus or a Jewish Zealot named Barabbas in honor of Passover. But still, the screaming Jewish crowd wants Jesus to die.

These accounts are absurd for several reasons. First, there was no Roman custom of releasing Jewish prisoners on Passover. Indeed, Romans were not in the habit of freeing seditious prisoners on holidays or any other day. They were ruthless and maintained order by the sword. Second, the story has Pontius Pilate actually going to bat for Jesus and trying to convince the Jews to free him, as though Pilate, whom historians regard as one of the most barbaric Romans of all time, would worry about killing a Jew. Third, after Pilate supposedly "washes his hands" of the affair, the Jews scream, "His blood be upon us and upon our children." Again, it is hard to imagine the Jews cursing themselves. It is much easier to believe that if they had a chance to save Jesus, whom many thought was the Messiah, the Jews would have jumped at the chance.

From this fabricated story, the Catholic Church would declare with right-eous indignation, "The Jews killed Jesus." This was standard Catholic rheto-ric until 1962, a mere forty-seven years ago, when the second **Pope John XXIII** officially exonerated the Jews from responsibility for killing Jesus (recall that the first Pope John XXIII was declared an anti-pope for piracy, murder, rape, sodomy, and incest). Prior to this pronouncement, the Catholics were loath to address, let alone assist, the Jews who were systematically spurned from every Christian nation for centuries on end. The Appendix lists the relentless expulsion of Jews by various nations, known as the **Diaspora**.

Indeed, the Catholic Church fueled the despicable treatment of the Jews. For instance, in 1215 C.E. during **Lateran Council IV**, the Church adopted a variety of oppressive rules aimed at suppressing the Jews. As a result, Jews were forced to wear distinctive clothing so that Christians could avoid dealing with them. In addition, Jewish books were burned, Jews were prohibited from hold-ing public office, and Jews had to stay indoors on Palm Sunday. Thereafter, the Jews were a favorite target of the Inquisition, which forced them either to con-vert to Christianity or forfeit their properties. Another prime example of Christian anti-Semitism occurred in 1556 C.E., when **Pope Paul IV** established a Jewish ghetto in Italy to further isolate the Jews. This novel approach to con-taining the Jewish populace would later be adopted by other Christian nations, including Germany under Adolf Hitler, who used ghettos to round up Jews for slaughter in furtherance of the "The Final Solution."

In fact, the Catholic Church did absolutely nothing to stop the **Holocaust**. On the contrary, **Pope Pius XII** entered into an agreement with several fascist regimes, including Nazi Germany, and even endorsed Hitler's government in order to protect Vatican City. Thereafter, the Church stayed abhorrently silent during the Holocaust, which resulted in the death of six million Jews. Incidentally, the Catholic Church currently is in the process of making Pope Pius XII a Saint. Needless to say, the Jewish people view the canonization of Pope Pius XII as monstrous.

In conclusion and for innumerable reasons, it is apparent that the Catholic Church has continuously and habitually committed unspeakable atrocities against mankind and performed unforgivable acts of depravity, all of which constitute a pattern and practice of immoral behavior in total violation of *Rule Number 3*. Furthermore, to the extent that the other Christian sects have denounced the sordid history of Christianity and now adhere to the moral les-sons taught by Jesus, I applaud them for their rebellion against the Catholic Church and their compliance with the ethical mandates of *Rule Number 3*.

Lastly, before we leave *Rule Number 4* concerning the supremacy of God's law, we must address the doctrine of Papal Infallibility, which purports to make the pope the final arbiter of all issues involving God. This man-made law has been attacked by so many respected theologians, philosophers, and spiritualists, and also caused so many divisions within the Church, it is hard to believe that Catholics still hold onto it as an article of faith. Nevertheless, I will take the time to argue the obvious: *Roman Catholic popes do not, by virtue of their office, speak for God.*

To begin with, the doctrine of Papal Infallibility is based on the false premise that the Roman popes can trace their predecessors all the way back to the apostle Peter, who the Catholic Church claims was the first pope ordained by Jesus. This succession theory for the Roman papacy is patently absurd for a whole host of reasons. First, as discussed in Chapter Two, Jesus' brother James the Just not only was the first Bishop of Jerusalem, he was the uncontested leader of the Christian movement after Jesus died. Regarding the other two "pillars of the church," Peter likely was second or third in command along with John. Nevertheless, the Catholic Church retroactively named Peter the first "Pope of Rome," despite the fact that there is no evidence that Peter ever went to Rome. In fact, history reveals that the first documented Bishop of Rome was a preacher named Clement, who lived around 90 C.E. and who wrote the *Epistle of Clement*, an apocryphal scripture that was originally included and then rejected as part of the *New Testament*. Once again, independent historians find the Catholic Church guilty of trying to rewrite history by retroactively retitling the first Bishop of Rome the fourth Pope of Rome, **Pope Clement I.**

Moreover, even if Clement knew Peter, as Catholics like to opine, the Bishop of Rome was not a powerful figure in the Christian movement. Recall that at the Church's inception, Rome no longer was the locus of power, as Emperor Constantine had moved his capital to Constantinople. Consequently, the bishops of Constantinople, Jerusalem, Antioch, and Alexandria had much more power than the Bishop of Rome, who did not even bother to attend some of the most important Church councils, such as the Council of Nicaea in 325 C.E., the Council of Constantinople in 381 C.E., and the 2nd Council of Ephesus in 449 C.E. Indeed, when Bishop Leo of Rome sent representatives to the Ephesus council using his newly adopted title, Pope Leo I, his envoys were summarily rejected by the other more powerful bishops. In sum, independent historians agree that the Roman papacy has absolutely no connection to any of the original apostles and that the title "Pope" was adopted by the Bishop of Rome around 450 C.E. Frankly, the first man to rightfully use this supreme title was **Pope Victor II**, the first pope elected *after* the Great Schism of 1054 C.E., when the Roman Catholic Church split from the Eastern Orthodox Church.

The doctrine of Papal Infallibility was discussed at numerous Church councils, and many clergy disputed the doctrine, including Wycliffe, Hus, and Luther. As a result, the Church did not officially adopt this man-made doctrine until 1870 C.E., at **Vatican Council I**. Specifically, the doctrine asserts that when the pope speaks from his chair, "his primacy includes the supreme teaching power to which Jesus Christ added the prerogative of infallibility, whereby the pope is preserved, free from error, when he teaches definitively that a doctrine concerning faith or morals is to be believed by the whole Church." Hence, the doctrine of Papal Infallibility states that the pope has perfect clarity regarding God's law, a potential challenge but not necessarily a violation of *Rule Number 4*, if it were true. However, it is quite easy to prove that the doctrine does indeed violate *Rule Number 4*. All we need do is review the history of the papacy to see that the Infallibility doctrine is indeed fallible.

Let us begin by examining how some of the popes achieved their rank. Historically, it was quite common for a powerful bishop to seize the title of pope. Thereafter, popes passed the title to their children or other relatives as though it were a birthright. It was even more common for popes to name their children and relatives to high posts within the Church. Noteworthy examples of these methods of succession include: **Pope Sergius III**, who managed to have his son named **Pope John XI**; and **Pope Sixtus IV**, who had three of his nephews named cardinals and then, in a related story, assisted in the assassination of two Medici nobles. Usually, however, a pope gained office as a gift from a powerful monarch. Indeed, Duke Alberic II of Spoleto, the ruler of Rome, selected no less than five popes, including his son, Octavian, who became **Pope John XII**.

It is equally shocking to examine how some of the popes lost their position. Many popes were murdered, either because they were on the wrong side of politics, or because they were deemed too corrupt for the office of Holy See. Examples of abruptly ended papacies abound, including: **Pope John VIII**, who was bludgeoned to death by his own entourage; **Pope Stephen VI**, who was strangled; and **Pope Leo V**, who was murdered by his successor, **Pope Sergius III**. In addition: **Pope John X** was suffocated to death; **Pope Stephen VIII** was horribly mutilated prior to his assassination; and **Pope John XVI** had his eyes gouged out, his nose cut off, his lips and tongue removed, and his hands cut off during the course of his murder. If God is involved with the appointment and removal of popes, then God must enjoy high drama. On the other hand, perhaps it is more logical for us to conclude that God has little to do with either the selection or termination of popes.

Finally, Catholic history is replete with "anti-popes." These men controlled the Church for a period of time, were deposed or murdered, then were defrocked while still alive or posthumously. In total, more than thirty popes were stripped of the title and declared anti-popes by the Catholic Church. There also were instances when as many as three men all claimed to be the pope at the same time.

In sum, the doctrine of Papal Infallibility clearly runs afoul of *Rule Number 4*, since not only is it patently ridiculous, as evidenced by the corrupt nature of so many popes, it also is blasphemous and an effrontery to God, whose authority over mankind is absolute and not subject to the whims of any man or any man-made religion.

Let us now consider whether Christianity satisfies *Rule Number 5*, which requires a good religion to welcome everyone who shares a faith in God and love for others. In my opinion, fundamentalist Christians are the greatest violators of this rule, as they staunchly assert that only those people who accept Jesus as God may enter heaven. We already have examined the origin of this misplaced belief at great length, so I will simply add the following. If you are a Christian who still thinks access to heaven is based on a "Jesus litmus test," it might behoove you to recall the most basic lesson of Jesus Christ: *Love thy neighbor.* By viewing heaven as the sole province of Christians as opposed to all good people, you are not loving your neighbor. Indeed, you are judging your neighbor – an act clearly reserved for God. In other words, you will not make it to heaven if you ignore the Golden Rule, which Jesus presented as God's Eleventh Commandment.

Frankly, the traditional Christian view of heaven – that it is a reward for those who believe that Jesus is God – is intolerant. If true, it would render most of the world's population unfit for spiritual salvation. Obviously, this is an insult to those people who subscribe to other religions and who act in a "Christian" manner. Ironically, being a "Christian" no longer relates or equates to any standard of conduct. *Rather, Christianity has become a mere label for those people who believe that Jesus died for their sins and opened up the gates of heaven.* Consequently, not only has Christianity become divisive and offensive to those who practice different religions, it also now fails to promote a meaningful moral compass, other than faith in Jesus, as though faith in Jesus' well-earned divinity somehow magically causes Christians to act morally and ethically.

As a result, the orthodox Christian view of heaven has taken mankind backward in terms of spiritual evolution. Recall that both Buddha and Jesus rejected the notion espoused by the earlier religions that only certain people are worthy of salvation. To this day, Hindus continue to believe that only their top caste members may ascend to the heavens, and Jews are taught that they will receive special treatment when their Messiah arrives. In stark contrast, Buddha and Jesus taught that *anyone* may attain enlightenment and salvation, but only if one does the hard work of searching for and communing directly with God through the process known as *Saddha*. Thus, the later Prophets taught that anyone and everyone who seeks the Truth about God and performs selfless acts of love may achieve divine enlightenment and rejoice in the Ethereal plane.

Unfortunately, Paul came along and reintroduced the pagan idea that gods crave worship. Hence, the orthodox Christian formula that mere faith in Jesus' divinity gets us to heaven (i.e., Jesus will save us if we worship him as a god). In his defense, it appears that Paul thought it was the end of the world, so he was trying to convert as many people as possible. But he warped the true message of Christ by instructing the Gentiles that salvation requires no moral, charitable, or spiritual work. Recall that Paul both ridiculed and abandoned the Jewish Ten Commandments. He also ignored the Eleventh Commandment. In sum, Paul's view of Christianity was tailor-made for the Gentiles, who liked multiple deities, loved virgin births, and expected their gods and goddesses to perform miracles. Thus, the reason Paul's version of Christianity survived was that it was modeled on pagan concepts and mythology and consistent with Roman culture.

Thereafter, the fledgling Catholic Church seized upon Paul's view – that faith in Jesus is paramount – to buttress their outrageous claim that a similar faith should be extended to them as God's administrators on the Earth plane. *In other words, Paul used faith to establish the laity, and the Catholics used blind faith to control the laity.* It also is ironic that the Church's adoption of the seemingly more inclusive Pauline Christianity has led to an exclusive form of fundamentalist Christianity. In sum, the elementary concept of faith which Paul used to amass followers is now the tenet used by fundamentalist Christians to exclude good people from other religions who have the utmost faith in God and who, strictly speaking, are good Christians because they adhere to the Eleventh Commandment. Ironically, this was exactly the type of religious hypocrisy that Jesus sought to expose and overcome.

Because the Catholic Church was so successful in controlling the dissemination of information pertaining to the historical person Jesus and because evangelical Christians also limit the scope of biblical and historical discussions, most Christians today seem unaware of the true underpinnings of their own religion. Sadly, most Christians are now taught that a cursory belief in Jesus' divinity *prior* to his resurrection is the only requirement for salvation. In Truth, they are spiritually confused. Otherwise, they would know that loving and compassionate people of other religions are just as worthy of ascending to heaven.

The Catholic and fundamentalist Christian concept that only those people who wear the Christian label may enter heaven is a flagrant violation of *Rule Number 5*, which holds that good people of all faiths may one day join with God.

Another way in which many Christians violate *Rule Number 5* is by their appalling treatment of homosexuals. In particular, during the 2000 and 2004 United States presidential elections, Christian leaders repeatedly denounced homosexuality. Therefore, let us take a moment to analyze how well some of these sects are adhering to the Golden Rule.

The **Baptist Church** through its group "Focus on the Family" supports a constitutional amendment banning gay marriage. In addition, the Southern Baptist Convention voted to leave the Baptist World Alliance, which is the international organization of Baptist churches. The stated reason for the withdrawal is that Southern Baptists disagree with the growing tolerance of homosexuality and support for women in the clergy.

The **Episcopal Church**, after electing its first gay bishop in 2003, placed a moratorium on any further ordinations after conservative Episcopalians threatened to leave the church. Rather than lose homophobic members, the Episcopal Church decided to denounce gays. They failed to act quickly enough, however, since one Episcopal church in the United States immediately withdrew and started a new church, the Anglican Mission in America, whose members believe that homosexuality is a sin.

The **Methodist Church** also has officially condemned homosexuality and refused to adopt a moderate pronouncement that good Christians can disagree on this issue. Instead, the church voted to declare, "The United Methodist Church does not condone the practice of homosexuality and considers this practice incompatible with Christian teaching." In addition, the church's high court defrocked a lesbian minister and agreed that ministers may exclude gays from services.

The **Lutheran Church** voted in 2005 to continue its ban on homosexual clergy. Afterward, the presiding bishop said that he hoped gay and lesbian people would not take the vote as a sign that they are not welcome in the church.

And lastly, **Evangelical Christians** are even more vehement that gay people are sinful and should be excluded from Christian worship. Recently, the despotic icon Jimmy Swaggart said, "And I'm going to be blunt and plain: If one ever looks at me like that, I'm going to kill him and tell God he died." Apparently, Swaggart was concerned that a gay man might find him appealing.

As usual, we can credit the Catholic Church with misinterpreting Jesus, this time, by discriminating against homosexuals. Although the *New Testament* is silent on this issue (except for the homophobic references in some of Paul's letters), the Catholic Church has long taken the position that gays are sinful and an offense to God. This judgmental position contradicts the very crux of Jesus' mission, which was to perfectly model non-judgment, total acceptance, and love.

A brave nun by the name of **Jeannine Gramick** and a priest named **Father Robert Nugent** have challenged the Church's position toward homosexuals. For the last thirty years, Sister Gramick and Father Nugent have ministered to gay Catholics, despite the Church's ban on homosexuality. In response, the CDF instructed them to label homosexual behavior as "intrinsically evil" and to stop inviting gay people into the Church. For a while, Sister Gramick and Father Nugent simply ignored the CDF censorship, but in 1999 they received formal notification from then Cardinal Ratzinger (currently pope Benedict XVI), ordering them to stop ministering to homosexuals. Still, they continued. In 2000, Sister Gramick and Father Nugent were summoned to Rome for a CDF hearing, during which they were forbidden to write or speak in public about homosexuality and the 1999 gag order. Nevertheless, Sister Gramick has refused to be silenced. Currently, she is facing excommunication for participating in a documentary about her struggle to minister to gay Catholics.

In conclusion, many Christian sects violate *Rule Number 5* by excluding homosexuals from their congregations and denouncing them as unworthy and defective Christians, in direct opposition to Jesus' model of total love and acceptance.

The only rule left to discuss is *Rule Number 7*, which requires a good religion to meet the emotional needs of and inspire its followers. For many

Christians, the belief that Jesus is God and that he died for mankind's sins brings them great joy and solace, so I do not wish to trample on this conviction anymore. In fact, out of fairness I will quote the two passages from the *Gospel of John* which orthodox Christians typically cite to support their belief that Jesus and God are one.

> So the Jews gathered around him and said to him, "How long are you going to keep us in suspense? If you are the Messiah, tell us plainly."
>
> Jesus answered them, "I told you and you do not believe. The works I do in my Father's name testify to me. But you do not believe, because you are not among my sheep. My sheep hear my voice; I know them, and they follow me. I give them eternal life, and they shall never perish. No one can take them out of my hand. My Father, who has given them to me, is greater than all, and no one can take them out of the Father's hand. **The Father and I are one.**" [Emphasis added]

Gospel of John, Chapter 10:24–30

> I am the way and the truth and the life. **No one comes to the Father except through me.** If you know me, then you will also know my Father. From now on you do know Him and have seen Him. [Emphasis added]

Gospel of John, Chapter 14:6

Admittedly, Jesus seems to blur the line between himself and God in the above passages. However, is Jesus really saying anything different than Buddha said? Remember, Buddha told us that if we follow his example, we too can reach *nirvana*, which he defined as enlightenment and the end of "self," not heaven. Perhaps Jesus was saying that if we follow his example, we too can reach the stage after *nirvana*, namely heaven. This would make sense if Jesus already had achieved enlightenment, gone to heaven and joined with God, but returned to Earth as a *bodhisattva* to teach mankind. Then, the above passages also would no longer conflict with Jesus' other statements in which he clearly views himself as separate and subordinate to God. Additionally, the above passages would no longer conflict with the Second Commandment, which states that there is only one God, nor the other scripture in the *Old Testament* which states that only God has the power to grant salvation.

> It is I, I the Lord; **There is no savior but me.** It is I who foretold, I who saved; I made it known, not any strange god among you. You are my witnesses, says the Lord. I am God, yes, from eternity I am He; there is none who can deliver from my hand. Who can countermand what I do? [Emphasis added]

Isaiah, Chapter 43:11

It is more reasonable, therefore, to conclude that Jesus came to Earth as an enlightened soul to provide mankind with the next layer to our Tower of Truth: *Spiritual enlightenment brings union with the Supreme Being.* Because Jesus relayed this Truth, it is natural to associate him with heaven and even confuse him with God. However, we should look to Jesus for guidance only. None of the Prophets, including Jesus, promised us heaven. Rather, the later Prophets told us it was possible to reach heaven, and they modeled for us the correct path. We still are free to choose whether or not we want to do the spiritual work necessary to gain access to heaven. Quite simply, we reach God based on our own merit and through the process of soul growth known as *Saddha.*

Finally, Chapter 10 of the *Gospel of John* ends with Jesus explaining what it means to be a "son of God." He does not claim this title exclusively for himself, but uses it to describe anyone who comes to know God. In the following passage, Jesus rebukes the Jews who are about to stone him for blasphemy by explaining to them that we each have the potential to become divine. Christians should take special note of this passage, since it completely contradicts the doctrine of original sin and also the dogma that we are hopeless and perpetual sinners.

> *The Jews again picked up rocks to stone him. Jesus answered them, "I have shown you many good works from my Father, for which of these are you stoning me?"*
>
> *The Jews answered him, "We are not stoning you for good work but for blasphemy. You, a man, are making yourself God."*
>
> *Jesus answered them, "Is it not written in your law, 'I said, "You are gods"?' If it calls them gods to whom the word of God came, and scripture cannot be set aside, can you say that the one whom the Father has consecrated and sent into the world blasphemes because I said, 'I am the Son of God?'" [Emphasis added]*

Gospel of John, Chapter 10:31–36

Lastly, it is important to remember that the *Gospel of John* is the most mystical of the four gospels, it was the last gospel written (*circa* 100 C.E.), and it was drafted for a pagan audience. It also is the only gospel in which Jesus refers to himself as the "son of God," as opposed to the "son of Man." Regardless, the above language makes clear that Jesus thought of himself as a "god" only because he had reached the level of spiritual enlightenment that Buddha had reached and that each of us may reach if we commit to perfecting ourselves.

To summarize, despite my Christian upbringing, independent research leads me to draw the following conclusions regarding the soul known as Jesus:

1. Jesus was sent here by God, just like the other Prophets, to add to our Tower of Truth and to update us on God's plan for mankind;

2. In order to speak effectively to the Jews (the only monotheistic culture at the time), Jesus appeared to fulfill the Messiah prophecies;

3. Jesus knew his true mission, however, which was to guide us to the Ethereal plane, not rule us on the Earth plane.

4. Jesus taught that we attain salvation by maintaining faith in God, honoring God's laws, and loving our neighbors through the performance of good works while on the Earth plane;

5. Jesus' mission was to let us know we are worthy of joining God in heaven and to model for us how to get there on our own;

6. To underscore his teachings, Jesus allowed himself to be martyred and then he (possibly) resurrected; and

7. Jesus was Divine, not because he was the literal or only son of God, but because he had perfected himself.

In sum, whether a god or not, Jesus is one of the most inspiring souls to ever visit the Earth plane, as his messages have influenced mankind for the last two thousand years and continue to emotionally uplift and spiritually motivate people of all faiths, in complete concordance with *Rule Number 7*.

On the other hand, I have concluded that some of the core tenets of man-made Christianity are emotionally damaging and spiritually harmful. Most notably, the Catholic Church's historical treatment of women is woefully disheartening and nearly devoid of positive emotional sustenance. As a female who was born into the Church, I believe I have the credentials to testify on this issue. Even as a small child, I felt negated and minimized based on the mythological account of Eve committing original sin and due to the Church's systemic subjugation of my gender. We all know the basics, like the fact that the Catholic Church won't accept female priests and that girls may not be altar attendants (except in rogue U.S. parishes). But do you know the true history of and the real motivation behind the endemic misogyny of the Catholic Church?

To start, let me underscore that the Catholic disdain for women did not stem from Jesus, who went further than Buddha in his appreciation and acceptance of women in his movement. Historians count at least six female disciples who were close followers of Jesus and often traveled with the men. Most of them were apostles' wives, but others were not. Indeed, even if we accept the orthodox account of Mary Magdalene as an unmarried woman, she still regularly met with Jesus. Likewise, even if we restrict ourselves to the four canonical gospels, it is still clear that Mary Magdalene played an important role in Jesus' mission. For example, she was present at the crucifixion and she was the first person to recognize and talk with Jesus after the resurrection. Consequently, the *New Testament* confirms that Mary's status was at least equal to that of the male apostles.

However, the *Gnostic Gospels* elevate Mary's stature even more, by disclosing that Jesus especially enjoyed discussions with her. For example, in the *Gnostic Gospel* the **Pistis Sophia**, Mary speaks to Jesus seventy-two times, as compared to Peter who only speaks six times. More telling still is the Gnostic **Gospel of Philip**, which describes Mary as the "companion" of Jesus and discloses that Jesus kissed her in front of the male apostles. For now, let us presume that Jesus and Mary were just friends, as their marital status is completely irrelevant to the point I am trying to make. The Truth is that Jesus valued women and obviously appreciated Mary for her mind and her spirit. Indeed, the depth of the discussions between Jesus and Mary in the *Gnostic Gospels* greatly exceeds the simple parables and the elementary spiritual lessons set forth in the *New Testament*.

> The Lord said, "Whatever is born of Truth does not die. Whatever is born of woman dies."
>
> Mary said, "Tell me, Lord, why I have come to this place to profit or to forfeit?"
>
> The Lord said, "You make clear the abundance of the revealer!"
>
> Mary said to him, "Lord, is there then a place which is ^ or lacking truth?"
>
> The Lord said, "The place where I am not!"...
>
> Mary said, "I want to understand all things, just as they are."
>
> *Dialogue of the Savior*, Verses 59–69

The above passage is a good example of the more complex discourses between Jesus and Mary Magdalene in the *Gnostic Gospels*. In it, Jesus confirms that the only way to attain eternal life is by seeking Truth. Jesus also commends Mary for bravely facing this challenge when he exclaims that she has grasped the "abundance of the revealer."

The question remains, then: *Why did the Catholic Church choose to subjugate women?* As usual, we can lay some of the blame at Paul's doorstep. Most historians believe that Paul was celibate his entire life and a few think he was gay. Either way, in his *New Testament* letters, Paul isn't shy about revealing his thoughts on women. For example, he wrote that a husband is "the head of his wife," because man is the "image and glory of God" and woman was made from man. He also instructed women on proper church behavior as follows, "Women should keep silent in the churches, for they are not allowed to speak, but should be subordinate, as even the law says." Here are some more precious quotes from Saint Paul.

> *Are you free of a wife? Then do not look for a wife. If you marry, however, you do not sin, nor does an unmarried woman sin if she marries; but such people will experience affliction in their earthly life, and I would like to spare you that. I tell you, brothers, the time is running out. From now on, let those having wives act as not having them .... So then, the one who marries his virgin does well; the one who does not marry her will do better.*

1st Letter to the Corinthians, Chapter 7:27–38

With Paul as a starting point, it was fairly easy for those Christian men who were obsessed with greed and power to stifle the female members of the Christian movement. Although Jesus elevated the status of women, this would be yet another forgotten lesson. Instead, male leaders seized the opportunity to diminish women and, thereby, efficiently subjugate half of their laity. Thus, Paul's misogynist theme was readily adopted by later church leaders, including **Tertullian**, a priest who lived around 190 C.E. In the following passage, Tertullian is chastising women for speaking at Gnostic meetings.

> *These heretical women – how audacious they are! They have no modesty; they are bold enough to teach, to engage in argument, to enact exorcisms, to undertake cures, and, it may be, even to baptize.*
>
> *It is not permitted for a woman to speak in the church, nor is it permitted for her to teach, nor to baptize, not to offer Eucharist, nor to claim for herself a share in any masculine function – not to mention any priestly office. [Emphasis added]*

Tertullian, *De Virginibus Velandis,* Chapter 9

As previously mentioned, the Gnostic Christians took Jesus' lessons to heart and allowed women to perform all the "masculine" functions at their church meetings. However, the orthodox Christian leaders were staunchly opposed to such inclusiveness. Battles over the gospels, the deification of Jesus, female participation, and the evolving church hierarchy continued to rage during the 2nd and 3rd Centuries. Finally, Roman Emperor Constantine ordered the bishops to adopt one universal religion during the Council of Nicaea in 325 C.E. The end result was that Gnostic Christianity was banned and female influence within the new Catholic Church was snuffed out.

Thereafter, women were not permitted to participate in the development of Catholic Church rules or doctrine. Instead, the bishops began to formulate policies that excluded women, and they also began to minimize the importance of the women who surrounded Jesus. Most notably, the Church revisited and then formalized the doctrine of **"Original Sin,"** casting Eve, the first woman, as the source of mankind's misery. It was **Saint Augustine**, the Bishop of Hippo and a pagan for the first half of his life, who officially enunciated this disastrous doctrine in 421 C.E.

> *Banished after his sin, Adam bound his offspring also with the penalty*
> *of death and damnation ... so that whatever progeny was born ... from*
> *himself and his spouse – who was the cause of his sin and the*
> *companion of his damnation – would drag through the ages the burden*
> *of Original Sin.*

> Saint Augustine, *Enchyridion*

By the 5th Century, the Church fathers were on a roll. They knew they still had a problem with the vexing Mary Magdalene, so they took additional steps to eradicate her from Christian history. In 591 C.E., **Pope Gregory I** announced that "the Magdalene," Mary of Bethany, and the female sinner described in Chapter 7 of the *Gospel of Luke*, were all the same person, thereby reducing Mary Magdalene to the status of a prostitute. Despite her crucial role in Jesus' life, the Catholic Church would propagate this myth – that Mary Magdalene was of a sordid and venal nature – for fourteen hundred years! Finally, in 1969 C.E., Pope Paul VI admitted that the Church had unduly and erroneously stigmatized this disciple and retracted all negative dicta about Mary Magdalene.

The Catholic Church's treatment of the other biblical Mary characters also is devilish. Remember *Jesus' Second "Official" Family Tree* from Chapter Two? There are so many women named Mary and so much confusion about which of them were with Jesus at the crucifixion and the resurrection that even our best scholars can't agree on how to sort out the mess. Suffice it to say, though, many historians believe the confusion surrounding the Marys was no accident.

It appears, for instance, that Mary the mother of Jesus, Mary Magdalene, and Jesus' sister Mary were purposely homogenized, as illustrated by the confusing description of the three Marys at the crucifixion. There also was another Mary, described as "the mother of James," who was present at Jesus' tomb along with Mary Magdalene just before the resurrection. Since we now know for certain that James was Jesus' brother, then the "mother of James" at the tomb probably was just another reference to Jesus' mother Mary. We will never know for sure, though, and that is the point. By heaping all of Jesus' female followers into one big "Mary pile," the Church effectively discounted their various personalities and the distinct roles they played in Jesus' life. When in doubt, call the women Mary and be done with it.

Also, please do not suppose that the Catholic Church's obsession with the virginity of Jesus' mother places Mary in a unique or prominent position within religious history. Recall that virgin births and gods mating with human females to produce demigods were common beliefs during that time. Indeed, Sumerian, Babylonian, Egyptian, Indian, Greek, and Roman mythology are chock full of such stories. For example, Augustus Caesar was worshiped both as the son of a god and as a god himself. Likewise, the Hindu god Karna was born of a virgin. Finally, Buddha's mother, although not described as a virgin, also was impregnated by a god. In sum, the miracle of a virgin birth may seem a unique honor to us today, but in biblical times it was practically expected. Incidentally, the virginity of Jesus' mother Mary was another hotly debated topic by the early Catholic bishops, who were unable to agree on the issue until 680 C.E., when an official decree was issued proclaiming Mary "the blessed, immaculate, ever-virgin."

Besides which, the entire topic of sexual relations between men and women is hypocritical within the context of the Catholic Church, as the early popes and bishops rarely hesitated to satisfy themselves with carnal pleasure. In fact, celibacy was not even an issue in the Church until the **Council of Elvira** in 306 C.E., at which time the Western bishops met and voted to institutionalize celibacy. However, the Eastern bishops did not attend this council and refused to go along with its decision. *Thus, the Eastern branch of the Catholic Church and the Eastern Orthodox Church which exists today have always allowed priests to marry and have children.*

The Catholic Church did not revisit the issue of celibacy again until 1049 C.E., right before the Great Schism, when **Pope Leo IX** imposed celibacy on all clergy from the rank of deacon up. The issue was addressed again after the Great Schism in a local synod convened in 1059 C.E., at which time the Church banned priests from having concubines as well as wives.

Nevertheless, the Catholic clergy ignored the early celibacy rules and continued to marry and father children. Not until 1139 C.E., at **Lateran Council II**, did the Catholic Church officially and forever ban priests from getting married. The formal decree also specified that the priests' wives would be considered "concubines" and that the priests' children would revert to Church property as "slaves." Thereafter, even though the Church formally imposed celibacy on its clergy, the rule was not followed nor enforced for another few hundred years. In fact, the rule was restated for the fifth time in 1512 C.E. at **Lateran Council V,** since many priests still were ignoring the prohibition.

It also is important to understand why the Catholic Church forced celibacy on its clergy. It was not because the pope viewed celibacy as a divine act or a necessary detachment from the physical plane. And it was not because sexual intimacy with women was considered too great a distraction from more important Church functions and obligations. Rather, the Catholic Church adopted the celibacy rule in order to preserve Church property and wealth. The Church did not want the property owned by its clergy to be inherited by the clergy member's family. *Thus, the Catholic Church became the heir of its clergy, not by choice but by edict.*

Apparently, though, popes were exempt from the celibacy rule. Here are some of the more titillating examples of papal sexual misconduct. **Pope John X** had a famous mistress named Theodora who eventually betrayed her lover and helped select his successor. Theodora also had a daughter named Marozia, who was a papal mistress. Marozia and **Pope Sergius III** had an illegitimate son together who later became **Pope John XI.** Additionally, Marozia's grandson, Octavian, became **Pope John XII** at the age of eighteen. And notably, **Pope John XII** died in 964 C.E. at the age of twenty-seven in bed with a married woman.

Another famous "papal family" began in 1455 C.E., with the relatives of **Pope Calixtus III.** This pope appointed his nephew as **Pope Alexander VI** in 1492 C.E. While pope, Alexander had eight illegitimate children by at least three different women, including the infamous offspring Cesare and Lucrezia Borgia. Cesare became Archbishop of Valencia at age sixteen, he was made a cardinal at seventeen, and at age twenty-three he was made general of the Vatican guard. Unfortunately, Cesare had to murder his own brother in order to acquire the position. Thereafter, Cesare killed his sister's husband, who was a member of the Naples royal family. Lucrezia, who was then without a sexual partner, reportedly had incestuous relations with both her father and her brother.

I also would be remiss if I failed to mention the rampant pedophilia within the Catholic Church. Hardly a month goes by that I don't read in my local newspaper yet another account of a priest being tried for molesting children, a priest admitting to such charges, an archdiocese settling such claims with victims out of court, or a diocese seeking the protection of the bankruptcy laws in order to avoid paying such damages. What can I say? Obviously, the system is broken, it's been broken for over a thousand years, but still the Catholics refuse to fix it.

Psychologists theorize that repressed homosexuals are drawn to the priest-hood in the vain hope that the forced celibacy rule will contain or eliminate their desires. However, in 2005 over 5,000 priests were accused of sexual abuse in the United States alone. In addition: 714 priests were accused of sex-ual abuse in 2006; 692 were accused in 2007; and another 803 complaints were filed in 2008 against priests in the U.S. In sum, since 1950 there have been over 14,000 claims of sexual abuse against priests in the U.S. Moreover, as of this writing, the U.S. Catholic Bishops' Conference site reports that the Church has spent a total of 2.3 billion dollars on settling sexual abuse claims. *That's two billion dollars, folks.* What a shame that this money needed to be spent on helping victims of the Catholic Church and not the poor. Incidentally, in addition to the staggering number of sexual predators within the Church, the priesthood suffers from unusually high rates of alcoholism, yet another indication of systemic pathologies related to celibacy.

Lastly, I want to comment on the Vatican's repeated declaration that con-doms do not protect against the spread of the AIDS virus. To date, more than 25 million people have died from AIDS, approximately 35 million people are presently infected, and yet the Catholic Church doesn't have the common sense nor the compassion to advise its laity about how to prevent the spread of this dreaded disease. Here is a short list of the many incredulous political leaders and disheartened medical experts who have criticized the Vatican for undermining worldwide efforts to halt this epidemic: U.S. former Secretary of State Colin Powell, Lutheran Bishop Gunnar Staalseth, representatives of the Nobel Peace Prize committee, doctors at the U.S. Center for Disease Control, and spokespersons from the World Health Organization.

Of course, ultimate responsibility for the direction of the Catholic Church rests with its laity. Until Catholics demand it, men of power at the Vatican will not change course. Unfortunately, the Catholic laity appears unwilling to demand positive change. For example, the Diocese of Arlington in Virginia recently sought to instruct its youth on the topic of sexual abuse. This diocese, one of the most conservative in the United States, realized that such education would be beneficial given the high rate of sexual abuse within the Church and the United States, generally. Believe it or not, the congregation protested. Parents actually denounced the Bishop of Arlington for endorsing "good touch/bad touch" classes. And the reason the parents objected: The priests might scare the children. Like lambs to the slaughter ...

For all these reasons, we may readily conclude that the Roman Catholic Church is physically, emotionally, and spiritually devoid of inspiration, which means that it fails to provide a positive environment for its laity, in direct contravention of *Rule Number 7* of *The Seven Rules of Any Good Religion.*

Once again, to the extent that the other sects of Christianity have managed to separate from their dysfunctional family of origin – the Catholic Church – they deserve credit. As I pointed out at the beginning of this section, there are so many different sects of Christianity today, it is beyond the scope of this book for me to "grade" each one against the objective template set forth in *The Seven Rules of Any Good Religion.* Therefore, I wish to acknowledge that some Christian congregations are doing wonderful work in the world, including many Catholic parishes.

Therefore, in spite of the failed leadership of the male clergy of the Catholic Church, and despite my personal disgust with the ingrained misogyny of my ex-religion, I sincerely want to end this section on a more positive note and give credit to those true Christians who do their utmost to emulate Jesus and follow his lessons of love. Specifically, I wish to focus on three female souls who stayed loyal to the Catholic Church in an effort to keep Jesus' messages alive. When I first read about these women, I marveled at their bravery, tenacity, and purity. They truly understood Jesus' lessons and perfectly modeled both his valor and humility. Even the male leaders of the Catholic Church were able to see the light emanating from these amazing female souls, as all three have earned double accolades: *They each have been declared a Saint and a Doctor of the Catholic Church.*

Saint Catherine of Sienna was born in 1347 C.E., at a time when the Church was rife with corruption. In fact, the French kings had appropriated the papacy after the massacre of the Knights Templar and started appointing French popes. These popes were afraid to challenge the French monarchy until Catherine convinced Pope Gregory XI to return to Rome and take proper control of the Church. Catherine also received messages from the Ethereal plane and wrote an autobiography in which she detailed her conversations with God. Although God spoke with her on numerous topics, the messages often focused on the abuses of the Catholic Church. Specifically, God was offended by the abuses of the male clergy and specifically denounced the cardinal sins of greed and pride, as set forth in the following quote.

Sin is both in the mind and in the act. ... Bodily cruelty springs from
greed, *which not only refuses to share what is one's own but takes what*
belongs to others, robbing the poor, playing the overlord, cheating,
defrauding, putting up one's neighbor's goods – and often their very
persons – for ransom. ...

    And who is hurt by the offspring of **pride**? *Only your neighbors. For you*
harm them when your exalted opinion of yourself leads you to consider
yourself superior and therefore to despise them. And if pride is in a position
of authority, it gives birth to injustice and cruelty and becomes a dealer in
human flesh. ...

    Every scandal, hatred, cruelty, and everything unbecoming springs
from this root of selfish love. **It has poisoned the whole world and**
sickened the mystic body of holy Church and the universal body of
Christianity. *For all virtues are built on charity for your neighbors. So I*
have told you and such is the **Truth**. *[Emphasis added]*

Saint Catherine of Sienna, *The Dialogue*

Another Doctor of the Church is **Saint Thérèse of Lisieux,** who was born
in 1873 C.E., and who is known as the "Little Flower." She was the embodiment of humility, as she never tired of menial or difficult tasks and she never
complained to her superiors. Like Saint Catherine, the Little Flower worked
hard to attain a state of grace with God, and she was rewarded for her spiritual efforts by eventually speaking directly with the Almighty. Saint Thérèse
believed with childlike innocence that her unquestioning loyalty to the Church
would help her to achieve salvation. She wished to ascend to heaven in accordance with Jesus' instructions regarding children in the *Gospel of Matthew,*
"Whoever humbles himself like this child is the greatest in the kingdom of
heaven." Saint Thérèse's prayers were answered, as she died at the tender age
of twenty-four with her innocence intact, a stark contrast to our last female
Doctor of the Church.

I must confess at the outset that **Saint Teresa of Avila** is my favorite hero-
ine of all time. When I read her autobiography, *The Life,* I laughed, I cried,
and I felt like I had met my twin soul. Saint Teresa was born in Spain in 1515
C.E., during the heyday of the Spanish Inquisition. Her grandparents were
Jewish and were victims of the Inquisition. Thus, her ancestors chose to convert to Christianity rather than lose their possessions or their lives. Indeed, it
was because of the Inquisition that Teresa was forced to write. She was
brought before the Inquisition because she claimed that she talked with Jesus
and with God. She was a nun, but that didn't matter, as even nuns were
deemed unworthy of talking directly with God. Consequently, she was

ordered to write about her mystical experiences so that her inquisitors could determine whether she was talking to the "devil" or to the Supreme Being.

Saint Teresa is the Catholic "Patron Saint of Prayer," which strikes me as humorous now that I have read her work. It is funny because Saint Teresa did not, in fact, "pray." Rather, she meditated in the same fashion that most people are taught to meditate today. There is a big difference between prayer and meditation, which I discovered long ago thanks to my ex-guru Sam. Prayer is supplication to a third party deity which resides *outside* of ourselves and which is viewed as so omnipotent that he or she is deemed entirely beyond our scope of reason. Conversely, meditation is the process of turning *inside* for answers based on the belief that God resides in each of us and that each of us has the tools we need to perfect our own divinity and join with God. Consider Saint Teresa's description of meditation, through which she saw a vision of Jesus.

> This vision seems to me very profitable to recollected persons, for it teaches them to think of the Lord as being in the very innermost part of the soul. This is a meditation which penetrates most deeply and, as I have previously said, is much more fruitful than the thought of Him as outside us, which one finds in certain books about prayer that tell us where we are to seek God. ... This is quite clearly the best way. There is no need to climb up to heaven, nor to go any further than to our own selves; to do so troubles the spirit, distracts the soul, and brings little fruit.
>
> Saint Teresa of Avila, *The Life*

Hence, people who pray usually ask God for help, as though they have little or no control over their destiny. People who pray also tend to view God as a father figure, as opposed to a source of divine energy, and they often think that God will grant their wishes if they are good. On the other hand, people who meditate usually have come to understand that they are responsible for their own salvation and have started to view themselves as true children of God. In addition, people who meditate have started the *Saddha* process of soul growth and know this elementary Truth: *Each of us is a part of God and God is a part of each one of us, as Jesus explained to us nearly two thousand years ago.*

In sum, I have learned a lot over the years while researching Christianity, which wasn't an easy task given the massive quantities of misinformation promulgated by the Catholic Church. In particular, I enjoyed reading the work of Saint Teresa, who was smart and confident enough to meditate her way to God – what the Catholic clergy today reluctantly calls "mental prayer." Unfortunately and through no fault of his own, Jesus' history and messages were hijacked and twisted by greedy and prideful men who stripped away the deeper meaning of his life and then repackaged his death for the masses. I can only imagine Jesus' horror over the religion that he inadvertently spawned.

Once you eliminate all the man-made rules and erroneous interpretations of Christianity, you discover that Jesus was a glorious messenger who spoke new Truths about the nature of God and about how mankind may achieve an everlasting spiritual life in the Ethereal plane. Moreover, Jesus was uncommonly loving, generous, brave, imaginative, and inspiring. We should honor and remember him for his compassionate acts and for his divine wisdom, not his untimely death. Whether a Prophet or a god, Jesus was one of the greatest teachers the Earth has ever seen. We should be a lot less concerned with where Jesus sits in heaven and a lot more concerned about whether our own thoughts, words, and deeds will earn us a seat in heaven as well.

The bottom line is: *There is no short cut to heaven.* The Almighty expects each of us to earn our own divinity. Luckily, Jesus came to tell us that we each have the potential to meet God's expectations by perfecting our souls. In order to attain that mystical and blissful eternity, however, each of us must do our best at all times and practice the *Saddha* process of soul growth.

Therefore, may we remember Jesus' lessons on how to achieve union with God. And may we also continue on our respective spiritual paths with open eyes, open minds, and open hearts. As a critical first step to spiritual enlightenment, let us no longer be fooled by corrupt and hypocritical men of power who claim false dominion over the rest of us. Rather let us seek God in an atmosphere of Truth, Love, and Light and without the distraction of man-made impediments, just as Jesus instructed:

> *Obstacles to Faith are sure to arise, but beware to the one who creates them. It would be better for that person to be thrown into the sea with a millstone tied around the neck than for that person to mislead one of my followers.*

> The Lost Gospel Q, Verse 76

Now, it is time to explore what happened after the Prophet of the world's last major religion left the Earth plane and joined God. Please, as you read the last section of this chapter, continue to ponder the theory that each of the Prophets built upon the foundation left by earlier teachers, and that each of them progressively refined and clarified the Truth about God.

ISLAM

At this juncture, I am hopeful that the reader agrees with me on the following two points. First, each successive Prophet gave us a message that progressively got us a little closer to the Truth about God. Second, the religions that evolved after the Prophets died no longer accurately reflect the lessons which they taught. The religions are flawed because they are man-made. However, none of the Prophets were flawed because they spoke for God, at God's direction, and with God's blessing. Muhammad certainly is no exception.

I am convinced that Muhammad, just like the other major Prophets, received divine messages of Truth which he appropriately shared with his people. Let us pause for a moment to clearly define his audience: *Muhammad was speaking to all Arabs, including the Jews.* Recall that after the Jewish uprising in 70 C.E., the Romans destroyed Jerusalem and scattered the Jews. Thereafter, Germanic tribes invaded the Roman Empire and by 476 C.E., the Romans controlled only the territory around Constantinople, which became known as the Byzantine Empire. Consequently, by the time Muhammad was preaching around 600 C.E., the Jews were living amongst the other nomadic and tribal cultures in Egypt, Palestine, and Arabia. In sum, all of these people were of Arab descent and they all were feuding. Thus, Muhammad had a very big mission. With God's authority, Muhammad was charged with the task of spiritually uniting all the Arabs, including the pagans, the Jews, and even the Christians.

Next, it is important to realize that Muhammad viewed all these warring Arab factions as true brothers. Muhammad was right; they were all related, and not simply because of their shared geographic origin. This Truth is clearly recited in *The Holy Bible.* The account of Abraham's offspring, if not historically true, at least provides us with the parable to drive this point home. Recall that in the *Old Testament*, God tells Abraham that both of his sons will father great nations. Muhammad, who studied Judaism and Christianity, believed that the *Old Testament* account was literally true. He believed that Abraham's first son, **Ishmael**, fathered one Arab line, which he called the children of Islam, and that Abraham's second son, **Isaac**, fathered another Arab line, the children of Israel. Therefore, Muhammad correctly concluded that Muslims and Jews are related by blood and should not be divided along religious lines. Sadly, what we've been witnessing for thousands of years is brother killing brother.

Muhammad also understood that the Jewish belief in monotheism was divinely inspired and relayed to the Hebrews by Abraham and Moses.

Moreover, Muhammad believed that Jesus was divinely inspired and that Christianity further clarified the nature of God and our obligations to each other while on the Earth plane. However, recall that Muhammad did not accept the Christian view of Jesus as a god. Indeed, Muhammad found the deification of Jesus preposterous, since he believed that there is only one God, Allah, who possesses such glory and magnificence that mankind can only begin to comprehend such power. Thus, Muhammad correctly viewed Jesus as another Prophet.

> *If not Him, ye worship nothing but names which ye have named – ye and your fathers – for which Allah hath sent down no authority. The command is for none but Allah: He hath commanded that ye worship none but Him: That is the right religion, but most men understand not.*
>
> The Holy Quran, Sura XII, Verse 40

Furthermore, Muhammad clearly understood mankind's connectedness to God and to each other. He rationally concluded that each of the major Prophets was a divine messenger sent to guide humanity, and he willingly accepted that God had sent different Prophets for different races and cultures in order to better disseminate Truth.

Because Muhammad realized that we all come from the same Supreme Being, and because he clearly understood the significance of the Prophets before him, Islam meets the philosophical requirements of *Rule Number 1* of *The Seven Rules of Any Good Religion.*

Muhammad also taught that mankind's personification of God is unnecessary, childish, self-aggrandizing, and even dangerous. He argued that God is so omnipotent that mankind can not and should not attempt to depict God in human terms. In keeping with the Jewish Second Commandment against graven images, Muhammad forbade Muslims from attempting to produce Allah's image, since man-made idols could not possibly encompass the full glory of God's energy. Consequently, Muslim mosques contain no portraits, statues, or other depictions of God. Muslims believe such idolatry is sacrilegious, if not just plain stupid. Instead, Muslims believe that Allah should be pondered and praised as an intangible yet exceedingly benevolent entity. Hence, viewing God as a "father figure" was way too simplistic for Muhammad.

> *It is not befitting to the majesty of Allah that He should beget a son. Glory be to Him! When He determines a matter, He only says to it, "Be", and it is.*
>
> The Holy Quran, Sura XIX, Verse 35

The reason Muhammad viewed the personification of God as potentially dangerous is that humanizing God limits our imagination and can make us spiritually lazy. In addition, Muhammad rejected the notion that God is male or that only men were created in God's image. As a result, Muslims are free to conceptualize God as either genderless or as comprising of both masculine and feminine energies. It appears, therefore, that Muhammad understood the true meaning behind the Biblical parable of Adam and Eve: *God divided its unified yet dual nature and manifested two genders of human beings – some with male and others with female genes.*

Notwithstanding the prohibition against idolatry, *The Holy Quran* does use the allegory of "light" to describe God. Consequently, Muslims often envision God as light or pure energy.

> *Allah is the Light of the heavens and the earth. The parable of His Light is as if there were a Niche and within it a Lamp: The Lamp enclosed in Glass.... Light upon Light! Allah doth guide whom He will to His Light: Allah doth set forth parables for men: and Allah doth know all things.*

> *The Holy Quran*, Sura XXIV, Verse 35

Similarly, throughout the ages our most inspiring philosophers, theologians, and mystics have asserted that while faith and hard work may lead one closer to God, the Supreme Being still is beyond mere mortal comprehension. Consequently, most spiritualists resist the urge to personify God because they recognize it as a futile exercise designed to make us feel "special." Therefore, as semi-enlightened beings poised to redefine ourselves and God for the 21st Century, we should admit that we have a limited understanding of God's composition and power, and also that we may not be the only intelligent and soulful life form created by God. Of course, such an admission would mean rejecting the Judeo-Christian myth that mankind literally was created in God's image. Needless to say, God fully intended for mankind to proudly walk upright as the most "godlike" species on this planet. However, we are not special because we look like God. We are special because God made us creatures of Truth, Love, and Light.

Because Muslims view God as an abundant and unfathomable energy source which both fuels and preserves the Universe, Islam passes the logic mandates of *Rule Number 1* and the scientific requirements of *Rule Number 2*.

In addition, Islam is the only one of the five primary religions to truly embrace the concept that God is a singular and complete entity. If God both predates creation and is the sole source of all creation then, by definition, God must contain all energy necessary to manifest the Universe. Therefore, God must contain both masculine and feminine energy. Unfortunately, the patriarchal view of God – which Judaism suggests and Christianity promotes – presumes that God is comprised of male energy alone or that male energy is dominant or that male energy is more divine. Obviously, if God is a singular entity, a point on which most of us supposedly agree, then God must not only encompass both masculine and feminine energies, God must also appreciate the value, relationship, and sanctity of both men and women. Only then does the Judeo-Christian parable of creation make sense. God did not create "man" in God's image. Rather, God split its own energies between the sexes. The Truth is that men and women represent the two equal halves of God's unified yet dually genderful nature.

Because Muslims correctly view men and women as physical expressions of God's unified yet dualistic nature, Islam again passes the philosophical and scientific prescriptions of *Rule Number 1* and *Rule Number 2*.

Islam also recognizes the scientific principle of *karma*, that our good actions produce positive outcomes, and that our bad actions produce negative results. Specifically, Muhammad taught that our salvation is dependent on a positive record of charity and good works, not on which Prophet we might prefer. *Thus, Muhammad, just like Buddha and Jesus before him, taught that we will be judged by God based on our karmic record, not on our chosen religion.*

> *And the Earth will shine with the glory of its Lord: The Record of Deeds will be placed open; the prophets and the witnesses will be brought forward; and a just decision pronounced between them; and they will not be wronged in the least. And to every soul will be paid in full the fruit of its deeds; and Allah knoweth best all that they do.*
>
> *The Holy Quran*, Sura XXXIX, Verses 69-70

Thus, Islam again meets the dictates of *Rule Number 2* of *The Seven Rules of Any Good Religion*, because the religion embraces the scientific and spiritual principle of cause and effect (i.e., *karma*).

Finally with regard to science, *The Holy Quran* appears to grasp the Truth of evolution. Although during Muhammad's time mankind had no concept of human evolution, there are portions of the *Quran* which not only allude to mankind growing in stages but which actually recite that life started from water. Consider the Darwinist foreshadowing of the following *suras*.

*What is the matter with you, that ye place not your hope for kindness and long-suffering in God – seeing that it is He that has **created you in diverse stages**? ... And God has produced you from the earth **growing gradually**. [Emphasis added]*

The Holy Quran, Sura LXXI, Verses 13, 14, 17

*O thou man! Verily thou art ever toiling on towards thy Lord – painfully toiling – but thou shalt meet Him. ... **Ye shall surely travel from stage to stage**. [Emphasis added]*

The Holy Quran, Sura LXXXIV, Verses 6, 19

***And Allah has created every animal from water:** Of them there are some that creep on their bellies; Some that walk on two legs; And some that walk on four. [Emphasis added].*

The Holy Quran, Sura XXIV, Verse 45

It is He who has created man from water; *Then He established relationships of lineage and marriage; for thy Lord has power over all things. [Emphasis added].*

The Holy Quran, Sura XXV, Verse 54

Today, scientists agree that all life on Earth started in the oceans and that through the process of evolution mankind evolved over the course of five million years. Thus, it appears that God expressed the basics of evolution to Muhammad, who faithfully recited this Truth for inclusion in *The Holy Quran* and for posterity.

Because *The Holy Quran* described the process of evolution in simple terms for the uneducated people of Muhammad's era, Islam originally complied with *Rule Number 2*.

Before proceeding with my analysis of Islam, I need to stop for a moment to acknowledge that many Islamic nations have fallen on dark times. Consequently, for the purposes of this chapter, I now must draw a clear distinction between the revolutionary teachings of the Prophet Muhammad and the current state of the religion of Islam. Just as I had to separate Jesus from the Catholics and current fundamentalist Christian dogma, I must now separate Muhammad from the terrorists and fundamentalist clerics who now dominate Islam. Indeed, I imagine that both Jesus and Muhammad would be greatly perplexed, disappointed, and likely disgusted by the current actions and harmful belief systems of their misguided followers.

Although the present conflict in the Middle East poses overwhelming challenges, that is no excuse for choosing violence as a method for conflict resolution. The frustrated Arabs can and should elect a better method of resolving their disputes with each other and with their oppressors. Meeting force with force is not working. For one thing, the military strength of the United States and Israel is too great. Consequently, Muslims must find a better way to preserve their lands, their culture, and their religion. Continuing to shame their oppressors by appealing to the international community, the justice system, and the United Nations tribunals is a better means of achieving justice. For example, the Israeli Supreme Court ruled in the summer of 2004 that the wall around Jerusalem violates the rights of Palestinians. This ruling from Israel's highest court shows that peaceful means of redressing injustice will bring greater benefits to displaced and dispossessed Arabs.

Unfortunately, many Muslim men have chosen violence as the means to obtain freedom from both internal and foreign aggressors. The results of this decision have been disastrous for everyone involved, but especially for the Muslim people who no longer enjoy peace nor even comprehend such a state of harmonious existence. Thus, as we begin to analyze the morality of Islam against the requirements of *Rule Number 3* of *The Seven Rules of Any Good Religion*, we must be careful to separate the teachings contained in *The Holy Quran* from the violent fundamentalist groups that have twisted the meaning of that holy book.

As previously discussed in Chapter Two, Islam presents a clear moral code to its followers. *The Holy Quran* poetically and accurately presents Allah's expectations for mankind. One may argue that certain punishments for immoral behavior are too severe or that war is never justified. However, the moral code contained in the *Quran* is easy to comprehend, correctly delineates between right and wrong, reiterates that charity is the key to salvation, clearly states that Muslims should never be the aggressors in war, and applies these moral rules uniformly to all.

Thus, Islam in its pure form comports with *Rule Number 3*, as it presents its followers with an updated moral code of conduct.

The *New Testament* actually provides less guidance on appropriate moral behavior. Rather than setting forth a detailed description of Jesus' life and the lessons he taught, the *New Testament* focuses on Jesus' death and strangely turns that tragic event into Jesus' crowning achievement. The *New Testament* is slanted in this manner for two reasons.

First, Jesus died so young and the Roman occupation and then destruction of Jerusalem were so fierce that Jesus' immediate followers were unable to fully process or safely record his life history or his messages of Truth. In addition, Jesus' followers were unable to watch him practice the Golden Rule, a template for compassionate living, over a full and complete lifetime. Consequently, the orthodox accounts of his ministry, which are contained in the four sanctioned gospels, are sketchy and incomplete. Only when you add the other accounts of his life, which are contained in the *Lost Gospels*, the *Gnostic Gospels*, the *Dead Sea Scrolls*, and other historical records of that era, do you get a truer picture of Jesus' life mission and lessons.

Second, the *New Testament* is slanted because of the teachings of Paul, a man who never met Jesus and who consistently opposed the true leaders of the early Christian movement. Sadly, Paul misappropriated and misquoted Jesus when he left to preach to the Gentiles. His pagan version of Christianity was based on blind faith in Jesus as a savior god, a theology which eventually undermined God's Eleventh Commandment (i.e., the Golden Rule). Additionally, because he was obsessed with the notion of End Times and besting James and Peter in Jerusalem, Paul's primary goal became converting as many pagans as possible, not disseminating Truth. The net result is that Jesus' life mission was poorly documented and his martyrdom, not his messages, became the focal point of orthodox Christianity. Consequently, Jesus' moral lessons are often ignored today by those Christians who would rather believe that simple Jesus worship, as opposed to good works, is the key to salvation.

Luckily, in the case of Buddha and Muhammad the world has received relatively untainted accounts of their missions and their lessons. In addition, Buddha and Muhammad lived full lives, which meant that multiple generations were able to study and accurately record these Prophets' life events. As a result, we know how Buddha and Muhammad resolved the difficult and complex moral issues of their day. In particular, we know how Muhammad treated people of diverse cultures and religions, even during times of war.

Recall that Muhammad taught that war is an act of last resort, undertaken only after Muslims have been harmed by "Unbelievers." That is why *The Holy Quran* instructs Muslims not to be aggressors, but only to retaliate for harms committed against them by others. In other words, war is acceptable as a means of self defense.

> *To those against whom war is made, permission is given to fight,*
> *because they are wronged …. They are those who have been expelled*
> *from their homes in defiance of right – for no cause except they say,*
> *"Our Lord is Allah."*
>
> The Holy Quran, Sura XXII, Verses 39- 40

> *And if one has retaliated to no greater extent than the injury he received,*
> *and is again set upon inordinately, Allah will help him: For Allah is One*
> *that blots out sins and forgives again and again.*
>
> The Holy Quran, Sura XXII, Verse 60

Under no circumstances were Muslims to fight other "Believers" (i.e. Jews or Christians). In fact, *The Holy Quran* sets forth penalties if another Believer is killed accidentally. Specifically, Muhammad recited that it is wrong to kill a Believer who belongs to another sect with whom the Muslims may be at war. The ultimate sin, according the *Quran*, is if a Muslim intentionally kills another Believer.

> **Never should a Believer kill a Believer: but if it happens by mistake,**
> **compensation is due.** *… If the deceased belonged to a people at war*
> *with you, and he was a Believer, the freeing of a Believing slave is*
> *enough. If he belonged to a people with whom ye have a treaty of*
> *mutual alliance, compensation should be paid to his family … by way of*
> *repentance to Allah: For Allah hath all knowledge and all wisdom.*

> **If a man kills a Believer intentionally, his recompense is Hell, to abide**
> **therein forever:** *and the wrath and the curse of Allah are upon him, and*
> *a dreadful penalty is prepared for him. [Emphasis added]*
>
> The Holy Quran, Sura IV, Verses 92–93

Thus, *The Holy Quran* offers guidance on how to practice compasion even in the midst of trying and frustrating circumstances, including war, which is yet another example of how the religion of Islam meets the moral requirements of *Rule Number 3*.

Today, when Muslims read *The Holy Quran* and the historical accounts of how Muhammad responded to the challenges of racial diversity and religious differences, they should receive helpful guidance when presented with similar moral dilemmas. In other words, because their holy book specifies and insists upon moral action even during difficult times, and because Muhammad modeled such moral behavior, the men of Islam know how they should be acting. *Unfortunately, fundamentalist Muslim men are not practicing their own religion.*

Many of us understand the frustration and anger Muslim people feel. Those of us who have the ability to empathize feel their pain at the hands of unjust neighbors, such as the Israelis, and arrogant interlopers, such as the United States. However, two wrongs do not beget a right, and Muslim men need to come to this obvious conclusion before it is too late. The Truth is that *The Holy Quran* does not give Muslim men permission to declare war on the world. By doing so, they are mostly hurting themselves, their women, and their children. Moreover, they are jeopardizing what they claim to love the most – their relationship with Allah.

> *Say: "We believe in Allah, and in what has been revealed to us and what was revealed to Abraham, Ishmael, Isaac, Jacob, and the Tribes, and in the Books given to Moses, Jesus, and the Prophets from the Lord. We make no distinction between one and another among them, and to God do we bow our will in Islam." [Emphasis added]*
>
> *The Holy Quran*, Sura III, Verse 84

In sum, I find that fundamentalist Muslims, including especially the Wahhabi sect led by Osama bin Laden, are rightfully *out-raged* but wrongfully *raging-out* against both their own people and people of other faiths. They were sent a glorious Prophet who preached unity and who showed them how to handle complex moral dilemmas. They also were blessed with an astounding holy book that prescribes tolerance first and war last, especially during dark times. Indeed, Muslim men should know better.

Tragically, fundamentalist Muslims are purposefully killing other Believers who may have gone astray within their own religions, but who still worship the one God. Rather than rely on Islamic law to help them rise above this dilemma, an alarming number of Muslim fundamentalists have embraced hatred and twisted their own religion to suit their aggressive and vengeful desires. They now resemble their enemies, who are heartless and cruel. Just like their oppressors, fundamentalist Muslims wage war out of wrath, rather than righteousness.

Regretfully, I am forced to conclude that the religion of Islam, as currently practiced by many angry and frustrated Muslim men, has degenerated into a brutal and vengeful movement in clear violation of *Rule Number 3*.

Before I wrote this section on the current morality of Islam, I read Osama bin Laden's *Declaration of War Against the Americans Occupying the Land of the Two Holy Places*, which he authored in 1996, and *Jihad Against Jews and Crusaders*, which he co-authored in 1998. These *fatwas* (i.e., religious

edicts) contain well-written and coherent explanations for Bin Laden's declaration of war against my country, the nation of Israel, and "apostate" leaders
of Muslim countries (i.e., degenerate Muslim monarchs). Needless to say, the
fatwas are extremely disturbing, and I carefully processed Bin Laden's views
before I attempted to write this section.

To summarize, both documents cogently set forth Bin Laden's reasons for
declaring a military *jihad*. He starts by referencing his support of the Muslims
in Afghanistan, who were able to beat back the Russians who invaded that
country in 1979. He also recounts how the U.S. would not leave the region
after providing him and the Afghan rebels military support. Ironically, the U.S.
helped train and arm Bin Laden in the 1980s, during a time when we feared
the Russians more than we feared fundamentalist Muslims.

Bin Laden also writes about the **First Gulf War** (a/k/a Desert Storm). When
Iraq invaded Kuwait in 1990, Bin Laden disagreed with his government's decision to allow U.S. troops to stage military maneuvers from Saudi Arabia.
Instead, he wanted to protect his country and blames the U.S. for killing
600,000 civilians and plundering Iraq. Bin Laden also criticizes the Saudis for
allowing U.S. troops to remain in his country and suggests that the Americans
will never leave. Indeed, U.S. military forces stayed in Saudi Arabia until
2003, after the start of the **Second Gulf War**. Regarding the current war in
Iraq, the U.S. Congress now has confirmed that the military campaign against
Saddam Hussein was based on faulty (or possibly manufactured) intelligence
which incorrectly indicated that Iraq had weapons of mass destruction. We
also now know that there was no link between Iraq and the terrorist attack
on September 11, 2001. Consequently, I wonder whether Bin Laden is correct.
Will the U.S. ever leave the Middle East?

Next, Bin Laden recites how numerous petitions were sent to **King Fahd**
of Saudi Arabia, requesting that the king expel the Americans troops, which
at that point had built permanent military bases near Mecca and Medina,
the two Muslim holy cities. In addition, Bin Laden lists the diplomatic chan-
nels that were exhausted in an attempt to avoid armed conflict. The result
of this letter writing campaign, backed by Muslim clerics, doctors, scholars,
and merchants, was that many influential Saudis were imprisoned or
expelled from the country. In 1994, Bin Laden himself was declared an
enemy of Saudi Arabia and his citizenship was revoked. Thus, Bin Laden's
peaceful attempts at freeing his country from the presence and influence of
the U.S. had failed.

Lastly, Bin Laden lists all the reasons why he no longer trusts the Saudi royal family. Recall that Muhammad's (and Jesus') most sacred message is that Allah wants us to care for our less fortunate brothers and sisters through charity. Bin Laden believes that the Saudi king and princes have been corrupted by greed and pride – the same two sins identified in this book as the most harmful to mankind. In sum, Bin Laden believes that the Saudi royals care more about lining their pockets (greed), and enjoying their international power and prestige (pride), than they care about ordinary Muslim citizens, whom they are charged with protecting.

It is important to keep in mind that Bin Laden is a member of the Wahhabi sect of the Sunni branch of Islam. Recall that the Sunnis rejected the Shiite notion that Muhammad's descendants were ordained leaders. Instead, the Sunnis believe that the *ummah* (community) has the moral right to overthrow a corrupt ruler. Consequently, Bin Laden believes that the Saudi royal family should be deposed because they have proven themselves to be selfish and dictatorial leaders. Strangely, the more I studied and pondered Bin Laden's declaration of war and the more I researched and learned about the Saudi royals, the more I began to understand Bin Laden.

At this point, I think it will be helpful to briefly detour into the history of the Middle East. Without this history, it is impossible to understand the current frustration of the Muslim people or the political and religious dynamics that presently are spiraling out of control. In addition, Americans need to understand that Osama bin Laden originally possessed altruistic motives, as he was not a terrorist when he first began his quest on behalf of the beleaguered and degraded Muslim people. Lastly, we need to comprehend the horrendous problems that resulted when the nation of Israel was formed. Otherwise, there simply is no way to understand what is happening in the Middle East, a region of the world that now threatens the entire globe.

Let me state in advance that it is my sincere hope that this brief history lesson will help everyone empathize and sympathize with the ongoing plight of both the Muslim and Jewish people. Until we step into their shoes, we will never understand their pain nor fathom why the suffering in the Middle East has spilled over and now impacts us all. To make this history lesson as easy as possible, maps are provided in the Appendix. Let's begin.

By the 1300s, the Muslim Empire was controlled by Turkish Muslims, known as the Ottoman Empire. Prior to the Christian Crusades, the Muslim Empire was the most dominant, progressive, and enlightened society ever to rule on planet Earth. However, by the start of the 20th Century, the Ottoman Empire had lost both ground and power. Most notably, Great Britain had taken control of Egypt in 1882 due to international trade concerns over access to the Suez Canal. As a result, the Ottoman Empire was on the verge of collapse. As a last ditch effort to save their empire, the Muslim Turks chose to back the Germans in **World War I**. Unfortunately for the Ottomans, the Axis nations lost the war, which meant that the Middle East was up for grabs. *After reigning in the Middle East for nearly fourteen hundred years, the Muslim Empire was history.*

One of the first things the victorious Allies did was sign the **Treaty of Sevres** in 1920, which officially dissolved the Ottoman Empire. Thereafter, Great Britain and France controlled the Middle East under mandates from the League of Nations (predecessor to the United Nations). The **British Mandate** of 1922 assigned Great Britain the regions known today as Palestine, Israel, Jordan, and Iraq. Similarly, the **French Mandate** gave control of Syria and Lebanon to the French. Thereafter, the Allies began to create new Muslim nations. The conquered Ottoman Turks retained the area around Constantinople (renamed Istanbul), and they named their new nation Turkey. Also, the country of Trans-Jordan was carved out and given to Abdullah bin Husayn, who had backed the Allies during the war. He later crowned himself **King Abdullah** and his grandson, **King Abdullah II**, rules Jordan today.

The Allies also helped create the Kingdom of Saudi Arabia by supporting another powerful tribal leader named Abdul Aziz ibn Saud. Ibn Saud was a devout Wahhabist Muslim who had opposed Ottoman rule. He managed to capture the Arabian peninsula and, in 1932, pronounced himself king of a new nation which he called Saudi Arabia. **King Saud** reportedly married as many as two hundred wives (divorcing them as necessary so as not to exceed the *Quran's* prohibition against having more than four wives). As a result, King Saud aligned himself with numerous Arab tribes and produced over one hundred male heirs. It was one of his sons, King Fahd, who Bin Laden labeled an apostate Muslim ruler in his declaration of war. King Fahd died in 2005, and today the country is ruled by another of the princes, **King Abdullah**.

With the help of American businessmen, King Saud discovered oil in 1938. The company that discovered and drilled the oil, California Arabian Standard Oil Company, was owned by Americans and later renamed Chevron. By 1948, Texaco, Exxon, and Mobil also had a piece of the action. Not until 1973 did the Saudi government acquire a 25% interest in the company. Then in 1980, the Saudis acquired 100% of the company, which now is called the Saudi Arabian Oil Company, the world's largest producer of oil. *Hence, the royal family of Saudi Arabia is the wealthiest family in the world with sole control over the world's largest supply of oil.*

After World War I, the Allies realized that the Jews needed a homeland. In 1903, the Jewish Zionist Theodor Herzl had proposed that the Jews be given the African nation of Uganda, which the Jews rejected. Then, in 1917 the British government proposed that the Jews receive territory in Palestine (despite the fact that the Ottoman Empire still controlled the region). However, after the fall of the Ottoman Empire, the British submitted their plan, entitled the **Balfour Declaration,** to the League of Nations, which endorsed the plan in 1922. Thereafter, the British allowed mass migration of Jewish settlers into Palestine.

Immediately, the Muslim Palestinians protested their loss of sovereignty. For a short time, the British army was able to maintain some semblance of order by restricting Jewish immigration. Nevertheless, the Jewish migration could not be stopped. The Jews finally had a place to call home after centuries of mistreatment and expulsion by European Christian nations, as more fully detailed in the Appendix. This mass migration of Jews into Palestine marked the beginning of a new Jewish homeland. It also marked the end of Muslim control of Palestine.

In retrospect, it appears that no one in a position of power was empathizing with the Arabs, who were being systematically displaced after controlling the region for nearly fourteen hundred years. Not surprisingly, violence erupted in the Middle East. The British, now overwhelmed by the magnitude of the passions involved, decided to change course. In 1939, Great Britain issued the **White Paper,** which capped Jewish immigration and stated, "His Majesty's Government therefore now declare unequivocally that it is not part of their policy that Palestine should become a Jewish State." In response, the Zionist wing of the Jewish movement attacked the occupying British army. By 1947, the British had had enough and announced that they would be departing, thereby leaving the foreign policy quagmire in the hands of the newly formed United Nations.

As an obvious and, hopefully, instructive analogy, I cannot help but draw a parallel between Great Britain's decision to "help" the people of Palestine after World War I and the United States' decision to "help" the people of Iraq by starting the Second Gulf War. Similarly, Great Britain's abrupt departure from Palestine at a critical moment in history naturally reminds me of my own country's awkward attempts to now extricate itself from Iraq. As of this writing, it appears that the United Nations will inherit the chaos caused by the

United States' unilateral decision to invade Iraq, just as it inherited Britain's Palestine policy fiasco seventy years ago.

After **World War II** ended, the Jewish population in Palestine soared even higher, despite British restrictions on immigration. The Holocaust not only fueled another wave of Jewish migration, it also underscored the centuries of racial and religious prejudice suffered by the Jews. It now seemed obvious to the entire world: *The Jews needed and deserved a homeland.*

In 1947, as the British prepared to evacuate Palestine, the United Nations passed **Resolution 181**, which was a plan for partitioning the region into two independent states. Unfortunately, the Arabs rejected the resolution, even though most Jews accepted the newly proposed boundaries. Thereafter, the day before the British Mandate was set to expire in 1948, the Jews unilaterally declared their independence and the nation of Israel was born again. Since then, there has been sixty years of holy war in Palestine. Surely, it now must be obvious to the entire world: *The Palestinians need and deserve a homeland too.*

Which brings us back to the topic at hand: *How do we fairly judge the morality of Islam and the actions of fundamentalist Muslim men, like Osama bin Laden?* Hopefully, this short history lesson on the Middle East, which also is summarized in the Appendix, has helped the reader understand the complicated nature of the ongoing Palestinian conflict. Yet, I feel we should dig even deeper if we truly want to comprehend the emotions and the suffering involved. Of course, I could label Bin Laden a religious fanatic, as most other commentators have done. However, that seems a little too simplistic. It also feels wrong to me.

The Truth is that until we start to empathize with the plight of the Muslim people and until we admit how we have added to their misery, we have no right to judge them at all. Once again, I am reminded of the wisdom of the great Prophet Jesus, who said:

> *Why do you notice the speck of sawdust in your brother's eye and not the wooden plank in your own? How can you say to your brother, "Let me take out the sawdust from your eye," when you cannot see the plank in your own?*
>
> *Hypocrite! Remove the plank from your own eye first: then you will see clearly enough to remove the sawdust from your brother's eye.*
>
> The Lost Gospel Q, Quote 20

In accordance with this sage advice, I want to propose an exercise. Although it may be difficult, particularly for Jews and Christians who now are under attack by radical Muslims, this exercise will do us all immense good. It also will help us fathom why the man we call a "terrorist" is considered a hero by his Muslim followers, whose numbers are estimated to be over two million and growing. Therefore, I fervently request that you allow your mind to wander, as I have allowed mine, in an attempt to seek the Truth. For the purpose of this exercise, please assume the following:

1. You are a highly intelligent and well educated Muslim man who believes in the teachings of the Prophet Muhammad, including: (i) charity is the path to salvation; (ii) the admonition against excess; and (iii) war is an act of last resort, sanctioned only if and when your religion and your homeland are threatened;

2. The most wealthy, powerful, and greedy nation in the world has occupied your country for more than a decade and won't leave the Middle East because it wants and needs your country's only natural resource, which happens to be very valuable;

3. You see your country's only natural resource being sold to outsiders on terms which seem to benefit them more than your own people, some of whom are poor, uneducated, suppressed, and begging for help;

4. You have concluded that your king is corrupt and that your government is run by greedy and power hungry souls; and

5. You have the personal strength and financial resources to help your people, which you feel obligated to do based on the many gifts bestowed upon you by God.

In short, imagine that you are Osama bin Laden. This would mean that you were born in 1957, into a very wealthy and religious Saudi Arabian family. In 1979, you graduate from college at the age of twenty-two, expecting to join your father's construction company, which has proudly assumed the task of rebuilding the two holiest Islamic mosques, located in your country's cities of Mecca and Medina. However, another Muslim country has just been invaded by a superpower and your Muslim brothers need help.

Despite the fact that your family possesses an immense fortune and you have the ability to live an opulent and privileged lifestyle, you choose to go to war against the Soviet Union and assist Afghanistan, a Muslim nation struggling to maintain its independence. During the war, you receive military help from the world's other superpower, the United States, even though you have doubts about U.S. intentions in the Middle East. Against all odds, you and your compatriots are victorious! The Russians withdraw from Afghanistan in 1989 and you come home.

However, just as you return to Saudi Arabia, you witness the start of yet another war. This time, the conflict is between Muslim countries, caused by Iraq invading Kuwait in 1990. Nevertheless, the United States intervenes on the behest of your king. You agree that Iraq must be checked, but you begin to wonder what is going on. *Why are the superpowers invading Muslim countries? And why isn't your wealthy and powerful Muslim country defending itself?*

You conclude that the invading superpowers need and want your country's only natural resource – oil. So you and other Muslim leaders write your king to share your concerns and to respectfully question the decision to rely on foreigners for protection. Your letters are ignored. When the Americans build permanent military bases in your country, you and other like-minded Muslims write more letters. These letters, too, are ignored. Finally, when the First Gulf War is long over and U.S. troops still occupy parts of your country, you and some of the most respected Muslims in Saudi Arabia petition the king to expel the Americans. This time, you are branded a "militant." As a result, you and many of the honored clerics and prominent citizens of Saudi Arabia now face imprisonment or worse.

So in 1992 you flee to Sudan, a country in Africa that also is experiencing religious strife. By this time, you realize that your country is no longer faithful to the messages of Muhammad, the charitable prescriptions of *The Holy Quran*, or the devout practices required by Islamic law. After searching your heart and soul and after asking Allah for spiritual guidance, you conclude that you have a moral and religious obligation to overthrow the corrupt leaders of Saudi Arabia. You begin to formulate a plan. In furtherance of this plan, you invite like-minded souls to join you in Sudan, to figure out what should be done about the oppression of the Muslim people.

Meanwhile, you help the Muslims in Sudan by using your incredible wealth to build roads, power plants, schools, and hospitals. You also decide to build a military base from which you hope to launch assaults against apostate Muslim leaders. However, the Americans figure out what you're up to, they accurately predict that you are a threat to their supply of oil, and they force you to leave Sudan. Your disgust with the United States now turns to full scale rage, as you deduce that U.S. interference in the Middle East has become the primary cause of problems for Muslim nations.

For example, you believe that while the U.S. backs Israel with money and arms, it ignores the human rights of Palestinians. In addition, you have evidence that U.S. covert operations have toppled Muslim leaders who disregard U.S. policies and demands. Finally, you believe that it is the influence and power of the U.S. that has corrupted the Muslim leaders of Saudi Arabia, Egypt, and Jordan. Ultimately, you come to the conclusion that the U.S. routinely undermines Muslim interests around the world. At this point, you have founded a resistance group called Al Qaeda and you believe you have no choice but to declare military *jihad*.

The year is 1996. You are back in Afghanistan where you are viewed as a hero. You still believe that your own country is being misled and mismanaged, but you no longer think that the root of the problem is your king, who long ago succumbed to material plane temptations. Instead, after further analysis, you conclude that the crux of the problem is the parasitic United States of America and the egocentric nation of Israel. Consequently, rather than add to the chaos in the Middle East by attacking apostate Muslims, you decide that it will be more effective to target the cause of all your pain, the U. S. and Israel, against whom you now declare war.

The rest, as they say, is history – as is our exercise in empathy. For who among us doesn't cringe when we hear the name Osama bin Laden or his terrorist group Al Qaeda? More to the point, who among us feels safe anymore? Given what Bin Laden chose to do next, it will be nearly impossible for most people in the West to ever feel empathy for him or his cause again.

Among other atrocities, Al Qaeda attacked the U.S. embassies in Kenya and Tanzania in 1998, killing 257 and wounding over 5,000 people. In 2000, Al Qaeda bombed the USS Cole, killing 17 and wounding 39 American sailors. In 2001, Saudi men (possibly Al Qaeda) flew airplanes into the Twin Towers in New York City and the Pentagon in Washington, D.C., killing nearly 3,000 people. In 2004, Muslim terrorists (possibly Al Qaeda) bombed trains in Spain, causing 191 deaths. And in 2005, British Muslims (with no proven link to Al Qaeda) bombed London subways, killing 53 people.

On the one hand, I congratulate Bin Laden: *He wanted to engage the Western World in a holy war and he has succeeded.* However, it is unlikely that Bin Laden will achieve his primary goal of forcing the U.S. and Israel to leave the Middle East. It is even more unlikely that his soul will receive the salvation he seeks, given the evil he has wrought. So on the other hand, I pity Bin Laden: *He wanted Allah to approve a holy war, but there is no such thing.* **All war is unholy.**

In Truth, Bin Laden already has failed. God gave him incredible talent, untold riches, immense power, and a keen sense of purpose. However, he now has misused all of these gifts. By his own choice, he has succumbed to the two cardinal sins of greed and pride. He makes his money by selling lethal narcotics, and he flatters his ego by twisting the minds of Muslim youth. In short, he has forfeited his connection to God.

At this juncture in history, God has sent us numerous Prophets and provided us with adequate spiritual messages to help us peacefully resolve any problem. Consequently, we may no longer plead ignorance or feign misunderstanding regarding our Earth plane obligations, either to God or to each other. I won't pretend to know exactly how to unlock a fair solution to the Middle East conflict, but I suspect that the key is *forgiveness*. Forgiveness breeds empathy. Empathy stirs compassion. And compassion blossoms into love. Once we are united by love, we will be able to resolve the Middle East conflict.

> *Whatever ye are given here is but a convenience of this Life: but that which is with Allah is better and more lasting: It is for those who believe and put their trust in their Lord: Those who avoid the greater crimes and shameful deeds, and, **when they are angry even then forgive**;*
>
> *The recompense for an injury is an injury equal thereto: but if a person forgives and makes reconciliation, his reward is due from Allah .... But indeed if any show patience and forgive, that would truly be an exercise of courageous will and resolution in the conduct of affairs.*
> [Emphasis added]

The Holy Quran, Sura XLII, Verses 36, 37, 40, 43

The Truth is that both the Jews and the Muslims need safe havens in which to live and flourish as God intended. It won't be easy, but we all have been taught and we all possess the ability to transform hatred into love. I say again, the key is forgiveness. *May I also humbly suggest that we make Jerusalem an international city, where Jews, Christians, Muslims, and the entire world may enjoy our shared heritage of faith in the Supreme Being.*

Let us now turn our attention to Islamic law to determine whether Muslims are justly interpreting and applying God's law. Originally, Islamic law was intended to help guide Muslims toward the "straight path" as prescribed by Allah. Recall that Islamic law (*Shariah*) is comprised of the moral lessons contained in *The Holy Quran* and the traditions of the Prophet (*Hadith*, his words; and *Sunnah*, his deeds). Moreover, Islamic law is supposed to be applied fairly and uniformly. The laws themselves are strict but in most respects fair. The rules pertaining to women are a little more vague, but they could be interpreted to fit modern day circumstances in an equitable manner. At the very least, Islamic law was extremely progressive for its time and it continues to provide a healthy framework for ethical and moral conduct.

However, just because the laws were fair when written does not mean that they are fairly interpreted or applied today. In fact, the opposite is true in many Muslim nations. Sadly, Muslim men are twisting and reinterpreting the *Shariah* to the detriment of Muslim women. In fact, the trend is toward misogynist interpretations of *The Holy Quran*, both inside Muslim countries and even in Muslim communities around the world. Consider the following examples:

1. In Muslim mosques, women are not permitted to pray in the same room with men. Usually, the women are placed behind a curtain or, at best, positioned behind the men in the back of the mosque. Consequently, families do not pray together. Despite this widespread practice of spiritual segregation, there is absolutely no basis for the tradition in *The Holy Quran*. In fact, in Muhammad's day, men and women prayed together. Muhammad once stated, "Do not stop the female servants of Allah from attending the mosques of Allah."

2. Even in the United States, Muslim women are not permitted to join men in prayer. Recently, a Muslim woman in West Virginia tried to enter the front door of her mosque and join the men in the main prayer room. The Muslim men refused to conduct the service and ordered her to leave. The men then voted to ban women from the main prayer room and restrict them to using the back door of the mosque.

3. In 2003, the Nobel Peace Prize was awarded to an Iranian woman, **Shirin Ebadi,** who was a judge until **Ayatollah Khomeini** rose to power in 1979. Since then, Ebadi has bravely defied the Shiite jurists who have imposed drastic interpretations of Islamic law, such as: (i) women who seek a divorce may only keep male children until age two and female children until age seven; (ii) women may not work in certain occupations; (iii) women must stay covered or risk imprisonment; and (iv) women may not leave Iran without their husband's written permission.

4. In 2004, Canada began sanctioning Islamic courts to resolve family matters such as divorce and inheritance. Although parties "voluntarily" submit to the jurisdiction of the new court, Muslim women now feel pressure to forego their Canadian civil rights in favor of unknown interpretations of the Muslim *Shariah*.

5. In 2004, the new Iraqi governing council, which the U.S. helped form, repealed the civil laws that had expanded women's rights in favor of the *Shariah*. As a result, the newly "liberated" Iraqi women have fewer rights than when Saddam Hussein ruled.

6. The dreaded *burqa* (hooded ensemble that covers a woman from head to toe) is back in vogue. Muslim women all over the world are being "encouraged" to wear this outrageous garment. In the parts of Afghanistan where the Taliban still rule, women must wear a *burqa*. They also are not permitted to leave the house without a male escort, speak to men unless they are related, nor attend school. The penalty for violating these rules is death.

7. In Africa, where Christian versus Muslim wars rage in numerous countries, the treatment of all women is barbaric. A prime example is the war in Sudan which technically ended in 2005 but which still persists in the Darfur region. During the twenty-one year civil war, the cruelty of the ruling Muslim men was unparalleled. In addition to their campaign of ethnic cleansing, Muslim men engaged in ethnic insemination (i.e., rape) of both Muslim and Christian women. The Muslim men believe their offspring are Muslim, as the mother's religion and ethnicity are deemed irrelevant.

8. In 2005, the monarchy of Saudi Arabia sanctioned limited municipal elections. Women, however, were not allowed to vote.

9. *Sharia* has been interpreted in some Muslim countries to permit the genital mutilation of women. For example, although Egypt banned the practice in 2008, over 90% of Egyptian women are "circumcised."

The abhorrent treatment inflicted by Muslim men on their own women, which now exceeds the misogyny of Catholic men, finds absolutely no support in *The Holy Quran*. In fact, the *Quran* is quite vague on matters such as how women should dress and behave, dealing instead with protecting women and improving their status. With regard to female attire, the *Quran* suggests only that women dress modestly and take care when out in public. Here are the *suras* that have been twisted by male Muslim jurists to subjugate women.

> And say to the believing women that they should lower their gaze and guard their modesty; that they should not display beauty and ornaments except what must ordinarily appear thereof; that they should draw their veils over their bosoms and not display their beauty except to their [male relatives].
>
> The Holy Quran, Sura XXIV, Verse 31

> *O Prophet! Tell thy wives and daughters, and the believing women, that*
> *they should cast their outer garments over their persons when abroad:*
> *that is most convenient, that they should be known as such and not*
> *molested.*

> *The Holy Quran*, Sura XXXIII, Verse 59

Frankly, *The Holy Quran* seems much more concerned with how men –
not women – behave in public. With regard to how Muslim women are
expected to conduct themselves, I have found nothing in the *Quran* that pre-
cludes women from enjoying an unfettered existence. Indeed, there are no
suras which forbid women from: (i) talking to men (either inside or outside
their family); (ii) leaving their homes (with or without permission); (iii) going
to school; (iv) voting; or (v) working in certain professions.

Nevertheless, Muslim men have purposely crafted and interpreted Islamic
law in ways which harm women. Another good example is the sexist interpretation of the following *sura*, which Shiite jurists view as permitting men to
contract for a "temporary marriage" (*nikah mutah*).

> *Except for these [prohibitions against marriage], all others are lawful,*
> *provided you seek them in marriage with gifts from your property –*
> *desiring chastity, not lust.* **Seeing that you derive benefit from them**, *give*
> *them their dowers at least as prescribed; but if after a dower is*
> *prescribed,* **ye agree mutually to vary it,** *there is no blame on you, and*
> *Allah is All-knowing, All-wise. [Emphasis added]*

> *The Holy Quran*, Sura IV, Verse 24

Shockingly, the above bolded language has been interpreted by Shiite
imams, including **Grand Ayatollah Seestani**, the leading cleric in Iraq, to allow
men to temporarily take a wife. Such women typically are viewed as concubines, even in Shiite Muslim countries. The women have no rights and may be
abandoned even before the contract expires by the man "gifting" her back the
time remaining under the marriage contract. Moreover, these women are not
entitled to any financial support, even during the term of the marriage. If a
child is born, however, the man is expected to financially provide for the child,
but still not for the mother. Thus, temporary marriage is nothing more than a
cover for men to have sex in an otherwise sexually repressive culture.

Suffice it to say that I find grave problems with the way that Muslim men
are dictating and interpreting Islamic laws, especially as those laws pertain to
women and young children, the most vulnerable members of Muslim society.
As an ex-attorney, I see the arbitrary manner in which the laws are manipu-

lated and enforced to accommodate Muslim men, and it leaves me stymied and sickened. My deepest sympathies flow to Muslim women who are forced to endure such abominable treatment by their own men. I wish them the blessings of Allah as they struggle for their God-given rights.

After reviewing Islamic law as currently practiced by Muslim men, I sadly conclude that *Shariah* no longer meets the egalitarian principles of *Rule Number 4*, as the laws now are unfairly and unjustly used to dominate and suppress Muslim women.

Just as I fear that hatred has putrefied the hearts of fundamentalist Muslim men, I now fear that despair has overtaken the hearts of Muslim women. *My Muslim sisters must be so tired.* When I think of the Palestinian mothers who have lost children and who have been repeatedly dislodged from their homes due to the incessant fighting between the PLO and the Israelis, the women of Afghanistan who are prisoners in their own homes wherever the Taliban rule, the Iranian women who still are forced to wear the *burqa* in many parts of their country, and the Iraqi women who may now lose hard won civil rights – my heart is heavy. Not only have these women lost judicial protection due to misinterpretations of the *Shariah*, they also stand to lose their children, their husbands, and their homes in senseless battles ordered by militant and misguided male Muslim leaders.

Even in democratic societies, Muslim women are being minimized and subjugated. Recently a Muslim woman living in Canada wrote a book entitled *The Trouble with Islam: A Wake-up Call for Honesty and Change*. In her book, author Irshad Manji identifies the prevalent misuse and misinterpretation of *The Holy Quran*, and she encourages Muslims to exercise *ijtihad*, which means independent thinking. After her book was published, she received multiple death threats and was forced to accept the protection of the Royal Canadian Mounted Police.

How any soul can take flight under such repressive circumstances is a miracle to me and further evidence that *Allah* remains strong and true in the hearts of faithful Muslim women. Yet, they should not be tested in this manner. Their talent, their intellect, and their spiritual power is being wasted. Allah would not approve of such foul conditions. Consequently, as a woman and as an admirer of the Prophet Muhammad, I must conclude that at this time Islam is not a source of spiritual inspiration so much as a burden that Muslims, particularly Muslim women, must bear.

Although the teachings of Muhammad and the beauty of *The Holy Quran* bring much joy and inspiration both to Muslims and people of other faiths, the religion of Islam, as practiced and administered today, clearly violates *Rule Number 7*, which sets forth the spirituality requirements which are necessary for any good religion.

Next, let's consider whether Allah, as depicted by the religion of Islam, loves all of mankind or just the children of Islam. From Chapter Two, we know, at a minimum, that Islam was supposed to embrace all "Believers" (a/k/a "People of the Book"). Thus, Muhammad preached the inclusive message that all Jews, Christians, and Muslims are blessed by Allah.

> *Say: Oh People of the Book! Ye have no ground to stand upon unless ye stand fast by the Law, the Gospel, and all the revelations that have come to you from your Lord. ... Those who believe in the Quran, those who follow the Jewish scriptures, and the Sabians and the Christians – any who believe in Allah and the Last Day, and work righteousness – on them shall be no fear, nor shall they grieve.*
>
> The Holy Quran, Sura V, Verses 71, 72

Moreover, Muhammad correctly deduced that the other Prophets were valid messengers of Allah and that the other monotheistic religions were earlier manifestations of Allah's plan.

> *And We sent Noah and Abraham, and established in their line Prophethood and Revelation: and some of them were on right guidance, but many of them became rebellious transgressors.*
> *Then, in their wake, We followed them up with others of Our apostles: We sent after them Jesus the son of Mary, and bestowed on him the Gospel; and We ordained in the hearts of those who followed him Compassion and Mercy.*
>
> The Holy Quran, Sura LVII, Verses 26–27

Because Muhammad revered the earlier Prophets, he also accepted the religions that they spawned. He definitely would have preferred for his entire Arab audience to convert to Islam, and he did try to convert the Jews and Christians in Arabia, but he never punished people of other monotheistic religions for holding fast to their distinct beliefs. As a result, the Muslim Empire had a long and fairly harmonious history of practicing religious tolerance, even when Arab rulers sought to expand Muslim territories. Recall that this practice of religious tolerance is mandated by Allah, who instructs in *The Holy Quran* that there should be "no compulsion in religion."

Moreover, Muhammad preached that people of all religions can join Allah in heaven, provided they worship the one true God and live a good and charitable life in Allah's service. Thus, Muhammad made crystal clear a Truth that Jesus only alluded to: *God loves us all and doesn't care what religion we subscribe to, so long as we attempt to model God's divine nature through moral, chaste, and compassionate behavior.*

Thus, in its original and unadulterated form, Islam easily satisfies *Rule Number 5* because it teaches that Allah loves us all the same and will fairly review and judge our past behavior on Judgment Day, regardless of our chosen religion.

Unfortunately, the actions of Muslim extremists now cloud the issue of whether Islam is an inclusive religion. To comport with *Rule Number 5*, a religion must welcome outsiders and view them as worthy of a spiritual afterlife. Clearly, the Muslim fundamentalists who are terrorizing the world believe that the Christian "Crusaders" in the U.S., the Jewish "Zionists" in Israel, and "apostate" Muslim leaders throughout the Middle East are evil and unworthy of living, let alone joining Allah in heaven. Moreover, the number of terrorists increases daily. Therefore, it seems evident that Islam is following the same trajectory as Christianity – toward divisiveness and intolerance. Many Muslims no longer seem to subscribe to the basic Truth espoused by Muhammad: *All righteous people are children of God.*

While I readily agree that the United States has increased tensions in the Middle East and that Israel has repeatedly sabotaged the peace process with the Palestinians, war is not the answer. Muslims need to acknowledge that the Jews also need a place to live, a reality specifically addressed by Muhammad in *The Holy Quran.*

> *Then after them sent We Moses and Aaron to Pharaoh and his chiefs with Our Signs. But they were arrogant: They were a people in sin. ... We took the Children of Israel across the sea; Pharaoh and his hosts followed them in insolence and spite. ... **We settled the Children of Israel in a beautiful dwelling-place, and provided for them sustenance of the best.** [Emphasis added]*

The Holy Quran, Sura X, Verses 75, 90, 93

Thus, the Muslim holy book recites that God wanted the people of Israel to have a home, yet another reason why the military *jihad* against the Jews would never be sanctioned by Allah. Nevertheless, Muslim extremists have demonized Christians and Jews, in order to garner support for their unholy war and convince Muslim youth that lethal force is necessary to solve the problems in the Middle East. Muslim terrorists are forgetting, however, that the moment they embrace violence as a means to an end, they risk offending Allah. Muhammad specifically denounced religious intolerance and divisiveness. Therefore, just as Catholics offended God when they initiated the crusades and the Inquisition, Muslims now offend Allah with their military *jihad*.

Muslim men need to remember that Muhammad was sent to Earth to promote the unification of all faiths under the banner of Islam, not the extermination of other religions. *Tragically, fundamentalist Muslims have forgotten that the sacred mission of Islam was Unity.*

> *If Allah had so willed, He would have made you a single people, but His plan is to test you in what he hath given you: so strive as in a race in all virtues. The goal of you all is to Allah; It is He that will show you the truth of the matters in which ye dispute.*
>
> The Holy Quran, Sura V, Verse 48

Like Muhammad, I believe that it is God's plan to one day have humanity unite under a global spiritual belief system. When mankind is ready for this universal Truth, we will undergo the prophesied Fifth Spiritual Paradigm and enter a new age of peace and enlightenment (a/k/a the New Millennium). Unfortunately, that day has yet to come, a topic we will discuss in detail in the last chapter of this book. Meanwhile, mankind needs to minimize religious tensions, learn to tolerate our differences, and do our best to promote inclusiveness and worldwide unity. We can start this process be admitting that war is never the solution – an elementary Truth expressed by our greatest Prophets. Indeed, war only serves to postpone our passage into the New Millennium. Therefore, in order to help us get to utopia a little faster, let me repeat the following spiritual Truth:

The ends never justify the means.

Consequently, I implore Muslim men to stay true to their Prophet's teachings. In addition, they should study the powerful yet passive methods employed by Mahatma Gandhi in India, Martin Luther King in the United States, and Nelson Mandela in Africa. These spiritual leaders mounted full scale revolutions for their people to regain lost dignity, to obtain safe havens in which to live and thrive, and to inspire the next generation. Most importantly, though, not one of these leaders used military weapons to vanquish or destroy their enemies. Instead, each one used his heart, his mind, and his faith in God as weapons of Truth.

Until Muslim leaders reach this level of understanding, there will be no peace in the Middle East. Sadly, Muslim intolerance is growing even within their own communities, since the two main Muslim sects, Sunni and Shiite, are fractured and fighting each other in many areas. Male Muslim leaders have allowed their masculine "can do" energy to run rampant. Instead, they need to tap into their feminine "should do" energy to arrive at just and wise solutions to their problems. Then the Muslims will win the backing of the international community, which also has grown tired of the United States unilaterally playing policeman to the world whenever it suits U.S. interests. If Muslims can remember the inclusive and compassionate foundation of their religion, new and unimagined possibilities for peace in the Middle East will be discovered.

However, so long as Muslims vainly attempt to exclude other races and religious groups from participating in a peaceful resolution to the Middle East conflict, Islam will continue to violate *Rule Number 5*, which requires us to embrace those outside our chosen religion.

Lastly, let's analyze whether Islam is open to new information, a necessary ingredient for both intellectual and spiritual growth. Recall that Muhammad believed he was supposed to share Allah's divine revelations with all of mankind. At first, Muhammad was reluctant to accept this mission, but later he was able to do so by relying on the encouragement and support of his first wife, Khadija. In addition, recall that Muhammad believed he was receiving the final layer of Truth from Allah. In other words, he thought he would be the last great Prophet and that his Truth about God was the ultimate and final interpretation.

Because he believed himself to be the final Prophet, Muhammad naturally preferred the universal religion he was founding over the other religions being practiced in his part of the world. He correctly stated that: (i) Judaism and Christianity were based on older information from God; (ii) the Jewish and Christian holy books were incomplete; and (iii) some man-made errors had been added to the Prophets' lessons (e.g., the pagan fallacy of the Christian Holy Trinity). Therefore, Muhammad assumed that once he revealed the next layer of Truth from God, people from all religions would welcome this new information and update their faith by joining Islam.

Unfortunately, Muhammad's dream of religious unification failed for a whole host of reasons. First, even though most of mankind finally shared a belief in one God – the same God – monotheism was not a strong enough foundation to bring us together. Second, although Muhammad added a divine next layer to our Tower of Truth by teaching that righteous souls from every cultural and religious background may attain salvation, this new information also was not enough of an impetus to unite us. Instead, the barbaric state of the human condition during the European Dark Ages perpetuated economic destitution, racial discrimination, and spiritual disunity among the masses.

Primarily, though, Muhammad's goal of uniting mankind was thwarted by greedy and prideful men who refused to adopt a religion that required them to relinquish their actual Earth plane power in exchange for mere Ethereal plane promises. Consequently, most Jewish and Christian leaders simply lied to their laity regarding the true nature of Islam, while those who never bothered to study Islam negligently misinformed their followers about this newer religion. As a result, most Jews and Christians have remained loyal to their more archaic and flawed religions, thereby proving, yet again, that ignorance benefits men of power.

Although Muhammad was unsuccessful in manifesting the Fifth Spiritual Paradigm, I greatly admire his noble goal. I also applaud his prophetic understanding of the central tenet of this book: *Each Prophet came from God with successively more refined Truths in an attempt to gradually increase our understanding of God and help us achieve spiritual enlightenment.* Moreover, I agree with his conclusion that Judaism and Christianity are in dire need of updating. But I'll go even further than Muhammad and state this core conviction even more emphatically:

All the primary religions, including Islam, are at this point hopelessly out of date.

Therefore, to the extent that Muhammad recognized God's pattern of sending us great teachers at critical moments in history, I humbly validate his observation. However, I disagree that he was God's last messenger. It has been nearly fifteen hundred years since Muhammad died. Obviously, much had happened since his death, and mankind has learned additional Truths which need to be incorporated into the fabric of our collective soul. Indeed, we have learned so much more about God and about ourselves that the religion of Islam – at one time the most progressive and modern of the monotheistic religions – has now become just another ancient religion.

Today, most Islamic leaders are closed to change, but that has not always been the case. In fact, during the last millennium the Muslim Empire thrived and was one of the most open and productive societies mankind has ever built. In the 800s during the reign of **Caliph Mamun**, the Muslim Empire reached unparalleled heights and Baghdad was the center of the civilized world. The Muslims not only protected mankind's accumulated store of knowledge, they also expanded upon earlier achievements by promoting and patronizing the best and brightest minds of that era. In sum, the Muslim rulers embraced philosophy, mathematics, sciences, the arts, and literature for centuries, and we owe them a debt of gratitude for being such meticulous and loving caretakers of humanity's collective wisdom.

During the same time that the Muslims were pushing the intellectual and scientific envelope in their altruistic search for Truth, the greedy European monarchs and corrupt Catholic Church lusted after wealth and power. As a result, the Christians undermined their societies. Consider these stupendous examples of Muslim openness and invention as compared to the oppressive conditions which existed in the Christian world:

1. While the Muslims were reviving the classic Greek fields of study and hiring teachers from all over the world to educate their citizens, the Catholic popes and European monarchs were terrorizing their citizens by keeping them destitute, uneducated, and fearful.
2. While Muslim scientist Al Razi was amassing a twenty volume treatise on the current state of medicine and Al Kindi was writing over 250 other scientific books, the despot King Henry III of Germany consolidated his power by deposing three rival popes and naming his relative Pope Leo IX.
3. While the Muslims were contemplating and writing about the complex nature of the one true God, the Roman Catholic Church and the Greek Orthodox Church were still arguing over whether there was a second god named Jesus.
4. While poetry blossomed and the celebrated *Arabian Nights* was being written, the Catholic Inquisition was burning both heretics and books.
5. While the Muslims were extending the scope of mathematics, medicine, and astronomy, the Catholics were imprisoning and torturing scientists who were trying to bring enlightenment to the West.

Today, though, these roles seem to have flip-flopped. Over time, the Christian crusades, the Mongolian invasions, and internal strife amongst competing Muslim rulers took its toll on the Muslim Empire. Sadly, the Arab nations that were formed after the World Wars still have not recovered from the fall of the their once great empire. Although they like to point to the West, the Truth is that fundamentalist Muslims primarily have themselves and their corrupt leaders to blame for the current suppression of the Muslim people.

On the bright side, we should all be thankful that the Catholic pope and the few remaining European monarchs no longer pose a serious threat to intellectuals and spiritualists in the West. Currently, there are many bearers of light in the West who are free to pursue Truth. However, we need our Muslim brothers and sisters to be free, too, so that they may contribute once again to the edification of the collective consciousness. I know this will be difficult, particularly given the aggressive actions of Israel and my own country. Admittedly, Muslim anger is justified. However, until one side begins to model the appropriate method for resolving conflict, we will have no peace in the Middle East and certainly no spiritual unification on this planet.

Thus, the dark side now threatens the people of Islam, who are desperately needed if we are to achieve God's plan for mankind. In Truth, it is the Muslim leaders, both political and religious, who now are the most to blame for their own society's oppression and pain. Moreover, it is the Muslim culture, with its unduly harsh moral code, that now suffers the most from its own stifling environment and lack of freedom. Similarly, it is the Muslim community, with its unjust and unpredictable legal system, which now subjugates its own citizens. And it is the Muslim children, who are taught to hate Christians and Jews, who now are devolving into suicidal warriors based on their own lack of education. Finally, it is the Muslim women, who secretly and silently endure physical abuse, emotional torment, and spiritual chaos, who can no longer trust their own men. What a tragedy it will be for all of us if the Muslim people continue to follow the men of power who have tainted their once glorious religion.

Regretfully, at this juncture in history I am forced to conclude that Islam violates *Rule Number 6*, since the leaders of this religion no longer promote freedom of thought, accept new information, nor are open to positive change.

I feel such a sadness over the current state of Islam. It was the religion I knew the least about when I embarked on my spiritual quest fifteen years ago, and my soul grew immensely after reading *The Holy Quran*. If only Muslims had stayed open over the centuries and allowed their religion to continue growing and assimilating new Truths, Islam may have fulfilled its avowed and sacred purpose of uniting mankind. Unfortunately, just as the other four primary religions have been compromised by greedy and prideful souls, men of power have seized control of Islam. Alas, I guess I'm not a Muslim either.

CONCLUSIONS

After studying the five primary religions, I sadly conclude that mankind's religious history is fraught with error and corruption. Rather than building the Tower of Truth that God wanted us to construct, we created a Tower of Babel, which unnecessarily divides and separates us. In sum, religion has become a divisive tool, not the uniting force intended by God and the Prophets. Here is a quick review of how and why the five primary religions have failed humanity:

1. Before the Big Bang and the advent of human consciousness, there was a period of perfect equipoise when everything – both ethereal and material – resided in unity. This was the **First Spiritual Paradigm**. God was all that existed, and humans were an unmanifested thought form within the Divine consciousness.

2. After the Big Bang, the illusion of separation began and with it the development of the man-made religions. Early man believed in the Great Mother, a goddess who gave life to all things. This was the **Second Spiritual Paradigm**, an era of female monotheism which lasted roughly twenty thousand years.

3. Thereafter, mankind started to believe in a variety of gods and goddesses who ruled the Universe. This was the **Third Spiritual Paradigm**, an era of polytheism that lasted approximately five thousand years. **Hinduism** is the only religion of that era which is still practiced today.

4. Then the major Prophets arrived, and they all pronounced the seminal Truth that there is one Supreme Being. The Prophets also delivered progressively more sophisticated messages about our collective Earth plane obligations and our individual Ethereal plane potential. However, men crafted the new theologies and masculine energy came to dominate the **Fourth Spiritual Paradigm**. As a result, for the past two thousand years male monotheism has characterized the other four primary religions: **Judaism, Buddhism, Christianity,** and **Islam**.

5. Thereafter, men utilized masculine energy to build new institutions to God. In the process, feminine energy was marginalized and God's messages were minimized. Thus it was that humanity started to lose the deeper meaning and wisdom behind the Prophets' messages. This led to all sorts of problems:

   (i) Man-made rules and rituals led to the creation of church hierarchy and positions of authority – which excluded women;

    (ii) Positions of authority led to the exercise of actual power by a few "chosen" men (i.e., the clergy) over the masses;

    (iii) The growing authority of the clergy often attracted men who were susceptible to the cardinal sins of greed and pride;

    (iv) The clergy's craving for wealth and power led to the intermingling of religion and politics – which also was dominated by men;

    (v) The intermingling of religion and politics allowed the clergy to gain absolute control over the masses – particularly women;

    (vi) Absolute control by the clergy led to the oppression and manipulation of the masses – especially women; and

    (vii) The masses became like herd animals, accustomed to being physically impoverished and spiritually confused, to the point that if a holy war were declared in God's name, the masses would fight each other to the death.

6. Today, orthodox religion is tainted by men of power and the lopsided application of masculine energy. As a result, the five primary religions are not:

    (i)   Mirroring the teachings of their respective Prophet;

    (ii) Synthesizing the collective wisdom imparted by all the Prophets; or

    (iii) Leading mankind to the state of spiritual unity that God intended, made possible, and still wants for us.

7. As further proof that orthodox religion has failed to spiritually guide us, only one of the five primary religions (Buddhism) currently satisfies the objective requirements of *The Seven Rules of Any Good Religion.*

8. Therefore, it appears that our continued blind faith in the five man-made religions is serving only to perpetuate and prolong our collective spiritual blindness.

9. It has been almost fifteen hundred years since a major Prophet has explained what God expects from us. Nevertheless, we have all the information we need to lead peaceful and purposeful lives on the Earth plane and to achieve eternal life in the Ethereal plane.

10. Thus, we should have faith in God and we should assume that God has faith in us. Put another way, we should have *Saddha* – confidence in our own ability to achieve spiritual enlightenment.

11. In sum, the five "new" religions created by mankind during the past two Spiritual Paradigms are now "ancient." None of them are leading us toward the prophesied **Fifth Spiritual Paradigm** of **Truth, Love,** and **Light.**

Across the world, men and women of all faiths are eagerly awaiting the prophesied Fifth Spiritual Paradigm, which will arrive once we re-embrace feminine energy and decide to either update (or simply discard) the ancient man-made religions which have failed us. Today, there are many people like me who have concluded that the five primary religions are hampering both our collective spiritual growth and our ability to attain individual enlightenment. As a result, many people have left their synagogues, temples, churches, and mosques to commence private spiritual journeys. Indeed, a 2009 *Newsweek* poll revealed that 30% of Americans now call themselves "spiritual" not "religious," up from 24% in 2005 when I wrote the first edition of this book. Moreover, one-quarter of all Americans now believe in reincarnation, according to a 2008 *Harris* poll. Thus, many souls are discovering the *Saddha* process of soul growth, as I did roughly fifteen years ago.

Strangely, though, there seem to be just as many people clinging to the ancient religions as there are people who have abandoned them. While half the world is reverting to religious fundamentalism, the other half is embracing New Age theologies. *Clearly, mankind has become spiritually polarized.* In the last chapter, I will attempt to explain why some of us still prefer the religions created during the Third and Fourth Spiritual Paradigms, while others of us are eager to embrace the Fifth Paradigm and enter the prophesied New Millennium.

COMPARATIVE RELIGIONS REPORT CARD

	Hinduism	Judaism	Buddhism	Christianity	Islam
Rule Number 1 Philosophy	D	D	B	D	C
Rule Number 2 Science	D	D	B	F	C
Rule Number 3 Morality	F	C-	A	D	D
Rule Number 4 Justice	F	F	C	F	F
Rule Number 5 Inclusiveness	F	F	C	F	D
Rule Number 6 Openness	F	C	C	F	F
Rule Number 7 Spirituality	F	D	C-	F	F
New Millennium GPA	F	D	C+	F	D

Before we proceed, however, let us take a final look at how the five primary religions practiced on the Earth today stack up against the *Seven Rules of Any Good Religion*. The following chart is a graphic illustration of how these religions are faring in the 21st Century.

The **New Millennium Grade Point Average** is based on the current performance of the five primary religions as objectively measured against: (i) how well the leaders of each religion are adhering to the messages of their Prophet; and (ii) *The Seven Rules of Any Good Religion*. Hence, the GPA is not an evaluation of the Prophets, all of whom delivered Truths from God.

For fun, I am providing a blank report card below. I encourage you to grade each of the five man-made religions for yourself to determine what GPA you feel is fair. Also, whenever your religious leaders speak on controversial moral or spiritual issues, use the objective template – *The Seven Rules of Any Good Religion* – to decide for yourself whether your clergy are adequately mirroring God's lessons, as relayed by your favorite Prophet. Better yet, grade your clergy to see if they are accurately representing your beliefs, as dictated by your own conscience. In short, it is time for all of us to think and seek spiritual Truth for ourselves.

COMPARATIVE RELIGIONS REPORT CARD

	Hinduism	Judaism	Buddhism	Christianity	Islam
Rule Number 1 **Philosophy**					
Rule Number 2 **Science**					
Rule Number 3 **Morality**					
Rule Number 4 **Justice**					
Rule Number 5 **Inclusiveness**					
Rule Number 6 **Openness**					
Rule Number 7 **Spirituality**					
New Millennium GPA					

*If they say to you, "Where did you come from?" say to them,
"We came from the light, the place where the light came into
being on its own accord and established itself and
became manifest through their image."
If they say to you, "Is it you?" say,
"We are children, and we are the elect of the living father."*

Gospel of Thomas, Verse 50

The above quote attributable to Jesus is one of my favorites. To me, it is a reminder of the most fundamental Truth of all:

We all share a common origin and we all share a common destiny.

Put another way, we are all connected. We may mature physically, evolve intellectually, and grow spiritually at different rates, but we remain connected to God ... *and to each other* ... forever.

The five primary religions correctly espouse the first half of this formula, that our souls are connected to God. Indeed, the man-made religions all claim to bring their laity closer to God through their respective doctrines and rituals. However, as shown in Chapter Four, the man-made religions are neglecting the second half of this equation: *Our souls are connected to each other.* Tragically, the man-made religions have devolved into divisive institutions that separate mankind along absurd and fractious lines in God's name. Intentional or not, the situation is blasphemous.

By failing to stress our connectedness to each other, the five primary religions are spinning humanity in circles. As a result, we currently are not making much spiritual progress. In fact, some believe that the resurgence of religious fundamentalism is a sign that we are losing ground. However, for the reasons set forth in the remainder of this book, I resolutely believe otherwise. Although mankind appears to have reached a spiritual "stalemate," we truly are on the verge of the Fifth Spiritual Paradigm.

It is true, though, that the intense polarization we are experiencing is a sign of prophetic magnitude. Consider these examples of spiritual chaos: (i) the "red state" versus "blue state" debates on moral values in the United States; (ii) the ever-widening worldwide gap between the rich and the poor, despite our professed compassion for our fellow man; (iii) the continued use of violence as our primary method of dispute resolution; and (iv) the glaring difference between the "blind faith" formula for *afterlife* salvation taught by fundamentalist clergy (e.g., Christian and Muslim) and the "good works" or *Saddha* method of soul growth taught by more advanced spiritualists (e.g., Buddhist and New Age) who understand the Truth – that souls may reach spiritual enlightenment and connect to God *at any time*. This extreme polarization of theological beliefs and practices indicates that mankind is in a **Great Cusp,** which is the period of intense spiritual vibration and increased social turbulence that immediately precedes a Spiritual Paradigm shift.

Certainly, most of the souls on Earth want the Fifth Spiritual Paradigm to arrive. Indeed, some people yearn to reach this next level of spirituality so much that they are willing to embrace catastrophic End Times prophecies – even if it means their own death – in the hope of witnessing the birth of the next phase of God's plan for mankind.

But such doomsday prophecies miss the mark, as do the fundamentalist preachers who literally interpret them. The next Spiritual Paradigm will not occur when God destroys the Earth or when Jesus reincarnates. Rather, the New Millennium will arrive when mankind collectively decides to manifest the Fifth Spiritual Paradigm. Then we will select only those religious and political leaders who have studied and assimilated God's Tower of Truth as built by our greatest Prophets, embellished by our brightest philosophers, and enhanced by our most brilliant scientists. *Oh, what a glorious day that will be ... heaven on Earth!*

Unfortunately, many religious leaders have ingrained in their laity the false premise that blind faith in a man-made religion or mere worship of a Divine soul (e.g., Jesus) guarantees one everlasting unity with the Almighty. These misguided clerics also preach the erroneous conclusion that heaven is a reward that one receives after death by picking the "right" religion. These false teachings have confused many souls and have produced an "every man for himself" approach to life as opposed to the compassionate model depicted by the Prophets. Once enough souls finally comprehend the Truth – that heaven is a state of consciousness and not a destination – the Great Cusp will end, the prophesied New Millennium will commence, and we will experience the heartfelt beauty of the Fifth Spiritual Paradigm.

It also is unfortunate that those people who still subscribe to the ancient religions worry that their souls may be at risk if they question their belief system or their spiritual leader. I had this same fear when I first started to question orthodox Christianity. But I found the courage to search my soul, study all the religions, and ponder the biggest question of all: *Why are we here?* And eventually the answer came to me: *Our souls are on the Earth plane to learn about love.*

In order to achieve this heavenly state of everlasting peace and harmony, we need not die. We need only learn how to love. We should love ourselves by caring for our bodies, improving our minds, and inspiring our souls. We also show love of self by accepting personal responsibility for our actions and by realizing that they produce *karmic* consequences that impact the Universe. We should love God by being grateful for the gift of life, enjoying the beauty of the Earth plane, and striving to be Divine ourselves. And we should love each other, which for some reason seems to be the hardest love for us to grasp. Your clergy may be telling you that blind faith alone or mere love of God will suffice to earn your salvation, but that is not what the Prophets said.

> *So you too must befriend the alien, for you were once aliens yourself in the land of Egypt.*
>
> Moses, *Deuteronomy*, Chapter 10:19

> *Hatreds do not cease in this world by hating, but by love: this is an eternal Truth.*
>
> Buddha, *The Dhammapada*, Sutra 1, Verse 5

Do to others whatever you would have them do to you. This is the law and the prophets.

Jesus, Gospel of Matthew, Chapter 7:12

Those who believe, and do deeds of righteousness, and establish regular prayers and regular charity, will have their reward with their Lord: On them shall be no fear, nor shall they grieve.

Muhammad, The Holy Quran, Sura II, Verse 277

More to the point, it is not what God said.

*You shall not bear hatred for your fellow man in your heart. Though you may have to reprove your fellow man, do not incur sin because of him. Take no revenge and cherish no grudge against your fellow countryman. **You shall love your neighbor as yourself.** I am the Lord. [Emphasis added]*

God, Leviticus, Chapter 19:8

Thus, if the soul focuses *only* on love of God, the soul fails its Earth plane mission, since we are here to learn about our connectedness to all things. Put another way, if we can't achieve unity on the Earth plane, how can we possibly be ready to unite with God in the Ethereal plane?

The resurgence of religious intolerance and divisiveness is not a sign that mankind is doomed. However, the overtly judgmental attitude and aggressive posture emanating from fundamentalist sects does constitute horrifying evidence that orthodox religious leaders are misguiding their laity. Ironically, it is the clergy who now are blocking our collective spiritual development. As proof, consider how the worldwide polarization that has occurred amongst "people of faith" is preventing us from achieving the level of spiritual enlightenment which the Prophets modeled and which God intended for us. Sadly, we seem to have forgotten an important corollary to the most basic Truth:

Whatever happens to the least of us happens to us all.

We are suffering because we have yet to accept the fact that we all share the same destiny. We are suffering because we are not taking care of each other or our beautiful planet Earth. Nevertheless, according to New Age Christians, we soon will achieve the "Christ Consciousness." Similarly, New Age Jews optimistically opine that our collective consciousness soon will manifest the "Messianic Age." These are just different ways of describing the prophesied New Millennium – an era when humanity will finally synthesize and assimilate God's Tower of Truth.

But before we attain this next level of our collective spiritual evolution, we must first navigate our way through the current Great Cusp, which is the difficult and chaotic period that always precedes a new millennium. Once we make it through this challenging stage of our collective Earth plane mission, we will experience the spiritual awakening that almost all of us, regardless of where we fall on the religious continuum, are so eager to embrace.

One of the main reasons that the Great Cusp is being prolonged is that mankind is worshiping only half of God's energy. Recall that during the Fourth Spiritual Paradigm, most of mankind rejected polytheism and re-embraced the Truth of monotheism. Unfortunately, the clerics of the last millennium mistakenly (or purposely) concluded that the sole source of all creation was a male deity. As a result, mankind spurned goddess worship and supplicated itself to a single patriarchal god. Thereafter, mankind began to glorify masculine energy and minimize feminine energy. Indeed, men of power went even further. Not only did they negate the existence of sublime feminine energy, they also subdued Earth plane females.

In order to properly analyze the spiritual dynamic of the last millennium, we need to accept the fact that God possesses dualistic components. The Chinese philosopher Laozi referred to this duality as Yin (female) and Yang (male) energy. So let us explore this Truth – that God is composed of a unified yet dual nature – since it will help us understand how the patriarchal religions that were created during the last millennium first helped but now hinder mankind.

At the outset, we need to know how the masculine and feminine halves of God differ. Mystics refer to the masculine half of God as **creation energy,** which encompasses conscious action, problem solving, invention, and productivity. In sum, masculine energy is concerned with *"what can be done."* The feminine half of God, on the other hand, is viewed as **wisdom energy,** which throughout the ages has been described as encompassing the unconscious mind, intuition, morality, and priority setting. Thus, feminine energy concentrates on *"what should be done."*

When masculine and feminine energies are balanced, blended, and harmonized, as they function in the Supreme Being, these energies produce stupendous results (a/k/a miracles). However, when these energies are bisected, disconnected, or oppositional, as may occur within human beings, the results can be disastrous. It is important to understand, however, that each of us possesses both masculine and feminine energy, regardless of our gender. In other words, men have a "feminine side" to their nature which inspires them to resolve moral dilemmas, just as women have a "masculine side" to their nature which motivates them to devise concrete applications.

With these concepts in mind, we now are ready to take a look at the last two thousand years of human history, which astrologers call the **Age of Pisces**. In astrological terms, a millennium lasts approximately two thousand years. Currently, mankind is passing from the Age of Pisces into the **Age of Aquarius**, concepts which we will discuss in more detail shortly. *For now, let us examine what happened during the Age of Pisces, when masculine "can do" energy was given free reign to create, without the complementary and counterbalancing wisdom of feminine "should do" energy.*

To begin with, after mankind fought its way through the last Great Cusp (which was exceedingly bloody) and finally progressed into the Fourth Spiritual Paradigm, men of power seized upon the opportunity to harness and exploit masculine energy. One of the first things they did was summarily exclude women from political and religious discourse. They also assigned women an inferior status both on the Earth plane and in the Ethereal plane. The Catholic treatment of women is a prime example of this purposeful female oppression, which shockingly continues to this day. Hence, one of the immediate consequences of making God male and worshiping masculine energy was that women were deemed not as worthy or Divine as men.

Next, the fixed concentration of masculine energy fueled all sorts of creative endeavors. Mankind designed advanced civilizations, built architectural wonders, invented machinery, conquered long distance travel, implemented mass communication, and learned to harness various sources of energy. Today, mankind has learned how to clone humans, a *very* godlike power. Hence, many wondrous discoveries and beneficial applications were made possible through the utilization of masculine energy. However, without the balance of feminine energy, some of our creations now have come back to haunt us. For example, it has been almost three hundred years since the start of the Industrial Revolution and we now understand the cumulative effects of the resulting pollution. Nevertheless, we continue to delay drawing on feminine energy to arrive at a wise solution to global warming. Thus, inadvertent dangers may result when masculine energy is given free reign.

The net results of the Fourth Spiritual Paradigm are fascinating. On the one hand, masculine energy established order on planet Earth, since practical achievements were deemed paramount. During the Age of Pisces, men of power vied with each other to build vast empires and organize religious institutions. They may have callously used the common people, who were forced to fight in the requisite wars and furnish the necessary labor to build these new societies, but the leaders of the last millennium successfully propelled humanity into a more productive existence.

By the end of this era, men of power were so focused on science and technology that they were able to create almost everything they could imagine, such as advanced medicine, computers, spaceships, nuclear power, and weapons of mass destruction. Also, greed was running rampant. Consequently, the leaders of the last millennium had little regard for public safety, our ecosystem, or the moral imperative of distributing scarce resources fairly. Nevertheless, even though the masses were herded like animals and manipulated by men of power during the Age of Pisces, many common people did begin to earn fair wages, purchase modest homes, and reap the benefits of the revolutionary technologies that improved our standard of living.

On the other hand, the political and religious leaders of the last millennium stymied our spiritual growth by choosing a path which minimized the importance of the common man and our collective consciousness. These men enjoyed their positions of power and they quickly realized that religion was an effective tool for controlling the poor and uneducated masses. As a result, the traditional bond between politics and religion was cemented during the Age of Pisces, despite the periodic challenges posed by philosophers, scientists, and true spiritualists. These brave souls tried to educate and enlighten the masses, but they didn't stand a chance. The aristocrats decided to preserve their wealth and social superiority by supporting the clergy. And the clergy determined to protect their riches and rank by inventing ingenious methods for controlling the masses.

First, religious men of power clouded the word of God by perpetuating mythological fantasies, adopting strict doctrine, and instituting inane rules of worship. Second, they convinced their laity to place blind faith in them as God's representatives on Earth. Third, they made false promises of absolution and salvation, as though they were the judges of our soul's fate. Last, if need be, the clergy was willing to torture and kill.

However, by the end of this era religious men of power faced a new threat: *education*. To the clergy's abject horror, during the 20th Century the masses began to study philosophy, science, and history. Moreover, ordinary people began to ponder and discuss the nature of God and mankind's place in the Universe. Finally, we had begun to think for ourselves, which left religious men of power with two choices: (i) admit that the five man-made religions no longer serve humanity, make the necessary changes, then lead us into the Fifth Spiritual Paradigm; or (ii) face extinction. Tragically, rather than accepting the next phase of God's plan for mankind, orthodox clergy have decided to protect their turf at all costs, which is why they now are reverting to proven methods of crowd control, such as attacking scientists, restricting basic human rights, and pronouncing holy wars in God's name. In short, religious fundamentalism is spiritually polarizing planet Earth and prolonging the current Great Cusp.

Today, there is overwhelming proof that the orthodox clergy of the five primary religions are failing to embrace the New Millennium. Fundamentalism has infected nearly every religion. Indeed, fundamentalist clerics of every ilk are instructing their laity to literally interpret ancient parables written for our unsophisticated ancestors and doomsday prophecies composed by bereft prophets from the past. Obviously, all of the ancient holy texts deserve reverence, as they were written by some of the best and most noble minds of bygone eras. However, the Truth is that these holy books were written by men – not God. Consequently, these texts do not have the power to control our fate. Rather, we have that power because God gave it to us. In sum, the time has come for us to start thinking for ourselves, exercising our free will in a loving manner, and crafting the utopian existence that God intended for us.

Finally, I would be remiss if I failed to underscore what I view as the primary barrier to the Fifth Spiritual Paradigm. Currently, religious men of power all over the planet are reverting to one of their favorite tools for maintaining the *status quo*. In fact, it has proven to be their most effective tool for controlling the masses. In my opinion, the current Great Cusp polarization is being purposely prolonged by orthodox male clergy who have made the calculated decision to continue oppressing over half of the world's inhabitants: *women*.

Please realize that by excluding women from positions of leadership and authority, the five primary religions are ignoring the wisdom of 50% of the population and the accompanying feminine energy which we need in order to birth the New Millennium.

Remarkably, these strategies for controlling the masses, particularly women, have worked for the last two thousand years! Doubtless, I am a late-comer to this realization, as I was fortunate enough to be born, raised, and educated in the United States. However, even in the U.S., many people are being duped by tainted religious leaders. Karl Marx and Friedrich Nietzsche wrote about this issue extensively in the 1800s, attempting to warn the populace that religion was being used to sedate, contain, and manipulate them ... but to no avail. In short, we were spiritual pawns during the Age of Pisces, blindly following outdated belief systems and pledging allegiance to hypocritical religious leaders who were more concerned with Earth plane power than synthesizing God's Tower of Truth.

As the Age of Pisces drew to a close, however, this pattern of abuse toward the masses started to wane. The spiritual tide really started to turn during the second half of the 20th Century, when mankind collectively began to value human rights, women's rights, and the inalienable rights and freedoms given to us by God. As a result, we witnessed for the first time political and religious movements intended to protect the rights of the oppressed. For example, in the United States we saw the civil rights movement, the feminist movement, the creation of the Peace Corps, and political backlash against unethical leaders and immoral wars. Eventually, our politicians codified some of these innate freedoms, although the benign Equal Rights Amendment, which simply promised women equal protection under the law, never passed. In addition, our judges bravely enforced these new laws which were geared to protect the weakest members of society. Finally, the world was rediscovering a precious and priceless commodity: *feminine energy.*

These social changes marked the beginning of the Fifth Spiritual Paradigm and our full entry into the chaos of a Great Cusp. It started gloriously in the United States around 1960. I am fortunate because I was born at the beginning of this era. My primary school already had been desegregated, so I never knew a time when African Americans ("black people" back then) were limited to inferior public schools. In fact, I didn't even know about racial discrimination until I was about ten years old, when I learned about the Civil War and saw shows on TV about the civil rights movement. Even then, I thought the TV reels of marches, police with fire hoses, Martin Luther King's assassination, and the loathsome Ku Klux Klan were clips from another era. As it later came to pass, my best girlfriend in high school was African American. I thank God that I lived during a time when I could get to know and love Toni, who still is in my life.

The Great Cusp also was a time when religion was banned from our public institutions, since we had begun to value the individuality of faith. As a result, public classrooms became sacred places of learning where science finally was untethered to and unfettered by religion. Consequently, I was taught the Truth of human evolution. I also studied Greek and Egyptian mythology regarding the origin of mankind, but teachers never asserted that these ancient creation stories were true science. Of course, I did learn about Adam and Eve during Catechism class, which I attended once a week *after* school. I also heard a modern interpretation of the Jewish creation myth that was consistent with what I was learning from my science teacher, when my Jewish girlfriend invited me to Hebrew class. Incidentally, Janet's religious training also was administered *outside* of the public classroom.

Back then, I never questioned the equal status of my gender (except at church), since I was told from birth that I should be a lawyer. I had no brothers, so there was never any discussion of "girl" versus "boy" chores in my home. In fact, I was expected to do everything. On TV, I saw liberated, self-confident, and self-sufficient working women, such as Marlo Thomas in *That Girl* and Mary Tyler Moore in the show which bore her name. And secretly, I dreamed that it was I (instead of Kim Darby) who was on the adventure of a lifetime with John Wayne in my most favorite movie, *True Grit*.

Moreover, by the time I got to law school in the early 1980s, half of my incoming class was female. As a result, it never occurred to me that I was inferior to men or that my destiny was not my own. Only lately, when I read about Arab women struggling for their innate rights, Indian women being forced to marry strangers, and Chinese women involuntarily aborting female babies, have I started to comprehend the precarious nature of my own civil rights and social freedoms. Additionally, the recent restrictions on civil liberties imposed by my own government (e.g., the *Patriot Act*), make me wonder whether my own civil rights are slowly slipping away. Consequently, I have a newfound respect and appreciation for the strides and sacrifices made by the leaders of the feminist movement. I salute Bella Abzug and Gloria Steinem, despite the one downside which resulted from their good work – the "superwoman" myth. As I learned firsthand, mothers who work outside the home need help to properly raise their children. It is not possible for anyone, male or female, to perform two full-time jobs.

I also saw the nightly news coverage of the Vietnam War when I was a child. We always watched CBS, as my father was a loyal Walter Cronkite fan. For those readers who are my age or older, recall that in the 1970s, reporters could follow soldiers anywhere, including through the jungle and on village raids. Back then, the news stations also broadcast anything caught on film. Consequently, as a young child I saw American men and Vietnamese men, women, and children suffer and die almost every night. I also had a few girlfriends who lost older brothers in the war, and we all wore silver POW and MIA bracelets. Lately, I am reminded of those sad silver bands whenever I see the rubber Lance Armstrong bracelet on my youngest son's wrist. I wish we had bought our bands to support charities instead of the missing and imprisoned souls who were forced or fooled into fighting that pointless and unnecessary war.

By the time I was a pre-teen, I was aware of the Vietnam War protesters and the hippies. My father said they were stoned out of their minds and he called them "commies." When I asked him about communism, he said it was a form of government that forced its citizens to share everything. I remember thinking to myself, "But isn't that what Jesus told us to do?" I also remember daydreaming about joining the hippies, going to Woodstock, and wearing a headband. In fact, my mother bought me a headband and I wore it for years. Somehow, I intuitively knew that the hippies were trying to accomplish something new and good. Today, I understand that the hippies were promoting an honest political dialogue, a pacifist approach to conflict, and a simpler existence. They also stood for non-judgment, non-violence, and compassionate living. In short, the much maligned hippies simply were trying to create a more loving environment, along the same lines prescribed by Buddha, Jesus, and Muhammad.

To summarize, the start of the Great Cusp was an exciting and terrifying time for many people, as the hippies squared off against the men of power. Our nation was spiritually polarized, just as it is today. We were in the throes of a Great Cusp and we were so close to embracing the Fifth Spiritual Paradigm!

Then suddenly, the Great Cusp lost steam. I am speaking, of course, about the 1980s, when political and religious men of power managed to herd us like animals, once again. But this time they used a new technique. This time, they used the cardinal sin of greed (to which they already had succumbed) to bribe the masses. There was plenty of money to go around, as the stock market rally of the 1980s was unprecedented. Never mind that our budget deficit and national debt soared as well. And never mind that our government was cutting benefits to the weakest members of our society. After all, the newly formed Christian Coalition assured us that it was perfectly fine to implement welfare reform, despite the devastating impact on millions of women and children. Yes, I, too, was fooled by "compassionate conservatism." Or, maybe I was just having too much fun being part of the "Me Generation." Either way, I was one of the souls who helped get us stuck in the Great Cusp, which is yet another reason for my writing this book.

But why, you may ask? Why would anyone want to undermine the next phase of mankind's spiritual evolution? Don't our political and religious leaders want to lead us into the New Millennium and the state of brotherly love prescribed by God through the Prophets?

The answers to these questions are obvious, once we understand what will happen after mankind accepts and absorbs the Fifth Spiritual Paradigm. Therefore, let us spend a little more time exploring what the Great Cusp represents and exactly what the New Millennium will look and feel like once it arrives.

To astrologers the term "millennium" does not mean 1,000 years. Rather, an astronomical millennium lasts 2,160 years, based on the time it takes the Earth to travel around the Sun *and* reach the exact same directional point from whence it started. Most of us probably would guess that it takes only 365 days for the Earth to rotate to the same relative position around the Sun. However, because the Earth's axis has a wobble, it takes much longer than a year for any point on Earth to reach the same directional position. Thus, the North Pole does not arrive at the same set point in the sky at the end of each year. To be precise, it takes us close to 26,000 years to complete the precessional cycle, when the North Pole returns to set point.

Therefore, both astronomers and astrologers use the 26,000 year precessional period to track the Earth's cycle around the Sun, rather than our solar year. To compute a millennium, astrologers divide the Earth's processional cycle by twelve, which is the number of quadrants used to divide the celestial sky. It is interesting to note that in 1925, astronomers accepted the ancient practice of dividing the heavens into regions and they assigned twelve sections of 30 degrees each to the central band. When you divide the 360 degree central skyline into 30 degree sections, you get twelve constellations, which now officially match the twelve houses of the zodiac used by ancient man. And when you divide the 26,000 year precessional period by the twelve constellations, you get astrological ages that last 2,160 years. For simplicity's sake, though, we will round-off the astronomical millennia to 2,000 years each. The following is a list of the astronomical ages that mankind has passed through in recent history, along with their assigned zodiac names.

10,000	B.C.E.	Age of Leo
8,000	B.C.E.	Age of Cancer
6,000	B.C.E.	Age of Gemini
4,000	B.C.E.	Age of Taurus
2,000	B.C.E.	Age of Aries
1	C.E.	Age of Pisces
2,000	C.E.	Age of Aquarius

It is worth repeating that ancient man knew about the Earth's processional cycle. Historians have verified that the Sumerians created accurate astrological charts by 4000 B.C.E. This means that the Sumerians knew the Earth was spherical. It also means that they somehow graphed the 360 degree skyline surrounding Earth. However, the most interesting issue is: *How did the Sumerians know that the Earth takes 26,000 years to fully complete one wobbly cycle around the Sun?*

In their legends, the Sumerians recorded that their gods and goddesses gave them this knowledge, which begs the question whether aliens have ever visited us. Regardless, when 15th and 16th Century scientists learned that the Earth was not flat and that we move around the Sun, they actually were rediscovering Truths that the Sumerians had discovered six thousand years earlier.

Now, let's examine the term Great Cusp in more detail. A Great Cusp occurs whenever we exit one astrological age and enter a new one. Accordingly, we are in a Great Cusp right now because we are crossing the bridge between the outgoing millennium, the Age of Pisces, and the incoming millennium, the Age of Aquarius. Although mankind chronologically is entering the Age of Aquarius (a/k/a the New Millennium), some people have yet to fully embrace the majesty of this next stage of our evolution and empowerment. As a result, we are spiritually polarized. This is common during paradigm shifts because it takes a while for our collective consciousness to absorb the impact of shifting energies. Thus, Great Cusps are times of spiritual turbulence, since some souls are more open to the influx of new astrological aspects and influences than are others.

In addition, the term "cusp" is used by astrologers to describe the one or two day transitional period between solar astrological signs. For example, my Sun sign is Libra, which is represented by the scales. This is interesting synchronicity considering that I seemed destined to practice law. However, if I had been born on September 23rd, my Sun sign would have been on the cusp between Virgo and Libra. In such a case, at least one house in my astrological chart would have been subject to the influences of two different astrological aspects.

Similarly, whenever our planet undergoes a millennium change, mankind experiences a Great Cusp that can last up to one hundred years. This is a highly vibrational time, as mankind is thrust, willingly or not, into a new phase of spiritual development. It is a birthing process and it is part of God's "life-death-life" cycle. Thus, planet Earth and its inhabitants currently are feeling the effects of being "born again" into the Age of Aquarius.

Unfortunately, because many religious leaders are obsessed with maintaining their positions of authority, they are encouraging their laity to resist the upcoming changes. Therefore, rather than leading their members into the New Millennium, the men of power who control the five man-made religions are confusing their laity by reintroducing ancient fundamentalist dogma. The result is the spiritual polarization we are witnessing between: (i) those souls who are clinging to the ancient religions and who have been taught that heaven requires death and God's mercy; and (ii) those souls who have synthesized God's Tower of Truth and who understand that humanity has the divine potential to create heaven right here on Earth, as God intended.

As previously discussed, the Great Cusp started in the United States in the 1960s. If the Great Cusp had gone smoothly, we would have accepted the Fifth Spiritual Paradigm by now. In other words, we would have rejected the fiction that God is male and embraced this Truth: *The Supreme Being is a singular entity which contains both masculine and feminine energies.* The assimilation of this essential Truth will be the hallmark of the Fifth Spiritual Paradigm. Then, during the next stage of our spiritual evolution, human beings will learn how to balance and blend masculine and feminine energies, just like the Supreme Being. Once we start to combine creation and wisdom energies, the Great Cusp will be over, we will pass into the New Millennium, and we will live an exceedingly more compassionate existence. Furthermore, once we embrace the Fifth Spiritual Paradigm, God's grace will be upon us. However, we first have to get through the Great Cusp.

The good news is that the Great Cusp birth of the New Millennium is almost over.

The bad news is that the Great Cusp birth is now breech.

The Great Cusp has lingered into the 21st Century due to increased spiritual polarization. In other words, we are experiencing severe labor pains. On the bright side, however, polarization is very common during a millennium change and it should not be interpreted as a sign that we will fail in our collective Earth plane mission. Polarization occurs as a result of the tensions created between the astrological age that is ending and the new age that is beginning. To better illustrate the concept of polarization, let's examine some of the differences between the Age of Pisces, the outgoing age, and the newly forming Age of Aquarius.

The astrological sign Pisces is represented by two fish swimming in opposite directions. This symbol connotes opposing forces flowing in diametrically different directions. Put simply, the symbol underscores the **Duality** of the Universe (i.e., Yin-Yang forces). In spiritual terms, duality suggests that mankind and God are not intrinsically connected and that the Supreme Being is separate from us, exalted over us, and beyond our breadth of understanding. Consequently, a religion based on duality assumes that mankind is subservient to and separated from the primordial Source most of us call God.

Jesus was born during the last Great Cusp which began the Age of Pisces. Therefore, it should come as no surprise that the Christian symbol for Jesus is the fish. Jesus ignited the shift into the Fourth Spiritual Paradigm, the seeds of which were planted during the Age of Aries by the Persian Prophet Zarathustra and the Jewish Prophet Abraham. Thus, the last Great Cusp, which spanned from roughly 50 B.C.E. to 50 C.E., was another period of intense spiritual vibration. Indeed, after the advent of the Fourth Spiritual Paradigm our collective consciousness changed radically, as mankind rejected polytheism in favor of monotheism. However, because mankind reasoned that God must be either all masculine or all feminine energy, we erroneously assigned the male gender to God. Apparently, God wanted us to learn about the duality of the Universe during the Fourth Spiritual Paradigm so that we would later appreciate the more advanced Truth available to us now: *God is composed of and perfectly balanced by opposing forces.*

The first Christians held fast to their Jewish heritage and, as a result, correctly interpreted most of Jesus' teachings. However, the pagan influence of the Roman Empire severely muddled Jesus' mission. Eventually, religious men of power totally absconded with the Jesus movement and bastardized Jesus' messages from God. Consequently, the first religion formed during the Age of Pisces contained some rather strange and erroneous doctrine. Most notably, Christians came to believe: (i) mankind cannot earn salvation because we are innately sinful; (ii) Jesus died to pay for our sins and to allow us to reach heaven despite our lack of merit; and (iii) salvation will be granted only to those people who worship a new deity – God's son/alter ego – Jesus Christ.

Thereafter, Muhammad arrived with additional divine messages from God, which were intended to correct some of the theological errors made by the Christians. Nevertheless, during the Age of Pisces, most of mankind continued to believe that we are perpetually unworthy of joining with God absent salvation. Moreover, both Christianity and Islam view God as a remote entity that desires our supplication and surrender. Finally, both of these religions view heaven as a reward for those who worship and place blind faith in God (or Jesus, in the case of Christians), although Islam correctly adds the necessary element of good works. Thus, Christianity and Islam are Piscean religions because they focus on the differences between human beings and the Supreme Being, rather than our connectedness.

Piscean duality also led men of power to separate humanity among various man-made classes and foster a herd instinct among the bottom caste members. For example, the nobility dominated and exploited their serfs and the priestly caste dictated to and spirituality restricted their laity. Thus, in the Age of Pisces, elite class members sought control over the masses and began to implement social and supposedly spiritual hierarchies designed to preserve their dominant positions. In the religious realm, the clergy asserted themselves as mediators between the people and God. Those who refused to conform to this model were labeled "heretics" and systematically eliminated. It is important to note that the obsession with rules and structure is another Piscean trait, which just happens to foster the herd instinct in most humans and make the populace much easier to manage.

Piscean duality also pitted "good" against "evil" and led the Christians to create another deity known as Satan. This fictional fellow cannot be viewed as anything other than a fourth deity behind God, Jesus, and the Holy Spirit.

Sadly, Satan became a permanent fixture in the Pauline version of Christianity adopted by the Romans, which further underscores the pagan origins of the Roman Catholic Church. Indeed, fundamentalist Christian preachers today seem to desperately need this demon in order to invoke fear and conformity within their congregations. Moreover, some evangelical preachers are telling their laity that the anti-Christ is here on Earth. They even seem to relish guessing his Earth plane identity. Once again, I shudder to think what Jesus would say about the pagan religion he inadvertently spawned. Truly, the only way I can make sense out of orthodox Christianity is to have faith that this two thousand year detour around the Truth is all part of God's plan and necessary preparation for the Fifth Spiritual Paradigm.

Yet, by far the most damaging consequence of our viewing the Universe in dualistic terms was the personification of God as a male deity. Gone were the ancient wisdom goddesses, all of whom balanced and informed the masculine half of God. Instead, man was pitted against woman, and masculine energy was deemed supreme. As a result, social order during the last millennium was not based on compassion, but on the male propensity to dominate and subjugate those who are physically weaker. Another byproduct of this era was the demonization of sex for any purpose other than procreation and the misogynist fear that women use their sexuality to manipulate men. Forced celibacy by the Catholic Church, disputes over gender roles, attacks on homosexuals, and the current debate over "moral values" are just some of the confusing legacies resulting from Piscean views on women and sex.

Incidentally, astrologists also describe Pisces as a "water sign." This is interesting because the oceans themselves underscore duality, since their vastness divides the continents of the Earth. At the beginning of the last millennium, the oceans separated and greatly restricted mankind both in terms of travel and communication. However, masculine creation energy met and conquered these challenges, as faster and more powerful ships were constructed. Indeed, water soon became the primary means of both mass travel and mass communication during the Age of Pisces.

Lastly, during the Age of Pisces mankind did not fully appreciate either the beauty of planet Earth or the grandeur of other species that live here with us. This ecological apathy primarily stemmed from two faulty religious beliefs: (i) the Earth is at the center of the Universe; and (ii) mankind is God's most precious creation. Scientists already have disproved the first of these egocentric assumptions and they soon may debunk the second by finding evidence of intelligent life on other planets. In short, these narcissistic views led us to believe that we could perpetually abuse and neglect both our environment and the other animals on planet Earth. Furthermore, religious End Times prophecies have only added to our ecological irresponsibility by condoning a destructive demise for planet Earth. Indeed, orthodox Jews, evangelical Christians, and Shiite Muslims all believe that a Messiah figure will come to Earth to spiritually save us, but that our planet will be massively damaged or, in the case of Christianity and Islam, totally destroyed in the process. Obviously, such a belief system does not foster love of our vibrant yet delicately balanced planet. It also has the potential to become a self-fulfilling prophecy if we fail to protect our environment.

Clearly, it is time for us to replace the outmoded spiritual belief in duality.

By way of contrast, the Age of Aquarius and the Aquarian Sun sign are symbolized by an angel pouring water from a jug onto the parched Earth. This symbol connotes relief, restoration, revival, and recovery. Spiritually, the angel signifies synthesis of the lessons of the ancient Prophets into a unified belief system that recognizes mankind's connectedness to each other, to planet Earth, and to all living things. The Aquarian angel also emphasizes the internal link between human beings and the Supreme Being. In sum, the Age of Aquarius will be a time when mankind finally acknowledges the spiritual significance of **Unity.**

For example, while the Piscean Age painted life in dualistic terms, such as the strong versus the weak, nobility against slaves, men controlling women, and mankind juxtaposed against an external God, the Aquarian Age envisions life that is connected, harmonious, and unified. Once humanity embraces the Fifth Spiritual Paradigm, we will assimilate and promote unitarian concepts like equality, sharing, compassion, and inner spirituality. Thus, after we pass into the Age of Aquarius, we will replace the "win-lose" dichotomy of duality with the "win-win" dynamic of unity. Moreover, once the collective consciousness fully grasps the principle of unity, mankind also will comprehend the Truth that we are intrinsically connected to God. No longer will we view God as a removed paternalistic deity, as described by the dualistic Piscean religions. Instead, the updated Aquarian religions will teach the Truth delivered by Jesus and quoted at the beginning of this chapter:

Mankind is innately Divine because our souls are created from and are part of the primordial Light.

Therefore, in the Age of Aquarius mankind will understand that everyone and everything in the Universe is related and interdependent. As a result, we will find it much easier to love our neighbor as the great Prophets instructed. We will know that if there are "losers" in our society, then we all lose. Consequently, we will want to share our resources and care for those who need our help because we will value all souls, regardless of the divisions previously drawn by dualistic governments and religions.

In the New Millennium, we also will reject outdated laws, be they civil or religious, which infringe upon or impede the soul's journey toward Truth, Love, and Light. We will elect only wise and plainspoken representatives, and we will not tolerate hypocritical leaders who tell us one thing and do another, or who think the rules of a just society apply to the masses but not to them. Moreover, because we will respect the individual nature of each soul's journey of faith, there will be no state sponsored religions nor even state preferred religions. In fact, the entire concept of separation between church and state will become obsolete, as everyone will revel in the spiritual advice and accomplishments of his or her neighbor. Finally, we as a people will only accept those political and religious leaders who acknowledge that each one of us has the inalienable right and internal wisdom to make our own life and death decisions, such as those involving birth control, abortion, euthanasia, and the artificial extension of life. In sum, during the Age of Aquarius humanity will choose to utilize both masculine and feminine energies to build the advanced society that God knew we would one day have the capacity and the clarity to create.

The way we accomplish this sacred task is by perfecting ourselves. The *Saddha* process of soul growth helps us tune in to our higher self and feel our connection to God and to others. *Saddha* is nothing more than a meditative method of communing with the Supreme Being by tapping into our own divinity. Eventually, *Saddha* helps us comprehend that our ability to reach God in the Ethereal plane is not dependent on any man-made religion, blind worship of deities, or even our physical death. Instead, *Saddha* teaches that our ability to rejoin with the Light is contingent on our own spiritual enlightenment, as evidenced by our compassionate acts on the Earth plane which serve to increase unity.

On the other hand, trying to reach God through traditional prayer and worship tends to be an unproductive exercise for most people. Admittedly, I do remember moments when I was inspired at church and times when I felt that my prayers brought me closer to God. However, mere prayer has never brought me as close to the Supreme Being as my meditations take me. That's because prayer and worship are outdated Piscean methods of reaching out to God. Furthermore, prayer typically is used by people who are imploring God to intervene in their lives. In sum, prayer and worship imply only one-way communication with God. In contrast, meditation is an Aquarian tool for connecting to Source, as it promotes a two-way dialogue. In my meditations, I literally see a white light and I talk to it. I know that this white light is the Light of God, which shines in two directions – both in to and out of me.

Astrologers refer to Aquarius as an "air sign." Recall that Pisces is a water sign and that during the Age of Pisces mankind conquered the great oceans which used to separate and isolate civilizations. Similarly, one might expect mankind to conquer the sky during the Age of Aquarius. And we did! Just consider that as the Age of Aquarius approached, mankind began to develop new technologies that were not hindered by land or water limitations. Hence, during the current Great Cusp mankind invented cell phones, satellites, and the internet, which are all air methods of communication. In addition, we built airplanes, jets, and rockets as air methods of travel for the Aquarian Age. We can expect technology to continue expanding at phenomenally rapid rates as we get further into the New Millennium. Indeed, scientists seem to be pulling technology out of thin air (no pun intended). But the trick will be managing these advanced technologies during the Great Cusp, as we learn how to perfect our use of feminine energy.

Lastly, once mankind embraces the Fifth Spiritual Paradigm, not only will we realize that all human beings are connected, we also will comprehend that the entire Universe is connected. This realization will usher in an era of austere ecological protection of our plant and animal life. We finally will admit to ourselves how vulnerable we are to pollution and how desperately the other life forms are searching for safe and healthy habitats. In the New Millennium, humanity will gladly accept the responsibility of taking care of planet Earth and protecting the other creatures that now rely upon us – not God – for their continued survival. Assuming there is enough time, once we learn how to combine our creation and wisdom energies, we will be able to arrive at miraculous solutions to all our ecological challenges.

To summarize, the New Millennium will be a time of love and sharing on an unprecedented level. Mankind finally will accept the Truth that each of us has the ability to perfect our own divinity and the obligation to help others reach their spiritual potential. However, in accordance with God's plan for humanity, the Fifth Spiritual Paradigm will not arrive until we collectively manifest it.

Thus, it is up to us to add the next layer to God's Tower of Truth. No Messiah is coming to "save" us. Rather, it is our birthright and our soul responsibility to synthesize all the new philosophical, scientific, moral, and spiritual lessons that we have accumulated since the time of the great Prophets. Then we will comprehend that the Fifth Spiritual Paradigm is about unity, and we will feel like ethereal beings in the material world. Best of all, though, once we navigate through the current Great Cusp, our collective consciousness will be much closer to God.

So now that we have a good idea of what the Age of Aquarius will look and feel like, who on Earth would object to its arrival? The answer should now be obvious. The souls who are fighting the Fifth Spiritual Paradigm are those who: (i) feel no compassion for their fellow man; (ii) love to hoard wealth; (iii) hate to share; (iv) enjoy controlling others; (v) judge and condemn others using a set of standards they never apply to themselves; and (vi) think they are superior to the common man. In a nutshell, the souls who are prolonging the Great Cusp are the ones who have succumbed to the cardinal sins of greed and pride.

In sum, because they think they will "lose" in the New Millennium, men of power have been working overtime to keep the rest of us spinning in the Great Cusp.

Selfishly, they cling to Piscean duality. Shamelessly, they undermine Aquarian unity. And stupidly, they delude themselves into believing that they can permanently forestall God's plan for mankind (or at least postpone the Fifth Spiritual Paradigm until they are gone and have no more need of Earth plane riches and power).

Thus, I sincerely believe that the masses are being duped, yet again, by men of power who have fallen prey to the sins of greed and pride. These men love money and themselves more than they love their fellow man and God. I also believe that these corrupt souls will do anything to prevent a new reality based on Truth, Love, and Light.

So how did men of power get us stuck in the Great Cusp and throw the New Millennium into a breech birth? Quite simply, our politicians and clergy were able to temporarily delay the Fifth Spiritual Paradigm by delivering an incredibly effective one-two punch to the masses:

First, they used the cardinal sins of greed and pride to tempt us.

Second, they resurrected the concept of "blind faith" to control us.

To start, men of power correctly assumed that many of us would succumb to the same temptations that have corrupted their souls. It was a pretty good bet, particularly since most of us had never experienced wealth before. So in the 1980s, we were taught that being selfish is okay, which is the very opposite of the Golden Rule. As a result, we started to focus more on ourselves and we forgot our less fortunate neighbors. Officially, we entered a phase of American excess: *God became green.*

I came out of law school in the mid-1980s and I will never forget my father's reaction to my starting salary. Boy, did I think I was hot stuff! Instead of hippies we bred yuppies, who were demographically described as young, upwardly mobile, and self-indulgent. In sum, the United States had spawned the "Me Generation." As the stock market soared, the rich got richer, the poor got poorer, and we started to lose our middle class.

Consider that since the "Reagan Revolution," the disparity of wealth and income between the most and least fortunate Americans has increased steadily. Today, this gap is at an all-time high, surpassing even the disparity reached during the Roaring Twenties ... right before the Great Depression. Presently, Americans in the top 1% take home 24% of all income and possess roughly 40% of all wealth. The top 10% receive nearly 50% of all income and hold almost 75% of all wealth. And during the Bush "economic expansion," Americans in the top 1% captured 65% of all income growth. So what about the other 99% of Americans? Well, the bottom 50% earn roughly 14% of all income and hold less than 3% of the wealth, with 13% of all Americans living below the poverty line (defined as a family of four living on less than $22,050 per year). Moreover, 18% of our children live in poverty, with our poorest citizens being Native Americans, 26% of whom live in poverty. In sum, during the Bush years, six million more Americans fell into poverty. Thus, it is undeniable that during this most recent phase of "compassionate conservatism," the polarization of wealth and income has gotten more extreme and our middle class has all but disappeared.

In addition, the 1980s began a phase of American hubris and imperialism. We were told that communism remained an imminent threat, so we built expensive nuclear arsenals as a deterrent, even though the Soviet Union and the Berlin Wall were about to crumble. Later, we were told that Muslim terrorists in Iraq were an imminent threat and that we needed to go to war, even though Saddam Hussein had no connection with either Osama bin Laden or the bombings on September 11, 2001. Hence, men of power convinced us that the United States has the right to impose its military might over the rest of the world, despite the fact that we have not been attacked by any foreign government since the beginning of the Great Cusp

While I agree that it is proper for the United States to intervene internationally when we are attacked or when oppressed human beings seek our assistance, those are not the reasons we have been interjecting ourselves into other countries' affairs. Quite frankly, if we really cared about human rights, our soldiers would be in the African continent instead of the Middle East. The Truth is that the Middle East is the locus of our attention because of our unnecessary but continued dependence on fossil fuels, not because the Arab nations pose a dire domestic threat. Not surprisingly, at this stage of the Great Cusp, the United States is viewed suspiciously by the rest of the world, including even our Allies, who now may be forced to pick up the gauntlet that we dropped when we ceased leading humanity into the New Millennium.

Men of power also have prolonged the Great Cusp by reindoctrinating us with the concept of "blind faith." In the political spectrum, men of power have been telling us that it is unpatriotic to challenge the actions of our government and that we should trust that they are protecting us. This position is fundamentally at odds with our democratic form of government and is a blatant attempt to water down the civil rights recognized by our founding fathers, like freedom of speech.

Similarly, in the religious realm, men of power have crafted a modern definition of "heretic." They tell us that souls who have moral values never question orthodox Christianity and that only souls who lack spiritual grounding disagree with their brand of theology. Additionally, evangelical ministers urge their laity to protect Christian beliefs (as though they were threatened) by imposing fundamentalist dogma on enlightened Christians and people of other faiths, and by introducing Christian literature, symbols, and mythology into public institutions. This position, too, is fundamentally at odds with our form of government and is an overt attempt to erode the separation between church and state and promote just one form of religion.

Incidentally, for those Americans who mistakenly believe that our founding fathers wanted Christian theology to dominate their new nation, I refer them to *An Act for the Establishment of Religious Freedom*, drafted by Thomas Jefferson, endorsed by James Madison, and passed by the Virginia General Assembly in 1786, a copy of which is reproduced at the end of this work. The Truth is that our founding fathers were disdainful of any leader who mixed politics with religion (or *vice versa*). In particular, they were contemptuous of King George III, who was the King of England when they commenced the War of Independence, since our founding fathers believed that leadership is an honor to be earned, not a birthright. Thankfully, Mr. Jefferson's *Act for Religious Freedom* still stands as a beacon of light and the law of the land in my home state, the Commonwealth of Virginia.

Thus, since the 1980s, many U.S. politicians and preachers have been insisting that we honor them with blind faith by promising that they know what is best and that they will protect us. For example, to garner our support, career politicians joined with orthodox Christian clerics to incessantly remind us of the many horrors resulting from Muslim terrorism and Islamic fundamentalism. Through the use of state scare tactics and pulpit bullying, these men have convinced us that if we follow their lead, we will be pledging allegiance to policies which protect American lives and values. However, the Truth is that most of our political and religious leaders have another agenda. Instead of preserving our civil and spiritual freedoms, these men of power are merely exploiting the chaos in the Arab world in order to fuel American economic imperialism and Christian fundamentalism. The result is more money for the politicians and more power for the orthodox Christian clergy. Indeed, our holy books have a name for such men: *hypocrites*.

Similarly, U.S. politicians and evangelical pastors are keen to discuss the pro-life ethics involved with the most private and personal of medical decisions, such as abortion and euthanasia (e.g., the Terry Schiavo case), but these men have yet to create a national health care system that covers all Americans, as provided by other industrialized nations around the world. Moreover, although our Christian statesmen and clergy claim to respect all of God's creation, they offer little, if any, support for the preservation of our planet or the other species that coexist with us. They also are remarkably silent when it comes to promoting the clean solar and hydrogen technologies which scientists developed at the start of the Great Cusp and which would solve many of our environmental problems. Instead, half of these men slowly plan for the obsolescence of their oily cash cow, while the other half gleefully predict the Earth's destruction by our greatest Prince of Peace, who they claim will return any day to start the final war between good and evil. The bottom line is: *Our leaders have betrayed us.*

Do I sound paranoid? I hope not. For, I have spent the last fifteen years of my life studying the parasitic relationship between politics and religion and its malignant effects on civilization and the collective consciousness. For my own peace of mind, I have tried hard to deduce otherwise, but I simply cannot avert my mind from the painful yet patent conclusion that we are all being manipulated by men of power.

Truly, if they had our best interests at heart, our political and religious leaders would be guiding us through the turbulence of the Great Cusp. Instead, they are purposely prolonging it.

Now, it may be that some of these men honestly believe that they are helping us. Moreover, some of them may believe that it is mere fortuity that they are getting richer and more powerful as the masses get poorer and more confused. However, I believe in non-coincidence (a/k/a the Universal law of synchronicity). Consequently, I see a connection between the $1.8 trillion in tax breaks that Congress recently gave our highest income earners and the increased wealth of our already richest citizens. Strangely, I also see a connection between the reduction in our welfare rolls and the most recent poverty statistics, which show that the U.S. ranks 2nd out of the 22 industrialized nations for the most children living in poverty.

Thank you, gentlemen, for all your help, but I for one would rather know the Truth than be treated like a fool. And the Truth is that our political and religious leaders currently are enjoying unprecedented wealth and power.

Now, it also may be that some of these men honestly believe that they are protecting us. Moreover, some of them may believe that the results they are attempting to achieve outweigh their miscalculations and their misdeeds. However, I believe that the ends never justify the means (a/k/a the Universal law of *karma*). Therefore, I feel profound shame when my government harms another human being under the banner of the American flag and yet takes no responsibility. Curiously, I also feel immense embarrassment when Christian missionaries from the U.S. proselytize overseas about the lessons of the Prophet Jesus, about whom they have so little understanding.

Thank you, gentlemen, for all your concern, but I for one would rather know the Truth than be treated like a child. And the Truth is that our political and religious leaders currently are unworthy of acting on our behalf because they do not comprehend the grave responsibilities associated with their positions of authority, nor do they respect the people whom they are charged with serving.

At this point, I will not write anymore about the political men of power who consciously abuse their positions of authority. They know who they are, they know they have sold their souls, and they probably are too far gone in this lifetime to benefit from this book.

However, I do wish to address the men of power who control the five primary religions. Initially at least, the vast majority of these men joined their respective religions to do God's work. In the vernacular of Christianity, these men felt the Holy Spirit and willingly surrendered to its calling. Thereafter, these novitiates were taught faulty man-made doctrine, just like the rest of us. Their superiors instructed them to have blind faith in the same orthodox interpretations of the Prophets and the same man-made constructs about God that their predecessors taught them. And so it goes.

Therefore, I earnestly wish to believe that most of our current religious leaders have not been tainted by the cardinal sins of greed and pride. I also trust that most clergy are frustrated, as I am, that they have not been allowed to update God's Tower of Truth. Furthermore, I suspect that the youngest members of the clergy are too frightened to challenge their superiors, who are the real men of power and the ones who should be leading us into the Fifth Spiritual Paradigm.

To those orthodox religious leaders who have the courage to read this book, I wish for you even more courage. May each of you find it within yourself to listen to your conscience and to hear God as you grapple with the Truths contained in this book. Take solace in the fact that you are not responsible for the mistakes made by your predecessors. You need not defend them nor maintain their lies anymore. You have the opportunity now to change the course of your chosen religion and the course of mankind's destiny. Join those of us who are ready for Truth. We need strong spiritual leaders now more than ever.

Please, for your own sake and for the sake of humanity, turn toward Truth, Love, and Light and help usher in the Fifth Spiritual Paradigm.

If you choose not to lead mankind into the New Millennium, though, know this Truth: *Mankind soon will experience the Fifth Spiritual Paradigm, with or without your help.* However, it might come faster if you help guide us. So please, stay true to your blessed calling, feel the presence of God within you, and lead your laity toward the next layer of Truth: **Unity.**

Don't you see? There simply is too much new and advanced information for you to maintain the orthodox positions of the five ancient religions. In Truth, the five primary religions will not survive much longer in their present form. Evidence abounds that God now wants us to progress to the next level of spiritual enlightenment. Just consider how the following discoveries are impacting the state of mankind's intellectual, scientific, moral, and spiritual development:

1. The recently discovered *Dead Sea Scrolls* and *Gnostic Gospels* clarify the meaning of Jesus' life and reveal that his death, although history's most painful martyrdom, was not the reason he came here.

2. Scientific explanations to some of our greatest mysteries, such as human evolution and the basic components and structure of life, already have replaced ancient mythology in the minds of educated people all over the world.

3. Moral and philosophical arguments about our duty to our fellow man, which currently reek of hypocrisy, ultimately will lead mankind to share the abundance of the Earth plane, regardless of which Prophet enunciated this Truth first.

4. Spiritual breakthroughs into the unseen world, such as those made by clairvoyants, holistic healers, and channelers are revealing fascinating new information from and about the Ethereal plane.

Based on all this new information, it is only a matter of time before the Great Cusp ends. Indeed, the Fifth Spiritual Paradigm is just around the corner. However, this generation is facing a monumental test of faith and of hard work. We must be brave enough to reject the outdated and faulty man-made constructs upon which our ancestors relied. We must be wise enough to add the next layer to God's Tower of Truth. And we must be strong enough, both physically and spiritually, to survive the current Great Cusp. Make no mistake, we stand at a critical juncture in our collective history and there is little margin for error.

Now is the time for us to synthesize God's past messages, add the next level of Truth, and transform ourselves into the godlike creatures God intended for us to one day become. Now is the time for us to appreciate both masculine and feminine energies and wisely create a utopian society for the New Millennium.

Therefore, let us rejoice at the fact that we are more knowledgeable than we were thousands of years ago when the five primary religions were created by less sophisticated souls. And let us eagerly assume the sacred obligation of updating the Earth's religions and adding the next layer to God's Tower of Truth. This is a solemn duty that we owe ourselves, our children, our planet, and our one true God.

*For those people who are **Hindu** and who believe in both masculine and feminine Divine energies*: Please help those who believe that God the Father created the Universe understand that it is God the Mother who sustains the Universe.

*For those people who are **Jewish** and who believe that the Messianic Age will be a time of compassionate and cooperative living for all of mankind, as foretold by the great Jewish Prophets*: Please help those who believe that the Earth plane will be destroyed as part of God's plan understand that it is our destiny to recreate the Garden of Eden.

*For those people who are **Buddhist** and who believe that the process of reincarnation is how the soul eventually ascends to the permanence and pre-eminence of the Ethereal plane*: Please help those who believe in just one life cycle understand the critical importance of mankind's spiritual rebirth into the New Millennium.

*For those people who are **Christian** and who believe that the Christ Consciousness is nearly here*: Please help those who believe that the sacrifice on the cross opened the gates to heaven understand that we are all children of God and that we must love our enemy before we can join Jesus in the Ethereal plane.

*For those people who are **Muslim** and who believe that spiritual unity is possible*: Please help those who believe that there is only one path to God understand that Muhammad's vision of uniting all people of faith was the most glorious prophecy ever relayed to mankind.

And for those **Religious Men of Power** *who made a pledge to teach others about God*: Please accept the Truth that your oath to the Almighty supercedes your loyalty to any man-made religion. Liberate yourselves from these institutions if need be so that you will be free to lead humanity toward the Fifth Spiritual Paradigm. Simply recall and recommit to the origins of your calling: **Truth, Love, and Light.**

> *Now I am going to Him who sent me .... It is for your good that I am*
> *going away. Unless I go away, the Counselor will not come to you; but*
> *if I go, I will send him to you. When he comes, he will prove the world*
> *wrong about sin and righteousness and judgment; about sin because*
> *men do not believe in me; about righteousness, because I am going to*
> *the Father, where you can see me no longer; and about judgment,*
> *because the prince of this world now stands condemned.*

> *Gospel of John*, Chapter 16:5–11

Is that not why advanced souls come to the Earth plane – to spiritually counsel others? Indeed, the Oracles of the future already are here and they are exhibiting Divine gifts and wisdom previously ascribed only to the Prophets. Likely, many of our most profound teachers are locked inside orthodox temples, synagogues, churches, and mosques, afraid to tell their superiors about their Ethereal plane insights and visions. If so, I implore these veiled masters of the New Age:

Please, wait no longer to share your advanced knowledge from and about the Supreme Being.

And so it mote be.

Appendix

Brief History of The Major Events in Human Evolution, Politics, and Religion

"Those who cannot remember the past are condemned to repeat it."

George Santayana, *The Life of Reason*

My burning desire to better understand God and my relationship to God led me to do a lot of research on religion. Allow me to share one of my most important discoveries:

The history of religion is inexorably enmeshed with the history of politics.

Throughout the ages, men of power have used religion and politics to control the masses. They also have used religion and politics as weapons, just like guns and knives, to conquer and manipulate those who are physically weaker and educationally disadvantaged. Moreover, corrupt religious and political leaders have helped each other build and fortify their tainted churches and governments whenever an alliance furthered their mutual quest for wealth and world domination. Thus, the five man-made religions and the world's dominant civilizations always have been symbiotically linked. Consequently, it is no accident that the messages of the Prophets have been bastardized whenever men of power have deemed it necessary to accommodate their ambitions. To prove this point, I present the following chronology of major world events.

The Appendix starts by presenting the most recent findings on the birth of the Universe and the evolution of life on planet Earth. This information is critical, as we must convince those religious fundamentalists who refuse to accept modern science that they are inhibiting mankind's collective spiritual progress. Thereafter, the Appendix condenses mankind's religious and political history. Finally, it lists mankind's major technological advancements to underscore the fearsome possibility that our intellectual cunning (i.e., applied masculine energy) now vastly exceeds our spiritual understanding (i.e., suppressed feminine energy).

May we find the wisdom to correct course for the New Millennium.

CHRONOLOGY OF MAJOR EVENTS KNOWN TO HUMANS

YEAR	EVENT
Pre-Big Bang	There exists a multi-faceted yet singular force which includes all things – both ethereal and material. This "God" possesses the omniscience and omnipotence to create life. Perfect unity characterizes the **First Spiritual Paradigm**. *God is everything and everything is God.*
13,700,000,000 B.C.E.	Our Universe is created in accordance with the Big Bang theory. The illusion of separation from God begins.
4,600,000,000 B.C.E.	Earth is formed.
3,500,000,000 B.C.E.	Life begins on Earth. Most of the Earth is covered by sea water, which is where the earliest life forms (algae, fungi, and bacteria) are spawned.
550,000,000 B.C.E.	**Paleozoic Era** of life. Worms, jellyfish, and seaweed live in the oceans.
500,000,000 B.C.E.	Fish start to evolve in the oceans.
450,000,000 B.C.E.	Plants begin to grow on dry land.
400,000,000 B.C.E.	Amphibians begin to crawl out of the oceans. Reptiles and insects evolve.
250,000,000 B.C.E.	**Mesozoic Era** of life. The land on Earth is one mass called Pangaea and the climate is warm and humid in most areas. In the first stage of this era, the **Triassic Period**, the dinosaurs and mammals start to evolve.
200,000,000 B.C.E.	**Jurassic Period.** Pangaea begins to break apart. Dinosaurs, sea reptiles, and flying reptiles become huge. Mammals, insects, and lizards live on the forest floor. Birds begin to evolve.
145,000,000 B.C.E.	**Cretaceous Period.** The Earth's continents fully separate and the climate becomes harsher. Animals start to die. By the end of this era, the dinosaurs, flying reptiles, and sea serpents are extinct.
65,000,000 B.C.E.	**Cenozoic Era** of life. The Earth's continents are relatively fixed as they are today and the mountains are forming. The climate is still warm and humid in most places. In the oceans, fish are abundant and whales evolve. On land, carnivore and herbivore mammals flourish, as elephants, rhinos, saber-toothed cats, and horses evolve. The only surviving reptiles on Earth are the crocodiles, lizards, snakes, and turtles.
6,000,000 B.C.E.	**Human evolution begins.** Based on DNA tests, most scientists believe that humans evolved from one *hominid* species in Africa, *Sahelanthropus tchadensis*, the oldest known human ancestor after the split of our line from chimpanzees.
4,000,000 B.C.E.	*Australopithecus* evolves. They are the first human-like mammals to walk upright. They live in Africa. Their brain size is 500 cc.
2,500,000 B.C.E.	**Paleolithic Age** of man (a/k/a **Stone Age**). *Homo habilis* evolves (discovered by Mary Leakey in 1964). They live in Africa. Their brain size is 750 cc. They are the first humans to make tools.
1,800,000 B.C.E.	*Homo erectus* evolves. They live in Africa, Asia, and Europe. Their brain size is 1,000 cc. They are the first humans to speak and make fire.
1,500,000 B.C.E.	Ice Age kills many animals. Scientists believe this is when *Homo habilis* goes extinct, but *Homo erectus* survives.

Pangaea

250,000,000 B.C.E.

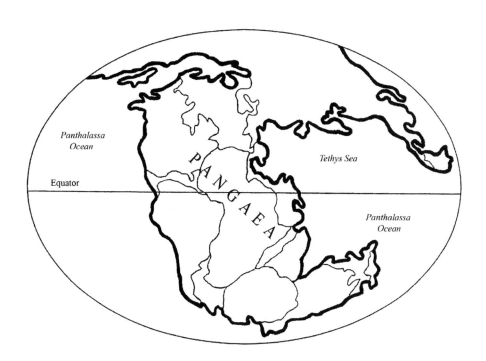

300,000 B.C.E.	Homo sapiens evolves. Early man lives in Africa, Asia, and Europe. Our brain size starts at 1150 cc and increases to 1400 cc over the next 200,000 years. Some scientists refer to this dramatic increase in our brain capacity as the "missing link."
200,000 B.C.E.	*Homo sapiens neanderthalensis* evolves. They live in Africa, Asia, and Europe. Their brain size is 1,450 cc. Scientists believe they are the first humans to practice religion, since they perform ritual burials. However, Neanderthals probably are not our ancestors, as proven through DNA testing done in 1997.
130,000 B.C.E.	*Homo sapiens sapiens* evolves. This is mankind's current scientific classification. Our brain capacity reaches 1400 cc. We can speak, create art, and bury our dead.
30,000 B.C.E.	*Neanderthals* die out. Scientists don't know why they went extinct.
25,000 B.C.E.	*Homo sapiens sapiens* rules planet Earth. Humans subsist as "hunters and gatherers." Cave drawings and sculptures indicate that early man worships a creation Goddess who gives birth to all life. Thus, humanity consciously attempts to reconnect to the Divine and initiates the **Second Spiritual Paradigm** by practicing female monotheism.
	God is viewed as a feminine deity.
8000 B.C.E.	**Neolithic Age** (a/k/a **New Stone Age**). Mankind still exists in small tribal groups. They refine stone tools, invent pottery, and learn to plant and farm.
5000 B.C.E.	**Agricultural Age.** The first civilization of Sumer forms along the Tigris and Euphrates Rivers in Mesopotamia (Iraq). The Sumerians invent the first written language and later record their creation myth. They believe gods and goddesses visit Earth from the "heavens," the god **Enki** created humans from clay, and the god **Enlil** tried to kill us in a great flood. Hence, the Sumerians spawn the **Third Spiritual Paradigm**, during which humanity replaces female monotheism with polytheism.
	Gods are viewed as masculine and Goddesses as feminine deities.
4000 B.C.E.	Three more societies evolve: (i) one along the Nile River in the African continent, known as the Egyptians; (ii) one in the Indus Valley in India; and (iii) another along the Yellow River in China. Together, the four early river cultures are referred to as the "Cradles of Civilization."
3761 B.C.E.	Mythological date for God's creation of the Universe, the Earth, and the first humans, **Adam** and **Eve** (based on Jewish calendar). Orthodox Jews and fundamentalist Christians still use this date for creation of the Universe and all life on planet Earth.
3500 B.C.E.	**Bronze Age.** The Sumerians are the most advanced society on Earth. They invent the wheel and learn how to smelt copper and make metal tools.
3000 B.C.E.	The Sumerians start to record stories about their gods and goddesses. They also create the first lunar and solar calendars based on the advanced state of their astronomy and mathematics, which they claim were given to them by their deities.
2600 B.C.E.	Egyptians build the pyramids at Giza (new evidence suggests date of 10,000 B.C.E. for Great Pyramid). Egyptian Empire is now the most dominant society on Earth. They believe in multiple deities, that their rulers are gods, and in reincarnation. Their primary god is **Osiris** and their primary goddess is **Isis**.
2500 B.C.E.	Approximate date the **Hindu religion** begins. Hindu holy texts are composed over time and include: the *Vedas* (*circa* 1500 B.C.E.); the *Upanishads* (*circa* 800 B.C.E.); and the *Bhagavad Gita* (*circa* 300 B.C.E.). Hindus believe in multiple deities, reincarnation, and that a soul is born into a defined caste. Through reincarnation and the internal search for *Dharma* (Truth or the law), the soul is reborn into higher castes and, eventually, ascends to the lower levels of heaven.

THE CRADLES OF CIVILIZATION

The Four Great River Valley Civilizations
4000 B.C.E.

2000 B.C.E.	Approximate birth date of **Zarathustra** (legendary date 6,000 B.C.E.). He believes in one benevolent God and a dark force, and he starts the **Zoroastrian religion**.
	Approximate birth date of **Abraham**. He rejects polytheism and worships one God, thereby starting the **Jewish religion**. By tradition, God promises Abraham the land known as Canaan. Abraham has two sons: **Ishmael,** who is banished but who fathers the Islamic religion; and **Isaac,** whose son **Jacob** is renamed **Israel** by God. The Jews view God as a single entity with masculine characteristics, but most of humanity still believes in multiple deities.
1500 B.C.E.	**Iron Age.** The Hittites (in present day Turkey) are the first society to learn how to make lighter metal and stronger weapons.
1250 B.C.E.	Egyptian Empire releases the Jews from slavery (Exodus may date to 1450 B.C.E.). The Jews are led by **Moses** back to Canaan, the land previously promised to them by God. Moses receives the Ten Commandments on Mount Sinai.
1200 B.C.E.	The Jews fight and conquer other Semitic (Arab) tribes living in Canaan. However, the Philistines, who are the ancestors of present-day Palestinians, continue to control the southern coastline of the Middle East.
1000 B.C.E.	Jewish King David unifies the 12 Jewish tribes in Canaan.
950 B.C.E.	King Solomon builds the first Temple in Jerusalem. The first 5 books of the *Old Testament* are written (the *Pentateuch*). The Jews borrow the Sumerian creation myth to write *Genesis*.
920 B.C.E.	Jewish Kingdom divides into the Kingdom of Israel in the north and the Kingdom of Judah in the south, which still is ruled by House of David.
800 B.C.E.	The Greek civilization prospers. They believe in multiple deities and that their primary god and goddess **Zeus** and **Hera** live on **Mount Olympus**.
722 B.C.E.	The Assyrians overtake the northern Kingdom of Israel. The Jewish tribes are scattered and referred to as the "Ten Lost Tribes of Israel."
586 B.C.E.	The Babylonians overtake the southern Kingdom of Judah. The Temple is destroyed and the Jews deported. The region becomes known as Palestine.
563 B.C.E.	**Siddhartha Gautama** is born in the land now known as Nepal. He is an Indian prince who becomes the enlightened **Buddha** and founder of the **Buddhist religion**. The Buddhist holy text, the *Pali Canon*, is compiled over time. By 100 B.C.E., the Tripitaka is completed (accepted translation of the *Pali Canon*). Buddhists believe that through the process of reincarnation a person can perfect his soul and reach the state of *nirvana* (peaceful release from the Earth plane).
552 B.C.E.	Approximate birth date for **Confucius** and **Laozi**. These Chinese philosophers inspire the theosophies of **Confucianism** and **Daoism**. They believe in a moral code, duality of God (Yin and Yang energy), and the Five Agents (water, fire, wood, metal, earth), and by 200 B.C.E., in heaven and the immortality of the soul.
538 B.C.E.	Persian Empire conquers the Babylonians and takes the southern part of Palestine (i.e., the old Kingdom of Judah). Zoroastrianism becomes the official religion of the Persian Empire. The Persians allow the Jews to return to Jerusalem.
516 B.C.E.	The Jews rebuild the Temple in Jerusalem and remain there until 70 C.E.
500 B.C.E.	Roman Republic begins its ascent. The Romans believe in multiple deities, and they call their primary god and goddess **Jupiter** and **Juno**.
469 B.C.E.	**Socrates** is born in Greece. He asserts that man has a soul and should strive for intellectual and spiritual perfection.

THE MIDDLE EAST

3000 B.C.E. to 1200 C.E.

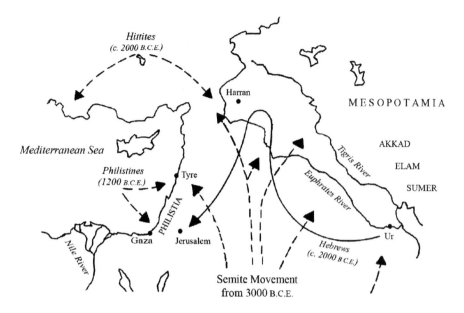

Hittites
(c. 2000 B.C.E.)

Harran

MESOPOTAMIA

Mediterranean Sea

AKKAD

ELAM

SUMER

Philistines
(1200 B.C.E.)

Tyre

PHILISTIA

Tigris River

Euphrates River

Gaza

Jerusalem

Nile River

Ur

Hebrews
(c. 2000 B.C.E.)

Semite Movement
from 3000 B.C.E.

THE MIDDLE EAST

900 C.E.

Tyre

PHOENICIA

GALILEE

Sea of
Galilee

Mediterranean Sea

ISRAEL

River Jordan

PHILISTIA

Jericho

Jerusalem

JUDAH

Dead
Sea

AMMON

Gaza

MOAB

332 B.C.E.	Alexander the Great expands the Greek Empire and conquers the Assyrians, the Persians, Palestine, and Egypt. He kills many Zoroastrian priests (called *magi*).
265 B.C.E.	Roman Republic overtakes the Greek Empire and becomes the dominant society on Earth.
250 B.C.E.	The Buddhist religion splits into **Hinayana** and **Mahayana** Buddhism.
63 B.C.E.	Roman Republic conquers Syria and Palestine.
44 B.C.E.	Julius Caesar is assassinated.
37 B.C.E.	The Romans place Herod the Great in charge of the Kingdom of Judea. He calls himself King of the Jews and rebuilds the Temple in Jerusalem.
27 B.C.E.	Augustus Caesar takes absolute control of the Roman Republic and transforms it into the Roman Empire.
6 B.C.E.	Approximate birth date of **Jesus**. He is a Jew and descendent from the House of David (Jewish Kings). He never promotes a new religion.
4 B.C.E.	Herod the Great dies and his sons divide the Kingdom of Judea.
30 C.E.	Jesus is crucified and Judaism splinters into 3 new sects: (i) **Jewish Christians** led by the original apostles and Jesus' brother **James**, who is Bishop of Jerusalem for the next 20 years; (ii) **Gnostic Christians** who believe Jesus was sent to reveal a spiritual path to heaven; and (iii) **Gentile Christens** led by Paul, a Roman Jew who never met Jesus, begins to deify Jesus, and starts a new **Christian religion**.
48 C.E.	The early Christians convene the Council of Jerusalem and decide to admit Gentiles (i.e., non-Jewish pagans) into the expanding religion. Paul leaves to do missionary work with the Gentiles, who still believe in multiple deities.
50 C.E.	Approximate starting date for the writings collectively known as the Christian gospels. More than 60 gospels are written over the course of the next 300 years, but only 4 gospels will be deemed "orthodox" and included in the *New Testament*, which also contains the letters of James and Paul. Humanity starts to re-embrace monotheism and the **Fourth Spiritual Paradigm** begins. But this time, mankind worships a male God.
	God is viewed as a masculine deity.
62 C.E.	Jesus' brother James is killed in Jerusalem.
64 C.E.	Roman Emperor Nero begins the persecution of the Christians. Paul is arrested and taken to Rome. By tradition, Peter also is imprisoned and both are executed.
70 C.E.	Jerusalem and the Jewish Temple are destroyed by Roman Emperor Titus after a Jewish revolt. The Jews will not control Palestine again until 1948 C.E.
90 C.E.	The Jewish Council of Jamnia meets to determine the composition of the *Old Testament*. The 24 books of the *Old Testament* are chosen by 135 C.E.
95 C.E.	Roman Emperor Domitian intensifies the persecution of Christians.
180 C.E.	Roman Emperor Marcus Aurelius dies. The Roman Empire starts to decline.
220 C.E.	Buddhism flourishes in China, competing with the philosophies of Confucianism and Daoism.
284 C.E.	The Goths (Germanic tribes) begin raiding the Roman Empire. They attack Rome, Gaul, Britain, and Spain.
303 C.E.	Roman Emperor Diocletian renews persecutions, destroys the Christian churches and many Christian books. Much history on the early Christians is lost.

ROMAN EMPIRE

44 B.C.E. to 180 C.E.

312 C.E.	Roman Co-Emperor Constantine the Great defeats the Goths and regains control of and consolidates what is left of the Roman Empire.
313 C.E.	Co-Emperor Constantine issues the Edict of Milan in which he grants universal religious freedom to pagans, Christians, and Jews.
323 C.E.	Constantine the Great becomes sole emperor of the Roman Empire.
325 C.E.	Constantine the Great consolidates his power by convening the Council of Nicaea to unify the Christians and end the "Arian Controversy." Arius proposed that Jesus was a man who became Divine *after* the crucifixion. The bishops debate Jesus' divinity, vote to make him a human manifestation of God, and adopt the **Holy Trinity** (God the Father, God the Son, and God the Holy Ghost). The bishops define "orthodox" Christianity and ban all other interpretations of Jesus' life. The **Roman Catholic Church** is born.
330 C.E.	Constantine the Great moves the capital of the Roman Empire to Constantinople (Istanbul in modern day Turkey).
337 C.E.	Constantine the Great is baptized as a Christian on his death bed.
359 C.E.	Roman Emperor Constantius (Constantine's son) backs the Arian bishops who believe that Jesus is subordinate to God. The Catholic Church rejects the Nicene Creed (i.e., the Holy Trinity), and adopts the Creed of Rimini-Seleucia, which states that Jesus is "like" God but not the "same nature."
364 C.E.	Christian bishops convene the Council of Laodicea, which meets to decide which gospels should be included in the *New Testament*. Four are chosen from over 60 available gospels, and 44 of the rejected gospels are ordered destroyed. Some of the banned gospels will be found in 1945. They are called the *Gnostic Gospels*.
381 C.E.	Roman Emperor Theodosius convenes the First Council of Constantinople and the bishops readopt the Nicene Creed. Christianity is the official religion of the Roman Empire and all other religions, including paganism, Judaism, and religions based on reincarnation, are banned.
410 C.E.	Rome is attacked by the Visigoths and the Roman Empire loses Britain.
451 C.E.	The Council of Chalcedon continues to debate the nature of Christ and to discuss the hierarchy of the Catholic Church. The Bishop of Rome starts to use the designation "Pope," while the Bishop of Constantinople uses the designation "Patriarch." The Council ranks the pope and patriarch as co-equals, but the bishops disagree on the nature of Christ. Thereafter, the **Coptic Church** of Egypt, the **Jacobite Church** in Syria, and the **Armenian Church** are founded.
452 C.E.	Bishop Leo of Rome (a/k/a Pope Leo the Great) saves Rome by persuading Attila the Hun (Mongolian) not to invade the city.
476 C.E.	Roman Empire is finally lost to the Ostrogoths. Only the territory around Constantinople remains safely under the Roman emperor's control. The empire is now known as the Byzantine Empire.
553 C.E.	Roman Emperor Justinian convenes the Second Council of Constantinople. The Holy Trinity is officially defined and Arius' view of Jesus condemned.
570 C.E.	**Muhammad** is born. He starts the **religion of Islam.** Muslims believe in one God, Allah, the same God described by the Jews and Christians in *The Holy Bible*. They also believe in the Jewish and Christian Prophets, but do not accept Jesus as god or the son of God. Like Christians, the Muslims believe that mankind may join God in heaven, but that salvation is dependent on charity, not worship of Jesus as a deity. Muhammad's teachings are contained in *The Holy Quran*.
600 C.E.	Buddhism becomes the official religion of Korea, Tibet, and Burma.

GERMANIC INVASION

Goths, Visigoths, Ostrogoths, Vandals
40 C.E. to 600 C.E.

630 C.E.	All the tribes of Arabia pledge allegiance to Muhammad and Islam.
638 C.E.	Muslim Empire conquers Jerusalem and Iran. The Muslims also kill the last Zoroastrian king. Some Zoroastrians flee to India where they become **Parsis**.
710 C.E.	Buddhism becomes the official religion of Japan.
732 C.E.	Muslim Empire is the dominant society on Earth. All the Arab nations are consolidated and the Muslims conquer northern Africa, western Asia, Spain, and part of France.
754 C.E.	Pope Stephen II anoints Pepin III as King of the Franks in return for Pepin protecting Rome from attacks by the Lombards. Baghdad is made the capital of the Muslim Empire.
800 C.E.	Pope Leo III crowns Pepin's son Charlemagne as the first Holy Roman Emperor and assumes authority to crown future emperors.
840 C.E.	Tibetan and Chinese emperors persecute Buddhism in favor of Daoism.
1046 C.E.	Emperor Henry III (Germany) deposes 3 rival "anti-popes" and installs the next 3 German popes. The third pope, Pope Leo IX, is a close relative of the emperor.
1054 C.E.	The **Great Schism** marks the formal break between the **Roman Catholic Church** and the **Eastern Orthodox Church**. The schism occurs due to continuing debate over the meaning of the Holy Trinity and the claim by Pope Leo IX in Rome for primacy over all other bishops, including the patriarch of Constantinople. The patriarch refuses to submit to the pope and Pope Leo IX excommunicates him. In return, the patriarch of Constantinople excommunicates the pope.
1059 C.E.	The now splintered Roman Catholic Church decides that popes will be elected by cardinals and approved by the emperor. However, for the next 120 years, the Catholics disagree on who should be pope and multiple anti-popes vie for control.
1073 C.E.	Pope Gregory VII forbids the Holy Roman Emperor from appointing bishops. In retaliation, Emperor Henry IV (Germany) deposes Pope Gregory VII and the pope excommunicates the emperor. As a result, civil war breaks out in Germany and the emperor solicits the pope's support by granting that Gregory VII is the true pope.
1084 C.E.	Emperor Henry IV (Germany) changes his mind again, deposes Gregory VII, and installs Clement III as pope, who is later declared an anti-pope.
1095 C.E.	Pope Urban II calls for the **First Crusade** to take Jerusalem from the Muslims.
1099 C.E.	European crusaders capture Jerusalem and other Muslim lands, calling them Crusader States. French nobleman Godfroi de Bouillon is ruler of Jerusalem.
1118 C.E.	The **Knights Templar** are formed by King Baudoin I, the second Christian king of Jerusalem, and by the Catholic Church to protect Christian pilgrims in Jerusalem. The Knights Templar dig under the Jewish Temple ruins for 9 years and possibly find the Jewish treasury, including the **"Holy Grail."**
1144 C.E.	Muslim Empire retakes some of the Crusader States.
1146 C.E.	Saint Bernard, a Christian bishop, rallies the **Second Crusade** which fails to retake Crusader States. Jerusalem is in peril.
1150 C.E.	Muslim Empire conquers India and Islam becomes the dominant religion.
1154 C.E.	Pope Adrian IV authorizes King Henry II of England to invade Ireland.
1187 C.E.	The crusaders are defeated by Muslim Sultan Saladin and lose Jerusalem.
1189 C.E.	Emperor Frederick Barbarossa (Germany), King Philip Augustus (France), and King Richard the Lionhearted (England) order the **Third Crusade** which fails.

MUSLIM EMPIRE

750 C.E.

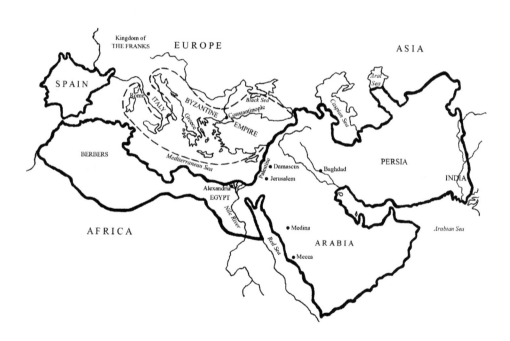

1201 C.E.	Pope Innocent III orders the **Fourth Crusade** which is unsuccessful. The European knights sack Constantinople (a co-Christian territory).
1208 C.E.	Pope Innocent III begins the **Albigensian Crusade** against the **Cathar (Gnostic) Christians** who are exterminated. Unofficial start of the **Catholic Inquisition.**
1212 C.E.	Pope Innocent III endorses a spontaneous **Children's Crusade** against the Muslims. Thousands of children are killed or sold into slavery.
1213 C.E.	King John concedes England and Ireland to Pope Innocent III as fiefs of the papacy and agrees to pay annual taxes to Rome. The king makes this concession to avoid invasion from King Philip Augustus (France).
1215 C.E.	King John is forced to sign the *Magna Carta* which, for the first time, holds the king accountable to the people. It also contains the earliest rules for taxation and imprisonment, which later will lead to democracy.
1219 C.E.	Pope Innocent III and European kings undertake the unsuccessful **Fifth Crusade.**
1221 C.E.	Mongolian Empire (Asians) invades the Muslim Empire (Arabs). The Mongolian Empire temporarily captures Baghdad.
1228 C.E.	King Frederick II (Italy) leads the **Sixth Crusade** and temporarily recovers Jerusalem by signing a 10 year treaty with the Muslim Empire.
1231 C.E.	Pope Gregory IX officially establishes the **Inquisition** to eliminate all who oppose the Catholic Church. Inquisitors confiscate property, torture, and kill the accused. For the next 600 years, millions are killed for heresy or refusing to convert.
1236 C.E.	Korean Buddhists complete their version of the holy book, the *Tripitaka.*
1244 C.E.	The Christians lose Jerusalem for the final time to the Muslims, soon known as the Ottoman Empire. The Muslims will rule Jerusalem until 1920, when the British take control of Palestine after World War I.
1249 C.E.	The **Seventh Crusade** led by King Louis IX (France) fails.
1253 C.E.	Mongolian Emperor Kublai Khan adopts Buddhism as the official religion of the Mongolian Empire, which includes China.
1270 C.E.	The **Eighth Crusade** initiated by King Louis IX (France) fails.
1290 C.E.	The Christians expel the Jews from England.
1291 C.E.	The Christians lose the remaining Crusader States in Palestine.
1307 C.E.	On October **Friday the 13th**, Pope Clement V and King Philip IV (France) arrest and imprison thousands of Knights Templar. The knights are tortured and killed by the Inquisition. Later, King Philip IV removes the papacy from Rome to Avignon. The papacy is controlled by French monarchs until 1378.
1312 C.E.	King Philip IV kills Jacques de Molay, the grand master of the Knights Templar, by burning him at the stake. King Philip IV also arrests the Jews, takes their property, and expels them from France.
1348 C.E.	The Black Death (bubonic plague) kills 1/3 of the European population. Jews are blamed and massacred throughout Europe.
1366 C.E.	The Muslim Ottoman Empire expands into Europe.
1378 C.E.	The papacy returns to Rome. However, two lines of rival "anti-popes" evolve for the next 71 years. This causes another major schism in the Catholic Church until 1449, when Pope Nicholas V assumes the papacy.
1391 C.E.	**Gendun Drub** is born. He is the first **Dalai Lama** sanctioned by Mongolia and he begins the **Tibetan Buddhist religion,** which asserts that the Dalai Lama reincarnates over and over to help mankind.

1431 C.E.	Joan of Arc is burned at the stake after the Catholic Inquisition condemns her.
1454 C.E.	Gutenberg invents the printing press and prints *The Holy Bible.*
1469 C.E.	**Guru Nanuk** is born in India. He starts the **Sikh religion** and is its first guru. Their sacred text is the *Adi Granth.*
1473 C.E.	Pope Sixtus IV builds the Sistine Chapel. To pay for construction, he begins the practice of selling Indulgences, which is a payment of money for remission of sins (and quicker admittance to heaven). The pope also extends the Inquisition to Spain.
1483 C.E.	**Martin Luther** is born in Germany. He challenges the corrupt practices of the Catholic Church and leads the **Protestant Reformation.** He also starts the **Lutheran religion.** In 1542, Luther writes *Of Jews and Their Lies,* a book which advocates the suppression of Jewish doctrine and destruction of Jewish temples.
1484 C.E.	Pope Innocent VIII expands the Inquisition and begins persecuting "witches." Over 100,000 heretics are killed, 80% of whom are women. Ironically, he is the first pope to acknowledge his bastard children.
1492 C.E.	Columbus discovers the "New World" for Spain. The Christians expel the Jews from Spain.
1493 C.E.	The Christians expel the Jews from Sicily.
1497 C.E.	The Christians expel the Jews from Portugal.
1506 C.E.	Pope Julius II begins the construction of St. Peter's Basilica at the Vatican and pays for the structure by selling Indulgences.
1509 C.E.	**John Calvin** is born in France. He challenges the corrupt Catholic Church along with Martin Luther. King Henry VIII is crowned King of England.
1516 C.E.	Ottoman Empire conquers Egypt and Syria to become the dominant civilization in the world. For the next 250 years, the Ottoman Empire will control all the Arab nations and parts of Africa, Europe, and Asia. Islam is the accepted religion.
1517 C.E.	**Martin Luther** publishes a paper against the Catholic practice of Indulgences. Pope Leo X excommunicates Luther and declares British King Henry VIII the "Defender of the Faith."
1527 C.E.	The Christians expel the Jews from Florence.
1530 C.E.	King Henry VIII breaks from the Catholic Church and declares himself head of the **Church of England** (a/k/a the Anglican Church).
1620 C.E.	Christian pilgrims leave England on the Mayflower for the New World.
1624 C.E.	**George Fox** is born in England. He starts the **Quaker religion.**
1633 C.E.	Catholic Inquisition, under Pope Urban VIII, condemns and threatens to torture Galileo for his teaching that the Earth is not the center of the Universe.
1635 C.E.	The Japanese Tokugawa Dynasty renounces Christianity, orders all Japanese citizens to register at Buddhist temples, and closes the Japanese borders until 1853.
1642 C.E.	Isaac Newton is born. He posits many scientific theories such as the law of gravity.
1703 C.E.	**John Wesley** is born in England. He and his brother start the Christian sect called the **Methodist religion.**
1720 C.E.	India is overtaken by the British East India Company.
1721 C.E.	Emperor K'ang Hsi of China bans Christianity.
1763 C.E.	**Industrial Age** begins with the invention of the steam engine.
1775 C.E.	Americans begin the War of Independence.

OTTOMAN EMPIRE

1500 C.E. to 1700 C.E.

1776 C.E.	American *Declaration of Independence* is published.
1789 C.E.	The French Revolution begins and King Louis XVI is later executed.
1800 C.E.	Emperor Napoleon expands the French territories throughout Europe and takes Italy after making an accord with the pope.
1805 C.E.	**Joseph Smith** is born in the U.S. He claims to find metal plates in 1827 (buried by the prophet Moroni in 421 C.E.). Smith translates the tablets into the *Book of Mormon* and starts the **Mormon religion.**
1816 C.E.	Pope Pius VII issues an edict forbidding torture in Inquisition tribunals. The Inquisition officially ends after 585 years. However, the Inquisition in Spain continues to torture and kill heretics until 1834.
1825 C.E	George Stephenson builds first public steam train for a British railroad company.
1831 C.E.	Michael Faraday invents mechanically produced electricity.
1848 C.E.	German activist Karl Marx publishes his *Communist Manifesto.*
1852 C.E.	Harriet Beecher Stowe writes *Uncle Tom's Cabin.*
1854 C.E.	Pope Pius IX declares the **Doctrine of the Immaculate Conception** which states that Jesus' mother Mary was conceived and born without the stain of original sin.
1858 C.E.	The British colonize India, formerly under Muslim control.
1859 C.E.	Charles Darwin writes *On the Origin of Species,* on the theory of evolution.
1861 C.E.	American Civil War begins. Over 620,000 people die.
1868 C.E.	Japan renounces Buddhism and adopts **Shinto** as the official religion.
1870 C.E.	The First Vatican Council pronounces the **Doctrine of Papal Supremacy and Infallibility** (i.e., popes are ordained by God and never make mistakes). The Vatican falls to the Italian government and the pope is confined to the Vatican.
1876 C.E.	**Technology Age.** Alexander Graham Bell invents the telephone and mankind embarks on an unprecedented era of technological invention.
1877 C.E.	Ottoman Empire loses much of Europe and the Balkans.
1879 C.E.	Thomas Edison invents the light bulb.
1882 C.E.	Ottoman Empire loses Egypt to the British, who seize the Suez Canal.
1890 C.E.	Radio is invented.
1903 C.E.	The Wright Brothers fly the first airplane.
1905 C.E.	Albert Einstein revolutionizes the field of physics with his theories on relativity, space-time continuum, and quantum mechanics.
1908 C.E.	Henry Ford mass produces the Model T automobile.
1911 C.E.	Last Chinese emperor is exiled and China becomes a republic. New Chinese government bans Confucianism, Daoism, and Buddhism, and dismantles temples.
1914 C.E.	Start of World War I. 15,000,000 people die.
1915 C.E.	Ottoman Empire exterminates 1,500,000 Armenians.
1917 C.E.	Russian Revolution starts and the Romanov Dynasty ends. 12,000,000 are killed.
1919 C.E.	League of Nations is formed at the end of World War I as an international body to resolve disputes without war. Later it is replaced with the United Nations.
1920 C.E.	The *Treaty of Sevre* is signed and the Ottoman Empire falls. Great Britain takes over Palestine, Jordan, and Iraq. France takes over Lebanon and Syria.
	U.S. passes the 19th Amendment and women obtain the right to vote.

1922 C.E.	Union of Soviet Socialist Republics is formed. The new communist government closes all churches and kills or imprisons thousands of clergy.
	League of Nations endorses Great Britain's *Balfour Declaration*, which supports the creation of a new nation (Israel) for the Jewish people in Palestine.
1925 C.E.	U.S state court rules in *Tennessee v. Scopes* that a public school teacher may not teach Darwin's theory of evolution.
1928 C.E.	Alexander Fleming discovers penicillin.
1929 C.E.	Start of the Great Depression.
	Italy recognizes the independence of Vatican City in Rome.
1930 C.E.	The Protestant Church sanctions birth control. Pope Pius XI condemns it.
1932 C.E.	U.S. and British scientists split the atom.
1933 C.E.	The Nazi government gains control of Germany.
1934 C.E.	Russian peasants revolt after Soviet leader Joseph Stalin collectivizes their land (by seizing 96% of Russian farms), imposes forced migration, and builds forced labor camps in Siberia. Over 20,000,000 Russians die.
1935 C.E.	**Tenzin Gyatso** is born. He is ordained the **14th Dalai Lama** of Tibetan Buddhism.
1937 C.E.	Japan invades China.
1939 C.E.	Start of World War II. 58,000,000 people are killed by the end of the war.
1942 C.E.	U.S. starts to build the first atomic bomb (Manhattan Project led by Robert Oppenheimer).
1945 C.E.	World War II ends after Germany surrenders and U.S. drops two atomic bombs on Japan killing 400,000 people. 6,000,000 Jews are killed during the Holocaust.
	The Japanese government ends religious restrictions.
	The *Gnostic Gospels* are found in Nag Hammadi, Egypt. They contain over 52 lost gospels which the early Catholic Church excluded from the *New Testament* and ordered destroyed.
1947 C.E.	United Nations passes *Resolution 81,* which divides Palestine between the Jews and Arabs. The Arabs reject the proposed boundaries.
	India regains independence after 227 years of British rule through a non-violent protest led by **Mahatma Gandhi**. India is partitioned and Pakistan is created. Conflict between Hindus in India and Muslims in Pakistan kills 500,000.
	Dead Sea Scrolls are found in Egypt and studied by a research team composed of Catholic priests. The Catholics refuse to release the scrolls, but they are leaked in 1991. Some of the scrolls appear to relate to Jesus and his brother James.
1948 C.E.	The British leave Palestine and Israel declares independence. Palestinians and surrounding Arab nations attack Israel. Fighting continues to this day.
1949 C.E.	The first Arab Israeli war officially ends. Israel conquers more than 3/4 of the former Palestine nation, creating 700,000 Palestinian refugees.
	Communist People's Republic of China is formed ending 4 years of civil war in which 2,500,000 are killed. Mao Zedong's regime kills another 40,000,000 people over the next 25 years. Religion is banned and missionaries are expelled.
	The Soviet Union is the second country to develop the atomic bomb.
1950 C.E.	Communist China invades Tibet. The Dalai Lama goes into exile. 1,200,000 Tibetan Buddhists are killed and 6,000 temples are destroyed.
1952 C.E.	U.S. builds the first hydrogen bomb.

INDIA AND PAKISTAN

1947 C.E.

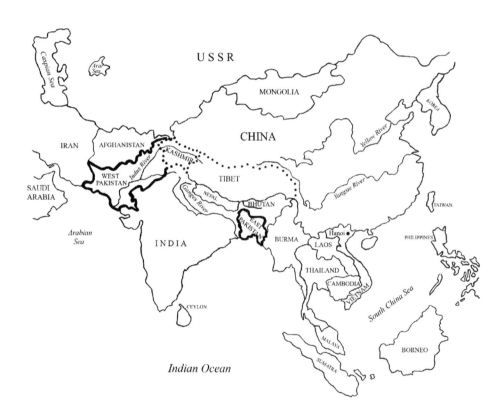

1953 C.E.	Korean War ends. 3,000,000 are killed.
1954 C.E.	U.S. Supreme Court in *Brown v. the Board of Education* ends segregation in public schools by declaring the policy unconstitutional.
1955 C.E.	U.S. operates first nuclear power plant.
	Soviet Union is the second world power to test a hydrogen bomb.
1963 C.E.	U.S. Supreme Court in *Abington School District v. Schempp* rules that reading the Ten Commandments in public schools violates the 1st Amendment.
1964 C.E.	U.S. passes the *Civil Rights Act* which ends discrimination based on race, color, religion, or national origin. Martin Luther King, Jr. wins the Nobel Peace Prize.
	Chinese build a nuclear bomb and acquire nuclear power.
1967 C.E.	Israel invades Egypt, Jordan, and Syria and seizes more Arab land in Six-Day War.
1968 C.E.	Pope Paul VI reasserts the Catholic ban on birth control.
1969 C.E.	U.S. astronaut Neil Armstrong is the first man to walk on the Moon.
	The Catholic Church retracts its designation of Mary Magdalene as a "sinner" and admits that she is not the prostitute mentioned in the gospels.
1971 C.E.	East Pakistan secedes from Pakistan to form the new Islamic country of Bangladesh. 1,200,000 are killed during the civil war.
1972 C.E.	**Information Age.** The first personal computers are built.
	U.S. builds the first 150 megaton thermonuclear weapon (25,000 times more powerful than the bombs dropped on Japan).
	Equal Rights Amendment passes both houses of U.S. Congress and goes to states for ratification. It guarantees full and equal rights without discrimination based on gender, but it fails (35 states ratify the Amendment, but 38 are needed).
1973 C.E.	The Vietnam War ends. 2,100,000 people are killed during the war. The Khmer Rouge regime kills another 1,500,000 in Cambodia.
1976 C.E.	U.S. Supreme Court in *Roe v. Wade* acknowledges that women have a constitutional right to an abortion during the first trimester of pregnancy.
1978 C.E.	Pope John Paul II reasserts the doctrine of celibacy for priests.
1979 C.E.	Israel and Egypt sign a treaty and the Sinai is returned to Egypt. Prime Minister Menachem Begin and President Anwar al Sadat win the 1978 Nobel Peace Prize.
	Muslim fundamentalists overthrow the Shah of Iran.
	Soviet Union invades Afghanistan. U.S. backs mujahedeen in Afghanistan.
1981 C.E.	AIDS is diagnosed.
	IBM markets the first personal computers to the general public.
1986 C.E.	Soviet Union's Chernobyl nuclear reactor disaster releases radioactive material.
1987 C.E.	Pope John Paul II condemns test-tube fertilization.
1988 C.E.	**Osama bin Laden** starts the Muslim terrorist group **Al Qaeda.**
1989 C.E.	The Berlin Wall is dismantled, and East and West Germany are reunited.
	The Soviet Union leaves Afghanistan and civil war erupts.
	Tenzin Gyatso, the 14th Dalai Lama, wins the Nobel Peace Prize.
1990 C.E.	Nelson Mandela is released from jail after 27 years for his Apartheid protest (racist system of white rule in South Africa). He wins the 1993 Nobel Peace Prize.

THE MIDDLE EAST

1948 C.E.

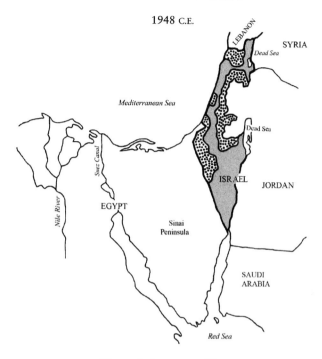

THE MIDDLE EAST

1967 C.E.

1991 C.E.	Soviet Union crumbles ending 74 years of Communist rule. 10 Soviet republics declare independence. Nuclear weapons now are located in fragile governments.
	U.S. invades Iraq in the First Gulf War.
1992 C.E.	The *Maastricht Treaty* is signed to form the European Union (EU). The new Euro currency becomes effective 10 years later in 2002.
1993 C.E.	Israel and Palestine sign the *Oslo Peace Accord* to return Gaza Strip and West Bank to Palestinians. Prime Minister Yitzhak Rabin and Yasser Arafat win 1994 Nobel Peace Prize. However, 12 years pass before Israel starts to honor the treaty.
1994 C.E.	Israel and Jordan sign a peace treaty.
1995 C.E.	Israeli Prime Minister Yitzhak Rabin is assassinated by a Zionist Jew.
1996 C.E.	Scottish scientists clone the first mammal, a sheep named Dolly.
1998 C.E.	Pakistan develops nuclear power and nuclear bombs.
	Al Qaeda bombs U.S. embassies in Kenya and Tanzania, killing 300 people.
1999 C.E.	Afghanistan civil war ends with 1,400,000 deaths. Muslim fundamentalists called the Taliban control the country.
	China bans the **Falun Gong spiritualist movement,** which has 70,000,000 members (more than the Communist Party). 3,000 are killed and 100,000 sent to labor camps.
2000 C.E.	The New Millennium starts and the world anticipates Y2K computer disasters.
	U.S. Supreme Court in *Bush v. Gore* decides the fate of the presidential election. George Bush is declared the winner by 537 votes in Florida.
	Al Qaeda bombs the USS Cole, killing 19 soldiers.
2001 C.E.	The Twin Towers in New York City and the Pentagon in Washington, D.C. are attacked, killing 3,000 people. Al Qaeda is blamed.
2002 C.E.	Israel starts the construction of a wall around Jerusalem and through the West Bank. The wall violates previously agreed borders.
2003 C.E.	U.S. invades Iraq in the Second Gulf War and topples Saddam Hussein. No weapons of mass destruction are found.
	An international team of scientists complete the Human Genome Project, which maps the DNA blueprint for humans.
	A deadly strain of Bird Flu (H5N1) mutates and kills 4 humans.
2004 C.E.	U.S. *September 11 Commission Report* determines that Saddam Hussein had no connection to Osama bin Laden, Al Qaeda, or the bombing of the Twin Towers and the Pentagon.
	Muslim terrorists bomb 4 trains in Spain killing 191 people.
	Palestinian leader Yasser Arafat dies.
	A tsunami hits Southeast Asia and kills 250,000 people. The earthquake shifts the Earth's axis 2.5 cm, causing our planet to spin .000003 seconds faster.
	U.S. successfully lands an unmanned spacecraft on Mars.
	South Korean and Chinese scientists clone human embryos.
	1,083 new sex-abuse claims filed against the Catholic Church. Settlements reach $600,000,000. Since 1950, 5,148 priests are accused of abusing 11,750 victims.
	44,000,000 people have AIDS, but the Catholic Church forbids the use of condoms.
	1,083 sex-abuse claims are filed against the Catholic Church and settlements reach $600,000,000. Since 1950, 5,148 priests are accused of abusing 11,750 victims.

2005 C.E.	John Roberts, Jr. replaces U.S. Supreme Court Chief Justice William Rehnquist. Samuel Alito, Jr replaces Sandra Day O'Connor. The Supreme Court has 5 Catholics.
	Iraqis hold democratic elections and adopt a constitution.
	Mohammed ElBaradei of the Int. Atomic Energy Agency wins Nobel Peace Prize. Before U.S. invaded Iraq, he reported to U.N. that Iraq had no atomic weapons.
	Al Qaeda kills 60 in Jordan; Muslim terrorists bomb London subway killing 53.
	Israeli Prime Minister Ariel Sharon and new Palestinian President Mahmoud Abbas agree to a truce. Israel vacates the Gaza Strip and parts of the West Bank.
	Iran elects fundamentalist president Mahmoud Ahmadinejad who denies the Holocaust, says "Israel should be wiped off the map," and declares that the Mahdi (Muslim Messiah) will soon appear.
	Egypt holds mock elections. President Hosni Mubarek imprisons his opponents.
	Syria ends 29 year military occupation of Lebanon. Lebanese Prime Minister Rafiq Hariri is assassinated. Syrian Muslim fundamentalists are blamed.
	Sudan's 21 year Muslim-Christian civil war ends. 2,000,000 die and 4,000,000 displaced.
	156 countries sign the *Kyoto Treaty*. The U.S. and Australia are the only industrialized nations that refuse to sign the treaty.
	Hurricanes Katrina and Rita destroy Gulf Coast, the worst natural disaster in U.S. history, 1,300 people die and 2,000,000 are homeless. Earthquake in Pakistan kills 87,000 people and leaves 3,500,000 homeless.
	Bird Flu spreads from Asia to Europe killing over 150,000 birds and 70 humans.
	43 public school systems in the U.S. debate the theory of "Intelligent Design." Kansas court rules that Intelligent Design can be taught in public schools. Pennsylvania rules that Intelligent Design is religious and may not be taught.
	Massachusetts legalizes same-sex marriage.
	Pope John Paul II dies and Cardinal Joseph Ratzinger, former head of the Congregation for the Doctrine of the Faith, is elected **Pope Benedict XVI**. The Catholic Church has spent one billion dollars to settle priest sex-abuse cases.
2006 C.E.	Former Iraqi President Saddam Hussein is executed in Baghdad. Al Qaeda leader Abu Musab al-Zarqawi and 7 aides are killed in Iraq.
	Ariel Sharon suffers a stroke and Ehud Olmert becomes Israeli Prime Minister. Israeli troops invade Lebanon after the kidnapping of two Israeli soldiers. Hamas wins the majority of seats in the Palestinian Legislative elections.
	North Korea claims to have tested its first nuclear weapon.
	Earthquake in Indonesia kills 6,000 people and leaves 1,500,000 homeless.
	NASA reclassifies both Eris (discovered in 2005) and Pluto as "dwarf planets," leaving 8 planets in our solar system.
2007 C.E.	Nancy Pelosi becomes first female Speaker of the U.S. House of Representatives.
	Islamic fundamentalist party Hamas takes control of Gaza. The PLO Fatah party takes control of West Bank.
	Former U.S. Vice President Al Gore wins Nobel Peace Prize for environmental work.
	Winter storms bring record rains and flooding to U.S. Pacific Northwest. Worst recorded flooding in England and Sudan, and heat wave in Greece. Cyclone Sidr hits Bangladesh and kills 5,000 people.
	Bird Flu spreads to a turkey farm in England.
	First potentially habitable planet Gliese (581-d) is discovered in the constellation Libra.

2008 C.E.   U.S. sub-prime mortgage and derivative bubbles burst causing a global financial crisis. Congress passes *Emergency Economic Stabilization Act* authorizing a bank bail-out of $700 billion. The first $350 billion payment is made with no oversight. In total, $50 trillion in wealth is lost worldwide.

Israel invades Gaza, killing 1,400 Palestinians and leaving 51,000 homeless.
Russia invades Georgia, killing 300 and leaving 158,000 homeless.
China cracks down on Tibetan Buddhists, killing 220 and arresting 7,000.
Mumbai is bombed, killing 175 people; India accuses Pakistani terrorists.

Fidel Castro resigns as President of Cuba and his brother Raul takes his place.

President Pervez Musharraf of Pakistan resigns and is replaced by Asi Ali Zardari following the assassination of former Pakistani Prime Minister Benazir Bhutto.

In Antarctica, 1000 sq. mi. of the Wilkins Ice Shelf breaks; the remaining 5,000 sq. mi. will soon detach.
In the Arctic, the Northwest Passage is open for the first time in recorded history.

Cyclones kill 140,000 people in Myanmar (Burma); 2,400,000 are left homeless.
Earthquakes kill 109,000 people in China; 2,800,000 are left homeless.

British scientists create a hybrid human/cow embryo which lives 3 days.
British surgeons successfully insert the first bionic eyes in 2 blind people.

International team at CERN Switzerland shoots proton beam in Hadron Collider.

Frozen water is discovered on Mars indicating Mars once had ability to sustain life.

2009 C.E.   **POLITICAL ISSUES:**

U.S. inaugurates its 44th (and 1st African American) President, Barack Hussein Obama II. President Obama wins the Nobel Peace Prize.

U.S. Supreme Court Justice David Souter retires and is replaced by Sonia Sotomayor. 6 of the 9 Supreme Court Justices are Catholic.

Global financial crisis continues with numerous countries technically bankrupt.
U.S. Congress fails to address the Wall Street practices that caused the collapse.
U.S. national debt hits $11.9 trillion, and Congress raises debt ceiling to $12.4 trillion.

The European Union now includes 27 European countries. Belgian Herman Van Rompuy becomes the first permanent president of the EU.

The Sri Lankan civil war ends after more than 25 years, resulting in 80,000 deaths.

Wars and political unrest consume much of the world:
U.S. enters 7th year of war in Iraq; death toll reaches 1,200,000.
U.S. enters 9th year of war in Afghanistan; death toll reaches 58,000.
U.S. military and CIA employ mercenaries (e.g.: Blackwater) in these conflicts.
U.S. beats back Al Qaeda in Pakistan, but tribal leaders fight to control country.
Al Qaeda moves base of operations to Yemen; U.S. faces another "terror" front.
In the Middle East, Israel continues to build illegal settlements in the West Bank and east Jerusalem, resulting in riots.
The reelection of Iranian president Mahmoud Ahmadinejad results in accusations of voter fraud and spawns riots.
In Africa, 17 of the 53 countries are fighting internal or cross border wars, creating an estimated 9,000,000 refugees in that continent.
In Asia, wars continue in Myanmar (Burma), Thailand, and the Philippines.
Russian and Chechen conflict continues.
In South America, Colombia continues 45 year civil war with rebel guerillas, and the Mexican drug war escalates with 16,000 killed.

Summary of deaths and homelessness due to war over the past 15 years:
Conflict deaths (military and civilian):   Over 12,480,000
Homelessness: Over 25,600,000

Nuclear warheads on planet Earth estimated to exceed 23,375:

U.S.:	9,400 nuclear weapons
Russia:	13,000 nuclear weapons
China:	240 nuclear weapons
England:	185 nuclear weapons
France:	300 nuclear weapons
Israel:	80 nuclear weapons
India:	80 nuclear weapons
Pakistan:	90 nuclear weapons
North Korea:	Claims to have nuclear weapons capability
Iran:	Suspected of building nuclear weapons

435 Nuclear power plants are operating globally, with 53 more in construction.

SOCIAL ISSUES:

Population of Earth is 6.8 billion people.

Worldwide, poverty is growing at an unprecedented rate:
1.4 billion people live in abject poverty with less than $1.25 per day.
3 billion people (almost half the population) live on less than $2.50 per day.
9,125,000 children die from poverty annually, with 44% of these deaths in Africa.

In the U.S., poverty rates also increase:
13.2 % of Americans and 18% of all children live below the poverty line.
Of the top 22 industrialized nations, U.S. ranks 2nd for child poverty.
1 in 6 Americans suffers from hunger, with low or very low food security.
1 in 8 Americans is on food stamps.
1 in 5 Americans is unemployed; 25 states have spent all unemployment funds.
1 in 8 American mortgages are in default or foreclosure.
1 in 50 American children are homeless.

But the U.S. still has the highest *per capita* consumer spending rate in the world:
American purchases constitute 20% of the global economy.
70% of U.S. gross domestic product (GDP) is spent on consumer goods.
Americans finance much of their consumerism through debt.
Americans' savings rate is the lowest in the industrialized world.
Of the top 22 industrialized nations, U.S. ranks last *per capita* for aid to others.

Worldwide, the literacy rate in developing countries is 62%.

In the U.S., the high school graduation rate is 69%, with 1,200,000 students dropping out annually. 75% of homeless children will not graduate high school.

Worldwide, same-sex marriage is legal in The Netherlands, Belgium, Canada, Spain, South Africa, Sweden, Norway, and Mexico City.

In the U.S., same sex marriage is legal in Massachusetts, Connecticut, Iowa, Vermont, New Hampshire, and D.C.; 4 states allow civil unions; 11 allow domestic partnerships.

HEALTH ISSUES:

Physical and emotional abuse of women continues:
46% of women in Africa are subjected to genital mutilation (90% in Egypt).
48% of girls in least developed countries are subjected to child marriage.
2,000,000 girls are forced into the commercial sex-trade every year.
5,000 women are killed every year in religious "honor killings."

135,000,000 babies are born this year, but many will not survive:
8,800,000 of these babies will die before their 5th birthday.
In Africa, 1 in 3 babies dies in the first month of life.
In India, 10,000,000 female fetuses have been aborted in the past 20 years.
In China, female fetuses are still routinely aborted to comply with 1 child rule.

In the U.S., health problems are on the rise:
> Of the top 22 industrialized nations, U.S. ranks 21st in overall child wellbeing.
> Of the top 22 industrialized nations, U.S ranks 2nd in infant mortality.
> 73% of Americans are overweight, with 40% obese or highly obese.
> Annual health care costs for obesity exceed $90 billion.
> Autism rates explode with 1 in 91 children and 1 in 58 boys autistic.

U.S. Congress rejects universal healthcare. U.S. is the only industrialized nation without universal healthcare. 46,000,000 Americans have no health insurance.

35,000,000 people have AIDS worldwide. 25,000,000 people have died from AIDS since 1981. AIDS rate in D.C. is 3% (higher than Africa). Africa has 14,000,000 AIDS orphans. Catholic Church continues to forbid the use of condoms.

Bird Flu (H5N1) has killed 250 people globally since 2003.
Swine flu (H1N1), a combination of bird, swine, and human genes, kills 12,000.

ENVIRONMENTAL ISSUES:

Scientists report that the effects of global warming are undeniable:
> This decade has been the warmest on record.
> Farmers contend with the highest temperatures in 7,000 years.
> Australia suffers its 12th year of drought and most wild fires ever recorded.
> Melting polar ice caps have produced more water than in Lakes Huron, Superior, Erie, and Ontario.
> 1,000,000 sq. mi. of Arctic ice has melted, reducing it to 1/2 its normal size.
> The Arctic is predicted to have no summer sea ice by 2030.
> 85% of Mt. Kilimanjaro snow has melted; it will totally disappear by 2015.
> Over 67% of the glaciers in the U.S. Glacier National Park have melted and remaining glaciers are expected to melt by 2020.
> By 2100, sea level rise from melting ice is expected to flood Pacific Ocean islands and coastal regions to displace 200,000,000 people.
> U.S. produces 20% of the world's greenhouse gases; China produces 22%.

During the United Nations Conference on Climate Change, member nations fail to agree on binding emissions targets.

Humanity consumes 40% more resources than the Earth can generate:
> 99% of the Earth's water is unsafe or unavailable for drinking.
> 40% of Earth is threatened by desertification.
> Topsoil loss is 135,000 sq. mi. per year; it takes 500 years to produce one inch of topsoil.
> Rainforests are lost at the rate of 60,000 sq. mi. per year; only 2,600,000 sq. mi. of rainforest remain.
> If everyone lived like Americans, it would take 5 planets to sustain us.

Deaths and illnesses related to climate change and pollution are increasing:
> On average, climate change due to heat waves, floods, storms, and fires results in 300,000 deaths per year and 350,000 severe illnesses.
> 99% of those who die from climate change live in developing countries which produce less than 1% of the world's greenhouse gases.
> Air pollution kills 2,400,000 people worldwide per year.
> Another 5,000,000 people die each year due to water pollution and water related diseases caused by typhoid, intestinal parasites, and diarrhea.
> A garbage patch twice the size of Texas is floating in the Pacific Ocean.

Scientists believe the "Sixth Great Extinction" has started:
> 25% of mammals, 12% of birds, and 33% of amphibians face extinction.
> 51% of reptiles, 52% of insects, and 73% of plants face extinction.
> 90% of the large predatory fish are already extinct.
> In total, 40% of all remaining species on Earth are at risk of extinction.

SCIENCE ISSUES:

The oldest skeleton of a pre-human hominid, *Ardipithecus ramidus*, is discovered. She lived 4,400,000 years ago and is the descendent of the last common ancestor shared by humans and chimps.

Scientists have mapped the genetic code for bacteria, yeast, worms, flies, rats, mice, goats, sheep, cows, dogs, horses, woolly mammoths, and humans.
Scientists have now cloned 22 animals.

U.S. lifts the ban on stem-cell research for the study of stem-cell lines in existence.

Nanotechnology inventory has grown by 379% since 2006. New evidence shows that these unbound particles poison the environment and accumulate in our organs.

U.S. and 24 other countries accept genetically modified organism (GMO) seed and allow corporations to patent GMO products. Natural farmers unsuccessfully fight the cross pollination of these "terminator seeds." In the U.S., 86% of all corn, 90% of all soybean, and 90% of all cotton is now GMO.

The deepest underwater volcano is discovered beneath Pacific Ocean near Samoa. Lava samples resemble 1,000,000 year old specimens from extinct volcanoes.

Water vapor and ice are discovered on the Moon.

For the first time, scientists use a telescope to directly observe a planet-like object (GJ 758 B) orbiting a star much like ours, 50 light-years from Earth.

RELIGIOUS ISSUES:

4.9 billion people still subscribe to the 5 primary religions:

Hinduism:	911,000,000 followers	(3rd place)
Judaism:	15,000,000 followers	(5th place)
Buddhism:	385,000,000 followers	(4th place)
Christianity:	2,100,000,000 followers	(1st place)
Islam:	1,500,000,000 followers	(2nd place)

The Anglican Church splits over the issues of ordination of female priests and gay bishops. The Catholic Church invites disaffected Anglicans to join the church, agreeing to allow their priests to continue as Catholic priests even though married. The Catholic Church has spent $2 billion to settle priest sex-abuse cases.
The Vatican's Pontifical Academy of Sciences hosts a conference on alien life.

Worldwide, 2 billion people seek spiritual sanctuary in New Age theosophies.

In U.S., the religious landscape is changing:
28% of Americans have left their birth religion, with the defection of Catholics the greatest.
38% of Americans attend religious services once a week, and 28% of these people also attend services of other faiths.
27% of Americans do not attend service at all.
Eastern and New Age beliefs are growing: 24% of Americans believe in reincarnation (including 22% of Christians), 29% report contact with the dead; 26% believe in spiritual energy; 25% believe in astrology; 23% use yoga to meditate; and 15% consult psychic intuitives.
16% of Americans report no religious affiliation (up from 8% in 1990).

2010 C.E.   Humanity is poised to enter the **Fifth Spiritual Paradigm**, which will arrive once we:
Assimilate the Tower of Truth built by God's messengers;
Add information from our best philosophers, scientists, historians, and mystics;
Acknowledge our spiritual connectedness by unifying the five primary religions;
Accept responsibility for the perfection of our souls; and
Adopt a more sophisticated belief system about ourselves and the Supreme Being.

God is viewed as a unified force composed of both masculine & feminine energies.

BIBLIOGRAPHY
Twelve Years of Research

COMPARATIVE RELIGIOUS READINGS:

Armstrong, Karen. *A History of God*. New York, NY: Random House, Inc., 1993.

The Book of Mormon. Translated by Joseph Smith. Salt Lake City, UT: Intellectual Reserve, Inc., 1981.

Borg, Marcus, Editor. *Jesus and Buddha: The Parallel Sayings*. Berkeley, CA: Ulysses Press, 1977.

Bowker, John. *God: A Brief History*. New York, NY: DK Publishing, Inc., 2002.

Bowker, John., Editor. *The Cambridge Illustrated History of Religions*. Cambridge, UK: Cambridge University Press, 2002.

Braden, Charles S. *The World's Religions*. Nashville, TN: Abingdon Press, 1954.

Campbell, Joseph. *Creative Mythology: The Masks of God*. New York, NY: Penguin Putnam, Inc., 1976.

Feiler, Bruce. *Abraham: A Journey to the Heart of the Three Faiths*. New York, NY: HarperCollins Publishers, Inc., 2002.

Kriwaczek, Paul. *In Search of Zarathustra*. New York, NY: Alfred A. Knopf Publishers, Random House, Inc., 2003.

Markale, Jean. *The Great Goddess*. Vermont: Inner Traditions International, 1999.

Nielson, Niels C., Jr.; Hein, Norvin; Reynolds, Frank E.; Miller, Alan, L.; Karff, Samuel, E.; Cochran, Alice C.; and McLean, Paul. *Religions of the World*. New York, NY: St. Martin's Press, Inc., 1983.

Samuel, E.; Cochran, Alice C.; and McLean, Paul. *Religions of the World*. New York, NY: St. Martin's Press, Inc., 1983.

Smith, Huston. *The World's Religions*. New York, NY: HarperCollins Publishers, Inc., 1991.

HINDU READINGS:

The Bhagavad Gita. Translated by Juan Mascaro. London, UK: Penguin Books, Ltd., 1962.

Copley, Antony. *Gandhi*. New York, NY: Basil Blackwell Inc., 1987.

Flood, Gavin. *An Introduction to Hinduism*. New York, NY: Cambridge University Press, 1996.

Hindu Scriptures. Edited and partially translated by Dominic Goodall. Los Angeles, CA: University of California Press, 1996.

Hindu Scriptures: Hymns from the Rigveda, Five Upanishads, The Bhagavadgita. Edited by Nicol Macnicol. New York, NY: E.P. Dutton & Company, Inc., 1957.

Mann, Gurinder Singh; Numrich, Paul David; & Williams, Raymond B. *Buddhists, Hindus, and Sikhs in America*. New York, NY: Oxford University Press, 2001.

Morgan, Diane. *The Best Guide to Eastern Philosophy and Religion*. Los Angeles, CA: Renaissance Media, Inc., 2001.

Renou, Louis. *Hinduism*. New York, NY: Washington Square Press, 1971.

The Rig Veda. Translated by Ralph T. H. Griffith, Edited by Jaroslav Pelikan. New York, NY: Motilal Banarsidass Publishers, Ltd., 1992.

JEWISH READINGS:

Anderson, Bernard W. *Understanding the Old Testament*. 2nd Ed. Englewood Cliffs, NJ: Prentice Hall, Inc., 1996.

Baigent, Michael and Leigh, Richard. *The Dead Sea Scrolls Deception*. New York, NY: Touchstone, 1993.

Dimont, Max I. *Jews, God and History*. New York, NY: Simon and Schuster, Inc., 1962.

Eisenman, Robert and Wise, Michael. *The Dead Sea Scrolls Uncovered*. New York, NY: Barnes and Noble, Inc., 1994.

Golb, Norman. *Who Wrote the Dead Sea Scrolls? The Search for the Secret of Qumran*. New York, NY: Scribner, 1995.

Josephus. *The Jewish War*. Translated by G.A. Williamson. New York, NY: Penguin Books, Ltd., 1981.

Kertzer, Morris N. and Hoffman, Lawrence A. *What is a Jew?* New York, NY: Simon & Schuster, Inc., 1996.

Mansfield, Peter. *A History of the Middle East*. New York, NY: Penguin Books, 1992.

Marks, John J.; Gray, John; Milgrom, Jacob; Guthrie, Harvey H. Jr.; Gottwald, Norman K.; and Laymon, Charles M., Editors. *The Pentateuch: A Commentary on Genesis, Exodus, Leviticus, Numbers, Deuteronomy*. Nashville, TN: Abingdon Press, 1983.

The Pentateuch and Haftorahs. 2nd Ed. Edited by Hertz, J. H. London, UK: Soncino Press, 1961.

Wise, Michael; Abegg, Martin Jr.; and Cook, Edward. *The Dead Sea Scrolls: A New Translation*. New York, NY: HarperCollins Publishers, Inc., 1996.

BUDDHIST READINGS:

Allione, Tsultrim. *Women of Wisdom*. London, UK: Routledge & Kegan Paul, PLC, 1984.

Buddhaghosa, Bhadantacariya. *The Path of Purification (Visuddhimagga)*. Translated by Bhikkhu Nyanamoli. Berkeley, CA: Shambhala Publications, Inc., 1976.

Cleary, Thomas. *Dhammapada: The Sayings of Buddha*. Bantam Books, 1994.

Dalai Lama XIV. *The Four Noble Truths*. New York, NY: HarperCollins Publishers, 1997.

The Dhammapada: The Sayings of the Buddha. Translated by John Ross Carter and Mahinda Palihawadana. New York, NY: Oxford University Press, 1987.

Harvey, Peter. *Introduction to Buddhism: Teachings, History and Practices*. Cambridge, NY: Cambridge University Press, 1990.

Kahula, Wapola. *What the Buddha Taught*. Grove/Atlantic Inc., 1987.

Kornfield, Jack. *After the Ecstacy, the Laundry*. New York, NY: Random House, Inc., 2000.

Lopez, Donald S. Jr. *The Story of Buddhism*. New York, NY: HarperCollins Publishers, 2001.

Mackenzie, Vicki. *Reborn in the West*. London, UK: Bloomsbury Publishing, Inc., 1995.

Ray, Reginald A. *Indestructible Truth*. Boston, MA: Shambhala Publications, Inc., 2000.

Tarantha, Jo Nang. *The Origin of Tara Tantra*. Translated by David Templeman. Kangra, India: Library of Tibetan Works & Archives, 1995.

CHRISTIAN READINGS:

Baldwin, Marshall W. *The Mediaeval Church*. Ithaca, NY: Cornell University Press, 1953.

Bauckham, Richard. *Gospel Women: Studies of the Named Women in the Gospels*. Grand Rapids, MI/Cambridge, UK: Wm. B. Eerdmans Publishing Co., 2002.

Bellitto, Christopher M. *The General Councils: A History of the Twenty-One Church Councils from Nicaea to Vatican II*. New York, NY: Paulist Press, 2002.

Borg, Marcus, consulting editor. *The Lost Gospel Q: The Original Sayings of Jesus*. Berkeley, CA: Ulysses Press, 1996.

Bower, William C. *The Living Bible*. Ayer Company Publishers, Inc., 1977.

Butz, Jeffrey J. *The Brother of Jesus and the Lost Teachings of Christianity*. Rochester, VT: Inner Traditions, 2005.

Carroll, James. *Constantine's Sword: The Church and the Jews*. New York, NY: Houghton Mifflin Company, 2001.

Saint Catherine of Siena. *The Dialogue*. Translated by Suzanne Nofske, O.P. New York, NY: Paulist Press, Inc., 1980.

Cheetham, Nicolas. *A History of the Popes*. Barnes and Noble, Inc., 1992.

Chidester, David. *Christianity: A Global History*. New York, NY: HarperCollins Publishers, 2000.

Collins, Paul. *The Modern Inquisition: Seven Prominent Catholics and Their Struggles with the Vatican*. New York, NY: The Overlook Press, Inc., 2002.

Crossan, John Dominic. *The Birth of Christianity*. New York, NY: Harper Collins Publishers, Inc., 1998.

Dart, John and Riegert, Ray. *Unearthing the Lost Words of Jesus: The Discovery and Text of the Gospel of Thomas*. Berkley, CA: Ulysses Press, 1998.

Duffy, Eamon. *Saints and Sinners: A History of the Popes*. Yale University Press, 1997.

Edwards, David L. *Christianity: The First Two Thousand Years*. Maryknoll, NY: Orbis Books, 1997.

Ehrman, Bart D. *Lost Christianities: Battles for Scripture and the Faiths We Never Knew*. New York, NY: Oxford University Press, Inc, 2003.

Ehrman, Bart D. *Lost Scriptures*. New York, NY: Oxford University Press, Inc, 2003.

Eisenman, Robert. *James the Brother of Jesus*. New York, NY: Penguin Putnam, Inc., 1998.

Eusebius. *The History of The Church*. Translated by G.A. Williamson. New York, NY: Marlboro Books Corporation, 1984.

Fredriksen, Paula. *Jesus of Nazareth, King of the Jews: A Jewish Life and the Emergence of Christianity*. New York, NY: Alfred A. Knopf, 1999.

Freke, Timothy and Gandy, Peter. *Jesus and the Lost Goddess: The Secret Teachings of the Original Christians*. New York, NY: Harmony Books, 2001.

Friedman, Richard Elliott. *Who Wrote the Bible?* New York, NY: Summit Books, 1987.

Gager, John G. *Reinventing Paul*. New York, NY: Oxford University Press, 2000.

The Gospel of Judas. Edited by Rodolphe Kasser, Marvin Meyer, and Gregor Wurst. Washington, D.C.: National Geographic Society, 2006.

The Holy Bible: King James Version.

The Holy Bible: New American Bible.

Jordan, Michael. *The Historical Mary: Revealing the Pagan Identity of the Virgin Mother.* Berkely, CA: Ulysses Press, 2003.

Kugel, James L. *The Bible As It Was.* Cambridge, MA: Harvard University Press, 1997.

Kung, Hans. *The Catholic Church.* New York, NY: Random House, Inc., 2001.

The Lost Books of the Bible and The Forgotten Books of Eden. World Bible Publishers, Inc., 1926.

Mack, Burton. *The Lost Gospel: The Book of Q and Christian Origins.* San Francisco, CA: HarperSanFrancisco, 1994.

Maxwell-Stuart, P.G. *Chronicle of the Popes: The Reign-by-Reign Record of the Papacy from St. Peter to the Present.* New York, NY: Thames and Hudson Inc., 1997.

Moynahan, Brian. *The Faith: A History of Christianity.* New York, NY: Random House, Inc., 2002.

Nelson-Pallmeyer, Jack. *Jesus Against Christianity: Reclaiming the Missing Jesus.* Harrisburg, PA: Trinity Press International, 2001.

The New International Version; Interlinear Greek-English New Testament. Translated by Reverend Alfred Marshall. Grand Rapids, MI: Zondervan Corporation, 1980.

The New Open Bible; New American Standard Bible. Nashville, TN: Thomas Nelson, Inc., 1990.

Pagels, Elaine. *Beyond Belief: The Secret Gospel of Thomas.* New York, NY: Random House, Inc., 2003.

Pagels, Elaine. *The Gnostic Gospels.* New York, NY: Random House, Inc., 1979.

Patzia, Arthur G. *The Making of the New Testament.* Downers Grove, IL: Inter Varsity Press, 1995.

Pelikan, Jaroslav. *Mary Through the Centuries: Her Place in the History of Culture.* New Haven and London, UK: Yale University Press, 1996.

Picknett, Lynn. *Mary Magdalene: Christianity's Hidden Goddess.* New York, NY: Carroll & Graf Publishers, 2003.

Porter, J.R. *Jesus Christ: The Jesus of History, The Christ of Faith.* New York, NY: Oxford University Press, 1999.

Powelson, Mark; Riegert, Ray; and Borg, Marcus, Editors. *The Lost Gospel Q: The Original Sayings of Jesus.* Berkeley, CA: Ulysses Press, 1999.

Robinson, James M., Editor. *The Nag Hammadi Library in English.* Revised Ed. New York, NY: HarperCollins, Publishers, 1990.

Rubenstein, Richard E. *When Jesus Became God.* New York, NY: Harcourt, Inc., 1999.

Schonfield, Hugh J. *The Passover Plot.* New York, NY: Random House, Inc., 1965.

Sheler, Jeffery L. *Is the Bible True?: How Modern Debates and Discoveries Affirm the Essence of the Scriptures.* New York, NY: HarperCollins Publishers, Inc., 1999.

Spong, John Shelby. *Here I Stand: My Struggle for a Christianity of Integrity, Love, and Equality.* New York, NY: HarperSanFrancisco, 2000.

Spong, John Shelby. *Jesus for the Non-Religious.* New York, NY: HarperSanFrancisco, 2007.

Spong, John Shelby. *Liberating The Gospels: Reading the Gospels with Jewish Eyes.* New York, NY: HarperSanFrancisco, 1996.

Starbird, Margaret. *The Woman With the Alabaster Jar.* Rochester, VT: Bear & Company, 1993.

Saint Teresa of Avila. *The Life*. Translated by J.M. Cohen. London, UK: Penguin Books, Ltd., 1957.

Saint Thérèse of Lisieux. *The Story of A Soul*. Translated by Michael Day. Rockford, IL: Tan Books and Publishers, Inc., 1997.

Thiering, Barbara. *Jesus and the Riddle of the Dead Sea Scrolls*. New York, NY: HarperCollins Publishers, Inc., 1992.

ISLAMIC READINGS:

Ali, Maulana Muhammad. *The Religion of Islam*. 7th Ed. Dublin, OH: The Ahmadiyya Anjuman Ishaat Islam, 1995.

Armstrong, Karen. *Muhammad: A Biography of the Prophet*. New York, NY: HarperCollins Publishers, Inc., 1992.

Armstrong, Karen. *Islam: A Short History*. New York, NY: Random House, Inc., 2000.

Bleany, Heather and Lawless, Richard. *The Middle East Since 1945*. London, UK: B.T. Batsford, Ltd., 1989.

Esposito, John L. *Islam: The Straight Path*. 3rd Ed. New York, NY: Oxford University Press, 1988.

Firestone, Reuven. *Jihad: The Origin of Holy War in Islam*. New York, NY: Oxford University Press, Inc., 1999.

Fromkin, David; Hawass, Zahi; Halevi, Yossi Klein; Mackey, Sandra; Sennott, Charles M.; Viorst, Milton and Wheatcroft, Andrew. *Cradle & Crucible: History and Faith in the Middle East*. Washington, D.C.: National Geographic Society, 2002.

The Holy Quran. Translated by Abdullah Yusuf Ali. Cairo, Egypt: Al-Manar Publishing & Distributing House, 1934.

Nasr, Seyyed Hossein. *Islam: Religion, History, and Civilization*. New York, NY: HarperCollins Publishers, Inc., 2003.

Seestani, Ayatullah al Uzama Syed Ali al-Husaini. *Islamic Laws*. Stanmore Middlesex, UK: The World Federation of K.S.I. Muslim Communities, 1994.

Williams, Paul L. *Al Qaeda: Brotherhood of Terror*. U.S: Pearson Education, Inc., 2002.

NEW AGE READINGS & FICTION:

Alford, Alan. *Gods of the New Millennium*. London, UK: Hodder and Stoughton, 1997.

Blavatsky, H.P. *The Secret Doctrine*. Theosophical University Press, 1999.

Blavatsky, H.P. *Isis Unveiled*. Theosophical University Press, 1999.

Brown, Dan. *The Da Vinci Code*. New York, NY: Random House, Inc., 2003.

Chopra, Deepak. *The Seven Spiritual Laws of Success*. San Rafael, CA: Amber-Allen Publishing and New World Library, 1994.

Estes, Clarissa Pinkola. *Women Who Run with the Wolves*. New York, NY: Random House, Inc., 1992.

Fisher, Joseph. *The Case for Reincarnation*. Carol Publishing Group, 1992.

Gawain, Shakti. *Creative Visualization*. New York, NY: MJF Books, 1978.

Gray, John. *Men are from Mars, Women are from Venus*. New York, NY: HarperCollins, Publishers, 1992.

Head, Joseph and Cranston, Sylvia. *Reincarnation: The Phoenix Fire Mystery*. Theosophical University Press, Inc., 1998.

Kingston, Maxine Hong. *The Fifth Book of Peace*. New York, NY: Alfred A. Knopf Publishers, Random House, Inc., 2003.

Langley, Noel; Cayce, Hugh Lynn. *Edgar Cayce on Reincarnation*. New York, NY: Warner Books., Inc., 1967.

Mandeville, Michael Wells. *Return of the Phoenix: A Trilogy of the World Epic*. Black Canyon City, AZ: MetaSyn Media, 2000.

McAfee, John. *Into the Heart of Truth*. Woodland Park, CO: Woodland Publications, 2001.

Redfield, James. *The Celestine Prophesy*. New York, NY: Warner Books, Inc., 1993.

Simms, Maria Kay. *The Witch's Circle*. St. Paul, MN: Llewellyn Publications, 1997.

Sitchen, Zecharia. *The 12th Planet*. New York, NY: HarperCollins Publishers, Inc., 1976.

Weinstein, Marion. *Positive Magic*. 3rd Ed. New York, NY: Earth Magic Productions, Inc., 1994.

HISTORICAL, PHILOSOPHICAL, AND SCIENTIFIC READINGS:

Baigent, Michael; Leigh, Richard; & Lincoln, Henry. *Holy Blood, Holy Grail*. New York, NY: Dell Publishing Group, Inc., 1982.

Brinton, Crane; Christopher, John B.; and Wolff, Robert Lee. *A History of Civilization: Volume One (Prehistory to 1715)*. 3rd Ed. Englewood Cliffs, NJ: Prentice-Hall, Inc., 1967.

Brinton, Crane; Christopher, John B.; and Wolff, Robert Lee. *A History of Civilization: Volume Two: (1715 to the Present)*. 3rd Ed. Englewood Cliffs, NJ: Prentice-Hall, Inc., 1967.

Craig, Albert M.; Graham, William A.; Kagan, Donald; Ozment, Steven; and Turner, Frank M. *The Heritage of World Civilizations*. New York, NY: Macmillan Publishing Company, 1986.

Freedman, Jonathan L. *Introductory Psychology*. Reading, MA: Addison-Wesley Publishing Company, Inc., 1978.

Goble, Frank G. *The Third Force: The Psychology of Abraham Maslow*. New York, NY: Washington Square Press Publications, 1970.

The I Ching or Book of Changes. 3rd Ed. Translated by Richard Wilhelm and Cary F. Baynes. Princeton, NJ: Princeton University Press, 1977.

Nietzsche, Friedrich. *The Genealogy of Morals*. Translated by Francis Golffing. New York, NY: Doubleday Dell Publishing, Inc., 1956

Nietzsche, Friedrich. *Thus Spoke Zarathustra*. Translated by Walter Kaufmann. New York, NY: Viking Penguin, Inc., 1978.

Nietzsche, Friedrich. *The Will To Power*. Translated by Walter Kaufmann and R. J. Hollingdale. New York, NY: Random House, Inc., 1967.

Read, Piers Paul. *The Templars*. New York, NY: St Martin's Press, 1999.

Robinson, Charles Alexander Jr. *Ancient History: From Prehistoric Times to the Death of Justinian*. New York, NY: The Macmillan Company, 1956.

Index

A

Aaron (brother of Moses), 44, 66, 71, 72
Abbas, Mahmoud, 251
Abram, see Abraham
Adam & Eve, 39, 42, 52,71, 146, 157, 159,
    189-191, 207, 228-233, 235-237, 240,
    246, 268, 318, 329, 370
Abraham, 40-43, 52, 71, 127-128, 146, 156,
    158, 164, 239-245, 247, 249, 327, 329, 375
Abu Bakr, 150, 170
Age of Aquarius, 366, 373-381
Age of Pisces, 366-369, 373-381
Ahura Mazda, see Zoroastrianism
Aisha (wife of Muhhamad), 170
Akasha, 58, 160
Akhenaten (Egyptian pharoah), 38, 243
Al Adawiyya, Rabia, 172-173
Al Aqsa Mosque, 159
Al Basri, Hasan, 172
Al Kindi, 354
Al Qaeda, 171, 343
Al Razi, 354
Allah, see Islam
Ali ibn Abi Talib (cousin/son-in-law
    of Muhammad), 170
Allegro, John, 271-272, 293
Ananda (cousin of Buddha), 56-57
Ananias, High Priest, 137
Anne (mother of Mary), 71-75, 89
Anti-popes, see Popes
Apostles: 85-88
    Peter (a/k/a Simon), 64, 86, 106-107, 115,
        117, 308
    Andrew, 64, 86
    James, son of Zebedee (a/k/a James "the
        Greater"), 74-75, 86, 89
    John, son of Zebedee, 78, 86, 115, 117
    Philip, 87
    Bartholomew (a/k/a Nathanael), 87
    Matthew (a/k/a/ Levi), 78, 87
    James, son of Alphaeus (a/k/a James
        "the Lesser"), 74-75, 87, see also
        James the Just
    Simon the Cananean (a/k/a Simon "the
        Zealot"), 72, 74, 87-89, 105-107, 137
    Thomas (a/k/a Judas Thomas), 72, 74, 81,
        88-89, 111
    Thaddeus (a/k/a Judas "not Iscariot"), 88
    Judas Iscariot, 88, 99, 101
Arafat, Yasser, 251
Arhat, 57, 62, 256
Arian Controversy, 286
Aristotle, 175
Arius, 286
Ark of the Covenant, 45, 47, 293
Armageddon, 50, 68, 243
Aryans, 30, 47, 223

Assyrians, 47-48
Atman, 31
Atrahasis, 190
Aung San Suu Kyi, 258
Ayatollah Khomeini, 345
Ayatollah Seestani, 347

B

Babylonians, 47-49, 66, 238, 320
Balfour Declaration, 339
Bhagavad Gita, see Hinduism
Bin Laden, Osama, 171,335, 337, 340-344
Black Madonna, 290, 292-293, 295, 301-305
Bodhisattvas, 16, 62, 143, 256, 259-262, 314
Book of Q, see Christianity
Borgia, Caesar & Borgia, Lucrezia, 321
Brahmin, 31-32, 34, 58-59, 223
Brown, Dan, 143, 276, 301, 303
Buddha (a/k/a Siddhartha Gautama),
    see Buddhism
Buddhism: 54-62, 181, 252-264, 356, 358
    Prophet:
        Buddha, 14, 27, 54-62, 112, 114, 141-
            143, 172, 252-264, 267, 276, 363
        Birth, 54
        Childhood, 44-45
        Death, 56, 256
        Enlightenment, 55-56
    Key Persons:
        Ananda (cousin), see Ananda
        Mahaprajapati (aunt/stepmother),
            see Mahaprajapati
        Maya (mother), see Maya
    Deities: 181, 267
        Brahma, 57, 59, 253, 267
        Tara, 260
    Holy Scriptures:
        Pali Canon, 57
        Sutra Pitaka, 57
        Dhammapada, 57, 59-60, 252-254,
            262-263, 363
        Vinaya Pitaka, 57
        Abhidharma Pitaka, 57
        Tripitaka, 57-58, 259
    Councils:
        First Buddhist Council, 57
        Second Buddhist Council, 61
        Third Buddhist Council, 256
    Buddhist sects:
        Hinayana (a/k/a Theravada), 256, 259
        Mahayana, 256-257
    Views on women: 56, 61-62, 258-261

C

Caiaphas, High Priest, 99, 109, 123, 137
Caliph Mamun, 353
Cardinal sins, 26, 34-35, 93-95, 114, 179, 193,
    218, 284, 298, 323-324, 344, 371, 381-382

Carolingian Dynasty, 301-302, 305
Caste system, 32-33, 35, 58, 223-225
Cathars, 139, 289-298, 301-306
Cayce, Edgar, 255
Charlemagne (Charles I, Holy Roman Emporer), 302, 304
Christ Consciousness, 364, 388
Christianity: 63-145, 181, 265-326, 356, 358
    Prophets:
        Jesus Christ, 14, 19, 36-37, 48-51, 56,
            63-145, 296, 300, 332-333
        Baptism, 65
        Birth, 54-55, 65-70
        Childhood, 68, 80-82
        Death, 69, 100-107, 121, see also
            Passover Plot
        Deification, 73,109, 111, 115, 122,
            126-128, 135, see also Paul
        Family trees, 71-72, 74, 89
        Genealogy, 70-75
        Good works, 91-92, 94, 111, 119, 130,
            142, 202, 280-282
        Last Supper, 88, 99-101, 107, 277, 291,
            300
        as Messiah, 37, 47-51, 64, 68-69, 96-98,
            102,109-110, 117, 127
        the Nazorean, 89, 97
        the Prophet, 107-114, 156-158, 161-162,
            171
        Resurrection, 70, 104-106
        Son of Man, 100, 109, 127, 315
        Son of God, 77-78, 92, 109, 126-127,
            157-158, 313-315
        Trials, 99, 109-110, 306
        John the Baptist, 64-65, 68, 72
    Key Persons:
        Anne (mother of Mary), see Anne
        Apostles, see Apostles
        Caiaphas, High Priest, see Caiaphas
        Herod the Great, see King Herod the
            Great
        James (brother), see James the Just
        Joseph (father), see Joseph
        Mary (mother), see Mary
        Mary Magdalene, see Mary Magdalene
        Paul (a/k/a Saul of Tarsus), see Paul
        Pontius Pilate, see Pontius Pilate
    Deities: 181, 266-267
        The Holy Trinity, 100,139-141, 157,
            158, 286, 330, 376
        Satan, see Satan
    Holy Scriptures:
        The Holy Bible, 28, 76-79, 269, 277-278
        New Testament, 28, 36, 65, 70, 77-79,
            86, 202, 332-333, see Gospels
        1st Corinthians, 107, 131, 133-134, 318
        2nd Corinthians, 127, 132
        Letter to Galatians, 129, 132, 281
        Letter of James, 79, 87, 130
        Letter of Jude, 88

        Letter to Romans, 128-129, 134
        Book of Q, 77, 326, 340
        Sayings Source, 77-79, 88, 130
    Church Councils:
        First Jerusalem Council, 132
        Second Jerusalem Council, 136
        Lateran Council II, 320
        Lateran Council IV, 307
        Lateran Council V, 320
        Council of Constance, 279
        Council of Constantinople, 308
        Council of Ephesus, 308
        Council of Elvira, 320
        Council of Laodicea, 78, 140
        Council of Nicaea, 73, 75-77, 139,
            286-287, 308, 318
        Council of Trent, 78, 140,278
        Vatican Council I, 309
        Vatican Council II, 278
    Holy Days:
        Christmas, 70
        Easter, 69-70
    Early Christian sects: 114
        Gentile Christians, 115, 130-132, 135,
            138-139
        Gnostic Christians, 112-113, 115-116,
            135, 138-139, 171, 231, 274, 290
        Jewish Christians, 77, 108, 114-115,
            117-126, 135, 138, 273-274
        Roman Catholic Church, 74, 87,109,
            113, 134, 139, 265-266, 268-272,
            274-275, 277-326, 377
    Later Christian sects:
        Anglican Church, see Appendix
        Armenian Church, see Appendix
        Baptist Church, 312
        Coptic Church of Egypt, 84
        Eastern Orthodox Church, 77, 84, 86,
            287-288
        Episcopal Church, 312
        Evangelical/Fundamentalist, 36, 129,
            161, 191-194, 233-235, 267, 280,
            282, 310-312, 377-378, 384
        Lutheran Church, 289, 312
        Methodist Church, 312
        Mormons, see Appendix
    Views on sin: 4, 39, 65, 93-95, 100, 128,
        217, 229, 235, 318
    Views on women (the "fall of mankind"):
        114, 143, 285, 316-318, 320-321
Clement, Bishop of Alexandria, 16
Clement, Bishop of Rome (a/k/a Pope Clement I),
    123, 308
Comparative Religions Chart, 181
Congregation for the Doctrine of Faith, 270
Confucius, 7, 56, 175-176
Constantine, Roman Emperor, 73-74, 76, 139,
    284, 286-287, 308, 318
Copernicus (a/k/a Koperik, Mikolaj), 206, 274-275
Cradles of Civilization, 30, 244

Creed of Rimini-Selucia, 140
Crusades: 285-286, 351
    Albigensian Crusade, 295
    First Crusade, 292
    Fourth Crusade, 288
Curran, Father Charles, 270

D

Da Vinci, Leonardo, 188, 277, 303
Dalai Lama, 16, 22, 62, 258
Dhammapada, see Buddhism
Darwin, Charles, 268
Dead Sea Scrolls, see Judaism
De Bouillon, Godfroi, 292, 302, 304
De Gellone, Guilhelm, 302, 304
De Molay, Jacques, 297
Descartes, René, 275-276
Dharma (Truth), 10, 16, 30-31, 55, 59, 252-257,
    263, 264
Dome of the Rock, 159, 293
Dossiers Secrets, 303

E

Eastern Orthodox Church, see Christianity
Ebadi, Shirin, 345
Ecole Biblique, 269, 271-272
Egyptian Empire, 40, 247-249
Eight-Fold Path, 58
Eisenman, Robert, 17
Eleventh Commandment, 119, 130, 280-282,
    310, 333
Elijah, 48, 51, 64, 156
Elohim, see Judaism
End Times, 121, 123, 171, 333, 362, 378
Enki & Enlil, 190, 206-207, 228, 232
Enuma Elish, 190
Epic of Gilgamesh, 190
Esau (son of Isaac), 42, 240
Essenes/Ossene, 67, 89, 124, 271
Eusebius, Bishop, 126
Evolution (see also Appendix), 20, 191-195, 205,
    207, 233-235, 267-269, 330-331, 370, 387
Exodus, 44-45, 72
Ezekiel, 49, 99

F

Family Charts:
    Grail Family Tree, 304
    Jesus' Ancestors, 71
    Jesus' First Family Tree, 72
    Jesus' Second Family Tree, 74, 89, 240
    Jewish Family Tree, 42, 240
Fatima (daughter of Muhammad), 170
Five Pillars of Islam, 163
Four Noble Truths, 7, 58
Freemasons, 294
Friday, the 13th, 297

G

Galileo Galilei, 275
Gandhi, Mahatma, 7, 35-36, 224-225, 351
Gentile Christians, see Christianity

Goddess, 29, 220, 231, 243-244, 356
Good works, 18, 20-21, 29, 36-37, 52, 78, 91-92,
    94, 111, 130, 142, 177, 202
Gospels:
    Canonical Gospels:
        Acts of the Apostles, 77-78, 86-87, 107,
            115, 118-120, 122-125
        Gospel of Matthew, 64, 71, 73, 78,
            86-87, 91, 94-95, 100, 102-104,
            110, 120, 130, 282, 324
        Gospel of Mark, 65, 78, 86, 93, 100, 364
        Gospel of Luke, 19, 71, 73, 78, 86,
            92-95, 100, 104-105, 142-143
        Gospel of John, 64, 78, 86, 103-104,
            106-107, 109-110, 147, 266,
            313-315, 389,
         Revelation to John, 50, 77, 217, 230
    Gnostic Gospels: 28, 79-80, 112, 140, 172,
        202, 273, 387
        Apocalypse of Peter, 139
        Apocryphon of James, 112
        Children of Salvation and the Mystery
           of Existence, 274
        Dialogue of the Savior, 273, 317
        Gospel of Judas, 99
        Gospel of Mary, 144-145
        Gospel of Philip, 113, 144, 273, 317
        Gospel of Thomas, 12, 88, 112, 116,
           143, 361
        Gospel of Truth, 113
        Pistis Sophia, 317
        The Testimony of Truth, 113
    Lost Gospels:
        Infancy Gospel of James, 81-82, 84
        Infancy Gospel of Thomas, 81
        Protovangelium of James, 72
Gnostic Christians, see Christianity
Gnostic Gospels, see Gospels
Gramick, Sister Jeannine, 313
Gregorian Calendar, 70
Great Cusp, 362-387
Great Mother, 29, 230, 243, 356
Great Schism (of 1054), 77, 86, 287, 308
Gulf War I and II 336
Gyalwa Karmapa, 258

H

Hagar, 41, 146, 239
Hajj, 154, 163
Hamas, see Islam
Hebrew/Habiru, 40-41, 43, 241
Hezbollah, see Islam
Hijra, 150
Hinayana Buddhism (a/k/a Theravada),
    see Buddhism
Hinduism: 30-36, 181, 220-227, 356, 358
    Prophets:
        Manu, 32, 224, 226
        Guru Nanuk, 34, see also Sikhs
    Key Persons:
        Mahatma Gandhi, see Gandhi

Swami Satchidanda, see Satchidanda
Deities: 33-35, 181, 220-221, 266
  Brahma, 33, 220, 267
  Brahman (a/k/a Prajapati), 31, 33, 262
  Durga, 33
  Ganesha, 221
  Krishna, 31-33, 320
  Lakshmi, 33
  Lalita, 220
  Mahadevi, 33
  Parvati, 33, 221
  Sarasvati, 33
  Shiva, 33, 220-221
  Varuna, 220
  Vishnu, 33, 220
  Kali (a/k/a Tara), 33, 260
Holy Scriptures:
  The Bhagavad Gita, 7, 10, 15, 31-32,
    35, 222
  Mahabharata, 31
  Manava-Dharma-Sastra (a/k/a Laws
    of Manu), 32, 224, 226
  Manu Smrti, 33, 226
  The Rig Veda, 30, 222, 223
  Vedas, 30-31, 223
  Upanishads, 30-31
Views on women: 32, 34, 226-227
Holocaust, 307, 340
The Holy Bible, see Christianity
Holy Grail, 291-293, 298-305
The Holy Quran, see Islam
Holy Trinity, 100, 139-141, 157-158, 181,
  266-267, 286
Hus, John, 277-279, 288-289
Hussein, Saddam, 336

I
Immaculate Conception, 74-75
Inquisition, 270, 275-279, 283-285, 288-291,
  324, 351
Intelligent Design, 192-195, 207
Iraneus, Bishop, 16, 139
Isaac (son of Abraham), 41-42, 71, 128, 156,
  158, 240-241, 327
Isaiah, 48, 51, 239-241
Ishmael, 41-42, 146, 156, 158, 164, 239-241,
  327
Islam: 146-173, 181, 327-356, 358
  Prophet:
    Muhammad ibn Abdallah, ix, 13-14,
      16, 20, 146, 291, 327-331
    Birth, 146
    Childhood, 146-147
    Death, 155
    Early persecution, 150-151
    Good works/charity, 161, 163-164,
      330, 337
    Hashim tribe, 146-150
    Hijra, 150
    Islam expansion, 151-155, 164, 352
    Khadija (wife), 147, 150, 169, 352

Revelations, 147-151, 155, 162, 352
  Shariah, 162-169, 171, 344-345, 348
  Sunnah, 163, 344-346
  Treatment of Jews, 150-154, 156, 349
  Tribal wars, 152-154, 327
  View on other Prophets, 156-157,
    161-162, 171, 328, 349
Key Persons:
  Abraham, see Abraham
  Abu Baker, see Abu Baker
  Ali ibn Abi Talib (cousin/son-in-law),
    see Ali ibn Abi Talib
  Aisha (wife), see Aisha
  Hagar (wife of Abraham), see Hagar
  Ishmael (son of Abraham), see Ishmael
  Mahdi (a/k/a Twelfth Imam), see Mahdi
Deity: 181
  Allah, 146-149, 155, 162, 328-330, 350
Holy Scripture:
  The Holy Quran, ix, 13, 20, 25, 28, 39,
    147-149, 151-152, 155-169, 171,
    328-332, 334-335, 344, 346-347,
    349-351, 364
  Hadith, 163, 170-171, 344
Holy Days:
  Hajj, 154, 163
  Ramadan, 152, 163
Muslim Sects:
  Hamas, 251
  Hezbollah, 251
  Shiite, 170-171, 337, 347, 352, 378
  Sufi, 171-173
  Sunni, 170-171, 337, 352
  Wahhabi, 171, 335, 337
  Fundamentalist/Extremist, 171, 331-332,
    334-335, 350-351, 355
Five Pillars of Islam, 163
Views on sin: 151, 159-160, 165, 236, 334,
  350
Views on women: 164, 168-170, 345-348,
  355
Israel (nation), 43, 48, 79, 171, 248-251, 332,
  336-337, 339, 350

J
Jacob (a/k/a Israel), 42-43, 71, 156, 158, 240-241
James the Just (brother of Jesus), 17, 74-75, 81,
  89, 106-107, 123, 136, 202, 307-308
  Death, 125, 137
  First Bishop of Jerusalem, 75, 87, 117,
    124-126, 131-132
  Good works, 79, 91-92, 94, 111, 130, 136,
    142, 202
  Righteous Teacher, 136
Jehovah, see Judaism
Jeremiah, 48
Jesus Christ, see Christianity
Jetsunma, 260-261
Jewish Christians, see Christianity
Jewish Temple, 12, 16, 37, 45, 47-49, 66-67,

88, 99, 137, 159, 249, 272, 292
Jihad, 165-168, 248, 336, 343, 350
Joachim (father of Mary), 71-74, 89
John the Baptist, 64-65, 68, 72
Jonah, 23, 156
Joseph (son of Jacob), 42, 240
Joseph of Arimathea, 102-104, 300
Joseph (father of Jesus), 69-74, 81-82, 89, 156
Josephus, Flavius, 16, 87
Joshua, 45-47
Judaism: 37-53, 181, 228-251, 356, 358
    Prophets:
        Abraham, 40-43, 52, 71, 127-128, 146,
            156-158, 164, 239-247, 249, 375
        Elijah, 48, 51, 64, 156
        Ezekiel, 49, 99
        Isaac (son of Abraham), 41-42, 71, 128,
            156, 158, 240-241, 327
        Isaiah, 48, 51, 314, 339-241
        Jacob (a/k/a Israel; son of Isaac), 42-43,
            71, 158, 240-241
        Jeremiah, 48
        Jonah, 23, 156
        Malachi, 48, 64
        Messiah, 37, 48-51, 64, 68, 96-98,
            117-118, 120, 241-243, 246, 262,
            378, 381
        Micah, 299
        Moses, 27, 38, 42-45, 66, 147-148,
            155-156, 158-159, 162, 228,
            240-241, 247-249, 363
        Noah, 39-40, 42, 71, 156
        Zechariah, 49-50, 98, 156, 243
    Key Persons:
        Ishmael (son of Abraham), see Ishmael
        Joseph (son of Jacob), see Joseph
        Joshua, see Joshua
        King David, see King David
        Sarah (wife of Abraham), see Sarah
    Deity: 181, 266
        God (a/k/a Yahweh/Elohim/Jehovah),
            39-40, 52, 140, 147-148, 90,
            228-233, 235-239, 245-247, 328
    Holy Scriptures:
        Old Testament/Tanach, 30, 38, 43, 189,
            228, 269
        Ketuvim, 38
        Nevi'im, 38
        Pentateuch/Torah, 38-45, 228, 237
        Genesis, 38-42, 52, 190-191, 215,
            228-233, 239-241
        Exodus, 43-44
        Leviticus, 45, 364
        Numbers, 45
        Deuteronomy, 11, 45-46, 241, 363
        Joshua, 46
        Judges, 46-47
        Kings, 238
        Mishna, 45, 162
        Talmud, 45

Zohar, 52, 156
Dead Sea Scrolls, 8, 17, 28, 67-68,
    79-80, 90, 123-124, 136, 202,
    270-273, 293, 387
Copper Scroll, 272, 293
Damascus Document, 136, 269
Habakkuk Pesher, 136
Manual of Discipline, 136
Holy Days:
    Hanukkah, 66
    Passover, 44, 98, 152
    Rosh Hashana, 235
    Sabbath, 45, 141
    Yom Kippur, 235
Jewish Sects:
    Orthodox, 52-53, 233-234, 246, 378
    Reform, 237, 246
Views on sin: 39, 229-233, 235-237, 246
Views on women (the "fall of mankind"): 45,
    52-53, 229, 232, 246
Judgment Day, 37, 49-51, 120-121, 158,
    160-162, 171-172, 242
Julian Calendar, 69
Jung, Dr. Carl, 7, 84

K
Ka'ba, 146, 150, 154, 158-159, 163
Kabbalah, see Judaism
Karma, 31, 33, 58, 159-160, 177, 222-223,
    252-255, 330, 385
Khadija (wife of Muhammad), 147, 149, 169, 352
King Abdullah II (Jordan), 338
King Baudouin I (Jerusalem), 292, 302, 304
King Charles I (Franks), see Charlemagne
King Dagobert II (Merovingian), 301, 304
King David, 47, 69, 71, 72, 156
King Faud (Saudi Arabia), 336, 338
King George III (Great Britain), 384
King Henry III (Germany), 354
King Herod the Great, 64,66-68, 80-81, 97
King Herod Antipas, 64, 68, 98, 109
King Philip IV (France), 297
King Saud (Saudi Arabia), 338
King Seigbert IV (Merovingian), 302, 304
King Soloman, 47-48, 71-72, 156, 228
King Theodoric IV (Merovingian), 302, 304
Kingdom of Israel, 46-48
Kingdom of Jerusalem, 292
Kingdom of Judah, 46-48
Kingdom of Septimania, 290-291, 302, 304
Kingston, Maxine Hong, 14
Knights Templar, 292-298, 301-305, 323
Kublai Khan, 257
Kung, Hans, 270

L
Lao Tzu (a/k/a Laozi), 176, 365
Lost Gospels, see Gospels
Lot (nephew of Abraham), 41-42, 46, 155,
    240-241
Luther, Martin, 288-289

M

Maccabee Dynasty, 66-67, 97, 272
Mahaprajapati (aunt/stepmother of Buddha), 54-56
Mahayana Buddhism, see Buddhism
Mahdi (a/k/a Twelfth Imam), 171
Maimonides, Moses, 45
Malachi, 48, 64
Manu, 32, 224-226
Mary (mother of Jesus), 54, 69-76, 81-82, 89, 104-105, 157-158, 320
Mary Magdalene: 75, 79, 96, 319
   a/k/a Mary of Bethany, 96, 144, 298
   the *Magdaleder*, 298-299
   as Apostle, 96, 143-145, 277, 296, 316, 319
   Crucifixion, 319
   Resurrection, 104-106, 144
   Wedding at Cana, 143, 300
   Holy Grail, 96, 143, 276, 298, 300-305, 317
   Black Madonna, 301, 304
Marx, Karl, 369
Masada, 68, 137
Maslow, Dr. Abraham, 13-15, 19, 31, 172, 245
Maya (mother of Buddha), 54, 259, 320
Merovingian Dynasty, 290-292, 297-298, 301-305
Messiah, 37, 48-51, 64, 68, 96-98, 117-118, 120, 241-243, 246, 262, 378, 381
Messianic Age, 50, 242, 247, 364, 388
Mishna, see Judaism
Mithras, 70, 74
Moksha, 30-31
Moses, 27,28, 42-45, 66, 147-148, 155-156, 158-159, 162, 228, 240-241, 247-249, 363
Moses of Leon, 52
Muhammad, see Islam
Muslim Empire, 155, 274, 290-292, 295-296, 353-354

N

Nanuk, Guru, 34, see also Sikhs
Nazoreans, 89-90, 124, 138
Neitzsche, Friedrich, 369
Nephilim, 191
New Age Movement, viii, 15, 18-19, 22, 211
New Millennium, 213, 216-217, 351, 361-389
New Millennium Grade Point Average, 358-359
New Testament, see Christianity
Newton, Sir Isaac, 276, 303
Nicene Creed, 100, 139
Nicodemus, 104
Nirvana, 55-60, 114, 143, 161, 252-256, 261-262, 314
Noah, 39-40, 42, 71, 240-241
Nugent, Father Robert, 313

O

Old Testament, see Judasim
Order of Sion, 292, 301, 304-305
Original sin, 235, 318, see also Christianity
   and Paul
Ossene, see Essenes
Ottoman Empire, 337-339, 341-344

P

Pagan deities:
   Apollo, 128; Athena, 231; Baal (a/k/a El), 43, 46, 48; Eostre, 70; Hades, 230; Hercules, 238; Ishtar, 231; Isis, 128, 231; Mithros, 70, 74; Osiris, 128; Ra, 128; Sophia, 231, 172; Venus, 238; Zeus, 128, 135, 217, 238
Palestine, 46-49, 65-67, 248-251
   Balfour Declaration, 339
   Oslo Peace Accord, 250
   Resolution 181, 340
   White Paper, 339
Pali Canon, see Buddhism
Panchen Lama, 258
Papal Infallibility, 269-270, 277-279, 307-309
Parsis, 37
Passover Plot, 100-107
Patriarch, 287
Paul (a/k/a Saul of Tarsus), 79, 115, 122-137, 280, 312
   Church hierarchy, 131, 133-134, 311
   Conversion, 115,123
   Death, 137
   Deification of Jesus, 115, 122, 126-128, 135
   Faith vs. good works, 72, 79, 91,92, 115, 126, 129-131, 202, 280, 289, 311
   Gentile conversion, 125, 13-132, 135, 311, 333
   Persecution of Christian Jews, 122-125, 136-137,
   Spouter of Lies, 136
   The Way, 123-124, 136
   Views on sin, 128-129
   Views on women, 133-134, 317-318
Pentateuch, see Judaism
Pepin II, 301-302, 304
Pepin III, 301-302, 304
Persian Empire, 37, 47-49,66
Peter (a/k/a Simon), see Apostles
Philistines, 46-47
Plato, 174
Pontifical Biblical Commission, 268-269
Pontius Pilate, 83, 99, 102, 109-110, 306
Popes: 287, 308
   Alexander VI, 321; Benedict XIII (anti-pope), 280; Benedict XVI (Cardinal Joseph Ratzinger), 270; Calixtus III, 321; Clement I, 123, 308 (see also Clement, Bishop of Rome); Pope Clement V, 297; Gregory I, 319; Gregory IX, 275, 283, 296; Gregory XI, 278, 323; Gregory XII, 279; Innocent II, 293; Innocent III (anti-pope), 284; Innocent IV, 285; Innocent VIII, 285; John VIII, 309; John X, 309, 321; John XI, 309, 321; John XII, 309, 321; John XVI, 310; John XXIII (1st; anti-pope), 279-280, 307; John XXIII (2nd), 280, 307; John Paul II, 270, 275; Leo I (a/k/a Leo the Great), 140, 287; Leo III, 302; Leo V, 309; Leo IX, 320, 354; Leo XIII, 268; Lucius III, 283; Nicholas

II, 287; Paul III, 275; Paul IV, 307; Paul VI, 270,144; Pius VII, 284; Pius IX, 76, 269, 284; Pius XII, 307; Sergius III, 309, 321; Sixtus IV, 309; Stephen II, 301; Stephen VI, 309; Stephen VIII, 309; Urban II, 292; Victor II, 309
Priory of Sion, 276-277, 295, 302-305

Q
Qumran (Damascus), 67-68, 79, 86, 88, 124, 137-138

R
Rabia, 172-173
Ratzinger, Cardinal Joseph (Pope Benedict XVI), 270
Redfield, James, 7
Reformation, 289
Reincarnation, 31, 34, 254, 388
Renan, Ernest, 269
Resurrection, 49, 58-59, 62, 70, 104-106, 160, 242, 248, 262
Righteous Teacher, 136
Roman Catholic Church, see Christianity
Roman Empire, 11, 48, 65-67, 74, 7683, 284, 291, 306, 327, 376
Rumi, Jalaluddin, 172

S
Sacred Feminine, 173, 180
Saddha, ix, 9-10, 14-16, 29, 52,58, 61, 172, 175, 178, 211, 233, 237, 252, 256, 264, 362, 379
Saint Augustine, 319
Saint Bernard, 290, 293
Saint Catherine of Sienna, 323-324
Saint Jerome, 74
Saint Teresa of Avila, 324-325
Saint Thérèse of Lisieux, 324
Samsara, 31, 33, 260
Sangha, 56-57, 59, 256, 258-259
Sanhedrin Council, 58, 65-66, 68, 83-84, 95, 99, 118, 121-125, 283, 289
Sarah (wife of Abraham), 41, 240
Sarah (Jewish princess), 301
Satan, 84-85, 181, 230, 376-377
Satchidanda (Hindu swami), 36
Saunier, Father, 303
Sayings Source, see Christianity
Schonfield, Hugh, 101
Second Jerusalem Council, see Judaism
Sermon on the Mount, 91
Seven Rules of Any Good Religion, 184-213, 356-359
Shariah, 162-169, 171, 344-345, 348
Sharon, Ariel, 251
Shiite Muslims, see Islam
Sikhs, 34,225
Socrates, 56, 174
Sons of Zodak, 89-90, 124
Spiritual Paradigm: 29, 179-180, 356-357, 362
    First Spiritual Paradigm, 29, 232, 356
    Second Spiritual Paradigm, 29, 220, 232, 356

Third Spiritual Paradigm, 29, 220, 231, 244, 356
Fourth Spiritual Paradigm, 29, 220, 245, 245, 356, 358, 365-366, 375
Fifth Spiritual Paradigm, 29, 216-217, 232, 247, 264, 306, 351-358, 362-389
Spouter of Lies, 136
Sufi Muslims, see Islam
Sumerians, 189-190, 206, 228, 231, 320, 373
Sunnah, 163, 344-346
Sunni Muslims, see Islam
Synchronicity, 7-8, 16, 84, 385

T
Taliban, 225
Talmud, see Judaism
Tanach, see Judasim
Ten Commandments, 20, 43-44, 93, 129, 141,189, 247, 280-282, 293
Ten Lost Tribes of Israel, 47
Tertullian, 318
Theodosius, Emperor, 74
Three Jewels, 59
Three Pillars, 86-87, 107, 115
Torah, see Judasim
Tower of Babel, 180, 203, 216, 218, 234
Tower of Truth, x, 20-21, 28-29, 62, 110, 130, 143, 177-178, 180, 203, 216-217, 234, 262, 314, 324, 362, 364, 369, 381, 386-388
Tridentine Index, 275-276
Twelve Tribes of Israel, 42

U
Ummah, 150-151, 153-154, 170, 337
Upanishads, see Hinduism

V
Valentinus, 16
Vedas, see Hinduism

W
Wahhabist Muslims, see Islam
Wailing Wall, 48, 159
The Way, 123-124
Wicked Priest, 136-137
World War I, 1-3, 338-339
World War II, 2, 48, 340, 354
Wycliffe, John, 277-278, 288

Y
Yin Yang, 176, 365, 375

Z
Zarathustra, 8, 37, 49, 243-244, 375
Zealots (a/k/a Zionists), 67-68, 90, 97, 121, 124, 138, 197, 198, 283
Zechariah, 49-50, 98, 156, 243
Zohar, see Judaism
Zoroastrianism: 7-8, 37-38, 47, 69, 146
    Ahura Mazda, 37
    Parsis, 37

AN ACT FOR ESTABLISHING RELIGIOUS FREEDOM

Authored by Thomas Jefferson in 1777
Adopted by the Virginia General Assembly in 1786

The Oracle Institute Mission Statement

As adapted from Virginia Code Section 57–1

Whereas, the Almighty hath created the mind free; and

Whereas, all attempts to influence mankind tend only to beget habits of hypocrisy and meanness and are a departure from the plan of the Holy Author of our existence who, being the Source of body, mind, and spirit, yet chose not to undermine freedom by coercions thereon; and

Whereas, the impious presumption of legislators and rulers, civil as well as ecclesiastical, who, being themselves fallible and uninspired men, have assumed dominion over the faith of others, setting up their own opinions and modes of thinking as the only true and infallible views, have established and maintained false religions over the greatest part of the world, thereby depriving mankind of comfortable liberty and spiritual freedom; and

Whereas, our civil rights have no dependence on our religious opinions any more than our opinions in physics or geometry; and

Whereas, Truth is great and will prevail if left to herself as the proper and sufficient antagonist to error and has nothing to fear from conflict unless, by human interposition, Truth is disarmed of her natural weapons - free argument and debate; errors ceasing to be dangerous when Truth is permitted freely to contradict them.

Now Therefore, The Oracle Institute is free to declare and does hereby declare:

(i)   That the purest faith is based in **Truth,** which sets us free;

(ii)   That the strongest force in the Universe is **Love,** which makes us whole; and

(iii)   That the guiding power of God is **Light,** which leads us toward one shared destiny.

To Wit, the Mission of The Oracle Institute shall be to serve as an Advocate for Enlightenment and a Vanguard for Spiritual Evolution.

THE ORACLE INSTITUTE

An Advocate for Enlightenment and a Vanguard for Spiritual Evolution

THE TRUTH:

The founders of The Oracle Institute are gravely concerned that the greatest crisis currently facing mankind is the resurgence of religious fundamentalism and the divisive nature of the five primary religions: Hinduism, Judaism, Buddhism, Christianity, and Islam. We believe that the time has come for humanity to shed archaic belief systems about the Supreme Being and acknowledge that the only path to God is spiritual enlightenment.

THE LOVE:

The *Saddha* process of soul growth, which is described in this work, accomplishes this goal by encouraging spiritual freedom and promoting private journeys of faith. Such an introspective path leads the soul to seek perfection and to perform compassionate acts for the benefit of others. By transforming the self and acknowledging a connection to everyone and everything, we prepare ourselves to enter a new spiritual paradigm.

THE LIGHT:

Many people are now ready to manifest the Fifth Spiritual Paradigm – the era of abundance, peace, and harmony foretold by the prophets of every religion and the elders of every indigenous culture. To that end, The Oracle Institute offers educational books, spirituality classes, and holistic products that are donated by authors and artists who wish to foster this next phase of our collective spiritual evolution.

We invite you to join us on our journey of Truth, Love, and Light

Donations may be made to:

THE ORACLE INSTITUTE
a 501(c)(3) educational charity
P.O. Box 368
Hamilton, VA 20159
www.TheOracleInstitute.org
(540)882-9252

**All donations and proceeds from our books and classes are used
to further our educational mission and to build
a sustainable spiritual community in Independence, Virginia.**